Asian Journalism

A SELECTED BIBLIOGRAPHY OF SOURCES ON JOURNALISM IN CHINA AND SOUTHEAST ASIA

Elliott S. Parker and
Emelia M. Parker

The Scarecrow Press, Inc.
Metuchen, N.J., & London
1979

PN
5360
P37

Library of Congress Cataloging in Publication Data

Parker, Elliott S
  Asian journalism.

  Includes index.
  1. Journalism--Asia--Bibliography.
  2. Journalism--China--Bibliography. I. Parker,
  Emelia M., joint author. II. Title.
  Z6940.P28   [PN5360]   016.079'5   79-22785
  ISBN 0-8108-1269-X

Contents

Introduction

Journalism in Asia has not been a particularly fertile field of historical endeavor, although in the past few decades, many books and articles have been written about such subjects as development communication, the use of media in population planning and the place of media in contemporary Asian society. But, general descriptive and historical works are lacking.

This bibliography attempts to open an additional area of research to scholars interested in the years of Asian journalism prior to about 1960.

The bibliography is eclectic and its' scope ambiguous. It is addressed to the researcher in journalism who has little background in the Asian area and little knowledge of the bibliographical complexity of the Asian field. The scope is hedged by generalities and the careful reader will find many exceptions; however, the main emphasis is asymptotically defined by the following parameters:

1. pre-1960
2. historical and descriptive
3. newspapers
4. China
5. Southeast Asia, primarily Malaysia, Singapore, and Indonesia
6. Chinese press in the United States
7. secondary materials

Topics generally not included are:

1. post-1960
2. use of the media in population and family planning
3. development communication
4. most theses and dissertations
5. fugitive materials and materials no longer extant
6. most primary material

Articles in such specialized journals as *Media Asia, Asian Messenger,* and *Media,* also are not included. This is not because they are unimportant, but because the publications are reasonably accessible to the researcher and a bibliography would be primarily an index.

This bibliography may be viewed as an entry to some sources. It is not meant to be, nor should it be expected to be, comprehensive. For instance, picking two newspapers in different time periods and countries, 218 articles on the press appeared in the *Peiping Chronicle* between 1934 and 1936, and between 1973 and 1975, more than 300 articles on media appeared in the Malaysian *Straits Times.* The inclusion of this type of material was beyond the physical scope of this volume. The area studies specialist will, no doubt, also find items missing.

We would suggest that researchers newly interested in this field, begin with the traditional bibliographical aids: *New York Times Index*, *Palmer's Index to the (London) Times*, and the *Index to the (London) Times*, *Subject Index to the Christian Science Monitor*, *Business Periodicals Index* (for the later issues of *Editor & Publisher*), and *Journalism Abstracts*.

Three other sources should also be consulted: G. William Skinner's *Modern Chinese Society: An Analytical Bibliography* (S00982) and John A. Lent's *Asian Mass Communications: A Comprehensive Bibliography* (L00718) and *Supplement* (L02746).

Skinner's work is central to any research on journalism in China. In three volumes, one each for English-, Chinese-, and Japanese-language sources, this massive compilation defines the bibliography of the field. Some entries in the present bibliography refer to Skinner's work, especially if they deal with electronic media or have complicated bibliographic definitions.

Lent's two bibliographies are also essential since they are the only available source on all media throughout Asia.

The present bibliography, although primarily dealing with print, does not exclude other communication media such as radio, television, or film. These non-print items were noted and entered, but remain secondary to the main work.

The authors believe that many people who would otherwise like to investigate the "early" period of Asian journalism are put off by the inaccuracy and paucity of citations and sources.

Some of these bibliographic inaccuracies are minor, in that the item is still locatable. These might include inaccurate volume numbers or incorrect spelling of the authors' name.

Other mistakes might be called "fatal" for they eliminate the possibility of finding the items with the information given. Under this category are instances of confusing Chinese surnames and given names, citation of journal names which have been used by several publications in different parts of the world, and perhaps most discouraging and typical of the field; the citation of sources with no indication that the original was not in English.

This is particularly prevalent in the field of journalism. We have compiled a long list of cited items that cannot be found. We know that by keeping notes and keeping our eyes open, many of these items will be "re-discovered" in some non-English language source because only a very free translation was cited.

The second problem perceived is a lack of secondary material on the descriptive aspect of the media. This bibliography does not pretend to systematically cover the area, but rather to suggest other areas of search and investigation. Certainly, abundant material in English on the development of the Chinese press is available, awaiting only the interested person to use it. Investigators fluent in languages such as Indonesian and Chinese, will uncover unbelievable amounts of material on topics of interest.

This bibliography is designed for mass media students and scholars of mass media. Its' emphasis is on the communication *process in Asia,* rather than the *content.* For instance, a roundup of editorial comment—"What the Chinese Press thinks of the Japanese Situation"—is not included, nor is the article, "Will Roger's Son Edits Paper in Beverly Hills." However, interest will not be limited to journalism researchers, and scholars in other fields may find it useful.

One aspect of this work, therefore, is that the compilers attempt to give all the information required to find the item listed. To some researchers, this may, at times, appear redundant. But in too many previous cases, references have been made to journals, only to find that the journal, was in fact, a book; other references were to a book with "communications" in the title, but the word was used in the broad sense of shipping and transportation with nothing on media; or references, to a "story" only to find out that it was only one of a series of letters-to-the-editor.

To a very great degree, the compilers have not forced any new bibliographic consistency. In fact, it may appear that there is little consistency. But we have kept in mind our own frustrations at locating the material and have attempted to quote the material as it is written *in the original*, and add any explanatory notes which would help in locating the item. Therefore, some volume numbers are in Arabic numerals, and some are in Roman numerals. This may be a small thing, but it was felt that more accuracy would be achieved.

Another seeming inconsistency is that of the names of authors.

In the case of Chinese authors, the entry is made exactly as it was in the book or article. Previously, names have been transliterated into Mandarin, with no indication that the author pronounced, and signed, his name in one of the other Chinese dialects, thereby making it impossible to find in a catalog. In the case of Southeast Asian names, we have attempted to use as the main entry, the form of the name under which a person working in the field would first expect to find it.

Some librarians may disagree with our approach. Many libraries, for example, did not recognize the difference between the *Straits Times* in Singapore and the new *Straits Times* in Malaysia, even though for some years they have been different companies and the issues carry very different news. In the present work, if no edition is cited, the items refer to the Malaysian edition. In addition, we have indicated the Sunday issue. Ostensibly a separate paper, (for instance, the *Straits Times* and the *Sunday Times*) most microfilm copies of these papers integrate the Sunday papers with the rest of the week.

We feel strongly that this very literal approach is the most useful at this time. In most cases, we have attempted to go to the original publication, so as to keep our entry as close to the original as possible. This has been done because of our belief that it was best to be faithful, rather than to impose yet more bibliographic problems, and cause further confusion.

Also important is the fact that no single library will have all the citations given here, and only a half-dozen in the world would have most.

This then, implies that the researcher must use interlibrary loan. Helpful as many librarians are, they are not inclined to search a journal volume, page by page, to find a letter to the editor, not an article as the request stated, written by Tan and not by Chen.

In addition, many articles appeared in periodicals which were never indexed, or even noted in the standard verification tools of the librarian, making the exact citation even more important.

In the case of sources in the various Asian languages, few union catalogs exist. This makes a search even more difficult if the bibliographic citation does not give enough information to start with. Computers, of course, are increasingly used to search large quantities of data. But such searches must be made with a very clear understanding of the rules of the particular computer ("close" will not score a "hit") and with the realization that the data bases, for the most part, are not retrospective. History begins when that data base became operational.

Transliterations from Chinese generally follow a modified Wade-Giles system, while Russian entries follow the *Government Printing Office Style Manual*. Unfortunately, given the restraints of the project, it was not possible to include tonal and diacritical marks.

EXPLANATORY NOTES

Citation structure:

1) Main entry   07 A01234
   Main entry continued, if needed

2) Title
   Title continued, if needed.

3) Imprint
   Bibliographic information, continued.
   Bibliographic information, continued.

4) Comments
   Comments continued, if needed.

5) Medium: Lang:

6) Chron: Verif:

7) Meth:

8) Geog:

9) Subj:

The *main entry* begins the citation. Usually this will be a person, but occasionally an institution, government, or book title may be used. The number at the right hand margin (A01234) is the citation number. The two digits (07) immediately preceding the letter, show the number of strokes in the Chinese character for the first part of the main entry. A comma indicates that the portions of the name are "reversed". No comma indicates the name has not been rearranged by the present authors.

The citations are in alphabetical order, but, due to the nature of the sort program on the computer, names with hyphens or apostrophes precede names without them regardless of alphabetic order, i.e., the sequence would be Ch'en, Ch'eng, Chai, Chao, Chen, Cheng.

The *title,* line 2, is the title of either the book or the article. It may be indented and continued.

The *imprint,* line 3, follows the sequence: place of publication, publisher, and date. For an article, the imprint would be substituted by the periodical title (if this was not the main entry), volume: number (and series, if appropriate), date (in parentheses), followed by the pages. If more is given, this line may also be indented and continued.

Comments begin on line 4. Primarily, this field expands on the preceding information, which may be cryptic or misleading, or gives additional information more fully explaining the item: for example, the series and catalog number of a government document. To the non-specialist, comments, in turn, may be cryptic. A comment to the "Herald affair" under an entry about Singapore assumes knowledge on the part of the user of the closing of the Singapore *Herald* in 1971. Comprehensive annotation would have been impractical. Translations of the title may also be given here, in parentheses, if it was too long to fit in the main entry field.

The comments field is followed by various other fields which help to annotate the citation.

Medium indicates which medium the citation is most concerned with, and if not print, books and newspapers, primarily, is specified as:
Electronic, including radio, television and satellite
Film
Other, including usch media as *dalangs* or wall posters
General, including, for instance, a survey of the media of a country or countries; mass communications

Language, on the same line as medium, indicates the primary language of the citation. This is English unless specified as :
Malay/Indonesian
Chinese
Russian
Other Asian language
Other European language
Other language, not specified above, or a combination of languages

Chronological is found on the next line, line 6 above, referring either to the date of the citation or the historical period with which it deals. The distinction is usually obvious from the remainder of the entry. The divisions are:
Before 1910
1910 to 1946
1946 to 1960
1960 to 1970
1970 to 1980
Survey, if the item is a historical survey or covers more than one of the above categories.

Verification, if noted, follows chronological. All items are "verified" unless noted. Verification is used in a very restrictive, perhaps constrictive, sense. Items are only accepted as verified if the item has been seen and checked by the present authors. In the case of books only, verification is assumed if it is listed in the *National Union Catalog.* Unverified implies nothing of the quality or existence of the item.

Methodology, if applicable and known, is indicated:
Survey research
Content analysis
Historical
Numerical, including mathematical and statistical studies
Other methods, not included above, or a combination of methods

The *geographical* field, unlike the preceding fields, may have more than one entry. The geographical divisions are:
Burma
Thailand
Malaysia
Singapore
Indonesia
Brunei
Vietnam, both North and South
Cambodia (Khmer Republic)
Laos
Hong Kong
Macao
Philippines
Taiwan
Oseas Chinese; the Chinese press outside China, Hong Kong, or Taiwan

China

East Asia, including Japan, and North and South Korea

Australasia, including the Pacific Islands, Micronesia, Australia, and New Zealand

South/West Asia, including the Indian sub-continent, West Asia, and North Africa

Europe

Russia

U.S., including American correspondents in Asia

Western Hemisphere, including Canada, Central and South America

Several Asia; either the Asian area in general or more than three individual
countries

Other; specific countries not named above

World; the world in general

The *subject* field carries descriptors and is meant to be explanatory; not an index. These descriptors add information to the entry, but do not analyze it. They are:

For Corr; foreign correspondence, its role and practice

Control, including censorship and freedom of the press

Propaganda

Development and the role of the media in modernization

Research aids, including bibliographies, literature reviews, and other guides
to research

Flow/agency, including items dealing with wire services and the flow of information between countries

Jrn History

Description; the most common category and usually an account of the press
at a given time

Law/ethics, includes not only law, but what the media "should" be doing

Biography indicates the citation has details of a journalist or journalists

Crosscultural, includes items that have a specific interest in the problems of
crosscultural communication

Education includes items dealing both with journalism education and the use
of media in general education

Printing includes items dealing with the practice of printing and typography

Publishing includes items concerned with publishing and the business of
printing

Language includes items dealing with the use and role of language in the media

Other jrn includes subjects of interest to the mass communication, but not
specifically identified above, such as advertising or public relations

Literature

Gen History; general, not journalistic, history

Political Science

Sociology/anthropology

Other; items of general interest, not dealing specifically with journalism or
the media

The subject field should not be considered as a full annotation with closely defined categories. For this reason, a full index across all the subjects and other fields was not included.

This type of index can be generated by a computer in seconds but was not included because this would have tended to give the bibliography a deceptive sense of resolution.

PUNCTUATION AND ABBREVIATIONS

The character set and computer program imposed some limitations on punctuation:
1. Arrows (< >) are used to indicate underlining (italics).
2. Single quotation marks are used for both single and double quotation marks.
3. Square brackets ([ ]) indicate additions by the current authors.
4. Parentheses indicate translations or additions by the author of the citation or previous bibliographers.
5. All diacritical and tonal marks are omitted.

Because of possible ambiguity, abbreviations have been kept to a minimum. The following have , however, been used:

CSM *Christian Science Monitor* newspaper
FEER *Far Eastern Economic Review*
HKG Hong Kong
JQ *Journalism Quarterly*
JMBRAS *Journal* of the Malayan Branch, Royal Asiatic Society
JRNL Journal
N.G. not given
N.P. no place or publisher given in source
NST *New Serials Titles* or supplements (vol. no.:page)
NUC *National Union Catalog* or supplements (vol. no.: page)
NYT *New York Times* newspaper
RAS Royal Asiatic Society
SIN Singapore
ULS *Union List of Serials*

COMPUTERIZATION

A computer, used in its fullest and most elegant way, can produce something on the scale of Skinner's bibliography, but a note may be of interest here. This bibliography is essentially a formatted printout of the authors' data. The computer used was the general purpose Univac 1106 system. A fact itself of little importance, except to demonstrate the comparative ease with which a general purpose computer can be used to print a bibliography. This bibliography, which began as a personal file, has several shortcomings and has neither the bibliographic or typographic elegance of Skinner's bibliography, but the method is available to almost any scholar. The authors highly recommend this approach to other researchers in the field. The method is extremely efficient: it allows infinite and easy corrections; and can be readily updated, and permits extensive cross referencing.

Introduction   xi

ACKNOWLEDGEMENTS

The authors wish to thank: Joyce Abler, Systems Analyst, at Central Michigan University, who wrote the program and helped us through the inevitable problems with the computer;

Joy Pastucha, Interlibrary Loan Librarian, at Park Library (and the many libraries and unknown librarians at the other end who made heroic efforts to locate material with inaccurate or incomplete citations);

Kay Dittenber and staff in the Grawn Hall Computer Center for help with the practical details of running the program;

Stanford Bradshaw and Guy Meiss who made many suggestions and comments on the manuscript.

The authors themselves are responsible for the inevitable inaccuracies and shortcomings in this work. They can blame neither their colleagues nor the computer (however tempting it may be to have an electronic scapegoat).

Corrections, comments or suggestions are actively solicited and may be addressed to the authors, Department of Journalism, Central Michigan University, Mt. Pleasant, Michigan 48859.

July 1979

Elliott S. Parker
Emelia M. Parker

A. GHANI ISMAIL   A00483
    SUDDENLY, OUT OF THE BLUE, A TREASURY OF OLD
        BAHASA FROM SRI LANKA
    MALAY MAIL 22 MAY 1975
    ##/MAL
    CHRON: BEFORE 1910
    GEOG: MALAYSIA   SO/WEST ASI
    SUBJ: LITERATURE LANGUAGE

ABDUL MANAF SULONG   A02155
    KONSEP KOMUNIKASI PEMBANGUNAN DI NEGARA-NEGARA
        MEMBANGUN
    SARINA [KUALA LUMPUR] 3:29(AUG 1978), 69-73.
    ##/MAL-3
    MEDIUM: GENERAL   LANG: MALAY/INDONESIAN
    CHRON: 1970-1980
    GEOG: MALAYSIA
    SUBJ: DEVELOPMENT

ABDUL AZIZ BIN MAT TON   A00101
    AL IMAM SEPINTAS LALU [AL-IMAM AT A GLANCE]
    JERNAL SEJARAH XI(1972/73), 29-40.
                           LANG: MALAY/INDONESIAN
    CHRON: 1910-1946
    GEOG: MALAYSIA
    SUBJ: JRN HISTORY

ABEND, HALLETT   A01744
    MY LIFE IN CHINA, 1926-1941
    NEW YORK, HARCOURT, BRACE, 1943.
    CHRON: 1910-1946
    GEOG: CHINA
    SUBJ: PROPAGANDA JRN HISTORY BIOGRAPHY

ABU-LUGHOD, IBRAHIM   A00102
    INTERNATIONAL NEWS IN THE ARABIC PRESS:
        A COMPARATIVE CONTENT ANALYSIS
    PUBLIC OPINION QUARTERLY XXVI:4(1962),
        600-612.
    CHRON: 1946-1960
    METH: CONTENT ANALYSIS
    GEOG: SO/WEST ASI
    SUBJ: FLOW/AGENCY DESCRIPTION

ADIBAH AMIN   A00103
    FILLING THE GAPS IN OUR HISTORY
    STRAITS TIMES (SUN) 11 APR 1976
    ##/MAL
    CHRON: BEFORE 1910
    GEOG: MALAYSIA
    SUBJ: GEN HISTORY LITERATURE

ADINEGORO, DJAMALUDIN   A00654
      PUBLISISTIK & DJURNALISTIK
      DJAKARTA, GUNUNG AGUNG, 1963-1966, 2 VOLS.
      NUC 56-67 1:414.
                              LANG: MALAY/INDONESIAN
      CHRON: 1960-1970
      GEOG: INDONESIA
      SUBJ: DESCRIPTION EDUCATION

ADJI, OEMAR SENO   A01309
      PERS: ASPEK--ASPEK HUKUM
      DJAKARTA, ERLANGA, 1974.
                              LANG: MALAY/INDONESIAN
      CHRON: 1970-1980
      GEOG: INDONESIA
      SUBJ: LAW/ETHICS

AFRO-ASIAN JOURNALIST   A02072
      SUHARTO FEARS 'JOURNALIST'S PEN'
      9:3(SEPT 1972), 33.
      CHRON: 1970-1980
      GEOG: INDONESIA
      SUBJ: CONTROL   DESCRIPTION

AFRO-ASIAN JOURNALIST   A02071
      LETTER TO DPRK JOURNALISTS
      11:3(NOV 1974), 29.
      CHRON: 1970-1980
      GEOG: EAST ASIA
      SUBJ: DESCRIPTION

AFRO-ASIAN JOURNALIST   A02070
      PRESS CIRCLES AGAINST THIEU CLIQUE'S
            FASCIST ACTS
      11:3(NOV 1974), 38.
      CHRON: 1970-1980
      GEOG: VIETNAM
      SUBJ: PROPAGANDA DESCRIPTION

AFRO-ASIAN JOURNALISTS ASSOCIATION,   A01980
            EDITOR
      SELECTIONS OF AFRO-ASIAN PEOPLE'S
            ANTI-IMPERIALIST CARICATURES
      PEKING, REN MIN MEI SHANG CHU PAN SHE, 1967.
                              LANG: OTHER OR COMB.
      CHRON: 1970-1980
      GEOG: CHINA   WORLD
      SUBJ: PROPAGANDA   OTHER JRN

AGASSI, JUDITH B.   A00104
    MASS MEDIA IN INDONESIA
    CAMBRIDGE, MASS, CENTER FOR INTL. STUDIES,
        1969.
    C/69-27; NUC 68-72 1:537.
    MEDIUM: GENERAL
    CHRON: 1960-1970
    METH: OTHER OR COMB
    GEOG: INDONESIA
    SUBJ: DESCRIPTION

AHMAD A. HAMID   A01981
    WUJUKAH BADAN PERUSHAHAAN FILEM BUMIPUTERA
    NADAMINGGU (12 MAR 1978), 8.
    ##/MAL-3; NADAMINGGU IS SUPPLEMENT
        TO <BERITA MINGGU>.
    MEDIUM: FILM   LANG: MALAY/INDONESIAN
    CHRON: 1970-1980
    GEOG: MALAYSIA
    SUBJ: OTHER JRN

AHMAT, ADAM   A02500
    THE VERNACULAR PRESS IN PADANG, 1865-1913
    AKADEMICA [KUALA LUMPUR] NO. 7(JULY 1975),
        75-99.
    ##/MAL-4
    CHRON: BEFORE 1910
    METH: HISTORICAL
    GEOG: INDONESIA
    SUBJ: DEVELOPMENT JRN HISTORY

AINON HAJI KUNTOM   A01366
    LEADING THE PATH TO FREEDOM
    LEADER MALAYSIAN JOURNALISM REVIEW
        3:1(1974), 39-41.
    CHRON: 1910-1946
    METH: HISTORICAL
    GEOG: MALAYSIA
    SUBJ: JRN HISTORY

AKKEREN, DR. PH. VAN   A02724
    MOCTAR LUBIS WINNER OF THE FIRST JEFFERSON
        FELLOWSHIP IN JOURNALISM
    REVIEW OF INDONESIAN AND MALAYAN AFFAIRS
        1:3(OCT 1967), 47-8.
    CHRON: 1960-1970
    GEOG: INDONESIA
    SUBJ: BIOGRAPHY

ALCOCK, RUTHERFORD   A00108
    THE <PEKING GAZETTE>
    FRASER'S MAGAZINE VII N.S.(FEB 1873), 245-56;
        PART 2 (MAR 1873),341-57.
    ##/CHIN-4; ULS 2:1630
    CHRON: BEFORE 1910
    METH: HISTORICAL
    GEOG: CHINA
    SUBJ: JRN HISTORY

```
ALCOTT, C. D.                                              A01345
     <CHINA PRESS> MEN OF OLDEN DAYS
     IN CHINA PRESS C02568, PP. 79, 88.
     ##/FILM
     CHRON: 1910-1946
     GEOG:  CHINA
     SUBJ:  JRN HISTORY


ALCOTT, CAROLL                                             A01745
     MY WAR WITH JAPAN
     NEW YORK, HENRY HOLT, 1943.
     CHRON: 1910-1946
     GEOG:  CHINA        EAST ASIA
     SUBJ:  FOR CORR     JRN HISTORY


ALI, SALAMAT                                               A02250
     RETURN TO THE LEAN TIMES
     FEER 100:25(23 JUNE 1978), 30.
     ##/SwAS
     CHRON: 1970-1980
     GEOG:  SO/WEST ASI
     SUBJ:  CONTROL


ALI, SALAMAT                                               A02249
     SAGA OF THE FOUR JUST MEN
     FEER 100:24(16 JUNE 1978), 32-3.
     ##/SwAS
     CHRON: 1970-1980
     GEOG:  SO/WEST ASI
     SUBJ:  CONTROL


ALIAS RAHIM                                                A00109
     FILM STARS SET UP $5MIL. COMPANY
     STRAITS TIMES 24 OCT 1972
     ##/MAL-2
     MEDIUM:  FILM
     CHRON: 1970-1980
     GEOG:  MALAYSIA
     SUBJ:  DESCRIPTION


ALIAS RAHIM                                                A00592
     TELLING ISLAM'S TRUE STORY
     STRAITS TIMES 17 AUG 1972
     ##/MALSP
     MEDIUM:  GENERAL
     CHRON: 1970-1980
     GEOG:  MALAYSIA     WORLD
     SUBJ:  FLOW/AGENCY
```

ALLEN, CHARLES L.   A00110
    COMMUNICATION PATTERNS IN HONG KONG
    HONG KONG, CHINESE UNIVERSITY OF HONG KONG,
        1970.
    MEDIUM: GENERAL
    CHRON: 1960-1970
    METH: OTHER OR COMB
    GEOG: HONG KONG
    SUBJ: DESCRIPTION

ALLEN, LAFE FRANKLIN   A02213
    A STUDY OF THE JAPANESE PRESS DURING THE
        FIRST YEAR OF ALLIED OCCUPATION
    MASTERS THESIS, UNIVERSITY OF MISSOURI, 1947.
    CHRON: 1946-1960
    METH: OTHER OR COMB
    GEOG: EAST ASIA
    SUBJ: DESCRIPTION

ALLEN, RILEY H.   A00111
    INTERCHANGE OF NEWS IN THE PACIFIC
    IN WILLIAMS W01152, PP. 433-9.
    #3
    MEDIUM: GENERAL
    CHRON: 1910-1946
    GEOG: AUSTRALASIA EAST ASIA
    SUBJ: FLOW/AGENCY DESCRIPTION

ALLEN, T. HARRELL   A00112
    U. S.-CHINESE DIALOGUE, 1969-72
    JRNL OF COMMUNICATION 26:1(WINTER 1976), 81-6.
    ##/US
    CHRON: SURVEY
    METH: CONTENT ANALYSIS
    GEOG: CHINA   U.S.
    SUBJ: CROSS CULTU FLOW/AGENCY

ALMANEY, ADNAN   A00113
    GOVERNMENTS' RESISTANCE TO THE FREE FLOW OF
        INTERNATIONAL COMMUNICATION
    JRNL OF COMMUNICATION 22:1(MAR 1972), 77-88.
    ##/INTL
    MEDIUM: GENERAL
    CHRON: 1960-1970
    GEOG: WORLD
    SUBJ: CONTROL

ALPHA MONTHLY   A00107
    MASS MEDIA IN SOUTHEAST ASIA
    (MAY-JUNE 1973), 32-4.
    ##/ASIA; ARTS ON INDON, KOREA, ROC, VN AND
        FILMS; NST(70) 1:230.
    MEDIUM: GENERAL
    CHRON: 1970-1980
    GEOG: SEV ASIA
    SUBJ: DESCRIPTION

ALSAGOFF, HUSSEIN A.   A00114
     VERNACULAR PRESS HAS GONE AHEAD IN PAST 8
          YEARS
     WORLD'S PRESS NEWS (MALAYAN SURVEY SUPPLEMENT)
          17:428(13 MAY 1937), XIII
     ##/MAL-3
     CHRON: 1910-1946
     GEOG: MALAYSIA   SINGAPORE
     SUBJ: DESCRIPTION

ALVAREZ, MAX   A02073
     THEIR BEAT IS THE WORLD
     HORIZONS [USIS] 20:8(1971), 38-45.
     MEDIUM: ELECTRONIC
     CHRON: 1970-1980
     GEOG: SEV ASIA   WORLD
     SUBJ: FOR CORR

AMAT MAT TOP   A01685
     MAJALAH TIMES DIBANTAH SIAR RENCANA 'RACUN'
     BERITA HARIAN (MALAYSIA) 25 DEC 1977
     ##/MAL-4
                            LANG: MALAY/INDONESIAN
     CHRON: 1970-1980
     GEOG: MALAYSIA   U.S.
     SUBJ: FOR CORR   FLOW/AGENCY LAW/ETHICS

AMBION, B. C.   A01003
     LIABILITY FOR LIBEL UNDER THE PRESENT STATE OF
          PHILIPPINES JURISPRUDENCE
     PHILIPPINE LAW JOURNAL (JAN 1940).
     CHRON: 1910-1946   VERIF: UNVERIFIED
     GEOG: PHILIPPINES
     SUBJ: LAW/ETHICS

AMERASIA   A01780
     CHINESE PAPER BOMBS
     2:6(AUG 1938), 297-7.
     CHRON: 1910-1946
     GEOG: CHINA   EAST ASIA
     SUBJ: PROPAGANDA

AMERASIA   A01424
     CHINESE CENSORSHIP AND THE FOREIGN PRESS
     8:5 (3 MAR 1944), 67-8.
     ##/CHIN-5
     CHRON: 1910-1946
     GEOG: CHINA
     SUBJ: FOR CORR   CONTROL   FLOW/AGENCY

AMERASIA   A01426
      CORRESPONDENTS IN ROUTE TO YENAN
      9:13(23 JUNE 1949), 195-6.
      ##/CHIN-5
      CHRON: 1910-1946
      GEOG: CHINA
      SUBJ: FOR CORR   DESCRIPTION

AMERASIA   A01425
      CENSORSHIP OF NEWS FROM CHINA
      8:8(14 APR 1944), 116.
      ##/CHIN-5
      CHRON: 1910-1946
      GEOG: CHINA
      SUBJ: FOR CORR   CONTROL   FLOW/AGENCY

AMERICAN JOURNAL OF INTERNATIONAL LAW   A01781
      RADIO CORPORATION OF AMERICA VS. CHINA
      XXX:3(JULY 1936), 535-51.
      MEDIUM: ELECTRONIC
      CHRON: 1910-1946
      GEOG: CHINA   U.S.
      SUBJ: LAW/ETHICS

AMERICAN PRINTER & BOOKMAKER, THE   A02807
      FIRST CHINESE DAILY NEWSPAPER IN AMERICA
      24(FEB 1900), 322-3.
      ##/CHIN-US; <CHUNG SAI YAT PO>; FROM ST. LOUIS
          <GLOBE DEMOCRAT>.
      CHRON: BEFORE 1910
      GEOG: OSEAS CHIN   U.S.
      SUBJ: DESCRIPTION

AMERICAN REVIEW OF REVIEWS, THE   A01983
      SOME PECULIARITIES OF CHINESE JOURNALISM
      32:2(AUG 1905), 242-3.
      ##/CHIN-6
      CHRON: BEFORE 1910
      GEOG: CHINA
      SUBJ: DESCRIPTION

AMERICAN REVIEW OF REVIEWS, THE   A01982
      NEWSPAPER ENTERPRISE IN CHINA
      43:1(JAN 1911), 110-12.
      ##/CHIN-6
      CHRON: 1910-1946
      GEOG: CHINA
      SUBJ: DESCRIPTION

AMERICAN UNIVERSITY (BUREAU OF SOCIAL   A01427
        SCIENCE RESEARCH)
COMMUNICATIONS AND PUBLIC OPINION IN THE
        PHILIPPINES: A SURVEY OF SELECTED SOURCES
WASHINGTON, D. C., OFFICE OF RESEARCH AND
        DEVELOPMENT, USIA, 1955.
NO. 674
MEDIUM: GENERAL
CHRON: SURVEY
GEOG: PHILIPPINES
SUBJ: RESEARCH

AMIC SECRETARIAT, COMPILER.   A02608
MASS COMMUNICATION IN SINGAPORE: AN
        ANNOTATED BIBLIOGRAPHY
SINGAPORE, AMIC, 1977.
BIBLIOGRAPHY SERIES 6
MEDIUM: GENERAL
CHRON: SURVEY
METH: OTHER OR COMB
GEOG: SINGAPORE
SUBJ: RESEARCH

AN I   06   A01782
SHENG-LI HOU TI PEI-PING PAO-CHIH (NEWSPAPERS
        IN PEIPING AFTER V-J DAY)
MIN-CHU CHOU K'AN NO. 3(27 OCT 1945), 84-5.
##/CHIN-6
                        LANG: CHINESE
CHRON: 1910-1946
GEOG: CHINA
SUBJ: DESCRIPTION

ANDELMAN, DAVID A.   A00115
SINGAPORE PREMIER ADDS TO HIS POWER
NYT 6 FEB 1977
FEER/HO KWON PING CASE
CHRON: 1970-1980
GEOG: SINGAPORE
SUBJ: CONTROL

ANDELMAN, DAVID A.   A00116
IN SINGAPORE, A COMMUNIST SPY DRAMA FEATURES
        BALLERINA, PETER PAN AND SISTER FONG
NYT 20 JUNE 1976
##/SIN
CHRON: 1970-1980
GEOG: SINGAPORE
SUBJ: CONTROL   LAW/ETHICS

ANDELMAN, DAVID A.   A00118
SATELLITE SYSTEM HAS LITTLE EFFECT ON
        INDONESIANS
NYT 20 FEB 1977
##/INDO
MEDIUM: ELECTRONIC
CHRON: 1970-1980
GEOG: INDONESIA
SUBJ: DESCRIPTION DEVELOPMENT

ANDELMAN, DAVID A.   A00117
    INDONESIAN GOVERNMENT IS ATTEMPTING TO GAIN
        BROADER POPULAR SUPPORT AS NATIONAL
        ELECTIONS APPROACH
    NYT 27 JUNE 1976
    ##/INDON
    CHRON: 1970-1980
    GEOG: INDONESIA
    SUBJ: POLIT SCI

ANETA   A01310
    PERSBUREAU
    BATAVIA, G. KOLFF, 1931.
                               LANG: OTHER EUROPEAN
    CHRON: 1910-1946
    GEOG: INDONESIA
    SUBJ: DESCRIPTION

ANG, PSEUD.   09   A00119
    SHANG-HAI PAO YEH TA PA KUNG (THE GREAT
        STRIKE OF NEWSPAPER WORKERS IN SHANGHAI)
    IN CHANG 07C02193, VOL. 1, PP. 116-26.
                         LANG: CHINESE
    CHRON: 1910-1946   VERIF: UNVERIFIED
    GEOG: CHINA
    SUBJ: JRN HISTORY PUBLISHING

ANGLO-INDIAN   A01686
    THE NATIVE PRESS OF INDIA
    ASIATIC QUARTERLY REVIEW X N. S.:19(JULY
        1895), 16-28.
    CHRON: BEFORE 1910
    GEOG: SO/WEST ASI
    SUBJ: DESCRIPTION

ANWAR, H. ROSIHAN   A01311
    IHWAL JURNALISTIK
    JAKARTA, PERSATUAN WARTAWAN INDONESIA, 1974.
                         LANG: MALAY/INDONESIAN
    CHRON: 1970-1980
    GEOG: INDONESIA
    SUBJ: EDUCATION

ANWAR, ROSIHAN   A01984
    THE SOUNDS OF SILENCE
    ASIAWEEK 4:22(9 JUNE 1978), 90.
    ##/INDON
    CHRON: 1970-1980
    GEOG: INDONESIA
    SUBJ: CONTROL

```
AP LOG                                                    A02501
     RODERICK, GRAHAM TO STAFF PEKING BUREAU
     19 MAR 1976
     ##/CHIN-8
     MEDIUM:  GENERAL
     CHRON: 1970-1980
     GEOG:  CHINA
     SUBJ:  FOR CORR      FLOW/AGENCY


AP LOG                                                    A01212
     AP FIRST IN MACAO WITH TELETYPE REPORT
     22 AUG 1977
     ##/HKG
     MEDIUM:  GENERAL
     CHRON: 1970-1980
     GEOG:  MACAO
     SUBJ:  FLOW/AGENCY


AP LOG                                                    A00124
     [IN TOP OF THE REPORT, HONG KONG WATCHING]
     7 JUNE 1976
     ##/HKG
     MEDIUM:  GENERAL
     CHRON: 1970-1980
     GEOG:  HONG KONG    CHINA
     SUBJ:  FOR CORR      FLOW/AGENCY


AP LOG                                                    A00123
     BUREAU CHIEF ZEITLIN BARRED BY PHILIPPINES
     15 NOV 1976
     ##/PHIL
     MEDIUM:  GENERAL
     CHRON: 1970-1980
     GEOG:  PHILIPPINES
     SUBJ:  CONTROL       FOR CORR      FLOW/AGENCY


AP LOG                                                    A00122
     [HONG KONG AS A LISTENING POST]
     7 JUNE 1976
     ##/HKG
     MEDIUM:  GENERAL
     CHRON: 1970-1980
     GEOG:  HONG KONG    CHINA
     SUBJ:  FOR CORR      DESCRIPTION


AP WORLD, THE                                             A01746
     VISIT TO CHINA
     34:3(DEC 1977), 17-19.
     ##/CHIN-5
     CHRON: 1970-1980
     GEOG:  CHINA
     SUBJ:  FOR CORR      FLOW/AGENCY
```

AP WORLD, THE   A02592
    FOR OPENERS, IT'S RODERICK AND GRAHAM IN
        PEKING
    NO. 1(1979), 6-7.
    ##/CHIN-9
    MEDIUM: GENERAL
    CHRON: 1970-1980
    GEOG: CHINA
    SUBJ: FLOW/AGENCY BIOGRAPHY

ARLINGTON, L. C.   A02156
    CHINESE SIGN-BOARD SYMBOLISM
    DIGEST OF THE SYNODAL COMMISSION (CATHOLIC
        CHURCH IN CHINA), 5:3(MAR 1932), 213-23.
    MEDIUM: OTHER
    CHRON: SURVEY
    METH: HISTORICAL
    GEOG: CHINA
    SUBJ: DESCRIPTION

ARMBRUSTER, WILLIAM   A00125
    TAIWAN SHUTS DOWN MAGAZINE
    CSM 3 DEC 1976
    ##/TAI; <TAIWAN POLITICAL REVIEW>.
    CHRON: 1970-1980
    GEOG: TAIWAN
    SUBJ: CONTROL

ARMBRUSTER, WILLIAM   A00126
    TAIWAN BANS PUBLICATION OF NEW POLITICAL
        MAGAZINE
    CSM 6 FEB 1976
    ##/TAI
    CHRON: 1970-1980
    GEOG: TAIWAN
    SUBJ: CONTROL

ARMBRUSTER, WILLIAM   A00412
    EDITOR GOES DOWN WITH HIS JOURNAL
    FEER 94:47(19 NOV 1976), 19.
    ##/TAI; <TAIWAN POLITICAL REVIEW>.
    CHRON: 1970-1980
    GEOG: TAIWAN
    SUBJ: CONTROL   LAW/ETHICS

ARNALDO, CARLOS A.   A00120
    PHILLIPINE MASS MEDIA
    SOLIDARITY 4(JAN 1969), 69-100.
    MEDIUM: GENERAL
                            VERIF: UNVERIFIED
    GEOG: PHILIPPINES
    SUBJ: DESCRIPTION

```
ARNETT, PETER                                          A01261
    THE MISSING 2: A HOPE AND A NEED
    DATELINE [OPC, NEW YORK] 18:1(1974), 68-9.
    ##/FOCO
    MEDIUM:  GENERAL
    CHRON: 1970-1980
    GEOG:  VIETNAM       CAMBODIA    LAOS
    SUBJ:  FOR CORR


ARNETT, PETER                                          A00129
    ARNETT RETURNS TO VIETNAM . . . BRIEFLY
    AP LOG (28 MAR 1977), 1, 4.
    ##/VN
    MEDIUM:  GENERAL
    CHRON: 1970-1980
    GEOG:  VIETNAM
    SUBJ:  FOR CORR


ARNETT, PETER                                          A02191
    GOSH, WAR IS HELL
    DATELINE [OPC, NEW YORK] 13:1(APR 1969), 68-9.
    CHRON: 1960-1970
    GEOG:  VIETNAM       U.S.
    SUBJ:  FOR CORR


ARNETT, PETER                                          A01643
    TET COVERAGE: A DEBATE RENEWED
    COL JRN REVIEW XVI:5(JAN/FEB 1978), 44-7.
    ##/VN; REVIEW OF <BIG STORY> BRAESTRUP B01368.
    MEDIUM:  GENERAL
    CHRON: 1970-1980
    GEOG:  VIETNAM       U.S.
    SUBJ:  FOR CORR      FLOW/AGENCY JRN HISTORY


ARNOT, SANDFORD                                        A01428
    A SKETCH OF THE HISTORY OF THE INDIAN PRESS
        . . .WITH A DISCLOSURE OF THE TRUE CAUSES
    LONDON, WILLIAM LOW, 1829.
    CHRON: BEFORE 1910
    GEOG:  SO/WEST ASI
    SUBJ:  CONTROL       DESCRIPTION


ASIA FOUNDATION PROGRAM QUARTERLY                      A00128
    SEA PRESS CENTER
    (SEPT 1968), 12.
    CHRON: 1960-1970        VERIF:  UNVERIFIED
    GEOG:  SEV ASIA
    SUBJ:  DESCRIPTION EDUCATION    FOR CORR
```

ASIAN ALMANAC   A00132
     MALAYSIA: INAUGURATION OF BERNAMA'S NEWS
          SERVICE
     6:30(27 JULY 1968), 2835.
     MEDIUM: GENERAL
     CHRON: 1960-1970   VERIF: UNVERIFIED
     GEOG: MALAYSIA
     SUBJ: FLOW/AGENCY

ASIAN ALMANAC   A00131
     MALAYSIA: CONTROL OF PUBLICATIONS
     3:35(FEB 27-MAR 5, 1966),1447.
     CHRON: 1960-1970   VERIF: UNVERIFIED
     GEOG: MALAYSIA
     SUBJ: CONTROL

ASIAN MASS COMMUNICATION RESEARCH AND   A00133
          INFORMATION CENTRE
     COMMUNICATIONS AND CHANGE IN RURAL ASIA; A
          SELECT BIBLIOGRAPHY
     SINGAPORE, AMIC, 1973.
     #3;, 50 PP.
     MEDIUM: GENERAL
     CHRON: SURVEY
     GEOG: SEV ASIA
     SUBJ: RESEARCH   DEVELOPMENT

ASIAN MASS COMMUNICATION RESEARCH AND   A01215
          INFORMATION CENTRE
     LIST OF THESES 1973 AND 1974
     SINGAPORE, AMIC, 1976.
     MEDIUM: GENERAL
     CHRON: 1970-1980
     GEOG: SEV ASIA
     SUBJ: RESEARCH

ASIAN MASS COMMUNICATION RESEARCH AND   A01214
          INFORMATION CENTRE
     LIST OF THESES 1972
     SINGAPORE, AMIC, 1974.
     MEDIUM: GENERAL
     CHRON: 1970-1980
     GEOG: SEV ASIA
     SUBJ: RESEARCH

ASIAN MASS COMMUNICATION RESEARCH AND   A01213
          INFORMATION CENTRE
     LIST OF THESES 1971
     SINGAPORE, AMIC, 1973.
     MEDIUM: GENERAL
     CHRON: 1970-1980
     GEOG: SEV ASIA
     SUBJ: RESEARCH

ASIAN PRESS, THE   A00134
        SEOUL, READERSHIP RESEARCH CENTER, PFA,
              INSTITUTE FOR COMMUNICATION RESEARCH,
              SEOUL NATIONAL UNIVERSITY, SEOUL, ANNUAL.
        ##/ASIA
        CHRON: 1970-1980
        GEOG: SEV ASIA
        SUBJ: DESCRIPTION

ASIAN PRINTER, THE   A02076
        COLOR REPRODUCTION IN JAPANESE NEWSPAPERS
        9:2(1969), 56-7.
        CHRON: 1960-1970
        GEOG: EAST ASIA
        SUBJ: DESCRIPTION PRINTING

ASIAN PRINTER, THE   A02075
        MASS COMMUNICATION IN JAPAN
        I:3(DEC 1958), 69-70.
        MEDIUM: GENERAL
        CHRON: 1946-1960
        GEOG: EAST ASIA
        SUBJ: DESCRIPTION

ASIAN PRINTER, THE   A02450
        LAOTIAN STUDENTS OF BROTHER AND SISTER
              TRAINING IN MONOTYPE OPERATION IN JAPAN
        2:2(1959), 37-8.
        CHRON: 1946-1960
        GEOG: LAOS   EAST ASIA
        SUBJ: EDUCATION   PRINTING

ASIAN, THE   A00127
        CAMBODIAN CENSORS STILL DOG THE PRESS
        13-19 FEB 1972
        ##/CAMB
        CHRON: 1970-1980
        GEOG: VIETNAM
        SUBJ: CONTROL   FOR CORR   DESCRIPTION

ASIAN-AFRICAN JOURNALISTS CONFERENCE   A02074
        THE PRELIMINARY SESSION OF THE FIRST
              ASIAN-AFRICAN JOURNALISTS CONFERENCE
        DJAKARTA, INDONESIA, DEPARTMENT OF
              INFORMATION, 1963.
        CHRON: 1960-1970
        GEOG: INDONESIA   SEV ASIA
        SUBJ: DESCRIPTION

ASIATIC JOURNAL, THE   A01313
      THE BOMBAY PRESS
      XXIII O. S.:CXXXVI(APR 1827), 491-4.
      CHRON: BEFORE 1910
      GEOG: SO/WEST ASI
      SUBJ: CONTROL   LAW/ETHICS

ASIATIC JOURNAL, THE   A01312
      THE BOMBAY PRESS
      XXIII O. S.:CXXXV(MAR 1827), 309-11.
      CHRON: BEFORE 1910
      GEOG: SO/WEST ASI
      SUBJ: CONTROL   · LAW/ETHICS

ASIATIC JOURNAL, THE   A01316
      MALACCA: THE MALACCA OBSERVER
      XXIV O. S.:CXLII(OCT 1827), 508.
      CHRON: BEFORE 1910
      GEOG: MALAYSIA
      SUBJ: DESCRIPTION

ASIATIC JOURNAL, THE   A01315
      SINGAPORE: THE PRESS
      XXIV O. S.:CXLI(SEPT 1827), 380-1.
      CHRON: BEFORE 1910
      GEOG: SINGAPORE
      SUBJ: CONTROL   DESCRIPTION

ASIATIC JOURNAL, THE   A01314
      MALACCA: CHINESE NEWSPAPER.
      XXIV O. S.:CXL(AUG 1827), 250-1.
      CHRON: BEFORE 1910
      GEOG: MALAYSIA
      SUBJ: DESCRIPTION

ASIATIC QUARTERLY REVIEW   A01687
      EDUCATION BY NEWSPAPER
      XIV 3RD SERIES:27(JULY 1902), 61-75.
      CHRON: BEFORE 1910
      GEOG: SO/WEST ASI
      SUBJ: CROSS CULTU EDUCATION

```
ASIAWEEK                                        A01583
    PAPER TIGER
    4:6(17 FEB 1978), 14-5.
    ##/SIN-2; LEE EU SENG.
    CHRON: 1970-1980
    GEOG:   SINGAPORE
    SUBJ:   CONTROL      LAW/ETHICS


ASIAWEEK                                        A02157
    OFFERS INVITED: ONE TV STATION
    4:35(8 SEPT 1978), 63-5.
    ##/HKG
    MEDIUM:  ELECTRONIC
    CHRON: 1970-1980
    GEOG:   HONG KONG
    SUBJ:   OTHER JRN


ASIAWEEK                                        A02257
    UPS AND DOWNS OF A CIRCULATION WAR
    4:51/52(29 DEC-5 JAN 1979), 11.
    ##/PHIL
    CHRON: 1970-1980
    GEOG:   PHILIPPINES
    SUBJ:   DESCRIPTION OTHER JRN


ASIAWEEK                                        A02256
    PAPER CHASE
    4:49(15 DEC 1978), 9.
    ##/PHIL; <MANILA JOURNAL>.
    CHRON: 1970-1980
    GEOG:   PHILIPPINES
    SUBJ:   DESCRIPTION OTHER JRN


ASIAWEEK                                        A02255
    STOP THE PRESSES
    4:39(6 OCT 1978), 9.
    ##/PHIL; <FINANCIAL TIMES>.
    CHRON: 1970-1980
    GEOG:   PHILIPPINES
    SUBJ:   DESCRIPTION OTHER JRN


ASIAWEEK                                        A02254
    COMEBACK FOR THE KISS
    4:25(30 JUNE 1978), 53.
    I ##/SWAS
    MEDIUM:  FILM
    CHRON: 1970-1980
    GEOG:   SO/WEST ASI
    SUBJ:   CONTROL      CROSS CULTU
```

ASIAWEEK   A02253
     AMERICA'S NO. 5 BUYS MALAYSIAN
     4:19(19 MAY 1978), 39-40.
     ##/MAL-3
     CHRON: 1970-1980
     GEOG: MALAYSIA
     SUBJ: DESCRIPTION OTHER JRN

ASIAWEEK   A02252
     AN INSTITUTION TURNS '30'
     4:12(31 MAR 1978), 44-5.
     ##/HKG; <TA KUNG PAO>.
     CHRON: 1970-1980
     GEOG: HONG KONG
     SUBJ: DESCRIPTION

ASIAWEEK   A02251
     WHERE 'D' MEANS DON'T PUBLISH
     4:12(31 MAR 1978), 18-19.
     ##/ASIA
     CHRON: 1970-1980
     GEOG: AUSTRALASIA
     SUBJ: CONTROL

ASIAWEEK   A02537
     A SUDDEN, SURPRISING AMNESTY
     4:47(1 DEC 1978), 18-19.
     ##/SIN-2; SAID ZAHARI.
     CHRON: 1970-1980
     GEOG: SINGAPORE
     SUBJ: CONTROL   LAW/ETHICS BIOGRAPHY

ASIAWEEK   A02503
     SINGING IN THE WAR
     5:3(26 JAN 1979), 6.
     ##/THAI
     MEDIUM: GENERAL
     CHRON: 1970-1980
     GEOG: THAILAND   VIETNAM   CAMBODIA
     SUBJ: FOR CORR

ASIAWEEK   A02502
     NEWS ON THE LEVEL
     5:6(16 FEB 1979), 10-11.
     ##/ASIA
     MEDIUM: GENERAL
     CHRON: 1970-1980
     GEOG: MALAYSIA   SEV ASIA
     SUBJ: CONTROL   FLOW/AGENCY

ASIAWEEK   A02802
        TELEVISION: HEYDAY OF THE ROBOTS
        5:26(6 JULY 1979), 8.
        ##/PHIL
        MEDIUM: ELECTRONIC
        CHRON: 1970-1980
        GEOG: OSEAS CHIN   EAST ASIA
        SUBJ: DESCRIPTION OTHER JRN

ASIAWEEK   A02801
        STAYING TUNED
        5:18(11 MAY 1979), 18.
        ##/TAI
        MEDIUM: ELECTRONIC
        CHRON: 1970-1980
        GEOG: TAIWAN
        SUBJ: DESCRIPTION

ASIAWEEK   A02819
        CHINESE REVERSAL FOR SINGAPORE
        5:28(20 JULY 1979), 16.
        ##/SIN-2
        CHRON: 1970-1980
        GEOG: SINGAPORE   OSEAS CHIN
        SUBJ: DESCRIPTION LANGUAGE

ASIAWEEK   A01216
        THE WORD IS CREDIBILITY
        (15 JULY 1977), 42-3.
        ##/HKG; RADIO TV HONG KONG.
        MEDIUM: ELECTRONIC
        CHRON: 1970-1980
        GEOG: HONG KONG
        SUBJ: DESCRIPTION

ASPIRAS, JOSE D.   A00136
        THE PHILIPPINES PRESS TODAY
        IN FOOKIEN F02714, P. 242.
        CHRON: 1960-1970
        GEOG: PHILIPPINES
        SUBJ: DESCRIPTION

ASPIRAS, JOSE D.   A00135
        THE PRESS IN NATION-BUILDING
        IN FOOKIEN F02714
        CHRON: 1960-1970   VERIF: UNVERIFIED
        GEOG: PHILIPPINES
        SUBJ: DEVELOPMENT

ASSEGAFF, D. H.   A00138
    HIGHER EDUCATION IN JOURNALISM COMMUNICATION
    DEN PASAR, SEM. ON COMM. TEACHING AND
        TRAINING, 1972.
    ##/INDO; MIMEO, 10 PP.
    MEDIUM: GENERAL
    CHRON: 1970-1980
    GEOG: INDONESIA
    SUBJ: EDUCATION

ASSEGAFF,D. H. AND ASTRID SUSANTO   A00137
    COUNTRY REPORT--INDONESIA
    KUALA LUMPUR, SEM. ON COMM. TEACHING AND
        TRAINING, 1972.
    ##/INDO; MIMEO, 13 PP.
    MEDIUM: GENERAL
    CHRON: 1970-1980
    GEOG: INDONESIA
    SUBJ: EDUCATION

ASSOCIATED PRESS(PHIL. EVENING   A00139
        BULLETIN)
    1 ST TV WOWS TRIBESMEN IN BORNEO JUNGLE
    18 JULY 1976
    ##/BRU
    MEDIUM: ELECTRONIC
    CHRON: 1970-1980
    GEOG: BRUNEI
    SUBJ: DESCRIPTION DEVELOPMENT

ATLAS   A00140
    MOVIES ARE BETTER . . . IN THAILAND, ANYWAY
    19:12(DEC 1970), 58-9.
    ##/THAI; FROM <THE INVESTOR>, 1970.
    MEDIUM: FILM
    CHRON: 1960-1970
    GEOG: THAILAND
    SUBJ: DESCRIPTION

ATLAS WORLD PRESS REVIEW   A00141
    ASIAN FILMS: ART, GORE, AND SKIN
    23:9(SEPT 1976), 50-1.
    ##/ASIA; FROM <ASIAWEEK>, 12 MARCH.
    MEDIUM: FILM
    CHRON: 1970-1980
    GEOG: SEV ASIA
    SUBJ: DESCRIPTION

AUSTRALIAN NATIONAL LIBRARY   A01747
    CHECKLIST OF SOUTHEAST ASIAN NEWSPAPERS
    CANBERRA, AUSTRALIAN NATIONAL LIBRARY, 1970.
    CHRON: SURVEY
    GEOG: SEV ASIA
    SUBJ: RESEARCH

AVELING, HARRY   A00142
     THE IMPORTANCE OF LITERATURE
     STRAITS TIMES 2 JUNE 1973
     ##/MAL-2
     CHRON: SURVEY
     GEOG: MALAYSIA
     SUBJ: LITERATURE

AW BOON HAW   A02158
     NEARLY SIXTY YEARS OF CHINESE JOURNALISM
     WORLD'S PRESS NEWS (MALAYAN SURVEY
          SUPPLEMENT) 17:428(13 MAY 1937), XII.
     ##/MAL-3
     CHRON: 1910-1946
     GEOG: MALAYSIA   SINGAPORE
     SUBJ: DESCRIPTION

AWANOHARA, SUSUMU   A02552
     IN SEARCH OF A GENERATION
     FEER 103:10(9 MAR 1979), 26.
     ##/SIN-2
     CHRON: 1970-1980
     GEOG: SINGAPORE
     SUBJ: DESCRIPTION LANGUAGE

AWANOHARA, SUSUMU   A01953
     STORY WITH A CATCH IN IT
     FEER 99:11(17 MAR 1978), 33-4.
     ##/EASI
     CHRON: 1970-1980
     GEOG: EAST ASIA
     SUBJ: LAW/ETHICS

AYER, FREDERIC L.   A01430
     QUANTIFYING THAI OPINION
     UNITED ASIA XVI:16(NOV-DEC 1964), 351-5.
     ##/THAI
     MEDIUM: GENERAL
     CHRON: 1960-1970
     METH: SURVEY
     GEOG: THAILAND
     SUBJ: CROSS CULTU OTHER JRN

BA THAN, U   B00144
     THE PRESS: EARLIER NEWSPAPERS IN BURMA IN
          <BURMESE YEARBOOK: 1957-8> 29-33, 35.
     RANGOON, STUDENT PRESS, 1957.
     ##/BURMA
     CHRON: 1910-1946
     GEOG: BURMA
     SUBJ: JRN HISTORY

BA THEIN, U   B02609
    BURMESE NEWSPAPERS AND THE BURMESE LANGUAGE
    BURMESE REVIEW (29 JULY 1946), 6.
    ##/BUR; REPRINTED IN WAIZZA W02586;
        PSEUDONYM IS SHWE-U-DAUNG.
    CHRON: SURVEY
    GEOG: BURMA
    SUBJ: JRN HISTORY LANGUAGE   LITERATURE

BACZYNSKYJ, BORIS   B00145
    BANNING FRIENDS
    FEER LXXI:7(13 FEB 1971), 26-7.
    ##/CAMB; CLOSING OF 3 CAMBODIAN PAPERS.
    CHRON: 1970-1980
    GEOG: CAMBODIA
    SUBJ: CONTROL

BAILEY, GEORGE ARTHUR   B00146
    THE VIETNAM WAR ACCORDING TO CHET, DAVID,
        . . .:A CONTENT ANALYSIS OF JOURNALISTIC
        PERFORMANCES BY NETWORK TELEVISION. . .
        ANCHORMEN . . .
    PHD DISS, UNIVERSITY OF WISCONSIN, 1973.
    INTL DISS 34-4182A
    MEDIUM: ELECTRONIC
    CHRON: 1960-1970   VERIF: UNVERIFIED
    METH: OTHER OR COMB
    GEOG: VIETNAM   U.S.
    SUBJ: DESCRIPTION

BALK, ALFRED   B02159
    MISSING INGREDIENT: A VILLAIN
    DATELINE [OPC, NEW YORK] XII:1(1968), 41-3.
    MEDIUM: GENERAL
    CHRON: 1960-1970
    GEOG: VIETNAM   U.S.
    SUBJ: FOR CORR   OTHER JRN

BALL, JAMES DYER   B00147
    NEWSPAPERS AND PERIODICALS IN <THINGS CHINESE
        OR, NOTES CONNECTED WITH CHINA>
    LONDON, JOHN MURRAY, 1926, 5TH ED.
    ##/CHIN-2; PP422-427, THIS ED REPUB. BY TOWER
        BOOK, DETROIT, 1971
        NUC<56, 32:328.
    CHRON: BEFORE 1910
    GEOG: CHINA
    SUBJ: JRN HISTORY

BAND, R. W. I.   B01985
    'OPERATION NEWSPAPER' IN A CAMP ON THE 'DEATH
        RAILWAY'
    MALAYSIA (MAR 1970), 13-15.
    CHRON: 1910-1946
    GEOG: THAILAND   MALAYSIA
    SUBJ: JRN HISTORY DESCRIPTION

BANGALORE CORRESONDENT   B01688
     THE MYSORE PRESS ACT: HOW TO DEAL WITH INDIAN
          SEDITIOUS WRITING
     ASIATIC QUARTERLY REVIEW XXVII:54(APR 1909),
          280-9.
     CHRON: BEFORE 1910
     GEOG: SO/WEST ASI
     SUBJ: CONTROL   LAW/ETHICS

BANNING, WILLIAM P.   B02077
     STARTING AN AMERICAN NEWSPAPER IN CHINA
     PUBLISHERS' GUIDE [ADVERTISING NEWS] XXI
          (1912), 39-41, 45.
     ##/CHIN-7
     CHRON: 1910-1946
     GEOG: CHINA   OTHER
     SUBJ: DESCRIPTION

BARBER, STEPHEN   B00148
     'DISINFORMATION' ON THE REBOUND
     FEER 91:5(30 JAN 1976), 14.
     ##/OTHR
     MEDIUM: GENERAL
     CHRON: 1970-1980
     GEOG: SEV ASIA
     SUBJ: PROPAGANDA FOR CORR   FLOW/AGENCY

BARNETT, SUZANNE W.   B02610
     SILENT EVANGELISM: PRESBYTERIANS AND THE
          MISSION PRESS IN CHINA, 1807-1860.
     JOURNAL OF PRESBYTERIAN HISTORY 49:4(WINTER
          1971), 287-302.
     CHRON: BEFORE 1910
     METH: HISTORICAL
     GEOG: CHINA
     SUBJ: JRN HISTORY PRINTING   PUBLISHING

BAROOAH, RENEE   B00149
     MECHANISM OF A CHINESE NEWSPAPER
     VIDURA (JUNE 1973), 201,203.
     ##/CHIN-3; FROM MCFARQUHAR M00775.
     CHRON: 1970-1980
     GEOG: CHINA
     SUBJ: DESCRIPTION PUBLISHING

BARUNG, E. U.   B02288
     JAPANESE-OWNED PAPERS LOSE CIRCULATION
     THE CHINA WEEKLY REVIEW 57:13(29 AUG 1931),
          512.
     CHRON: 1910-1946
     GEOG: CHINA   OTHER
     SUBJ: DESCRIPTION OTHER JRN

BAUTISTA, JOSE P.   B00150
     THE PHILIPPINE PRESS TODAY
     IN <FOOKIEN TIMES YEARBOOK 1961>
     CHRON: 1960-1970   VERIF: UNVERIFIED
     GEOG: PHILIPPINES
     SUBJ: DESCRIPTION

BEAGARIE, MAX   B00151
     READ ALL ABOUT IT
     NEW CHINA II:2(SEPT 1976), 14-6.
     ##/CHIN-2
     CHRON: 1970-1980
     GEOG: CHINA
     SUBJ: DESCRIPTION

BEECH, KEYES   B00152
     DATELINE: TOKYO
     ESQUIRE XXXVIII:6(DEC 1952), 126, 7, 198,
          200, 202.
     ##/EASI
     MEDIUM: GENERAL
     CHRON: 1946-1960
     GEOG: EAST ASIA
     SUBJ: FOR CORR   DESCRIPTION

BEECH, KEYES   B00154
     DATELINE: TOKYO
     THE ASIA MAIL I:6(MARCH 1977).
     ##/EASI; FROM <ESQUIRE> BEECH B00152.
     MEDIUM: GENERAL
     CHRON: 1946-1960
     GEOG: EAST ASIA
     SUBJ: FOR CORR   DESCRIPTION

BEECH, KEYES   B00153
     TOKYO AND POINTS EAST
     GARDEN CITY, N. Y., DOUBLEDAY, 1954.
     MEDIUM: GENERAL
     CHRON: 1946-1960
     GEOG: EAST ASIA
     SUBJ: FOR CORR   DESCRIPTION

BEECH, KEYES   B02160
     NUMBER 1 SHIMBUN ALLEY
     DATELINE [OPC, NEW YORK] 3:1(1959), 23.
     CHRON: 1946-1960
     GEOG: EAST ASIA
     SUBJ: FOR CORR

BELL, HENRY HESKETH   B01431
    FOREIGN COLONIAL ADMINISTRATION IN, THE FAR
        EAST
    LONDON, E. ARNOLD & CO., 1928.
    ##/INDON-2; CINEMA, PP. 120-4.
    MEDIUM: FILM
    CHRON: 1910-1946
    GEOG: SEV ASIA
    SUBJ: DESCRIPTION CROSS CULTU

BENNETT, ADRIAN A.   B00692
    RESEARCH GUIDE TO THE <WAN-KUO KUNG PAO>(THE
        GLOBE MAGAZINE), 1874-1883
    SAN FRANCISCO, CHINESE MATERIALS CENTER, 1976.
    CHRON: BEFORE 1910   VERIF: UNVERIFIED
    METH: HISTORICAL
    GEOG: CHINA
    SUBJ: RESEARCH

BENNETT, ADRIAN A.   B00156
    RESEARCH GUIDE TO THE <CHIAO-HUI SHIN-PAO>(THE
        CHURCH NEWS) 1868-1874
    SAN FRANCISCO, CHINESE MATERIALS CENTER, 1975.
    CHRON: BEFORE 1910
    METH: HISTORICAL
    GEOG: CHINA
    SUBJ: RESEARCH   JRN HISTORY

BENNETT, ADRIAN A. AND   B00155
        KWANG-CHING LIU
    CHRISTIANITY IN THE CHINESE IDIOM: YOUNG J.
        ALLEN AND THE EARLY CHAO-HUI HSIN-PAO,
        1868-1870
    IN FAIRBANK F02558, PP. 159-96.
    CHRON: BEFORE 1910
    METH: HISTORICAL
    GEOG: CHINA
    SUBJ: JRN HISTORY

BENNETT, ADRIAN ARTHUR, III   B01333
    MISSIONARY JOURNALISM IN NINETEENTH-CENTURY
        CHINA: YOUNG J. ALLEN AND THE EARLY
        'WAN-KUO KUNG-PAO' [GLOBE MAGAZINE]
    PHD DISS, UNIVERSITY OF CALIFORNIA/DAVIS,
        1970.
    U. MICROFILMS, 71-15,519.
    CHRON: BEFORE 1910
    METH: HISTORICAL
    GEOG: CHINA
    SUBJ: JRN HISTORY

BERGER, VIRGIL   B02161
    HOW RED CHINA GETS THE MESSAGE
    DATELINE [OPC, NEW YORK] XI:1(1967), 38-40.
    WALL POSTERS
    MEDIUM: OTHER
    CHRON: 1960-1970
    GEOG: CHINA
    SUBJ: DESCRIPTION

BERITA HARIAN   B01986
    100 WARTAWAN, AKADEMIS SERTAI SIDANG
        JOURNALISME
    19 MAR 1978
    ##/MAL-3; SUNDAY MALAYSIAN EDITION.
                              LANG: MALAY/INDONESIAN
    CHRON: 1970-1980
    GEOG: MALAYSIA
    SUBJ: EDUCATION

BERITA HARIAN   B01814
    2 AKHBAR JAKARTA DIBENTAR TERBIT SEMULA
    5 FEB 1978
    ##/INDON; SUNDAY MALAYSIA EDITION.
                              LANG: MALAY/INDONESIAN
    CHRON: 1970-1980
    GEOG: INDONESIA
    SUBJ: CONTROL

BERITA HARIAN   B00158
    HUSSEIN, AZMI DEDAHKAN KOMPLOT DI TV S'PURA
    27 JUNE 1976
    ##/MAL; SUNDAY MALAYSIA EDITION.
    MEDIUM: GENERAL   LANG: MALAY/INDONESIAN
    CHRON: 1970-1980
    GEOG: SINGAPORE   MALAYSIA
    SUBJ: CONTROL   LAW/ETHICS

BERITA HARIAN   B00157
    6 DIKURNIA 'PEJUANG SASTRA'
    30 MAY 1976
    ##/MAL; SAMAD ISMAIL; SUNDAY MALAYSIA EDITION.
                              LANG: MALAY/INDONESIAN
    CHRON: 1970-1980
    GEOG: MALAYSIA
    SUBJ: LITERATURE CONTROL   LAW/ETHICS

BERITA HARIAN   B00161
    PERANAN AKHBAR2 CHINA DI BIDANG BAHASA,
        SASTRA MELAYU
    5 SEPT 1976
    ##/MAL; SUNDAY MALAYSIA EDITION.
                              LANG: MALAY/INDONESIAN
    CHRON: 1970-1980
    GEOG: MALAYSIA
    SUBJ: DESCRIPTION LITERATURE

BERITA HARIAN   B00160
    SAMAD DAN SAMANI DIHARAM KE S'PURA
    15 AUG 1976
    ##/MAL; SUNDAY MALAYSIA EDITION.
    MEDIUM: GENERAL   LANG: MALAY/INDONESIAN
    CHRON: 1970-1980
    GEOG: MALAYSIA   SINGAPORE
    SUBJ: LAW/ETHICS CONTROL

BERITA HARIAN   B00159
        IKLAN TAK JUJUR: KERAJAAN DISERU AWASI
        1 AUG 1976
        ##/MAL; SUNDAY MALAYSIA EDITION.
        MEDIUM: OTHER   LANG: MALAY/INDONESIAN
        CHRON: 1970-1980
        GEOG: MALAYSIA
        SUBJ: OTHER JRN

BERITA MINGGU   B02058
        SHOOTING FILEM KE-2 PERFIMA MINGGU DEPAN
        16 APR 1978
        ##/MAL-3;SUNDAY, MALAYSIAN EDITION.
        MEDIUM: FILM   LANG: MALAY/INDONESIAN
        CHRON: 1970-1980
        GEOG: MALAYSIA
        SUBJ: DESCRIPTION

BERNAMA   B00162
        [ACT OF PARLIAMENT ESTABLISHING BERNAMA]
        KUALA LUMPUR, NP, 1967.
        ##/MAL-2; 12 PP PAMPHLET, ACT OF PARLIAMENT
             ESTABLISHING BERNAMA
        MEDIUM: GENERAL
        CHRON: 1960-1970
        GEOG: MALAYSIA
        SUBJ: FLOW/AGENCY DESCRIPTION

BERNAMA   B00164
        BERNAMA TO LAUNCH NEWS SERVICE IN MAY:
             MALAYSIAN NATIONAL NEWS AGENCY HAS
             MULTI-RACIAL STAFF
        NP, NP, [1968?].
        MIMEO
        MEDIUM: GENERAL
        CHRON: 1960-1970
        GEOG: MALAYSIA
        SUBJ: FLOW/AGENCY

BERNAMA   B00163
        BERNAMA: MALAYSIAN NATIONAL NEWS AGENCY
        KUALA LUMPUR, NP, 1968.
        ##/MAL; 12 PP; BROCHURE INCLUDES COPY OF
             FORMATION LAW
        MEDIUM: GENERAL
        CHRON: 1960-1970
        GEOG: MALAYSIA
        SUBJ: FLOW/AGENCY LAW/ETHICS

BERNSTEIN, STANLEY O.   B00165
        CHINESE COMMUNIST PRESS
        FOI CENTER REPORT, NO. 84 (AUG 1962).
        ##/CHIN-2
        CHRON: SURVEY
        GEOG: CHINA
        SUBJ: DESCRIPTION CONTROL

BERTON, PETER AND EUGENE WU   B01432
    CONTEMPORARY CHINA: A RESEARCH GUIDE
    STANFORD, CAL., HOOVER INSTITUTION, 1967.
    SELECTED SERIAL PUBLICATIONS, PP. 333-481.
    CHRON: SURVEY
    GEOG: CHINA
    SUBJ: RESEARCH

BETTS, RUSSELL H.   B00166
    THE MASS MEDIA OF MALAYA AND SINGAPORE AS
        OF 1965: A SURVEY OF THE LITERATURE
    CAMBRIDGE, MIT/CENTER FOR INTL. STUDIES, 1969.
    ##/VF
    MEDIUM: GENERAL
    CHRON: 1960-1970
    GEOG: MALAYSIA   SINGAPORE
    SUBJ: RESEARCH

BETTS, T. J.   B01783
    CHINESE PUBLIC OPINION
    FOREIGN AFFAIRS 11:3(APR 1933), 470-7.
    CHRON: 1910-1946
    GEOG: CHINA
    SUBJ: DESCRIPTION

BHATHAL, R. S.   B00167
    POWER AND STABILITY
    FEER 77:32(5 AUG 1972), 12, 13.
    ##/SIN
    MEDIUM: GENERAL
    CHRON: 1970-1980
    GEOG: SINGAPORE
    SUBJ: CONTROL

BIGGERSTAFF, KNIGHT   B00738
    THE NANKING PRESS: APRIL-SEPTEMBER 1949
    FAR EASTERN SURVEY 19(8 MAR 1950), 50-4.
    ##/CHIN-5
    CHRON: 1910-1946
    GEOG: CHINA
    SUBJ: DESCRIPTION

BILAINKIN, GEORGE   B01433
    HAIL PENANG
    LONDON, S. LOW, MARSTON & CO., 1932.
    ##/MAL-2; CINEMA, PP. 58-66.
    MEDIUM: FILM
    CHRON: 1910-1946
    GEOG: MALAYSIA
    SUBJ: DESCRIPTION

BILAINKIN, GEORGE   B01367
    MORE ABOUT THE CINEMA AND THE ORIENT
    BRITISH MALAYA VIII:12(APR 1934), 263.
    ##/MAL-3; SEE WEAIT W01418 AND HARLOFF H01392.
    MEDIUM: FILM
    CHRON: 1910-1946
    GEOG: SEV ASIA
    SUBJ: CONTROL   DESCRIPTION

BIRCH, E. W.   B00169
    THE VERNACULAR PRESS IN THE STRAITS
    JOURNAL STRAITS BRANCH, RAS 2[?]:4
        (DEC 1879), 51-4.
    ##/MAL
    CHRON: BEFORE 1910
    GEOG: SINGAPORE   MALAYSIA
    SUBJ: DESCRIPTION

BIRD, KAI   B00170
    BHUTTO TIGHTENS THE SCREWS
    FEER 91:12(MAR 1976), 32-3.
    ##/SwAS
    CHRON: 1970-1980
    GEOG: SO/WEST ASI
    SUBJ: CONTROL

BITZ, IRA   B01434
    A BIBLIOGRAPHY OF ENGLISH LANGUAGE SOURCE
        MATERIALS ON THAILAND IN THE HUMANITIES,
        SOCIAL SCIENCES, AND PHYSICAL SCIENCES
    WASHINGTON, D. C., AMERICAN U. CENTER FOR
        RESEARCH IN SOCIAL SYSTEMS, 1968.
    MEDIUM: GENERAL
    CHRON: SURVEY
    GEOG: THAILAND
    SUBJ: RESEARCH

BLACKMAN, SAMUEL G.   B02162
    EVOLUTION OF THE NEWS SERVICES
    DATELINE [OPC, NEW YORK] 19:1(1976), 30-2.
    MEDIUM: GENERAL
    CHRON: 1970-1980
    GEOG: SEV ASIA   WORLD
    SUBJ: FOR CORR   FLOW/AGENCY

BLAKER, JAMES ROLAND   B02504
    THE CHINESE NEWSPAPER IN THE PHILIPPINES:
        TOWARDS THE DEFINITION OF A TOOL
    ASIAN STUDIES [QUEZON CITY] 3:2(AUG 1965),
        243-61.
    ##/PHIL
    CHRON: SURVEY
    METH: OTHER OR COMB
    GEOG: OSEAS CHIN OTHER
    SUBJ: RESEARCH

BLOCKER, JOEL   B00171
     THE BAD NEWS FROM UNESCO
     COL JRN REVIEW (MAR/APR 1976), 57-60.
     ##/INTL
     MEDIUM: GENERAL
     CHRON: 1970-1980
     GEOG: WORLD
     SUBJ: CONTROL   FLOW/AGENCY

BLUMBERG, NATHAN B.   B02078
     IN BANGKOK: THE ANTENNAE ARE UP
     MONTANA JOURNALISM REVIEW NO. 5 (1962), 30-2.
     MEDIUM: GENERAL
     CHRON: 1960-1970
     GEOG: THAILAND
     SUBJ: DESCRIPTION

BOCCARDI, LOUIS D.   B01279
     A LOOK AT CHINA: MONGOLIA TO CANTON
     AP LOG (26 SEPT 1977), 1, 4.
     ##/CHIN-4
     MEDIUM: GENERAL
     CHRON: 1970-1980
     GEOG: CHINA
     SUBJ: FOR CORR   FLOW/AGENCY DESCRIPTION

BOGART, LEO   B00174
     THE OVERSEAS NEWSMAN: A 1967 PROFILE STUDY
     JQ 45:2(SUMMER 1968), 293-306.
     ##/FOCO
     MEDIUM: GENERAL
     CHRON: 1960-1970
     METH: SURVEY
     GEOG: WORLD
     SUBJ: FOR CORR

BOGUSLAV, DAVID   B00175
     RECOLLECTIONS OF 30 YEARS OF PHILIPPINES
          JOURNALISM
     IN <FOOKIEN TIMES YEARBOOK 1956>, P. 51.
     FAMOUS PHIL. JOURNALISTS, 1926-56.
     CHRON: SURVEY   VERIF: UNVERIFIED
     GEOG: PHILIPPINES
     SUBJ: BIOGRAPHY   JRN HISTORY

BOJESEN, C. C. AND REWI ALLEY   B01672
     CHINA'S RURAL PAPER INDUSTRY
     THE CHINA JOURNAL XXVIII:5(MAY 1938), 233-43.
     PRECEDED BY PHOTOS
     CHRON: 1910-1946
     GEOG: CHINA
     SUBJ: PRINTING

BONAVIA, DAVID   B02258
      TRAVELER'S TALES
      FEER 100:23(9 JUNE 1978), 17.
      ##/CHIN-8
      MEDIUM: OTHER
      CHRON: 1970-1980
      GEOG: CHINA
      SUBJ: PROPAGANDA DESCRIPTION

BONAVIA, DAVID   B02555
      OL'MAN RIVER AND MICKEY MOUSE WIN THE CHINESE
      FEER 103:11(16 MAR 1979), 83-4.
      ##/CHIN-9
      MEDIUM: GENERAL
      CHRON: 1970-1980
      GEOG: CHINA   U.S.
      SUBJ: FOR CORR   CROSS CULTU

BONAVIA, DAVID   B02554
      PEKING FEELS A BREATH OF SPRING
      FEER 103:11(16 MAR 1979), 37, 39.
      ##/CHIN-9
      CHRON: 1970-1980
      GEOG: CHINA
      SUBJ: CONTROL   DESCRIPTION

BONAVIA, DAVID   B02553
      A ZHANGE OUT OF ZHONGGUO
      FEER 103:2(12 JAN 1979), 26.
      ##/CHIN-9
      CHRON: 1970-1980
      GEOG: CHINA
      SUBJ: LANGUAGE

BONAVIA, DAVID   B00177
      CHINA'S WINDOW ON THE WORLD
      FEER 93:29(16 JULY 1976), 28.
      ##/CHIN; REFERENCE NEWS.
      CHRON: SURVEY
      GEOG: CHINA
      SUBJ: DESCRIPTION FOR CORR

BONAVIA, DAVID   B00176
      EXODUS FROM PEKING
      FEER 92:20(14 MAY 1977), 35.
      ##/CHIN-2
      MEDIUM: GENERAL
      CHRON: 1970-1980
      GEOG: CHINA
      SUBJ: FOR CORR   DESCRIPTION

BONAVIA, DAVID   B00179
    RESTRICTED ACCESS TO INFORMATION IN PEKING
    IPI REPORT 25:9(SEPT 1976), 7.
    ##/CHIN-2
    MEDIUM: GENERAL
    CHRON: 1970-1980
    GEOG: CHINA
    SUBJ: CONTROL   FOR CORR   DESCRIPTION

BONAVIA, DAVID   B00178
    EXODUS FROM PEKING
    ATLAS WORLD PRESS REVIEW 23:9(SEPT 1976), 53.
    FROM FEER, 14 MAY 1976
    MEDIUM: GENERAL
    CHRON: 1970-1980
    GEOG: CHINA
    SUBJ: FOR CORR   DESCRIPTION

BOOKER, EDNA LEE   B00180
    NEWS IS MY JOB: A CORRESPONDENT IN WAR-TORN
        CHINA
    NEW YORK, MACMILLAN, 1940.
    CHRON: 1910-1946
    GEOG: CHINA
    SUBJ: FOR CORR   DESCRIPTION

BORDERS, WILLIAM   B00181
    INDIAN PRESS CONTROLS, DESIGNED TO HALT
        RUMORS, SEEM TO FOSTER MORE RUMORS
    NYT 18 JAN 1976
    ##/SWAS
    CHRON: 1970-1980
    GEOG: SO/WEST ASI
    SUBJ: CONTROL   FOR CORR   DESCRIPTION

BORDERS, WILLIAM   B00183
    IN YEAR AND A HALF, INDIA'S PRESS MOVES FROM
        ACCEPTING CENSORSHIP TO ACTIVELY
        PROMOTING REGIME'S VIEWS
    NYT 5 DEC 1976
    ##/SWAS
    CHRON: 1970-1980
    GEOG: SO/WEST ASI
    SUBJ: CONTROL   DEVELOPMENT

BORDERS, WILLIAM   B01911
    KISSES IN NEW FILM IN INDIA FUEL CENSORSHIP
        DEBATE
    NYT 28 MAY 1978
    ##/SWAS
    MEDIUM: FILM
    CHRON: 1970-1980
    GEOG: SO/WEST ASI
    SUBJ: CONTROL

BORDERS, WILLIAM   B01217
    MATRIMONIAL ADVERTISING IN INDIA'S SUNDAY
        PAPERS ADAPTS ITSELF TO CHANGING
        ECONOMIES AND MORES
    NYT 28 AUG 1977
    ##/SWAS
    CHRON: 1970-1980
    GEOG: SO/WEST ASI
    SUBJ: DESCRIPTION

BORDWELL, CONSTANCE   B00184
    EDUCATIONAL TV SCORES IN SINGAPORE
    CSM 24 JULY 1971
    ##/SIN
    MEDIUM: ELECTRONIC
    CHRON: 1970-1980
    GEOG: SINGAPORE
    SUBJ: EDUCATION   DEVELOPMENT

BOROP, MIRIAM JEAN   B02214
    EDITORIAL TREATMENT OF THE WAR IN
        VIETNAM IN <THE JAPAN TIMES> 1964-1967
    MASTERS THESIS, UNIVERSITY OF MISSOURI, 1969.
    CHRON: 1960-1970
    METH: OTHER OR COMB
    GEOG: VIETNAM   EAST ASIA
    SUBJ: DESCRIPTION

BORSUK, RICHARD   B01435
    THE PUSH-BUTTON NEWSPAPER LIBRARY
    MEDIA [HONG KONG] 3:6(JUNE 1976), 10-11.
    <HONG KONG STANDARD>
    CHRON: 1970-1980
    GEOG: HONG KONG
    SUBJ: OTHER JRN

BORSUK, RICHARD   B01436
    DRIVING THE WRONG WAY ON JOURNALISM ROAD
    MEDIA [HONG KONG] 3:8(AUG 1976), 24-5.
    INTERVIEW WITH JOHN MITCHELL
    CHRON: 1970-1980
    GEOG: HONG KONG
    SUBJ: DEVELOPMENT DESCRIPTION

BOWRING, PHILIP   B00413
    CONFLICT OF EVIDENCE
    FEER 95:12(25 MAR 1977), 17.
    ##/SIN; ARUN.
    CHRON: 1970-1980
    GEOG: SINGAPORE
    SUBJ: FOR CORR   CONTROL   LAW/ETHICS

BOX, ERNEST   B01317
    NATIVE NEWSPAPERS AND THEIR VALUE FOR OR
        AGAINST CHRISTIAN WORK
    THE MESSENGER [SHANGHAI] VII:3(MAR 1895),PP.
        37-8; VII:4(APR 1895),PP. 49-52;VII:6(MAY
        1895),PP. 75-7;VII:7(JUNE 1895),PP. 83-4.
    CHRON: BEFORE 1910
    GEOG: CHINA
    SUBJ: DESCRIPTION

BOYLAN, JAMES   B00187
    A SALISBURY CHRONICLE
    COL JRN REVIEW (WINTER 1966/67), 10-15.
    CHRON: 1960-1970
    GEOG: VIETNAM
    SUBJ: FOR CORR

BOYLE, RICHARD   B02578
    THE FLOWER OF THE DRAGON: THE BREAKDOWN OF
        THE U. S. ARMY IN VIETNAM
    SAN FRANCISCO, RAMPARTS, 1972.
    CHRON: 1960-1970
    GEOG: VIETNAM
    SUBJ: FOR CORR

BRAESTRUP, PETER   B02556
    BIG STORY: HOW THE AMERICAN PRESS AND
        TELEVISION REPORTED AND INTERPRETED THE
        CRISIS OF TET 1968 IN VIETNAM AND
        WASHINGTON
    GARDEN CITY, N. Y., ANCHOR, 1978.
    ONE VOLUME EDITION OF BRAESTRUP B01368
    MEDIUM: GENERAL
    CHRON: 1960-1970
    METH: OTHER OR COMB
    GEOG: VIETNAM   U.S.
    SUBJ: FOR CORR   CONTROL   FLOW/AGENCY

BRAESTRUP, PETER   B01368
    BIG STORY: HOW THE AMERICAN PRESS AND
        TELEVISION REPORTED AND INTERPRETED THE
        CRISIS OF TET 1968 IN VIETNAM AND
        WASHINGTON
    BOULDER, COLO., WESTVIEW, 1977, 2 VOLS.
    MEDIUM: GENERAL
    CHRON: 1960-1970
    GEOG: VIETNAM   U.S.
    SUBJ: FOR CORR   CONTROL   FLOW/AGENCY

BRAESTRUP, PETER   B01644
    <BIG STORY>: THE AUTHOR RESPONDS
    COL JRN REVIEW XVI:6(MAR/APR 1978), 67-8.
    ##/VN; LETTER TO EDITOR; SEE ARNETT A01643.
    MEDIUM: GENERAL
    CHRON: 1970-1980
    GEOG: VIETNAM   U.S.
    SUBJ: FOR CORR   FLOW/AGENCY JRN HISTORY

BRAESTRUP, PETER   B00188
     COVERING THE VIETNAM WAR
     NIEMAN REPORTS XXIII:14(DEC 1969), 8-13.
     ##/VN
     MEDIUM: GENERAL
     CHRON: 1960-1970
     GEOG: VIETNAM   U.S.
     SUBJ: FOR CORR

BRANNIGAN, BILL   B02163
     BRANNIGAN'S STEW IN VIETNAM
     DATELINE [OPC, NEW YORK] (1970), 56-9.
     CHRON: 1970-1980
     GEOG: VIETNAM
     SUBJ: FOR CORR

BRESNAHAN, MARY I.   B02550
     ENGLISH IN THE PHILIPPINES
     JOURNAL OF COMMUNICATION 29:2(SPRING 1979),
         64-71.
     MEDIUM: GENERAL
     CHRON: SURVEY
     METH: OTHER OR COMB
     GEOG: PHILIPPINES
     SUBJ: LANGUAGE

BRILLER, BERT   B01689
     INSIDIOUS PROPAGANDA--STREAMLINED
     CHINESE STUDENT III:4(APR 1940), 9, 17.
     CHRON: 1910-1946
     GEOG: CHINA   EAST ASIA
     SUBJ: PROPAGANDA

BRINES, BARBARA   B00486
     JAPANESE FILM INDUSTRY HAS NO USE FOR
         HOLLYWOOD FRILLS
     THE PEIPING CHRONICLE 23 FEB 1940
     MEDIUM: FILM
     CHRON: 1910-1946
     GEOG: EAST ASIA
     SUBJ: DESCRIPTION

BRINK, DIRK   B02505
     'IDENTITHINK'
     ASIAWEEK 5:14(13 APR 1979), 49.
     ##/ASIA
     MEDIUM: GENERAL
     CHRON: 1970-1980
     GEOG: WORLD
     SUBJ: FOR CORR   FLOW/AGENCY

BRITISH MALAYA   B01370
        THE MALAYAN <PUNCH>
        II:5(SEPT 1927), 131.
        ##/MAL-3; <STRAITS PRODUCE>.
        CHRON: 1910-1946
        GEOG: MALAYSIA   SINGAPORE
        SUBJ: DESCRIPTION

BRITISH MALAYA   B01369
        FILM PRODUCTION IN MALAYA
        VI:3(JULY 1931), 64.
        ##/MAL-3; EDITORIAL.
        MEDIUM: FILM
        CHRON: 1910-1946
        GEOG: MALAYSIA
        SUBJ: DEVELOPMENT DESCRIPTION

BRITTON, ROSWELL   B00189
        ANCIENT CHINA VERSUS MODERN JOURNALISM
        THE QUILL XIII:3(MAY 1925), 10-11.
        ##/CHIN-3; ULS 4:3512.
        CHRON: 1910-1946
        GEOG: CHINA
        SUBJ: DESCRIPTION

BRITTON, ROSWELL S.   B00190
        THE CHINESE PERIODICAL PRESS: 1800-1912
        SHANGHAI, KELLY AND WALSH, 1933.
        REPRINT BY CHENGWEN PUB. CO., TAIPEI, 1966.
        CHRON: BEFORE 1910
        METH: HISTORICAL
        GEOG: CHINA
        SUBJ: JRN HISTORY

BRITTON, ROSWELL S.   B01437
        A HORN PRINTING BLOCK
        HARVARD JOURNAL OF ASIATIC STUDIES III(JULY
            1938), 99-102.
        ##/CHIN-5
        CHRON: BEFORE 1910
        METH: HISTORICAL
        GEOG: CHINA
        SUBJ: PRINTING

BRITTON, ROSWELL SESSOMS   B00191
        CHINESE NEWS INTERESTS
        PACIFIC AFFAIRS 7:2(JUNE 1934), 181-93.
        ##/CHIN-3
        CHRON: 1910-1946
        GEOG: CHINA
        SUBJ: DESCRIPTION

BROMAN, BARRY M.   B00192
    TATZEPAO: MEDIUM OF CONFLICT IN CHINA'S
        'CULTURAL REVOLUTION'
    JQ 46:1(SPRING 1969), 100-4, 127.
    ##/CHIN
    MEDIUM: OTHER
    CHRON: 1960-1970
    METH: OTHER OR COMB
    GEOG: CHINA
    SUBJ: PROPAGANDA OTHER JRN

BROWN, CHARLES B.   B00193
    A WOMAN'S ODYSSEY: THE WAR CORRESPONDENCE
        OF ANNA BENJAMIN
    JQ 46:3(AUTUMN 1969), 522-30.
    ##/FOCO
    CHRON: BEFORE 1910
    METH: HISTORICAL
    GEOG: PHILIPPINES U.S.
    SUBJ: FOR CORR

BROWNE, DONALD   B00194
    INTERNATIONAL BROADCASTING IN ASIA--A
        COMPARATIVE STUDY
    CALIFORNIA?, ICA CONFERENCE, 1970.
    ##/ASIA; MIMEO, 13 PP.
    MEDIUM: ELECTRONIC
    CHRON: 1970-1980
    METH: CONTENT ANALYSIS
    GEOG: SEV ASIA
    SUBJ: DESCRIPTION

BROWNE, MALCOLM W.   B00195
    VIET NAM REPORTING: THREE YEARS OF CRISIS
    COL JRN REVIEW (FALL 1964), 4-9.
    ##/VN
    MEDIUM: GENERAL
    CHRON: 1960-1970
    GEOG: VIETNAM   U.S.
    SUBJ: FOR CORR   FLOW/AGENCY DESCRIPTION

BRYAN, R. J., JR.   B02326
    TRADE-MARKS IN CHINA
    THE CHINA WEEKLY REVIEW XI:1, 3, 4, 10,
        11(DEC-FEB 1920),41-7, 136-43, 184-8,
        496-500, 550-5.
    CHRON: 1910-1946
    GEOG: CHINA
    SUBJ: OTHER JRN

BRYANT, CHARLES R.   B00196
    SURVEY OF SELECTED CURRENT AND RECENT
        RESEARCH MATERIALS ON SOUTHEAST ASIA
    MICROFORM REVIEW II:1(JAN 1973), 14-22.
    ##/BIB
    CHRON: SURVEY
    GEOG: SEV ASIA
    SUBJ: RESEARCH

BUCHLER, WALTER   B01371
     THE MALAYAN READING PUBLIC
     BRITISH MALAYA VII:4(AUG 1932), 89-90.
     BOOKS
     CHRON: 1910-1946
     GEOG: MALAYSIA
     SUBJ: OTHER JRN   LITERATURE

BUREAU OF SOCIAL SCIENCE RESEARCH   B00488
     POLITICAL AWARENESS IN LAOS, JANUARY-FEBRUARY
          1959
     WASHINGTON, D. C., BUREAU OF SOCIAL SCIENCE
          RESEARCH, 1959.
     RAYMOND FINK, STUDY DIRECTOR; PREPARED FOR
          USIA, OFFICE OF RESEARCH AND INTELLIGENCE
     MEDIUM: GENERAL
     CHRON: 1946-1960
     METH: SURVEY
     GEOG: LAOS
     SUBJ: DESCRIPTION OTHER JRN   POLIT SCI

BUREAU OF SOCIAL SCIENCE RESEARCH   B00197
     COMMUNICATIONS AND PUBLIC OPINION IN MALAYA:
          A SURVEY OF SELECTED SOURCES
     WASHINGTON, D. C., AMERICAN U., 1954.
     S. K. BIGMAN, PROJECT DIRECTOR; PREPARED FOR
          USIA, OFFICE OF RESEARCH
          AND INTELLIGENCE
     MEDIUM: GENERAL
     CHRON: 1946-1960
     GEOG: MALAYSIA   SINGAPORE
     SUBJ: DESCRIPTION OTHER JRN   OTHER NON-J

BURMA   B01004
     STATEMENT OF NEWSPAPER AND PERIODICALS IN
          THE PROVINCES OF BURMA
     RANGOON, SUPT. OF GOVERNMENT PRINTING AND
          STATIONERY, ANNUAL.
     CHRON: SURVEY   VERIF: UNVERIFIED
     GEOG: BURMA
     SUBJ: RESEARCH

BURNS, JOHN   B00199
     THE CHINESE ARE TOLD LITTLE, AND ACCEPT IT
     NYT 15 FEB 1976
     MEDIUM: GENERAL
     CHRON: 1970-1980
     GEOG: CHINA
     SUBJ: DESCRIPTION CONTROL   PROPAGANDA

BURNS, JOHN   B00201
     INSIDE <PEOPLE'S DAILY>
     ATLAS WORLD PRESS REVIEW 22:2(FEB 1975), 60-1.
     ##/CHIN-2; FROM TORONTO GLOBE AND MAIL
          2 OCT 1975.
     CHRON: 1970-1980
     GEOG: CHINA
     SUBJ: DESCRIPTION

BURNS, JOHN   B00200
    A NIGHT OF TV IN CHINA
    CSM 27 JAN 1975
    ##/CHIN
    MEDIUM: ELECTRONIC
    CHRON: 1970-1980
    GEOG: CHINA
    SUBJ: DESCRIPTION

BURNS, JOHN   B00203
    BEHIND THE PEKING POSTER WAR
    ATLAS WORLD PRESS REVIEW 21:8(SEPT 1974),
        39-40.
    ##/CHIN-2
    MEDIUM: OTHER
    CHRON: 1970-1980
    GEOG: CHINA
    SUBJ: DESCRIPTION PROPAGANDA

BURNS, JOHN   B00202
    CHINA'S 'NEWSPAPER' WITH NO REPORTERS
    CSM 24 OCT 1974
    ##/CHIN
    CHRON: 1970-1980
    GEOG: CHINA
    SUBJ: DESCRIPTION

BURNS, P.   B00204
    THE ENGLISH-LANGUAGE PAPERS OF SINGAPORE:
        1915-1951
    B. A. (HONS) EXERCISE, 1957, U. OF MALAYA
        AT SINGAPORE.
    CHRON: SURVEY   VERIF: UNVERIFIED
    GEOG: SINGAPORE
    SUBJ: JRN HISTORY

BURROWS, LARRY   B02164
    MAN WITH A CAMERA
    DATELINE [OPC, NEW YORK] 7:1(1963), 29-31.
    CHRON: 1960-1970
    GEOG: VIETNAM   SEV ASIA   WORLD
    SUBJ: FOR CORR

BURTON, WILBUR   B01690
    CHINESE REACTIONS TO THE CINEMA
    ASIA XXXIV:10(OCT 1934), 594-600.
    MEDIUM: FILM
    CHRON: 1910-1946
    GEOG: CHINA
    SUBJ: DESCRIPTION CROSS CULTU

BUSINESS WEEK   B00205
     THEY KEEP U. S. TRAVELERS POSTED
     NO. 2022(1 JUNE 1968), 112-14.
     ##/INTL
     CHRON: 1960-1970
     GEOG: WORLD
     SUBJ: DESCRIPTION FLOW/AGENCY

BUTTERFIELD, FOX   B00206
     CHINESE PAPERS TAKE DIFFERING ROADS IN DRIVE
          AGAINST 'CAPITALIST ROADERS'
     NYT JUNE 1976
     ##/CHIN
     CHRON: 1970-1980
     GEOG: CHINA
     SUBJ: PROPAGANDA DESCRIPTION

BUTTERFIELD, FOX   B02215
     CHINA'S PRESS AGENCY PLANS OWN ROMAN SPELLING
     NYT 3 DEC 1978
     ##/CHIN-8
     CHRON: 1970-1980
     GEOG: CHINA
     SUBJ: DESCRIPTION LANGUAGE

BUTTERFIELD, FOX   B02506
     INSIDE CHINA--MORE THAN A PERSPECTIVE IS
          CHANGED
     NYT 21 JAN 1979
     ##/CHIN-8
     MEDIUM: OTHER
     CHRON: 1970-1980
     GEOG: CHINA
     SUBJ: DESCRIPTION

BYRD, CECIL K.   B00207
     EARLY PRINTING IN THE STRAITS SETTLEMENTS,
          1806-1858
     SINGAPORE, SINGAPORE NATIONAL LIBRARY, 1970.
     CHRON: BEFORE 1910
     METH: HISTORICAL
     GEOG: SINGAPORE   MALAYSIA
     SUBJ: PRINTING

C., G. F.   C02289
     THE CABLE MONOPOLY IN THE FAR EAST
     THE CHINA WEEKLY REVIEW XLIX:4(22 JUNE
          1929), 162.
     MEDIUM: ELECTRONIC
     CHRON: 1910-1946
     GEOG: CHINA   SEV ASIA
     SUBJ: OTHER JRN

CABINET INFORMATION BUREAU   C01784
     MOTION PICTURES IN JAPAN
     TOKYO GAZETTE III:4(OCT 1939), 133-42.
     MEDIUM: FILM
     CHRON: 1910-1946
     GEOG: EAST ASIA
     SUBJ: DESCRIPTION

CAMERON, W. H. MORTON-   C00208
     PRESENT DAY IMPRESSIONS OF THE FAR EAST AND
          PROMINENT AND PROGRESSIVE CHINESE AT
          HOME AND ABROAD
     LONDON, GLOBE ENCYCLOPEDIA CO., 1917.
     ##/CHIN-3; EUROPEAN AND NATIVE PRESS IN
          CHINA, PP. 110-113;
          MALAYA/SIN, SEE MAKEPEACE M00780; DUTCH
          EAST INDIES, SEE VAN LOON
          L00755; NUC<56 91:608.
     CHRON: 1910-1946
     METH: HISTORICAL
     GEOG: SINGAPORE   INDONESIA   CHINA
     SUBJ: JRN HISTORY DESCRIPTION

CARBALLO, TITO V.   C00210
     ASIAN PRESS SEMINAR '70
     WASHINGTON, D.C., EMBASSY OF VIET-NAM, 1970.
     ##/ASIA; 12 PP.
     CHRON: 1960-1970
     GEOG: SEV ASIA
     SUBJ: FOR CORR   CONTROL   EDUCATION

CAREEM, NICKY   C01440
     REGIONAL JOURNALS IN ASIA
     MEDIA [HONG KONG] 4:5(MAY 1977), 2-7.
     CHRON: 1970-1980
     GEOG: HONG KONG   SEV ASIA
     SUBJ: DESCRIPTION

CAREEM, NICKY   C01439
     A NEW WORLD FOR NANCY KWAN
     MEDIA [HONG KONG] 4:1(JAN 1977), 12-15.
     MEDIUM: FILM
     CHRON: 1970-1980
     GEOG: HONG KONG
     SUBJ: DESCRIPTION BIOGRAPHY

CAREEM, NICKY   C01438
     FRANK FISCHBECK: DEDICATION TO THE RECORDING
          OF LIFE
     MEDIA [HONG KONG] 4:11(NOV 1976), 8-9.
     CHRON: 1970-1980
     GEOG: HONG KONG   SEV ASIA
     SUBJ: BIOGRAPHY

CARNELL, FRANCIS   C01005
     MALAYA AND THE ENGLISH PRESS
     SPECTATOR NO. 6544(27 NOV 1953), 632-3.
     ##/MAL-2; LETTER TO EDITOR IN REPLY TO
          CORRY C01015.
     CHRON: 1946-1960
     GEOG: MALAYSIA
     SUBJ: DESCRIPTION

CARROLL, JOHN   C02507
     A HUNDRED AND GOING STRONG
     ASIAWEEK 5:14(13 APR 1979), 19-20.
     ##/EASI; ASAHI SHIMBUN.
     CHRON: SURVEY
     GEOG: EAST ASIA
     SUBJ: JRN HISTORY

CASADY, SIMON   C01155
     PURGING THE PRESS
     INDEX ON CENSORSHIP 4:3(AUTUMN 1975), 3-7.
     ##/SIN
     CHRON: 1970-1980
     GEOG: SINGAPORE
     SUBJ: CONTROL

CASEY, JOHN H.   C01372
     CHINA AND THE AMERICAN NEWSPAPER EDITORS
     THE CHINA WEEKLY REVIEW V:14(31 AUG 1918),
          543-4.
     CHRON: 1910-1946
     GEOG: CHINA
     SUBJ: FOR CORR   DESCRIPTION

CASTRO, JOSE LUNA   C00211
     THE MANILA TIMES HANDBOOK OF JOURNALISM
     MANILA, MANILA TIMES PRESS, 1966.
     ORIG PUB AS <THE MANILA TIMES JOURNALISM
          MANUAL>, 1963.
     CHRON: 1960-1970
     GEOG: PHILIPPINES
     SUBJ: EDUCATION

CELESTIAL EMPIRE, THE   C02154
     CHINESE NEWSPAPERS AND THE PRESENT SITUATION
     CXIIII:1(3 APR 1915), 23.
     LETTER TO EDITOR, ONE WHO LOVES PEACE.
     CHRON: 1910-1946
     GEOG: CHINA   EAST ASIA
     SUBJ: DESCRIPTION

```
CELESTIAL EMPIRE, THE                                    C02085
     A NEW NORTHERN NEWSPAPER
     CXIII:6(6 FEB 1915), 217.
     <NORTH CHINA DAILY MAIL>
     CHRON: 1910-1946
     GEOG:  CHINA
     SUBJ:  DESCRIPTION


CELESTIAL EMPIRE, THE                                    C02084
     SHANGHAI JOURNALISTS AND BELGIAN COLLEAGUES
     CXIII:7(13 FEB 1915), 256.
     CHRON: 1910-1946
     GEOG:  CHINA
     SUBJ:  DESCRIPTION


CELESTIAL EMPIRE, THE                                    C02083
     NEWSPAPERS IN CHINA
     CXIII:9(27 FEB 1915), 327.
     CHRON: 1910-1946
     GEOG:  CHINA
     SUBJ:  DESCRIPTION


CELESTIAL EMPIRE, THE                                    C02082
     SHANGHAI NEWSPAPERS
     CXX:3(21 OCT 1916), 89.
     CHRON: 1910-1946
     GEOG:  CHINA
     SUBJ:  DESCRIPTION


CELESTIAL EMPIRE, THE                                    C02081
     GERMAN NEWSPAPERS IN JAPAN: PUBLICATION
        PROHIBITED
     CXI:13(26 SEPT 1914), 516-7.
     <JAPAN HERALD>, <DEUTSCHE-JAPAN-POST>
     CHRON: 1910-1946
     GEOG:  EAST ASIA    OTHER
     SUBJ:  CONTROL


CELESTIAL EMPIRE, THE                                    C02080
     CHINESE NEWSPAPERS IN SHANGHAI
     CXIII:9(29 MAY 1915), 367.
     LETTER TO EDITOR
     CHRON: 1910-1946
     GEOG:  CHINA
     SUBJ:  DESCRIPTION
```

CELESTIAL EMPIRE, THE   C02079
    JAPANESE NEWSPAPERS AND FOREIGN AFFAIRS
    CXI:13(26 SEPT 1914), SUPPLEMENT PAGE 52.
    CHRON: 1910-1946
    GEOG: EAST ASIA
    SUBJ: DESCRIPTION OTHER JRN

CENTER FOR RESEARCH LIBRARIES   C00212
    MICROFORM HOLDINGS LIST AND GUIDE TO OTHER
         SOUTHEAST ASIAN MATERIAL AT CRL
    CHICAGO, CRL, SEPT 1976.
    ##/BIB; SEAM/NAP; MIMEO 9 PP.
    MEDIUM: GENERAL
    CHRON: SURVEY
    GEOG: SEV ASIA
    SUBJ: RESEARCH

CH'ANG CH'UNG-PAO   11   C00215
    WANG K'ANG-NIEN YU CH'I MENG SHIH CH'I CHIH
         CHUNG-KUO PAO YEH (WANG K'ANG NIEN AND
         THE CHINESE PRESS IN THE PERIOD OF
         ENLIGHTENMENT
    UNPUB MASTERS THESIS IN JOURNALISM
    SKINNER S00982 II:41754
                       LANG: CHINESE
    CHRON: BEFORE 1910 VERIF: UNVERIFIED
    GEOG: CHINA
    SUBJ: BIOGRAPHY

CH'EN CHI-YING   11   C00231
    CHANG CHI-LUAN HSIEN SHENG YU CHUNG-KUO
         PAO YEH (CHANG CHI-LUAN AND CHINESE
         JOURNALISM)
    CHUNG YANG JIH PAO (TAIPEI) (12 MAR 1957).
    REPRINTED IN CH'EN 11C01815
                       LANG: CHINESE
    CHRON: 1910-1946   VERIF: UNVERIFIED
    GEOG: CHINA   TAIWAN
    SUBJ: BIOGRAPHY

CH'EN CHI-YING   11   C00230
    TIAO 'TA KUNG PAO'
         (IN MEMORY OF THE NEWSPAPER TA-KUNG PAO)
    HSIN WEN T'IEN TI 81(6 SEPT 1949), 35-50.
    REPRINTED IN CH'EN 11C01815
                       LANG: CHINESE
    CHRON: 1910-1946   VERIF: UNVERIFIED
    GEOG: CHINA
    SUBJ: DESCRIPTION BIOGRAPHY

CH'EN CHI-YING   11   C02059
    HU CHENG-CHIH YU TA KUNG PAO [HU CHENG-CHIH
         AND THE <TA KUNG PAO>]
    HONG KONG, CHANG KU YUEH K'AN SHE, 1974.
                       LANG: CHINESE
    CHRON: BEFORE 1910
    METH: HISTORICAL
    GEOG: CHINA
    SUBJ: JRN HISTORY BIOGRAPHY

CH'EN CHI-YING   11   C01815
     PAO JEN CHANG CHI-LUAN [CHANG CHI-LUAN,
          JOURNALIST]
     TAIPEI, WEN U CH'U PAN SHE, 1957.
     #3
                         LANG: CHINESE
     CHRON: 1910-1946
     METH: HISTORICAL
     GEOG: CHINA
     SUBJ: BIOGRAPHY

CH'EN CHIH-P'ING   11   C00232
     T'AI-WAN KAO CHUNG HSUEH SHENG HSIN WEN
          T'ING TU HSI KUAN CHIH TIAO CH'A YU
          FEN HSI
     UNPUB MASTERS THESIS IN JOURNALISM, 1959.
     SKINNER S00982 II:46524; (SENIOR-MIDDLE-SCHOOL
          STUDENTS IN TAIWAN AND
          THE NEWS MEDIA: SURVEY AND ANALYSIS
          OF READING AND LISTENING HABITS
          SEE CHEN 11C02729.
     MEDIUM: GENERAL   LANG: CHINESE
     CHRON: 1946-1960   VERIF: UNVERIFIED
     GEOG: TAIWAN
     SUBJ: DESCRIPTION

CH'EN LANG   11   C02090
     CHAN-HOU CHUNG-KUO TI HSIN-WEN SHIH-YEH
          (CHINESE JOURNALISM AFTER THE WAR)
     SHIH-TAI P'I-P'ING 4:86(1 JULY 1947), 28-30.
     ##/CHIN-7
                         LANG: CHINESE
     CHRON: 1910-1946
     GEOG: CHINA
     SUBJ: DESCRIPTION

CH'EN SHENG-SHIH   11   C00235
     CHIN TAI CHUNG-KUO PAO CHIH SHE LUN CHIH YEN
          PIEN (CHANGES IN THE EDITORIALS
          PUBLISHED IN CHINA'S MODERN NEWSPAPERS)
     UNPUB MASTERS THESIS IN JOURNALISM, 1958.
     SKINNER S00982 II:50910; SEE CHEN 11C02731.
                         LANG: CHINESE
     CHRON: 1946-1960   VERIF: UNVERIFIED
     GEOG: TAIWAN
     SUBJ: DESCRIPTION

CH'EN TSU-HUA   11   C00236
     YU YU-JEN HSIEN SHENG CH'UANG PAN KO MING PAO
          CHIH CHIH CHING KUO CHI CH'I YING HSIANG
          CHIH YEN CHIU
     UNPUB MASTERS THESIS, 1966.
     SKINNER II:41755; (AN ACCOUNT OF THE
          REVOLUTIONARY NEWSPAPERS
          FOUNDED BY YU YU-JEN AND THEIR
          INFLUENCE)
                         LANG: CHINESE
     CHRON: BEFORE 1910   VERIF: UNVERIFIED
     METH: HISTORICAL
     GEOG: CHINA
     SUBJ: BIOGRAPHY

CH'EN TZU HSIANG   11   C00237
    THE ENGLISH-LANGUAGE DAILY PRESS IN CHINA
    DIGEST OF THE SYNODAL COMMISSION (CATHOLIC
        CHURCH IN CHINA)10:11(NOV 1937),
        900-25.
    ##/CHIN-3
    CHRON: 1910-1946
    GEOG: CHINA
    SUBJ: RESEARCH

CH'EN YU-SUNG   11   C01008
    NAN-YANG TI I PAO JEN (THE FOREMOST
        JOURNALIST OF NANYANG)
    SINGAPORE, SHIH CHIEH SHU CHU, 1958.
    YEH CHI-YUN, EDITOR OF <LI PAO>
                            LANG: CHINESE
    CHRON: SURVEY   VERIF: UNVERIFIED
    METH: HISTORICAL
    GEOG: SINGAPORE
    SUBJ: BIOGRAPHY

CH'EN YUAN-HSIUNG   11   C01376
    CHIAO-T'UNG TE LI-LUN YU SHIH-CHI [THEORIES
        AND PRACTICE OF COMMUNICATION SYSTEMS]
    TAIPEI, N. G., 1977.
    MEDIUM: GENERAL   LANG: CHINESE
    CHRON: 1970-1980   VERIF: UNVERIFIED
    GEOG: TAIWAN
    SUBJ: DESCRIPTION

CH'EN, HUNG-SHUN   11   C01375
    THE TAOIST PRESS IN CHINA
    DIGEST OF THE SYNODAL COMMISSION (CATHOLIC
        CHURCH IN CHINA) 11(MAY 1938), 484-97.
    ##/CHIN-5
    CHRON: 1910-1946
    GEOG: CHINA
    SUBJ: DESCRIPTION

CH'EN, SHIH-AN   11   C01449
    PAO HSUEH KAI LUN [INTRODUCTION TO JOURNALISM]
    TAIPEI, JEN YIN CH'U PAN SHE, 1968.
    ##/CHIN-5
                            LANG: CHINESE
    CHRON: 1960-1970
    GEOG: TAIWAN
    SUBJ: EDUCATION

CH'ENG CH'ANG-PO   12   C01007
    WARTIME PRESS IN CHINA
    THE CHINA QUARTERLY IV:4(AUTUMN 1939), 615-21.
    ##/CHIN-4
    CHRON: 1910-1946
    GEOG: CHINA
    SUBJ: DESCRIPTION

CH'ENG CH'I-HENG   C02595
     CHAN SHIH CHUNG-KUO PAO YEH (CHINESE WARTIME
          JOURNALISM)
     KWELIN, MING TAN CHU PEN SHE, 1944.
     MA SHING-YEH; NUC<56 105:351.
     CHRON: 1910-1946   LANG: CHINESE
     GEOG: CHINA
     SUBJ: DESCRIPTION BIOGRAPHY

CH'ENG CHI-HENG AND JUNG   C02594
          YU-MING, EDITORS.
     CHI-CHE CHING-YEN T'AN (JOURNALISTS PERSONAL
          EXPERIENCES)
     KWELIN, MING TAN CHU PEN SHE, 1943.
     NUC<56 105:351
                          LANG: CHINESE
     CHRON: 1910-1946
     GEOG: CHINA
     SUBJ: BIOGRAPHY

CH'ENG SHE-WO   C02596
     PAO-HSUEH TSA-CHU (NOTES ON JOURNALISM)
     TAIPEI, CHUNG YANG WEN WU KUNG, 1956.
     NUC 1956-67 22:18
                          LANG: CHINESE
     CHRON: 1910-1946
     GEOG: TAIWAN   CHINA
     SUBJ: DESCRIPTION BIOGRAPHY

CH'IEN CH'I-CH'EN   16   C00251
     WO KUO TIEN HSIN CHIEN SHE CHIH KUO CH'ENG
          (THE DEVELOPMENT OF TELECOMMUNICATIONS
          IN CHINA)
     IN TIEN HSIN KAI LUN (INTRODUCTION TO
          TELECOMMUNICATIONS), BY CH'IEN CH'I-CHEN.
          TAIPEI, CHUNG-KUO CHIAO T'UNG CHIEN
          SHE HSUEH HUI, 1958.
     MEDIUM: ELECTRONIC   LANG: CHINESE
     CHRON: SURVEY   VERIF: UNVERIFIED
     GEOG: CHINA
     SUBJ: JRN HISTORY

CH'IU JUNG-KUANG   08   C00328
     T'AI-PEI KO PAO SHIH CHANG CHING HSUAN HSIN
          WEN CHIH FEN HSI (AN ANALYSIS OF
          MAYORALITY ELECTION REPORTS IN TAIPEI
          NEWSPAPERS)
     UNPUB MASTERS THESIS IN JOURNALISM, 1965.
                          LANG: CHINESE
     CHRON: 1970-1980   VERIF: UNVERIFIED
     GEOG: TAIWAN
     SUBJ: DESCRIPTION POLIT SCI

CHAI, TRONG R.   C01785
     A CONTENT ANALYSIS OF THE OBITUARY NOTICES
          ON MAO TSE-TUNG
     PUBLIC OPINION QUARTERLY 41:4(WINTER
          1977/1978), 475-87.
     CHRON: 1970-1980
     METH: CONTENT ANALYSIS
     GEOG: CHINA
     SUBJ: DESCRIPTION

CHAN, HENG CHEE   C01441
     COMMENT
     COMMENTARY [SINGAPORE] 4:1(SEPT 1971), 39-41.
     ##/SIN-2; SEE KWA K01396.
     MEDIUM: GENERAL
     CHRON: 1970-1980
     GEOG: SINGAPORE
     SUBJ: DEVELOPMENT DESCRIPTION

CHANCE, NORMAN, CHRIS GILMARTIN   C01998
         AND FRANK KEHL
     RED MENACE OR YELLOW JOURNALISM
     NEW CHINA FIRST ISSUE (1974), 25-8.
     ##/CHIN-7
     MEDIUM: GENERAL
     CHRON: 1970-1980
     GEOG: CHINA
     SUBJ: FOR CORR   PROPAGANDA FLOW/AGENCY

CHANDRA, A. M.   C00213
     MASS COMMUNICATION IN INDONESIA
     SINGAPORE, AMIC, 23 NOV 1973.
     ##/INDO; PAPER
     MEDIUM: GENERAL
     CHRON: 1970-1980
     GEOG: INDONESIA
     SUBJ: DESCRIPTION

CHANG CHI-LUAN   C00487
     WHY DO YOU WANT TO BE A JOURNALIST?
     THE NEW CHINA [PEKING] (JUNE 1931), 196-8.
     #3/NEW CHINA
     CHRON: 1910-1946
     GEOG: CHINA
     SUBJ: DESCRIPTION EDUCATION

CHANG CHING LU   07   C01691
     CHUNG KUO TI HSIN WEN CHIH   CHINESE
          JOURNALISM]
     SHANGHAI, KUANG HUA SHU CHU, 1927.
     #3
                              LANG: CHINESE
     CHRON: 1910-1946
     GEOG: CHINA
     SUBJ: JRN HISTORY DESCRIPTION

CHANG CHING-LU   07   C02193
     CHUNG-KUO HSIEN-TAI' CH'U-PAN SHIH-LIAO
          (MATERIALS FOR A HISTORY OF MODERN
          PUBLISHING IN CHINA)
     PEKING, CHUNG HUA SHU-CHU, 1954.
     SEE SKINNER S00982 II:49372 AND HSIEH H08311,
          PP. 105-6.
                              LANG: CHINESE
     CHRON: SURVEY
     METH: HISTORICAL
     GEOG: CHINA
     SUBJ: PUBLISHING

CHANG CHING-LU   C02593
     TSAI CH'U-PAN CHIEH ERH-SHIH NIEN (TWENTY
        YEARS IN THE PUBLISHING BUSINESS)
     HANKOW, SHANG HAI TSA CHIH, 1938.
                          LANG: CHINESE
     CHRON: 1910-1946
     GEOG: CHINA
     SUBJ: PUBLISHING

CHANG CHING-LU, EDITOR   07   C02192
     CHUNG-KUO CHIN-TAI CH'U-PAN SHIH-LIAO
        (MATERIALS ON THE HISTORY OF CONTEMPORARY
        PUBLISHING IN CHINA)
     SHANGHAI, SHANG-HAI CH'U PAN SHE, 1953.
                          LANG: CHINESE
     CHRON: 1946-1960
     GEOG: CHINA
     SUBJ: DESCRIPTION PUBLISHING

CHANG HSIAO-LU   C02087
     YEN-LUN YU TZU-PEN [THE PRESS AND THE CAPITAL]
     SHIH YU WEN NO. 17 (30 JAN 1948), 6-8.
                          LANG: CHINESE
     CHRON: 1910-1946
     GEOG: CHINA
     SUBJ: DESCRIPTION

CHANG HSU-HUI   11   C00216
     SHIH CHIU SHIH CHI HSIA PAN CH'I HSIANG-KANG
        CH'U PAN CHIH HSI WEN SHU CHI PAO CHANG
     UNPUB.SENIOR THESIS IN CHINESE, HONG KONG U.
     (THE PUBLICATION OF FOREIGN BOOKS, PERIODICALS
        AND NEWSPAPERS
        IN HONG KONG IN THE LATTER HALF OF THE
        NINETEENTH CENTURY);
        SKINNER S00982 II:51205.
                          LANG: CHINESE
     CHRON: BEFORE 1910   VERIF: UNVERIFIED
     GEOG: HONG KONG
     SUBJ: PUBLISHING JRN HISTORY

CHANG I-WEI   11   C02088
     HUA-PEI HSIN-WEN CHIEN (JOURNALISM IN NORTH
        CHINA)
     PAO-HSUEH YUEH-K'AN 1:2(1929), 64-74.
                          LANG: CHINESE
     CHRON: 1910-1946
     GEOG: CHINA
     SUBJ: DESCRIPTION

CHANG JO-YIN   11   C02089
     CHUNG-KUO HSIN-WEN CHI-CHE TSUI-CH'U TI
        HSI-SHENG CHE-- SHEN CHIN (THE FIRST
        MARTYR AMONG CHINESE JOURNALISTS--
        SHEN CHIN
     HSIN JEN-SHIH NO. 2 (20 SEPT 1936), 96-7.
                          LANG: CHINESE
     CHRON: 1910-1946
     GEOG: CHINA
     SUBJ: BIOGRAPHY

CHANG KUO-HSING   11   C00220
     CHUNG WEN PAO CHIH KAI KUAN (CHINESE-LANGUAGE
          NEWSPAPERS, AN OVERVIEW)
     HONG KONG, KUO CHI HSIN WEN HSIEH HUI, 1968.
     FOR ENGLISH LANGUAGE SEE CHANG 11C00229.
                         LANG: CHINESE
     CHRON: SURVEY
     GEOG: HONG KONG
     SUBJ: DESCRIPTION

CHANG KUO-SIN   C00219
     INVESTIGATIVE REPORT SHUTS CAMPUS PAPER
     IPI REPORT 25:9(SEPT 1976).
     CHINESE UNIVERSITY OF HONG KONG
     CHRON: 1970-1980
     GEOG: HONG KONG
     SUBJ: CONTROL

CHANG KUO-SIN   11   C00218
     WORLD NEWS READ ONLY BY CHINA'S SELECTED FEW
     IPI REPORT 25:2(FEB 1976), 1, 2, 7.
     REFERENCE NEWS
     CHRON: 1970-1980
     GEOG: CHINA
     SUBJ: DESCRIPTION CONTROL

CHANG MING-FANG   11   C00221
     CH'ING MO 'SHIH WU PAO' CHIH YEN CHIU
          (SHIH-WU PAO <CHINESE PROGRESS>, A
          JOURNAL OF THE LATE CH'ING PERIOD)
     UNPUB MASTERS THESIS IN JOURNALISM, 1968.
     SKINNER S00982 II:41753
                         LANG: CHINESE
     CHRON: BEFORE 1910   VERIF: UNVERIFIED
     METH: HISTORICAL
     GEOG: CHINA
     SUBJ: JRN HISTORY

CHANG P'ENG-YUAN   C02611
     SHIH PAO-WEI HSIN PAI HSUAN CH'UAN CHI KUAN
          CHIH I (<SHIH PAO> (THE EASTERN TIMES)--
          THE PROPAGANDA ORGAN OF THE REFORMERS
     CHUNG YANG YEN CHIU YUAN   BULLETIN OF
          THE INSTITUTE OF MODERN HISTORY, TAIWAN]
          4:1(1974), 151-75.
                         LANG: CHINESE
     CHRON: BEFORE 1910   VERIF: UNVERIFIED
     METH: HISTORICAL
     GEOG: CHINA
     SUBJ: PROPAGANDA   JRN HISTORY

CHANG PEI-HEI   11   C01318
     MOTION PICTURES
     IN <THE CHINESE YEARBOOK 1937>, PP. 1111-15.
     MEDIUM: FILM
     CHRON: 1910-1946
     GEOG: CHINA
     SUBJ: DESCRIPTION

CHANG PO-MIN   11   C00222
    HSIN WEN SHIH YEH TSAI FA LU SHANG CHIH TSE
        JEN (THE LEGAL LIABILITY OF THE PRESS)
    UNPUB MASTERS THESIS IN JOURNALISM, 1965.
    SKINNER S00982 II:46522
                            LANG: CHINESE
    CHRON: 1960-1970   VERIF: UNVERIFIED
    GEOG: HONG KONG   CHINA
    SUBJ: LAW/ETHICS

CHANG T'IEN-HU   C02167
    THE FRENCH PRESS IN CHINA
    DIGEST OF THE SYNODAL COMMISSION (CATHOLIC
        CHURCH IN CHINA) 10:9-10(SEPT-OCT 1937),
        803-9.
    CHRON: 1910-1946
    GEOG: CHINA
    SUBJ: DESCRIPTION

CHANG T. B.   11   C01006
    THE CHINESE PRESS SINCE 1925
    THE CHINA WEEKLY REVIEW 71:7(12 JAN 1935),
        227-8.
    ##/CHIN-4
    CHRON: SURVEY
    GEOG: CHINA
    SUBJ: DESCRIPTION

CHANG YONG   C01442
    TELECOMMUNICATIONS AND POSTAL SERVICES IN
        KOREA
    KOREA JOURNAL 8:1(JAN 1968), 13-17.
    MEDIUM: GENERAL
    CHRON: 1960-1970
    GEOG: EAST ASIA
    SUBJ: DESCRIPTION

CHANG YOW TONG   C01987
    WHAT THE PEOPLE READ IN CHINA
    THE AMERICAN REVIEW OF REVIEWS 30:4(OCT
        1904), 464-6.
    ##/CHIN-6
    CHRON: BEFORE 1910
    GEOG: CHINA
    SUBJ: DESCRIPTION

CHANG, CHUH-HA   C00214
    MY LIFE WITH MAGAZINES
    SOLIDARITY X:1(JAN/FEB 1976), 5-11.
    ##/PHIL
    CHRON: SURVEY
    GEOG: PHILIPPINES
    SUBJ: BIOGRAPHY   JRN HISTORY

CHANG, JAMES B.   C02290
     HONGKONG BATTLEGROUND OF BITTER WAR BETWEEN
          FASCIST, BOLSHEVIK PAPERS
     THE CHINA WEEKLY REVIEW 102:5(29 JUNE 1946),
          96-7.
     CHRON: 1946-1960
     GEOG: HONG KONG
     SUBJ: DESCRIPTION OTHER JRN

CHANG, JOSEPHINE   C00217
     BEATEN TO DEATH?
     STRAITS TIMES (UPI) 2 NOV 1973
     ##/HKG
     MEDIUM: FILM
     CHRON: 1970-1980
     GEOG: WORLD
     SUBJ: DESCRIPTION

CHANG, JOSEPHINE   C00593
     SCHOOL FOR FILM STARS
     MALAY MAIL (UPI) 16 JAN 1974
     ##/MALSP
     MEDIUM: FILM
     CHRON: 1970-1980
     GEOG: HONG KONG   SEV ASIA
     SUBJ: DESCRIPTION EDUCATION

CHANG, KUO-SIN   11   C00229
     A SURVEY OF THE CHINESE LANGUAGE DAILY PRESS
     HONG KONG, IPI, 1968.
     FOR CHINESE VERSION, SEE CHANG 11C00220
     CHRON: 1960-1970
     GEOG: OTHER
     SUBJ: DESCRIPTION FLOW/AGENCY

CHANG, LI-HSIUNG   11   C01584
     PAO YEH YU SHE HUI TI TSE JEN CHIH YEN CHIU
          [RESEARCH ON JOURNALISM AND ITS
          RESPONSIBILITY TO SOCIETY]
     TAIPEI, M. A. THESIS, 1964.
     ##/CHIN-5
                         LANG: CHINESE
     CHRON: 1960-1970
     GEOG: TAIWAN
     SUBJ: LAW/ETHICS

CHANG, RAYMOND   C01363
     A MOVABLE FEAST OF WORDS
     CSM 8 NOV 1977
     ##/CHIN-5
     CHRON: SURVEY
     GEOG: CHINA
     SUBJ: PRINTING

CHANG, Y. L.   C02327
    CHINESE OWN AND OPERATE LARGEST PUBLISHING
        HOUSE IN CHINA
    THE CHINA WEEKLY REVIEW 5:13(24 AUG 1918),
        526-7.
    COMMERCIAL PRESS
    CHRON: 1910-1946
    GEOG: CHINA
    SUBJ: PUBLISHING

CHANG, YONG   C02216
    SURVEY OF KOREAN NEWSPAPERS: STUDY OF
        RHEE AND THE PRESS
    MASTERS THESIS, UNIVERSITY OF MISSOURI, 1958.
    CHRON: 1946-1960
    METH: OTHER OR COMB
    GEOG: EAST ASIA
    SUBJ: CONTROL   DESCRIPTION

CHAO CHAN-YUAN   14   C02793
    KUO-FANG HSIN WEN SHIH-YEH CHIN T'UNG CHIH
        (PROTECTING THE COUNTRY AND CONTROLLING
        THE PRESS)
    SHANGHAI, HAN HSIEH SHU TIEN, 1937.
                            LANG: CHINESE
    CHRON: 1910-1946
    GEOG: CHINA
    SUBJ: CONTROL

CHAO CHUN-HAO   14   C00655
    SHANG-HAI PAO JEN TI FEN TOU THE STRUGGLING
        SHANGHAI JOURNALISTS]
    CHUNGKING, ERH YA SHU TIEN, 1944.
    NUC<56 103:388
                            LANG: CHINESE
    CHRON: 1910-1946
    GEOG: CHINA
    SUBJ: DESCRIPTION BIOGRAPHY

CHAO CHUN-HAO   14   C00223
    CHUNG-KUO CHIN TAI CHIH PAO YEH (JOURNALISM
        IN MODERN CHINA)
    HONG KONG, SHEN PAO KUAN, 1938.
    NUC<56 103:388
                            LANG: CHINESE
    CHRON: 1910-1946
    GEOG: CHINA
    SUBJ: DESCRIPTION

CHAO MING-HENG   C01319
    THE PRESS
    IN <THE CHINESE YEARBOOK 1937>, PP. 1090-1100.
    ##/CHIN-7
    CHRON: 1910-1946
    GEOG: CHINA
    SUBJ: CONTROL   FLOW/AGENCY DESCRIPTION

CHAO, M. H.   C01373
     PRESS
     IN <THE CHINESE YEARBOOK 1936-7>, PP. 524-34.
     ##/CHIN-5
     CHRON: 1910-1946
     GEOG: CHINA
     SUBJ: DESCRIPTION

CHAO, MIN-HENG   14   C01443
     WAI JEN TSAI HUA TI HSIN WEN SHIH YEH
          [FOREIGNERS IN CHINESE JOURNALISM]
     SHANGHAI, CHUNG KUO T'AI PING YANG KUO CHI
          HSUEH HUI, 1932.
     #3
     CHRON: SURVEY
     METH: HISTORICAL
     GEOG: CHINA
     SUBJ: JRN HISTORY DESCRIPTION BIOGRAPHY

CHAO, MING-HENG   C01374
     THE WAR-TIME PRESS
     IN <CHINESE YEARBOOK 1938-39>, PP. 698-705.
     ##/CHIN-5
     CHRON: 1910-1946
     GEOG: CHINA
     SUBJ: CONTROL   DESCRIPTION

CHAO, THOMAS M. H.   C01673
     I 'COVER' CHUNGKING
     THE CHINA QUARTERLY V:1(WINTER 1939), 103-111.
     CHRON: 1910-1946
     GEOG: CHINA
     SUBJ: DESCRIPTION BIOGRAPHY

CHAO, THOMAS MING-HENG   14   C01445
     PRESS LAWS WANTED
     THE CHINA CRITIC III:19(8 MAY 1930), 437-9.
     ##/FILM
     CHRON: 1910-1946
     GEOG: CHINA
     SUBJ: LAW/ETHICS

CHAO, THOMAS MING-HENG   14   C01444
     PROPAGANDA
     THE CHINA CRITIC II:11(14 MAR 1929), 211-2.
     CHRON: 1910-1946
     GEOG: CHINA
     SUBJ: PROPAGANDA

CHAO, THOMAS MING-HENG   14   C00224
    THE FOREIGN PRESS OF CHINA
    SHANGHAI, CHINA INSTITUTE OF PACIFIC
        RELATIONS, 1931.
    #3
    CHRON: SURVEY
    GEOG: CHINA   OTHER
    SUBJ: DESCRIPTION JRN HISTORY

CHATTERJIE, S.   C00225
    FOREIGN NEWS AGENCIES IN <BURMESE YEARBOOK:
        1957-8>, PP. 37,9.
    RANGOON, STUDENT PRESS, 1957.
    ##/BURMA
    CHRON: 1946-1960
    GEOG: BURMA
    SUBJ: FLOW/AGENCY

CHATURVEDI, RAM NIHORE   C01446
    THE PRESS BEFORE THE MUTINY
    JOURNAL OF INDIAN HISTORY 17(1938), 360-79.
    ##/ASIA
    CHRON: BEFORE 1910
    GEOG: SEV ASIA
    SUBJ: JRN HISTORY

CHEAH, FREDDIE   C00227
    JOURNALISTS FINED: COUNSEL TO FILE APPEAL
    STRAITS TIMES 19 JUNE 1971
    ##/MAL-2
    CHRON: 1970-1980
    GEOG: MALAYSIA
    SUBJ: LAW/ETHICS

CHEAH, FREDDIE AND CHIN FAH SIN   C00226
    EDITOR IS LIABLE, COURT IS TOLD
    STRAITS TIMES 10 JUNE 1971
    ##/MAL-2; MELAN CASE.
    CHRON: 1970-1980
    GEOG: MALAYSIA
    SUBJ: LAW/ETHICS

CHEAH, FREDDIE AND CHIN FAH SHIN   C00594
    EDITOR DIDN'T KNOW ABOUT HEADING, TRIAL IS
        TOLD
    STRAITS TIMES 9 JUNE 1971
    ##/MALSP
    CHRON: 1970-1980
    GEOG: MALAYSIA
    SUBJ: LAW/ETHICS

CHEE OI CHIN   C02217
    MENGAPA LEBIH RAMAI WANITA DALAM KAJIAN
        SEBARAN AM?
    BERITA HARIAN (SUNDAY, MALAYSIA EDITION)
        3 SEPT 1978.
    MEDIUM: GENERAL   LANG: MALAY/INDONESIAN
    CHRON: 1970-1980
    GEOG: MALAYSIA
    SUBJ: EDUCATION

CHEESEMAN, H. A. R.   C00228
    BIBLIOGRAPHY OF MALAYA
    LONDON, LONGMAN, GREEN, 1957.
    ##/MAL; PERIODICALS, PP. 135-7;
        NUC<56 105:136.
    CHRON: SURVEY
    GEOG: MALAYSIA   SINGAPORE
    SUBJ: RESEARCH

CHEN CHIH-PING   11   C02729
    T'AI WAN KAO CHUNG HSUEH SHENG HSING WEN
        TING TU HSI KUAN CHIH TIAO CH'A YU
        FEN SHI
    PAO HSUEH [TAIPEI] II:6(APR 1960), 40-60.
    SEE CH'EN 11C00232; (A SURVEY AND ANALYSIS
        OF NEWS READING AND
        LISTENING HABITS OF TAIWAN SENIOR
        MIDDLE SCHOOL STUDENTS).
    MEDIUM: GENERAL   LANG: CHINESE
    CHRON: 1946-1960
    METH: OTHER OR COMB
    GEOG: TAIWAN
    SUBJ: DESCRIPTION

CHEN CHIN-JEN   11   C01447
    AN APPRAISAL OF CHINESE NEWSPAPERS
    THE CHINA CRITIC VI:24(15 JUNE 1933), 593-4.
    CHRON: 1910-1946
    GEOG: CHINA
    SUBJ: DESCRIPTION

CHEN HSIAO-CHI   11   C02730
    NAN YANG TI YI PAO JEN YEH LI-YUN (MR. YEH
        CHI-YUN, NO. 1 CHINESE NEWSMAN IN
        SINGAPORE)
    PAO HSUEH [TAIPEI] II:2(DEC 1957), 23-5.
                            LANG: CHINESE
    CHRON: 1946-1960
    GEOG: SINGAPORE   OSEAS CHIN
    SUBJ: DESCRIPTION BIOGRAPHY

CHEN MONG HOCK   C00234
    THE EARLY CHINESE NEWSPAPERS OF SINGAPORE:
        1881-1912
    SINGAPORE, U. OF MALAYA PRESS, 1967.
    CHRON: BEFORE 1910
    METH: HISTORICAL
    GEOG: SINGAPORE
    SUBJ: JRN HISTORY

CHEN PAO-LIANG   C02328
    PHOTOGRAPHIC REGULATIONS NEED AMENDMENT
    THE CHINA WEEKLY REVIEW 80:5(3 APR 1937), 164.
    CHRON: 1910-1946
    GEOG: CHINA
    SUBJ: LAW/ETHICS

CHEN SHENG-SHIH   11   C02731
    CHIN TAI CHUNG KUO CHIH SHE LUN CHIH YEN
         PIEN (THE EVOLUTION OF EDITORIALS IN
         MODERN CHINESE NEWSPAPERS)
    PAO HSUEH [TAIPEI] II:3(AUG 1958), 8-15.
    SEE CH'EN 11C00235
                          LANG: CHINESE
    CHRON: SURVEY
    METH: HISTORICAL
    GEOG: TAIWAN   CHINA
    SUBJ: DESCRIPTION

CHEN YUN-LO   C00238
    A HISTORICAL ACCOUNT OF THE LOCAL CHINESE
          PRESS
    NANYANG SIANG PAU (JAN 1962)
    CHRON: SURVEY   VERIF: UNVERIFIED
    GEOG: MALAYSIA   SINGAPORE
    SUBJ: JRN HISTORY

CHEN, DURHAM S. F.   11   C01448
    WHAT AILS THE PRESS OF SHANGHAI
    THE CHINA CRITIC III:10(6 MAR 1930), 221-5.
    ##/FILM
    CHRON: 1910-1946
    GEOG: CHINA
    SUBJ: DESCRIPTION

CHEN, HERMIA   C02630
    THE XIAFENG OF CADRES: A MEANS OF MASS
         COMMUNICATION
    THE CHINA MAINLAND REVIEW II:4(MAR
         1967), 257-61.
    MEDIUM: OTHER
    CHRON: 1960-1970
    METH: OTHER OR COMB
    GEOG: CHINA
    SUBJ: PROPAGANDA   OTHER NON-J

CHEN, KINGLU S.   C02168
    CHINESE PAPERS AS ADVERTISING MEDIUMS
    THE CHINA WEEKLY REVIEW XLVI:1(1 SEPT 1928),
         15, 18, 20.
    CHRON: 1910-1946
    GEOG: CHINA
    SUBJ: OTHER JRN

CHEN, MIN   C00233
    CHINESE COMMUNIST PRESS (II)
    FOI CENTER PUBLICATION·NO. 123 (MAY 1964).
    ##/CHIN
    CHRON: 1960-1970
    GEOG: CHINA
    SUBJ: DESCRIPTION CONTROL

CHEN, PAUL   C02291
    LOCAL BRITISH PAPERS MAINTAIN INTERNATIONAL
        'LOVE-MART' FOR THE LONELY
    THE CHINA WEEKLY REVIEW 76:9(2 MAY 1936), 293.
    CHRON: 1910-1946
    GEOG: CHINA
    SUBJ: DESCRIPTION OTHER JRN

CHEN, YIH   C02218
    PRESS OPINION IN FAR EASTERN CRISIS
    MASTERS THESIS, UNIVERSITY OF MISSOURI, 1941.
    NYT, KANSAS CITY STAR, INDEPENDENCE EXAMINER,
        SEDALIA DEMOCRAT
    CHRON: 1910-1946
    METH: CONTENT ANALYSIS
    GEOG: CHINA   EAST ASIA   U.S.
    SUBJ: DESCRIPTION

CHENG CHANG-PO   12   C02732
    CHUNG KUO TZU YU SHIH SHANG YI WEI TO LI TI
        CHI CHE--CHENG SHE-WO SHIEN SHENG
    PAO SHUEH [TAIPEI] II:1(JUNE 1957), 6-8.
    (MR. CHENG SHE-WO: AN INDEPENDENT
        NEWSPAPERMAN IN THE CHINESE HISTORY OF
        FREEDOM)
    CHRON: SURVEY   LANG: CHINESE
    METH: HISTORICAL
    GEOG: TAIWAN   CHINA
    SUBJ: CONTROL   DESCRIPTION

CHENG CHEN-MING   16   C00239
    HSIEN CHIEH TUAN CHUNG-KUO TA HSUEH TI HSIN
        WEN CHIAO YU (PRESENT DAY JOURNALISM
        INSTRUCTION IN CHINESE COLLEGES)
    TAIPEI, CHIA HSIN SHUI NI KUNG SSU, WEN HUA
        CHI HSIN HUI, 1964.
    SKINNER II:44202; IN CHUNG-KUO TA HSUEH HSIN
        WEN CHIAO YU CHIH
        YEN CHIU (STUDIES OF JOURNALISM
        INSTRUCTION IN CHINESE COLLEGES),
        62-119.
    CHRON: 1960-1970   LANG: CHINESE
    GEOG: TAIWAN   VERIF: UNVERIFIED
    SUBJ: EDUCATION

CHENG CHEN-MING   16   C00240
    CHUNG-KUO HSIN WEN CHIAO YU TI FA CHAN' (THE
        DEVELOPMENT OF JOURNALISM INSTRUCTION
        IN CHINA)
    TAIPEI, CHIA HSIN SHUI NI KUNG SSU, WEN HUA
        CHI CHIN HUI, 1964.
    SKINNER II:44143; IN CHUNG-KUO TA HSUEH HSIN
        WEN CHIAO YU CHIH
        YEN CHIU (STUDIES IN
        JOURNALISM INSTRUCTION IN CHINESE
        COLLEGES), 24-34.
                            LANG: CHINESE
    CHRON: 1960-1970   VERIF: UNVERIFIED
    GEOG: TAIWAN
    SUBJ: EDUCATION   JRN HISTORY

CHENG CHIH   09   C02091
     CHUNG-KUO WEI-SHEN-MO MEI-YU YU-LUN [WHY IS
          THERE NO PUBLIC OPINION IN CHINA?]
     KUO-WEN CHOU-PAO 11:2(1 JAN 1934), 1-5.
     ##/CHIN-7
                         LANG: CHINESE
     CHRON: 1910-1946
     GEOG: CHINA
     SUBJ: DESCRIPTION OTHER JRN

CHENG CHU-YUAN   C00241
     CHINESE COMMUNIST INFILTRATION OF THE
          MAINLAND PRESS, 1927-1949; IN <COMMUNIST
          PENETRATION AND EXPLOITATION OF THE FREE
          PRESS>, PP. 22-8.
     WASHINGTON, D. C., U. S. CONGRESS JUDICIARY
          COMM., USGPO, 1962.
     ##/CHIN-3; Y4.J89/2:C73/42
     CHRON: 1946-1960
     GEOG: CHINA
     SUBJ: PROPAGANDA

CHENG HENG-HSIUNG, COMPILER.   13   C01585
     CH'UAN KUO TSO-CHIH CHIH-NAN MIN-KUO
          LIU-SHIH-LIU NIEN CHIH LIU-SHIH-CH'I NIEN
          PAN (GUIDE TO CHINESE PERIODICALS,
          1977-78
     TAIPEI, N. G., 1977.
                         LANG: CHINESE
     CHRON: 1970-1980   VERIF: UNVERIFIED
     GEOG: TAIWAN
     SUBJ: RESEARCH

CHENG HSI CHANG   C01569
     THE CHILDREN'S PAGE IN CHINESE NEWSPAPERS
     THE NEW CHINA [PEKING] (FEB 1931), 103-4.
     CHRON: 1910-1946
     GEOG: CHINA
     SUBJ: DEVELOPMENT DESCRIPTION EDUCATION

CHENG HUAN   C00242
     CHINA'S TV GAINS
     FEER 77:30(22 JULY 1972), 35.
     MEDIUM: ELECTRONIC
     CHRON: 1970-1980
     GEOG: CHINA
     SUBJ: DEVELOPMENT DESCRIPTION

CHENG JEN MING   15   C01749
     TA CHUNG CH'UAN PO HSUEH LI [MASS
          COMMUNICATIONS]
     TAIPEI, HUA HSIN HSUEH SHU TS'UNG SHU, 1976.
     MEDIUM: GENERAL   LANG: CHINESE
     CHRON: SURVEY
     GEOG: TAIWAN   CHINA
     SUBJ: DESCRIPTION

CHENG JENG-CHIEH   C02166
    THE FUTURE OF RADIO IN CHINA
    THE CHINA WEEKLY REVIEW XLVI:7(10 OCT 1928),
        19.
    MEDIUM: ELECTRONIC
    CHRON: 1910-1946
    GEOG: CHINA
    SUBJ: DESCRIPTION

CHENG YI   06   C02733
    T'AI PEI SHIH PAO YEH TI HSIN FA CHAN (THE
        DEVELOPMENT OF THE PRESS IN TAIPEI)
    PAO HSUEH [TAIPEI] III:8(JUNE 1967), 40-5.
                         LANG: CHINESE
    CHRON: SURVEY
    METH: HISTORICAL
    GEOG: TAIWAN
    SUBJ: JRN HISTORY

CHENG, JASON (JU-SHIEN)   C01748
    WALTER WILLIAMS AND CHINA, HIS INFLUENCE ON
        CHINESE JOURNALISM
    MASTERS THESIS, UNIVERSITY OF MISSOURI, 1963.
    #3
    CHRON: 1910-1946
    METH: HISTORICAL
    GEOG: CHINA   U.S.
    SUBJ: JRN HISTORY BIOGRAPHY   EDUCATION

CHENG, NAN WEI   C02219
    A HIGHLIGHT ON THE AMERICAN PRESS PICTURE OF
        CHINA: THE STEREOTYPE OF THE NORTH CHINA
        PROBLEM AS MOLDED BY THE NEW YORK TIMES
    MASTERS THESIS, UNIVERSITY OF MISSOURI, 1937.
    CHRON: 1910-1946
    METH: OTHER OR COMB
    GEOG: CHINA   EAST ASIA
    SUBJ: DESCRIPTION

CHENG, PAUL P. W., COMPILER.   C02261
    AN ANNOTATED GUIDE TO CURRENT CHINESE
        PERIODICALS IN HONG KONG
    TAIPEI, CHINESE MATERIALS AND RESEARCH AIDS
        SERVICE CENTER, 1978.
    CHRON: 1970-1980   VERIF: UNVERIFIED
    GEOG: HONG KONG
    SUBJ: RESEARCH

CHENG, PHILIP HUI-HO   C00243
    THE FUNCTION OF CHINESE OPERA IN SOCIAL
        CONTROL AND CHANGE
    PHD DISS, SOUTHERN ILLINOIS UNIVERSITY, 1974.
    INTL. DISS. 35:7933A; 151 PP.
    MEDIUM: OTHER
    CHRON: 1970-1980   VERIF: UNVERIFIED
    GEOG: CHINA
    SUBJ: PROPAGANDA CONTROL

CHEONG MEI SUI   C00244
    $60,000 SURPRISE FOR OUR WRITERS
    STRAITS TIMES (SUN) 30 MAY 1976
    ##/MAL; SAMAD ISMAIL
    CHRON: 1970-1980
    GEOG: MALAYSIA
    SUBJ: LITERATURE   CONTROL   LAW/ETHICS

CHEONG MEI SUI   C00595
    NOW 50 PER CENT LEVY ON FOREIGN TV ADS
    STRAITS TIMES (SUN) 22 JAN 1973
    ##/MALSP
    MEDIUM: ELECTRONIC
    CHRON: 1970-1980
    GEOG: MALAYSIA
    SUBJ: DESCRIPTION LAW/ETHICS

CHERRY, BENJAMIN   C00245
    DEATH OF CONSCIENCE
    FEER 77:34(19 AUG 1972), 14-5.
    ##/VN
    CHRON: 1970-1980
    GEOG: VIETNAM
    SUBJ: CONTROL

CHI CH'A CHENG WU WEI YUAN HUI.   16   C00246
    TISAN K'O, EDITOR.
    CHI CH'A P'ING CHIN HSIN WEN SHIH YEH T'UNG
        CHI (STATISTICS ON JOURNALISM IN HOPEI,
        CHAHAR, PEIPING, AND TIENTSIN)
    CHI CH'A TIAO CH'A T'UNG CHI TS'UNG
        K'AN 1:1(JULY 1936),57-85; 1:2(AUG
        1936), 61-75.
    SKINNER II:46455
                            LANG: CHINESE
    CHRON: 1910-1946   VERIF: UNVERIFIED
    GEOG: CHINA
    SUBJ: DESCRIPTION

CHIANG CHAN-K'UEI   09   C00247
    FAN TSUI HSIN WEN CHIH YEN CHIU (CRIME
        REPORTING)
    UNPUB MASTERS THESIS, 1959.
    SKINNER S00982 II:46525
    MEDIUM: GENERAL   LANG: CHINESE
    CHRON: 1946-1960   VERIF: UNVERIFIED
    GEOG: TAIWAN
    SUBJ: DESCRIPTION

CHIANG CHAO-CHI   .C02092
    I-CHIU-SAN-SSU NIEN WO-KUO HSIN-WEN SHIH-YEH
        LIAO K'AN (A BIRD'S EYE VIEW OF CHINESE
        JOURNALISM, 1934)
    PAO-HSUEH CHI K'AN 1:2(JAN 1935), 39-50.
                            LANG: CHINESE
    CHRON: 1910-1946
    GEOG: CHINA
    SUBJ: DESCRIPTION

CHIANG KUEI-LIN   09   C01692
    HSIN HUA SHE SHIH ERH NIEN (TWELVE YEARS WITH
        THE NCNA)
    TAIPEI, CHENG SHENG BROADCASTING CORP., 1962.
    MEDIUM: ELECTRONIC   LANG: CHINESE
    CHRON: 1946-1960
    GEOG: CHINA
    SUBJ: JRN HISTORY DESCRIPTION

CHIANG SHEN-WU   15   C00248
    <SU PAO> AN SHIH MO (THE SU PAO CASE)
    IN SHANG-HAI T'UNG SHE 03S02607, PP. 71-143.
    SKINNER S00982 II:48490
                            LANG: CHINESE
    CHRON: 1910-1946   VERIF: UNVERIFIED
    GEOG: CHINA
    SUBJ: JRN HISTORY LAW/ETHICS

CHIANG YEN, MA HSIUNG-FAN AND CHANG   C00249
         WAN-YANG
    WALL NEWSPAPERS IN THE RURAL AREAS (TRANS. OF
        TA TZU PAO TSAI NUNG TS'UN CHUNG)
    HUNG-CH'I 5(1 AUG 1958), 4-6.
    IN <SELECTED TRANSLATIONS FROM 'HUNG CHI'>,
        JUNE-AUG 1958, USJPRS,21 APR 1961, 93-100
        (JPRS 7837:MC 5498/1962).
    SKINNER 1:16994; CHINESE VERSION, SKINNER
        II:46526
    MEDIUM: OTHER
    CHRON: 1946-1960   VERIF: UNVERIFIED
    GEOG: CHINA
    SUBJ: DESCRIPTION

CHICO, SILVANO P.   C00250
    HISTORY OF THE PRESS AND PUBLIC OPINION IN
        THE PHILIPPINE ISLANDS
    MASTERS THESIS, UC/BERKELEY, 1956.
    CHRON: SURVEY   VERIF: UNVERIFIED
    GEOG: PHILIPPINES
    SUBJ: JRN HISTORY

CHIEH FU   15   C02734
    TS'UNG TU HUI HSIN WEN SHIH YEH SHUO TAO NEI
        TI HSIN WEN SHIH YEH TI WEI CHI HO
        FA CHAN
    PAO HSUEH CHI KAN [SHANGHAI] 1:2(JAN 1935),
        80-3.
                            LANG: CHINESE
    CHRON: 1910-1946
    METH: HISTORICAL
    GEOG: CHINA
    SUBJ: DEVELOPMENT DESCRIPTION LAW/ETHICS

CHIEN, HSUIN YUI   C02811
    DAS ALTE CHINESISCHE NACHRICHTENWESEN UND
        DIE CHINESISCHE STAATSPRESSE
    BERLIN, FAHRMANN, 1934.
                            LANG: OTHER EUROPEAN
    CHRON: SURVEY
    METH: HISTORICAL
    GEOG: CHINA
    SUBJ: JRN HISTORY DESCRIPTION

CHIEN, P. Y.   C02329
    CHINA'S FILM MAGNATE, T. J. HOLT, TO SEEK
        IDEAS ABROAD FOR DEVELOPMENT OF MOVING
        PICTURE INDUSTRY
    THE CHINA WEEKLY REVIEW 79:13(27 FEB 1937),
        437-8.
    MEDIUM: FILM
    CHRON: 1910-1946
    GEOG: CHINA
    SUBJ: DESCRIPTION

CHIN HSIANG LIN AND KUANG YUAN HSI   07   C01750
    WU CHUNG PAO CHIH TI KUANG KAO FEN HSI [A
        (QUANTITATIVE) ANALYSIS OF NEWSPAPER ADS]
    CH'ING HUA HSUEH PAO II:2(DEC 1925), 643-49.
                        LANG: CHINESE
    CHRON: 1910-1946
    METH: CONTENT ANALYSIS
    GEOG: CHINA
    SUBJ: OTHER JRN

CHIN PAO-MIN   10   C02735
    SAO TANG CHIEN PAO TI SHENG HO T'IEN CHE
        (OF SAO TANG PAO, TABLOID)
    PAO HSUEH [TAIPEI] II:7(DEC 1960), 89-91.
                        LANG: CHINESE
    CHRON: 1960-1970
    GEOG: TAIWAN
    SUBJ: DESCRIPTION

CHIN TA-K'AI   08   C01450
    CHUNG-KUNG TI CH'U-PAN KUNG-CHIH (THE CHINESE
        COMMUNIST CONTROL ON PUBLICATIONS)
    TSU-KUO CHOU-K'AN (CHINA WEEKLY) [HONG KONG]
        NO. 56 (25 JAN 1954), 7-9.
                        LANG: CHINESE
    CHRON: 1946-1960
    GEOG: CHINA
    SUBJ: CONTROL

CHIN, CHIEN   C00252
    A CHINESE PRINTING MANUAL, 1776
    LOS ANGELES, WARD RITCHIE PRESS, 1954.
    #3; PRINTED FOR MEMBERS OF TYPOPHILES IN
        LIMITED EDS. (1 OF 360,
        1 OF 100).
    CHRON: BEFORE 1910
    GEOG: CHINA
    SUBJ: PRINTING

CHINA AT WAR   C01754
    JAPANESE CINEMA STAR DIES
    IV:4(MAY 1940), 114.
    ##/CHIN-5; YAMAMOTO.
    MEDIUM: FILM
    CHRON: 1910-1946
    GEOG: CHINA   EAST ASIA
    SUBJ: DESCRIPTION BIOGRAPHY

CHINA AT WAR   C01753
    ASSASSINATED JOURNALIST'S FAREWELL
    III:4(NOV 1939), 60-3.
    ##/CHIN-5; CHU HSIN-KONG.
    CHRON: 1910-1946
    GEOG: CHINA
    SUBJ: DESCRIPTION BIOGRAPHY

CHINA AT WAR   C01752
    MODERN JOURNALISM FOR SINKIANG
    III:2(SEPT 1939), 19-20.
    ##/CHIN-5
    CHRON: 1910-1946
    GEOG: CHINA
    SUBJ: DESCRIPTION

CHINA AT WAR   C01751
    ODYSSEY OF A CHINESE DAILY
    1:3(JUNE 1938), 60.
    ##/CHIN-5; <THE CHINA TIMES>.
    CHRON: 1910-1946
    GEOG: CHINA
    SUBJ: DESCRIPTION

CHINA CRITIC, THE   C01923
    FOR A HIGHER JOURNALISTIC STANDARD
    I:2(7 JUNE 1928), 26.
    FILM
    CHRON: 1910-1946
    GEOG: CHINA
    SUBJ: EDUCATION

CHINA CRITIC, THE   C01927
    BOYCOTT OF JAPANESE PAPERS
    I:18(27 SEPT 1928), 345.
    CHRON: 1910-1946
    GEOG: CHINA   EAST ASIA
    SUBJ: CONTROL   DESCRIPTION

CHINA CRITIC, THE   C01926
    FOREIGN PAPERS AND EXTRATERRITORIALITY
    I:18(27 SEPT 1928), 343.
    CHRON: 1910-1946
    GEOG: CHINA
    SUBJ: DESCRIPTION LAW/ETHICS

CHINA CRITIC, THE   C01925
        SECOND-HAND REPORTING
        I:12(16 AUG 1928), 226-7.
        CHRON: 1910-1946
        GEOG: CHINA
        SUBJ: DESCRIPTION LAW/ETHICS

CHINA CRITIC, THE   C01924
        DEAN WILLIAMS AND THE PRESS IN CHINA
        I:11(9 AUG 1928), 205-6.
        FILM
        CHRON: 1910-1946
        GEOG: CHINA
        SUBJ: DESCRIPTION BIOGRAPHY

CHINA CRITIC, THE   C01949
        PURGING THE PRESS
        VI:45(9 NOV 1933), 1095.
        FILM
        CHRON: 1910-1946
        GEOG: CHINA
        SUBJ: CONTROL   LAW/ETHICS

CHINA CRITIC, THE   C01948
        ONE WAY OF NEWS REPORTING
        VI:41(12 OCT 1933), 999.
        FILM
        CHRON: 1910-1946
        GEOG: CHINA
        SUBJ: DESCRIPTION LAW/ETHICS

CHINA CRITIC, THE   C01947
        CHEN AND WOODHEAD
        VI:14(6 APR 1933), 349.
        FILM
        CHRON: 1910-1946
        GEOG: CHINA
        SUBJ: DESCRIPTION

CHINA CRITIC, THE   C01946
        BANNING THE FAR EASTERN REVIEW
        V:52(29 DEC 1932), 1377.
        FILM
        CHRON: 1910-1946
        GEOG: PHILIPPINES CHINA
        SUBJ: CONTROL

CHINA CRITIC, THE   C01945
       SCREEN CHINESE VS. REAL CHINESE
       V:30(28 JULY 1932), 758.
       FILM
       MEDIUM: FILM
       CHRON: 1910-1946
       GEOG: CHINA
       SUBJ: CROSS CULTU

CHINA CRITIC, THE   C01944
       REPORTED JAPANESE BRIBERY OF SHANGHAI PAPERS
       V:12(24 MAR 1932), 269.
       FILM
       CHRON: 1910-1946
       GEOG: CHINA   EAST ASIA
       SUBJ: CONTROL   DESCRIPTION LAW/ETHICS

CHINA CRITIC, THE   C01943
       THE HUSHED PRESS
       V:7(18 FEB 1937), 165-6.
       FILM
       CHRON: 1910-1946
       GEOG: CHINA
       SUBJ: CONTROL

CHINA CRITIC, THE   C01942
       JAPANESE CENSORSHIP IN MANCHURIA
       IV:46(12 NOV 1931), 1095-6.
       FILM
       CHRON: 1910-1946
       GEOG: CHINA   EAST ASIA
       SUBJ: CONTROL

CHINA CRITIC, THE   C01941
       PRESS REGAINS FREEDOM
       IV:44(29 OCT 1931), 1047-8.
       FILM
       CHRON: 1910-1946
       GEOG: CHINA
       SUBJ: CONTROL

CHINA CRITIC, THE   C01940
       KWEI [C. S.] JOINS POST
       IV:34(20 AUG 1931), 795.
       FILM
       CHRON: 1910-1946
       GEOG: CHINA
       SUBJ: DESCRIPTION BIOGRAPHY

CHINA CRITIC, THE   C01939
        THE RENGO NEWS AGENCY
        IV:17(23 APR 1931), 389.
        FILM
        CHRON: 1910-1946
        GEOG: CHINA   EAST ASIA
        SUBJ: PROPAGANDA FLOW/AGENCY DESCRIPTION

CHINA CRITIC, THE   C01938
        FILM CENSORSHIP AND <THE STORM OVER ASIA>
        IV:15(9 APR 1931), 339.
        FILM
        MEDIUM: FILM
        CHRON: 1910-1946
        GEOG: CHINA
        SUBJ: CONTROL

CHINA CRITIC, THE   C01937
        FILM CENSORSHIP
        III:2(9 JAN 1930), 26-7.
        FILM
        MEDIUM: FILM
        CHRON: 1910-1946
        GEOG: CHINA
        SUBJ: CONTROL

CHINA CRITIC, THE   C01936
        TALKING PICTURES IN CHINA
        II:40(3 OCT 1929), 788-9.
        FILM
        MEDIUM: FILM
        CHRON: 1910-1946
        GEOG: CHINA
        SUBJ: DESCRIPTION

CHINA CRITIC, THE   C01935
        THE SHANGHAI EVENING POST
        II:39(26 SEPT 1929), 766.
        FILM
        CHRON: 1910-1946
        GEOG: CHINA
        SUBJ: CONTROL

CHINA CRITIC, THE   C01934
        FREEDOM OF THE PRESS
        II:35(27 AUG 1929), 687.
        FILM
        CHRON: 1910-1946
        GEOG: CHINA
        SUBJ: CONTROL

CHINA CRITIC, THE   C01933
    AMERICAN JOURNALIST SEES CHINA THROUGH
        JAPANESE SPECTACLES
    II:34(27 AUG 1929), 668-9.
    FILM; G. A. LYONS, WASHINGTON STAR.
    CHRON: 1910-1946
    GEOG: CHINA   U.S.
    SUBJ: FOR CORR   DESCRIPTION

CHINA CRITIC, THE   C01932
    NANKING AND THE NORTH CHINA DAILY NEWS
    II:19(9 MAY 1929), 366-7.
    CHRON: 1910-1946
    GEOG: CHINA
    SUBJ: CONTROL

CHINA CRITIC, THE   C01931
    A SCHOOL OF JOURNALISM FOR CHINA
    I:16(18 APR 1929), 307-8.
    CHRON: 1910-1946
    GEOG: CHINA
    SUBJ: EDUCATION

CHINA CRITIC, THE   C01930
    JOURNALISTIC ETHICS
    I:31(27 DEC 1928), 606-7.
    FILM
    CHRON: 1910-1946
    GEOG: CHINA
    SUBJ: LAW/ETHICS

CHINA CRITIC, THE   C01928
    ABUSE OF PRESS PRIVLEGES
    I:23(1 NOV 1928), 443.
    FILM
    CHRON: 1910-1946
    GEOG: CHINA
    SUBJ: LAW/ETHICS

CHINA CRITIC, THE   C01377
    THE DEPORTATION OF MR. SOKOLSKY
    11:17(25 APR 1929), 327.
    ##/CHIN-5
    CHRON: 1910-1946
    GEOG: CHINA
    SUBJ: CONTROL

CHINA HANDBOOK 1937-1944   C01397

    CHUNGKING, CHINESE MINISTRY OF INFORMATION,
        1944.
    ##/CHIN-5; THE PRESS, PP. 415-27; REV. ED. OF
        1943 ED., SEE C01389.
    CHRON: 1910-1946
    GEOG: CHINA
    SUBJ: DESCRIPTION

CHINA HANDBOOK EDITORIAL BOARD,   C01398
        COMPILER.
    CHINA HANDBOOK 1950
    NEW YORK, ROCKPORT, 1950.
    ##/CHIN-5; PRESS, PP. 678-82.
    CHRON: 1910-1946
    GEOG: CHINA
    SUBJ: DESCRIPTION

CHINA INSTITUTE BULLETIN   C01786
    CHINESE CURRENT PERIODICALS
    3:3(DEC 1938), 87-96; PART 2, 3:4(JAN 1939),
        125-8.
    CHRON: 1910-1946
    GEOG: CHINA
    SUBJ: RESEARCH

CHINA JOURNAL, THE   C01787
    THE PRINTED WORD IN SHANGHAI
    XII:5(MAY 1930), 240-2.
    ##/CHIN-6
    CHRON: 1910-1946
    GEOG: CHINA
    SUBJ: DESCRIPTION PRINTING

CHINA MAGAZINE, THE   C01755
    INFORMATION AGAINST THE <CHINA MAIL>
    I(1868), 202.
    ##/CHIN-6
    CHRON: BEFORE 1910
    GEOG: HONG KONG   CHINA
    SUBJ: LAW/ETHICS

CHINA NEWS ANALYSIS   C01693
    NEWSPAPERS [A NEW THEME: HONESTY]
    1101(2 DEC 1977), 1-3.
    LADISLAO LA DANY
    CHRON: 1970-1980
    GEOG: CHINA
    SUBJ: LAW/ETHICS

```
CHINA NEWS ANALYSIS                                    C01009
    FILMS
    1070(18 FEB 1977), 7.
    ##/CHIN-4; LADISLAO LA DANY.
    MEDIUM:   FILM
    CHRON: 1970-1980
    GEOG:   CHINA
    SUBJ:   DESCRIPTION


CHINA NEWS ANALYSIS                                    C01011
    BEWARE OF PHOTOGRAPHS
    1076(15 APR 1977).
    ##-CHIN-4; LADISLAO LA DANY; 6 PP.
    CHRON: 1970-1980
    GEOG:   CHINA
    SUBJ:   DESCRIPTION


CHINA NEWS ANALYSIS                                    C01010
    THE MASS MEDIA
    1070(18 FEB 1977), 2-3.
    ##/CHIN-4; LADISLAO LA DANY.
    MEDIUM:   GENERAL
    CHRON: 1970-1980
    GEOG:   CHINA
    SUBJ:   DESCRIPTION


CHINA NEWS ANALYSIS                                    C00334
    THE BOOK
    744/745(14 FEB 1969), 7-13.
    ##/CHIN-2; LADISLAO LA DANY
    CHRON: 1960-1970
    GEOG:   CHINA
    SUBJ:   LITERATURE   PUBLISHING   DESCRIPTION


CHINA NEWS ANALYSIS                                    C00253
    NEWSPAPERS
    94(5 AUG 1955), 1-7.
    ##/CHIN-4; LADISLAO LA DANY
    CHRON: 1946-1960
    GEOG:   CHINA
    SUBJ:   DESCRIPTION


CHINA NEWS ANALYSIS                                    C00257
    NEW TONE IN PEOPLE'S DAILY
    157(16 NOV 1956), 5-7.
    ##/CHIN-4; LADISLO LA DANY
    CHRON: 1946-1960
    GEOG:   CHINA
    SUBJ:   DESCRIPTION
```

CHINA NEWS ANALYSIS   C00256
     READERS AND READING MATTER
     123(9 MAR 1956), 2-7.
     ##/CHIN-4; LADISLAO LA DANY
     CHRON: 1946-1960
     GEOG: CHINA
     SUBJ: DESCRIPTION LITERATURE

CHINA NEWS ANALYSIS   C00255
     BOOKS, MIRRORS OF THE NATIONS' SOUL
     123(9 MAR 1956), 1.
     ##/CHIN-4; LADISLAO LA DANY
     CHRON: 1946-1960
     GEOG: CHINA
     SUBJ: DESCRIPTION LITERATURE

CHINA NEWS ANALYSIS   C00254
     JOURNALISM
     104(14 OCT 1955), 2-7.
     ##/CHIN-4; LADISLAO LA DANY
     CHRON: 1946-1960
     GEOG: CHINA
     SUBJ: DESCRIPTION

CHINA NEWS ANALYSIS   C00265
     SOURCES OF NEWS DRYING UP?
     570(2 JULY 1965), 1-7.
     ##/CHIN-2; LADISLAO LA DANY
     MEDIUM: GENERAL
     CHRON: 1960-1970
     GEOG: CHINA
     SUBJ: CONTROL   FOR CORR

CHINA NEWS ANALYSIS   C00264
     A FILM: 'EARLY SPRING IN FEBRUARY'
     552(19 FEB 1965).
     LADISLAO LA DANY
     MEDIUM: FILM
     CHRON: 1960-1970
     GEOG: CHINA
     SUBJ: DESCRIPTION

CHINA NEWS ANALYSIS   C00263
     TELECOMMUNICATIONS
     514(1 MAY 1964), 1-7.
     ##/CHIN-2; LADISLAO LA DANY
     MEDIUM: ELECTRONIC
     CHRON: 1960-1970
     GEOG: CHINA
     SUBJ: DESCRIPTION

CHINA NEWS ANALYSIS   C00262
     WHAT THE 'RED FLAG' TEACHES
     440(5 OCT 1962), 1-7.
     ##/CHIN-2; LADISLAO LA DANY
     CHRON: 1960-1970
     GEOG: CHINA
     SUBJ: PROPAGANDA EDUCATION   DESCRIPTION

CHINA NEWS ANALYSIS   C00261
     CHANGING BOOKMARKET
     170(1 MAR 1957), 1-2.
     ##/CHIN-4; LADISLAO LA DANY
     CHRON: 1946-1960
     GEOG: CHINA
     SUBJ: PUBLISHING LITERATURE DESCRIPTION

CHINA NEWS ANALYSIS   C00260
     PUBLISHERS, EDITORS, LIBRARIES, BOOKSHOPS
     170(1 MAR 1957), 2-7.
     ##/CHIN-4; LADISLAO LA DANY
     CHRON: 1946-1960
     GEOG: CHINA
     SUBJ: PUBLISHING DESCRIPTION PRINTING

CHINA NEWS ANALYSIS   C00259
     CHANGES IN THE NEWSPAPER
     157(16 NOV 1956), 1.
     ##/CHIN-4; LADISLAO LA DANY
     CHRON: 1946-1960
     GEOG: CHINA
     SUBJ: DESCRIPTION

CHINA NEWS ANALYSIS   C00258
     THE CONQUEST OF READERS
     157(16 NOV 1956), 2-5.
     ##/CHIN-4; LADISLAO LA DANY
     CHRON: 1946-1960
     GEOG: CHINA
     SUBJ: DESCRIPTION LITERATURE PROPAGANDA

CHINA NEWS ANALYSIS   C00271
     IN THE CINEMA
     1041(21 MAY 1976), 1-7.
     LASISLAO LA DANY
     MEDIUM: FILM
     CHRON: 1970-1980
     GEOG: CHINA
     SUBJ: DESCRIPTION

CHINA NEWS ANALYSIS   C00270
     PUBLISHING TRADE
     920(18 MAY 1973), 1-7.
     LADISLAO LA DANY
     CHRON: 1970-1980
     GEOG: CHINA
     SUBJ: PUBLISHING

CHINA NEWS ANALYSIS   C00269
     LITERATURE AND PUBLICATIONS IN 1971
     867(14 MAR 1972), 1-7.
     ##/CHIN-2; LADISLAO LA DANY
     CHRON: 1970-1980
     GEOG: CHINA
     SUBJ: LITERATURE PUBLISHING

CHINA NEWS ANALYSIS   C00268
     NEWSPAPERS AND JOURNALISM
     828(15 JAN 1971), 1-7.
     ##/CHIN; LADISLAO LA DANY
     CHRON: 1970-1980
     GEOG: CHINA
     SUBJ: DESCRIPTION

CHINA NEWS ANALYSIS   C00267
     THE PEOPLE'S DAILY TODAY
     744/745(14 FEB 1969), 2-6.
     ##/CHIN-2; LADISLAO LA DANY
     CHRON: 1960-1970
     GEOG: CHINA
     SUBJ: DESCRIPTION

CHINA NEWS ANALYSIS   C00266
     NEWSPAPERS AND JOURNALISM
     631(7 OCT 1966), 1-7.
     ##/CHIN-2; LADISLAO LA DANY; SAYINGS OF MAO,
          THE HEADS OF
          PROPAGANDA, THE CANTON EVENING
          PAPER, IN DEEP WATERS,
          NEWSPAPERS, BEFORE AND AFTER
     CHRON: 1960-1970
     GEOG: CHINA
     SUBJ: DESCRIPTION

CHINA NEWS ANALYSIS   C02337
     A NEW STEP IN WRITING REFORM
     1119(12 MAY 1978), 1-7.
     CHRON: 1970-1980
     GEOG: CHINA
     SUBJ: LANGUAGE

CHINA PICTORIAL   C01694
    THE PRINTERS AIM HIGH
    NO. 7-8(1971), 24-6.
    CHRON: 1970-1980
    GEOG: CHINA
    SUBJ: PRINTING

CHINA PRESS, THE   C02268
    CHINESE TALKIE WELCOMED IN N. Y.
    (8 APR 1936), 9, 12.
    MEDIUM: FILM
    CHRON: 1910-1946
    GEOG: CHINA   U.S.
    SUBJ: DESCRIPTION

CHINA PRESS, THE   C02267
    DR. SWEN NELOTS, THE OLD RASCAL, TURNS UP
        IN JAPAN
    (8 APR 1936), 9.
    CHRON: 1910-1946
    GEOG: CHINA   EAST ASIA
    SUBJ: LAW/ETHICS

CHINA PRESS, THE   C02266
    NANKING RULES ON FILMS MADE BY FOREIGNERS
    (8 APR 1936), 2.
    MEDIUM: FILM
    CHRON: 1910-1946
    GEOG: CHINA
    SUBJ: CONTROL

CHINA PRESS, THE   C02265
    PEIPING CHEN PAO REORGANIZED
    (28 MAR 1936), 10.
    EDITORIAL FROM <TA WAN PAO>
    CHRON: 1910-1946
    GEOG: CHINA
    SUBJ: OTHER JRN

CHINA PRESS, THE   C02264
    WOO KYA-TANG ARRIVES ABROAD S. S. PRESIDENT
        LINCOLN
    (28 MAR 1936), 1.
    CHRON: 1910-1946
    GEOG: CHINA
    SUBJ: BIOGRAPHY

CHINA PRESS, THE   C02263
        PEIPING 4TH ESTATE MEMBERS CHIDE TIME FOR
              ERROR IN PHOTO
        (3 MAR 1936), 9.
        CHRON: 1910-1946
        GEOG: CHINA
        SUBJ: DESCRIPTION LAW/ETHICS

CHINA PRESS, THE   C02568
        THE CHINA PRESS JUBILEE EDITION
        SHANGHAI, THE CHINA PRESS, 1936.
        ##/FILM; NUC<56 107:339.
        CHRON: SURVEY
        GEOG: CHINA
        SUBJ: JRN HISTORY DESCRIPTION

CHINA TODAY   C01988
        THE CHINA NEWS AGENCY--IN CELEBRATION OF THE
              44TH FOUNDING ANNIVERSARY, APRIL 1, 1967
        10:6(JUNE 1967), 26-7.
        ##/TAI
        MEDIUM: GENERAL
        CHRON: SURVEY
        GEOG: TAIWAN   CHINA
        SUBJ: FLOW/AGENCY

CHINA TRUTH, THE   C01451
        HOW COME 'CHINA MAIL'?
        1:7(1 JUNE 1929), 2-3.
        ##/FILM
        CHRON: 1910-1946
        GEOG: CHINA
        SUBJ: LAW/ETHICS

CHINA TRUTH, THE   C01453
        THE CHINESE PRESS AMERICANIZED
        1:42-3(8 FEB 1930), 3.
        ##/FILM
        CHRON: 1910-1946
        GEOG: CHINA
        SUBJ: DESCRIPTION

CHINA TRUTH, THE   C01452
        A JOURNALIST WHO MISLEADS
        1:34(7 DEC 1929), 5-6.
        ##/FILM
        CHRON: 1910-1946
        GEOG: CHINA
        SUBJ: LAW/ETHICS

CHINA YEAR BOOK 1913, THE   C01218
    NEWSPAPERS, P. 662.
    LONDON, GEORGE ROUTLEDGE, 1913.
    ##/CHIN-4; BELL, H. T. MONTAGUE AND
        H. G. W. WOODHEAD, EDITORS.
    CHRON: 1910-1946
    GEOG: CHINA
    SUBJ: RESEARCH   DESCRIPTION

CHINA YEAR BOOK 1914, THE   C01219
    NEWSPAPERS, P. 720.
    LONDON, GEORGE ROUTLEDGE, 1914.
    ##/CHIN-4; WOODHEAD, H. G. W. AND H. T.
        MONTAGUE BELL, EDITORS.
    CHRON: 1910-1946
    GEOG: CHINA
    SUBJ: RESEARCH   DESCRIPTION

CHINA YEAR BOOK 1916, THE   C01220
    NEWSPAPERS, P. 693.
    LONDON, GEORGE ROUTLEDGE, 1916.
    BELL, H. T. MONTAGUE AND H. G. W.
        WOODHEAD, EDITORS.
    CHRON: 1910-1946
    GEOG: CHINA
    SUBJ: RESEARCH   DESCRIPTION

CHINA YEAR BOOK 1919-1920, THE   C01221
    NEWSPAPERS, P. 697.
    LONDON, GEORGE ROUTLEDGE, 1920.
    ##/CHIN-4; BELL, H. T. MONTAGUE AND H. G. W.
        WOODHEAD, EDITORS.
    CHRON: 1910-1946
    GEOG: CHINA
    SUBJ: RESEARCH   DESCRIPTION

CHINA YEAR BOOK 1921-1922, THE   C01320
    NEWSPAPERS AND PERIODICALS IN CHINA, PP.
        93-130.
    TIENTSIN, TIENTSIN PRESS, 1922.
    ##/CHIN-5; H. G. W. WOODHEAD, ED., COMPLETE
        LIST OF PAPERS.
    CHRON: 1910-1946
    GEOG: CHINA
    SUBJ: RESEARCH   DESCRIPTION

CHINA YEAR BOOK 1923, THE   C01222
    NEWSPAPERS AND PERIODICALS IN CHINA, PP.
        152-99.
    TIENTSIN, TIENTSIN PRESS, 1923.
    ##/CHIN-4; H. G. W. WOODHEAD, ED.; COMPLETE
        LIST OF PAPERS.
    CHRON: 1910-1946
    GEOG: CHINA
    SUBJ: RESEARCH   DESCRIPTION

CHINA YEAR BOOK 1924-25, THE   C01223
    NEWSPAPERS AND PERIODICALS IN CHINA,
        PP. 1156-7.
    TIENTSIN, TIENTSIN PRESS, 1924.
    ##/CHIN-4; WOODHEAD, H. G. W., ED.
    CHRON: 1910-1946
    GEOG: CHINA
    SUBJ: RESEARCH   DESCRIPTION

CHINA YEAR BOOK 1925-26, THE   C01224
    NEWSPAPERS AND PERIODICALS IN CHINA, PP.
        1057-1110.
    TIENTSIN, TIENTSIN PRESS, 1926.
    ##/CHIN-4; WOODHEAD, H. G. W., ED.;
        COMPLETE LIST OF PAPERS.
    CHRON: 1910-1946
    GEOG: CHINA
    SUBJ: RESEARCH   DESCRIPTION

CHINA YEAR BOOK 1928, THE   C01225
    NEWSPAPERS AND PERIODICALS IN CHINA, PP.
        1212-3.
    TIENTSIN, TIENTSIN PRESS, 1928.
    ##/CHIN-4; H. G. W. WOODHEAD, ED.
    CHRON: 1910-1946
    GEOG: CHINA
    SUBJ: RESEARCH   DESCRIPTION

CHINA YEAR BOOK 1929-1930, THE   C01226
    NEWSPAPERS AND PERIODICALS IN CHINA, PP.
        1124-5.
    TIENTSIN, TIENTSIN PRESS, 1930.
    ##/CHIN-4; WOODHEAD, H. G. W., ED.
    CHRON: 1910-1946
    GEOG: CHINA
    SUBJ: RESEARCH   DESCRIPTION

CHINA YEAR BOOK 1931, THE   C01227
    NEWSPAPERS AND PERIODICALS IN CHINA, PP.
        657, 659.
    SHANGHAI, THE NORTH-CHINA DAILY NEWS &
        HERALD, 1931.
    ##/CHIN-4; WOODHEAD, H. G. W., ED.
    CHRON: 1910-1946
    GEOG: CHINA
    SUBJ: RESEARCH   DESCRIPTION

CHINA YEAR BOOK 1932, THE   C01228
    NEWSPAPERS AND PERIODICALS IN CHINA, P. 789.
    SHANGHAI, THE NORTH-CHINA DAILY NEWS &
        HERALD, 1932.
    ##/CHIN-4; WOODHEAD, H. G. W., ED.
    CHRON: 1910-1946
    GEOG: CHINA
    SUBJ: RESEARCH   DESCRIPTION

CHINA YEAR BOOK 1933, THE   C01229
    NEWSPAPERS AND PERIODICALS IN CHINA, PP.715,
        717.
    SHANGHAI, THE NORTH-CHINA DAILY NEWS & HERALD,
        1933.
    ##/CHIN-4; WOODHEAD, H. G. W., ED.
    CHRON: 1910-1946
    GEOG: CHINA
    SUBJ: RESEARCH   DESCRIPTION

CHINA YEAR BOOK 1934, THE   C01230
    NEWSPAPERS AND PERIODICALS IN CHINA, PP.
        817, 819.
    SHANGHAI, THE NORTH-CHINA DAILY NEWS &
        HERALD, 1934.
    ##/CHIN-4; WOODHEAD, H. G. W., ED.
    CHRON: 1910-1946
    GEOG: CHINA
    SUBJ: RESEARCH   DESCRIPTION

CHINA YEAR BOOK 1935, THE   C01231
    NEWSPAPERS AND PERIODICALS IN CHINA, P. 591.
    SHANGHAI, THE NORTH-CHINA DAILY NEWS &
        HERALD, 1935.
    ##/CHIN-4; WOODHEAD, H. G. W., ED.
    CHRON: 1910-1946
    GEOG: CHINA
    SUBJ: RESEARCH   DESCRIPTION

CHINA YEAR BOOK 1936, THE   C01234
    CHINESE DAILY NEWSPAPERS, P. 473; CHINESE
        LAW, 473, 5, 7, 9; FOREIGN NEWSPAPERS
        AND PERIODICALS IN CHINA,
    SHANGHAI, THE NORTH-CHINA DAILY NEWS &
        HERALD, 1936.
    ##/CHIN-4; WOODHEAD, H. G. W., ED.
    CHRON: 1910-1946
    GEOG: CHINA
    SUBJ: RESEARCH   DESCRIPTION

CHINA YEAR BOOK 1938, THE   C01235
    CHINESE DAILY NEWSPAPERS, PP. 559, 561;
        FOREIGN NEWSPAPERS AND PERIODICALS IN
        CHINA, 561.
    SHANGHAI, THE NORTH-CHINA DAILY NEWS &
        HERALD, 1938.
    CHRON: 1910-1946
    GEOG: CHINA
    SUBJ: RESEARCH   DESCRIPTION

CHINA YEAR BOOK 1939, THE   C01236
    FOREIGN NEWSPAPERS AND PERIODICALS IN CHINA,
        P. 591.
    SHANGHAI, THE NORTH-CHINA DAILY NEWS & HERALD,
        1939.
    CHRON: 1910-1946
    GEOG: CHINA
    SUBJ: RESEARCH   DESCRIPTION

CHINESE CHRISTIAN INTELLIGENCER, THE   C00324
      CHRISTIAN JOURNALISM IN CHINA AT THE
          PRESENT DAY
      CHINESE RECORDER 43:1(JAN 1912), 16-23.
      AUTHOR SEEMS TO BE I. S. WOODBRIDGE
      CHRON: 1910-1946
      GEOG: CHINA
      SUBJ: DESCRIPTION

CHINESE ECONOMIC MONTHLY   C00326
      AN ANALYTICAL STUDY OF ADVERTISEMENTS IN
          CHINESE NEWSPAPERS
      3:4(APR 1926), 139-143.
      TRANS OF PARTIAL STUDY, SEE FOOTNOTE IN
          BRITTON B00191
      CHRON: 1910-1946
      METH: CONTENT ANALYSIS
      GEOG: CHINA
      SUBJ: OTHER JRN

CHINESE LANGUAGE PRESS INSTITUTE, THE   C00327
      HONG KONG
      IN ASIAN PRESS A00134.
      ##/ASIA
      CHRON: 1970-1980
      GEOG: HONG KONG
      SUBJ: DESCRIPTION

CHINESE MINISTRY OF INFORMATION,   C01389
          COMPILER.
      CHINA HANDBOOK 1937-1943
      NEW YORK, MACMILLAN, 1943.
      ##/CHIN-5; THE PRESS, PP. 696-711; SEE CHINA
          HANDBOOK C01397.
      CHRON: 1910-1946
      GEOG: CHINA
      SUBJ: DESCRIPTION

CHINESE NATION, THE   C01978
      MR. WOODHEAD AND THE SHANGHAI EVENING POST
      I:8(6 AUG 1930), 116-17.
      FILM
      CHRON: 1910-1946
      GEOG: CHINA
      SUBJ: CONTROL   LAW/ETHICS

CHINESE NATION, THE   C01959
      AN EXAMPLE OF NEWSPAPER CENSORSHIP
      II:25(2 DEC 1931), 855-6.
      FILM
      CHRON: 1910-1946
      GEOG: CHINA   EAST ASIA
      SUBJ: CONTROL   PROPAGANDA FLOW/AGENCY

CHINESE NATION, THE   C01958
     NEWSPAPER PREJUDICE
     I:43(8 APR 1931), 1130, 1156.
     FILM
     CHRON: 1910-1946
     GEOG: CHINA
     SUBJ: DESCRIPTION LAW/ETHICS

CHINESE NATION, THE   C01955
     SIMPSON THE MAN
     I:9(13 AUG 1930), 136.
     FILM
     CHRON: 1910-1946
     GEOG: CHINA
     SUBJ: DESCRIPTION BIOGRAPHY

CHINESE NATION, THE   C01957
     NEWSPAPER TASTES
     I:40(18 MAR 1931), 1034, 1051.
     FILM
     CHRON: 1910-1946
     GEOG: CHINA
     SUBJ: DESCRIPTION

CHINESE NATION, THE   C01956
     RENGO 'NEWS' AGENCY
     I:40(18 MAR 1931), 1029-30.
     FILM
     CHRON: 1910-1946
     GEOG: CHINA   EAST ASIA
     SUBJ: PROPAGANDA   FLOW/AGENCY

CHINESE RECORDER AND MISSIONARY   C00274
          JOURNAL
     THE PEKING GAZETTES
     XIII:1(JUNE 1870), 10-12.
     CHRON: BEFORE 1910
     GEOG: CHINA
     SUBJ: DESCRIPTION

CHINESE RECORDER AND MISSIONARY   C00273
          JOURNAL
     THE PRESBYTERIAN MISSION PRESS AT SHANGHAI
     I:8(DEC 1868), 167-68.
     MENTIONS <THE CHINESE NEWSPAPER> BY
          Y. J. ALLEN
     CHRON: BEFORE 1910
     GEOG: CHINA
     SUBJ: DESCRIPTION

CHINESE RECORDER AND MISSIONARY   C00276
          JOURNAL
     HANGCHOW COLLOQUIAL PAPER
     XXXII:9(SEPT 1901), 459-460.
     BY 'J. C. G.'
     CHRON: BEFORE 1910
     GEOG: CHINA
     SUBJ: DESCRIPTION

CHINESE RECORDER AND MISSIONARY   C00275
          JOURNAL
     THE PRESS IN CHINA
     III:3(AUG 1870), 81-2.
     CORRESPONDENCE FROM 'F. H. E.'
     CHRON: BEFORE 1910
     GEOG: CHINA
     SUBJ: DESCRIPTION

CHINESE REPOSITORY   C00280
     MAGAZINES
     I:12(APR 1833), 508.
     CHRON: BEFORE 1910
     GEOG: CHINA
     SUBJ: DESCRIPTION

CHINESE REPOSITORY   C00278
     RELIGIOUS INTELLIGENCE: MALACCA; THE PRESS
     I:3(JULY 1832), 106-7.
     CHRON: BEFORE 1910
     GEOG: MALAYSIA   CHINA
     SUBJ: PRINTING   PUBLISHING

CHINESE REPOSITORY   C00284
     THE <INDO-CHINESE GLEANER>
     II:5(SEPT 1833), 186.
     CHRON: BEFORE 1910
     GEOG: CHINA   SEV ASIA
     SUBJ: DESCRIPTION

CHINESE REPOSITORY   C00283
     A MONTHLY PERIODICAL
     II:4(AUG 1833), 186.
     CHARLES GUTZLAFF PUB/ED
     CHRON: BEFORE 1910
     GEOG: CHINA
     SUBJ: DESCRIPTION

CHINESE REPOSITORY   C00282
    THE <EVANGELIST>
    II:1(MAY 1833), 46-7.
    CHRON: BEFORE 1910
    GEOG: CHINA
    SUBJ: DESCRIPTION

CHINESE REPOSITORY   C00281
    INTRODUCTORY REMARKS
    II:1(MAY 1833), 6-7.
    5 PRINTING PRESSES MENTIONED
    CHRON: BEFORE 1910
    GEOG: CHINA
    SUBJ: PRINTING

CHINESE REPOSITORY   C00318
    ORDINANCES OF THE GOVERNMENT OF HONGKONG
        RELATING TO SEAMEN AND TO PRINTING
    XIII:3(MAR 1844), 164-5.
    CHRON: BEFORE 1910
    GEOG: HONG KONG   CHINA
    SUBJ: DESCRIPTION

CHINESE REPOSITORY   C00317
    <THE NORTH CHINA HERALD>
    XIX:8(AUG 1850), 462-4.
    CHRON: BEFORE 1910
    GEOG: CHINA
    SUBJ: DESCRIPTION

CHINESE REPOSITORY   C00316
    MEN AND THINGS IN SHANGHAI: PEKING GAZETTE
        IS POOR INDEX OF WHAT ACTUALLY OCCURS
    XIX:4(APR 1850), 229.
    CHRON: BEFORE 1910
    GEOG: CHINA
    SUBJ: DESCRIPTION

CHINESE REPOSITORY   C00315
    MEADOWS' COMMERCIAL REPORTER
    XVI:5(MAY 1847), 271.
    FOLDED
    CHRON: BEFORE 1910
    GEOG: CHINA
    SUBJ: DESCRIPTION

CHINESE REPOSITORY   C00314
    MEADOWS' COMMERCIAL REPORTER
    XVI:3(MAR 1847), 129-33.
    CHRON: BEFORE 1910
    GEOG: CHINA
    SUBJ: DESCRIPTION

CHINESE REPOSITORY   C00313
    MEADOWS' COMMERCIAL REPORTER
    XVI:2(FEB 1847), 104.
    STARTED
    CHRON: BEFORE 1910
    GEOG: CHINA
    SUBJ: DESCRIPTION

CHINESE REPOSITORY   C00312
    EXTRACTS FROM THE <PEKING GAZETTES>, NOS. 1
        TO 4
    XV:4(APR 1846), 221-3.
    CHRON: BEFORE 1910
    GEOG: CHINA
    SUBJ: DESCRIPTION

CHINESE REPOSITORY   C00311
    <THE CHINA MAIL>, NOS. 1-5.
    XIV:3(MAR 1845), 135-7.
    CHRON: BEFORE 1910
    GEOG: CHINA
    SUBJ: DESCRIPTION

CHINESE REPOSITORY   C00310
    <PEKING GAZETTES>
    XIII:12(DEC 1844), 656.
    CHRON: BEFORE 1910
    GEOG: CHINA
    SUBJ: DESCRIPTION

CHINESE REPOSITORY   C00309
    SPECIMEN OF CHINESE TYPE, AND CHARACTERS
        FORMED BY DIVISABLE TYPE
    XIII:12(DEC 1844), 656.
    CHRON: BEFORE 1910
    GEOG: CHINA
    SUBJ: PRINTING

CHINESE REPOSITORY   C00308
     REMOVAL OF THE OFFICE OF THE <CHINESE
          REPOSITORY> TO HONGKONG
     XIII:10(OCT 1844), 559.
     CHRON: BEFORE 1910
     GEOG: MACAO   CHINA
     SUBJ: DESCRIPTION

CHINESE REPOSITORY   C00307
     <THE CANTON PRESS>
     XIII:4(APR 1844), 224.
     CHRON: BEFORE 1910
     GEOG: CHINA
     SUBJ: DESCRIPTION

CHINESE REPOSITORY   C00306
     REMARKS UPON THE <PEKING GAZETTES>
     XIII:2(FEB 1844), 107-8.
     CHRON: BEFORE 1910
     GEOG: CHINA
     SUBJ: DESCRIPTION

CHINESE REPOSITORY   C00305
     <THE EASTERN GLOBE AND COMMERCIAL ADVERTISER>
     XII:6(JUNE 1843), 336.
     CHRON: BEFORE 1910
     GEOG: CHINA
     SUBJ: DESCRIPTION

CHINESE REPOSITORY   C00304
     A PERIODICAL IN CHINESE
     XII:2(FEB 1843), 111.
     <TELESCOPE> (TSIEN-LI-KING)
     CHRON: BEFORE 1910
     GEOG: CHINA
     SUBJ: DESCRIPTION

CHINESE REPOSITORY   C00303
     NEWSPAPERS IN MACAO AND MANILA
     XII:2(FEB 1843), 110-111.
     <A AURORA MACANENSE> AND <SEMINARIO FILIPINO>
     CHRON: BEFORE 1910
     GEOG: CHINA   PHILIPPINES
     SUBJ: DESCRIPTION

CHINESE REPOSITORY   C00302
    DONATION TO THE PORTUGUESE OF MACAO, BY
        JAMES MATHESON, ESQ.
    XI:3(MAR 1842), 181-2.
    MATHESON WAS ED. OF <CANTON REGISTER>
    CHRON: BEFORE 1910
    GEOG: MACAO   CHINA
    SUBJ: BIOGRAPHY   DESCRIPTION

CHINESE REPOSITORY   C00301
    RETROSPECTION, OR A REVIEW OF PUBLIC
        OCCURRENCES DURING THE LAST TEN YEARS,
        FROM 1832-1841
    XI:1(JAN 1842), 1-28.
    P. 19, GUTZLAFF'S MAGAZINE (1833)
    CHRON: BEFORE 1910
    GEOG: CHINA
    SUBJ: DESCRIPTION

CHINESE REPOSITORY   C00300
    THE <HONGKONG GAZETTE>
    X:5(MAY 1841), 286-9.
    SELECTIONS
    CHRON: BEFORE 1910
    GEOG: CHINA
    SUBJ: DESCRIPTION

CHINESE REPOSITORY   C00299
    CANTON NEWSPAPERS
    VIII:3(JULY 1839), 168.
    CHRON: BEFORE 1910
    GEOG: CHINA
    SUBJ: DESCRIPTION

CHINESE REPOSITORY   C00298
    THE <BOLETIM OFFICIAL>
    VII:6(OCT 1838), 335.
    CHRON: BEFORE 1910
    GEOG: MACAO   CHINA
    SUBJ: DESCRIPTION

CHINESE REPOSITORY   C00297
    <THE CHINESE MAGAZINE>
    V:12(APR 1837), 576-6.
    CHRON: BEFORE 1910
    GEOG: CHINA
    SUBJ: DESCRIPTION

CHINESE REPOSITORY   C00296
     EUROPEAN PERIODICALS BEYOND THE GANGES
     V:4(AUG 1836), 145-60.
     CHRON: BEFORE 1910
     GEOG: SEV ASIA
     SUBJ: DESCRIPTION

CHINESE REPOSITORY   C00295
     RELIGIOUS INTELLIGENCE: THE PRESS AT
          SINGAPORE; SIAM; BURMAH; AND BOMBAY
     V:2(JUNE 1836), 91.
     CHRON: BEFORE 1910
     GEOG: SEV ASIA
     SUBJ: PRINTING

CHINESE REPOSITORY   C00294
     LITERARY PIRACY
     V:2(JUNE 1836), 95.
     CHRON: BEFORE 1910
     GEOG: CHINA
     SUBJ: DESCRIPTION LITERATURE

CHINESE REPOSITORY   C00293
     <THE CANTON PRESS>
     IV:5(SEPT 1835), 247.
     CHRON: BEFORE 1910
     GEOG: CHINA
     SUBJ: DESCRIPTION

CHINESE REPOSITORY   C00292
     <FRIEND OF INDIA>
     IV:5(SEPT 1835), 246-7.
     CHRON: BEFORE 1910
     GEOG: CHINA   SO/WEST ASI
     SUBJ: DESCRIPTION

CHINESE REPOSITORY   C00291
     CHINESE CLASSICS, AND METALLIC TYPES FOR THE
          CHINESE LANGUAGE IN PARIS
     IV:1(MAY 1835), 42.
     CHRON: BEFORE 1910
     GEOG: CHINA   EUROPE
     SUBJ: PRINTING

CHINESE REPOSITORY   C00290
     <CHRONICA DE MACAO>
     III:11(MAR 1835), 536.
     CHRON: BEFORE 1910
     GEOG: MACAO   CHINA
     SUBJ: DESCRIPTION

CHINESE REPOSITORY   C00289
     <THE CHINESE MAGAZINE>
     III:4(AUG 1834), 185.
     CHRON: BEFORE 1910
     GEOG: CHINA
     SUBJ: DESCRIPTION

CHINESE REPOSITORY   C00288
     FOREIGN PRESSES IN CHINA
     III:1(MAY 1834), 43-4.
     CHRON: BEFORE 1910
     GEOG: CHINA
     SUBJ: PRINTING   DESCRIPTION

CHINESE REPOSITORY   C00287
     CHINESE METAL TYPES
     II:10(FEB 1834), 477-8.
     SAMUEL DYER
     CHRON: BEFORE 1910
     GEOG: CHINA   EUROPE
     SUBJ: PRINTING

CHINESE REPOSITORY   C00286
     PUBLICATIONS OF THE SOCIETY FOR THE DIFFUSION
          OF USEFUL KNOWLEDGE
     II:7(NOV 1833), 329-31.
     CHRON: BEFORE 1910
     GEOG: CHINA
     SUBJ: DESCRIPTION

CHINESE REPOSITORY   C00285
     <THE CHINESE MAGAZINE>
     II:5(SEPT 1833), 234-6.
     CHRON: BEFORE 1910
     GEOG: CHINA
     SUBJ: DESCRIPTION

CHINOY, MICHAEL   C02269
    THE CHARGE FOR FREEDOM
    FEER 101:32(11 AUG 1978), 30.
    ##/SWAS
    CHRON: 1970-1980
    GEOG: SO/WEST ASI
    SUBJ: CONTROL   LAW/ETHICS

CHOI CHANG-SUP   C01454
    IMPACT OF MASS MEDIA: SUGGESTIONS FOR
        IMPROVEMENT
    KOREA JOURNAL 15:3(MAR 1975), 27-38.
    CHRON: 1970-1980
    GEOG: EAST ASIA
    SUBJ: LAW/ETHICS

CHONG YUN-MU   C01455
    BASIC SURVEY ON POLITICAL FUNCTIONS OF
        TELEVISION IN KOREA (I)
    KOREA JOURNAL 15:1(JAN 1975), 11-7;
        PART II, 15:2 (FEB 1975), 16-30.
    MEDIUM: ELECTRONIC
    CHRON: 1970-1980
    METH: SURVEY
    GEOG: EAST ASIA
    SUBJ: DEVELOPMENT DESCRIPTION

CHOOI, BEBE   C00329
    COUNTRY REPORT ON THE PROPOSED SCHOOL OF
        MASS COMMUNICATIONS AT MARA INSTITUTE OF
        TECHNOLOGY
    KUALA LUMPUR, AMIC, 1972.
    ##/MAL; MIMEO
    CHRON: 1970-1980
    GEOG: MALAYSIA
    SUBJ: EDUCATION

CHOPRA, PRAN   C01456
    SINGAPORE SHOWS HOW TO CONTROL THE
        PRESS--BUY IT
    MEDIA [HONG KONG] 2:1(JAN 1975), 4.
    CHRON: 1970-1980
    GEOG: SINGAPORE
    SUBJ: CONTROL

CHOU HSIAO-HUNG   08   C02736
    TSAI CHIEN KU CHUNG CHENG CH'ANG TI MA TSU
        JIH PAO (MATSU JIH PAO-- A NEWSPAPER
        GROWN UP AMID DIFFICULTIES)
    PAO HSUEH [TAIPEI] II:7(DEC 1960), 92-5.
                        LANG: CHINESE
    CHRON: 1960-1970
    GEOG: TAIWAN
    SUBJ: DESCRIPTION

CHOU SHENG-SHENG   08   C02737
     WO KUO CHUN PAO SAO TANG PAO TI FA CHAN SHIH
          LUEH (A SKETCH OF CHINESE ARMY
          NEWSPAPER--SAO TANG APO)
     PAO HSUEH [TAIPEI] II:2(DEC 1957), 86-7.
                              LANG: CHINESE
     CHRON: 1946-1960
     GEOG: TAIWAN
     SUBJ: DESCRIPTION

CHOU, ERIC   C01779
     A MAN MUST CHOOSE
     NEW YORK, KNOPF, 1963.
     CHRON: SURVEY
     GEOG: CHINA
     SUBJ: DESCRIPTION BIOGRAPHY

CHOU, NELSON   C00330
     THE CHINESE LANGUAGE AND INFORMATION
          PROCESSING
     MEXICO CITY, 30TH INT. CONGRESS OF HUMAN
          SCIENCES IN ASIA AND NORTH AFRICA, 1976.
     CHIN LANG; MIMEO, 14 PP.
     CHRON: 1970-1980
     GEOG: CHINA
     SUBJ: LANGUAGE

CHOWDHURY, AMITABHA   C00331
     FIESTA OF ASIAN PRESS FREEDOM SEEN AT AN END
     IPI REPORT 25:7(JULY 1976), 1-2.
     ORIGINAL PAPER PRESENTED AT IPI/PHILADELPHIA,
          1976.
     CHRON: 1970-1980
     GEOG: SEV ASIA
     SUBJ: CONTROL

CHRISTIANSEN, SIBBY   C01788
     CHARTING THE CHINA SEAS
     THE AP WORLD 34:3(DEC 1977), 30-1.
     ##/CHIN-5
     CHRON: 1970-1980
     GEOG: CHINA   MACAO
     SUBJ: FOR CORR   FLOW/AGENCY

CHU CH'UAN-YU   06   C01960
     PAO-JEN, PAO-SHIH, PAO-HSUEH (JOURNALIST,
          HISTORY OF JOURNALISM, AND JOURNALISM)
     TAIPEI, TAI WAN SHANG WU YIN SHU KUAN, 1967.
                              LANG: CHINESE
     CHRON: SURVEY
     GEOG: TAIWAN   CHINA   WORLD
     SUBJ: DESCRIPTION BIOGRAPHY

CHU CH'UAN-YU   06   C02030
    HSIEN CH'IN CH'UAN PO SHIH YEH KAI YAO
        [OUTLINE OF PRE-CHIN DYNASTY
        COMMUNICATIONS]
    TAIPEI, COMMERCIAL PRESS, 1973.
    #3
    MEDIUM: GENERAL   LANG: CHINESE
    CHRON: BEFORE 1910
    METH: HISTORICAL
    GEOG: CHINA
    SUBJ: JRN HISTORY

CHU CHI-YING   C00341
    T'AI-WAN HSIANG TS'UN TU CHE TU PAO HSI KUAN
        TIAO CH'A
    TAIPEI, CHIA HSIN SHUI NI KUNG SSU, WEN HUA
        CHI CHIN HUI, 1964.
    (SURVEY OF NEWSPAPER-READING HABITS OF THE
        LITERATE POPULATION OF RURAL
        TAIWAN); SKINNER II:46528.
    CHRON: 1960-1970   VERIF: UNVERIFIED
    METH: SURVEY
    GEOG: TAIWAN
    SUBJ: DESCRIPTION

CHU CHUAN-YU   06   C02738
    SUNG DAI YU LUN YEN CHIU (THE PUBLIC
        OPINION IN THE SUNG DYNASTY)
    PAO HSUEH [TAIPEI] III:8(JUNE 1967), 48-65.
    MEDIUM: GENERAL   LANG: CHINESE
    CHRON: BEFORE 1910
    METH: HISTORICAL
    GEOG: CHINA
    SUBJ: JRN HISTORY OTHER JRN

CHU CHUANG-YU   06   C01237
    SUNG TAI HSIN WEN SHIH [SUNG JOURNALISM
        HISTORY]
    TAIPEI, CHUNG KUO HSUEH SHU CHU TSO CHIANG
        CHU WEI YUAN HUI, 1967.
                            LANG: CHINESE
    CHRON: BEFORE 1910
    METH: HISTORICAL
    GEOG: CHINA
    SUBJ: JRN HISTORY

CHU HSU-PAI   06   C02093
    TAI-WAN HSIN-WEN SHIH-YEH [NEWSPAPERS IN
        TAIWAN] IN <HSIN- SHENG TI T'AI-WAN>
        [TAIWAN UNDER A NEW LIFE]
    TAIPEI, HSIN-SHENG PAO, 1950.
    ##/CHIN-7; P. 81.
                            LANG: CHINESE
    CHRON: 1946-1960
    GEOG: TAIWAN
    SUBJ: DESCRIPTION

CHU WEI-YU   06   C00346
    T'AI-WAN CHING CHI FA CHAN CHUNG PAO CHIH
        KUNG NENG CHIH YEN CHIU (THE FUNCTION OF
        PRESS IN TAIWAN'S ECONOMIC DEVELOPMENT)
    UNPUB MASTERS THESIS IN JOURNALISM, 1969
    SKINNER S00982 II:46529
                            LANG: CHINESE
    CHRON: 1960-1970   VERIF: UNVERIFIED
    GEOG: TAIWAN
    SUBJ: DEVELOPMENT

CHU YU-LUNG   06   C00347
    T'AI-PEI PAO CHIH I CHIEN PU FEN CHIH PI
        CHIAO YEN CHIU (A COMPARATIVE STUDY OF
        EDITORIAL SECTIONS OF TAIPEI NEWSPAPERS)
    UNPUB MASTERS THESIS IN JOURNALISM, 1961.
    SKINNER S00982 II:46530
                         LANG: CHINESE
    CHRON: 1960-1970   VERIF: UNVERIFIED
    GEOG: TAIWAN
    SUBJ: DESCRIPTION

CHU, AUGUSTUS F.   C00340
    THE STUDY OF JOURNALISM IN FREE CHINA
    JQ 33:3(SUMMER 1956), 357-8.
    ##/CHIN
    CHRON: 1946-1960
    GEOG: TAIWAN
    SUBJ: EDUCATION

CHU, B. F.   C01789
    CHINESE CARTOONISTS IN WAR-TIME
    FAR EASTERN MIRROR I:4(21 APR 1938), 72-3.
    CHRON: 1910-1946
    GEOG: CHINA
    SUBJ: DESCRIPTION

CHU, GODWIN   C00344
    COMMUNICATION, SOCIAL STRUCTURAL CHANGE, AND
        CAPITAL FORMATION IN THE PEOPLES'
        REPUBLIC OF CHINA
    HONOLULU, EWCI, 1974.
    #3; PAPERS OF EWCI, 29 PP.
    MEDIUM: GENERAL
    CHRON: 1970-1980
    GEOG: CHINA
    SUBJ: DEVELOPMENT POLIT SCI   OTHER NON-J

CHU, GODWIN C.   C00343
    THE ROLES OF TATZEPAO IN THE CULTURAL
        REVOLUTION: FUNCTIONAL ANALYSIS
    CARBONDALE, ILL., SIU, 1972.
    ##/CHIN
    CHRON: 1960-1970
    METH: OTHER OR COMB
    GEOG: CHINA
    SUBJ: PROPAGANDA POLIT SCI   DESCRIPTION

CHU, GODWIN C., EDITOR.   C02273
    POPULAR MEDIA IN CHINA: SHAPING NEW
        CULTURAL PATTERNS
    HONOLULU, U. OF HAWAII, 1978.
    MEDIUM: OTHER
    CHRON: 1970-1980
    METH: OTHER OR COMB
    GEOG: CHINA
    SUBJ: DESCRIPTION

CHU, JAMES   10   C01790
     TA CHUNG CH'UAN PO HSUEH [MASS
          COMMUNICATIONS AND JOURNALISM]
     TAIPEI, HSUEH SHENG SHU CHU, 1973.
     MEDIUM: GENERAL
     CHRON: 1970-1980
     GEOG: U.S.
     SUBJ: DESCRIPTION

CHU, JAMES C. Y.   C01457
     THE PRC JOURNALIST AS CADRE
     CURRENT SCENE XIII:11(NOV 1975), 1-14.
     ##/CHIN-5
     CHRON: 1970-1980
     GEOG: CHINA
     SUBJ: PROPAGANDA DESCRIPTION

CHU, JAMES C. Y.   C00345
     TELEVISION IN TAIWAN: A CURRENT PROFILE
     PUBLIC TELECOMS REVIEW (OCT 1974), 12-16.
     ##/TAI
     MEDIUM: ELECTRONIC
     CHRON: 1970-1980
     GEOG: TAIWAN
     SUBJ: DESCRIPTION

CHUNG KWANG-HSING   17   C02739
     YIN NA HUA CH'IAO PAO SHIH LUEH (A SKETCH OF
          CHINESE NEWSPAPERS IN INDONESIA)
     PAO HSUEH [TAIPEI] III:3(JUNE 1964), 100-103.
                          LANG: CHINESE
     CHRON: 1960-1970
     GEOG: INDONESIA   OSEAS CHIN
     SUBJ: DESCRIPTION

CHUNG-CH'UNG, PSEUD.   06   C00348
     CH'UAN TANG PAN PAO SHIH PAO CHIH KUNG TSO
          TI KEN PEN FANG CHEN
     JEN MIN JIH PAO 12 JUNE 1960
     SKINNER S00982 II:48457; TRANS (FOR THE WHOLE
          PARTY TO RUN A NEWSPAPER
          IS THE BASIC POLICY ON JOURNALISTIC WORK)
          IN <CURRENT BACKGROUND>
          (8 AUG 1960), 19-28.
                          LANG: CHINESE
     CHRON: 1946-1960   VERIF: UNVERIFIED
     GEOG: CHINA
     SUBJ: DESCRIPTION·

CHUNG-KUO CH'ING-NIEN CHI-CHE   04   C02086
          HSUEH-HUI, EDITOR.
     CHAN-SHIH HSIN-WEN KUNG TSO-JU-MEN
          [INTRODUCTION TO WARTIME JOURNALISM]
     SHANGHAI, SHENG HWO SHU TIEN, 1940.
     #3; REPRINT.
                          LANG: CHINESE
     CHRON: 1910-1946
     GEOG: CHINA
     SUBJ: DESCRIPTION

CHUNG-KUO KUO MIN TANG.   04   C00349
        CHUNG YANGWEI YUAN HUI.
    JU HO KO CH'U SHE HUI HSIN WEN TI PI HAI: . .
    TAIPEI, SHE CHI K'AO HO WEI YUAN, 1961.
    SKINNER S00982 II:46533; (HOW TO ROOT OUT THE
        EVILS OF LOCAL NEWS
        REPORTS: A STUDY OF LOCAL NEWS REPORTS
        IN MAJOR NEWSPAPERS IN
        TAIWAN DURING THE PAST YEAR)
                        LANG: CHINESE
    CHRON: 1960-1970   VERIF: UNVERIFIED
    GEOG: TAIWAN
    SUBJ: DESCRIPTION PROPAGANDA

CHUNG-KUO WEN HUA CHIEN SHE HSIEH HUI   04   C02591
        EDITOR.
    SHIH NIEN LAI TI CHUNG-KUO KUANG PO SHIH YEH
        (CHINA DURING THE PAST DECADE)
    SHANGHAI, SHANG WU YIN SHU KUAN, 1937.
    SEE WU 08W01181, WANG 04W01138; SKINNER
        S00982 II:41887.
    MEDIUM: ELECTRONIC   LANG: CHINESE
    CHRON: 1910-1946   VERIF: UNVERIFIED
    GEOG: CHINA
    SUBJ: DESCRIPTION

CLANCY, PHYLLIS E.   C00350
    NEWS MANAGEMENT IN VIETNAM
    FOI CENTER REPORT NO. 228(SEPT 1969).
    ##/VN
    MEDIUM: GENERAL
    CHRON: 1960-1970
    GEOG: VIETNAM
    SUBJ: CONTROL

CLAYTON, CHARLES C.   C01791
    FORMOSA STAMP HAILS CHINESE PRESS HERO
    EDITOR & PUBLISHER (5 MAY 1962), 66.
    ##/CHIN-5; YU YU-JEN
    CHRON: 1910-1946
    GEOG: CHINA
    SUBJ: DESCRIPTION BIOGRAPHY

CLAYTON, CHARLES C.   C02633
    HONG KONG
    IN LENT L000708, PP. 55-64.
    CHRON: SURVEY
    METH: OTHER OR COMB
    GEOG: HONG KONG
    SUBJ: DESCRIPTION

CLAYTON, CHARLES C.   C02634
    TAIWAN
    IN LENT L00708, PP. 105-114.
    CHRON: SURVEY
    METH: OTHER OR COMB
    GEOG: TAIWAN
    SUBJ: DESCRIPTION

COATS, HOWARD AND FRANCES DYER   C02812
    THE PRINT AND BROADCASTING MEDIA IN MALAYSIA
    KUALA LUMPUR, SOUTH EAST ASIA PRESS CENTRE,
        1972.
    SEE GLATTBACH G02813
    MEDIUM: GENERAL
    CHRON: 1970-1980
    METH: OTHER OR COMB
    GEOG: MALAYSIA
    SUBJ: DESCRIPTION

COCKBURN, ALEXANDER   C01123
    CHINA AND THE LEFT PRESS
    VILLAGE VOICE XXI:23(7 JUNE 1976), 27.
    CHRON: 1970-1980
    GEOG: CHINA   U.S.
    SUBJ: PROPAGANDA

COCKBURN, ALEXANDER   C01122
    ASIAN STORIES
    VILLAGE VOICE XXI:3(19 JAN 1976), 29.
    ##/HKG; FEER AND WALL ST. JOURNAL.
    CHRON: 1970-1980
    GEOG: HONG KONG
    SUBJ: DESCRIPTION

COLQUHOUN, ARCHIBALD R.   C01816
    CHINESE NEWSPAPERS
    CURRENT LITERATURE [LONDON] 24(NOV 1898),
        452-3.
    CHRON: BEFORE 1910   VERIF: UNVERIFIED
    GEOG: CHINA
    SUBJ: DESCRIPTION

COLQUHOUN, ARCHIBALD R.   C01813
    THE CHINESE PRESS OF TODAY
    THE NORTH AMERICAN REVIEW 182:1(JAN 1906),
        97-104.
    ##/CHIN-5
    CHRON: BEFORE 1910
    GEOG: CHINA
    SUBJ: DESCRIPTION

COLQUHOUN, ARCHIBALD ROSS   C00351
    CHINA IN TRANSFORMATION
    NEW YORK AND LONDON, HARPER, 1912.
    ##/CHIN-3; CHAP. 5, THE NATIVE PRESS.
    CHRON: BEFORE 1910
    GEOG: CHINA
    SUBJ: DESCRIPTION

COLUMBIA JOURNALISM REVIEW   C00352
        BEHIND THE VIETNAM STORY
        (WINTER 1965), 14-18.
        ##/VN
        MEDIUM: GENERAL
        CHRON: 1960-1970
        GEOG: VIETNAM
        SUBJ: CONTROL   DESCRIPTION

COLUMBIA JOURNALISM REVIEW   C00354
        A VIET NAM REGISTER
        (WINTER 1966-1967), 4-15.
        ##/VN
        MEDIUM: GENERAL
        CHRON: 1960-1970
        GEOG: VIETNAM   U.S.
        SUBJ: FOR CORR

COLUMBIA JOURNALISM REVIEW   C00353
        ARE WE GETTING THROUGH?
        (FALL 1966), 41-5.
        ##/VN; BASED ON A NET PROGRAM, BROWNE,
              FOISIE, MOHR, BRELIS, NIVEN.
        MEDIUM: GENERAL
        CHRON: 1960-1970
        GEOG: VIETNAM   U.S.
        SUBJ: FOR CORR

COLUMBIA JOURNALISM REVIEW   C00355
        VIETNAM: WHAT LESSONS?
        IX:4(WINTER 1970-1)
        SPECIAL ISSUE
        MEDIUM: GENERAL
        CHRON: 1970-1980
        GEOG: VIETNAM   U.S.
        SUBJ: DESCRIPTION .

COMMUNICATION ARTS   C00356
        EDITORS COLUMN
        18:4(SEPT/OCT 1976), 2,8.
        PUBLISHING, DESIGN, HK POLYTECHNIC
        CHRON: 1970-1980
        GEOG: HONG KONG
        SUBJ: PUBLISHING   OTHER NON-J

COMMUNICATION ARTS   C00357
        HENRY STEINER
        18:4(SEPT/OCT 1976), 86-103.
        <ASIA MAGAZINE> REDESIGN
        CHRON: 1970-1980
        GEOG: HONG KONG   SEV ASIA
        SUBJ: DESCRIPTION PRINTING   PUBLISHING

CONLU, DR. FRANCISCO VILLANUEVA   C02169
    CHINESE NEWSPAPERS IN MANILA
    THE CHINA WEEKLY REVIEW XXXIII:9(1 AUG 1925),
        164-5.
    CHRON: 1910-1946
    GEOG: PHILIPPINES OSEAS CHIN
    SUBJ: DESCRIPTION

CONTEMPORARY CHINA INSTITUTE, EDITOR.   C00358
    A BIBLIOGRAPHY OF CHINESE NEWSPAPERS AND
        PERIODICALS IN EUROPEAN LIBRARIES
    NEW YORK, CAMBRIDGE U. PRESS, 1975.
    REV. IN <CHINA QUARTERLY> 68(DEC 1976), 866-8;
        U. K., FRANCE, ITALY,
        USSR, E. EUROPE; PINYIN; 1045 PP.
    CHRON: SURVEY
    GEOG: CHINA
    SUBJ: RESEARCH

COOKE, GEORGE WINGROVE   C01792
    CHINA: BEING 'THE TIMES' SPECIAL CORRESPONDENT
        FROM CHINA IN THE YEARS 1857-58
    NEW YORK, G. ROUTLEDGE, 1858.
    CHRON: BEFORE 1910
    GEOG: CHINA
    SUBJ: BIOGRAPHY

COOLEY, JOHN   C00359
    BRIDGING EAST-WEST NEWS GAP
    CSM 16 MAY 1972
    ##/SWAS; ARABIC.
    CHRON: 1970-1980
    GEOG: SO/WEST ASI
    SUBJ: FLOW/AGENCY LAW/ETHICS

CORNABY, W. ARTHUR   C00361
    NOTES ON RECENT NATIVE JOURNALISM
    CHINESE RECORDER XLI:3(MARCH 1910), 226-8.
    ##/CHIN-3
    CHRON: BEFORE 1910
    GEOG: CHINA
    SUBJ: DESCRIPTION

CORRESPONDENT   C02508
    BACK TO THE GOOD OLD DAYS
    FEER 102:48(1 DEC 1978), 22-3.
    ##/PHIL
    CHRON: 1970-1980
    GEOG: PHILIPPINES
    SUBJ: DESCRIPTION

CORRESPONDENT IN PEIPING   C01695
     HOW NORTH CHINA GETS NEWS
     ASIA XLI:1(JAN 1941), 25-6.
     CHRON: 1910-1946
     GEOG: CHINA
     SUBJ: CONTROL   FLOW/AGENCY DESCRIPTION

CORRESPONDENT, A   C01961
     A PEEK AT CAMBODIA
     FEER 100:17(28 APR 1978), 48.
     MEDIUM: FILM
     CHRON: 1970-1980
     GEOG: CHINA
     SUBJ: DESCRIPTION

CORRIE, J.   C02170
     FILM PROPAGANDA IN BRITISH MALAYA
     THE CROWN COLONIST 2:10(SEPT 1932), 112-4.
     ##/MAL-3
     MEDIUM: FILM
     CHRON: 1910-1946
     GEOG: MALAYSIA   SINGAPORE
     SUBJ: PROPAGANDA   OTHER JRN

CORRY, W. C. S.   C01015
     MALAYA AND THE ENGLISH PRESS
     SPECTATOR NO. 6542(13 NOV 1953), 537.
     LETTER TO EDITOR, FOR REPLY SEE CARNELL
          C01005.
     CHRON: 1946-1960
     GEOG: MALAYSIA
     SUBJ: DESCRIPTION

COSTENOBLE, EARL L.   C01458
     WHAT THIS WAR IS LIKE
     HORIZONS [USIS] XVII:11(1968-1970), 42-3.
     CHRON: 1960-1970
     GEOG: VIETNAM
     SUBJ: FOR CORR   DESCRIPTION

COUGHLIN, WILLIAM J.   C00362
     CONQUERED PRESS
     PALO ALTO, PACIFIC BOOKS, 1952.
     PRESS IN OCCUPIED JAPAN
     CHRON: 1946-1960
     GEOG: EAST ASIA
     SUBJ: DESCRIPTION

COUGHLIN, WILLIAM JAMES   C02715
     PRESS POLICIES OF THE OCCUPATION
     MASTERS THESIS, STANFORD, 1950.
     NUC<56 124:576.
     CHRON: 1946-1960
     METH: OTHER OR COMB
     GEOG: EAST ASIA   U.S.
     SUBJ: CONTROL

COULING, SAMUEL   C00363
     THE ENCYCLOPAEDIA SINICA
     SHANGHAI, KELLY AND WALSH, 1917.
     ##/CHIN-2; NUC<56 124:589; NEWSPAPERS,
          CHINESE, 397-8;
          PRESS, EUROPEAN, 459-461; PRINTING,
          461-2; ALSO SEE SPECIFIC PAPERS
          AND EDITORS.
     CHRON: SURVEY
     GEOG: CHINA
     SUBJ: JRN HISTORY PRINTING   PUBLISHING

COVENTRY-ISLAND ARGUS, EDITOR.   C01793
     COLONIAL JOURNALISM AND COLONIAL GOVERNMENT
     THE CHINA MAGAZINE III(1868), 93-7.
     ##/CHIN-6
     CHRON: BEFORE 1910
     GEOG: HONG KONG   CHINA
     SUBJ: DESCRIPTION

COX, THOMAS R.   C02612
     THE TREATY PORT PRESS AND THE HUNDRED DAYS
          REFORMS: A CROSS- CULTURAL CREDIBILITY
          GAP
     HISTORIAN 37:1(NOV 1974), 82-100.
     ##/CHIN-9
     CHRON: BEFORE 1910
     METH: HISTORICAL
     GEOG: HONG KONG   CHINA
     SUBJ: JRN HISTORY CROSS CULTU

CRABBE, ROBERT   C02509
     CHINESE ACCOMMODATE REPORTERS COVERING
          OPENING OF RELATIONS
     EDITOR & PUBLISHER 112:3(20 JAN 1979), 42.
     MEDIUM: GENERAL
     CHRON: 1970-1980
     GEOG: CHINA
     SUBJ: FLOW/AGENCY DESCRIPTION

CRABBE, ROBERT   C02510
     PEKING REPORTERS COPE WITH WORKING
          CONDITIONS
     EDITOR & PUBLISHER 112:17(28 APR 1979),
          24.
     MEDIUM: GENERAL
     CHRON: 1970-1980
     GEOG: CHINA
     SUBJ: FOR CORR   FLOW/AGENCY

CRANZ, GALEN   C02511
     PHOTOGRAPHY IN CHINESE POPULAR CULTURE
     EXPOSURE 16:4(WINTER 1979), 24-9.
     CHRON: 1970-1980
     METH: OTHER OR COMB
     GEOG: CHINA
     SUBJ: OTHER JRN

CRAWFORD, ROBERT   C02635
     INDONESIA
     IN LENT L00708, PP. 158-178.
     CHRON: SURVEY
     GEOG: INDONESIA
     SUBJ: JRN HISTORY DESCRIPTION

CRAWFORD, ROBERT HENRY   C00364
     THE DAILY INDONESIAN LANGUAGE PRESS OF
          DJAKARTA: AN ANALYSIS OF TWO RECENT
          PERIODS
     PHD DISS, SYRACUSE, 1967.
     JULY-DEC 1964 AND JULY-DEC 1966
     CHRON: 1960-1970
     METH: CONTENT ANALYSIS
     GEOG: INDONESIA
     SUBJ: DESCRIPTION

CREWDSON, JOHN M. AND JOSEPH B. TREAS   C01459
     THE C. I. A.'S 3-DECADE EFFORT TO MOLD THE
          WORLD'S VIEW
     NYT 25, 26, 27 DEC 1977
     ##/ASIA
     MEDIUM: GENERAL
     CHRON: SURVEY
     GEOG: SEV ASIA
     SUBJ: PROPAGANDA

CROW, CARL   C01460
     FOUR HUNDRED MILLION CUSTOMERS
     NEW YORK, HARPER AND BROS., 1937.
     ADVERTISING; REPRINT AVAILABLE.
     MEDIUM: GENERAL
     CHRON: 1910-1946
     GEOG: CHINA
     SUBJ: OTHER JRN

CROW, CARL   C01797
     FAREWELL TO SHANGHAI
     HARPERS 176:1051(DEC 1937), 38-47.
     ##/CHIN-6
     CHRON: 1910-1946
     GEOG: CHINA
     SUBJ: FOR CORR   DESCRIPTION BIOGRAPHY

CROW, CARL   C01796
    OFFICE MORALE AND CHINESE DEVILS
    HARPERS 174:1043(APR 1937), 537-43.
    ##/CHIN-6
    CHRON: 1910-1946
    GEOG: CHINA
    SUBJ: FOR CORR   DESCRIPTION BIOGRAPHY

CROW, CARL   C01795
    FREE SAMPLES IN CHINA
    HARPERS 174:1042(MAR 1937), 398-406.
    ##/CHIN-6
    CHRON: 1910-1946
    GEOG: CHINA
    SUBJ: OTHER JRN

CROW, CARL   C01794
    NEWSPAPER DIRECTORY OF CHINA (INCLUDING
        HONG KONG) WITH CHECKLIST OF NEWSPAPERS
        . . . PUBLISHED IN JAPAN, CHOSEN, BURMA .
    SHANGHAI, CARL CROW, 1931.
    CHRON: 1910-1946
    GEOG: CHINA   SEV ASIA
    SUBJ: RESEARCH   DESCRIPTION

CROW, CARL   C01989
    CHINA TAKES HER PLACE
    NEW YORK, HARPER AND BROS., 1944.
    CHRON: SURVEY
    GEOG: CHINA
    SUBJ: JRN HISTORY DESCRIPTION OTHER JRN

CURRENT SCENE   C01461
    INSIDE PEOPLE'S DAILY
    XI:1(JAN 1973), 19.
    ##/CHIN-5
    CHRON: 1970-1980
    GEOG: CHINA
    SUBJ: DESCRIPTION

CURRENT SCENE   C01469
    PRC MEDIA ON NATIONAL DEFENSE
    XV:3(MAR 1977), 20-1.
    MEDIUM: GENERAL
    CHRON: 1970-1980
    GEOG: CHINA
    SUBJ: DESCRIPTION

CURRENT SCENE   C01468
     'PROLETARIAN TELEVISION SERVICE' GROWS
     XIV:7(JULY 1976), 18-19.
     MEDIUM: ELECTRONIC
     CHRON: 1970-1980
     GEOG: CHINA
     SUBJ: DESCRIPTION

CURRENT SCENE   C01467
     FIVE NEW ARTS JOURNALS
     XIV:4(APR 1976), 25.
     <PEOPLE'S MUSIC>, <DANCE>, <FINE ARTS>,
          <PEOPLE'S THEATER>, <PEOPLE'S
          CINEMA>.
     CHRON: 1970-1980
     GEOG: CHINA
     SUBJ: DESCRIPTION

CURRENT SCENE   C01466
     NATIONAL LITERARY JOURNALS PUBLISHED
     XIV:3(MAR 1976), 15.
     <PEOPLE'S LITERATURE>, <POETRY>, <IDEOLOGICAL
          FRONT>.
     CHRON: 1970-1980
     GEOG: CHINA
     SUBJ: DESCRIPTION LITERATURE

CURRENT SCENE   C01465
     BOOK PUBLISHING IN THE PRC
     XIII:11(NOV 1975), 14-16.
     CHRON: 1970-1980
     GEOG: CHINA
     SUBJ: PUBLISHING

CURRENT SCENE   C01464
     PRC JOURNAL REVIVED
     XIII:1(JAN 1975), 19.
     <HISTORICAL STUDIES>
     CHRON: 1970-1980
     GEOG: CHINA
     SUBJ: DESCRIPTION

CURRENT SCENE   C01463
     NEW SHANGHAI JOURNAL
     XIII:1(JAN 1975), 25.
     <STUDY AND CRITICISM>
     CHRON: 1970-1980
     GEOG: CHINA
     SUBJ: DESCRIPTION

CURRENT SCENE   C01462
     SHANGHAI JOURNAL GOES PUBLIC
     XII:6(JUNE 1974), 18.
     <STUDY AND CRITICISM>
     CHRON: 1970-1980
     GEOG: CHINA
     SUBJ: DESCRIPTION

CURRENT SCENE   C00365
     YANG CHENG WAN PAO [CANTON EVENING NEWS]:
          A NEWSPAPER IN COMMUNIST CHINA
     2:16(1 JULY 1963), 1-14.
     ##/CHIN-3; REPRINTED AS 'A JOURNALIST AND
          HIS PAPER' IN <OUT
          OF CHINA>, FRANCIS HARPER, ED.,
          HONG KONG, DRAGONFLY BOOKS, 1964.
     CHRON: 1960-1970
     GEOG: CHINA
     SUBJ: DESCRIPTION PRINTING

CURRENT SCENE   C00367
     WITH BANNERS AND DRUMS: THE MASS CAMPAIGN
          IN CHINA'S DRIVE FOR DEVELOPMENT
     IV:9(1 MAY 1966), 1-12.
     CHRON: 1960-1970
     GEOG: CHINA
     SUBJ: DEVELOPMENT

CURRENT SCENE   C00366
     THE NEW CHINA NEWS AGENCY: MAO'S MESSENGERS
          AROUND THE WORLD
     IV:7(1 APR 1966), 1-14.
     ##/CHIN-3
     CHRON: 1960-1970
     GEOG: CHINA
     SUBJ: FLOW/AGENCY PROPAGANDA   DESCRIPTION

CURRENT SCENE   C00369
     THROUGH PEKING'S EYES: A SURVEY OF CHINESE
          MEDIA
     VIII:3(1 FEB 1970), 1-10.
     MEDIUM: GENERAL
     CHRON: 1970-1980
     GEOG: CHINA
     SUBJ: DESCRIPTION

CURRENT SCENE   C00368
     THE HANDWRITING ON THE WALL: POSTERS AND
          RED GUARD PAPERS SPEAK THE MIND OF CHINA
     5:9(31 MAY 1967), 1-17.
     ##/CHIN-3
     MEDIUM: GENERAL
     CHRON: 1960-1970
     GEOG: CHINA
     SUBJ: DESCRIPTION

CURZON, GEORGE N.   C01390
    PROBLEMS OF THE FAR EAST
    LONDON, LONGMANS GREEN, 1894.
    THE PRESS IN CHINA, PP. 362-4.
    CHRON: BEFORE 1910
    GEOG: CHINA
    SUBJ: DESCRIPTION

CUTTRISS, C. A.   C01321
    EARLY NEWSPAPERS IN BURMA IN <BURMA RESEARCH
            SOCIETY FIFTIETH ANNIVERSARY
            PUBLICATIONS NO. 2>.
    RANGOON, BURMA RESEARCH SOCIETY, 1960.
    REPRINT, SEE CUTTRISS C01016
    CHRON: BEFORE 1910
    GEOG: BURMA
    SUBJ: JRN HISTORY DESCRIPTION

CUTTRISS, C. A.   C01016
    EARLY NEWSPAPERS IN BURMA
    JRNL OF THE BURMA RESEARCH SOCIETY 27:3(DEC
            1937), 277-82.
    ULS 1:850
    CHRON: BEFORE 1910
    METH: HISTORICAL
    GEOG: BURMA
    SUBJ: DESCRIPTION

DAGGETT, EMERSON, SUPERVISOR.   D02094
    HISTORY OF JOURNALISM IN SAN FRANCISCO
    SAN FRANCISCO, W. P. A., 1939.
    VOL. 1, HISTORY OF FOREIGN JOURNALISM IN SAN
            FRANCISCO: CHINESE
            JOURNALISM IN SAN FRANCISCO, PP. 42-61;
            PROJECT 10008,
            O. P. 665-08-3-12.
    CHRON: SURVEY
    GEOG: OSEAS CHIN U.S.
    SUBJ: DESCRIPTION

DAHLAN, M. ALWI   D00370
    JOINT REGIONAL EFFORTS IN COMMUNICATION
            RESEARCH
    DEN PASAR, AMIC SEMINAR ON COMM TEACHING
            AND RESEARCH, 1972.
    ##/ASIA; MIMEO, 6 PP.
    MEDIUM: GENERAL
    CHRON: 1970-1980
    GEOG: SEV ASIA
    SUBJ: EDUCATION

DALAND, JUDSON   D01470
    THE EVOLUTION OF MODERN PRINTING AND THE
            DISCOVERY OF MOVABLE METAL TYPE BY THE
            CHINESE AND KOREANS IN THE FOURTEENTH
            CENTURY
    JRNL OF THE FRANKLIN INSTITUTE 212:2(AUG
            1931), 209-34.
    CHRON: 1910-1946
    METH: OTHER OR COMB
    GEOG: CHINA   EAST ASIA
    SUBJ: PRINTING

DALTON, JAMES JOSEPH   D00439
    FOOD FOR THE MIND
    FEER LXVIII:23(4 JUNE 1970), 19-22.
    OVERSEAS CHINESE MAGAZINES AND PAPERS
    CHRON: 1970-1980
    GEOG: OTHER   SEV ASIA
    SUBJ: PRINTING   PUBLISHING

DANIELS, JOSEPHUS   D00371
    A ROMP THROUGH ASIAN JOURNALISM
    HORIZONS [USIS] 19:12(1970), 2-6, 30-1;
        PART 2, 20:1(1971), 20-5.
    ##/ASIA; INTERVIEW WITH A. CHOWDHURY.
    CHRON: 1970-1980
    GEOG: SEV ASIA
    SUBJ: DESCRIPTION

DANIELS, JOSEPHUS   D00372
    AN EDITOR SPEAKS HIS MIND
    HORIZONS XX:12(N. D., DEC 1971?), 48-51.
    ##/THAI; INTERVIEW WITH SUTHICHE YOON,
        EDITOR OF <THE NATION>.
    CHRON: 1970-1980
    GEOG: THAILAND
    SUBJ: BIOGRAPHY   DESCRIPTION

DARROCH, J.   D00373
    CURRENT EVENTS AS SEEN THROUGH THE MEDIUM OF
        THE CHINESE NEWSPAPER
    CHINESE RECORDER 43:1(JAN 1912), 23-33.
    CHIN REC
    CHRON: 1910-1946
    GEOG: CHINA
    SUBJ: DESCRIPTION

DAS, K.   D00376
    BACKLASH OF THE PURGE
    FEER 93:28(9 JULY 1976), 10-12.
    ##/MAL-2; SAMAD ISMAIL
    CHRON: 1970-1980
    GEOG: MALAYSIA
    SUBJ: CONTROL   LAW/ETHICS   DESCRIPTION

DAS, K.   D00377
    MALAYSIA'S SAMAD: 'I DID IT MY WAY'
    FEER 93:38(17 SEPT 1976), 8-10, 15.
    ##/MAL-2
    CHRON: 1970-1980
    GEOG: MALAYSIA
    SUBJ: LAW/ETHICS   CONTROL

DAS, K.   D00375
    MALAYSIA: THE ENEMIES WITHIN
    FEER 93:27(2 JULY 1976), 8-9.
    ##/MAL
    CHRON: 1970-1980
    GEOG: MALAYSIA
    SUBJ: DESCRIPTION CONTROL   BIOGRAPHY

DAS, K.   D00374
    WAITING FOR THE NEWS ON RAZAK
    FEER 91:3(16 JAN 1976), 15-16.
    ##/MAL
    MEDIUM: GENERAL
    CHRON: 1970-1980
    GEOG: MALAYSIA
    SUBJ: CONTROL   DESCRIPTION

DAS, K.   D00379
    CONCERN ACROSS THE CAUSEWAY
    FEER 95:12(25 MAR 1977), 13.
    ##/MAL-2
    CHRON: 1970-1980
    GEOG: MALAYSIA   SINGAPORE
    SUBJ: PROPAGANDA

DAS, K.   D00378
    THE SUBTLE ART OF SUBVERSION
    FEER 95:8(25 FEB 1977), 14.
    ##/MAL-2; CHAN KIEN SIN/SIN CHEW JIT POH.
    CHRON: 1970-1980
    GEOG: MALAYSIA
    SUBJ: PROPAGANDA

DAS, K.   D01471
    THE RISING STAR OF THE PARTY
    FEER 97:35(2 SEPT 1977), 19-20.
    ##/MAL-2; <THE STAR>.
    CHRON: 1970-1980
    GEOG: MALAYSIA
    SUBJ: DESCRIPTION

DATELINE [OPC, NEW YORK]   D02172
    'MORE SENSATION THAN INFORMATION'
    5:1(1961), 12-13, 68-70.
    CHRON: 1960-1970
    GEOG: OTHER
    SUBJ: FOR CORR

DATELINE [OPC, NEW YORK]   D02171
    UNDER THE BAMBOO TREE
    3:1(1959), 18-21.
    CHRON: 1946-1960
    GEOG: HONG KONG
    SUBJ: FOR CORR   DESCRIPTION

DATELINE: ASIA, 25 YEARS OF HISTORY   D01472
        AS REPORTED BY PACIFIC
        STARS AND STRIPES
    TOKYO, PACIFIC STARS AND STRIPES, 1970.
    CHRON: SURVEY
    GEOG: SEV ASIA
    SUBJ: FOR CORR   DESCRIPTION OTHER JRN

DAVIES, DEREK   D00397
    TRAVELER'S TALES
    FEER 96:18(6 MAY 1977), 17.
    ##/SIN; HO KWON PING.
    CHRON: 1970-1980
    GEOG: SINGAPORE
    SUBJ: LAW/ETHICS   CONTROL

DAVIES, DEREK   D00396
    TRAVELER'S TALES
    FEER 96:17(29 APR 1977), 15.
    ##/HKG; TALK CRITICAL OF FEER.
    CHRON: 1970-1980
    GEOG: SEV ASIA
    SUBJ: DESCRIPTION LAW/ETHICS   FOR CORR

DAVIES, DEREK   D00395
    ANOTHER 'CONFESSION' IN SINGAPORE
    FEER 96:17(29 APR 1977), 12-13.
    ##/SIN; HO KWON PING.
    CHRON: 1970-1980
    GEOG: SINGAPORE
    SUBJ: LAW/ETHICS   FOR CORR   CONTROL

DAVIES, DEREK   D00394
    TRAVELER'S TALES
    FEER 96:14(8 APR 1977), 19.
    ##/AGEN
    CHRON: 1970-1980
    GEOG: SEV ASIA
    SUBJ: FLOW/AGENCY

DAVIES, DEREK   D00393
    POSTSCRIPT ON ARUN
    FEER 95:12(25 MAR 1977), 14, 17-18.
    ##/SIN
    CHRON: 1970-1980
    GEOG: SINGAPORE
    SUBJ: FOR CORR   CONTROL   LAW/ETHICS

DAVIES, DEREK   D00392
    MORE IN SORROW THAN ANGER
    FEER 95:12(25 MAR 1977), 12-13.
    ##/SIN; ARUN SENKUTTUVAN.
    CHRON: 1970-1980
    GEOG: SINGAPORE
    SUBJ: FOR CORR   CONTROL   LAW/ETHICS

DAVIES, DEREK   D00391
    PUTTING THE RECORD STRAIGHT
    FEER 95:12(25 MAR 1977), 10-11.
    ##/SIN; ARUN SENKUTTUVAN/HO KWON PING.
    CHRON: 1970-1980
    GEOG: SINGAPORE
    SUBJ: FOR CORR   CONTROL   LAW/ETHICS

DAVIES, DEREK   D00390
    TRAVELER'S TALES
    FEER 95:11(18 MAR 1977), 17.
    ##/CHIN-4; REN MIN JIH PAO.
    CHRON: 1970-1980
    GEOG: CHINA
    SUBJ: DESCRIPTION CONTROL

DAVIES, DEREK   D00389
    REVIEW MAN FINED $7,500
    FEER 95:6(11 FEB 1977), 15.
    ##/SIN; HO KWON PING.
    CHRON: 1970-1980
    GEOG: SINGAPORE
    SUBJ: LAW/ETHICS

DAVIES, DEREK   D00388
    TRAVELER'S TALES
    FEER 95:3(21 JAN 1977), 19.
    ##/HKG
    MEDIUM: GENERAL
    CHRON: 1970-1980
    GEOG: CHINA   HONG KONG
    SUBJ: FOR CORR   CONTROL

DAVIES, DEREK   D00387
    TRAVELER'S TALES
    FEER 94:47(19 NOV 1976), 27.
    ##/HKG; HISTORY OF FEER.
    CHRON: 1970-1980
    GEOG: HONG KONG
    SUBJ: DESCRIPTION JRN HISTORY

DAVIES, DEREK   D00386
    COMMENT
    FEER 93:33(13 AUG 1976), 25.
    ##/AGEN; THIRD WORLD NEWS AGENCY.
    CHRON: 1970-1980
    GEOG: WORLD
    SUBJ: FLOW/AGENCY

DAVIES, DEREK   D01473
    TRAVELLER'S TALES
    FEER 97:36(9 SEPT 1977), 25.
    ##/CHIN-5
    CHRON: 1910-1946
    GEOG: CHINA
    SUBJ: JRN HISTORY

DAVIES, DEREK   D00381
    TRAVELER'S TALES
    FEER 86:39(4 OCT 1974), 17.
    PFA AND DEVELOPMENT JOURNALISM
    CHRON: 1970-1980
    GEOG: SEV ASIA
    SUBJ: DEVELOPMENT EDUCATION

DAVIES, DEREK   D00385
    TRAVELER'S TALES
    FEER 93:30(23 JULY 1976), 17.
    ##/ESAI
    CHRON: 1970-1980
    GEOG: EAST ASIA
    SUBJ: FOR CORR

DAVIES, DEREK   D00383
    TRAVELER'S TALES
    FEER 91:12(19 MAR 1976), 29.
    ##/MAL
    CHRON: 1970-1980
    GEOG: SEV ASIA
    SUBJ: DESCRIPTION

DAVIES, DEREK   D00382
     TRAVELER'S TALES
     FEER 86:39(4 OCT 1974). 17.
     ##/ASIA; PFA.
     CHRON: 1970-1980
     GEOG: SEV ASIA
     SUBJ: DEVELOPMENT

DAVIES, DEREK   D02557
     TRAVELLER'S TALES
     FEER 102:49(8 DEC 1978), 31.
     ##/ASIA
     MEDIUM: GENERAL
     CHRON: 1970-1980
     GEOG: SEV ASIA
     SUBJ: CONTROL   FLOW/AGENCY

DAVIES, DEREK AND HARVEY STOCKWIN   D00384
     THE DEBATE IS ON AGAIN
     FEER 92:23(4 JUNE 1976), 20-3.
     ##/INDON
     CHRON: 1970-1980
     GEOG: INDONESIA
     SUBJ: CONTROL

DAVIES, DEREK AND LEO GOODSTADT,   D00380
          T. J. S. GEORGE
     THE ROMANCE OF THE PRESS (21-3); THE ROLE OF
          THE PRESS (23-4, 27-8); THE STATE OF THE
          PRESS (28, 50, 53-4)
     FEER LXXIV:41(9 OCT 1971).
     ##/ASIA
     CHRON: 1970-1980
     GEOG: SEV ASIA
     SUBJ: DESCRIPTION DEVELOPMENT

DAVIS, JOHN K.   D02053
     CHINESE PRINTING TYPE
     THE INLAND PRINTER XLVIII:4(JAN 1912), 575.
     ##/CHIN-7
     CHRON: 1910-1946
     GEOG: CHINA
     SUBJ: PRINTING

DAVIS, NEIL   D00398
     THE PEN-AND-PAPER WARRIORS
     FEER 86:42(18 OCT 1974), 32.
     ##/CAMB
     CHRON: 1970-1980
     GEOG: CAMBODIA
     SUBJ: FOR CORR

DAVISON, W. PHILLIPS   D00399
    MAKING SENSE OF VIET NAM NEWS
    COL JRN REVIEW (WINTER 1966/1967), 5-10.
    ##/VN
    CHRON: 1960-1970
    GEOG: VIETNAM   U.S.
    SUBJ: FOR CORR   FLOW/AGENCY

DAWSON, ALAN   D02512
    COVERAGE OF THE NEW CONFLICT IN INDOCHINA
    UPI REPORTER (1 MAR 1979), 1-2.
    ##/THAI
    MEDIUM: GENERAL
    CHRON: 1970-1980
    GEOG: THAILAND   VIETNAM   CHINA
    SUBJ: FOR CORR   FLOW/AGENCY

DAY, BILLIE   D02173
    PERSPECTIVES FROM THE ASIAN PRESS
    INTERCOM NO. 89(JUNE 1978), 24-8.
    CHRON: 1970-1980
    GEOG: SEV ASIA
    SUBJ: EDUCATION

DE LA CRUZ, JR., JOSE   D01798
    PRESS IN MANILA RUNS THREE NEWSPAPERS AT ONCE
    EDITOR & PUBLISHER (5 MAY 1962), 46.
    CHRON: 1970-1980
    GEOG: PHILIPPINES
    SUBJ: PRINTING   PUBLISHING

DE VERNEIL, ANDRE J.   D01474
    A CORRELATIONAL ANALYSIS OF INTERNATIONAL
        NEWSPAPER COVERAGE AND INTERNATIONAL,
        . . .RELATIONSHIPS
    IN RUBEN R02564
    CHRON: 1970-1980
    METH: NUMERICAL
    GEOG: WORLD
    SUBJ: DESCRIPTION OTHER JRN

DEANE, HUGH   D02293
    MACARTHUR WARS ON THE PRESS
    THE CHINA WEEKLY REVIEW 108:12(21 FEB 1948),
        346.
    CHRON: 1946-1960
    GEOG: EAST ASIA   OTHER
    SUBJ: FOR CORR   CONTROL

DEANE, HUGH   D02292
     AMERICAN CORRESPONDENT EXPELLED FROM JAPAN BY
          SCAP'S ORDER
     THE CHINA WEEKLY REVIEW 105:8(19 APR 1947),
          213.
     DAVID CONDE
     CHRON: 1946-1960
     GEOG: EAST ASIA
     SUBJ: FOR CORR   CONTROL

DEEN, THALIF   D02513
     A NEWS AGENCY FOR ASIA?
     ASIAWEEK 5:4(2 FEB 1979), 36.
     ##/ASIA
     MEDIUM: GENERAL
     CHRON: 1970-1980
     GEOG: SEV ASIA
     SUBJ: FLOW/AGENCY

DEEPE, BEVERLY   D02174
     THE WOMAN CORRESPONDENT
     DATELINE [OPC, NEW YORK] X:1(1966), 95-7.
     MEDIUM: GENERAL
     CHRON: 1960-1970
     GEOG: VIETNAM   U.S.
     SUBJ: FOR CORR

DEKA [PSEUD.?]   D00400
     NATIVE NEWSPAPERS
     NOTES AND QUERIES: ON CHINA AND JAPAN I:2(28
          FEB 1867), 19.
     ##/CHIN-3; ANSWER TO LETTER IN I:1(31 JAN
          1867), 7.
     CHRON: BEFORE 1910
     GEOG: CHINA
     SUBJ: DESCRIPTION

DEKKER, DOUWES E. F. E.   D01017
     THE PRESS
     IN WRIGHT W02565, PP. 261-7.
     ##/INDO; FOR OTHERS IN THIS SERIES, SEE
          WRIGHT W01174, W01175, W01678,
          W02565, W02589.
     CHRON: SURVEY
     GEOG: INDONESIA
     SUBJ: JRN HISTORY DESCRIPTION

DELIKHAN, GERALD A.   D00401
     LEE'S BLACK OPERATION
     INSIGHT 1:7(JULY 1971), 37-40.
     ##/SIN
     CHRON: 1970-1980
     GEOG: SINGAPORE
     SUBJ: CONTROL   PROPAGANDA   LAW/ETHICS

DELYUSIN, L.   D02716
     PECHAT' KITAIA SLUZHIT NARODU
     SOVETSKAIA PECHAT' 5(1957), 69-70.
                           LANG: RUSSIAN
     CHRON: 1946-1960   VERIF: UNVERIFIED
     GEOG: CHINA
     SUBJ: DESCRIPTION

DEVOSS, DAVID   D01645
     SOUTHEAST ASIA'S INTIMIDATED PRESS
     COL JRN REVIEW XVI:6(MAR/APR 1978), 37-9.
     ##/ASIA
     CHRON: 1970-1980
     GEOG: SEV ASIA
     SUBJ: CONTROL   DESCRIPTION

DEVOSS, DAVID   D02220
     INDONESIA UPDATE
     COL JRN REVIEW XVII:1(MAY/JUNE 1978), 68.
     ##/INDON-2; UPDATE TO DEVOSS D01645.
     CHRON: 1970-1980
     GEOG: INDONESIA
     SUBJ: CONTROL   DESCRIPTION

DHAR, ASHA   D02596
     INDIAN FILM INDUSTRY
     ASIAN REVIEW LIII:195(JULY 1957), 194-7.
     MEDIUM: FILM
     CHRON: 1946-1960
     GEOG: SO/WEST ASI
     SUBJ: DESCRIPTION-

DIAL, ROGER L.   D00403
     THE NEW CHINA NEWS AGENCY AND FOREIGN
          POLICY IN CHINA
     INTERNATIONAL JOURNAL XXXI:2(SPRING 1976),
          293-318.
     ##/CHIN-3
     MEDIUM: GENERAL
     CHRON: 1970-1980
     GEOG: CHINA
     SUBJ: FOR CORR   FLOW/AGENCY POLIT SCI   POLIT SCI

DIAMOND, EDWIN   D00404
     WHO IS THE 'ENEMY'
     COL JRN REVIEW IX:4(WINTER 1970-1), 38-9.
     MEDIUM: GENERAL
     CHRON: 1970-1980
     GEOG: VIETNAM   U.S.
     SUBJ: FOR CORR   FLOW/AGENCY

DIARIO, RUBEN   D00405
        MANAGING THE MEDIA FILIPINO STYLE
        BULLETIN OF CONCERNED ASIAN SCHOLARS
            6:1(JAN-MAR 1974), 32-5.
        ##/PHIL
        MEDIUM: GENERAL
        CHRON: 1970-1980
        GEOG: PHILIPPINES
        SUBJ: CONTROL

DIBBLE, ARNOLD   D00406
        MARCOS MUZZLES HIS FREE PRESS
        STRAITS TIMES 26 SEPT 1972 (UPI)
        ##/PHIL
        CHRON: 1970-1980
        GEOG: PHILIPPINES
        SUBJ: CONTROL

DIGEST OF THE SYNODAL COMMISSION   D02186
        CINEMA IN SINIS
        8:5-6(MAY-JUNE 1935), 508-9.
        CATHOLIC CHURCH IN CHINA, SYNODAL COMMISSION
            COLLECTANEA SYNODALIS
        MEDIUM: FILM
        CHRON: 1910-1946
        GEOG: CHINA
        SUBJ: DESCRIPTION

DIGEST OF THE SYNODAL COMMISSION   D02185
        NANKING BANNED FILMS NOT USING 'NATIONAL'
            LANGUAGE
        8:3(MAR 1935), 270-71.
        CATHOLIC CHURCH IN CHINA, SYNODAL COMMISSION
            COLLECTANEA SYNODALIS
        MEDIUM: FILM
        CHRON: 1910-1946
        GEOG: CHINA
        SUBJ: CONTROL   LANGUAGE

DIGEST OF THE SYNODAL COMMISSION   D02184
        76 CHINESE PAPERS PUBLISHED ABROAD
        7:11(NOV 1934), 906.
        CATHOLIC CHURCH IN CHINA, SYNODAL COMMISSION
            COLLECTANEA SYNODALIS
        CHRON: 1910-1946
        GEOG: OSEAS CHIN   WORLD
        SUBJ: DESCRIPTION

DIGEST OF THE SYNODAL COMMISSION   D02183
        THE LANGUAGE OF CHINESE NEWSPAPERS
        7:3(MAR 1934), 269-71.
        FROM <PEIPING CHRONICLE>, 10 JAN 1934;
            CATHOLIC CHURCH IN CHINA,
            SYNODAL COMMISSION COLLECTANEA SYNODALIS.
        CHRON: 1910-1946
        GEOG: CHINA
        SUBJ: DESCRIPTION LANGUAGE

DIGEST OF THE SYNODAL COMMISSION   D02182
    KINEMAS IN CANTON
    6:3(MAR 1933), 247.
    CATHOLIC CHURCH IN CHINA, SYNODAL COMMISSION
        COLLECTANEA SYNODALIS
    MEDIUM: FILM
    CHRON: 1910-1946
    GEOG: CHINA
    SUBJ: DESCRIPTION

DIGEST OF THE SYNODAL COMMISSION   D02181
    THE EXHIBITION OF MOTION PICTURES IN CHINA
    5:8/9(AUG/SEPT 1932), 780-82.
    FROM <CAPITAL AND TRADE>; CATHOLIC CHURCH
        IN CHINA, SYNODAL COMMISSION
        COLLECTANEA SYNODALIS.
    MEDIUM: FILM
    CHRON: 1910-1946
    GEOG: CHINA
    SUBJ: DESCRIPTION OTHER JRN

DIGEST OF THE SYNODAL COMMISSION   D02180
    THE LUCE MOVING PICTURE COMPANY: VALUE OF
        EDUCATIONAL FILMS
    5:2(FEB 1932), 143-7.
    CATHOLIC CHURCH IN CHINA, SYNODAL COMMISSION
        COLLECTANEA SYNODALIS
    MEDIUM: FILM
    CHRON: 1910-1946
    GEOG: CHINA
    SUBJ: EDUCATION

DIGEST OF THE SYNODAL COMMISSION   D02179
    MOTION PICTURE HOUSES IN CHINA
    4:5/6(MAY-JUNE 1931), 457.
    CATHOLIC CHURCH IN CHINA, SYNODAL COMMISSION
        COLLECTANEA SYNODALIS
    MEDIUM: FILM
    CHRON: 1910-1946
    GEOG: CHINA
    SUBJ: DESCRIPTION

DIGEST OF THE SYNODAL COMMISSION   D02178
    NEW PRESS LAWS
    3:12(DEC 1930), 1000.
    CATHOLIC CHURCH IN CHINA, SYNODAL COMMISSION
        COLLECTANEA SYNODALIS
    CHRON: 1910-1946
    GEOG: CHINA
    SUBJ: CONTROL

DIGEST OF THE SYNODAL COMMISSION   D02176
    CATHOLIC UNIVERSITY HERE HAS MOST COMPLETE
        LABORATORY FOR POTENTIAL NEWSMAN
    3:11(NOV 1930), 907-8.
    CATHOLIC CHURCH IN CHINA, SYNODAL COMMISSION
        COLLECTANEA SYNODALIS
    CHRON: 1910-1946
    GEOG: CHINA
    SUBJ: EDUCATION

DIGEST OF THE SYNODAL COMMISSION   D02175
      CENSORSHIP FOR CINEMA FILMS
      3:11(NOV 1930), 896-7.
      FROM <NORTH-CHINA DAILY NEWS>; CATHOLIC
          CHURCH IN CHINA, SYNODAL
          COMMISSION COLLECTANEA SYNODALIS.
      MEDIUM: FILM
      CHRON: 1910-1946
      GEOG: CHINA
      SUBJ: CONTROL

DIGEST OF THE SYNODAL   COMMISSION   D02177
      PRESS CENSORSHIP ENDED, BUT NEWSPAPERS MUST
          REGISTER
      3:12(DEC 1930), 999-1000.
      CATHOLIC CHURCH IN CHINA, SYNODAL COMMISSION
          COLLECTANEA SYNODALIS;
          FROM <NORTH-CHINA DAILY NEWS>.
      CHRON: 1910-1946
      GEOG: CHINA
      SUBJ: CONTROL

DILKE, CHARLES W.   D01280
      THE CHINESE PRINTING PRESS
      THE TIMES [LONDON](5 APR 1877), 6.
      LT; LETTER TO EDITOR, ANSWER TO MAULE M01281.
      CHRON: BEFORE 1910
      GEOG: CHINA
      SUBJ: PRINTING

DINH, TRAN VAN   D00407
      HO CHI MINH AS A COMMUNICATOR
      JRNL OF COMMUNICATION 26:4(AUTUMN 1976),
          142-7.
      ##/VN-2
      MEDIUM: OTHER
      CHRON: SURVEY
      GEOG: VIETNAM
      SUBJ: PROPAGANDA BIOGRAPHY

DIZARD, WILSON P.   D00408
      NCNA--REPORTER OF CORRECT NEWS
      CURRENT SCENE X:7(JULY 1972), 7-11.
      ##/CHIN-3
      MEDIUM: GENERAL
      CHRON: SURVEY
      GEOG: CHINA
      SUBJ: FLOW/AGENCY PROPAGANDA

DJAJANTO, WARIEF   D01475
      ROLLING AHEAD SLOWLY IN INDONESIA
      MEDIA [HONG KONG] 4:4(APR 1977), 7.
      CHRON: 1970-1980
      GEOG: INDONESIA
      SUBJ: PRINTING

DJASWADI,SOEPRATO, R.   D02096
    BRIEF TALK ABOUT INDONESIAN PRINTING
        INDUSTRY
    THE ASIAN PRINTER 5:3(1962), 53-4.
    CHRON: 1960-1970
    GEOG: INDONESIA
    SUBJ: PRINTING

DJAWADI SUPRAPTO   D02095
    GRAPHIC ARTS INDUSTRY OF INDONESIA: SOCIAL
        WELFARE AND LABOUR POLICY
    THE ASIAN PRINTER 7:3(1965), 58-61.
    CHRON: 1960-1970
    GEOG: INDONESIA
    SUBJ: PRINTING

DOBRA, BHARAT B.   D00409
    INDIA CINEMA AWAKENS
    ATLAS WORLD PRESS REVIEW 23:3(MAR 1976),
        34-5.
    FROM <PATRIOT> 16 NOV 1975
    MEDIUM: FILM
    CHRON: 1970-1980
    GEOG: SO/WEST ASI
    SUBJ: DESCRIPTION

DONALD, W. H.   D01238
    THE PRESS
    IN WRIGHT W02589, PP. 343-67.
    ##/HKG; FOR OTHERS IN THIS SERIES, SEE
        WRIGHT W01174, W01175, W01678,
        W02565.
    CHRON: BEFORE 1910
    GEOG: HONG KONG   CHINA
    SUBJ: DESCRIPTION

DONOVAN, JOHN PATRICK   D00411
    THE PRESS OF CHINA
    ASIATIC REVIEW NEW (4TH SERIES) 15:42(APRIL
        1919), 153-67.
    ##/ChIN-3
    CHRON: 1910-1946
    GEOG: CHINA
    SUBJ: DESCRIPTION

DUDMAN, RICHARD   D00415
    HEADLINES AND DEADLINES: CHINA STYLE
    NIEMAN REPORTS XXVIII:1,2(SPRING/SUMMER
        1974), 19-22.
    ##/ChIN
    CHRON: 1970-1980
    GEOG: CHINA
    SUBJ: DESCRIPTION

DUDMAN, RICHARD   D02097
     CHINA IN GENERAL
     MONTANA JOURNALISM REVIEW NO. 15 (1972), 2-6.
     CHRON: 1970-1980
     GEOG: CHINA
     SUBJ: DESCRIPTION

DUDMAN, RICHARD   D02054
     THE RESTRICTIVE SIDE OF VIETNAM
     NIEMAN REPORTS XXXII:2(SUMMER 1978), 38-40.
     ##/VN-2
     CHRON: 1970-1980
     GEOG: VIETNAM   U.S.
     SUBJ: FOR CORR   CONTROL   FLOW/AGENCY

DURDIN, F. T.   D00272
     TWENTY-FIVE YEARS OF <THE CHINA PRESS>
     IN CHINA PRESS C02568, P. 75.
     ##/FILM
     CHRON: 1910-1946
     GEOG: CHINA
     SUBJ: JRN HISTORY DESCRIPTION

EAPEN, K. E.   E00419
     THE ROLE OF MASS MEDIA IN INDONESIA'S
          DEVELOPMENT
     INDIAN PRESS 1:5(JULY 1974), 27-33.
     ##/INDON
     MEDIUM: GENERAL
     CHRON: 1970-1980
     GEOG: INDONESIA
     SUBJ: DEVELOPMENT

EAPEN, K. E.   E00418
     NEWS AGENCIES: THE INDONESIAN SCENE
     GAZETTE XIX:1(1973), 1-12.
     ##/INDON
     MEDIUM: GENERAL
     CHRON: 1970-1980
     GEOG: INDONESIA
     SUBJ: FLOW/AGENCY

EAPEN, KADAMATTU EAPEN   E00417
     JOURNALISM AS A PROFESSION IN INDIA: A STUDY
          OF TWO STATES AND TWO CITIES
     PHD DISS, UNIVERSITY OF WISCONSIN, 1969.
     U. MICROFILM, 70-3518; INTL DISS, 31A:1217;
          247 PP.
     CHRON: 1970-1980   VERIF: UNVERIFIED
     GEOG: SO/WEST ASI
     SUBJ: EDUCATION   DESCRIPTION

ECO, UNBERTO   E00420
    LITTLE RED COMIC BOOK
    ATLAS 20:10(NOV 1971), 36-8.
    ##/CHIN-2; FROM <L'ESPRESSO>.
    CHRON: 1970-1980
    GEOG: CHINA
    SUBJ: PROPAGANDA   DESCRIPTION

EDELSTEIN, ALEX S. AND ALAN   E00421
        PING-LIN LIU
    ANTI-AMERICANISM IN RED CHINA'S <PEOPLE'S
        DAILY>: A FUNCTIONAL ANALYSIS
    JQ 40:2(SPRING 1963), 187-195.
    ##/CHIN
    CHRON: 1960-1970
    METH: OTHER OR COMB
    GEOG: CHINA
    SUBJ: CONTROL   DESCRIPTION

EDITOR & PUBLISHER   E00427
    CALIFORNIA PUBLISHERS VISIT CHINA MAINLAND
    (9 JULY 1977), 9, 13.
    ##/CHIN-5
    CHRON: 1970-1980
    GEOG: CHINA
    SUBJ: DESCRIPTION

EDITOR & PUBLISHER   E00426
    CHINESE STILL NOT READY FOR U. S. BUREAUS
    (9 JULY 1977), 9.
    ##/CHIN-5
    MEDIUM: GENERAL
    CHRON: 1970-1980
    GEOG: CHINA
    SUBJ: FLOW/AGENCY DESCRIPTION

EDITOR & PUBLISHER   E00425
    CHINA DAILY GOES ROMAN IN NAME
    (22 JAN 1977), 42.
    'RENMIN RIBAO' ON MASTHEAD
    CHRON: 1970-1980
    GEOG: CHINA
    SUBJ: DESCRIPTION

EDITOR & PUBLISHER   E00424
    PRESS HIT BY MALAYSIA DELEGATE
    (25 OCT 1969), 34.
    ##/MAL; TENGKU ON PRESS DURING 1969 RIOTS.
    CHRON: 1960-1970
    GEOG: MALAYSIA
    SUBJ: FOR CORR

EDITOR & PUBLISHER   E00423
        AMERICAN GROUP BUYS PERCENTAGE OF BANGKOK
            DAILY
        (18 OCT 1969), 14.
        ##/THAI
        CHRON: 1960-1970
        GEOG: THAILAND
        SUBJ: PUBLISHING   DESCRIPTION

EDITOR & PUBLISHER   E02221
        CHINESE OFFICIALS SOFTEN POSITION ON
            CORRESPONDENTS
        (28 OCT 1978), 36.
        ##/CHIN-8
        MEDIUM: GENERAL
        CHRON: 1970-1980
        GEOG: CHINA   U.S.
        SUBJ: FOR CORR   CONTROL

EDITOR & PUBLISHER   E02098
        SINGAPORE PAPERS BUY TAL-STAR SYSTEM
        (29 JULY 1978), 22.
        ##/SIN-2
        CHRON: 1970-1980
        GEOG: SINGAPORE
        SUBJ: PRINTING

EDITOR & PUBLISHER   E01800
        CHINESE TO ESTABLISH JOURNALISM INSTITUTE
        (11 MAR 1978), 20.
        ##/CHIN-5
        CHRON: 1970-1980
        GEOG: CHINA
        SUBJ: EDUCATION

EDITOR & PUBLISHER   E01401
        CHINA MAY RELAX RULES FOR JOURNALISTS
        (10 DEC 1977), 14.
        CHRON: 1970-1980
        GEOG: CHINA
        SUBJ: FOR CORR   CONTROL   LAW/ETHICS

EDITOR & PUBLISHER   E01391
        MOVEMENT STARTED TO FREE JAILED EDITOR
        (19 NOV 1977), 25.
        ##/MAL-3; SAMAD ISMAIL.
        CHRON: 1970-1980
        GEOG: MALAYSIA
        SUBJ: CONTROL   LAW/ETHICS

EDITOR & PUBLISHER   E02669
     CONTINUOUS CENSORSHIP IN CHINA BARS
          U. S. GRASP OF EVENTS
     66:43(10 MAR 1934), 16.
     CHRON: 1910-1946
     GEOG: CHINA
     SUBJ: CONTROL   FLOW/AGENCY

EDITOR & PUBLISHER   E02668
     U. S. NEWSPAPER MEN UNDERWRITE JOURNALISM
          SCHOOL IN CHINA
     61:44(23 MAR 1929), 30.
     UNIVERSITY OF MISSOURI AND YENCHING UNIVERSITY
     CHRON: 1910-1946
     GEOG: CHINA
     SUBJ: EDUCATION

EDITOR & PUBLISHER   E02516
     PEKING NEWS EXECS VISIT U. S. PAPERS
     (27 JAN 1979), 40.
     ##/CHIN-8
     CHRON: 1970-1980
     GEOG: CHINA   U.S.
     SUBJ: DESCRIPTION

EDITOR & PUBLISHER   E02515
     AMERICAN TO TEACH AT CHINESE J-SCHOOL
     (20 JAN 1979), 42.
     ##/CHIN-8; JAMES ARONSON.
     CHRON: 1970-1980
     GEOG: CHINA
     SUBJ: EDUCATION

EDITOR & PUBLISHER   E02514
     WORD ON PEKING BUREAUS EXPECTED THIS MONTH
     (13 JAN 1979), 14, 23.
     ##/CHIN-8
     MEDIUM: GENERAL
     CHRON: 1970-1980
     GEOG: CHINA
     SUBJ: FLOW/AGENCY

EDKINS, J.   E01799
     ON THE ORIGIN OF PAPER MAKING IN CHINA
     NOTES AND QUERIES: ON CHINA AND JAPAN I:6(29
          JUNE 1867), 67-8.
     CHRON: BEFORE 1910
     GEOG: CHINA
     SUBJ: PRINTING

ELDERLY CHINA HAND   E01476
     SHANGHAI PUBLICATIONS
     FEER 98:40(7 OCT 1977), 7.
     ##/CHIN-5; LETTER.
     CHRON: 1910-1946
     GEOG: CHINA
     SUBJ: JRN HISTORY

ELEGANT, ROBERT S.   E01477
     'THE FEEL OF HONG KONG'
     THE ASIA MAIL 2:3(DEC 1977), 7, 14, 19.
     ##/FOCO
     CHRON: 1970-1980
     GEOG: HONG KONG   SEV ASIA
     SUBJ: FOR CORR   BIOGRAPHY

ELEGANT, ROBERT S.   E02187
     ON ASIA: FOOLS RUSH IN--AND PROGNOSTICATE
     DATELINE [OPC, NEW YORK] 15:1(1971), 51-3.
     MEDIUM: GENERAL
     CHRON: 1970-1980
     GEOG: SEV ASIA
     SUBJ: FOR CORR   DESCRIPTION

ELEGANT, ROBERT S.   E00430
     THE DRAGON'S SEED: PEKING AND THE OVERSEAS
          CHINESE
     NEW YORK, ST. MARTIN'S PRESS, 1959.
     CHINESE IN SEA, 1954-59, MALAYA AND INDONESIA
     CHRON: 1946-1960
     GEOG: OSEAS CHIN
     SUBJ: DESCRIPTION JRN HISTORY

ELLITHORPE, HAROLD   E01479
     THE MEDIA THEY LEFT BEHIND
     MEDIA [HONG KONG] 2:6(JUNE 1975), 4.
     MEDIUM: GENERAL
     CHRON: 1970-1980
     GEOG: VIETNAM
     SUBJ: DESCRIPTION

ELLITHORPE, HAROLD   E01478
     I WISH I'D DONE DIFFERENTLY SAYS EX-VIETNAM
          NEWS 'CZAR'
     MEDIA [HONG KONG] 2:1(JAN 1975), 6.
     B. ZORTHIAN
     MEDIUM: GENERAL
     CHRON: 1970-1980
     GEOG: VIETNAM
     SUBJ: FOR CORR   CONTROL   LAW/ETHICS

EMERSON, GLORIA   E00431
    WINNERS AND LOSERS
    NEW YORK, RANDOM HOUSE, 1977.
    CORRESPONDENT IN VN FOR NYT
    CHRON: SURVEY
    GEOG: VIETNAM   U.S.
    SUBJ: FOR CORR   OTHER JRN

ENGLISH, JOHN W.   E00432
    CHINA WATCHING
    GAZETTE XXII:4(1976), 230-9.
    ##/CHIN-2
    CHRON: 1970-1980
    GEOG: CHINA   HONG KONG
    SUBJ: FOR CORR   FLOW/AGENCY CONTROL

ERLANGER, STEVEN   E02222
    VIETNAM NOW
    COL JRN REVIEW XVII:2(JULY/AUG 1978), 27-31.
    ##/VN-2
    CHRON: 1970-1980
    GEOG: VIETNAM
    SUBJ: FOR CORR   DESCRIPTION

ESPIE, STEPHEN   E01480
    ACTION LINE
    HORIZONS [USIS] XVII:11(1968-70), 17-20.
    CHRON: 1970-1980
    GEOG: PHILIPPINES
    SUBJ: DESCRIPTION

EVERINGHAM, JOHN   E01481
    THE LAOTIAN CHARGE-SHEET
    FEER 97:28(15 JULY 1977), 34-9.
    ##/LAOS
    CHRON: 1970-1980
    GEOG: LAOS
    SUBJ: FOR CORR   CONTROL

EVERINGHAM, JOHN   E00434
    THE THAI PRESS GOES TO WAR
    FEER 96:16(22 APR 1977), 20-1.
    ##/THAI
    CHRON: 1970-1980
    GEOG: THAILAND
    SUBJ: DESCRIPTION

EVERINGHAM, JOHN   E00433
    PRESS WAR CREATES PROBLEM FOR LAOS
    FEER 93:30(23 JULY 1976), 18-20.
    ##/LAOS
    CHRON: 1970-1980
    GEOG: LAOS   THAILAND
    SUBJ: FOR CORR   DESCRIPTION

EVERS, HANS-DIETER   E00435
    THE FORMULATION OF A SOCIAL CLASS STRUCTURE:
        URBANIZATION, BUREAUCRATZATION AND
        SOCIAL MOBILITY IN THAILAND
    AMERICAN SOCIOLOGICAL REVIEW 31:4(1966),
        480-8.
    CHRON: 1960-1970
    GEOG: THAILAND
    SUBJ: DESCRIPTION DEVELOPMENT SOCIO/ANTHR

FAAS, HORST   F01362
    FAAS BACK IN VIETNAM: OLD FRIENDS TURN AWAY
    AP LOG(17 OCT 1977), 1, 4.
    ##/VN-2
    CHRON: 1970-1980
    GEOG: VIETNAM
    SUBJ: FOR CORR   DESCRIPTION

FABER, G. H. VON   F00436
    A SHORT HISTORY OF JOURNALISM IN THE DUTCH
        EAST INDIES
    SOURABAYA, JAVA, G. KOLFF & CO., N. D. [1930?]
    #3
    CHRON: SURVEY
    METH: HISTORICAL
    GEOG: INDONESIA
    SUBJ: JRN HISTORY DESCRIPTION

FAIRBANK, JOHN K., EDITOR.   F02558
    THE MISSIONARY ENTERPRISE IN CHINA AND
        AMERICA
    CAMBRIDGE, HARVARD U. P., 1974.
    ##/CHIN-4;   SEE BENNETT B00155.
    CHRON: BEFORE 1910
    METH: HISTORICAL
    GEOG: CHINA
    SUBJ: JRN HISTORY

FAIRBANK, JOHN KING AND   F01696
        KWANG-CHING LIU
    MODERN CHINA: A BIBLIOGRAPHICAL GUIDE TO
        CHINESE WORKS, 1898-1937
    CAMBRIDGE, HARVARD U. P., 1950.
    LIBERAL PERIODICALS, PP. 137-40; SELECTED
        NEWSPAPERS, PP. 502-9.
    CHRON: SURVEY
    GEOG: CHINA
    SUBJ: RESEARCH

FAIRPLAY   F01801
     JOURNALISM IN THE FAR EAST
     SATURDAY REVIEW [OF POLITICS, LITERATURE,
          SCIENCE AND ART. LONDON] 86(16 JULY
          1898), 79.
     ##/THAI; LETTER TO EDITOR, SEE LILLIE L01836.
     CHRON: 1910-1946
     GEOG: CHINA   SEV ASIA
     SUBJ: DESCRIPTION

FALCONER, ALUN   F02294
     CHANGES IN SHANGHAI'S PRESS
     THE CHINA WEEKLY REVIEW 117:2(11 MAR 1950),
          26-8.
     CHRON: 1946-1960
     GEOG: CHINA
     SUBJ: DESCRIPTION

FAN WEI, ET AL., EDITORS.   09   F00438
     SHU PAO SHIH YEH (PUBLISHING ACTIVITIES)
     CHUNG-HUA CHI-TU CHIAO HUI NIEN CHIEN
          2(1915), 195-239.
     SKINNER S00982 II:41800
     CHRON: 1910-1946   VERIF: UNVERIFIED
     GEOG: CHINA
     SUBJ: PUBLISHING

FANG FU-AN   F02295
     'MOSQUITO PAPERS' AND PUBLIC OPINION IN
          SHANGHAI
     THE CHINA WEEKLY REVIEW 51:7(18 JAN 1930),
          250, 256.
     CHRON: 1910-1946
     GEOG: CHINA
     SUBJ: DESCRIPTION OTHER JRN

FANG PAI   04   F02055
     PAO CHIH TI KU SHIH [NEWSPAPER INCIDENTS]
     SHANGHAI, K'AI MING SHU TIEN, 1950.
     #3
                         LANG: CHINESE
     CHRON: SURVEY
     METH: HISTORICAL
     GEOG: CHINA
     SUBJ: DESCRIPTION BIOGRAPHY

FANTANANGE, STEPHANE   F02517
     VOICES FROM THE UNDERGROUND
     ASIAWEEK 5:17(4 MAY 1979), 29-30.
     ##/CHIN-8
     CHRON: 1970-1980
     GEOG: CHINA
     SUBJ: DESCRIPTION

FAR EASTERN ECONOMIC REVIEW   F02806
    RUSHING INTO PRINT
    104:22(1 JUNE 1979), 7.
    ##/SIN-2
    CHRON: 1970-1980
    GEOG: SINGAPORE   OSEAS CHIN
    SUBJ: DESCRIPTION PUBLISHING

FAR EASTERN ECONOMIC REVIEW   F01962
    CHANGE OF COURSE
    100:18(5 MAY 1978), 5.
    ##/TAI; <FU PAO CHIH SHENG>.
    CHRON: 1970-1980
    GEOG: TAIWAN
    SUBJ: CONTROL

FAR EASTERN ECONOMIC REVIEW   F02272
    THE REVIEW AND JUAN PONCE ENRILE
    102:45(10 NOV 1978), 28.
    ##/PHIL
    CHRON: 1970-1980
    GEOG: PHILIPPINES
    SUBJ: CONTROL   LAW/ETHICS

FAR EASTERN ECONOMIC REVIEW   F02271
    NEW SCHOOLS FOR THOUGHT
    100:23(9 JUNE 1978), 23-4.
    ##/HKG
    CHRON: 1970-1980
    GEOG: HONG KONG
    SUBJ: DESCRIPTION

FAR EASTERN ECONOMIC REVIEW   F02270
    [COMMENT]
    100:21(26 MAY 1978), 8-9.
    ##/SWAS
    CHRON: 1970-1980
    GEOG: SO/WEST ASI
    SUBJ: CONTROL

FAR EASTERN ECONOMIC REVIEW   F01483
    DOGMA EATS DOGMA
    97:38(23 SEPT 1977), 12.
    ##/CHIN-5
    CHRON: 1970-1980
    GEOG: CHINA
    SUBJ: PROPAGANDA

FAR EASTERN ECONOMIC REVIEW   F01482
    NEWSMAN'S RELEASE
    97:35(2 SEPT 1977), 5.
    ##/MAL-2
    CHRON: 1970-1980
    GEOG: MALAYSIA
    SUBJ: CONTROL   LAW/ETHICS

FAR EASTERN ECONOMIC REVIEW   F01484
    COMMUNIST SING-SONG
    97:39(30 SEPT 1977), 7.
    ##/THAI; VOPT.
    MEDIUM: ELECTRONIC
    CHRON: 1970-1980
    GEOG: THAILAND
    SUBJ: PROPAGANDA DESCRIPTION

FAR EASTERN ECONOMIC REVIEW   F00476
    HO RELEASED
    96:19(13 MAY 1977), 14.
    ##/SIN
    CHRON: 1970-1980
    GEOG: SINGAPORE
    SUBJ: LAW/ETHICS CONTROL   FOR CORR

FAR EASTERN ECONOMIC REVIEW   F00475
    CHINA NOW AND THEN AGAIN . . .
    96:18(6 MAY 1977), 22-3.
    ##/CHIN-4; <CHINA NOW>.
    CHRON: 1970-1980
    GEOG: CHINA
    SUBJ: PROPAGANDA FOR CORR

FAR EASTERN ECONOMIC REVIEW   F00474
    JOURNALIST RELEASED
    96:16(22 APR 1977), 14.
    ##/SIN; ARUN.
    CHRON: 1970-1980
    GEOG: SINGAPORE
    SUBJ: LAW/ETHICS FOR CORR   CONTROL

FAR EASTERN ECONOMIC REVIEW   F00473
    REFUTING THE IMPLICATIONS
    95:12(25 MAR 1977), 14.
    ##/SIN
    CHRON: 1970-1980
    GEOG: SINGAPORE
    SUBJ: CONTROL   LAW/ETHICS FOR CORR

```
FAR EASTERN ECONOMIC REVIEW                          F00472
     REVIEW WRITER DEPORTED
     95:9(4 MAR 1977), 9.
     ##/THAI; N. PEAGAM.
     CHRON: 1970-1980
     GEOG:   THAILAND
     SUBJ:   FOR CORR      CONTROL      LAW/ETHICS


FAR EASTERN ECONOMIC REVIEW                          F00471
     COUP PHOTOGRAPHS
     95:5(4 FEB 1977), 7.
     ##/THAI; RETOUCHING PHOTOGRAPHS, LETTER FROM
        'ANOTHER WESTERN OBSERVER'
     CHRON: 1970-1980
     GEOG:   THAILAND
     SUBJ:   PROPAGANDA  DESCRIPTION


FAR EASTERN ECONOMIC REVIEW                          F00470
     REVIEW MAN CHARGED
     95:2(14 JAN 1977), 15.
     ##/SIN; HO KWON PING.
     CHRON: 1970-1980
     GEOG:   SINGAPORE
     SUBJ:   LAW/ETHICS  CONTROL      FOR CORR


FAR EASTERN ECONOMIC REVIEW                          F00469
     THE STRATEGY OF SUBVERSION: MALAYSIA
     94:48(31 DEC 1976), 22-34.
     ##/MAL-2;SAMAD ISMAIL, KGB.
     CHRON: 1970-1980
     GEOG:   MALAYSIA
     SUBJ:   PROPAGANDA  OTHER NON-J


FAR EASTERN ECONOMIC REVIEW                          F00468
     STOP-PRESS NEWS FROM SABAH
     94:45(5 NOV 1976), 24.
     ##/MAL-2
     CHRON: 1970-1980
     GEOG:   MALAYSIA
     SUBJ:   CONTROL


FAR EASTERN ECONOMIC REVIEW                          F00467
     PUBLISH--AND THEY'RE DAMNED
     94:44(29 OCT 1976), 14.
     ##/SWAS
     CHRON: 1970-1980
     GEOG:   SO/WEST ASI
     SUBJ:   CONTROL
```

FAR EASTERN ECONOMIC REVIEW   F00448
    A CLEAR CASE
    LXXIV:47(20 NOV 1971), 13.
    ##/MAL-2; UTUSAN MELAYU SEDITION CASE.
    CHRON: 1970-1980
    GEOG: MALAYSIA
    SUBJ: LAW/ETHICS

FAR EASTERN ECONOMIC REVIEW   F00447
    NO BANANA REPUBLIC
    LXXIII:32(7 AUG 1971), 3.
    ##/SIN
    CHRON: 1970-1980
    GEOG: SINGAPORE
    SUBJ: CONTROL

FAR EASTERN ECONOMIC REVIEW   F00446
    TRAVELER'S TALES
    LXXII:23(5 JUNE 1971), 13.
    DIGEST OF HERALD PRESS CONFERENCE
    CHRON: 1970-1980
    GEOG: SINGAPORE
    SUBJ: CONTROL

FAR EASTERN ECONOMIC REVIEW   F00445
    THE DAY A MAN CRIED
    XXXII:23(5 JUNE 1971), 5-6.
    ##/SIN; HERALD
    CHRON: 1970-1980
    GEOG: SINGAPORE
    SUBJ: CONTROL

FAR EASTERN ECONOMIC REVIEW   F00443
    WILD ABOUT HARRY
    LXXII:22(29 MAY 1971), 3.
    ##/SIN; EDITORIAL.
    CHRON: 1970-1980
    GEOG: SINGAPORE
    SUBJ: CONTROL

FAR EASTERN ECONOMIC REVIEW   F00442
    SINGAPORE: FREE-FOR-ALL
    LXXII:22(29 MAY 1971), 5.
    ##/SIN; HERALD.
    CHRON: 1970-1980
    GEOG: SINGAPORE
    SUBJ: CONTROL   LAW/ETHICS

FAR EASTERN ECONOMIC REVIEW   F00441
     MAYDAY, MAYDAY, MAYDAY.
     LXXII:21(22 MAY 1971), 5.
     ##/SIN
     CHRON: 1970-1980
     GEOG: SINGAPORE
     SUBJ: CONTROL   DESCRIPTION

FAR EASTERN ECONOMIC REVIEW   F00440
     PRINTING AND PUBLISHING IN ASIA
     LXXII:18(1 MAY 1971).
     ##/PRIN; SPECIAL SECTION.
     CHRON: 1970-1980
     GEOG: SEV ASIA
     SUBJ: PRINTING   PUBLISHING

FAR EASTERN ECONOMIC REVIEW   F00466
     JAIL FOR TAIWAN EDITOR
     94:44(29 OCT 1976), 5.
     ##/TAI; <TAIWAN POLITICAL REVIEW>.
     CHRON: 1970-1980
     GEOG: TAIWAN
     SUBJ: CONTROL   LAW/ETHICS POLIT SCI

FAR EASTERN ECONOMIC REVIEW   F00465
     DENYING POWER TO PUBLISH
     94:42(15 OCT 1976), 25.
     ##/SWAS
     CHRON: 1970-1980
     GEOG: SO/WEST ASI
     SUBJ: CONTROL

FAR EASTERN ECONOMIC REVIEW   F00462
     TUNING IN TO THE MASSES
     93:29(16 JULY 1976), 28-9.
     ##/SWAS
     MEDIUM: ELECTRONIC
     CHRON: 1970-1980
     GEOG: SO/WEST ASI
     SUBJ: DEVELOPMENT DESCRIPTION

FAR EASTERN ECONOMIC REVIEW   F00461
     FOREIGNERS LEARN THE HARD WAY
     93:29(16 JULY 1976), 22-3.
     ##/CHIN-4
     CHRON: 1970-1980
     GEOG: CHINA   HONG KONG
     SUBJ: EDUCATION   OTHER NON-J

```
FAR EASTERN ECONOMIC REVIEW                          F00460
     STIFLING A VOICE OF THE LIBERALS
     91:5(30 JAN 1976), 26.
     ##/TAI
     CHRON: 1970-1980
     GEOG:  TAIWAN
     SUBJ:  CONTROL


FAR EASTERN ECONOMIC REVIEW                          F00459
     COMMUNICATIONS IN ASIA '75
     87:10(7 MAR 1975).
     ##/ASIA; SPECIAL SECTION.
     MEDIUM:  GENERAL
     CHRON: 1970-1980
     GEOG:   SEV ASIA
     SUBJ:  DESCRIPTION


FAR EASTERN ECONOMIC REVIEW                          F00458
     SEOUL'S WATCHDOGS CLAW THE MUZZLE
     86:44(8 NOV 1974), 34.
     ##/PHIL
     CHRON: 1970-1980
     GEOG:  EAST ASIA
     SUBJ:  CONTROL


FAR EASTERN ECONOMIC REVIEW                          F00457
     THE DEATH OF A NEWSPAPER
     85:35(30 AUG 1974), 13.
     ##/HKG; CHINA MAIL.
     CHRON: 1970-1980
     GEOG:  HONG KONG
     SUBJ:  DESCRIPTION


FAR EASTERN ECONOMIC REVIEW                          F00456
     MALAYSIA IN ASIA '74
     85:35(30 AUG 1974).
     ##/MAL
     CHRON: 1970-1980
     GEOG:  MALAYSIA
     SUBJ:  OTHER NON-J


FAR EASTERN ECONOMIC REVIEW                          F00455
     THE LOUD SILENCE
     83:8(25 FEB 1974), 50.
     ##/SIN; A. C. SIMMONS.
     CHRON: 1970-1980
     GEOG:  SINGAPORE
     SUBJ:  DESCRIPTION
```

```
FAR EASTERN ECONOMIC REVIEW                          F00454
     SPREADING THE WORD
     83:7(18 FEB 1974), 24-5.
     ##/PHIL
     CHRON: 1970-1980
     GEOG:  PHILIPPINES
     SUBJ:  DESCRIPTION


FAR EASTERN ECONOMIC REVIEW                          F00453
     AND NOW, IN GLORIOUS COLOUR . . .
     82:49(10 DEC 1973), 29.
     ##/THAI
     CHRON: 1970-1980
     GEOG:  THAILAND
     SUBJ:  DESCRIPTION


FAR EASTERN ECONOMIC REVIEW                          F00452
     PREDICTING UNREST
     82:48(3 DEC 1973), 21.
     ##/SIN; LEE MAU SENG.
     CHRON: 1970-1980
     GEOG:  SINGAPORE
     SUBJ:  CONTROL      LAW/ETHICS


FAR EASTERN ECONOMIC REVIEW                          F00451
     RADIO LAMENT
     77:31(29 JULY 1972), 19-20.
     ##/HKG
     MEDIUM:  ELECTRONIC
     CHRON: 1970-1980
     GEOG:  HONG KONG
     SUBJ:  DESCRIPTION


FAR EASTERN ECONOMIC REVIEW                          F00450
     ASIA'S PRINT REVOLUTION
     LXXVI:19(6 MAY 1972).
     ##/PRIN; SPECIAL SECTION.
     CHRON: 1970-1980
     GEOG:  SEV ASIA
     SUBJ:  PRINTING      PUBLISHING


FAR EASTERN ECONOMIC REVIEW                          F00449
     BURMA CURBS PAPER IMPORTS
     LXXV:12(18 MAR 1972), 59.
     ##/BURMA
     CHRON: 1970-1980
     GEOG:  BURMA
     SUBJ:  DESCRIPTION PUBLISHING
```

FAR EASTERN FORTNIGHTLY, THE   F01697
    JAPAN'S FILM WAR
    VIII:1(3 JAN 1921), 1-2.
    MEDIUM: FILM
    CHRON: 1910-1946
    GEOG: SO/WEST ASI
    SUBJ: PROPAGANDA DESCRIPTION

FAR EASTERN INFORMATION BULLETIN   F01992
    NEWS AND PROPAGANDA
    I:13(15 OCT 1929), 6-9.
    ##/CHIN-6; REPRINTED FROM <THE CHINA CRITIC>
        (12 SEPT 1929) AND
        <JAPAN CHRONICLE>.
    CHRON: 1910-1946
    GEOG: CHINA   EAST ASIA
    SUBJ: CONTROL   FLOW/AGENCY

FAR EASTERN INFORMATION BULLETIN   F01993
    NANKING ABOLISHES PRESS CENSORSHIP
    I:12(1 OCT 1929), 15-16.
    ##/CHIN-6
    CHRON: 1910-1946
    GEOG: CHINA
    SUBJ: CONTROL

FAR EASTERN INFORMATION BUREAU   F01991
       BULLETIN
    CHINESE PUBLICATION BARRED FROM INDIA
    I:10(1 SEPT 1929), 1-2.
    ##/CHIN-6; <THE CHINA TRUTH>.
    CHRON: 1910-1946
    GEOG: CHINA   SO/WEST ASI
    SUBJ: CONTROL

FAR EASTERN INFORMATION BUREAU   F01990
       BULLETIN
    THE FOREIGN PRESS IN CHINA
    I:10(1 SEPT 1929), 2-3.
    ##/CHIN-6; FROM N. Y. <HERALD TRIBUNE>; NCDN.
    CHRON: 1910-1946
    GEOG: CHINA   OTHER
    SUBJ: DESCRIPTION

FAR EASTERN REVIEW, THE   F01803
    CHINESE OFFICIAL PUBLICITY
    27:4(APR 1931), 206.
    ##/CHIN-6
    CHRON: 1910-1946
    GEOG: CHINA   EAST ASIA
    SUBJ: DESCRIPTION OTHER JRN

FAR EASTERN REVIEW, THE   F01802
    RED JOURNALISM
    21:8(AUG 1925), 538-9.
    CHRON: 1910-1946
    GEOG: CHINA   EAST ASIA
    SUBJ: PROPAGANDA

FAR HORIZONS   F01586
    INTERNATIONAL COMMUNICATIONS: FREEDOM OF
        INFORMATION AND CULTURAL INTEGRITY
    VII:2(SPRING 1974), 1-4.
    MEDIUM: GENERAL
    CHRON: 1970-1980
    GEOG: SEV ASIA
    SUBJ: FLOW/AGENCY CROSS CULTU

FARIS, BARRY   F02519
    THE CORRESPONDENTS IN THE PACIFIC
    IN MOTT M02529, PP. 63-6.
    CHRON: SURVEY
    GEOG: SEV ASIA
    SUBJ: FOR CORR   ,DESCRIPTION

FASS, JOSEF   F00480
    CHINESE NEWSPAPERS
    IN LESLIE L02567, PP. 221-8.
    CHRON: SURVEY
    GEOG: CHINA
    SUBJ: RESEARCH

FELICIANO, GLORIA   F00481
    AN OVERVIEW OF COMMUNICATION RESEARCH IN
        ASIA: STATUS, PROBLEMS, AND NEEDS
    HONOLULU, EWCI, 1973.
    ##/ASIA; VF.
    MEDIUM: GENERAL
    CHRON: 1960-1970
    GEOG: SEV ASIA
    SUBJ: RESEARCH

FELLNER, FREDERICK VINCENT DE   F00482
    COMMUNICATIONS IN THE FAR EAST
    LONDON, P. S. KING & SON, 1934.
    NOTHING ON MEDIA
    GEOG: SEV ASIA
    SUBJ: OTHER NON-J

FENG AI-CHUN [EDITOR]   12   F00485
     CHUNG-KUO HSIN WEN SHIH (HISTORY OF CHINESE
          JOURNALISM)
     TAIPEI, HSUEH SHENG SHU CHU, 1967.
                              LANG: CHINESE
     CHRON: SURVEY
     METH: HISTORICAL
     GEOG: CHINA
     SUBJ: JRN HISTORY

FENG AI-CHUN [EDITOR]   12   F01698
     HUA CH'IAO PAO YEH SHIH [HISTORY OF THE
          OVERSEAS CHINESE PRESS]
     TAIPEI, HSUEH SHENG SHU CHU, 1967.
     #3
                              LANG: CHINESE
     CHRON: SURVEY
     METH: HISTORICAL
     GEOG: SEV ASIA   WORLD
     SUBJ: JRN HISTORY DESCRIPTION

FENG TZU-YU   12   F00489
     KO MING I SHIH (AN ANECDOTAL HISTORY OF THE
          REVOLUTION OF 1911)
     TAIPEI, COMMERICAL PRESS, 1969, 5 VOLS.
     #3; SEVERAL CHAPTERS ON JOURNALISM; SEE
          SKINNER S00982 FOR REPRINTS.
                              LANG: CHINESE
     CHRON: BEFORE 1910
     METH: HISTORICAL
     GEOG: CHINA   SEV ASIA
     SUBJ: JRN HISTORY

FERNANDEZ, T.   F00490
     ASIAN NEWS AGENCY
     GAZETTE 12:4(1966), 287-93.
     ##/ASIA
     MEDIUM: GENERAL
     CHRON: 1960-1970
     GEOG: SEV ASIA
     SUBJ: FLOW/AGENCY

FEUEREISEN, FRITZ AND ERNST SCHMACKE   F00491
     DIE PRESSEN IN ASIEN UND OZEANIEN: EIN
          HANDBUCH FUR WIRTSCHAFT UND WESBUNG
     MUNCHEN, VERLAG DOKUMENTATION, 1968.
     PRODUCTION DETAILS, ETC.
     CHRON: 1960-1970
     GEOG: SEV ASIA
     SUBJ: DESCRIPTION

FISHER, W. E. JR.   F01340
     PRESS PAGES WRITE THRILLING HISTORY
     IN CHINA PRESS C02568, PP. 78-9.
     ##/FILM
     CHRON: 1910-1946
     GEOG: CHINA
     SUBJ: JRN HISTORY DESCRIPTION

FLUG, K. K.   F01485
    IZ ISTORII KNIGOPECHATANIYA V KITAE: 10-13
        V. V. (HISTORY OF BOOKPRINTING IN CHINA
        FROM THE 10TH TO THE 13TH CENTURY)
    SOVETSKOE VOSTOKOVEDENIE I(1940).
                         LANG: RUSSIAN
    CHRON: BEFORE 1910   VERIF: UNVERIFIED
    METH: HISTORICAL
    GEOG: CHINA
    SUBJ: PRINTING

FONG, DAVID CHONG SIN   F00492
    A COMPARATIVE STUDY OF PUBLIC INFORMATION
        SERVICES IN MULTI-RACIAL SOCIETY OF
        MALAYSIA BEFORE AND AFTER INDEPENDENCE
    MASTERS THESIS, U. OF OKLAHOMA, 1968.
    MEDIUM: GENERAL
    CHRON: 1946-1960
    GEOG: MALAYSIA
    SUBJ: DESCRIPTION

FONG, LESLIE   F00493
    HO: I DISTORTED ARTICLES TO DISCREDIT GOVT
    STRAITS TIMES (SUN, SIN) 17 APR 1977
    ##/SIN
    CHRON: 1970-1980
    GEOG: SINGAPORE
    SUBJ: PROPAGANDA LAW/ETHICS

FONGALLAND, GUY DE   F00494
    A POWERFUL PRESS FALTERS IN SRI LANKA
    CSM 21 AUG 1973
    ##/SWAS
    CHRON: 1970-1980
    GEOG: SO/WEST ASI
    SUBJ: CONTROL

FOOCHOW CORRESPONDENT   F02296
    ARREST OF EDITOR AND BANNING OF A SOUTH
        FUKIEN NEWSPAPER
    THE CHINA WEEKLY REVIEW 78:9(31 OCT 1936),
        317.
    TSAI MIN-LIANG OF <SIANG PAO>
    CHRON: 1910-1946
    GEOG: CHINA
    SUBJ: CONTROL

FOOKIEN TIMES, EDITOR.   F02714
    FOOKIEN TIMES YEAR BOOK 1967
    MANILA, FOOKIEN TIMES, 1967.
    SEE ASPIRAS A00135, ASPIRAS A00136,
        ROSARIO R00934.
    CHRON: SURVEY
    GEOG: PHILIPPINES
    SUBJ: DESCRIPTION BIOGRAPHY   OTHER JRN

FORBIS, WILLIAM H.   F00656
    JAPAN TODAY: PEOPLE, PLACES, POWER
    NEW YORK, HARPER AND ROW, 1975.
    PP. 156-160; REPRINTED IN <MONTANA
        JOURNALISM REVIEW> NO. 18 (1975),
        9-11.
    CHRON: 1970-1980
    GEOG: EAST ASIA
    SUBJ: FOR CORR   DESCRIPTION

FORD, ALEXANDER HUME   F00495
    WHY A PERMANENT PAN-PACIFIC CONFERENCE BODY
    IN WILLIAMS W01152
    #3
    CHRON: 1910-1946
    GEOG: SEV ASIA
    SUBJ: FLOW/AGENCY

FOREIGN CORRESPONDENT, A   F01486
    TYPICAL PRESS CONFERENCE IN SHANGHAI
    AMERASIA III:2(APR 1939), 90-2.
    ##/CHIN-5
    CHRON: 1910-1946
    GEOG: CHINA
    SUBJ: FOR CORR   DESCRIPTION

FOSTER, DOUGLAS ZOLOTH   F01646
    PHOTOS OF 'HORROR' IN CAMBODIA: FAKE OR REAL?
    COL JRN REVIEW XVI:6(MAR/APR 1978), 46-7.
    ##/CAMB
    CHRON: 1970-1980
    GEOG: CAMBODIA
    SUBJ: PROPAGANDA   DESCRIPTION

FOWLER, JOHN A.   F02099
    NETHERLANDS EAST INDIES AND BRITISH MALAYA:
        A COMMERCIAL AND INDUSTRIAL HANDBOOK
    WASHINGTON, D. C., DEPARTMENT OF COMMERCE,
        BUREAU OF FOREIGN AND DOMESTIC COMMERCE,
        1923.
    SPECIAL AGENTS SERIES, NO. 218
    MEDIUM: GENERAL
    CHRON: 1910-1946
    GEOG: MALAYSIA   SINGAPORE   INDONESIA
    SUBJ: OTHER JRN

FOX, RICHARD W.   F00496
    PRAGMATISM, HONG KONG STYLE
    COMMONWEAL 378:13(14 JUNE 1968), 378-80.
    ##/CHIN-3; 1968 RIOTS; NOTHING ON MEDIA.
    CHRON: 1960-1970
    GEOG: HONG KONG
    SUBJ: OTHER NON-J

FOX, TOM   F00497
    THE WORD FROM THE FRONT
    COMMONWEAL XC:18(8 AUG 1969), 485-6.
    ##/VN-2
    CHRON: 1960-1970
    GEOG: VIETNAM   U.S.
    SUBJ: FOR CORR   CONTROL

FRANK, ROBERT S.   F00498
    THE IAS CASE AGAINST CBS
    JRNL OF COMMUNICATION 25:4(AUTUMN 1975),
        186-9.
    ##/VN
    MEDIUM: ELECTRONIC
    CHRON: SURVEY
    GEOG: VIETNAM   U.S.
    SUBJ: FOR CORR

FRASER, JOHN   F02223
    WESTERN NEWSMEN FACE DIFFERENT WORLD IN CHINA
    CSM 29 DEC 1978
    ##/CHIN-8
    MEDIUM: GENERAL
    CHRON: 1970-1980
    GEOG: CHINA   SEV ASIA
    SUBJ: FOR CORR   CROSS CULTU

FREE CHINA WEEKLY   F01994
    BREAKTHROUGH IN COMMUNICATIONS
    XIX:22(4 JUNE 1978), 1.
    ##/TAI
    CHRON: 1970-1980
    GEOG: TAIWAN   CHINA
    SUBJ: LANGUAGE

FREE CHINA WEEKLY   F00503
    KUNG-FU FADING; ROC MOVIES SEEK CHANGES
    12 SEPT 1976
    ##/TAI
    MEDIUM: FILM
    CHRON: 1970-1980
    GEOG: TAIWAN
    SUBJ: DESCRIPTION

FREE CHINA WEEKLY   F00502
    WESTERN NEWS AGENCIES TO PULL OUT OF MAINLAND
    20 MAR 1977
    ##/CHIN-3
    MEDIUM: GENERAL
    CHRON: 1970-1980
    GEOG: CHINA
    SUBJ: FOR CORR   FLOW/AGENCY

```
FREE CHINA WEEKLY                               F00501
    MACHINE TYPES CHINESE AND 18 OTHER LANGUAGES
    24 OCT 1976
    ##/TAI
    CHRON: 1970-1980
    GEOG:  TAIWAN      CHINA
    SUBJ:  PRINTING    PUBLISHING


FREE CHINA WEEKLY                               F00500
    TRADE WAR IN MAGAZINES FOR WOMEN
    26 SEPT 1976
    ##/TAI
    CHRON: 1970-1980
    GEOG:  TAIWAN
    SUBJ:  DESCRIPTION


FREE CHINA WEEKLY                               F02521
    PEIPING PLOT USES FOREIGN JOURNALISTS
    XX:10(18 MAR 1979), 1.
    ##/CHIN-8
    MEDIUM:  GENERAL
    CHRON: 1970-1980
    GEOG:  TAIWAN      CHINA
    SUBJ:  FOR CORR    PROPAGANDA  DESCRIPTION


FREE CHINA WEEKLY                               F02520
    FOREIGN REPORTERS IN PEIPING INVITED TO VISIT
        ROC
    XX:10(18 MAR 1979), 1.
    ##/CHIN-8
    MEDIUM:  GENERAL
    CHRON: 1970-1980
    GEOG:  TAIWAN      CHINA
    SUBJ:  FOR CORR    DESCRIPTION


FREE CHINA WEEKLY                               F02518
    ALIEN REPORTERS IN PEIPING INVITED TO ROC
    XX:12(1 APR 1979), 1.
    ##/CHIN-8
    MEDIUM:  GENERAL
    CHRON: 1970-1980
    GEOG:  TAIWAN      CHINA
    SUBJ:  FOR CORR    DESCRIPTION


FREEDOM OF INFORMATION CENTER                   F00505
    THE NEWS FROM CHINA
    NO. 12, (N. D.).
    ##/CHIN-2; 7PP.; THEODORE WHITE, JOHN FAIRBANK
    CHRON: SURVEY
    GEOG:  CHINA
    SUBJ:  CONTROL       FLOW/AGENCY DESCRIPTION
```

FREEDOM OF INFORMATION CENTER   F00504
    WORLD PRESS FREEDOM, 1967
    FOI CENTER REPORT NO. 201 (MAY 1968).
    ##/FREE; PICA; 6 PP.
    MEDIUM: GENERAL
    CHRON: 1960-1970
    METH: OTHER OR COMB
    GEOG: WORLD
    SUBJ: CONTROL   POLIT SCI

FREEMAN, ANDREW A.   F01487
    A TABLOID IN BANGKOK
    ASIA XXX:8(AUG 1930), 555-60, 599-601;
        PART 2, XXX:9(SEPT 1930),650-5, 665-6.
    ##/FILM
    CHRON: 1910-1946
    GEOG: THAILAND
    SUBJ: JRN HISTORY BIOGRAPHY

FRIENDLY, FRED W.   F00506
    TV AT THE TURNING POINT
    COL JRN REVIEW IX:4(WINTER 1970-1), 13-20.
    MEDIUM: ELECTRONIC
    CHRON: 1970-1980
    GEOG: VIETNAM   U.S.
    SUBJ: DESCRIPTION

FULBRIGHT, NEWTON H.   F02056
    CHINESE NEWSPAPERS FLOURISH, FORTIFYING
        BELIEF IN PEACE
    EDITOR & PUBLISHER (28 JUNE 1969), 15, 52.
    ##/CHIN-US
    CHRON: 1960-1970
    GEOG: CHINA   OTHER   WORLD
    SUBJ: DESCRIPTION

GALE, JOHN   G00507
    IPI IN TURBULENT ASSEMBLY CALLS FOR
        SINGAPORE PROBE
    EDITOR & PUBLISHER (19 JUNE 1971), 14-5, 21.
    CHRON: 1970-1980
    GEOG: SINGAPORE
    SUBJ: CONTROL

GALLAGHER, CHARLES F.   G00508
    LESSON FROM THE MODERNIZATION OF JAPAN:
        PART II, THE ROLE OF COMMUNICATIONS
    AUFS REPORTS, EAST ASIA SERIES XV:3(1968).
    MEDIUM: GENERAL
    CHRON: 1960-1970
    GEOG: EAST ASIA
    SUBJ: DEVELOPMENT

GALLINER, PETER   G01488
    IPI'S UPHILL TASK: FREE FLOW OF INFORMATION
    MEDIA [HONG KONG] 4:3(MAR 1977), 22-3.
    CHRON: 1970-1980
    GEOG: SEV ASIA   WORLD
    SUBJ: CONTROL

GARIS BESAR PERKEMBANGAN PERS   G01334
        INDONESIA
    DJAKARTA, SERIKAT PENERBIT SURATKABAR, 1971.
                        LANG: MALAY/INDONESIAN
    CHRON: 1970-1980
    GEOG: INDONESIA
    SUBJ: DESCRIPTION

GARVER, RICHARD A.   G00511
    COMMUNICATION PROBLEMS OF UNDERDEVELOPMENT:
        CHEJU-DO, KOREA,1962
    PUB OPINION QUARTERLY XXVI:4(1962), 613-25.
    ##/EASI
    MEDIUM: GENERAL
    CHRON: 1960-1970
    GEOG: EAST ASIA
    SUBJ: DEVELOPMENT

GARVER, RICHARD A.   G00510
    CONTENT OF KOREAN LANGUAGE DAILY NEWSPAPERS
    GAZETTE VIII:4(1962), 302-16.
    ##/EASI
    CHRON: 1960-1970
    METH: CONTENT ANALYSIS
    GEOG: EAST ASIA
    SUBJ: DESCRIPTION

GASPARD, ARMAND   G00512
    MISSION TO SINGAPORE
    IPI REPORT 8:5(1959), 1-5.
    CHRON: 1946-1960   VERIF: UNVERIFIED
    GEOG: SINGAPORE
    SUBJ: CONTROL

GEORGE, T. J. S. [THAMIL JACOB SONY]   G00514
    BRAVE NEW WORD
    FEER LXX:46(14 NOV 1970), 8, 11.
    ##/ASIA; INAUG. OF SINAPORE HERALD AND NEW
        NATION.
    CHRON: 1970-1980
    GEOG: SINGAPORE
    SUBJ: DESCRIPTION

GEORGE, T. J. S. [THAMIL JACOB SONY]   G00516
     THE PARTY'S OVER
     FEER 78:47(18 NOV 1972), 4.
     CHRON: 1970-1980
     GEOG: PHILIPPINES
     SUBJ: CONTROL

GEORGE, T. J. S. [THAMIL JACOB SONY]   G00515
     DAILY FERDINAND
     FEER 77:7(1 JULY 1972), 21.
     ##/PHIL
     CHRON: 1970-1980
     GEOG: PHILIPPINES
     SUBJ: CONTROL   DESCRIPTION

GEORGE, T. J. S. [THAMIL JACOB SONY]   G00517
     MEDIA MODERATION
     FEER 78:79(2 DEC 1972), 14.
     ##/PHIL
     MEDIUM: GENERAL
     CHRON: 1970-1980
     GEOG: PHILIPPINES
     SUBJ: CONTROL

GERBNER, GEORGE AND GEORGE MARVANYI   G00518
     THE MANY WORLDS OF THE WORLD'S PRESS
     JRNL OF COMMUNICATION 27:1(WINTER 1977),
          52-66.
     ##/INTL
     CHRON: 1970-1980
     GEOG: WORLD
     SUBJ: FLOW/AGENCY DESCRIPTION

GERMAN, R. L., COMPILER.   G01995
     THE MALAYAN INFORMATION AGENCY IN <HANDBOOK
          TO BRITISH MALAYA>
     LONDON, MALAYAN INFORMATION AGENCY, 1937.
     MEDIUM: GENERAL
     CHRON: 1910-1946
     GEOG: MALAYSIA   SINGAPORE
     SUBJ: DESCRIPTION

GERSHEN, MARTIN   G00520
     PRESS VS. MILITARY IN VIET NAM: A FURTHER
          VIEW
     COL JRN REVIEW (WINTER 1966/67), 62-3.
     ##/VN
     CHRON: 1960-1970
     GEOG: VIETNAM   U.S.
     SUBJ: CONTROL   LAW/ETHICS

GERSHEN, MARTIN   G00519
    THE 'RIGHT TO LIE'
    COL JRN REVIEW (WINTER 1966/67), 14-17.
    ##/FREE
    MEDIUM: GENERAL
    CHRON: 1960-1970
    GEOG: VIETNAM   U.S.
    SUBJ: CONTROL   LAW/ETHICS

GHAURI, S. R.   G01963
    PRESS FEELS THE WHIP
    FEER 99:11(17 MAR 1978), 34.
    ##/EASI
    CHRON: 1970-1980
    GEOG: SO/WEST ASI
    SUBJ: CONTROL

GIBSON-HILL, C. A.   G00521
    THE SINGAPORE CHRONICLE (1824-37)
    JMBRAS XXVI, PART 1(1953), 175-199.
    ##/SIN
    CHRON: BEFORE 1910
    METH: HISTORICAL
    GEOG: SINGAPORE
    SUBJ: JRN HISTORY

GIDLUND, CARL A.   G01996
    STRIDENT CRITIC OF THE U. S.: THE VIETNAM
        COURIER IN 1966
    MONTANA JOURNALISM REVIEW NO. 11(SPRING
        1968), 55-60.
    ##/VN-2
    CHRON: 1970-1980
    GEOG: VIETNAM   U.S.
    SUBJ: PROPAGANDA

GILES, HERBERT A.   G00522
    A HISTORY OF CHINESE LITERATURE
    NEW YORK, APPLETON, 1931.
    ##/CHIN-3; WALL LITERATURE AND JOURNALISM,
        PP. 425-8; NUC<56 199:630.
    CHRON: SURVEY
    GEOG: CHINA
    SUBJ: JRN HISTORY

GILES, LIONEL   G01489
    DATED CHINESE MANUSCRIPTS IN THE STEIN
        COLLECTION
    BULLETIN OF THE SCHOOL FOR ORIENTAL STUDIES
        (LONDON UNIVERSITY) VII(1935), 809-36.
    CHIN LAN
    CHRON: BEFORE 1910
    METH: HISTORICAL
    GEOG: CHINA
    SUBJ: OTHER JRN

GINSBOURG, ANNA   G01490
     WHY STRUGGLE FOR A FREE PRESS?
     THE CHINA CRITIC XII:12(19 MAR 1936), 272-4.
     ##/FILM
     CHRON: 1910-1946
     GEOG: CHINA
     SUBJ: CONTROL

GINSBOURG, ANNA   G02297
     CHINESE PRESS CONTROL
     THE CHINA WEEKLY REVIEW 74:1(7 SEPT 1935), 24.
     CHRON: 1910-1946
     GEOG: CHINA
     SUBJ: CONTROL   LAW/ETHICS

GLATTBACH, JACK   G01491
     HENRY STEINER, BLUE CHIP OF THE GRAPHIC
          DESIGN BUSINESS
     MEDIA [HONG KONG] 1:6(JUNE 1974), 14-5, 17.
     CHRON: 1970-1980
     GEOG: HONG KONG
     SUBJ: DESCRIPTION BIOGRAPHY

GLATTBACH, JACK AND MIKE ANDERSON   G02813
     THE PRINT AND BROADCASTING MEDIA IN MALAYSIA
     KUALA LUMPUR, SOUTH EAST ASIA PRESS CENTRE,
          1971.
     SEE COATS C02812.
     MEDIUM: GENERAL
     CHRON: 1970-1980
     METH: OTHER OR COMB
     GEOG: MALAYSIA
     SUBJ: DESCRIPTION

GOLDEN, NATHAN DANIEL [COMPILER]   G01587
     SHORT-SUBJECT FILM MARKET IN LATIN AMERICA,
          CANADA, THE FAR EAST, AFRICA, AND THE
          NEAR EAST
     WASHINGTON, D. C., FOREIGN AND DOMESTIC
          COMMERCE BUREAU, 1928.
     TRADE INFORMATION BULLETIN 544; C 18.25:544.
     MEDIUM: FILM
     CHRON: 1910-1946
     GEOG: SEV ASIA   WORLD
     SUBJ: DESCRIPTION

GOLDING, PETER   G00523
     MEDIA ROLE IN NATIONAL DEVELOPMENT: CRITIQUE
          OF A THEORETICAL ORTHODOXY
     JRNL OF COMMUNICATION 24:3(SUMMER 1974),
          39-53.
     ##/DEV
     MEDIUM: GENERAL
     CHRON: 1970-1980
     GEOG: WORLD
     SUBJ: DEVELOPMENT

GOLDSTONE, ANTHONY   G00525
    SUHARTO'S GUIDELINES
    FEER 83:9(4 MARCH 1974), 27-8.
    MEDIUM: GENERAL
    CHRON: 1970-1980
    GEOG: INDONESIA
    SUBJ: CONTROL

GOODMAN, DAVID S. G.   G02606
        AND TONY SAICH
    CHINESE LOCAL NEWSPAPERS AT SOAS
    LONDON, CONTEMPORARY CHINA INSTITUTE, 1979.
    RESEARCH NOTES AND STUDIES NO. 4
    CHRON: 1970-1980   VERIF: UNVERIFIED
    GEOG: CHINA
    SUBJ: RESEARCH

GOODMAN, DAVID S. G.   G00526
    RESEARCH GUIDE TO CHINESE PROVINCIAL AND
        REGIONAL PAPERS
    LONDON, CONTEMPORARY CHINA INSTITUTE, 1976.
    RESEARCH NOTES AND STUDIES NO. 2.
    CHRON: SURVEY
    GEOG: CHINA
    SUBJ: RESEARCH

GOODRICH, L. CARRINGTON   G00527
    THE DEVELOPMENT OF PRINTING IN CHINA AND
        ITS EFFECTS ON THE RENAISSANCE UNDER THE
        SUNG DYNASTY
    JRNL OF HK BRANCH, RAS 3(1963), 36-43.
    ##/CHIN-2
    CHRON: BEFORE 1910
    METH: HISTORICAL
    GEOG: CHINA
    SUBJ: PRINTING

GOODRICH, L. CARRINGTON   G00529
    CHINA'S EARLIEST PRINTING--A NOTE
    JRNL OF HK BRANCH, RAS 12(1972), 197-8.
    ##/CHIN-2
    CHRON: BEFORE 1910
    GEOG: CHINA
    SUBJ: PRINTING

GOODRICH, L. CARRINGTON   G00528
    PRINTING--A NEW DISCOVERY
    JRNL OF HK BRANCH, RAS 7(1967), 39-41.
    ##/CHIN-3
    CHRON: BEFORE 1910
    GEOG: CHINA   EAST ASIA
    SUBJ: PRINTING

GOULD, RANDALL   G02188
      IMPROVING CHINA'S COMMUNICATIONS
      THE CHINA WEEKLY REVIEW XLI:4(25 JUNE 1927),
         92.
      CHRON: 1910-1946
      GEOG: CHINA
      SUBJ: DESCRIPTION

GOULD, RANDALL   G01954
      NEWSPAPERS IN CHINA
      THE CHINESE NATION I:1(18 JUNE 1930), 9-10.
      FILM
      CHRON: 1910-1946
      GEOG: CHINA
      SUBJ: DESCRIPTION

GOULD, RANDALL   G01742
      EDITORIAL PROBLEMS OF AN AMERICAN NEWSPAPER
         IN CHINA
      THE PEOPLE'S TRIBUNE 1(N. S.):4(1 JAN 1932),
         108-11.
      ##/CHIN-5
      CHRON: 1910-1946
      GEOG: CHINA
      SUBJ: DESCRIPTION

GOULD, RANDALL   G01492
      FOREIGN JOURNALISM IN CHINA
      THE PEIPING CHRONICLE 13 OCT 1935.
      ##/CHIN-5;FROM <THE CHINA PRESS>.
      CHRON: 1910-1946
      GEOG: CHINA
      SUBJ: DESCRIPTION

GOULD, RANDALL   G01277
      THE FOREIGN PRESS IN CHINA
      CHINA CRITIC 10:9(29 AUG 1935), 202-4.
      ##/CHIN-4; MC/FILM.
      CHRON: 1910-1946
      GEOG: CHINA
      SUBJ: DESCRIPTION

GOW, GORDON   G00530
      WIFE VS. MISTRESS JAPANESE STYLE
      ATLAS 20:1(JAN 1971), 55.
      FROM <FILMS AND FILMING>
      MEDIUM: FILM
      CHRON: 1970-1980
      GEOG: EAST ASIA
      SUBJ: DESCRIPTION

```
GRAFF, H. J. DE                                          G00531
     THE SPREAD OF PRINTING: INDONESIA
     AMSTERDAM, VANGENDT & CO., 1969.
     CHRON: SURVEY
     METH:  HISTORICAL
     GEOG:  INDONESIA
     SUBJ:  PRINTING


GRAY, DENIS                                              G02522
     CAMBODIA: THE OLD AND THE NEW
     AP LOG (15 JAN 1979), 1.
     ##/CAMB
     MEDIUM:  GENERAL
     CHRON: 1970-1980
     GEOG:  THAILAND     CAMBODIA
     SUBJ:  FOR CORR     FLOW/AGENCY


GREEN, O. M. [OWEN MORTIMER]                             G01322
     THE ORGANIZATION OF NEWS FROM THE FAR EAST
     LONDON, ROYAL INSTITUTE OF INTERNATIONAL
          AFFAIRS, 1933.
     CHRON: 1910-1946
     GEOG:  CHINA
     SUBJ:  FOR CORR     CONTROL     FLOW/AGENCY


GRIGGS, (DAVID) THURSTON                                 G01493
     AMERICANS IN CHINA: SOME CHINESE VIEWS
     WASHINGTON, D. C., FOUNDATION FOR FOREIGN
          AFFAIRS, 1948.
     #3
     CHRON: 1910-1946
     METH:  CONTENT ANALYSIS
     GEOG:  CHINA
     SUBJ:  DESCRIPTION


GRIMES, PAUL                                             G00532
     REPORTING FROM ABROAD
     SUVA, FIJI, EWCI, 1972.
     ##/FOCO; EWCI PAPER NO. 2.
     CHRON: 1970-1980
     GEOG:  WORLD
     SUBJ:  FOR CORR


GRISOLA, MICHEL                                          G00533
     THE RISE OF CHOP SUEY EASTERNS
     ATLAS WORLD PRESS REVIEW 21:10(NOV 1974),
          45-6.
     ##/ASIA; FROM <LE NOUVEL OBSERVATEUR>.
     MEDIUM:  FILM
     CHRON: 1970-1980
     GEOG:  SEV ASIA
     SUBJ:  DESCRIPTION
```

GROFF, SAMUEL   G01570
    THE NEED OF ADVERTISING IN CHINA
    THE NEW CHINA [PEKING] (JAN 1931), 65-6.
    #3/NEW CHINA
    CHRON: 1910-1946
    GEOG: CHINA
    SUBJ: OTHER JRN

GUILLERMO, ARTEMIO RAMOS   G00537
    A READERSHIP SURVEY OF <TALIBA>, A
        PHILLIPPINE NEWSPAPER
    PHD DISS, SYRACUSE UNIVERSITY, 1972.
    668 PP., (73-19,815); INTL DISS 34:1306A.
    CHRON: 1970-1980   VERIF: UNVERIFIED
    METH: SURVEY
    GEOG: PHILIPPINES
    SUBJ: DESCRIPTION

GUIMARY, DONALD   G00538
    THE PRESS OF SOUTH VIETNAM: A RECENT
        PERSPECTIVE
    GAZETTE XXI:3(1975), 163-9.
    ##/VN
    CHRON: 1970-1980
    GEOG: VIETNAM
    SUBJ: DESCRIPTION

GUIMARY, DONALD L.   G00539
    INFORMATIONAL CAMPAIGNS IN A DEVELOPING
        NATION: MALAYSIA, A CASE STUDY
    COLLEGE PARK, MARYLAND, AEJ CONFERENCE, 1975.
    ##/MAL; MIMEO.
    MEDIUM: GENERAL
    CHRON: 1970-1980
    METH: OTHER OR COMB
    GEOG: MALAYSIA
    SUBJ: DEVELOPMENT

GULLICK, J. M.   G00540
    STYLE AND TRANSLATION IN THE MALAY PRESS
    JMBRAS XXVI, PART 1(JULY 1953), 14-23.
    CHRON: 1946-1960
    GEOG: MALAYSIA
    SUBJ: LANGUAGE   LITERATURE

GUNARATNE, SHELTON   G00541
    MALAYSIA'S PRESS CONTENT ANALYSED
    IPI REPORT 24:1(NOV 1975), 11.
    ##/MAL
    CHRON: 1970-1980
    METH: CONTENT ANALYSIS
    GEOG: MALAYSIA
    SUBJ: DESCRIPTION

GUPTA, UMA DAS   G02569
     THE INDIAN PRESS 1870-1880: A SMALL WORLD OF
          JOURNALISM
     MODERN ASIAN STUDIES 11:2(1977), 213-35.
     CHRON: BEFORE 1910
     METH: HISTORICAL
     GEOG: SO/WEST ASI
     SUBJ: JRN HISTORY

HAISMAN, STEPHEN FREDRIC   H00542
     TELEVISIONS' WORLD VIEW: ONE MONTH OF NETWORK
          INTERNATIONAL NEWS
     PHD DISS, UNIVERSITY OF IOWA, 1970.
     185 PP., (71-5745); INTL DISS 31 4807A;
          BASED ON 'TRIDEX', NOT
          ITEM COUNTS.
     MEDIUM: ELECTRONIC
     CHRON: 1970-1980
     METH: CONTENT ANALYSIS
     GEOG: WORLD
     SUBJ: FLOW/AGENCY DESCRIPTION

HALBERSTAM, DAVID   H00543
     GETTING THE STORY IN VIETNAM
     COMMENTARY 39:1(JAN 1965), 30-4.
     ##/VN
     CHRON: 1960-1970
     GEOG: VIETNAM   U.S.
     SUBJ: FOR CORR   CONTROL   DESCRIPTION

HALBERSTAM, DAVID   H01494
     TIME INC'S INTERNAL WAR OVER VIETNAM
     ESQUIRE (JAN 1977), 94-100+.
     ##/FOCO
     CHRON: 1970-1980
     GEOG: VIETNAM   CHINA   U.S.
     SUBJ: FOR CORR   CONTROL

HALBERSTAM, DAVID   H01392
     THE WAR WILL BE OVER BY CHRISTMAS
     ROLLING STONE (1 DEC 1977), 53-5.
     CHRON: 1970-1980
     GEOG: VIETNAM   U.S.
     SUBJ: FOR CORR   DESCRIPTION

HALBERSTAM, DAVID   H02189
     ANYBODY SEEN A MONTAGNARD?
     DATELINE [OPC, NEW YORK] 7:1(1963), 28.
     CHRON: 1960-1970
     GEOG: VIETNAM
     SUBJ: FOR CORR

HALE, KATHLEEN, COMPILER.   H01239
    REPRINTS AND MICROFORM MATERIALS IN ASIAN
        STUDIES
    N. P., ASSOCIATION FOR ASIAN STUDIES, 1972.
    JOURNALS AND NEWSPAPERS, PP. 178-220.
    CHRON: 1970-1980
    GEOG: SEV ASIA
    SUBJ: RESEARCH

HALLORAN, RICHARD   H00544
    CHRYSANTHEMUM CURTAIN
    COL URN REVIEW (FALL 1967), 39-42.
    ##/EASI
    CHRON: 1960-1970
    GEOG: EAST ASIA
    SUBJ: FOR CORR   CONTROL

HAMMOND, JAMES D.   H01341
    WORKERS BEHIND THE FRONT PAGE
    IN CHINA PRESS C02568.
    ##/FILM
    CHRON: 1910-1946
    GEOG: CHINA
    SUBJ: DESCRIPTION

HAN KI-UK   H01495
    INFLUENCE OF TRADITIONAL FACTORS ON
        EFFECTIVENESS OF MASS COMMUNICATIONS IN
        KOREA
    KOREA JOURNAL 8:2(FEB 1968), 18-25.
    MEDIUM: GENERAL
    CHRON: 1960-1970
    METH: SURVEY
    GEOG: EAST ASIA
    SUBJ: DEVELOPMENT

HANCOCK, ALAN   H00545
    UNESCO AND COMMUNICATION EDUCATION AND
        TRAINING IN MALAYSIA
    KUALA LUMPUR, AMIC SEMINAR ON COMM. TEACHING
        AND TRAINING, 1972.
    ##/MAL; MIMEO, 2 PP.
    MEDIUM: ELECTRONIC
    CHRON: 1970-1980
    GEOG: MALAYSIA
    SUBJ: EDUCATION

HANGEN, PAT   H02190
    THEY WILL WALK BACK
    DATELINE [OPC, NEW YORK] 16:1(1972), 12-13.
    CHRON: 1970-1980
    GEOG: VIETNAM   U.S.
    SUBJ: FOR CORR   BIOGRAPHY

HANGEN, PATRICIA   H00546
    TELL HIM THAT I HEARD
    NEW YORK, HARPER & ROW, 1977.
    MEDIUM: ELECTRONIC
    CHRON: SURVEY
    GEOG: VIETNAM   U.S.
    SUBJ: FOR CORR

HANI, GYO   H00547
    JAPAN'S CONTROVERSIAL MUCKRAKERS
    ATLAS WORLD PRESS REVIEW 23:5(MAY 1976), 52.
    FROM <JAPAN TIMES> 14 FEB.
    MEDIUM: GENERAL
    CHRON: 1970-1980
    GEOG: EAST ASIA
    SUBJ: DESCRIPTION

HANNA, WILLARD A.   H00548
    CHANGE IN CHIENGMAI, PART XII: PROVINCIAL
        EDITOR
    AUFS REPORTS, SEA SERIES XIII:16(1965).
    ##/ThAI
    CHRON: 1960-1970
    GEOG: THAILAND
    SUBJ: DESCRIPTION BIOGRAPHY

HANSEN, CARL C.   H01588
    SIAM, ENGLISH PRINTED LITERATURE NOW DESIRED
        IN <MONTHLY CONSULAR AND TRADE REPORTS>
    JUNE 1910, PT. 2, NO. 357, P. 37-8.
    ##/THAI; C 10.6:357.
    MEDIUM: FILM
    CHRON: BEFORE 1910
    GEOG: THAILAND
    SUBJ: PRINTING

HARAHAP, PARADA   H01496
    KEMERDEKAAN PERS
    MAKASSAR, INDO. NED. HANDEL MIJ EN DRUKKERIJ
        MAKASSAR, [1946?].
                          LANG: MALAY/INDONESIAN
    CHRON: 1910-1946
    GEOG: INDONESIA
    SUBJ: LAW/ETHICS

HARBEN, AYESHA   H00550
    TV--THE NEW FORMULA
    MALAY MAIL(SUN) 29 OCT 1972
    ##/MAL-2; PART 2 OF 2.
    MEDIUM: ELECTRONIC
    CHRON: 1970-1980
    GEOG: MALAYSIA
    SUBJ: DESCRIPTION

HARBEN, AYESHA   H00549
     WHAT'S WRONG WITH TV
     MALAY MAIL(SUN) 15 OCT 1972
     ##/MAL-2; PART 1 OF 2.
     MEDIUM: ELECTRONIC
     CHRON: 1970-1980
     GEOG: MALAYSIA
     SUBJ: DESCRIPTION

HARBIN CORRESPONDENT   H02298
     HOW 'MANCHURIA DAILY NEWS' AND 'KOKUTSU'
          DISTORT THE NEWS
     THE CHINA WEEKLY REVIEW 76:7(18 APR 1936),
          232.
     CHRON: 1910-1946
     GEOG: CHINA
     SUBJ: PROPAGANDA

HARIHARAN, A.   H00553
     THE PRESS BREATHES EASIER
     FEER 96:16(22 APR 1977), 27-8.
     ##/SWAS
     MEDIUM: ELECTRONIC
     CHRON: 1970-1980
     GEOG: SO/WEST ASI
     SUBJ: CONTROL

HARIHARAN, A.   H00552
     PRESSING FOR PRINT
     FEER 83:8(25 FEB 1974), 39-40.
     ##/SWAS
     CHRON: 1970-1980
     GEOG: WORLD
     SUBJ: FLOW/AGENCY

HARIMAU [PSEUD.]   H02100
     ONE YEAR OF THE 'VOICE OF THE MALAYAN
          REVOLUTION'
     THE AFRO-ASIAN JOURNALIST 7:4(DEC 1970),
          13-14.
     MEDIUM: ELECTRONIC
     CHRON: 1960-1970
     GEOG: MALAYSIA
     SUBJ: PROPAGANDA DESCRIPTION

HARLOFF, A. J. W.   H01743
     THE INFLUENCE OF THE CINEMA ON ORIENTAL
          PEOPLES
     BRITISH MALAYA VIII:10(FEB 1934), 213-6.
     ##/MAL-3; SEE BILAINKIN B01367 AND WEAIT
          W01418.
     MEDIUM: FILM
     CHRON: 1910-1946
     GEOG: MALAYSIA
     SUBJ: DESCRIPTION LAW/ETHICS CROSS CULTU

HART, DONN V. AND QUINTIN A. EALA   H00591
     AN ANNOTATED GUIDE TO CURRENT PHILIPPINES
          PERIODICALS
     NEW HAVEN, YALE U. PRESS, 1957.
     CHRON: 1946-1960   VERIF: UNVERIFIED
     GEOG: PHILIPPINES
     SUBJ: RESEARCH

HART, DONN VORHIS   H00657
     A PRELIMINARY LIST OF SOUTHEAST ASIAN
          BIBLIOGRAPHIES
     DEKALB, ILL.[?], N. P., 1959.
     NUC 56-67 47:405
     CHRON: SURVEY
     GEOG: SEV ASIA
     SUBJ: RESEARCH

HARTENDORP, A. V. H.   H00554
     TWENTYFIVE YEARS OF PHILIPPINE JOURNALISM
     IN <FOOKIEN TIMES YEARBOOK 1951>.
     CHRON: SURVEY   VERIF: UNVERIFIED
     GEOG: PHILIPPINES
     SUBJ: JRN HISTORY

HASIBUAN, ADAHAM   H00555
     GENESIS OF A PRESS: ECONOMIC ASPECTS OF THE
          NATIONAL PRESS IN INDONESIA
     GAZETTE III:1,2(1957), 29-46.
     ##/INDO
     CHRON: 1946-1960
     GEOG: INDONESIA
     SUBJ: DESCRIPTION

HAUSER, ERNEST O.   H00556
     NEWS OF THE FAR EAST IN U. S. DAILIES
     PUB OPINION QUARTERLY II:4(OCT 1938), 651-8.
     ##/ASIA
     CHRON: 1910-1946
     METH: CONTENT ANALYSIS
     GEOG: U.S.   SEV ASIA
     SUBJ: FOR CORR   FLOW/AGENCY

HAUSER, ERNEST O.   H01497
     THE PRESS AND THE WAR
     AMERASIA 1:7(SEPT 1937), 321-4.
     ##/CHIN-5
     CHRON: 1910-1946
     GEOG: CHINA   EAST ASIA
     SUBJ: FOR CORR   PROPAGANDA

HAYES, HAROLD B.   H00557
     INTERNATIONAL PERSUASION VARIABLES ARE
          TESTED ACROSS THREE CULTURES
     JQ 48:4(WINTER 1971), 714-24.
     ##/XCUL
     MEDIUM: GENERAL
     CHRON: 1970-1980
     METH: OTHER OR COMB
     GEOG: CHINA   EUROPE   W. HEMIS
     SUBJ: PROPAGANDA

HAYWARD, HENRY S.   H00559
     FOCUS ON JAKARTA'S PRESS SPLIT
     CSM 23 DEC 1970
     CHRON: 1970-1980   VERIF: UNVERIFIED
     GEOG: INDONESIA
     SUBJ: DESCRIPTION

HAYWARD, HENRY S.   H00558
     INDONESIA'S MATURING PRESS
     CSM 3 AUG 1973
     ##/INDO
     CHRON: 1970-1980
     GEOG: INDONESIA
     SUBJ: DESCRIPTION

HAYWARD, HENRY S.   H00561
     'BONANZA' ET AL BID GOOD-BYE TO SAIGON
     CSM 5 MAR 1973
     ##/VN
     MEDIUM: ELECTRONIC
     CHRON: 1970-1980
     GEOG: VIETNAM   U.S.
     SUBJ: CONTROL   DESCRIPTION

HAYWARD, HENRY. S.   H00560
     BAN DIMS VITALITY OF PHILIPPINE PRESS
     CSM 26 OCT 1972
     ##/PHIL
     CHRON: 1970-1980
     GEOG: PHILIPPINES
     SUBJ: CONTROL

HAZAMA, NAOKI   H02613
     LIU-SHIH-FU TO <MINSEI> (LIU SHIH-FU AND
          <MINSHENG>)
     SHISO 578(1972), 109-21.
                         LANG: OTHER ASIAN
     CHRON: 1910-1946   VERIF: UNVERIFIED
     METH: HISTORICAL
     GEOG: CHINA   EAST ASIA
     SUBJ: PROPAGANDA JRN HISTORY

HENDRICK, J.   H02299
    THE STORY OF VIET NAM VERSUS FRENCH PROPAGANDA
    THE CHINA WEEKLY REVIEW 108(17 JAN 1948),
        198-200.
    CHRON: 1946-1960
    GEOG: VIETNAM   EUROPE
    SUBJ: PROPAGANDA

HERR, MICHAEL   H01647
    HEARTS AND MINDS
    COL JRN REVIEW XVI:5(JAN/FEB 1978), 47-8.
    ##/VN; FROM <DISPATCHES> H01364.
    CHRON: 1970-1980
    GEOG: VIETNAM
    SUBJ: FOR CORR   DESCRIPTION

HERR, MICHAEL   H00565
    KHESANH
    ESQUIRE (SEPT 1969), 118-23+.
    ##/VN
    CHRON: 1960-1970
    GEOG: VIETNAM
    SUBJ: FOR CORR   OTHER NON-J

HERR, MICHAEL   H00564
    HELL SUCKS
    ESQUIRE (AUG 1968), 66-9+.
    ##/VN
    CHRON: 1960-1970
    GEOG: VIETNAM
    SUBJ: FOR CORR   OTHER NON-J

HERR, MICHAEL   H00568
    HIGH ON WAR
    ESQUIRE (JAN 1977), 82-8+.
    ##/VN-2
    CHRON: 1970-1980
    GEOG: VIETNAM
    SUBJ: FOR CORR   CONTROL

HERR, MICHAEL   H00567
    THE WAR CORRESPONDENT: A REAPPRAISAL
    ESQUIRE (APRIL 1970), 95-101+.
    ##/VN
    CHRON: 1970-1980
    GEOG: VIETNAM
    SUBJ: FOR CORR   CONTROL

HERR, MICHAEL   H00566
     CONCLUSION AT KHESANH
     ESQUIRE (OCT 1969), 118-23+.
     ##/VN
     CHRON: 1960-1970
     GEOG: VIETNAM
     SUBJ: FOR CORR   OTHER NON-J

HERR, MICHAEL   H01364
     DISPATCHES
     NEW YORK, KNOPF, 1977.
     MEDIUM: GENERAL
     CHRON: 1960-1970
     GEOG: VIETNAM   U.S.
     SUBJ: FOR CORR

HESTER, AL   H00569
     AN ANALYSIS OF NEWS FLOW FROM DEVELOPED AND
          DEVELOPING NATIONS
     GAZETTE XVII:1,2(1971), 29-43.
     ##/INTL
     MEDIUM: GENERAL
     CHRON: 1970-1980
     METH: OTHER OR COMB
     GEOG: WORLD
     SUBJ: FLOW/AGENCY

HILL, I. WILLIAM   H01804
     JOHN HUGHES--ASNE'S NEW PRESIDENT
     EDITOR & PUBLISHER (8 APR 1978), 20, 26.
     FOCO
     MEDIUM: GENERAL
     CHRON: 1970-1980
     GEOG: SEV ASIA
     SUBJ: FOR CORR   BIOGRAPHY

HILL, I. WILLIAM   H01589
     STUDY SHOWS FEWER U. S. FOREIGN CORRESPONDENTS
     EDITOR & PUBLISHER (18 FEB 1978), 46.
     ##/FOCO; BASED ON RUBIN R01624.
     MEDIUM: GENERAL
     CHRON: 1970-1980
     GEOG: WORLD
     SUBJ: FOR CORR

HILL, I. WILLIAM   H02523
     U.S.-CHINA AGREE TO EXCHANGE REPORTERS
     EDITOR & PUBLISHER 112:5(3 FEB 1979), 56.
     ##/CHIN-8
     MEDIUM: GENERAL
     CHRON: 1970-1980
     GEOG: CHINA   U.S.
     SUBJ: FOR CORR   FLOW/AGENCY

HILL, R. D.   H00571
    MATERIALS FOR HISTORICAL GEOGRAPHY AND
        ECONOMIC HISTORY OF SOUTHEAST ASIA IN
        NINETEENTH CENTURY MALAYAN NEWSPAPERS
    JMBRAS XLIV, PART 2(DEC 1971), 151-98.
    ##/MAL-2
    CHRON: 1970-1980
    METH: HISTORICAL
    GEOG: MALAYSIA   SINGAPORE
    SUBJ: RESEARCH

HIRO, DILID   H00572
    THE FILMS OF INDIA
    THE ASIA MAGAZINE (10 JUNE 1973), 18-20.
    ##/SWAS
    MEDIUM: FILM
    CHRON: 1970-1980
    GEOG: SO/WEST ASI
    SUBJ: DESCRIPTION

HIRTH, F.   H00573
    WESTERN APPLIANCES IN THE CHINESE PRINTING
        INDUSTRY
    JRNL OF CHINA BRANCH, RAS XX(N. S.)(1885),
        162-77.
    ##/CHIN-3
    CHRON: SURVEY
    METH: HISTORICAL
    GEOG: CHINA
    SUBJ: PRINTING

HITCHCOCK, DAVID, JR.   H02631
    PROVINCIAL PRESS AND NATIONAL DEVELOPMENT IN
        MALAYSIA AND THE PHILIPPINES
    SINGAPORE, AMIC, [1974?].
    CHRON: 1970-1980
    METH: OTHER OR COMB
    GEOG: MALAYSIA   PHILIPPINES
    SUBJ: DEVELOPMENT CROSS CULTU

HO LIN   H00574
    LUN HSIN CH'U PAN FA (THE NEW PUBLICATION LAW)
    FA LU P'ING LUN 18:6(JUNE 1952), 7-9;
        18:2(AUG 1952), 10-12.
    SKINNER S00982 II:46535
    CHRON: 1946-1960   VERIF: UNVERIFIED
    GEOG: CHINA
    SUBJ: LAW/ETHICS

HO TSANG-HSU   07   H02741
    KUANG CHOU SHIH HSIN WEN PAO CHIH TI TSUNG
        CHIEN YUEH [A REVIEW OF JOURNALISM IN
        CANTON]
    PAO HSUEH CHI KAN [SHANGHAI] 1:4(AUG 1936),
        73-83.
                             LANG: CHINESE
    CHRON: 1910-1946
    GEOG: CHINA
    SUBJ: DESCRIPTION

HOARE, J. E.   H02570
    THE 'BANKOKU SHIMBUN' AFFAIR
    MODERN ASIAN STUDIES 9:3(1975), 289-302.
    CHRON: BEFORE 1910
    METH: HISTORICAL
    GEOG: EAST ASIA
    SUBJ:

HOBBS, CECIL   H01356
    CURRENT PUBLICATIONS IN SOUTHEAST ASIA
    FAR EASTERN QUARTERLY VIII:3(MAY 1949),
        296-318.
    ##/BIB
    CHRON: 1946-1960
    METH: OTHER OR COMB
    GEOG: SEV ASIA
    SUBJ: RESEARCH   DESCRIPTION

HOBEN, LINDSAY   H02300
    AMERICAN JOURNALIST DESCRIBES ORIENTAL TOUR
        AS 'BLANKETY BLANK SOCIAL ENDURANCE
        CONTEST'
    THE CHINA WEEKLY REVIEW L:3(21 SEPT 1929),
        138-9.
    CHRON: 1910-1946
    GEOG: CHINA   SEV ASIA
    SUBJ: FOR CORR   DESCRIPTION

HOBERECHT, EARNEST   H00575
    ASIA IS MY BEAT
    RUTLAND, VT., CHARLES TUTTLE, 1961.
    MEDIUM: GENERAL
    CHRON: 1960-1970
    GEOG: EAST ASIA
    SUBJ: FOR CORR

HOC, KIM CHHEAN   H01997
    INFORMATION IN CAMBODIA AND THE KHMER PRESS
        AGENCY
    JOURNALISM [STRASBOURG] (SPRING 1966), 58-60.
    ##/CAMB
    MEDIUM: GENERAL
    CHRON: 1960-1970
    GEOG: CAMBODIA
    SUBJ: SERIALS   DESCRIPTION

HOFFER, THOMAS WILLIAM   H00576
    BROADCASTING IN AN INSURGENCY ENVIRONMENT:
        USIA IN VIETNAM, 1965-1970.
    PHD DISS, UNIVERSITY OF WISCONSIN, 1972.
    INTL DISS 33 6943A.
    MEDIUM: ELECTRONIC
    CHRON: 1960-1970   VERIF: UNVERIFIED
    METH: OTHER OR COMB
    GEOG: VIETNAM   U.S.
    SUBJ: PROPAGANDA DESCRIPTION

HOFFMAN, FRED S.   H02191
    THE CLOSE-MOUTHED PENTAGON
    DATELINE [OPC, NEW YORK] X:1(1966), 89-9.
    MEDIUM: GENERAL
    CHRON: 1960-1970
    GEOG: VIETNAM   U.S.
    SUBJ: FOR CORR   CONTROL

HOHENBERG, JOHN   H00578
    MAKE WAY FOR THE NEW CHINA HANDS
    SATURDAY REVIEW (8 JAN 1972), 14-5.
    ##/US
    MEDIUM: GENERAL
    CHRON: 1970-1980
    GEOG: CHINA
    SUBJ: FOR CORR

HOHENBERG, JOHN   H00577
    BETWEEN TWO WORLDS: POLICY, PRESS, AND
        PUBLIC OPINIONS IN ASIAN-AMERICAN
        RELATIONS
    NEW YORK, PRAEGER, 1967.
    CHRON: 1960-1970
    GEOG: SEV ASIA
    SUBJ: FOR CORR   DESCRIPTION POLIT SCI

HOLBERT, JOHN   H01498
    PROUD PUBLISHERS OF PENANG
    HORIZONS [USIS] XIX:6(1968-70), 42-5.
    CHRON: 1960-1970
    GEOG: MALAYSIA
    SUBJ: PRINTING   PUBLISHING

HOLDER, CHARLES F.   H01805
    CHINESE PRESS IN AMERICA
    SCIENTIFIC AMERICAN LXXXVII:15(11 OCT 1902),
        241.
    ##/CHIN-US
    CHRON: BEFORE 1910
    GEOG: OSEAS CHIN   U.S.
    SUBJ: DESCRIPTION

HOLLSTEIN, MILTON   H02636
    BURMA
    IN LENT L00708, PP. 138-157.
    CHRON: SURVEY
    GEOG: BURMA
    SUBJ: JRN HISTORY DESCRIPTION

HOLLSTEIN, MILTON   H00580
    THE PRESS IN BURMA: ITS HOPES AND PROBLEMS
    JQ 38:3(SUMMER 1961), 351-9.
    ##/BURMA
    CHRON: 1960-1970
    GEOG: BURMA
    SUBJ: DESCRIPTION

HOLLSTEIN, MILTON   H00579
    BURMA PRESS BATTLES VALIANTLY FOR ITS
        LIBERTIES
    IPI REPORT (JUNE 1961).
    CHRON: 1960-1970   VERIF: UNVERIFIED
    GEOG: BURMA
    SUBJ: CONTROL

HOLT, HAMILTON   H01806
    THE AMERICAN AND JAPANESE PRESS
    THE ORIENTAL REVIEW II:4(FEB 1912), 210-14.
    CHRON: 1910-1946
    GEOG: EAST ASIA   U.S.
    SUBJ: DESCRIPTION

HONG KONG DAILY PRESS, THE   H01807
    [PROSPECTUS FOR <THE UNIVERSAL CIRCULATING
        HERALD>]
    14 FEB 1874
    ##/CHIN-5; P. 3, COL. 2.
    CHRON: 1910-1946
    GEOG: HONG KONG   CHINA
    SUBJ: DESCRIPTION

HONG KONG DAILY PRESS, THE   H01808
    JAPANESE AND CHINESE NEWSPAPERS
    20 SEPT 1873
    ##/CHIN-5; FROM <PALL MALL GAZETTE>,
        4 AUG 1873, SEE P02199.
    CHRON: BEFORE 1910
    GEOG: CHINA   EAST ASIA   U.S.
    SUBJ: DESCRIPTION

HORIZONS [USIS]   H01499
    MALAYSIA: WHERE BROADCASTERS GO BACK TO SCHOOL
    XXII:7(1973), 10-15.
    MEDIUM: ELECTRONIC
    CHRON: 1970-1980
    GEOG: MALAYSIA
    SUBJ: EDUCATION

HORNE, NORMAN P.   H01571
    GUIDE TO PUBLISHED UNITED STATES GOVERNMENT
        DOCUMENTS PERTAINING TO SOUTHEAST ASIA,
        1893-1941.
    MASTERS THESIS, CATHOLIC UNIVERSITY, 1961.
    NUC 56-67 51:176
    MEDIUM: GENERAL
    CHRON: SURVEY
    METH: OTHER OR COMB
    GEOG: SEV ASIA
    SUBJ: RESEARCH

HORNIK, ROBERT C.   H00582
    MASS MEDIA USE AND THE 'REVOLUTION OF RISING
        FRUSTRATIONS': A RECONSIDERATION OF THE
        THEORY
    HONOLULU, EWCI, 1974.
    MEDIUM: GENERAL
    CHRON: 1970-1980
    GEOG: WORLD
    SUBJ: DEVELOPMENT

HORSLEY, WILLIAM   H00583
    MONTY PYTHON INVADES JAPAN
    ATLAS WORLD PRESS REVIEW 23:12(DEC 1976), 47.
    FROM <THE LISTENER>, 29 JULY.
    MEDIUM: ELECTRONIC
    CHRON: 1970-1980
    GEOG: EAST ASIA
    SUBJ: DESCRIPTION

HOWSE, HUGH   - H00584
    THE ROLE OF MASS MEDIA IN CHINA
    IN KLATT K02573, PP. 48-64.
    MEDIUM: GENERAL
    CHRON: 1960-1970
    GEOG: CHINA
    SUBJ: DEVELOPMENT DESCRIPTION

HSI KEN-LIN   10   H00588
    T'AI-WAN TIEN HSIN SHIH YEH CHIH YEN KO'
        (THE DEVELOPMENT OF TELECOMMUNICATIONS IN
        TAIWAN)
    T'AI-WAN TIEN HSIN YUEH K'AN 3:1(JAN 1952),
        31-9.
    SKINNER S00982 II:46418
    MEDIUM: ELECTRONIC   LANG: CHINESE
    CHRON: 1946-1960   VERIF: UNVERIFIED
    GEOG: TAIWAN
    SUBJ: JRN HISTORY DESCRIPTION

HSI, KUNG K'AI   H02224
    PROBLEMS OF CHINESE NEWSPAPER CIRCULATION
        AND ADVERTISING TO 1949 WITH SUGGESTED
        SOLUTIONS
    MASTERS THESIS, UNIVERSITY OF MISSOURI, 1951.
    ##
    CHRON: 1946-1960
    METH: OTHER OR COMB
    GEOG: CHINA
    SUBJ: DESCRIPTION OTHER JRN

HSIANG CHENG   06   H02742
    CHIN MA HUA WEN PAO TI KUO CH'U HO HSIEN
        TSAI (CHINESE NEWSPAPERS IN MALAYSIA)
    PAO HSUEH [TAIPEI] III:3(JUNE 1964), 104-8.
                            LANG: CHINESE
    CHRON: 1960-1970
    GEOG: MALAYSIA   OSEAS CHIN
    SUBJ: DESCRIPTION

HSIAO CHI'EN   H02192
    THE CHINESE PRESS
    THE ASIATIC REVIEW 38:134(1942), 192-204.
    ##/CHIN-8
    CHRON: 1910-1946
    GEOG: CHINA
    SUBJ: DESCRIPTION

HSIAO, I-WEN   H02225
    CENTRAL NEWS AGENCY OF CHINA: AN HISTORICAL
        STUDY 1924-1959
    MASTERS THESIS, UNIVERSITY OF MISSOURI, 1959.
    MEDIUM: GENERAL
    CHRON: SURVEY
    METH: HISTORICAL
    GEOG: TAIWAN   CHINA
    SUBJ: JRN HISTORY

HSIEH, ALICE LANGLEY   H00589
    CHINA'S SECRET MILITARY PAPERS: MILITARY
        DOCTRINE AND STRATEGY
    CHINA QUARTERLY NO. 18(APR/JUNE 1964), 79-89.
    ##/CHIN-2
    CHRON: 1960-1970
    GEOG: CHINA
    SUBJ: DESCRIPTION POLIT SCI

HSIEH, JAN-CHIH [MILTON J. T.]   17   H02101
    HSIN WEN HSUEH LUN TS'UNG [COLLECTION OF
        JOURNALISM ARTICLES]
    TAIPEI, KAI TSAO CHU PAN SHE, 1963.
    #3
                            LANG: CHINESE
    CHRON: 1960-1970
    GEOG: TAIWAN
    SUBJ: DESCRIPTION

HSIEH, JAN-SHIH [MILTON J. T.]   17   H01999
    T'AI-WAN HSIN SHENG PAO SHE [TENTH
        ANNIVERSARY OF <HSIN SHENG PAO>]
    IN T'AI-WAN 14T02574, PP. 273-9.
    ##/TAI
                            LANG: CHINESE
    CHRON: SURVEY
    GEOG: TAIWAN
    SUBJ: JRN HISTORY

HSIEH, JAN-SHIH   17   H01979
         [MILTON J. T.], EDITOR.
     PAO HSUEH LUN CHI (A SYMPOSIUM OF JOURNALISM)
     TAIPEI, HSIN WEN HSUEH HSI, 1965.
     MEDIUM: GENERAL   LANG: CHINESE
     CHRON: 1970-1980
     GEOG: TAIWAN   WORLD
     SUBJ: DESCRIPTION

HSIEH, WINSTON   H00831
     CHINESE HISTORIOGRAPHY ON THE REVOLUTION OF
         1911
     STANFORD, CAL., HOOVER INSTITUTION PRESS,
         1975.
     JOURNALS/NEWSPAPERS, PP. 134-8.
     CHRON: 1910-1946
     METH: HISTORICAL
     GEOG: CHINA
     SUBJ: RESEARCH

HSIN HUA JIH PAO SHE   13   H02102
     PIEN HSIEH YU TS'AI FAN [EDITING AND
          PUBLISHING]
     SHANSI, HSIN HUA SHE, 1946.
     #3
                          LANG: CHINESE
     CHRON: 1910-1946
     GEOG: CHINA
     SUBJ: BIOGRAPHY

HSING SUNG-WEN   07   H02743
     CHIEN HSIEN JIH PAO HUI YI LU (A RECALL ON
          THE CHIEN HSIEN JIH PAO)
     PAO HSUEH [TAIPEI] II:9(DEC 1961), 104-10.
                          LANG: CHINESE
     CHRON: SURVEY
     GEOG: CHINA
     SUBJ: DESCRIPTION JRN HISTORY

HSING SUNG-WEN   06   H02792
     TSAI YIN NA PAN PAO PA NIEN (AS A
          NEWSPAPERMAN IN INDONESIA IN EIGHT YEARS)
     PAO HSUEH [TAIPEI] II:7(DEC 1960), 80-5.
                          LANG: CHINESE
     CHRON: 1946-1960
     GEOG: INDONESIA   OSEAS CHIN
     SUBJ: DESCRIPTION LAW/ETHICS

HSING CHENG YUAN   H02104
     SAN SHIH NIEN LAI TI CHUNG KUO HSIN WEN SHIH
          YEH [THIRTY YEARS OF CHINESE JOURNALISM]
     TAIPEI, HSIN WEN CHU, 1961.
                          LANG: CHINESE
     CHRON: SURVEY
     GEOG: TAIWAN   CHINA
     SUBJ: JRN HISTORY

HSING CHENG YUAN   H02103
     HSIN WEN SHIH YEH [JOURNALISM]
     NANKING, N. P., 1947.
                         LANG: CHINESE
     CHRON: 1910-1946
     GEOG: CHINA
     SUBJ: DESCRIPTION

HSU CHAO-YUNG   H01393
     THE PRESS
     IN <THE CHINESE YEARBOOK 1943-1944>, PP.
        665-89.
     ##/CHIN-5
     CHRON: 1910-1946
     GEOG: CHINA
     SUBJ: DESCRIPTION

HSU HSU   H00585
     SHANG-HAI HSIAO SHU PAO T'AN TIAO CH'A'
          (SURVEY OF BOOK AND NEWSPAPER VENDORS IN
          SHANGHAI)
     IN HSU H02575, PP. 142-213.
                         LANG: CHINESE
     CHRON: 1946-1960   VERIF: UNVERIFIED
     METH: SURVEY
     GEOG: CHINA
     SUBJ: DESCRIPTION

HSU HSU   H02575
     T'U SHU KUAN YU MIN CHUNG CHIAO YU
          (LIBRARIES AND MASS EDUCATION)
     CHANGSHA, SHANG WU YIN SHU KUAN, 1941.
     SEE HSU H00585; SKINNER S00982 II:47724.
                         LANG: CHINESE
     CHRON: 1946-1960   VERIF: UNVERIFIED
     METH: SURVEY
     GEOG: CHINA
     SUBJ: DESCRIPTION

HSU YUN-CHIAO   11 H02744
     CHIN HSI SHENG TIEN HUA PAO T'AN TS'ANG
          SANG--WU SHIH NIEN LAI TI MA LAI YA
          HUA WEN PAO CHIH
     PAO HSUEH [TAIPEI] II:8(JULY 1960), 100-103.
          (JUBILEE ANNIVERSARY OF CHINESE NEWSPAPERS
          IN MALAYA)
                         LANG: CHINESE
     CHRON: SURVEY
     GEOG: MALAYSIA   SINGAPORE   OSEAS CHIN
     SUBJ: JRN HISTORY

HSU YUNG P'ING   10   H01809
     TS'AI SE P'ING PAN YIN PAO TI YEN CHIU
          [RESEARCH IN COLOR OFFSET PRINTING OF
          NEWSPAPERS]
     TAIPEI, LI MING WEN HUA SHIH YEH, 1974.
     CHRON: 1970-1980
     GEOG: TAIWAN
     SUBJ: PRINTING

HSU YUNG-PING   10   H02745
   CHUNG KUNG FEI PANG TI HSIN WEN CHENG TS'E
      (THE PRESS POLICY OF CHINESE REDS)
   PAO HSUEH [TAIPEI] II:1(JUNE 1957), 44-56.
                           LANG: CHINESE
   CHRON: 1946-1960
   GEOG: CHINA
   SUBJ: CONTROL

HSU, JABIN   H00586
   A MESSAGE FROM THE CHINESE PRESS
   IN WILLIAMS W01152, PP. 453-6.
   #3
   CHRON: 1910-1946
   GEOG: CHINA
   SUBJ: DESCRIPTION

HSU, PAO-HUANG   10   H01572
   HSIN WEN SHIH YEH [JOURNALISM]
   SHANGHAI, COMMERCIAL PRESS, 1924.
                           LANG: CHINESE
   CHRON: 1910-1946
   GEOG: CHINA
   SUBJ: DESCRIPTION

HSUEH, CHUN-TU   H01500
   PERSISTENT CIA SYNDROME
   THE ASIA MAIL 2:3(DEC 1977), 10.
   ##/ASIA; HERALD AFFAIR.
   CHRON: 1970-1980
   GEOG: SINGAPORE   SEV ASIA
   SUBJ: CONTROL

HU CHENG   H02301
   THE MOVIES AND CHINA
   THE CHINA WEEKLY REVIEW 54:10(8 NOV 1930),
      360.
   LETTER TO EDITOR
   MEDIUM: FILM
   CHRON: 1910-1946
   GEOG: CHINA
   SUBJ: DESCRIPTION

HU LIN   H02193
   JOURNALISM WEEK AT YENCHING
   DIGEST OF THE SYNODAL COMMISSION (CATHOLIC
      CHURCH IN CHINA) 5:6/7(JUNE-JULY 1932),
      630-2.
   CHRON: 1910-1946
   GEOG: CHINA
   SUBJ: EDUCATION

HU SHIH   09   H02798
     HU SHIH WEN TS'UN [HU SHIH ANTHOLOGY]
     TAIPEI, YUAN T'UNG T'U SHU KUNG SSU,
          1953.
     ##/CHIN-9;FA CH'I 'TU SHU TSA CHIH' TI YUAN
          CH'I [ORIGIN OF BOOKS AND
          MAGAZINES],
          VOLUME 2, PP. 19-20.
                              LANG: CHINESE
     CHRON: SURVEY
     GEOG: CHINA
     SUBJ: JRN HISTORY LANGUAGE

HU SHIH   09   H02797
     HU SHIH WEN TS'UN WAI PIEN [SELECTED
          ANTHOLOGY OF HU SHIH]
     TAIPEI, YUN T'IEN CH'U PAN SHE, 1970.
     ##/CHIN-9; TSUNG CH'UAN YUNG PAI HUA
          [NEWSPAPERS SHOULD USE
          PAI HUA],
          PP. 67-71.
                         LANG: CHINESE
     CHRON: SURVEY
     GEOG: CHINA
     SUBJ: LANGUAGE

HU SHIH   09   H00587
     SHIH CH'I NIEN TI HUI KU (REVIEW OF THE PAST
          SEVENTEEN YEARS [OF THE NEWSPAPER
          <SHIH PAO>])
     SHIH PAO (13 OCT.1921).
     SKINNER II:41761; REPRINT AVAILABLE.
                         LANG: CHINESE
     CHRON: 1910-1946   VERIF: UNVERIFIED
     GEOG: CHINA
     SUBJ: DESCRIPTION

HU TAO-CHING   09   H00596
     SHANG-HAI YU KUANG PO SHIH YEH (SHANGHAI AND
          THE BROADCASTING INDUSTRY)
     IN SHANG-HAI T'UNG SHE S02607, PP. 563-9.
     MEDIUM: ELECTRONIC LANG: CHINESE
     CHRON: 1910-1946   VERIF: UNVERIFIED
     GEOG: CHINA
     SUBJ: DESCRIPTION

HU TAO-CHING   09   H01574
     SHANG-HAI HSIN WEN SHIH YEH CHIH SHIH TI FA
          CHAN (THE DEVELOPMENT OF JOURNALISM IN
          SHANGHAI)
     SHANG-HAI SHIH T'UNG CHIH KUAN CH'I K'AN
          2:3(DEC 1934), 947-1034.
                         LANG: CHINESE
     CHRON: 1910-1946
     GEOG: CHINA
     SUBJ: DESCRIPTION

HU TAO-CHING   09   H01573
     SHANG-HAI TI JIH PAO (NEWSPAPERS IN SHANGHAI)
     SHANG-HAI SHIH T'UNG CHIH KUAN CH'I K'AN
          2:1(JUNE 1934), 219-326.
                         LANG: CHINESE
     CHRON: 1910-1946
     GEOG: CHINA
     SUBJ: DESCRIPTION

HUANG HO   12   H02274
    LI KUANG-YAO HSIN-WEN CHENG-TS'E YU
        HSIN-CHIA-P'O HUA-WEN PAO-YEH
    MASTERS THESIS, CHINESE COLLEGE OF CULTURE,
        1978.
    (LEE KUAN YEW'S NEWS POLICIES AND
        JOURNALISM IN SINGAPORE)
                        LANG: CHINESE
    CHRON: 1970-1980   VERIF: UNVERIFIED
    METH: OTHER OR COMB
    GEOG: SINGAPORE   OSEAS CHIN
    SUBJ: DESCRIPTION LAW/ETHICS

HUANG T'IEN-P'ENG   12   H00598
    CHUNG-KUO HSIN WEN SHIH YEH (JOURNALISM IN
        CHINA)
    SHANGHAI, HSIEN TAI SHU CHU, 1932.
    REPRINT; NUC<56 257:657.
                        LANG: CHINESE
    CHRON: SURVEY
    METH: HISTORICAL
    GEOG: CHINA
    SUBJ: JRN HISTORY

HUANG, NANCY LAI-SHEN   H02226
    A STUDY OF THE POSSIBILITIES OF TELEVISION
        IN FORMOSA
    MASTERS THESIS, UNIVERSITY OF MISSOURI, 1957.
    MEDIUM: ELECTRONIC
    CHRON: 1946-1960
    METH: OTHER OR COMB
    GEOG: TAIWAN
    SUBJ: DEVELOPMENT DESCRIPTION

HUANG, PAUL T. H.   H00597
    TIPAO, THE EARLIEST CHINESE NEWSPAPER
    CANADIAN LIBRARY JOURNAL 27(MAR 1970), 96-101.
    CHRON: BEFORE 1910
    METH: HISTORICAL
    GEOG: CHINA
    SUBJ: JRN HISTORY

HUANG, VERONICA   H00599
    HONG KONG'S '007' MIXES BRAZEN, BIZARRE IN
        SUCCESSFUL BLEND AT 'TONIGHT'S PAPER'
    WALL STREET JRNL 27 DEC 1976
    CHRON: 1970-1980
    GEOG: HONG KONG
    SUBJ: DESCRIPTION

HUFFMAN, JAMES L.   H02614
    THE MEIJI ROOTS AND CONTEMPORARY PRACTICES OF
        THE JAPANESE PRESS
    JAPAN INTERPRETER 11:4(SPRING 1977),
        448-66.
    CHRON: SURVEY
    METH: HISTORICAL
    GEOG: EAST ASIA
    SUBJ: DEVELOPMENT JRN HISTORY

HUGHES, JOHN   H00601
     PEKING'S PROPAGANDA MILL SPINS A POWERFUL WEB
     CSM 3 NOV 1972
     ##/CHIN
     MEDIUM: GENERAL
     CHRON: 1970-1980
     GEOG: CHINA
     SUBJ: PROPAGANDA

HUGHES, PENNETHORNE   H02105
     TRAINING COMMONWEALTH BROADCASTERS
     NEW COMMONWEALTH 39:9(SEPT 1961), 567-70.
     MEDIUM: ELECTRONIC
     CHRON: 1960-1970
     GEOG: WORLD
     SUBJ: EDUCATION

HUGHES, RICHARD   H02814
     [COLUMN]
     FEER 104:19(11 MAY 1979), 28-9.
     ##/ASIA; RICHARD APPLEGATE.
     MEDIUM: GENERAL
     CHRON: SURVEY
     GEOG: SEV ASIA
     SUBJ: FOR CORR   BIOGRAPHY

HUGHES, RICHARD   H00693
     [COLUMN]
     FEER 94:43(22 OCT 1976), 20.
     ##/HKG; CHINESE NEWS SUMMARY.
     CHRON: 1970-1980
     GEOG: HONG KONG   CHINA
     SUBJ: RESEARCH   SERIALS

HUGHES, RICHARD   H01501
     [COLUMN]
     FEER 98:45(11 NOV 1977), 31.
     ##/EASI
     CHRON: 1970-1980
     GEOG: EAST ASIA
     SUBJ: FOR CORR

HUGHES, RICHARD   H00694
     [COLUMN]
     FEER 95:4(28 JAN 1977), 20.
     ##/LAOS; CONSTELLATION.
     MEDIUM: GENERAL
     CHRON: 1970-1980
     GEOG: LAOS
     SUBJ: FOR CORR

HULSTON, LINDA   H01502
     NOT JUST A PASSING VISION
     HORIZONS [USIS] XVII:11(1968-1970), 32-5.
     CHRON: 1960-1970
     GEOG: THAILAND
     SUBJ: DESCRIPTION

HUNG KUEI-CHI   09   H02275
     T'AI-WAN PAO YEH SHIH TI YEN CHIU (AN
           HISTORICAL STUDY OF NEWSPAPERS IN TAIWAN)
     MASTERS THESIS, KUO LI CHENG CHIH TA HSUEH,
           1957.
     SKINNER S00982 II:46520
                           LANG: CHINESE
     CHRON: SURVEY   VERIF: UNVERIFIED
     METH: HISTORICAL
     GEOG: TAIWAN
     SUBJ: JRN HISTORY

HUNG KUEI-CHI   09   H00602
     T'AI-WAN PAO YEH SHIH TI YEN CHIU (AN
           HISTORICAL STUDY OF NEWSPAPERS IN TAIWAN)
     TAIPEI, T'AI PEI PU WEN HSIEN WEN YUAN HUI,
           1968.
                           LANG: CHINESE
     CHRON: SURVEY
     METH: HISTORICAL
     GEOG: TAIWAN   CHINA
     SUBJ: JRN HISTORY

HUNG, FREDERICK   09   H01503
     RACIAL MOCKERY IN MOTION PICTURES
     THE CHINA CRITIC III:52(25 DEC 1930), 1236-7.
     ##/FILM
     MEDIUM: FILM
     CHRON: 1910-1946
     GEOG: CHINA
     SUBJ: DESCRIPTION CROSS CULTU

HUNTER, DARD   H01812
     CHINESE CEREMONIAL PAPER
     CHILLICOTHE, OHIO, MOUNTAIN HOUSE PRESS, 1937.
     CHRON: 1910-1946
     GEOG: CHINA
     SUBJ: PRINTING

HUNTER, DARD   H01811
     OLD PAPERMAKING IN CHINA AND JAPAN
     CHILLICOTHE, OHIO, MOUNTAIN HOUSE PRESS, 1932.
     CHRON: 1910-1946
     GEOG: CHINA   EAST ASIA
     SUBJ: PRINTING

HUNTER, DARD   H01810
    PAPERMAKING IN INDO-CHINA
    CHILLICOTHE, OHIO, MOUNTAIN HOUSE PRESS, 1947.
    CHRON: 1960-1970
    GEOG: VIETNAM   CAMBODIA   LAOS
    SUBJ: PRINTING

HUNTER, EDWARD   H01817
    GETTING THE NEWS IN MANCHURIA
    THE CHINA REVIEW [LONDON] III:3(JULY-SEPT
        1934), 17-19.
    CHRON: 1910-1946
    GEOG: CHINA   EAST ASIA
    SUBJ: FOR CORR   CONTROL

HUNTER, WILLIAM C.   H00603
    BITS OF OLD CHINA
    LONDON, KEGAN PAUL, TRENCH & CO., 1855.
    ##/CHIN-3; ORIGIN OF PRINTING IN CHINA,
        PP. 211-17; REPRINTED
        BY CHENG-WEN PUB. CO., TAIPEI, 1966.
    CHRON: SURVEY
    METH: HISTORICAL
    GEOG: CHINA
    SUBJ: PRINTING

HWANG CHING-SHU   H02302
    SUSPENSION OF NEWSPAPERS IN CHINA
    THE CHINA WEEKLY REVIEW 54:10(8 NOV 1930),
        359-60.
    CHRON: 1910-1946
    GEOG: CHINA
    SUBJ: CONTROL

HWANG, JOHN C.   H02637
    <LIEN HUAN HUA>: REVOLUTIONARY SERIAL
        PICTURES
    IN CHU C02632, PP. 51-72.
    MEDIUM: OTHER
    CHRON: 1970-1980
    METH: OTHER OR COMB
    GEOG: CHINA
    SUBJ: DESCRIPTION OTHER JRN

I CHIH [PSEUD.] AND AI KANG   01   I00605
    TEN YEARS OF THE <SHANSI JIH-PAO>(TRANS. OF
        SHAN-HSI JIH-PAO SHIH NIEN)
    WASHINGTON, D. C., USJPRS, 1960.
    SKINNER S00982 I:17005; IN TRANSLATIONS OF
        CHINESE COMMUNIST ARTICLES ON
        NEWSPAPER AND BROADCASTING
        WORK>, MIMEO; JPRS 14 JULY 1960,
        15-34 (JPRS 3548; MC 14,260/1960).
    CHRON: 1946-1960   VERIF: UNVERIFIED
    GEOG: CHINA
    SUBJ: JRN HISTORY

I CHIH [PSEUD] AND AI KANG   01   I00606
    <SHAN-HSI JIH PAO> SHIH NIEN (A DECADE OF
       <SHAN-HSI JIH-PAO>)
    HSIN WEN CHAN HSIEN 1959 18(24 SEPT), 7-12.
    FOR TRANS., SEE SKINNER S00982 I:17005 OR
       01I006051
                        LANG: CHINESE
    CHRON: 1946-1960   VERIF: UNVERIFIED
    GEOG: CHINA
    SUBJ: JRN HISTORY

IBNU HANIFFAH   I02060
    [SERIES OF 15 ARTICLES ON EARLY NEWSPAPERS
        AND MAGAZINES]
    BERITA HARIAN [BERITA MINGGU, KUALA LUMPUR]
        (27 MAY; 3, 10, 17,24 JUNE; 1, 8, 15, 22,
        29 JULY; 5, 12, 19 AUG; 2, 9 SEPT 1962).
    #3/MAL-3
                        LANG: MALAY/INDONESIAN
    CHRON: SURVEY
    METH: HISTORICAL
    GEOG: MALAYSIA   SINGAPORE
    SUBJ: JRN HISTORY

IBRAHIM HAMID   I00604
    FILEM MELAYU BERTAPAK SEMULA TETAPI MUTUNYA
        PERLU DIJAGA
    BERITA MINGGU 26 SEPT 1976
    ##/MAL-2
    MEDIUM: ELECTRONIC   LANG: MALAY/INDONESIAN
    CHRON: 1970-1980
    GEOG: MALAYSIA
    SUBJ: CONTROL   DESCRIPTION

IMADA, SADAO   I01699
    MOVING PICTURE AND JAPAN
    ASIA XXII:5(MAY 1922), 345-51.
    MEDIUM: FILM
    CHRON: 1910-1946
    GEOG: EAST ASIA
    SUBJ: DESCRIPTION

INDEPENDENT, THE   I01818
    CHINESE JOURNALISM
    64:3105(4 JUNE 1908), 1224-25.
    ##/CHIN-6
    CHRON: BEFORE 1910
    GEOG: CHINA
    SUBJ: DESCRIPTION

INDOCHINA SOLIDARITY   I00607
    CONFERENCE [COMPILER]
    THE BRITISH PRESS AND VIETNAM
    LONDON, INDOCHINA SOLIDARITY CONF., 1973.
    ##/VN; INDOCHINA INFORMATION NO. 3.
    CHRON: 1970-1980
    GEOG: VIETNAM   EUROPE   U.S.
    SUBJ: CONTROL   PROPAGANDA DESCRIPTION

INGLESON, JOHN   I02106
    PERHIMPUNAN INDONESIA AND THE INDONESIAN
        NATIONALIST MOVEMENT, 1923-1928.
    MELBOURNE, CENTRE OF SOUTHEAST ASIAN
        STUDIES, MONASH UNIVERSITY, 1975.
    MONASH PAPERS IN SOUTHEAST ASIA NO. 4
    CHRON: 1910-1946
    GEOG: INDONESIA
    SUBJ: JRN HISTORY

INGRAM, DEREK   I00608
    THE LUXURY OF PRESS FREEDOM
    ATLAS WORLD PRESS REVIEW 23:11(NOV 1976), 45.
    FROM <CEYLON DAILY NEWS> 14 JULY 1976.
    CHRON: 1970-1980
    GEOG: SO/WEST ASI WORLD
    SUBJ: CONTROL

INLAND PRINTER, THE   I02062
    PROGRESS IN CHINESE JOURNALISM
    XLVI:3(DEC 1910), 387.
    ##/CHIN-7; FROM OHLINGER 000861.
    CHRON: BEFORE 1910
    GEOG:/ CHINA
    SUBJ: DESCRIPTION

INLAND PRINTER, THE   I02061
    CHINESE NEWSPAPERS
    III:12(AUG 1886), 738.
    ##/CHIN-7
    CHRON: BEFORE 1910
    GEOG: OSEAS CHIN U.S.
    SUBJ: DESCRIPTION

INLAND PRINTER, THE   I02058
    NEWSPAPERS 3609 YEARS OLD
    XLIII:2(MAY 1909), 244.
    ##/CHIN-7; FROM <CHICAGO EXAMINER>.
    CHRON: BEFORE 1910
    GEOG: CHINA   WORLD
    SUBJ: JRN HISTORY

INLAND PRINTER, THE   I02042
    THE CHINA BAPTIST PUBLICATION SOCIETY
    XLIII:2(MAY 1909), 253-4.
    ##/CHIN-7
    CHRON: BEFORE 1910
    GEOG: CHINA
    SUBJ: DESCRIPTION PRINTING

```
INLAND PRINTER, THE                                    I02041
    THE PRESS IN CHINA
    XXXVI:6(MAR 1906), 860-1.
    ##/CHIN-7; FROM COLQUHOUN C01813.
    CHRON: BEFORE 1910
    GEOG:   CHINA
    SUBJ:   DESCRIPTION


INLAND PRINTER, THE                                    I02040
    CHINESE THE FIRST PRINTERS
    XXXIV:4(1905), 542.
    ##/CHIN-7; FROM <MASTER PRINTER>.
    CHRON: BEFORE 1910
    GEOG:   CHINA
    SUBJ:   PRINTING


INLAND PRINTER, THE                                    I02039
    JOURNALISM IN CHINA
    XXXVII:1(APR 1906), 82-4.
    ##/CHIN-7
    CHRON: BEFORE 1910
    GEOG:   CHINA
    SUBJ:   DESCRIPTION


INLAND PRINTER, THE                                    I02038
    DAILY NEWSPAPERS IN CHINA
    XLIII:2(MAY 1909), 249-50.
    ##/CHIN-7
    CHRON: BEFORE 1910
    GEOG:   CHINA
    SUBJ:   DESCRIPTION


INLAND PRINTER, THE                                    I02037
    THE NEWSPAPERS OF JAPAN
    XXVII:5(AUG 1906), 740-1.
    ##/CHIN-7; FROM <LONDON EXPRESS>.
    CHRON: BEFORE 1910
    GEOG:   EAST ASIA
    SUBJ:   DESCRIPTION


INLAND PRINTER, THE                                    I02036
    CHINESE PRINTING
    XXIX:3(JUNE 1902), 447.
    ##/CHIN-7; FROM <SCIENTIFIC AMERICAN>.
    CHRON: BEFORE 1910
    GEOG:   CHINA
    SUBJ:   PRINTING
```

INLAND PRINTER, THE   I02035
     HOW NEWS IS FURNISHED BY THE PRESS OF
          CHINATOWN
     IX:11(AUG 1892), 968.
     ##/CHIN-7
     CHRON: BEFORE 1910
     GEOG: OSEAS CHIN U.S.
     SUBJ: DESCRIPTION

INLAND PRINTER, THE   I02034
     HOW THE CHINESE 'FOLLOW COPY'
     IX:5(FEB 1892), 445.
     ##/CHIN-7
     CHRON: BEFORE 1910
     GEOG: HONG KONG   CHINA
     SUBJ: DESCRIPTION PRINTING

INLAND PRINTER, THE   I02033
     A CHINESE PRINTING OFFICE
     III:8(MAY 1886), 506.
     ##/CHIN-7
     CHRON: BEFORE 1910
     GEOG: OSEAS CHIN U.S.
     SUBJ: DESCRIPTION PRINTING

INLAND PRINTER, THE   I02032
     CHINESE PAPER MAKERS
     III:8(MAY 1886), 507.
     ##/CHIN-7
     CHRON: BEFORE 1910
     GEOG: CHINA
     SUBJ: DESCRIPTION PRINTING

INLAND PRINTER, THE   I02031
     A CHINESE NEWSPAPER OFFICE
     III:1(OCT 1885), 52.
     ##/CHIN-7
     CHRON: BEFORE 1910
     GEOG: OSEAS CHIN U.S.
     SUBJ: DESCRIPTION PRINTING

INSIGHT   I00612
     <THE ASIAN>: ANTIDOTE TO PAROCHIAL
          PERVERSITY
     (NOV 1971), 50-1.
     CHRON: 1970-1980
     GEOG: HONG KONG   SEV ASIA
     SUBJ: DESCRIPTION

INSIGHT   I00611
    COMMENT
    (JULY 1971), 11-2.
    ##/SIN; EDITORIAL ON SINGAPORE HERALD.
    CHRON: 1970-1980
    GEOG: SINGAPORE
    SUBJ: CONTROL   LAW/ETHICS

INSTITUTE OF PACIFIC RELATIONS   I02727
    INTERNATIONAL EDUCATION AND COMMUNICATION
    HONOLULU, INSTITUTE OF PACIFIC
        RELATIONS, 1927.
    PROCEEDINGS OF SECOND CONFERENCE
    MEDIUM: GENERAL
    CHRON: 1910-1946
    GEOG: SEV ASIA
    SUBJ: EDUCATION

INTERNATIONAL CO-OPERATIVE ALLIANCE   I00613
    CO-OPERATIVE PRESS IN SOUTHEAST ASIA
    NEW DELHI, INTERNATIONAL CO-OPERATIVE
        ALLIANCE, N. D.
    CHRON: SURVEY
    GEOG: SEV ASIA
    SUBJ: FLOW/AGENCY DESCRIPTION

INTERNATIONAL PRESS INSTITUTE   I00614
    THE FLOW OF THE NEWS
    ZURICH, IPI, 1953.
    CHRON: 1946-1960
    METH: CONTENT ANALYSIS
    GEOG: WORLD
    SUBJ: FLOW/AGENCY DESCRIPTION

INTERNATIONAL PRESS INSTITUTE   I00616
    THE SINGAPORE GOVERNMENT AND THE PRESS
    ZURICH, IPI, 1971.
    MIMEO
    CHRON: 1970-1980
    GEOG: SINGAPORE
    SUBJ: CONTROL

INTERNATIONAL PRESS INSTITUTE   I00615
    NEWS IN ASIA
    ZURICH, IPI, 1956.
    CHRON: 1946-1960
    GEOG: SEV ASIA
    SUBJ: FLOW/AGENCY DESCRIPTION

INTERNATIONAL PRESS INSTITUTE   I00617
     THE ACTIVE NEWSROOM
     ZURICH, IPI, 1961.
     WRITING/EDITING FOR THIRD-WORLD NEWSPAPERS
     CHRON: 1960-1970
     GEOG: WORLD
     SUBJ: EDUCATION

INTERNATIONAL PRESS INSTITUTE   I01240
     IPI IN ASIA
     ZURICH, IPI, N. D. [1966?].
     CHRON: 1960-1970
     GEOG: SEV ASIA
     SUBJ: DESCRIPTION

IPI REPORT   I00659
     IPI APPEALS TO TAIWANESE PREMIER FOR MEDICAL
          AID FOR SERIOUSLY ILL JOURNALIST HELD
          IN PRISON SINCE 1971
     25:11(NOV 1976), 2.
     CHRON: 1970-1980
     GEOG: TAIWAN
     SUBJ: CONTROL

IPI REPORT   I00629
     LAOS CLOSES AFP OFFICE
     25:12(DEC 1976), 12.
     MEDIUM: GENERAL
     CHRON: 1970-1980
     GEOG: LAOS
     SUBJ: CONTROL

IPI REPORT   I00628
     THAILAND GIVES EDITOR BAIL FOR VISIT TO
          U. S. A.
     25:12(DEC 1976), 2.
     CHRON: 1970-1980
     GEOG: THAILAND
     SUBJ: CONTROL

IPI REPORT   I00627
     INDONESIA BANS NEWSWEEK
     25:12(DEC 1976), 8.
     CHRON: 1970-1980
     GEOG: INDONESIA
     SUBJ: CONTROL

IPI REPORT   I00626
    IPI PROTESTS AGAINST TAIWAN SENTENCE ON EDITOR
    25:12(DEC 1976), 10.
    CHRON: 1970-1980
    GEOG: TAIWAN
    SUBJ: CONTROL

IPI REPORT   I00618
    EDITORS ARE NEITHER COWARDS NOR BRAVE MEN
    24:7(JULY 1975), 3.
    ##/MAL
    CHRON: 1970-1980
    GEOG: MALAYSIA
    SUBJ: CONTROL

IPI REPORT   I00620
    THAILAND PRESS FREEDOM 'UNIQUE'
    24:9(SEPT 1975), 5.
    CHRON: 1970-1980
    GEOG: THAILAND
    SUBJ: CONTROL

IPI REPORT   I00619
    TAIWAN--'FREEDOM TO REPORT'
    24:8(AUG 1975), 7.
    CHRON: 1970-1980
    GEOG: TAIWAN
    SUBJ: CONTROL

IPI REPORT   I00625
    PHILIPPINES BARS AP MAN
    25:12(DEC 1976), 8.
    MEDIUM: GENERAL
    CHRON: 1970-1980
    GEOG: PHILIPPINES
    SUBJ: FOR CORR   CONTROL

IPI REPORT   I00624
    THAILAND BARS MEDIA FROM CRITICIZING NEW
        REGIME
    25:11(NOV 1976), 1, 12.
    MEDIUM: GENERAL
    CHRON: 1970-1980
    GEOG: THAILAND
    SUBJ: CONTROL

IPI REPORT   I00622
    TV FOR MACAU
    25:4(APR 1976), 7.
    MEDIUM: ELECTRONIC
    CHRON: 1970-1980
    GEOG: MACAO
    SUBJ: DESCRIPTION

IPI REPORT   I00621
    PRESS FREEDOM REPORT--12
    24:12(DEC 1975), 15-7, 19.
    CHRON: 1970-1980
    GEOG: SEV ASIA
    SUBJ: CONTROL

IRANI, C. R.   I00630
    NEW MOVES TO CONTROL THE INDIAN PRESS
    IPI REPORT 25:3(MAR 1976), 1-3.
    CHRON: 1970-1980
    GEOG: SO/WEST ASI
    SUBJ: CONTROL

IRICK, ROBERT L.   I00631
    AN ANNOTATED GUIDE TO TAIWAN PERIODICAL
        LITERATURE, 1972
    SAN FRANCISCO, CHINESE MATERIALS CENTER, 1973.
    CHRON: SURVEY   VERIF: UNVERIFIED
    GEOG: TAIWAN
    SUBJ: RESEARCH

IRICK, ROBERT L., YING-SHIH   I02579
        YU AND KWANG-CHING LIU
    AMERICAN-CHINESE RELATIONS, 1784-1941: A
        SURVEY OF CHINESE-LANGUAGE MATERIALS
        AT HARVARD
    CAMBRIDGE, HARVARD U. PRESS, 1960.
    ##/BIB
    CHRON: SURVEY
    GEOG: CHINA   U.S.
    SUBJ: RESEARCH

ISA, ZUBAIDAH   I01335
    PRINTING AND PUBLISHING IN INDONESIA:
        1602-1970
    PHD DISS, INDIANA UNIVERSITY, 1972.
    INTL. DISS. 33/8 4444A
    CHRON: SURVEY
    METH: HISTORICAL
    GEOG: INDONESIA
    SUBJ: PRINTING   PUBLISHING

ISAACS, HAROLD R.   I00632
    COVERING RED CHINA
    NIEMAN REPORTS XI:2(APR 1957), 9-10.
    ##/CHIN-2
    CHRON: 1946-1960
    GEOG: CHINA
    SUBJ: FOR CORR

ISAACS, NORMAN E.   I00634
    CHINA: CASTING OFF THE MYTHS
    COL JRN REVIEW (JAN/FEB 1973), 51-7.
    ##/CHIN
    CHRON: 1970-1980
    GEOG: CHINA   U.S.
    SUBJ: FOR CORR

ISHIBASHI, TANZAN   I01819
    PRESS AS GUARDIAN OF PEACE
    ORIENTAL ECONOMIST [TOKYO] III:11(NOV 1936),
        689-90.
    CHRON: 1910-1946
    GEOG: CHINA   EAST ASIA
    SUBJ: PROPAGANDA   DESCRIPTION

ISHII, AKIRA   I02728
    CHINA'S RADIO COMMUNICATION PROBLEM
    HONOLULU, INSTITUTE OF PACIFIC RELATIONS,
        1927.
    SECOND CONFERENCE OF INSTITUTE OF
        PACIFIC RELATIONS
    MEDIUM: ELECTRONIC
    CHRON: 1910-1946
    GEOG: CHINA
    SUBJ: DESCRIPTION

ISHIJIMA, NORIYUKI   I02615
    KONICHI MINZOKU TOITSU SENSEN TO
        CHISHIKKIJIN(THE NATIONAL UNITED FRONT
        AGAINST JAPAN AND THE INTELLECTUALS)
    REKISHI HYORON 256(1971), 22-50.
    TSOU TAO-FEN AND THE <SHENG HUO>
                        LANG: OTHER ASIAN
    CHRON: SURVEY   VERIF: UNVERIFIED
    METH: HISTORICAL
    GEOG: CHINA   EAST ASIA
    SUBJ: JRN HISTORY

ISHIKAWA, K.   I01820
    JOURNALISM IN JAPAN
    TRANSACTIONS AND PROCEEDINGS OF THE JAPAN
        SOCIETY [LONDON] XXXII(1935), 37-46.
    CHRON: 1910-1946
    GEOG: EAST ASIA
    SUBJ: DESCRIPTION

ISKANDAR HAJI AHMAD, A. M.   I02107
    PERSURATKHABARAN MELAYU, 1876-1968.
    KUALA LUMPUR, DEWAN BAHASA DAN PUSTAKA, 1973.
                        LANG: MALAY/INDONESIAN
    CHRON: SURVEY
    GEOG: MALAYSIA
    SUBJ: JRN HISTORY

ISMAIL HUSSEIN   I00636
    LITERATURE BY THE PEOPLE
    STRAITS TIMES 28 DEC 1973
    ##/MAL-2; SECOND OF TWO ARTICLES, SEE I00635.
    CHRON: 1970-1980
    GEOG: MALAYSIA
    SUBJ: LITERATURE

ISMAIL HUSSEIN   I00635
    TOWARDS A NEW LITERARY TRADITION
    STRAITS TIMES 27 DEC 1973
    ##/MAL-2; ONE OF TWO ARTICLES, SEE I00636.
    CHRON: 1970-1980
    GEOG: MALAYSIA
    SUBJ: LITERATURE

IWANAGA, Y.   I02642
    [ON FALSE RENGO REPORTS]
    THE NEW CHINA [PEKING] I:8(JUNE 1931),
        212-3.
    LETTER TO EDITOR
    CHRON: 1910-1946
    GEOG: CHINA   EAST ASIA
    SUBJ: FLOW/AGENCY LAW/ETHICS

J., J. A.   J01821
    JAPAN'S SUBSIDIZED PRESS IN CHINA
    THE CHINA WEEKLY REVIEW 42:10(5 NOV 1927),
        242-5.
    CHRON: 1910-1946
    GEOG: CHINA   EAST ASIA
    SUBJ: PROPAGANDA DESCRIPTION

JABLONS, PAMELA H.   J02227
    INDIA'S PRESS: CAN IT BECOME INDEPENDENT AT
        LAST
    COL JRN REVIEW XVII:2(JULY/AUG 1978), 33-6.
    CHRON: 1970-1980
    GEOG: SO/WEST ASI
    SUBJ: CONTROL

JACOBS, J. BRUCE   J00637
    TAIWAN'S PRESS: POLITICAL COMMUNICATIONS
        LINK AND RESEARCH RESOURCE
    CHINA QUARTERLY NO. 68(DEC 1976), 778-788.
    CHRON: 1970-1980
    METH: OTHER OR COMB
    GEOG: TAIWAN
    SUBJ: RESEARCH

JACOBS, MILTON   J00638
    A STUDY OF KEY COMMUNICATORS IN URBAN THAILAND
    SOCIAL FORCES 45:2(DEC 1966), 192-199.
    MEDIUM: GENERAL
    CHRON: 1960-1970
    METH: OTHER OR COMB
    GEOG: THAILAND
    SUBJ: DESCRIPTION OTHER JRN   OTHER NON-J

JACOBS, MILTON AND CHARLES E. RICE,   J01504
        L. SZALY
    THE STUDY OF COMMUNICATION IN THAILAND WITH
        EMPHASIS ON WORD-OF-MOUTH COMMUNICATION
    WASHINGTON, D. C., SPECIAL OPERATION'
        RESEARCH OFFICE, AMERICAN UNIVERSITY,
        1964.
    MEDIUM: OTHER
    CHRON: 1960-1970
    METH: SURVEY
    GEOG: THAILAND
    SUBJ: OTHER JRN

JAYEWARDENE, B. H. S.   J00695
    NEW TEETH FOR THE WATCH-DOG
    FEER 95:10(11 MAR 1977), 25.
    CHRON: 1970-1980
    GEOG: SO/WEST ASI
    SUBJ: CONTROL

JEBB, MARCIA   J00639
    BBC SUMMARY OF WORLD BROADCASTING
    MICROFORM REVIEW II:2(APR 1973), 115-7.
    REVIEW OF WEEKLY MICROFILM ED. (PART 3, THE
        FAR EAST), PUB. BY
        UNIVERSITY MICROFILMS, LTD (ENGLAND);
        DIFFERENT FROM FBIS.
    MEDIUM: ELECTRONIC
    CHRON: 1970-1980
    GEOG: SEV ASIA
    SUBJ: DESCRIPTION

JEE, LUTHER M.   J02195
    INTEREST IN MOTION PICTURES IN CHINA NOT
        FAR BEHIND WEST
    THE CHINA WEEKLY REVIEW (SUPPLEMENT)
        (4 DEC 1926), 12, 81.
    MEDIUM: FILM
    CHRON: 1910-1946
    GEOG: CHINA
    SUBJ: DESCRIPTION

JEE, LUTHER M.   J02194
    THE MOTION PICTURE INDUSTRY IN CHINA
    THE CHINA WEEKLY REVIEW XXXIV:4(26 SEPT
        1925), 81-2.
    MEDIUM: FILM
    CHRON: 1910-1946
    GEOG: CHINA
    SUBJ: DESCRIPTION

JEFFRES, LEO W.   J00640
    THE PRINT TRADITION IN A RURAL PHILIPPINE
        PROVINCE
    GAZETTE XIX:4(1973), 248-57.
    ##/PHIL
    CHRON: 1970-1980
    GEOG: PHILIPPINES
    SUBJ: DESCRIPTION LANGUAGE

JEN CHUNG   06   J01506
    CHUNG-KUNG PAO-CHIH TI NEI-JUNG CHI PIEN-P'AI
        (THE CONTENTS AND LAYOUTS OF CHINESE
        COMMUNIST NEWSPAPERS)
    TSU-KUO CHOU-K'AN (CHINA WEEKLY) [HKG]
        NO. 71(10 MAY 1954), 14-5.
    ##/CHIN-5
                        LANG: CHINESE
    CHRON: 1946-1960
    GEOG: CHINA
    SUBJ: DESCRIPTION OTHER JRN

JEN CHUNG   06   J01505
    TUN CHUNG-KUNG TI HSIN-WEN KUNG TAO (ON THE
        CHINESE COMMUNIST PRESS)
    TSU-KUO CHOU-K'AN (CHINA WEEKLY) [HKG]
        (29 MAR 1954), 7-9.
    ##/CHIN-5
                        LANG: CHINESE
    CHRON: 1946-1960
    GEOG: CHINA
    SUBJ: DESCRIPTION

JEN, RICHARD   06   J02638
    CHINA'S PUBLISHING PROBLEMS
    THE CHINA WEEKLY REVIEW 76:6(11 APR
        1936), 214-15.
    CHRON: 1910-1946
    GEOG: CHINA
    SUBJ: PROPAGANDA OTHER JRN

JEN, RICHARD L.   J01343
    DEVELOPMENT OF CHINESE NEWS AGENCIES
    IN CHINA PRESS C02568, PP. 87-8.
    ##/FILM
    CHRON: SURVEY
    METH: HISTORICAL
    GEOG: CHINA
    SUBJ: FLOW/AGENCY JRN HISTORY DESCRIPTION

JEN, RICHARD L.   J01508
    NEWS AGENCIES IN CHINA
    THE PEIPING CHRONICLE 18, 20, 22 OCT 1936
    ##/CHIN-5
    CHRON: 1910-1946
    GEOG: CHINA
    SUBJ: FLOW/AGENCY DESCRIPTION

JEN, RICHARD L.   J01507
    NEW JOURNALISM IN SHANGHAI
    THE PEIPING CHRONICLE 27 SEPT 1935
    ##/CHIN-5
    CHRON: 1910-1946
  . GEOG: CHINA
    SUBJ: DESCRIPTION

JENKINS, DAVID   J00698
    NEWSPAPER'S ELECTION CRUSADE
    FEER 96:16(22 APR 1977), 30.
    ##/INDO
    CHRON: 1970-1980
    GEOG: INDONESIA
    SUBJ: CONTROL

JENKINS, DAVID   J00697
    SUHARTO SLATES A CRITIC
    FEER 94:48(26 NOV 1976), 36.
    ##/INDO; NEWSWEEK.
    CHRON: 1970-1980
    GEOG: INDONESIA
    SUBJ: CONTROL

JENKINS, DAVID   J00696
    PULLING STRINGS FOR GOLKAR
    FEER 94:46(12 NOV 1976), 34.
    ##/INDO; DALANGS.
    MEDIUM: OTHER
    CHRON: 1970-1980
    GEOG: INDONESIA
    SUBJ: DESCRIPTION

JENKINS, DAVID   J01966
    PRESS FREEDOM, MILITARY STYLE
    FEER 9:7(17 FEB 1978), 19.
    ##/INDON-2
    CHRON: 1970-1980
    GEOG: INDONESIA
    SUBJ: CONTROL

JENKINS, DAVID   J01965
     PYRRHIC WIN FOR PRESS
     FEER 99:6(10 FEB 1978), 13-14.
     ##/INDON-2
     CHRON: 1970-1980
     GEOG: INDONESIA
     SUBJ: CONTROL

JENKINS, DAVID   J01964
     THE GENERALS FLEX THEIR MUSCLES
     FEER 99:5(3 FEB 1978), 8-10.
     ##/INDON-2
     CHRON: 1970-1980
     GEOG: INDONESIA
     SUBJ: CONTROL

JENKINS, DAVID   J02815
     THE MEDIA AND AN INSIDE STORY
     FEER 104:24(15 JUNE 1979), 48, 51.
     CHRON: 1970-1980
     GEOG: INDONESIA
     SUBJ: DESCRIPTION PRINTING

JENKINS, DAVID   J00641
     SPACE-AGE BOOST IN COMMUNICATION
     FEER 93:30(23 JULY 1976), 23.
     ##/INDO
     MEDIUM: ELECTRONIC
     CHRON: 1970-1980
     GEOG: INDONESIA
     SUBJ: DESCRIPTION

JOHNSON, ALBIN E.   J02639
     JOURNALISM IN CHINA UNDEVELOPED; CALLED
          MERCENARY AND COLORLESS
     EDITOR & PUBLISHER 62:17(14 SEPT 1929),
          32.
     CHRON: 1910-1946
     GEOG: CHINA
     SUBJ: DESCRIPTION

JOHNSON, DEWAYNE B.   J00881
     VIETNAM: REPORT CARD ON THE PRESS CORPS AT WAR
     JQ 46:1(SPRING 1969), 9-19.
     CHRON: 1960-1970
     METH: SURVEY
     GEOG: VIETNAM   U.S.
     SUBJ: FOR CORR

JOHNSON, MARTIN   J01509
    A CAMERA MAN IN BORNEO
    ASIA XXI:2(FEB 1921), 125-40.
    MEDIUM: FILM
    CHRON: 1910-1946
    GEOG: MALAYSIA
    SUBJ: DESCRIPTION BIOGRAPHY

JOHNSTON, DAVID   J02196
    THE TAIWAN CONNECTION
    FEED/BACK [SAN FRANCISCO] IV:11(WINTER
        1978), 6-9, 12.
    ##/CHIN-US
    CHRON: 1970-1980
    GEOG: OSEAS CHIN U.S.
    SUBJ: DESCRIPTION

JOHNSTON, WILLIAM   J01700
    SUPRESSION OF MAGAZINE RAISES PROTEST
    THE CHINA WEEKLY REVIEW 100:7(12 JAN 1946),
        115.
    CHRON: 1910-1946
    GEOG: CHINA
    SUBJ: CONTROL

JOHNSTON, WILLIAM   J01701
    'VOICE OF NEW CHINA' PUBLISHER CLAIMS HE
        WAS PATRIOT
    THE CHINA WEEKLY REVIEW 100:10(2 FEB 1946),
        166.
    CHRON: 1910-1946
    GEOG: OSEAS CHIN U.S.
    SUBJ: CONTROL   LAW/ETHICS

JONAS, F. M.   J01822
    FOREIGN INFLUENCE ON THE EARLY PRESS OF JAPAN
    TRANSACTIONS AND PROCEEDINGS OF THE JAPAN
        SOCIETY [LONDON] XXXII(1935), 47-62.
    CHRON: BEFORE 1910
    METH: HISTORICAL
    GEOG: EAST ASIA
    SUBJ: JRN HISTORY

JOSEY, ALEX   J00643
    JUDGEMENT: A WARNING TO CORRESPONDENTS
    FEER 86:49(13 DEC 1974), 30.
    ##/SIN
    MEDIUM: GENERAL
    CHRON: 1970-1980
    GEOG: SINGAPORE
    SUBJ: FOR CORR   CONTROL   LAW/ETHICS

JOURNALIST'S WORLD, THE   J02640
     CONTRIBUTIONS TO KOREAN JOURNALISM
     II:3(1964), 14-16.
     CHRON: 1960-1970
     GEOG: EAST ASIA
     SUBJ: DESCRIPTION

JU, WILLIAM C.[COMPILER]   J00644
     A UNION LIST OF CHINESE PERIODICALS IN
          UNIVERSITIES AND COLLEGES IN TAIWAN
     SAN FRANCISCO, CHINESE MATERIALS CENTER, 1975.
     CHRON: SURVEY
     GEOG: TAIWAN
     SUBJ: RESEARCH

JUSOF MANAF   J01823
     FILEM MELAYU MENGHADAPI ZAMAN MEROSAT?
     BERITA HARIAN (SUNDAY MALAYSIA EDITION)
          5 MAR 1978
     ##/MAL-3
     MEDIUM: FILM   LANG: MALAY/INDONESIAN
     CHRON: 1970-1980
     GEOG: MALAYSIA
     SUBJ: DESCRIPTION

KAIM, J. R.   K01510
     CHINESE FILMS
     THE CHINA JOURNAL XXXI:2(AUG 1939), 72-5.
     ##/CHIN-5
     MEDIUM: FILM
     CHRON: 1910-1946
     GEOG: CHINA
     SUBJ: DESCRIPTION

KALB, MARVIN   K02171
     CHINA: THE GREATEST STORY NEVER TOLD
     DATELINE [OPC, NEW YORK] 9:1(1965), 24-7.
     CHRON: 1960-1970
     GEOG: VIETNAM
     SUBJ: FOR CORR   CONTROL

KAM, JOHN   K00646
     DUTY OF MASS MEDIA TO BE OBJECTIVE
     MALAY MAIL 18 AUG 1972
     ##/MAL-2
     MEDIUM: GENERAL
     CHRON: 1970-1980
     GEOG: MALAYSIA
     SUBJ: PROPAGANDA   DEVELOPMENT

KAM, JOHN   K00647
     MORE TRAINED STAFF FOR ANGKASAPURI
     MALAY MAIL 15 SEPT 1972
     ##/MALSP
     MEDIUM: ELECTRONIC
     CHRON: 1970-1980
     GEOG: MALAYSIA
     SUBJ: DESCRIPTION EDUCATION

KAMM, HENRY   K01272
     INDIAN EDITOR, GRANDSON OF GANDHI, PROTESTS
          CURBS ON FREEDOM
     NYT 8 AUG 1976
     ##/SWAS
     CHRON: 1970-1980
     GEOG: SO/WEST ASI
     SUBJ: FOR CORR

KAMM, HENRY   K01824
     INDONESIA IS KEEPING A TIGHT REIN ON PRESS
     NYT 23 APR 1978
     ##/INDO-2
     CHRON: 1970-1980
     GEOG: INDONESIA
     SUBJ: CONTROL

KAN LAI-BING   K00651
     PRESENT DAY PUBLISHING IN HONG KONG
     MEXICO CITY, 30TH INTL. CONG. OF HUMAN
          SCIENCES IN ASIA AND NORTH AFRICA,
          5 AUG 1976.
     ##/HKG; MIMEO.
     CHRON: 1970-1980
     GEOG: HONG KONG
     SUBJ: PUBLISHING

KANAYSON, A.   K00650
     THE NEWSPAPERS OF SINGAPORE, 1824-1914
     JRNL OF THE SOUTH SEAS SOCIETY XVIII, PART 1
          AND 2(1963), 31-95.
     REPRINT OF B. A. (HONS) EXERCISE K00649
     CHRON: SURVEY
     METH: HISTORICAL
     GEOG: SINGAPORE
     SUBJ: JRN HISTORY

KANAYSON, A.   K00649
     THE NEWSPAPERS OF SINGAPORE:1824-1914
     B. A. (HONS) EXERCISE, 1956, U. OF MALAYA.
     REPRINTED IN <JOURNAL OF THE SOUTH SEAS
          SOCIETY>, SEE K00650.
     CHRON: SURVEY
     METH: HISTORICAL
     GEOG: SINGAPORE
     SUBJ: JRN HISTORY

KANG HUI-SU   K01511
    UTILIZATION OF MASS MEDIA FOR EDUCATION
    KOREA JOURNAL 8:1(JAN 1968), 10-12, 17.
    AUDIOVISUAL
    MEDIUM: OTHER
    CHRON: 1960-1970
    GEOG: EAST ASIA
    SUBJ: EDUCATION

KAO FENG-JUNG   10   K00652
    WO KUO MU CH'IEN HSIN WEN CHUAN YEH HUA TI
        T'AN T'AO
    UNPUB MASTERS THESIS IN JOURNALISM, 1969.
    (AN EXAMINATION OF THE PROFESSIONALIZATION
        OF JOURNALISM IN
        CONTEMPORARY CHINA);
        SKINNER S00982 II:46538.
                              LANG: CHINESE
    CHRON: 1960-1970   VERIF: UNVERIFIED
    GEOG: TAIWAN
    SUBJ: DESCRIPTION EDUCATION

KAO LIANG-TSO   10   K00653
    HSING CHUNG HUI CHI T'UNGMENGHUI SHIH TAI
        KO MING SHU PAO CHIH LUEH THE TIME OF THE
        HSING-CHUNG HUI [REVIVE CHINA SOCIETY]
    CHIEN KUO YUEH K'AN 11:2(AUG 1934), 1-14.
    ##/CHIN-7
                              LANG: CHINESE
    CHRON: BEFORE 1910
    GEOG: CHINA
    SUBJ: JRN HISTORY

KAO, IRVING KE-YUNG   K02228
    TA KUNG PAO: BEFORE AND AFTER COMMUNISM
    MASTERS THESIS, UNIVERSITY OF MISSOURI, 1951.
    ##
    CHRON: SURVEY
    METH: HISTORICAL
    GEOG: HONG KONG   CHINA
    SUBJ: JRN HISTORY

KAO, Y.   K01394
    MOTION PICTURES
    IN <CHINESE YEARBOOK 1935-36>, PP. 967-86.
    MEDIUM: FILM
    CHRON: 1910-1946
    GEOG: CHINA
    SUBJ: DESCRIPTION

KAO, Y.   K01344
    DEVELOPMENT OF MOTION PICTURES IN CHINA
    IN CHINA PRESS C02568, PP. 122-3.
    ##/FILM
    MEDIUM: FILM
    CHRON: SURVEY
    METH: HISTORICAL
    GEOG: CHINA
    SUBJ: JRN HISTORY

KARNOW, STANLEY   K00660
    SNARING THE DRAGON FROM AFAR
    NIEMAN REPORTS XIV:4(OCT 1960), 3-6.
    ##/CHIN
    MEDIUM: GENERAL
    CHRON: 1960-1970
    GEOG: HONG KONG   CHINA
    SUBJ: FOR CORR   FLOW/AGENCY DESCRIPTION

KARNOW, STANLEY   K00661
    THE NEWSMAN'S WAR IN VIETNAM
    NIEMAN REPORTS 17:4(DEC 1963), 3-8.
    ##/VN
    CHRON: 1960-1970
    GEOG: VIETNAM   U.S.
    SUBJ: FOR CORR   DESCRIPTION

KASAGI, MASAAKI   K02641
    THE ACCOMPLISHMENTS OF THE JAPANESE
        NEWSPAPER INDUSTRY
    THE JOURNALIST'S WORLD III:3(1965), 8-11.
    CHRON: 1960-1970
    GEOG: EAST ASIA
    SUBJ: DESCRIPTION PRINTING

KASNAKHEYEV, ALEKSANDR YURIEVICH   K00662
    COMMUNIST PENETRATION AND EXPLOITATION OF
        THE FREE PRESS
    WASHINGTON, D. C., U. S. G. P. O., 1962.
    ##/BURM; Y4.J89/2:C73/42; TESTIMONY ON
        SOVIET USE OF BURMESE PRESS
        BEFORE JUDICIARY COMMITTEE,
        U. S. CONGRESS.
    CHRON: 1960-1970
    GEOG: BURMA
    SUBJ: CONTROL   PROPAGANDA

KATALOGUS SURAT-KABAR: KOLEKSI   K00658
        PERPUSTAKAKAAN MUSEUM PUSAT 1810-1973

    JAKARTA, MUSEUM PUSAT, 1973.
    MUSEUM PUSAT, DEP. P & K, MERDEKA BARAT 12,
        JAKARTA.
                            LANG: MALAY/INDONESIAN
    CHRON: SURVEY
    GEOG: INDONESIA
    SUBJ: RESEARCH

KAVIYA, SOMKUAN AND DUANGLAJ   K02000
        NAEWBANJI
    THE ARMY, EDUCATION, AGRICULTURE, POLICE
        HAVE THEIR OWN RADIO
    JOURNALISME [STRASBOURG] NO. 30 (1966), 122-3.
    ##/THAI
    MEDIUM: GENERAL
    CHRON: 1960-1970
    GEOG: THAILAND
    SUBJ: DESCRIPTION

KAY, CHARLES S.   K02063
    HOW NEWSPAPERS OF THE ORIENT ARE HANDICAPPED
    THE OHIO NEWSPAPER 2:8(1921), 3, 6.
    ##/ASIA
    CHRON: SURVEY
    GEOG: SEV ASIA
    SUBJ: DESCRIPTION LANGUAGE

KAYSER, JACQUES   K00664
    ONE WEEKS NEWS: COMPARATIVE STUDY OF
        SEVENTEEN MAJOR DAILIES FOR A SEVEN DAY
        PERIOD
    PARIS, UNESCO, 1953.
    CHRON: 1946-1960
    METH: CONTENT ANALYSIS
    GEOG: WORLD
    SUBJ: DESCRIPTION

KAZER, BILL   K02276
    THE MEDIUM GETS THE MESSAGE
    FEER 101:38(22 SEPT 1978), 22.
    ##/TAI
    CHRON: 1970-1980
    GEOG: TAIWAN
    SUBJ: CONTROL

KAZER, BILL   K02524
    TAIWAN'S PRESS VOTES FOR FREEDOM
    FEER 102:51(22 DEC 1979), 22-3.
    ##/TAI
    CHRON: 1970-1980
    GEOG: TAIWAN
    SUBJ: CONTROL   DESCRIPTION

KEARNS, FRANK   K02172
    ALL FOR NOUGHT
    DATELINE [OPC, NEW YORK] 7:1(1963), 32.
    CHRON: 1960-1970
    GEOG: VIETNAM   U.S.
    SUBJ: FOR CORR   DESCRIPTION

KEHL, FRANK   K01825
    THE MESSAGE OF THE MEDIA
    NEW CHINA 4:1(SPRING 1978), 37-45.
    ##/CHIN-6
    CHRON: 1970-1980
    GEOG: CHINA
    SUBJ: FOR CORR   DESCRIPTION

KEITH, ORRIN   K01702
    'NEWS' FROM THE FAR EASTERN REPUBLIC
    THE CHINA WEEKLY REVIEW XVII:6(9 JULY 1921),
        280-2.
    MEDIUM: GENERAL
    CHRON: 1910-1946
    GEOG: SEV ASIA   WORLD
    SUBJ: FOR CORR   FLOW/AGENCY

KELANA, C. M.   K00665
    SUMBANGAN AKHBAR2 TIONGHUA KIAN BERTAMBAH
    BERITA MINGGU 10 OCT 1976
    ##/MAL-2
                        LANG: MALAY/INDONESIAN
    CHRON: 1970-1980
    GEOG: MALAYSIA   OTHER
    SUBJ: DESCRIPTION LANGUAGE

KENNARD, ALLINGTON   K00666
    A SURVEY ON ASIA'S NEWSPAPERS
    STRAITS TIMES 4 SEPT 1972
    ##/ASIA; REVIEW OF LENT L00708.
    CHRON: 1970-1980
    GEOG: SEV ASIA
    SUBJ: RESEARCH   DESCRIPTION

KENNEDY, M. D.   K01826
    BEHIND THE NEWS IN TOKIO
    TRANSACTIONS AND PROCEEDINGS OF THE JAPAN
        SOCIETY [LONDON] 33(1935),93-109.
    CHRON: 1910-1946
    GEOG: EAST ASIA
    SUBJ: FOR CORR   DESCRIPTION

KENNEDY, MALCOLM DUNCAN   K01703
    THE CHANGING FABRIC OF JAPAN
    LONDON, CONSTABLE, 1930.
    JAPANESE PRESS AND ITS INFLUENCE, PP. 180-203.
    CHRON: 1910-1946
    GEOG: EAST ASIA
    SUBJ: DESCRIPTION

KENNEDY, WILLIAM V.   K02229
    IT TAKES MORE THAN TALENT TO COVER A WAR
    ARMY 28:7(JULY 1978), 23-6.
    ##/VN-2
    MEDIUM: GENERAL
    CHRON: SURVEY
    GEOG: VIETNAM   U.S.
    SUBJ: FOR CORR

KERR, FRANCES   K01575
     ASIAN JOURNALISTS AT HARVARD
     HORIZONS [USIS] XVII:11(1968-70), 26-27.
     CHRON: 1960-1970
     GEOG: SEV ASIA
     SUBJ: EDUCATION

KERTAPATI, TON   K00667
     DASAR-DASAR PUBLISISTIK
     DJAKARTA, SOEROENGAN, 1968, 2 VOLS.
                              LANG: MALAY/INDONESIAN
     CHRON: 1960-1970
     GEOG: INDONESIA
     SUBJ: DESCRIPTION EDUCATION

KHAW, AMBROSE   K00668
     THE HERALD AFFAIR
     STRAITS TIMES(SIN) 25 MAY 1971
     ##/SINSP; LETTER TO EDITOR.
     CHRON: 1970-1980
     GEOG: SINGAPORE
     SUBJ: CONTROL

KHOO BOON CHOO   K00669
     LINKING THE PEOPLE THROUGH MASS MEDIA AIM OF
          SCHOOL OF HUMANITIES
     STRAITS TIMES 6 OCT 1972
     ##/MALSP
     MEDIUM: GENERAL
     CHRON: 1970-1980
     GEOG: MALAYSIA
     SUBJ: DEVELOPMENT DESCRIPTION

KHOUW GIOK PO [COMPILER]   K00670
     BOOKS ON JOURNALISM PUBLISHED IN INDONESIA
     GAZETTE II:3(1956), 190.
     CHRON: SURVEY
     GEOG: INDONESIA
     SUBJ: RESEARCH

KHURSHID, A. S.   K00671
     NEWSLETTERS IN THE ORIENT: WITH SPECIAL
          REFERENCE TO THE INDO - PAKISTAN
          SUB-CONTINENT
     ASSEN, NETHERLANDS, ROYAL VAN GORCOM,
          1956.
     CHRON: SURVEY
     METH: HISTORICAL
     GEOG: SO/WEST ASI
     SUBJ: JRN HISTORY

KIHSS, PETER   K00672
    UNESCO IS ACCUSED ON PRESS FREEDOM
    NYT 1 JULY 1976
    ##/FREE
    CHRON: 1970-1980
    GEOG: OTHER   WORLD
    SUBJ: CONTROL   FLOW/AGENCY

KIM, D. S.   K00673
    THE NEWSPAPER IN KOREA
    IN WILLIAMS W01152, PP. 459-60.
    #3
    CHRON: 1910-1946
    GEOG: EAST ASIA
    SUBJ: DESCRIPTION

KIM, DONG-SUNG   K00674
    JOURNALISM IN KOREA
    IN WILLIAMS W01152, PP. 521-4.
    #3
    CHRON: 1910-1946
    GEOG: EAST ASIA
    SUBJ: DESCRIPTION

KING, FRANK H. AND PRESCOTT CLARKE,   K00675
        EDITORS.
    A RESEARCH GUIDE TO CHINA-COAST NEWSPAPERS
        1822-1911.
    CAMBRIDGE, HARVARD U. PRESS, 1965.
    HARVARD EAST ASIAN MONOGRAPHS NO. 18
    CHRON: BEFORE 1910
    METH: HISTORICAL
    GEOG: HONG KONG   MACAO   CHINA
    SUBJ: RESEARCH

KING, VINCENT V. S.   K00676
    A GENERAL STUDY OF THE CHANNELS OF
        COMMUNICATION BETWEEN COMMUNIST CHINA
        AND THE WESTERN WORLD
    CAMBRIDGE, CENTER FOR INTERNATIONAL STUDIES,
        MIT, 1964.
    C/64-9, 94 PP., MIMEO.
    MEDIUM: GENERAL
    CHRON: SURVEY
    METH: OTHER OR COMB
    GEOG: CHINA   WORLD
    SUBJ: FLOW/AGENCY

KIRKHAM, BARRY   K01827
    ASIAWEEK TAKES A LOOK AT ITS READERS
    MEDIA [HONG KONG] (FEB 1978), 10.
    ##/HKG
    CHRON: 1970-1980
    METH: SURVEY
    GEOG: HONG KONG   SEV ASIA
    SUBJ: DESCRIPTION

KLATT, WERNER, EDITOR.   K02573
    THE CHINESE MODEL: A POLITICAL, ECONOMIC AND
         SOCIAL SURVEY
    HONG KONG, HONG KONG U. PRESS, 1965.
    SEE HOWSE H00584.
    CHRON: 1960-1970
    METH: OTHER OR COMB
    GEOG: CHINA
    SUBJ: DEVELOPMENT DESCRIPTION

KLIMLEY, APRIL   K00678
    'I DIDN'T DARE TELL YOU' BY TAIWAN FILMAKER
         WHO DARED
    CSM 13 AUG 1971
    ##/TAI
    MEDIUM: FILM
    CHRON: 1970-1980
    GEOG: TAIWAN
    SUBJ: DESCRIPTION BIOGRAPHY

KLIMLEY, APRIL   K00679
    CAN ART CONQUER AUDIENCES?
    FEER LXXIII:39(25 SEPT 1971), 34.
    ##/TAI
    MEDIUM: FILM
    CHRON: 1970-1980
    GEOG: TAIWAN
    SUBJ: DESCRIPTION

KO KUNG-CHEN   K00680
    CHUNG-KUO PAO HSUEH SHIH (HISTORY OF CHINESE
         JOURNALISM)
    SHANGHAI, SHANG WU YIN SHU KUAN, 1927.
    ##/VF; REPRINTED BY TAI PING SHU JU, HONG
         KONG, 1964; SKINNER S00982
         II:41804; NUC 56-67 62:353.
                        LANG: CHINESE
    CHRON: SURVEY
    METH: HISTORICAL
    GEOG: CHINA
    SUBJ: JRN HISTORY

KOH MYUNG-SHIK   K01512
    DEVELOPMENT OF THE KOREAN PRESS
    KOREA JOURNAL 8:1(JAN 1968), 5-9.
    CHRON: 1960-1970
    METH: HISTORICAL
    GEOG: EAST ASIA
    SUBJ: JRN HISTORY

KOH TAI ANN   K01513
    COMMENT
    COMMENTARY [SINGAPORE] 4:1(SEPT 1971), 24-9.
    ##/SIN-2; SEE TAN T01415.
    CHRON: 1970-1980
    GEOG: SINGAPORE
    SUBJ: DEVELOPMENT

KOJIMA, HARUKO   K00681
    JAPANESE PRESS SELF-CONTROL
    FOI CENTER PUB. NO. 102 (JUNE 1963).
    ##/EASI
    CHRON: 1960-1970
    GEOG: EAST ASIA
    SUBJ: CONTROL   DESCRIPTION

KON, HIDEMI   K01576
    WOMEN'S MAGAZINES ARE MUCH READ BY JAPANESE
    THE PEIPING CHRONICLE 4 OCT 1940
    CHRON: 1910-1946
    GEOG: EAST ASIA
    SUBJ: DESCRIPTION

KOREA JOURNAL   K02001
    JAPANESE CENSORSHIP EXTENDS TO WASHINGTON
    III:10(DEC 1921), 4.
    CHRON: 1910-1946
    GEOG: EAST ASIA   U.S.
    SUBJ: CONTROL

KOREA REVIEW   K02002
    THE KOREAN PRESS
    III:9(NOV 1921), 7-9.
    FROM <JAPANESE WEEKLY CHRONICLE>
    CHRON: 1910-1946
    GEOG: EAST ASIA
    SUBJ: DESCRIPTION

KOREA REVIEW   K02029
    JAPANESE PRESS AND LORD NORTHCLIFF
    IV:3(MAY 1922), 9-10.
    CHRON: 1910-1946
    GEOG: EAST ASIA
    SUBJ: DESCRIPTION OTHER JRN

KOREA REVIEW   K02004
    REPORT OF THE PRESS CONGRESS COMMITTEE
    IV:5(JULY 1922), 12.
    CHRON: 1910-1946
    GEOG: EAST ASIA   SEV ASIA
    SUBJ: DESCRIPTION EDUCATION   OTHER JRN

KOREA REVIEW   K02003
    A JAPANESE JOURNALIST DENOUNCES AMERICA
    IV:5(JULY 1922), 9-10.
    CHRON: 1910-1946
    GEOG: EAST ASIA   U.S.
    SUBJ: FOR CORR   DESCRIPTION

KORNER, FRITZ   K02799
    DAS CHINESISCHE ZEITUNGSWESEN DER GEGENWART
    ZEITUNGSWISSENSCHAFT 1:5(15 MAY 1926), 76-7.
    ##/CHIN-9
                        LANG: OTHER EUROPEAN
    CHRON: 1910-1946
    GEOG: CHINA
    SUBJ: DESCRIPTION

KRAUSZ, GEORGE   K00682
    WITH OUR COLLEGUES IN SOUTHEAST ASIA
    DEMOCRATIC JOURNALIST VI:10(1958), 8-9.
    CHRON: 1946-1960   VERIF: UNVERIFIED
    GEOG: SEV ASIA
    SUBJ: FOR CORR   DESCRIPTION

KROEF, JUSTUS M. VAN DER   K00683
    THE PRESS IN INDONESIA: BYPRODUCT OF
        NATIONALISM
    JQ 31:3(1954), 337-46.
    CHRON: 1946-1960
    GEOG: INDONESIA
    SUBJ: DEVELOPMENT DESCRIPTION

KU T'ING-CH'ANG   05   K02173
    THE PROTESTANT PERIODICAL PRESS IN CHINA
    DIGEST OF THE SYNODAL COMMISSION (CATHOLIC
        CHURCH IN CHINA) XI:3(MAR 1938),
        264-319.
    CHRON: 1910-1946
    GEOG: CHINA
    SUBJ: DESCRIPTION

KUANG-TUNG WEN WU CHAN LAN HUI,   15   K02590
        EDITOR.
    KUANG-TUNG WEN WU (THE CULTURE OF
        KWANGTUNG)
    HONG KONG, CHUNG-KUO WEN HUA HSIEH CHIN HUI,
        1941.
    SEE WU 08W01180; SKINNER S00982 II:46431.
                        LANG: CHINESE
    CHRON: 1910-1946
    GEOG: CHINA
    SUBJ: DESCRIPTION

KULKARNI, V. G.   K01515
    CHINA SNAPS UP (AND SEND OUT) CAMERAS
    MEDIA [HONG KONG] 4:10(NOV 1976), 12.
    MEDIUM: GENERAL
    CHRON: 1970-1980
    GEOG: CHINA
    SUBJ: OTHER JRN

KULKARNI, V. G.   K01514
    MAGIC OF THE JOURNAL: HOW WILL IT PERFORM IN
        ASIA
    MEDIA [HONG KONG] 4:9-10(SEPT-OCT 1976), 39.
    CHRON: 1970-1980
    GEOG: SEV ASIA
    SUBJ: DESCRIPTION

KUNAU, JOHN A.   K01828
    THE PUBLISHING BUSINESS IN CHINA
    THE AMERICAN MERCURY XXXVII:145(JAN 1936),
        98-100.
    ##/CHIN-6
    CHRON: 1910-1946
    GEOG: CHINA
    SUBJ: PUBLISHING

KUNG MIN-CHUNG   K02303
    NEW BOOKS PUBLISHED IN CHINA, 1946-48
    THE CHINA WEEKLY REVIEW 114:3(18 JUNE 1949),
        55-6.
    CHRON: 1946-1960
    GEOG: CHINA
    SUBJ: PUBLISHING

KUO WEI-HUNG   K01395
    CHINA'S NEED OF A NATIONAL AND INDEPENDENT
        NEWS SERVICE
    THE CHINA WEEKLY REVIEW 71:6(5 JAN 1935),
        196-8.
    ##/CHIN-5
    CHRON: 1910-1946
    GEOG: CHINA
    SUBJ: FLOW/AGENCY

KUO, EDDIE C. Y.   K02598
    MULTILINGUALISM AND MASS MEDIA IN SINGAPORE
    ASIAN SURVEY XVIII:10(OCT 1978), 1067-1083.
    ##/SIN-2
    MEDIUM: GENERAL
    CHRON: 1970-1980
    GEOG: SINGAPORE
    SUBJ: LANGUAGE

KUO, HELENA [CHING-CHIU]   K01262
I'VE COME A LONG WAY
NEW YORK, D. APPLETON-CENTURY, 1942.
CHRON: 1910-1946
GEOG: SEV ASIA
SUBJ: FOR CORR

KUO, T. L.   11   K01829
CHINESE VERNACULAR PRESS IN SAN FRANCISCO
THE CHINA WEEKLY REVIEW 63:8(21 JAN 1933),
    344.
##/CHIN-US
CHRON: 1910-1946
GEOG: OSEAS CHIN   U.S.
SUBJ: DESCRIPTION

KUO, WEI-HUNG   11   K02646
LET US ORGANIZE
THE CHINA WEEKLY REVIEW 73:9(27 JULY
    1935), 295.
CHRON: 1910-1946
GEOG: CHINA
SUBJ: DESCRIPTION

KUO-WEN CHOU-PAO   K02108
CHENG-CHU TO-PIEN CHUNG CHIH SHANG-HAI
    YU-LUN (PUBLIC OPINION IN SHANGHAI
    DURING THE POLITICAL CRISIS)
I:15(9 NOV 1924), 7-12.
                        LANG: CHINESE
CHRON: 1910-1946
GEOG: CHINA
SUBJ: OTHER JRN

KURODA, KAZUO   K00685
REPORTING ON COMMUNIST CHINA IN JAPAN
NIEMAN REPORTS XI:1(JAN 1957), 3-4.
##/EASI
MEDIUM: GENERAL
CHRON: 1946-1960
GEOG: CHINA   EAST ASIA
SUBJ: FOR CORR   DESCRIPTION

KUWABARA, TAKEO, HIDETOSHI KATO,   K02644
    MINORU YAMADA
THE INTELLECTUAL ROLE OF JOURNALISM
JAPANESE INTERPRETER II:1(APR 1964),
    48-53.
FROM <KINDAI NIHON SHISOSHI KOZA>
    V(1960), PP. 142-83.
CHRON: SURVEY
GEOG: EAST ASIA
SUBJ: DESCRIPTION LAW/ETHICS

KWA, CHONG GUAN   K01396
    THE MASS MEDIA AND NATION BUILDING
    COMMENTARY [SINGAPORE] 4:1(SEPT 1971), 30-8.
    ##/SIN-2; SEE CHAN C01441.
    MEDIUM: GENERAL
    CHRON: 1970-1980
    GEOG: SINGAPORE
    SUBJ: DEVELOPMENT

KWEI, CHUNGSHU   K01516
    MOTION PICTURES IN CHINA
    CHINA REVIEW V:2(AUG 1923), 34-6.
    ##/FILM
    MEDIUM: FILM
    CHRON: 1910-1946
    GEOG: CHINA
    SUBJ: DESCRIPTION

KYI, KHIN MAUNG AND ASSOCIATES   K02601
    PROCESS OF COMMUNICATION IN MODERNIZATION OF
        RURAL SOCIETY, A SURVEY REPORT ON TWO
        BURMESE VILLAGES
    MALAYAN ECONOMIC REVIEW 18(PT. 1) (1973),
        55-73.
    ##/BURM
    MEDIUM: GENERAL
    CHRON: SURVEY
    METH: OTHER OR COMB
    GEOG: BURMA
    SUBJ: DEVELOPMENT

LACEY, JOSEPH   L00686
    THE DEVELOPMENT OF THE PRESS IN THE
        PHILIPPINES, BURMA, AND INDONESIA: A
        COMPARATIVE STUDY
    MASTERS THESIS, STANFORD UNIVERSITY, 1963.
    CHRON: 1960-1970
    METH: CONTENT ANALYSIS
    GEOG: BURMA   INDONESIA   PHILIPPINES
    SUBJ: DESCRIPTION

LACHICA, EDUARDO   L00687
    TV: JAPAN PIONEERS IN SATELLITE TRANSMISSION
    CSM 13 AUG 1971
    ##/EASI
    MEDIUM: ELECTRONIC
    CHRON: 1970-1980
    GEOG: EAST ASIA
    SUBJ: DESCRIPTION

LAI KUANG-LIN   16   L00688
    LIANG CH'I-CH'AO YU CHIN TAI PAO YEH (LIANG
        CH'I CH'AO AND MODERN JOURNALISM)
    TAIPEI, SHANG WU YIN SHU KUAN, 1968.
                            LANG: CHINESE
    CHRON: 1910-1946
    METH: HISTORICAL
    GEOG: CHINA
    SUBJ: DESCRIPTION BIOGRAPHY

LAI MING-CHI   07   L02277
    MING-CHI T'AN PAO (MING-CHI ON NEWSPAPERS)
    TAIPEI, N. G., 1978.
                            LANG: CHINESE
    CHRON: 1970-1980   VERIF: UNVERIFIED
    GEOG: TAIWAN
    SUBJ: DESCRIPTION OTHER JRN

LAI, LESLIE K.   L02230
    FACSIMILE BROADCASTING AND CHINA
    MASTERS THESIS, UNIVERSITY OF MISSOURI, 1951.
    MEDIUM: ELECTRONIC
    CHRON: 1946-1960
    METH: OTHER OR COMB
    GEOG: TAIWAN
    SUBJ: DESCRIPTION

LANIAUSKAS, VICTOR   L00690
    FOREIGN PRESS GIVEN HARD TIME IN SOUTHEAST
        ASIA
    CSM 8 MAR 1977
    ##/ASIA
    CHRON: 1970-1980
    GEOG: SEV ASIA
    SUBJ: FOR CORR   CONTROL

LANNING, GEORGE   L00691
    OLD FORCES IN NEW CHINA
    SHANGHAI, 'THE NATIONAL REVIEW' OFFICE, 1912.
    ##/CHIN-3; CHAP. XXXIII, CHINESE NEWSPAPER
        PRESS; CHAP. XXXIV,
        THE POWER OF BOOKS; NUC<56 315:469.
    CHRON: SURVEY
    METH: HISTORICAL
    GEOG: CHINA
    SUBJ: JRN HISTORY DESCRIPTION LITERATURE

LASKER, BRUNO AND AGNES ROMAN   L01517
    PROPAGANDA FROM CHINA AND JAPAN
    NEW YORK, INSTITUTE OF PACIFIC RELATIONS,
        1938.
    MEDIUM: GENERAL
    CHRON: 1910-1946
    GEOG: CHINA   EAST ASIA
    SUBJ: PROPAGANDA

LATTIMORE, OWEN   L01830
    FACTS DO NOT SPEAK FOR THEMSELVES
    PACIFIC AFFAIRS 7:2(JUNE 1934), 202-5.
    ##/CHIN-6; REPRINTED IN <THE PEIPING
        CHRONICLE> P01971.
    CHRON: 1910-1946
    GEOG: CHINA   RUSSIA   WORLD
    SUBJ: FOR CORR

LAU TZU-CHING   15   L00699
    CHRONOLOGY OF NEWSPAPERS IN SOUTH-EAST ASIA
    JRNL OF SOUTH SEAS SOCIETY XIII:25, PART
        1(JUNE 1957), 58-68.
    ##/ASIA; AUTHOR IN WADE-GILES IS LIU.
                          LANG: CHINESE
    CHRON: SURVEY
    METH: HISTORICAL
    GEOG: SEV ASIA
    SUBJ: JRN HISTORY

LAU WEI-SAN   L01831
    THE UNIVERSITY OF MISSOURI AND JOURNALISM
        OF CHINA
    MASTERS THESIS, UNIVERSITY OF MISSOURI, 1949.
    CHRON: SURVEY
    METH: HISTORICAL
    GEOG: CHINA
    SUBJ: JRN HISTORY BIOGRAPHY

LAUFER, BERTHOLD   L01577
    PAPER AND PRINTING IN ANCIENT CHINA
    NEW YORK, BURT FRANKLIN, 1931.
    CHRON: BEFORE 1910
    METH: HISTORICAL
    GEOG: CHINA
    SUBJ: JRN HISTORY PRINTING

LEE HSING-CHU   L02231
    NEWS PRACTICES OF FORMOSA RADIO STATIONS
    MASTERS THESIS, UNIVERSITY OF MISSOURI,
        1960. ,
    MEDIUM: ELECTRONIC
    CHRON: 1960-1970
    METH: OTHER OR COMB
    GEOG: TAIWAN
    SUBJ: DESCRIPTION

LEE KUAN YEW   L01578
    WHEN THE FREEDOM OF THE PRESS AND OTHER NEWS
        MEDIA SHOULD BE SUBORDINATED
    MALAYSIA (JULY 1971), 7-10.
    TEXT OF SPEECH TO IPI/HELSINKI
    MEDIUM: GENERAL
    CHRON: 1970-1980
    GEOG: SINGAPORE
    SUBJ: CONTROL   DEVELOPMENT

LEE KUAN YEW   L01423
    THE MASS MEDIA AND NEW COUNTRIES
    ASIA PACIFIC RECORD 2:3(JUNE 1971), 15-8.
    ##/SIN-2
    MEDIUM: GENERAL
    CHRON: 1970-1980
    GEOG: SINGAPORE   WORLD
    SUBJ: CONTROL   DEVELOPMENT

LEE MAU-SENG   L01967
    BETTER RED THAN DEAD
    FEER 99:13(31 MAR 1978), 6.
    ##/SIN-2; LETTER TO EDITOR.
    CHRON: 1970-1980
    GEOG: SINGAPORE
    SUBJ: CONTROL   BIOGRAPHY

LEE SANG-HI   L01518.
    EDUCATION OF KOREAN JOURNALISTS
    KOREA JOURNAL 8:1(JAN 1968), 18-19, 21.
    CHRON: 1960-1970
    GEOG: EAST ASIA
    SUBJ: EDUCATION

LEE, B. Y.   L02304
    MODERN PAPER MANUFACTURING IN SHANGHAI
    THE CHINA WEEKLY REVIEW XLVII:10(2 FEB 1929),
        407.
    CHRON: 1910-1946
    GEOG: CHINA
    SUBJ: PRINTING

LEE, EDWARD BING-SHUEY   L01832
    CHINA'S LACK OF INTERNATIONAL PUBLICITY
    THE CHINA WEEKLY REVIEW 56:7(18 APR 1931),
        231, 238.
    CHRON: 1910-1946
    GEOG: CHINA
    SUBJ: PROPAGANDA

LEE, JOHN   L00700
    INTERNATIONAL NEWS FLOW IN EXPATRIATE
        ENGLISH LANGUAGE PRESS
    JQ 42:2(AUTUMN 1965), 632-8.
    ##/INTL
    CHRON: 1960-1970
    GEOG: WORLD
    SUBJ: FLOW/AGENCY

LEE, MARY   L02563
    SEE NOW, BUY LATER
    FEER 104:18(4 MAY 1979), 81-2.
    MEDIUM: GENERAL
    CHRON: 1970-1980
    GEOG: CHINA
    SUBJ: OTHER JRN

LEE, MARY   L02280
    A LICENCE TO LOSE MONEY
    FEER 101:36(8 SEPT 1978), 17-19.
    ##/HKG; COMMERCIAL TELEVISION.
    MEDIUM: ELECTRONIC
    CHRON: 1970-1980
    GEOG: HONG KONG
    SUBJ: DESCRIPTION OTHER JRN

LEE, MARY   L02279
    LOOKING FOR QUALITY CONTROL
    FEER 101:33(18 AUG 1978), 22-3.
    ##/SIN-2
    CHRON: 1970-1980
    GEOG: SINGAPORE
    SUBJ: DESCRIPTION OTHER JRN

LEE, MARY   L02278
    SHOUTING TO BE HEARD
    FEER 101:31(4 AUG 1978), 20-1.
    ##/HKG
    MEDIUM: OTHER
    CHRON: 1970-1980
    GEOG: HONG KONG
    SUBJ: OTHER JRN

LEE, T. T.   L02305
    ARE SHANGHAI EDITORS SUFFERING FROM
        'EXTRALITY COMPLEX'?
    THE CHINA WEEKLY REVIEW 54:12(22 NOV 1930),
        426, 449.
    CHRON: 1910-1946
    GEOG: CHINA
    SUBJ: DESCRIPTION

LEEPER, ETHEL M., EDITOR.   L00701
    TOWARDS BETTER COMMUNICATIONS
    KUALA LUMPUR, U. S. INFORMATION SERVICE, 1969.
    CHRON: 1960-1970
    GEOG: MALAYSIA
    SUBJ: LAW/ETHICS EDUCATION

LEFEVER, ERNEST W.   L00702
    CBS AND NATIONAL DEFENSE, 1972-73
    JRNL OF COMMUNICATION 25:4(AUTUMN 1975),
        181-5.
    ##/VN
    MEDIUM: ELECTRONIC
    CHRON: 1970-1980
    METH: OTHER OR COMB
    GEOG: VIETNAM   U.S.
    SUBJ: PROPAGANDA DESCRIPTION

LENT, JOHN A.   L00704
    HISTORY OF THE JAPANESE PRESS
    GAZETTE 14(1968), 7-36.
    ##/EASI
    CHRON: SURVEY
    METH: HISTORICAL
    GEOG: EAST ASIA
    SUBJ: JRN HISTORY

LENT, JOHN A.   L00703
    THE PRESS OF THE PHILIPPINES: ITS HISTORY
        AND PROBLEMS
    JQ 43:4(1966), 739-52.
    ##/PHIL
    CHRON: SURVEY
    METH: HISTORICAL
    GEOG: PHILIPPINES
    SUBJ: JRN HISTORY

LENT, JOHN A.   L00707
    PHILLIPINE MEDIA AND NATION BUILDING: AN
        OVERVIEW
    GAZETTE XVI:1(1970), 2-12.
    ##/PHIL
    CHRON: 1970-1980
    GEOG: PHILIPPINES
    SUBJ: DEVELOPMENT DESCRIPTION

LENT, JOHN A.   L00706
    THE TROUBLED CHINESE DAILIES OF THE
        PHILIPPINES
    JQ 47:1(SPRING 1970), 131-8.
    ##/PHIL
    CHRON: 1970-1980
    GEOG: PHILIPPINES OTHER
    SUBJ: DESCRIPTION

LENT, JOHN A.   L00705
    THE PHILIPPINES PROVINCIAL PRESS
    SILLIMAN JOURNAL 16:3(1969), 273-90.
    IN JAS BIBLIOGRAPHY 1969, NO. 5993
    CHRON: 1960-1970   VERIF: UNVERIFIED
    GEOG: PHILIPPINES
    SUBJ: DESCRIPTION

LENT, JOHN A.   L00716
    IN MALAYSIA MASS MEDIA ARE STATE BUSINESS!
    INDIAN PRESS (FEB 1975) 19-21, 24.
    ##/MAL
    CHRON: 1970-1980
    GEOG: MALAYSIA
    SUBJ: CONTROL

LENT, JOHN A.   L00715
    MALAYSIAN CHINESE AND THEIR MASS MEDIA:
        HISTORY AND SURVEY
    ASIAN PROFILE 2:4(AUG 1974), 397-412.
    ##/MAL
    CHRON: 1970-1980
    GEOG: MALAYSIA   OTHER
    SUBJ: DESCRIPTION

LENT, JOHN A.   L00714
    MALAYSIA'S GUIDED MEDIA
    INDEX ON CENSORSHIP (WINTER 1974), 65-75.
    ##/MAL
    CHRON: 1970-1980
    GEOG: MALAYSIA
    SUBJ: CONTROL

LENT, JOHN A.   L00713
    THE PHILIPPINE PRESS UNDER MARTIAL LAW
    INDEX ON CENSORSHIP (SPRING 1974), 47-59.
    ##/PHIL
    CHRON: 1970-1980
    GEOG: PHILIPPINES
    SUBJ: CONTROL

LENT, JOHN A.   L00712
    FOREIGN NEWS CONTENT OF UNITED STATES
        AND ASIAN PRINT MEDIA: A LITERATURE
        REVIEW AND PROBLEM ANALYSIS
    LEWISBURG, PENN., MID-ATLANTIC REGION, AAS,
        10 NOV 1974.
    ##/INTL; MIMEO, 21 PP.
    CHRON: 1970-1980
    METH: CONTENT ANALYSIS
    GEOG: U.S.   SEV ASIA
    SUBJ: RESEARCH   DESCRIPTION

LENT, JOHN A.   L00711
    MASS MEDIA IN LAOS
    GAZETTE XX:3(1974), 171-9.
    ##/LAOS
    MEDIUM: GENERAL
    CHRON: 1970-1980
    GEOG: LAOS
    SUBJ: DESCRIPTION

LENT, JOHN A.   L00710
    A RELUCTANT REVOLUTION AMONG ASIAN NEWSPAPERS
    GAZETTE XVIII:1(1972), 1-23.
    ##/ASIA
    CHRON: 1970-1980
    GEOG: SEV ASIA
    SUBJ: DESCRIPTION

LENT, JOHN A.   L00709
    PHILIPPINE MASS COMMUNICATIONS: BEFORE 1811,
        AFTER 1966
    MANILA, PHILIPPINES PRESS INSTITUTE, 1971.
    #3
    CHRON: SURVEY
    METH: HISTORICAL
    GEOG: PHILIPPINES
    SUBJ: JRN HISTORY

LENT, JOHN A.   L02109
    MASS MEDIA IN MALAYSIA
    ASIAN PROFILE 6:2(APR 1978), 153-61.
    MEDIUM: GENERAL
    CHRON: 1970-1980
    GEOG: MALAYSIA
    SUBJ: DESCRIPTION

LENT, JOHN A.   L01263
    THE TRAGEDY OF MASS MEDIA IN LAOS
    INDIAN PRESS II:3(MAR 1975), 19-22, 23.
    ##/LAOS
    CHRON: 1970-1980
    GEOG: LAOS
    SUBJ: CONTROL   DESCRIPTION

LENT, JOHN A.   L01156
    'PROTECTING THE PEOPLE'
    INDEX ON CENSORSHIP 4:3(AUTUMN 1975), 7-16.
    ##/SIN
    CHRON: 1970-1980
    GEOG: SINGAPORE
    SUBJ: CONTROL

LENT, JOHN A.   L00724
    FOREIGN NEWS IN AMERICAN MEDIA
    JRNL OF COMMUNICATION 27:1(WINTER 1977),
        46-51.
    ##/INTL
    MEDIUM: GENERAL
    CHRON: 1970-1980
    METH: CONTENT ANALYSIS
    GEOG: U.S.   WORLD
    SUBJ: FLOW/AGENCY DESCRIPTION

LENT, JOHN A.   L00723
    MOST PHILIPPINES PAPERS STICK TO GOVERNMENT
        LINE UNDER MARTIAL LAW
    IPI REPORT 25:11(NOV 1976), 5,12.
    CHRON: 1970-1980
    GEOG: PHILIPPINES
    SUBJ: CONTROL

LENT, JOHN A.   L00722
    TELEVISION IN MALAYSIA
    TELEVISION QUARTERLY XIII:2(MAY-JULY 1976),
        51-5.
    ##/MAL
    MEDIUM: FILM
    CHRON: 1970-1980
    GEOG: MALAYSIA
    SUBJ: DESCRIPTION

LENT, JOHN A.   L00721
    THE MOTION PICTURE OF MALAYSIA: HISTORY AND
        PROBLEMS
    ASIAN PROFILE 4:3(JUNE 1976), 261-270.
    ##/MAL-2
    CHRON: 1970-1980
    METH: HISTORICAL
    GEOG: MALAYSIA
    SUBJ: JRN HISTORY

LENT, JOHN A.   L00720
    FOREIGN NEWS CONTENT OF UNITED STATES
        AND ASIAN PRINT MEDIA: A LITERATURE
        REVIEW AND PROBLEM ANALYSIS
    GAZETTE XXII:3(1976), 169-82.
    ##/MISC
    CHRON: 1970-1980
    METH: CONTENT ANALYSIS
    GEOG: U.S.   SEV ASIA
    SUBJ: RESEARCH   DESCRIPTION

LENT, JOHN A.   L00719
    MALAYSIA SHORT ON MEDIA
    GRASSROOTS EDITOR (FALL 1976), 5-6.
    ##/MAL-2
    CHRON: 1970-1980
    GEOG: MALAYSIA
    SUBJ: DESCRIPTION

LENT, JOHN A.   L00718
    ASIAN MASS COMMUNICATION: A COMPREHENSIVE
        BIBLIOGRAPHY
    PHILADELPHIA, TEMPLE U., SCHOOL OF
        COMMUNICATIONS AND THEATER, 1975.
    ALSO SEE LENT L02746 1977 SUPPLEMENT
    MEDIUM: GENERAL
    CHRON: SURVEY
    GEOG: SEV ASIA
    SUBJ: RESEARCH

LENT, JOHN A.   L00717
    ENGLISH-LANGUAGE MASS MEDIA OF MALAYSIA:
        HISTORICAL AND CONTEMPORARY PERSPECTIVE
    GAZETTE XXI:2(1975), 95-113.
    ##/MAL
    MEDIUM: GENERAL
    CHRON: 1970-1980
    GEOG: MALAYSIA
    SUBJ: JRN HISTORY DESCRIPTION

LENT, JOHN A.   L02525
    PRESS FREEDOM IN ASIA: THE QUIET, BUT
        COMPLETED, REVOLUTION
    GAZETTE XXIV:1(1978), 41-60.
    ##/ASIA
    CHRON: 1970-1980
    GEOG: SEV ASIA
    SUBJ: CONTROL   DESCRIPTION

LENT, JOHN A.   L02746
    ASIAN MASS COMMUNICATIONS: A COMPREHENSIVE
        BIBLIOGRAPHY 1977 SUPPLEMENT
    PHILADELPHIA, SCHOOL OF COMMUNICATIONS AND
        THEATER, TEMPLE UNIVERSITY,1978.
    SEE ALSO LENT L00718
    MEDIUM: GENERAL
    CHRON: SURVEY
    METH: OTHER OR COMB
    GEOG: SEV ASIA
    SUBJ: RESEARCH

LENT, JOHN A.   L02647
    THE PHILIPPINES
    IN LENT L00708, PP. 191-209.
    CHRON: SURVEY
    METH: OTHER OR COMB
    GEOG: PHILIPPINES
    SUBJ: JRN HISTORY DESCRIPTION

LENT, JOHN A., EDITOR.   L01833
    CULTURAL PLURALISM IN MALAYSIA: POLITY,
        MILITARY, MASS MEDIA, EDUCATION,
        RELIGION AND SOCIAL CLASS
    DE KALB, ILL., CENTER FOR SOUTHEAST ASIAN
        STUDIES/NIU, 1977.
    ##/MAL-3
    MEDIUM: GENERAL
    CHRON: 1970-1980
    GEOG: MALAYSIA
    SUBJ: CONTROL   DEVELOPMENT DESCRIPTION

LENT, JOHN A., EDITOR.   L00708
    THE ASIAN NEWSPAPERS' RELUCTANT REVOLUTION
    AMES, IOWA, IOWA STATE U. PRESS, 1971.
    CHRON: SURVEY
    METH: OTHER OR COMB
    GEOG: SEV ASIA
    SUBJ: RESEARCH   DESCRIPTION

LESLIE, DONALD D., ET AL., EDITORS.   L02567
    ESSAYS ON THE SOURCES FOR CHINESE HISTORY
    CANBERRA, AUST. NATIONAL UNIVERSITY, 1973.
    SEE FASS F00480
    CHRON: SURVEY
    GEOG: CHINA
    SUBJ: RESEARCH

LETCHMIKANTHAN, R.   L01520
    KUALA LUMPUR'S COMPUTER NEWSROOM, THE FIRST
        OF ITS KIND EAST OF SUEZ
    MEDIA [HONG KONG] 4:2(FEB 1973), 18-19.
    CHRON: 1970-1980
    GEOG: MALAYSIA
    SUBJ: DESCRIPTION PUBLISHING

LETCHMIKANTHAN, R.   L01519
    MALAYSIA RECONSIDERS 'PRESS COUNCIL' PLAN
    MEDIA [HONG KONG] 4:1(JAN 1977), 21.
    CHRON: 1970-1980
    GEOG: MALAYSIA
    SUBJ: CONTROL   LAW/ETHICS

LETCHMIKANTHAN, R.   L01521
    NEW STRAITS TIMES PUSHES NORTHWARDS
    MEDIA [HONG KONG] 4:2(FEB 1977), 25.
    CHRON: 1970-1980
    GEOG: MALAYSIA
    SUBJ: DESCRIPTION

LEW TIEN   L02232
    THE RADIO BROADCASTING ENTERPRISE OF
        FREE CHINA
    MASTERS THESIS, UNIVERSITY OF MISSOURI, 1958.
    MEDIUM: ELECTRONIC
    CHRON: 1946-1960
    METH: OTHER OR COMB
    GEOG: TAIWAN
    SUBJ: DESCRIPTION

LEWIS, JOHN WILSON   L00727
    CHINA'S SECRET MILITARY PAPERS:
        'CONTINUITIES' AND 'REVELATIONS'
    CHINA QUARTERLY NO. 18(APR/JUNE 1964), 67-78.
    ##/CHIN-2
    CHRON: 1960-1970
    GEOG: CHINA
    SUBJ: OTHER JRN   POLIT SCI

LI CHAN   07   L00730
    KUANG PO T'ING CHUNG I CHIEN' YU 'KUANG PO
        HSIN WEN HSIAO KUO CH'A PAO KAO SHU
    TAIPEI, KUO LI CHENG CHIH TA HSUEH, MIN I TIAO
    (REPORT ON 'RADIO AUDIENCE OPINION' AND
        'ANALYSIS OF THE EFFECTS
    OF RADIO NEWS BROADCASTING'); MIMEO;
        SKINNER S00982 II:46540.
    MEDIUM: ELECTRONIC   LANG: CHINESE
    CHRON: 1970-1980   VERIF: UNVERIFIED
    METH: OTHER OR COMB
    GEOG: TAIWAN
    SUBJ: DESCRIPTION

LI CHAN   07   L00729
     CHUNG-KUO PAO YEH P'ING I HUI (THE CHINESE
          PRESS COUNCIL)
     IN LI L02576, PP. 237-56.
                         LANG: CHINESE
     CHRON: 1960-1970   VERIF: UNVERIFIED
     GEOG: TAIWAN
     SUBJ: LAW/ETHICS

LI CHAN   07   L02281
     WO KUO HSIN WEN CHENG TS'E (PRESS POLICY OF
          CHINA)
     TAIPEI, YU SHIH YUEH K'AN SHE, 1972.
                         LANG: CHINESE
     CHRON: 1970-1980
     GEOG: TAIWAN
     SUBJ: CONTROL   LAW/ETHICS

LI CHAN   07   L02576
     KO KUO YEH TZU LU PI CHIAO YEN CHIU (PRESS
          COUNCILS AND PRESS CODES IN VARIOUS
          COUNTRIES)
     TAIPEI, KUO LI CHENG CHIH TA HSUEH, 1969.
     SEE LI 07L00729
                         LANG: CHINESE
     CHRON: 1960-1970   VERIF: UNVERIFIED
     GEOG: TAIWAN
     SUBJ: LAW/ETHICS

LI CHUNG-FA   L02306
     PRESS FREEDOM AT GENEVA:EAST VS. WEST
     THE CHINA WEEKLY REVIEW 109:12(22 MAY 1948),
          369-71.
     CHRON: 1946-1960
     GEOG: CHINA   EUROPE
     SUBJ: CONTROL

LI LUNG-MU   07   L00731
     'WU SSU' SHIH CH'I PAO K'AN KUNG TSO TI KAI
          KO (REFORMS IN THE PUBLICATION OF
          PERIODICALS DURING THE MAY FOURTH PERIOD)
     CHIEH FANG 9(1959).
     SKINNER S00982 II:46486; REPRINT AVAILABLE.
                         LANG: CHINESE
     CHRON: 1910-1946   VERIF: UNVERIFIED
     METH: HISTORICAL
     GEOG: CHINA
     SUBJ: JRN HISTORY

LI SHENG-WEN   07   L00732
     TA HSUEH SHENG HSIN WEN T'ING TU HSI KUAN
          YEN CHIU
     UNPUB MASTERS THESIS IN JOURNALISM, 1962.
     (COLLEGE STUDENTS AND THE NEWS MEDIA: A STUDY
          OF READING AND LISTENING
          HABITS); SKINNER
          S00982 II:46541.
     MEDIUM: GENERAL   LANG: CHINESE
     CHRON: 1960-1970   VERIF: UNVERIFIED
     METH: OTHER OR COMB
     GEOG: TAIWAN
     SUBJ: DESCRIPTION

LI TIEN-YI   07   L02747
   CHINESE NEWSPAPER MANUAL
   NEW HAVEN, CONNECTICUT, FAR EASTERN
      PUBLICATIONS, YALE UNIVERSITY,1953.
   CHRON: SURVEY
   GEOG: CHINA
   SUBJ: RESEARCH   LANGUAGE

LI TZE-CHUNG   L00733
   BOOK PUBLISHING IN THE REPUBLIC OF CHINA
   MEXICO CITY, 30TH INTL. CONGRESS OF HUMAN
      SCIENCES IN ASIA AND NORTH AFRICA, 1976.
   ##/TAI; MIMEO, 9 PP.
   CHRON: 1970-1980
   GEOG: TAIWAN
   SUBJ: DESCRIPTION PUBLISHING

LI WEN-CH'ING   07   L02282
   HSIN-WEN P'ING-I SHIH-ERH-NIEN (TWELVE YEARS
      OF NEWSPAPER ARBITRATION)
   TAIPEI, N. G., 1975.
                         LANG: CHINESE
   CHRON: SURVEY   VERIF: UNVERIFIED
   GEOG: TAIWAN
   SUBJ: OTHER JRN

LI YU-NING   L02599
   'BOLSHEVIK': AN EARLY CCP ORGAN
   CHINESE STUDIES IN HISTORY VIII:4(SUMMER
      1975), 27-53.
   CHRON: 1910-1946
   GEOG: CHINA
   SUBJ: PROPAGANDA   DESCRIPTION

LI, CHAN   07   L01579
   SHIH CHIEH HSIN WEN SHIH [HISTORY OF WORLD
      JOURNALISM]
   TAIPEI, K'UO LI CHENG CHIH DA HSUEH
      YEN CHIU SO, 1966.
                         LANG: CHINESE
   CHRON: 1960-1970
   GEOG: WORLD
   SUBJ: DESCRIPTION

LI, TI-TSUN   L01355
   THE PRESS AND PRESS REGULATION
   IN CHINA PRESS C02568, P. 40.
   ##/FILM
   CHRON: 1910-1946
   GEOG: CHINA
   SUBJ: LAW/ETHICS

LIANG CHI-CHAO   11   L02174
    LIANG CHI CHAO'S COMMENTS ON JOURNALISM
    COLUMBIA, MISSOURI, PRESS OF THE CRIPPLED
        TURTLE, 1953.
    ##/CHIN-8; NUC<1956 331:392; C. Y. SHEN,
        TRANSLATOR.
    CHRON: 1910-1946
    GEOG: CHINA
    SUBJ: CONTROL   DESCRIPTION LAW/ETHICS

LIANG, H. S.   L02005
    MINISTER WANG ON THE FOREIGN PRESS IN CHINA
    FAR EASTERN INFORMATION BUREAU BULLETIN
        I:10(1 SEPT 1929), 6-7.
    ##/CHIN-6
    CHRON: 1910-1946
    GEOG: CHINA   OTHER
    SUBJ: DESCRIPTION

LIANG, HUBERT S.   L01834
    SPEAKING OF PRESS CENSORSHIP
    THE CHINA CRITIC 11:2(10 OCT 1935), 35.
    CHRON: 1910-1946
    GEOG: CHINA
    SUBJ: CONTROL

LIANG, HUBERT S.   L01835
    RECORD OF JOURNALISM EDUCATION IN CHINA AND
        ITS FUTURE NEED
    JQ 23:1(MAR 1946), 69-72, 130.
    ##/CHIN-5
    CHRON: 1910-1946
    GEOG: CHINA
    SUBJ: EDUCATION

LIANG, HUBERT S.   L01399
    JOURNALISTIC EDUCATION IN CHINA
    THE CHINA QUARTERLY (MAR 1936), 65-9.
    ##/CHIN-5
    CHRON: 1910-1946
    GEOG: CHINA
    SUBJ: EDUCATION

LIANG, HUBERT S.   L01353
    SOME SIGNIFICANT TRENDS IN CHINESE JOURNALISM
    CHINA CRITIC X:8(22 AUG 1935), 178-9.
    ##/CHIN-5
    CHRON: 1910-1946
    GEOG: CHINA
    SUBJ: DESCRIPTION

LIANG, HUBERT S.   L00728
    DEVELOPMENT OF THE MODERN CHINESE PRESS
    NANKING, COUNCIL OF INTERNATIONAL AFFAIRS,
        12 MAY 1937.
    ##/CHIN-2; INFORMATION BULLETIN 4:1; 19 PP.
    CHRON: SURVEY
    METH: HISTORICAL
    GEOG: CHINA
    SUBJ: JRN HISTORY DESCRIPTION

LIANG, HUBERT S.   L02307
    PEIPING-TIENTSIN JOURNALISTS ORGANIZE
        ASSOCIATION
    THE CHINA WEEKLY REVIEW 75:6(11 JAN 1936),
        202.
    CHRON: 1910-1946
    GEOG: CHINA
    SUBJ: DESCRIPTION

LIANG, WILLIAM W. Y.   11   L02175
    THE CHINESE PRESS IN THE TERRITORY OF HAWAII
    DIGEST OF THE SYNODAL COMMISSION (CATHOLIC
        CHURCH IN CHINA) 10:12(DEC 1937),
        1025-8.
    ##/CHIN-US
    CHRON: 1910-1946
    GEOG: OSEAS CHIN   U.S.
    SUBJ: DESCRIPTION

LIAO, KUAN-SHENG AND ALLEN S. WHITING   L00734
    CHINA PRESS PERCEPTIONS OF THREAT: THE
        U. S. AND INDIA, 1962
    CHINA QUARTERLY NO. 53(JAN/MAR 1973), 80-97.
    ##/CHIN
    CHRON: 1970-1980
    METH: CONTENT ANALYSIS
    GEOG: CHINA
    SUBJ: DESCRIPTION POLIT SCI

LIBRARY OF CONGRESS   L00735
    NEWSPAPERS IN MICROFILM: FOREIGN COUNTRIES,
        1948-1972
    WASHINGTON, D. C., LIBRARY OF CONGRESS, 1973.
    NEW ANNUAL SERIES BEGAN 1974 (ENTRIES TO
        1974) WITH DOMESTIC
        AND FOREIGN COMBINED
    CHRON: SURVEY
    GEOG: WORLD
    SUBJ: RESEARCH

LIEBERMAN, HENRY   L00736
    HOW THE 'NEW YORK TIMES' COVERS THE CHINESE
        PEOPLES' REPUBLIC AND THE U. S. S. R.
    GAZETTE III:1,2(1957), 9-14.
    ##/US
    CHRON: 1946-1960
    GEOG: CHINA   RUSSIA
    SUBJ: FOR CORR   DESCRIPTION

LIEBERTHAL, KENNETH   L01590
    THE FOREIGN POLICY DEBATE IN PEKING AS SEEN
        THROUGH ALLEGORICAL ARTICLES, 1973-1976
    LOS ANGELES, RAND CORP., 1977.
    RAND PAPER P-5768.
    CHRON: 1970-1980   VERIF: UNVERIFIED
    GEOG: CHINA
    SUBJ: PROPAGANDA POLIT SCI

LIFSHULTZ, LAWRENCE   L00737
    DATELINE DELHI--FOR THE LAST TIME
    FEER 91:8(20 FEB 1976), 25-8.
    ##/SWAS
    CHRON: 1970-1980
    GEOG: SO/WEST ASI
    SUBJ: FOR CORR   CONTROL

LILLIE, J. J.   L01836
    JOURNALISM IN THE FAR EAST
    SATURDAY REVIEW [OF POLITICS, LITERATURE,
        SCIENCE AND ART. LONDON] 86(2 JULY 1898),
        8-9.
    ##/THAI; <SIAM FREE PRESS>; SEE
        FAIRPLAY F01801 AND STANDING S01894.
    CHRON: BEFORE 1910
    GEOG: THAILAND
    SUBJ: CONTROL

LIM HUCK TEE, COMPILER.   L01241
    MASS COMMUNICATIONS IN MALAYSIA: AN
        ANNOTATED BIBLIOGRAPHY
    SINGAPORE, AMIC, 1975.
    BIBLIOGRAPHY SERIES 1
    MEDIUM: GENERAL
    CHRON: 1970-1980
    GEOG: MALAYSIA
    SUBJ: RESEARCH

LIM, PUI HUEN P.   L01341
    NEWSPAPERS PUBLISHED IN THE MALAYSIAN AREA;
        WITH A UNION LIST OF LOCAL HOLDINGS
    SINGAPORE, INSTITUTE OF SOUTHEAST ASIAN
        STUDIES, 1970.
    OCCASIONAL PAPER NO. 2
    CHRON: SURVEY
    GEOG: MALAYSIA   SINGAPORE
    SUBJ: RESEARCH

LIM, PUI HUEN P.   L01323
    NEWS RESOURCES ON SOUTHEAST ASIAN RESEARCH
    SINGAPORE, INSTITUTE OF SOUTHEAST ASIAN
        STUDIES, 1976.
    #3
    CHRON: SURVEY
    GEOG: SEV ASIA
    SUBJ: RESEARCH   DESCRIPTION

LIN YU   L01837
    CHINESE PERIODICALS
    THE CHINA REVIEW [LONDON] V:5(SEPT 1936),
        13-14.
    CHRON: 1910-1946
    GEOG: CHINA
    SUBJ: RESEARCH

LIN YU   08   L01522
    CHINESE DAILIES IN THE SOUTH SEAS
    THE CHINA CRITIC VII:35(30 AUG 1934), 860.
    ##/FILM
    CHRON: 1910-1946
    GEOG: OSEAS CHIN SEV ASIA
    SUBJ: DESCRIPTION

LIN YU   08   L01523
    CHINESE PERIODICALS
    THE CHINA CRITIC XII:10(5 MAR 1936), 229-31.
    ##/FILM
    CHRON: 1910-1946
    GEOG: CHINA
    SUBJ: DESCRIPTION

LIN YU, EDITOR.   L01354
    OVERSEA CHINESE: CHINESE READING PUBLIC IN
        KUALA LUMPUR
    CHINA CRITIC XI:11(12 DEC 1936), 256.
    ##/CHIN-5; LIBRARY USERS.
    CHRON: 1910-1946
    GEOG: MALAYSIA   OSEAS CHIN
    SUBJ: OTHER NON-J

LIN YU-LAN   08   L02748
    YI FEN PAI NIEN CHIEN TI HUA TZU JIH JAO (A
        CHINESE NEWSPAPER OF A CENTURY AGO)
    PAO HSUEH [TAIPEI] III:8(JUNE 1967), 84-91.
                        LANG: CHINESE
    CHRON: BEFORE 1910
    METH: HISTORICAL
    GEOG: CHINA
    SUBJ: JRN HISTORY DESCRIPTION

LIN YU-LAN   08   L02749
    HSIANG KANG PAO YEH CHAN SHIH LUEH (THE
        DEVELOPMENT OF THE PRESS IN HONGKONG)
    PAO HSUEH [TAIPEI] II:10(AUG 1962), 100-115.
                        LANG: CHINESE
    CHRON: SURVEY
    METH: HISTORICAL
    GEOG: HONG KONG
    SUBJ: JRN HISTORY

LIN YU-TANG   08   L01400
    MY EXPERIENCE IN READING A CHINESE DAILY
    THE CHINA WEEKLY REVIEW LII:5(30 MAR 1930),
        178, 180-1.
    ##/CHIN-5; FROM <THE CHINA CRITIC> LIN L01524.
    CHRON: 1910-1946
    GEOG: CHINA
    SUBJ: DESCRIPTION LANGUAGE

LIN YUAN-CH'I   08   L02526
    TI-PAO CHIH YEN-CHIU [STUDY OF THE PEKING
        GAZETTE]
    TAIPEI, HAN LIN CHU PAN SHE, 1977.
                        LANG: CHINESE
    CHRON: BEFORE 1910
    GEOG: CHINA
    SUBJ: JRN HISTORY

LIN YUTANG   08   L01524
    MY EXPERIENCE IN READING A CHINESE DAILY
    THE CHINA CRITIC III:11(13 MAR 1930),
        245-8.
    ##/FILM; REPRINTED IN LIN L01400.
    CHRON: 1910-1946
    GEOG: CHINA
    SUBJ: DESCRIPTION LITERATURE

LIN YUTANG   08   L00739
    A HISTORY OF THE PRESS AND PUBLIC OPINION IN
        CHINA
    LONDON, OXFORD U. PRESS, 1937.
    CHRON: SURVEY
    METH: HISTORICAL
    GEOG: CHINA
    SUBJ: PROPAGANDA DESCRIPTION

LIN YUTANG   08   L00740
    CONTEMPORARY CHINESE PERIODICAL LITERATURE
    T'IEN HSIA MONTHLY 2:3(MAR 1936), 225-44.
    ##/CHIN-2
    CHRON: 1910-1946
    GEOG: CHINA
    SUBJ: DESCRIPTION

LIN, MOUSHENG   L01648
    A GUIDE TO LEADING CHINESE PERIODICALS
    NEW YORK, CHINA INSTITUTE IN AMERICA, 1936.
    CHRON: 1910-1946
    GEOG: CHINA
    SUBJ: RESEARCH

LINANG, W.   L02110
     NORTH KALIMANTAN PEOPLE ARE SURE TO WIN
     THE AFRO-ASIAN JOURNALIST 7:1(MAR 1970),
          10-11.
     CHRON: 1970-1980
     GEOG: INDONESIA
     SUBJ: PROPAGANDA

LINDSTROM, SIEGFRIED F.   L01704
     THE CINEMA IN CINEMA-MINDED JAPAN
     ASIA XXXI:12(DEC 1931), 768-775.
     MEDIUM: FILM
     CHRON: 1910-1946
     GEOG: EAST ASIA
     SUBJ: DESCRIPTION

LINDT, A. R.   L01580
     SPECIAL CORRESPONDENT WITH BANDIT AND
          GENERAL IN MANCHURIA
     LONDON, COBDEN-SANDERSON, 1933.
     CHRON: 1910-1946
     GEOG: CHINA
     SUBJ: FOR CORR   DESCRIPTION

LING, C. P.   L02648
     EFFECTIVE ADVERTISING IN CHINA
     THE CHINA WEEKLY REVIEW (SUPPLEMENT) (10
          OCT 1928), 171, 184.
     CHRON: 1910-1946
     GEOG: CHINA
     SUBJ: OTHER JRN

LINGAT, R.   L02006
     LES TROIS BANGKOK RECORDERS
     THE JOURNAL OF THE SIAM SOCIETY XXVIII,
          PART 2(DEC 1935), 203-13.
     ##/THAI
                         LANG: OTHER EUROPEAN
     CHRON: BEFORE 1910
     GEOG: THAILAND
     SUBJ: RESEARCH   JRN HISTORY

LITERARY DIGEST   L01846
     CHINA'S 'MOSQUITO' NEWSPAPERS
     114:2(9 JULY 1932), 10.
     CHRON: 1910-1946
     GEOG: CHINA
     SUBJ: DESCRIPTION

LITERARY DIGEST   L01838
     GAGGING THE PRESS IN CHINA
     48(24 JAN 1914), 152.
     CHRON: 1910-1946
     GEOG: CHINA
     SUBJ: CONTROL

:LITERARY DIGEST   L01841
     PRESS CORRUPTION IN CHINA
     114:12(17 SEPT 1932), 12.
     CHRON: 1910-1946
     GEOG: CHINA
     SUBJ: PROPAGANDA DESCRIPTION

LITERARY DIGEST   L01840
     CHINA AND THE FOREIGN PRESS
     75:9(2 DEC 1922), 20.
     CHRON: 1910-1946
     GEOG: CHINA
     SUBJ: CONTROL   PROPAGANDA   DESCRIPTION

LITERARY DIGEST   L01839
     CHRISTIANITY'S JOURNALISTIC DOOR IN CHINA
     52:3(15 JAN 1916), 122.
     CHRON: 1910-1946
     GEOG: CHINA
     SUBJ: DESCRIPTION

LITERARY DIGEST, THE   L01063
     THE PRESS IN CHINA
     XCVII:13(30 JUNE 1928), 23-4.
     ##/CHIN-4
     CHRON: 1910-1946
     GEOG: CHINA
     SUBJ: DESCRIPTION

LIU CHIEN-SHUN   15   L02600
     HSIN WEN YU TA CHUNG CH'UAN PO [BROADCASTING
          AND JOURNALISM]
     TAIPEI [?], KUANG PO TIEN SHIH LI K'AN SHE,
          1972.
     MEDIUM: GENERAL   LANG: CHINESE
     CHRON: 1970-1980
     GEOG: TAIWAN
     SUBJ: DESCRIPTION

LIU HOH-HSUAN AND CHANG CHING-MING   15   L02176
    EDUCATION IN JOURNALISM AT YENCHING UNIVERSITY
    DIGEST OF THE SYNODAL COMMISSION (CATHOLIC
        CHURCH IN CHINA) XIV:3(MAR 1941), 223-45;
        PART 2, XIV:5(MAY 1941), 347-59.
    ##/CHIN-8
    CHRON: 1910-1946
    GEOG: CHINA
    SUBJ: EDUCATION

LIU KUANG-YEN   15   L02111
    HSIN WEN HSUEH CHIANG HUA [TALKS ON
        JOURNALISM]
    TAIPEI, CHUNG HUA WEN HUA CHU PAN
        CHIH YEH, 1952.
                        LANG: CHINESE
    CHRON: 1960-1970
    GEOG: TAIWAN
    SUBJ: DESCRIPTION

LIU KUANG-YEN   15   L02233
    HSIN WEN HSUEH [JOURNALISM]
    TAIPEI, TAIPEI LIAN HE CHU PAN SHE, 1951.
                        LANG: CHINESE
    CHRON: 1960-1970
    METH: OTHER OR COMB
    GEOG: TAIWAN
    SUBJ: EDUCATION

LIU KWANG-CHING   L00747
    AMERICANS AND CHINESE: A HISTORICAL ESSAY
        AND A BIBLIOGRAPHY
    CAMBRIDGE, HARVARD U. PRESS, 1963.
    NEWSPAPERS AND PERIODICALS, PP. 159-75;
        JOURNALISTS, PP. 132-3.
    CHRON: SURVEY
    METH: HISTORICAL
    GEOG: CHINA
    SUBJ: RESEARCH

LIU PU-T'UNG   15   L00748
    CHIN JIH CHIH TIEN-CHIN HSIN WEN CHIEH
        (JOURNALISM IN CONTEMPORARY TIENTSIN)
    HSIN PEI FANG 1:2(FEB 1931), 1-20.
                        LANG: CHINESE
    CHRON: 1910-1946
    GEOG: CHINA
    SUBJ: DESCRIPTION

LIU SHIH-HONG   L00749
    MAKING OF THE CHARACTERS
    FREE CHINA REVIEW XIX:3(MAR 1969), 19-25
        (PART 2); XIX:4(APR 1969), 20-6 (PART 3).
    ##/VF; PARTS 2 AND 3 ON USE OF CHARACTERS IN
        NEWSPAPERS.
    CHRON: SURVEY
    GEOG: CHINA
    SUBJ: LANGUAGE

LIU TZU CHENG   15   L00750
   CHRONOLOGY OF NEWSPAPERS IN SOUTHEAST ASIA
   SEE LAU TZU-CHING 15L00699
                              LANG: CHINESE
   CHRON: SURVEY
   METH: HISTORICAL
   GEOG: SEV ASIA
   SUBJ: JRN HISTORY

LIU TZU-CHENG   L00751
   CHINESE PUBLISHING ACTIVITIES IN SARAWAK
   JRNL OF SOUTH SEAS SOCIETY XX, PART 1 AND
      2(1965), 1-12.
                              LANG: CHINESE
   CHRON: 1960-1970
   GEOG: MALAYSIA   OSEAS CHIN
   SUBJ: DESCRIPTION

LIU WEN CH'U, EDITOR.   15   L01649
   CHE PAN KE SHIH CHI KUANG HUA JIH PAO
         CHIN SHIN CHI NIEN TSENG K'AN
   PENANG, KWONG WAH YIT POH, 1960.
   [THIS HALF CENTURY: GOLDEN ANNIVERSARY
         SUPPLEMENT TO <KWONG WAH YIT POH>]
                              LANG: CHINESE
   CHRON: 1960-1970
   GEOG: MALAYSIA
   SUBJ: JRN HISTORY DESCRIPTION

LIU, ALAN P. L.   L00745
   CONTROL OF PUBLIC INFORMATION AND ITS EFFECTS
         ON CHINA'S FOREIGN AFFAIRS
   ASIAN SURVEY XIV:10(OCT 1974), 936-51.
   MEDIUM: GENERAL
   CHRON: 1970-1980
   GEOG: CHINA
   SUBJ: CONTROL   PROPAGANDA POLIT SCI

LIU, ALAN P. L.   L00744
   IDEOLOGY AND INFORMATION: CORRESPONDENTS OF
         THE NEW CHINA NEWS AGENCY AND CHINESE
         FOREIGN POLICY MAKING
   JRNL OF INTERNATIONAL AFFAIRS XXVI(1972),
         131-145.
   MEDIUM: GENERAL
   CHRON: 1970-1980
   GEOG: CHINA
   SUBJ: FOR CORR   POLIT SCI

LIU, ALAN P. L.   L00743
   MASS COMMUNICATION AND MEDIA IN CHINA'S
         CULTURAL REVOLUTION
   JQ 46:2(SUMMER 1969), 314-9.
   ##/CHIN
   MEDIUM: GENERAL
   CHRON: 1960-1970
   GEOG: CHINA
   SUBJ: DESCRIPTION

LIU, ALAN P. L.   L00742
MOVIES AND MODERNIZATION IN COMMUNIST CHINA
JQ 43:2(SUMMER 1966), 319-24.
##/CHIN
MEDIUM: FILM
CHRON: 1960-1970
METH: OTHER OR COMB
GEOG: CHINA
SUBJ: DEVELOPMENT

LIU, ALAN P. L.   L01157
COMMUNICATIONS AND NATIONAL INTEGRATION IN
      COMMUNIST CHINA
BERKELEY, CALIF., U. OF CALIFORNIA, 1971.
MEDIUM: GENERAL
CHRON: 1970-1980
METH: OTHER OR COMB
GEOG: CHINA
SUBJ: DEVELOPMENT DESCRIPTION

LIU, ALAN P. L.   L01358
THE PRESS AND JOURNALS IN CHINA
CAMBRIDGE, MIT CENTER FOR INTERNATIONAL
      STUDIES, 1966.
C/66-9; NUC AUTHORS 68-72 57:354.
CHRON: 1960-1970
GEOG: CHINA
SUBJ: DESCRIPTION

LIU, ALAN P. L.   L01357
THE FILM INDUSTRY IN CHINA
CAMBRIDGE, MIT CENTER FOR INTERNATIONAL
      STUDIES, 1965.
C/65-5; NUC AUTHORS 68-72 57:354.
MEDIUM: FILM
CHRON: 1960-1970
GEOG: CHINA
SUBJ: DESCRIPTION

LIU, ALAN P. L.   L02649
COMMUNIST CHINA
IN LENT L00708, PP. 43-53.
CHRON: SURVEY
METH: HISTORICAL
GEOG: CHINA
SUBJ: JRN HISTORY DESCRIPTION

LIU, ALAN PING-LIU   L00741
GROWTH AND MODERNIZATION FUNCTIONS OF RURAL
      RADIO IN COMMUNIST CHINA
JQ 41:4(AUTUMN 1964), 573-7.
##/CHIN
MEDIUM: ELECTRONIC
CHRON: 1960-1970
METH: OTHER OR COMB
GEOG: CHINA
SUBJ: PROPAGANDA DEVELOPMENT DESCRIPTION

LIU, HAN C. AND SHELTON A. GUNARATNE   L00746
     FOREIGN NEWS IN TWO ASIAN DAILIES
     GAZETTE XVIII:1(1972), 37-41.
     ##/MISC; CEYLON DAILY NEWS (1970) AND TAIWAN
          DAILY NEWS (1967).
     CHRON: 1970-1980
     METH: CONTENT ANALYSIS
     GEOG: TAIWAN   SO/WEST ASI
     SUBJ: DESCRIPTION

LIU, HENRY Y.   L01581
     TAIWAN'S PRESS: POLITICAL COMMUNICATIONS
          LINK AND RESEARCH RESOURCE
     THE CHINA QUARTERLY NO. 71(SEPT 1977), 608.
     ##/CHIN-5; LETTER; SEE JACOBS J00637.
     CHRON: 1970-1980
     GEOG: TAIWAN
     SUBJ: RESEARCH

LIU, MELINDA   L01526
     CHANG RAISES A NEW GENERATION
     FEER 97:28(15 JULY 1977), 40-1.
     ##/LAOS; <THE NEW GENERATION>.
     CHRON: 1970-1980
     GEOG: TAIWAN
     SUBJ: DESCRIPTION

LIU, MELINDA   L01525
     THE <HUMANIST> TOUCH UPSETS THE CENSOR
     FEER 97:28(15 JULY 1977), 40.
     ##/LAOS; <CHINA HUMANIST MONTHLY>.
     CHRON: 1970-1980
     GEOG: TAIWAN
     SUBJ: CONTROL

LIU, MELINDA   L01968
     DELEGATES FULFILL A VITAL TASK
     FEER 99:13(31 MAR 1978), 6.
     ##/TAI
     CHRON: 1970-1980
     GEOG: TAIWAN
     SUBJ: CONTROL

LIU, MELINDA   L02064
     LETTER FROM TAIPEI [BOOK PIRATING]
     FEER 100:19(12 MAY 1978), 62.
     ##/TAI
     MEDIUM: OTHER
     CHRON: 1970-1980
     GEOG: TAIWAN
     SUBJ: PUBLISHING

LIU, MELINDA   L01969
    WRITERS FACE A FULL STOP
    FEER 100:15(14 APR 1978), 22-3.
    ##/TAI
    CHRON: 1970-1980
    GEOG: TAIWAN
    SUBJ: CONTROL

LIU, MELINDA   L02527
    HOW TO BE FIRST WITH THE NEWS
    FEER 102:51(22 DEC 1978), 21-3.
    ##/HKG
    CHRON: 1970-1980
    GEOG: HONG KONG
    SUBJ: DESCRIPTION

LIU, MELINDA   L02283
    LETTER FROM QUEMOY
    FEER 102:41(13 OCT 1978), 78.
    ##/TAI
    MEDIUM: OTHER
    CHRON: 1970-1980
    GEOG: TAIWAN
    SUBJ: PROPAGANDA

LIU, WEI-SEN   15 L01582
    HSIN WEN CHENG TS'E YEN CHIU [JOURNALISM
          POLICY RESEARCH]
    TAIPEI, CHUNG K'UO WEN KUNG YING SHE, 1954.
                          LANG: CHINESE
    CHRON: 1946-1960
    GEOG: TAIWAN
    SUBJ: DESCRIPTION LAW/ETHICS

LIVING AGE   L01842
    CENSORSHIP IN NORTH CHINA
    354:4461(JUNE 1938), 346-8.
    ##/CHIN-6; FROM <MANCHESTER GUARDIAN>.
    CHRON: 1910-1946
    GEOG: CHINA   EAST ASIA
    SUBJ: FOR CORR   CONTROL

LO.CHIA-LUN   19 L00752
    CHIN JIH CHUNG-KUO CHIH TSA CHIH CHIEN,
          I CHIU I CHIU NIEN (PERIODICALS IN
          CHINA, 1919)
    HSIN CH'AO 1:4(APR 1919), 623-32.
    SKINNER S00982 II:41859; REPRINT AVAILABLE.
                          LANG: CHINESE
                          VERIF: UNVERIFIED
    CHRON: 1910-1946
    GEOG: CHINA
    SUBJ: DESCRIPTION

LO HUI-MIN, EDITOR.   L00754
    THE CORRESPONDENCE OF G. E. MORRISON,
        1895-1912.
    NEW YORK, CAMBRIDGE U. PRESS, 1976, 2 VOLS.
    CHRON: SURVEY
    METH: HISTORICAL
    GEOG: CHINA
    SUBJ: FOR CORR   JRN HISTORY

LO LE   L02717
    KRATKAIA ISTORIA PECHATI V KITAI
    NARODNY KITAI 5(1957), 19-22, 27-29.
                           LANG: RUSSIAN
    CHRON: 1946-1960   VERIF: UNVERIFIED
    GEOG: CHINA
    SUBJ: DESCRIPTION

LO LIEH   08   L01705
    CHINA'S JOURNALISTIC EDUCATION IN TEN YEARS
    EXTRACTS FROM CHINESE MAGAZINES NO. 196(18
        JAN 1960), 8-13.
    FROM <HSIN-WEN CHAN-HSIEN> (NEWS FRONT)
        NO. 18 (24 SEPT 1959).
    MEDIUM: GENERAL
    CHRON: 1946-1960
    GEOG: CHINA
    SUBJ: EDUCATION

LO, KARL AND H. M. LAI, COMPILERS.   L02790
    CHINESE NEWSPAPERS PUBLISHED IN NORTH
        AMERICA, 1854-1975.
    WASHINGTON, D. C., CCRM/ARL, 1977.
    BIBLIOGRAPHIC SERIES NO. 16
    CHRON: SURVEY
    METH: OTHER OR COMB
    GEOG: OSEAS CHIN U.S.   W. HEMIS
    SUBJ: RESEARCH   JRN HISTORY

LONDON, MIRIAM AND IVAN D. LONDON   L02235
    CHINA'S 'BYROAD' NEWS LEAKS: A NEW PEOPLE'S
        CHANNEL
    FREEDOM AT ISSUE NO. 47(SEPT-OCT 1978), 9-12.
    ##/CHIN-8
    MEDIUM: OTHER
    CHRON: 1970-1980
    GEOG: CHINA
    SUBJ: DESCRIPTION

LONG, HWA SHU   L02234
    THE MODERN CHINESE PRESS ON TAIWAN
    MASTERS THESIS, UNIVERSITY OF MISSOURI, 1958.
    ##
    CHRON: 1946-1960
    METH: HISTORICAL
    GEOG: TAIWAN
    SUBJ: DESCRIPTION

LOON, G. VAN   L00755
    THE PRESS IN THE DUTCH EAST INDIES
    IN CAMERON C00208, PP. 902-3, 1014, 1018.
    ##/INDO
    CHRON: 1910-1946
    METH: HISTORICAL
    GEOG: INDONESIA   OSEAS CHIN
    SUBJ: JRN HISTORY DESCRIPTION

LOVING, GEORGE G.   L02178
    ON THE ENEMY AS A LEGITIMATE NEWS SOURCE
    DATELINE [OPC, NEW YORK] 14:1(1970), 62-5.
    MEDIUM: GENERAL
    CHRON: 1970-1980
    GEOG: VIETNAM   U.S.
    SUBJ: FOR CORR   LAW/ETHICS

LOWENTHAL, RUDOLF   L02179
    THE CATHOLIC PRESS IN CHINA
    DIGEST OF THE SYNODAL COMMISSION (CATHOLIC
        CHURCH IN CHINA)9:3(MAR 1936),
        272-312.
    CHRON: 1910-1946
    GEOG: CHINA
    SUBJ: DESCRIPTION

LOWENTHAL, RUDOLF   L01950
    THE PEIPING PRESS: A TECHNICAL SURVEY
    THE PEIPING CHRONICLE (14, 15 AUG 1934).
    ##/CHIN-6; PAGE 4.
    CHRON: 1910-1946
    GEOG: CHINA
    SUBJ: DESCRIPTION

LOWENTHAL, RUDOLF   L01706
    THE JEWISH PRESS IN CHINA
    NANKAI SOCIAL & ECONOMIC QUARTERLY X:1(APR
        1937), 104-13.
    CHRON: 1910-1946
    GEOG: CHINA
    SUBJ: DESCRIPTION

LOWENTHAL, RUDOLF   L01707
    THE COPYRIGHT IN CHINA
    THE YENCHING JOURNAL OF SOCIAL STUDIES
        III:2(AUG 1941), 145-73.
    CHRON: 1910-1946
    GEOG: CHINA
    SUBJ: LAW/ETHICS

LOWENTHAL, RUDOLF   L01527
     THE PRESENT STATUS OF THE FILM IN CHINA
     DIGEST OF THE SYNODAL COMMISSION (CATHOLIC
          CHURCH IN CHINA)9:1(JAN 1936),
          82-102; PART 2, 9:6(JUNE 1936), 545-551.
     ##/CHIN-5; ULS 2:945.
     MEDIUM: FILM
     CHRON: 1910-1946
     GEOG: CHINA
     SUBJ: DESCRIPTION

LOWENTHAL, RUDOLF   L01529
     WORK ON THE FAR EAST AND CENTRAL ASIA
          PUBLISHED IN THE U.S.S.R., 1937-47
     ITHACA, CORNELL U.P., 1949.
     FROM <FAR EASTERN QUARTERLY> VIII:2(FEB
          1949), 172-83.
     MEDIUM: OTHER
     CHRON: 1910-1946
     GEOG: CHINA   SEV ASIA
     SUBJ: RESEARCH

LOWENTHAL, RUDOLF   L01402
     THE CHINESE PRESS IN AUSTRALIA
     DIGEST OF THE SYNODAL COMMISSION (CATHOLIC
          CHURCH IN CHINA) 10:5(MAY 1937),
          427-30.
     ##/CHIN-5; ULS 2:945.
     CHRON: 1910-1946
     GEOG: OSEAS CHIN   AUSTRALASIA
     SUBJ: DESCRIPTION

LOWENTHAL, RUDOLF   L01359
     THE PRESENT STATUS OF THE PRESS IN CHINA
     DIGEST OF THE SYNODAL COMMISSION (CATHOLIC
          CHURCH IN CHINA) 8:11(NOV 1935),
          928-40.
     ##/CHIN-5; ULS 2:945.
     CHRON: 1910-1946
     GEOG: CHINA
     SUBJ: DESCRIPTION

LOWENTHAL, RUDOLF   L01405
     THE CONFUCIAN PRESS IN CHINA
     DIGEST OF THE SYNODAL COMMISSION (CATHOLIC
          CHURCH IN CHINA) 11:11(NOV 1938),
          1031-38.
     ##/CHIN-5; ULS 2:945.
     CHRON: 1910-1946
     GEOG: CHINA
     SUBJ: DESCRIPTION

LOWENTHAL, RUDOLF   L01404
     THE MOHAMMEDAN PRESS IN CHINA
     DIGEST OF THE SYNODAL COMMISSION (CATHOLIC
          CHURCH IN CHINA) 11:9-10(SEPT-OCT 1938),
          867-94.
     ##/CHIN-5; ULS 2:945.
     CHRON: 1910-1946
     GEOG: CHINA
     SUBJ: DESCRIPTION

LOWENTHAL, RUDOLF   L01403
    THE CATHOLIC PRESS IN MANCHURIA
    DIGEST OF THE SYNODAL COMMISSION (CATHOLIC
        CHURCH IN CHINA) 11:7(JULY 1938),
        750-9.
    ##/CHIN-5; ULS 2:945.
    CHRON: 1910-1946
    GEOG: CHINA
    SUBJ: DESCRIPTION

LOWENTHAL, RUDOLF   L00756
    WESTERN LITERATURE ON CHINESE JOURNALISM: A
        BIBLIOGRAPHY
    NANKAI SOCIAL & ECONOMIC QUARTERLY 9(JAN
        1937), 1007-66.
    #3; BEST BIBLIOGRAPHY TO 1936; TIENTSIN,
        NANKAI INSTITUTE OF ECONOMICS.
    CHRON: SURVEY
    METH: HISTORICAL
    GEOG: CHINA
    SUBJ: RESEARCH

LOWENTHAL, RUDOLF   L00758
    THE RELIGIOUS PERIODICAL PRESS IN CHINA
    PEKING, SYNODAL COMMISSION IN CHINA, 1940.
    #3; SINOLOGICAL SERIES, 57; REPRINT OF
        9 MONOGRAPHS.
    CHRON: 1910-1946
    GEOG: CHINA   OTHER
    SUBJ: DESCRIPTION

LOWENTHAL, RUDOLF   L00757
    THE RUSSIAN PRESS IN CHINA
    THE CHINESE SOCIAL AND POLITICAL SCIENCE
        REVIEW 21:3(OCT-DEC 1937),330-340.
    ##/CHIN-2; REPRINTED IN LOWENTHAL L02182.
    CHRON: 1910-1946
    GEOG: CHINA   OTHER
    SUBJ: DESCRIPTION

LOWENTHAL, RUDOLF   L01020
    PUBLIC COMMUNICATIONS IN CHINA BEFORE JULY,
        1937.
    CHINESE SOCIAL AND POLITICAL SCIENCE REVIEW
        22(APR-JUNE 1938), 42-58.
    ##/CHIN-4
    MEDIUM: GENERAL
    CHRON: 1910-1946
    GEOG: CHINA
    SUBJ: DESCRIPTION

LOWENTHAL, RUDOLF   L01019
    PRINTING PAPER: ITS SUPPLY AND DEMAND IN
        CHINA
    YENCHING JOURNAL OF SOCIAL STUDIES I(JUNE
        1938), 107-21.
    CHRON: 1910-1946
    GEOG: CHINA
    SUBJ: PRINTING

LOWENTHAL, RUDOLF   L01018
    THE TIENTSIN PRESS
    THE CHINESE SOCIAL AND POLITICAL SCIENCE
        REVIEW XIX:4(JAN 1936),543-58.
    ##/CHIN-4
    CHRON: 1910-1946
    GEOG: CHINA
    SUBJ: DESCRIPTION

LOWENTHAL, RUDOLF   L02183
    THE DEVELOPMENT OF COPYRIGHT IN CHINA
    DIGEST OF THE SYNODAL COMMISSION (CATHOLIC
        CHURCH IN CHINA) XIV:7-8(JULY-AUG 1941),
        676-86.
    CHRON: 1910-1946
    GEOG: CHINA
    SUBJ: LAW/ETHICS

LOWENTHAL, RUDOLF   L02182
    THE RUSSIAN DAILY PRESS IN CHINA
    DIGEST OF THE SYNODAL COMMISSION (CATHOLIC
        CHURCH IN CHINA) 11:4(APR 1938),
        375-83.
    FROM LOWENTHAL L00757
    CHRON: 1910-1946
    GEOG: CHINA   RUSSIA
    SUBJ: DESCRIPTION

LOWENTHAL, RUDOLF   L02181
    THE RUSSIAN ORTHODOX PRESS IN CHINA
    DIGEST OF THE SYNODAL COMMISSION (CATHOLIC
        CHURCH IN CHINA) 10:12(DEC 1937),
        1017-24.
    CHRON: 1910-1946
    GEOG: CHINA
    SUBJ: DESCRIPTION

LOWENTHAL, RUDOLF   L02180
    THE JEWISH PRESS IN CHINA
    DIGEST OF THE SYNODAL COMMISSION (CATHOLIC
        CHURCH IN CHINA) 10:7-8(1937), 684-91.
    CHRON: 1910-1946
    GEOG: CHINA
    SUBJ: DESCRIPTION

LOWENTHAL, RUDOLF AND WILLIAM   L01528
        A. Y. LIANG
    THE BUDDHIST PERIODICAL PRESS IN CHINA
    DIGEST OF THE SYNODAL COMMISSION (CATHOLIC
        CHURCH IN CHINA) 11:1(JAN 1938),
        50-63.
    ##/CHIN-5; ULS 2:945.
    CHRON: 1910-1946
    GEOG: CHINA
    SUBJ: DESCRIPTION

LU CHIH-CH'U   16   L00759
    WO KUO HSIN WEN P'ING I HUI CHIH YEN CHIU
      (THE CHINESE PRESS COUNCIL)
    UNPUB MASTERS THESIS IN JOURNALISM, 1969.
                        LANG: CHINESE
    CHRON: 1960-1970   VERIF: UNVERIFIED
    GEOG: TAIWAN
    SUBJ: LAW/ETHICS

LU K'ANG-YU   07   L00761
    CHUNG-KUO T'UNG HSUN SHE SHIH YEH TI HUI
        KU YU CH'IEN CHAN (CHINESE NEWS AGENCIES,
        RETROSPECT AND PROSPECT)
    UNPUB MASTERS THESIS IN JOURNALISM, 1962.
    SKINNER S00982 II:41902
                        LANG: CHINESE
    CHRON: 1960-1970   VERIF: UNVERIFIED
    GEOG: TAIWAN   CHINA
    SUBJ: FLOW/AGENCY

LU, DAVID CHI-HSIN   L00760
    GEMS FROM THE MOSQUITO PRESS
    T'IEN HSIA MONTHLY 6:1(JAN 1938), 7-17.
    TH
    CHRON: 1910-1946
    GEOG: CHINA
    SUBJ: DESCRIPTION

LU, DAVID CHI-HSIN   L02236
    THE SEIGE OF PEKING AS RECORDED IN THE
        LONDON TIMES
    MASTERS THESIS, UNIVERSITY OF MISSOURI, 1932.
    CHRON: BEFORE 1910
    METH: HISTORICAL
    GEOG: CHINA
    SUBJ: JRN HISTORY

LU, DAVID CHI-HSIN   L02308
    'SO THIS IS AMERICA'
    THE CHINA WEEKLY REVIEW 55:5(3 JAN 1931),
        180-1.
    CHRON: 1910-1946
    GEOG: CHINA   U.S.
    SUBJ: DESCRIPTION OTHER JRN

LUAN, JOSEPH I. C.   L02309
    PRESS FACES CRISIS IN TSINAN
    THE CHINA WEEKLY REVIEW 109:5(3 APR 1948),
        136.
    CHRON: 1910-1946
    GEOG: CHINA
    SUBJ: CONTROL

LUBIS, MOCHTAR   L00762
    THE PRESS IN INDONESIA
    FAR EASTERN SURVEY 21:9(4 JUNE 1952), 90-4.
    ##/INDO
    CHRON: 1946-1960
    GEOG: INDONESIA
    SUBJ: DESCRIPTION

LUBIS, MOCHTAR   L00764
    AFTER PRISON, NO BITTERNESS
    NIEMAN REPORTS 21:1(1967), 20-2.
    ##/INDO
    CHRON: 1960-1970
    GEOG: INDONESIA
    SUBJ: CONTROL   LAW/ETHICS BIOGRAPHY

LUBIS, MOCHTAR   L00763
    OF THINGS REMEMBERED FROM THE PAST
    QUADRANT XIII:5(OCT 1960), 11-23.
    CHRON: 1970-1980
    GEOG: INDONESIA
    SUBJ: BIOGRAPHY

LUBIS, MOCHTAR   L01324
    PERS DAN WARTAWAN
    DJAKARTA, BALAI PUSTAKA, 1963.
                        LANG: MALAY/INDONESIAN
    CHRON: 1960-1970
    GEOG: INDONESIA
    SUBJ: DESCRIPTION EDUCATION

LUBIS, MOCHTAR   L01530
    MASS MEDIA AND THE NEW NATIONS
    HORIZONS [USIS] XVII:11(1968-70), 14-16.
    MEDIUM: GENERAL
    CHRON: 1960-1970
    GEOG: SEV ASIA
    SUBJ: DEVELOPMENT

LUM, MAGDALENE   L00767
    ASSAULT CASE: VERDICT AGAINST DOCTOR UPHELD
    STRAITS TIMES 22 JAN 1972
    ##/MAL-2
    CHRON: 1970-1980
    GEOG: MALAYSIA
    SUBJ: LAW/ETHICS

LUM, MAGDALENE   L00766
    EDITOR CLEARED
    STRAITS TIMES 2 NOV 1971
    ##/MALSP; MELAN.
    CHRON: 1970-1980
    GEOG: MALAYSIA
    SUBJ: LAW/ETHICS

LUM, MAGDALENE   L00765
    TRIAL WAS 'IRREGULAR AND UNAUTHORIZED'
    STRAITS TIMES 14 SEPT 1971
    ##/MAL-2; FAN YEW TENG/ROCKET CASE.
    CHRON: 1970-1980
    GEOG: MALAYSIA
    SUBJ: CONTROL   LAW/ETHICS

LUNG CH'UNG-KUANG   12   L00768
    T'AI-PEI PAO CHIH SHE HUI FU WU CHIH YEN CHIU
         (SOCIAL SERVICES OF TAIPEI NEWSPAPERS)
    UNPUB MASTERS THESIS IN JOURNALISM, 1966.
    SKINNER S00982 II:48199
                              LANG: CHINESE
    CHRON: 1960-1970   VERIF: UNVERIFIED
    GEOG: TAIWAN
    SUBJ: DESCRIPTION OTHER JRN

LUNG CHUNG   L02616
    NEW TENDENCIES IN THE MOSCOW STRUGGLE: A
         COMPARATIVE STUDY OF THE PRESS BETWEEN
         MOSCOW AND PEIPING
    ISSUES AND STUDIES XI:2(DEC 1975), 68-83.
    CHRON: 1970-1980
    METH: CONTENT ANALYSIS
    GEOG: CHINA
    SUBJ: PROPAGANDA DESCRIPTION

MA YIN-LIANG   M01325
    A BRIEF HISTORY OF THE CHINESE PRESS
    SHANGHAI, SHUN PAO DAILY NEWS, 1937.
    ##/CHIN-5
    CHRON: 1910-1946
    GEOG: CHINA
    SUBJ: JRN HISTORY DESCRIPTION

MA, HSIN YE WEI   M00769
    THE FOREIGN PRESS: CHINA
    JQ XVI:3(SEPT 1939), 284-7.
    ##/CHIN
    CHRON: 1910-1946
    GEOG: CHINA
    SUBJ: DESCRIPTION

MA, HSIN-YE WEI   M00773
    THE FOREIGN PRESS: CHINA
    JQ XVII:3(SEPT 1940), 277-280.
    ##/CHIN
    CHRON: 1910-1946
    GEOG: CHINA
    SUBJ: DESCRIPTION

MA, HSIN-YE WEI   M00772
    THE FOREIGN PRESS: CHINA
    JQ XVII:2(JUNE 1940), 172-5.
    ##/CHIN
    CHRON: 1910-1946
    GEOG: CHINA
    SUBJ: DESCRIPTION

MA, HSIN-YE WEI   M00771
    THE FOREIGN PRESS: CHINA
    JQ XVII:1(MAR 1940),77-80.
    ##/CHIN
    CHRON: 1910-1946
    GEOG: CHINA
    SUBJ: DESCRIPTION

MA, SHIN-YE WEI   M00770
    THE FOREIGN PRESS: CHINA
    JQ XVI:4(DEC 1939), 393-5.
    ##/CHIN
    CHRON: 1910-1946
    GEOG: CHINA
    SUBJ: DESCRIPTION

MA, T. C., EDITOR.   M02007
    NEWS STORIES CLASSIFIED AND ILLUSTRATED
    TAIPEI, STUDENT BOOK CO., 1972.
                            LANG: CHINESE
    CHRON: 1970-1980
    GEOG: TAIWAN   CHINA
    SUBJ: EDUCATION

MA, W. Y.   M02184
    A CRITICISM OF THE PRESS IN SHANGHAI
    THE CHINA WEEKLY REVIEW 51:2(14 DEC 1929), 68.
    CHRON: 1910-1946
    GEOG: CHINA
    SUBJ: DESCRIPTION

MABBETT, HUGH   M01531
    KEEPING UP WITH THE TIMES
    HORIZONS [USIS] XVII:11(1968-70), 28-31.
    CHRON: 1960-1970
    GEOG: MALAYSIA
    SUBJ: DESCRIPTION

MAC GREGOR, GREG   M02185
    ALL FRIENDS OF CHINA
    DATELINE [OPC, NEW YORK] 3:1(1959), 25, 68.
    CHRON: 1946-1960
    GEOG: TAIWAN
    SUBJ: DESCRIPTION

MAC NAIR, H. F.   M01843
    [REVIEW NOTE OF BRITTON'S <THE CHINESE
        PERIODICAL PRESS>]
    AMERICAN HISTORICAL REVIEW XL:2(JAN 1935),
        394.
    CHRON: 1910-1946
    GEOG: CHINA
    SUBJ: RESEARCH

MACDONALD, ALEXANDER   M00776
    BANGKOK EDITOR
    NEW YORK, MACMILLAN, 1949.
    CHRON: SURVEY
    GEOG: THAILAND
    SUBJ: BIOGRAPHY

MACFARQUHAR, RODERICK   M00775
    A VISIT TO THE CHINESE PRESS
    CHINA QUARTERLY NO. 53(JAN/MAR 1973), 144-52.
    ##/CHIN
    CHRON: 1970-1980
    GEOG: CHINA
    SUBJ: DESCRIPTION PRINTING

MACFARQUHAR, RODERICK   M00774
    ON PHOTOGRAPHS
    CHINA QUARTERLY NO. 46(APR/JUNE 1971),
        289-307.
    ##/CHIN
    CHRON: 1970-1980
    METH: OTHER OR COMB
    GEOG: CHINA
    SUBJ: DESCRIPTION OTHER JRN

MADDOX, BRENDA   M00778
    TV COMES TO INDIA'S VILLAGES
    ATLAS WORLD PRESS REVIEW 22:10(OCT 1975),
        44-5.
    ##/SWAS; FROM MADDOX M00777.
    MEDIUM: ELECTRONIC
    CHRON: 1970-1980
    GEOG: SO/WEST ASI
    SUBJ: DEVELOPMENT DESCRIPTION

MADDOX, BRENDA   M00777
    INDIA'S SCHOOLROOM IN THE SKY
    NEW SCIENTIST 67:961(7 AUG 1975), 332-4.
    MADDOX M00778 IS EXCERPT.
    MEDIUM: ELECTRONIC
    CHRON: 1970-1980
    GEOG: SO/WEST ASI
    SUBJ: DEVELOPMENT DESCRIPTION

MAEDA, HISASHI   M00779
    A NATIONAL NEWSPAPER IN JAPAN
    NIEMAN REPORTS X:2(APR 1956), 9-13.
    ##/EASI
    CHRON: 1946-1960
    GEOG: SO/WEST ASI
    SUBJ: DESCRIPTION

MAKEPEACE, W. E., G. E. BROOKE AND   M00781
        R. ST. J. BRADDELL, EDS.
    ONE HUNDRED YEARS OF SINGAPORE
    LONDON, J. MURRAY, 1921, 2 VOLS.
    ##/SIN; THE PRESS, VOL. 2, 278-97.
    CHRON: 1910-1946   VERIF: UNVERIFIED
    GEOG: SINGAPORE
    SUBJ: JRN HISTORY DESCRIPTION

MAKEPEACE, WALTER   M00780
    THE PRESS
    IN CAMERON C00208, PP. 794-5.
    ##/SIN
    CHRON: 1910-1946
    GEOG: SINGAPORE
    SUBJ: JRN HISTORY DESCRIPTION

MALAY MAIL [MALAYSIA]   M02617
    MALAY MAIL FROM 1896 ON FILM IN NATIONAL
        ARCHIVES
    15 JULY 1972
    ##/MAL-2
    CHRON: SURVEY
    GEOG: MALAYSIA
    SUBJ: RESEARCH

MALAYA [BRITISH MALAYA, MALAYSIA]   M02009
    MALAYAN FILM UNIT
    (APR 1953), 212-13.
    ALL PHOTOS
    MEDIUM: FILM
    CHRON: 1946-1960
    GEOG: MALAYSIA
    SUBJ: DESCRIPTION

MALAYA [BRITISH MALAYA, MALAYSIA]   M02008
    FEDERATION OF MALAYA INFORMATION SERVICES
    (FEB 1953), 87-90.
    MEDIUM: GENERAL
    CHRON: 1946-1960
    GEOG: MALAYSIA
    SUBJ: DESCRIPTION

MALAYSIA [BRITISH MALAYA, MALAYA]   M01407
    THE ROLE OF MASS MEDIA
    (DEC 1967), 9.
    ##/MAL-3
    CHRON: 1960-1970
    GEOG: MALAYSIA
    SUBJ: DEVELOPMENT

MALAYSIA [BRITISH MALAYA, MALAYA]   M01406
    A NATIONAL NEWS SERVICE
    (JAN 1967), 10.
    ##/MAL-3
    CHRON: 1960-1970
    GEOG: MALAYSIA
    SUBJ: FLOW/AGENCY

MALAYSIAN BUSINESS   M01242
    THE IRRESISTABLE DRAW OF THE CINEMA
    (AUG 1977), 62-3, 65.
    ##/MAL-2
    MEDIUM: FILM
    CHRON: 1970-1980
    GEOG: MALAYSIA
    SUBJ: DESCRIPTION

MALCOLM, ANDREW H.   M01844
    ASAHI, WORLD'S LARGEST PAPER GIRDS FOR BATTLE
    NYT 19 MAR 1978
    ##/EASI
    CHRON: 1970-1980
    GEOG: EAST ASIA
    SUBJ: DESCRIPTION OTHER JRN

MALCOLM, ELIZABETH L.   M00782
    THE <CHINESE REPOSITORY> AND WESTERN
        LITERATURE ON CHINA, 1800-1850.
    MODERN ASIAN STUDIES 7:2(1973), 165-178.
    ##/CHIN-2
    CHRON: BEFORE 1910
    METH: HISTORICAL
    GEOG: CHINA
    SUBJ: JRN HISTORY

MALIK, HARJI   M00783
    NEW WAVE REMAINS A RIPPLE
    STRAITS TIMES 6 JULY 1974
    ##/SWAS
    MEDIUM: FILM
    CHRON: 1970-1980
    GEOG: SO/WEST ASI
    SUBJ: DESCRIPTION

MALLOY, MICHAEL T.   M00784
    LAOTIAN EDITOR FITS PRESS PIONEER IMAGE
    EDITOR & PUBLISHER (1 OCT 1966), 82.
    ##/LAOS
    CHRON: 1960-1970
    GEOG: LAOS
    SUBJ: DESCRIPTION BIOGRAPHY

MANGAHAS, FEDERICO   M01021
    CURRENT POLITICAL JOURNALISM IN THE
        PHILIPPINES
    AMERASIA 3(SEPT 1939), 310-14.
    ##/PHIL
    CHRON: 1910-1946
    GEOG: PHILIPPINES
    SUBJ: DESCRIPTION

MANKEKAR, D. R.   M01845
    THE INDIAN PRESS
    . JOURNAL OF EAST ASIATIC STUDIES [MANILA]
        III:4(JULY-OCT 1954), 416-9.
    CHRON: 1946-1960
    GEOG: SO/WEST ASI
    SUBJ: DESCRIPTION

MARKHAM, JAMES   M01532
    VOICES OF THE RED GIANTS
    AMES, IOWA, IOWA STATE UNIVERSITY PRESS, 1978.
    MEDIUM: GENERAL
    CHRON: 1960-1970
    GEOG: CHINA   RUSSIA
    SUBJ: DESCRIPTION

MARQUEZ, FLORDELINDO TINGSON   M00787
    A COMPARATIVE ANALYSIS OF CULTURE AND THE
        CULTURAL CONTENT OF PRINTED ADVERTISING
        IN THE PHILIPPINES AND THAILAND
    PHD DISS, UNIVERSITY OF WISCONSIN, 1973.
    343 PP., (74-9010); INTL DISS 34 7799A.
    CHRON: 1970-1980   VERIF: UNVERIFIED
    METH: OTHER OR COMB
    GEOG: THAILAND   PHILIPPINES
    SUBJ: DESCRIPTION CROSS CULTU OTHER JRN

MARSDALE, JAMES   M02010
    THE NEWSPAPERS OF CHINATOWN
    NATIONAL PRINTER-JOURNALIST [MAIL ORDER
        JOURNAL] 40(DEC 1922), 16-17.
    ##/CHIN-US
    CHRON: 1910-1946
    GEOG: OSEAS CHIN   U.S.
    SUBJ: DESCRIPTION

MARSHALL, S. L. A.   M00788
    PRESS FAILURE IN VIETNAM
    THE NEW LEADER XLIX:20(10 OCT 1966), 3-6.
    ##/VN
    CHRON: 1960-1970
    GEOG: VIETNAM   U.S.
    SUBJ: FOR CORR

MARTIN, DUDLEY B.   M02640
    WESTERN RACES MISUNDERSTAND EAST,
        KALTENBORN SAYS AFTER TOUR
    EDITOR & PUBLISHER 60:21(15 OCT 1927),
        50.
    CHRON: 1910-1946
    GEOG: CHINA   SEV ASIA   WORLD
    SUBJ: DESCRIPTION CROSS CULTU

MARTIN, ROBERT   M00789
    THE PEIPING CASE: HOW CHINESE COMMUNISTS
        TREAT CORRESPONDENTS
    NIEMAN REPORTS III:3(JULY 1949), 7-8.
    ##/CHIN
    CHRON: 1946-1960
    GEOG: CHINA
    SUBJ: FOR CORR

MARTONO   M02113
    INDONESIAN PRESS UNDER FASCIST MILITARY
        DICTATORSHIP
    THE AFRO-ASIAN JOURNALIST 7:4(DEC 1970),
        14-16.
    CHRON: 1970-1980
    GEOG: INDONESIA
    SUBJ: CONTROL

MASLOG, CRISPIN   M00790
     PROFILE OF THE PHILIPPINE COMMUNITY
          NEWSPAPER AND EDITOR
     JQ 46:2(SUMMER 1969), 337-42.
     ##/PHIL
     CHRON: 1960-1970
     METH: OTHER OR COMB
     GEOG: PHILIPPINES
     SUBJ: DESCRIPTION BIOGRAPHY

MASON, ISAAC   M01534
     TWO CHINESE MOSLEM MAGAZINES
     MOSLEM WORLD 15:4(OCT 1925), 385-7.
     ##/CHIN-5; <BRIGHT VIRTUE> AND <LIGHT OF
          ISLAM>.
     CHRON: 1910-1946
     GEOG: CHINA
     SUBJ: DESCRIPTION

MASON, ISAAC   M01533
     NOTES ON CHINESE MOHAMMEDAN LITERATURE
     ROYAL ASIATIC SOCIETY, JRNL OF THE
          NORTH-CHINA BRANCH 56(1925), 172-215.
     ##/CHIN-5
     CHRON: 1910-1946
     GEOG: CHINA
     SUBJ: RESEARCH

MATEER, ADA HAVEN   M00791
     NEW TERMS FOR NEW IDEAS: A STUDY OF THE
          CHINESE NEWSPAPER
     SHANGHAI, PRESBYTERIAN PRESS, 1924.
     ##/CHIN-3; NUC<56 368:662; LANGUAGE TEXT.
     CHRON: 1910-1946
     GEOG: CHINA
     SUBJ: LANGUAGE

MATIENZO, LORETO H,JR.   M01535
     THEY TUNED US IN TO THE WORLD
     HORIZONS [USIS] XVII:11(1968-70), 36-41.
     MEDIUM: ELECTRONIC
     CHRON: 1960-1970
     GEOG: SEV ASIA
     SUBJ: DESCRIPTION

MATIENZO, LORETO JR.   M00792
     TURN ON, TUNE IN, AND YOU WON'T DROP OUT
     HORIZONS [USIS] XX:9(1971), 14-21.
     ##/ASIA
     MEDIUM: ELECTRONIC
     CHRON: 1970-1980
     GEOG: SEV ASIA
     SUBJ: EDUCATION

MATSUYAMA, YUKIO   M00793
    JAPANESE PRESS AND JAPAN'S FOREIGN POLICY
    JRNL OF INTERNATIONAL AFFAIRS 26:2(1972),
        146-53.
    CHRON: 1970-1980
    GEOG: SO/WEST ASI
    SUBJ: OTHER JRN   POLIT SCI

MAULE, GEORGE B.   M01281
    THE CHINESE PRINTING PRESS
    THE TIMES [LONDON] (30 MAR 1877), 9.
    #=; LETTER TO EDITOR, SEE DILKE (D01280).
    CHRON: BEFORE 1910
    GEOG: CHINA
    SUBJ: PRINTING

MAWATARI, T.   M02114
    GRAPHIC ARTS INDUSTRIES IN SE ASIA
    THE ASIAN PRINTER 3:2(1960), 40-64, PART 1;
        3:3(1960), 36-57 PART 2; 4:1(1961),
        34-46, PART 3.
    CHRON: 1970-1980
    GEOG: INDONESIA
    SUBJ: PRINTING

MAYER, NORBERT   M02808
    DIE PRESSE IN CHINA
    ZEITUNGSWISSENSCHAFT 10:12(1 DEC 1935),
        589-606.
    ##/CHIN-9
                          LANG: OTHER EUROPEAN
    CHRON: SURVEY
    METH: HISTORICAL
    GEOG: CHINA
    SUBJ: JRN HISTORY DESCRIPTION

MAYERS, WILLIAM FREDERICK   M00795
    THE PEKING GAZETTE
    THE CHINA REVIEW [HONG KONG] III:1(JULY/AUG
        1874), 13-8.
    ##/CHIN-3
    CHRON: BEFORE 1910
    METH: HISTORICAL
    GEOG: CHINA
    SUBJ: JRN HISTORY

MC ANDREW, WILLIAM R.   M02186
    HOW WELL DOES TV COVER VIETNAM?
    DATELINE [OPC, NEW YORK] X:1(1967), 73-5.
    MEDIUM: ELECTRONIC
    CHRON: 1960-1970
    GEOG: VIETNAM   U.S.
    SUBJ: DESCRIPTION LAW/ETHICS

MC CABE, ROBERT KARR   M00796
    NO NEWS IS BAD NEWS: THE BAN ON AMERICAN
        REPORTING FROM COMMUNIST CHINA
    NIEMAN REPORTS XV:3(JULY 1961), 24-7.
    ##/CHIN-2
    MEDIUM: GENERAL
    CHRON: 1960-1970
    GEOG: CHINA
    SUBJ: FOR CORR

MC CARTNEY, JAMES   M00797
    CAN THE MEDIA COVER GUERILLA WARS?
    COL JRN REVIEW IX:4(WINTER 1970-1), 33-7.
    MEDIUM: GENERAL
    CHRON: 1970-1980
    GEOG: VIETNAM   U.S.
    SUBJ: FOR CORR

MC ELHENY, VICTOR K.   M00799
    INDONESIAN SATELLITE TO BE LAUNCHED
    NYT 8 JULY 1976
    ##/INDO
    MEDIUM: ELECTRONIC
    CHRON: 1970-1980
    GEOG: INDONESIA
    SUBJ: DESCRIPTION

MC KENZIE, VERNON   M00801
    CHINESE NEWSPAPERS AND THE MEN WHO MAKE THEM
    THE CHINA WEEKLY REVIEW L:11(9 NOV 1929),
        376, 397.
    ##/CHIN-3; REPRINT OF MC KENZIE M00800.
    CHRON: 1910-1946
    GEOG: CHINA
    SUBJ: DESCRIPTION BIOGRAPHY

MC KENZIE, VERNON   M00800
    CHINESE NEWSPAPERS AND THE MEN WHO MAKE THEM
    EDITOR & PUBLISHER (5 OCT 1929), 56.
    REPRINTED IN MC KENZIE M00801
    CHRON: 1910-1946
    GEOG: CHINA
    SUBJ: DESCRIPTION BIOGRAPHY

MC KENZIE, VERNON   M01847
    MANY EMPLOYEES OF CHINESE PAPERS HAVE THEIR
        HOMES IN PLANT
    EDITOR & PUBLISHER (5 OCT 1929), 56.
    ##/CHIN-6
    CHRON: 1910-1946
    GEOG: CHINA
    SUBJ: DESCRIPTION

MC LAUGHLIN, JOHN   M02187
    MAKING THE WAR WORSE THAN IT IS
    DATELINE [OPC, NEW YORK] 13:1(APR 1969), 66-7.
    CHRON: 1960-1970
    GEOG: VIETNAM   TAIWAN
    SUBJ: DESCRIPTION LAW/ETHICS

MC MURTRIE, DOUGLAS C.   M00802
    MEMORANDUM ON THE HISTORY OF PRINTING IN THE
        DUTCH EAST INDIES
    CHICAGO, PRIVATELY PRINTED AT CHICAGO
        SCHOOL OF PRINTING, 1935.
    ##/INDON; NUC<56 353:302.
    CHRON: SURVEY
    METH: HISTORICAL
    GEOG: INDONESIA
    SUBJ: PRINTING

MC NULTY, THOMAS M.   M00798
    VIETNAM SPECIALS: POLICY AND CONTENT
    JRNL OF COMMUNICATION 25:4(AUTUMN 1975),
        173-80.
    ##/VN
    MEDIUM: ELECTRONIC
    CHRON: 1970-1980
    METH: OTHER OR COMB
    GEOG: VIETNAM   U.S.
    SUBJ: FOR CORR   OTHER JRN

MC NULTY, THOMAS MICHAEL   M00803
    NETWORK TELEVISION DOCUMENTARY TREATMENT OF
        THE VIETNAM WAR, 1965-1969
    PHD DISS, INDIANA UNIVERSITY, 1974.
    INTL DISS 35 2210A.
    MEDIUM: ELECTRONIC
    CHRON: 1960-1970   VERIF: UNVERIFIED
    METH: OTHER OR COMB
    GEOG: VIETNAM   U.S.
    SUBJ: FOR CORR   DESCRIPTION

MEI CHI-CHU   M01591
    SELLING TO THE CHINESE MILLIONS: ADVERTISING
        IN CHINA
    CHINA REVIEW III:3(SEPT 1922), 82-3.
    ##/FILM
    CHRON: 1910-1946
    GEOG: CHINA
    SUBJ: OTHER JRN

MENEFEE, SELDEN C.   M01708
    JAPAN'S PROPAGANDA WAR
    ASIA XLIII:3(MAR 1943), 167-9.
    MEDIUM: GENERAL
    CHRON: 1910-1946
    GEOG: EAST ASIA
    SUBJ: PROPAGANDA

MENG, C. Y. W.   M02313
    POPULAR MAGAZINES VANISH
    THE CHINA WEEKLY REVIEW 112:9(29 JAN 1949),
        214-5.
    CHRON: 1910-1946
    GEOG: CHINA
    SUBJ: CONTROL

MENG, C. Y. W.   M02312
    CHINA'S FIGHT AGAINST THE PUBLICATION LAW
    THE CHINA WEEKLY REVIEW 110:13(28 AUG 1948),
        351-2.
    CHRON: 1910-1946
    GEOG: CHINA
    SUBJ: CONTROL   LAW/ETHICS

MENG, C. Y. W.   M02311
    INVESTIGATION SHOWS THAT REPORT OF PEIPING
        SHOOTING EPISODE WAS DISTORTED
    THE CHINA WEEKLY REVIEW 75:7(18 JAN 1936),
        238-9.
    CHRON: 1910-1946
    GEOG: CHINA
    SUBJ: PROPAGANDA LAW/ETHICS

MENG, C. Y. W.   M02310
    SOME IMPRESSIONS OF THE 'NEW LIFE MAGAZINE'
        CASE
    THE CHINA WEEKLY REVIEW 73:13(24 AUG 1935),
        440.
    CHRON: 1910-1946
    GEOG: CHINA
    SUBJ: LAW/ETHICS

MERRILL, JOHN C.   M00806
    THE ROLE OF THE MASS MEDIA IN NATIONAL
        DEVELOPMENT: AN OPEN QUESTION FOR
        SPECULATION
    GAZETTE XVII:4(1971), 236-243.
    ##/DEV
    MEDIUM: GENERAL
    CHRON: 1970-1980
    GEOG: WORLD
    SUBJ: DEVELOPMENT

MERRILL, JOHN C., ET AL.   M00805
    FOREIGN PRESS: A SURVEY OF THE WORLD'S
        JOURNALISM
    BATON ROUGE, L. S. U. PRESS, 1970.
    CHRON: 1970-1980
    GEOG: WORLD
    SUBJ: DESCRIPTION

MESNY'S CHINESE MISCELLANY   M01408
    A OFFICIAL NEWSPAPER FOR HUPEH PROVINCE
    IV:14(1 APR 1905), 279.
    ##/CHIN-5
    CHRON: BEFORE 1910
    GEOG: CHINA
    SUBJ: DESCRIPTION

MICHENER, CARROLL K.   M01022
    FROM CONFUCIUS TO <THE DAILY NEWS>
    THE CATHOLIC WORLD 123:733(APR 1926), 20-7.
    ##/CHIN-4
    CHRON: SURVEY
    GEOG: CHINA
    SUBJ: JRN HISTORY

MILLARD, THOMAS F.   M01346
    THE PRESS AND CHINESE DEVELOPMENT
    IN CHINA PRESS C02568, P. 74.
    ##/FILM
    CHRON: 1910-1946
    GEOG: CHINA
    SUBJ: DEVELOPMENT

MIN BYONG-GI   M01592
    THE GOVERNMENT, THE THE PRESS, AND THE
        PUBLIC IN JAPAN
    KOREA JOURNAL 8:5(MAY 1968), 30-3.
    CHRON: 1960-1970
    GEOG: EAST ASIA
    SUBJ: CONTROL   DEVELOPMENT DESCRIPTION

MINETRAKINETRA, BANCHA, KASEM   M01849
        SIRISUMPANDH AND JOHN D. MITCHELL
    MASS COMMUNICATION RESOURCES IN THAILAND:
        A SURVEY
    BANGKOK, DIV. OF JOURNALISM FACULTY OF
        SOCIAL ADMIN., THAMMASAT U., 1965
    CHRON: SURVEY
    GEOG: THAILAND
    SUBJ: RESEARCH

MING CHIEN-HUA   08   M00807
    T'AI-WAN PAO YEH KUANG KAO HSIEN CHUANG
        YEN CHIU (NEWSPAPER ADVERTISING IN
        PRESENT-DAY TAIWAN)
    TAIPEI, CHIA HSIN SHUI NI KUNG SSU, WEN HUA
        CHI CHIN HUI, 1968.
    SKINNER S00982 II:42258
                        LANG: CHINESE
    CHRON: 1960-1970   VERIF: UNVERIFIED
    GEOG: TAIWAN
    SUBJ: OTHER JRN

MISA, VERONICA   M00808
    VOICES OF THE PRESS
    THE ASIA MAGAZINE (27 AUG 1972), 21-3.
    ##/PHIL
    CHRON: 1970-1980
    GEOG: PHILIPPINES
    SUBJ: BIOGRAPHY

MITCHELL, JOHN D.   M00810
    SOCIALIZATION AND THE MASS MEDIA IN CHINA
        AND JAPAN
    JQ 46:3(AUTUMN 1969), 576-82.
    ##/MISC
    MEDIUM: GENERAL
    CHRON: 1960-1970
    GEOG: CHINA   SO/WEST ASI
    SUBJ: OTHER JRN   SOCIO/ANTHR

MITCHELL, JOHN D.   M00809
    THAILAND'S UNEXAMINED MEDIA: NON-DAILY
        NEWSPAPERS AND RADIO-TV
    JQ 42:1(1965), 87-97.
    ##/THAI
    MEDIUM: GENERAL
    CHRON: 1960-1970
    GEOG: THAILAND
    SUBJ: DESCRIPTION

MITCHELL, JOHN D.   M02651
    THAILAND
    IN LENT L00708, PP. 210-233.
    CHRON: SURVEY
    METH: OTHER OR COMB
    GEOG: THAILAND
    SUBJ: JRN HISTORY DESCRIPTION

MITCHELL, ROBERT EDWARD   M00811
    HOW HONG KONG NEWSPAPERS HAVE RESPONDED TO
        15 YEARS OF RAPID SOCIAL CHANGE
    ASIAN SURVEY IX:9(SEPT 1969), 669-81.
    ##/HKG
    CHRON: 1960-1970
    GEOG: HONG KONG
    SUBJ: DEVELOPMENT SOCIO/ANTHR

MIYOSHI, OSAMU   M02618
    HOW THE JAPANESE PRESS YIELDED TO PEKING
    SURVEY 18:4(AUTUMN 1972), 103-25.
    ##/CHIN-9
    CHRON: 1970-1980
    GEOG: CHINA   EAST ASIA
    SUBJ: CONTROL   DESCRIPTION LAW/ETHICS

MOHAMAD, GOENAWAN   M00813
    INDONESIAN FILMS: A DISTORTED MIRROR
    ATLAS WORLD PRESS REVIEW 22:10(OCT 1975), 53.
    ##/INDON
    MEDIUM: FILM
    CHRON: 1970-1980
    GEOG: INDONESIA
    SUBJ: DESCRIPTION

MOHAMED BIN ISMAIL   M00817
    'SUARA BENAR'--AKHBAR MELAYU TERAWAL DI
        MELAKA [FIRST MALAY NEWSPAPER IN MALACCA]
    JERNAL SEJARAH XI(1972-3), 49-54.
    HISTORY SOCIETY, UNIVERSITY OF MALAYA.
                            LANG: MALAY/INDONESIAN
    CHRON: BEFORE 1910
    METH: HISTORICAL
    GEOG: MALAYSIA
    SUBJ: JRN HISTORY

MOHAMED TAIB OSMAN   M00812
    THE LANGUAGE OF THE EDITORIALS IN MALAY
        VERNACULAR NEWSPAPERS UP TO 1941
    KUALA LUMPUR, DEWAN BAHASA DAN PUSTAKA, 1966.
    NUC AUTHORS 68-72 65:143
    CHRON: 1910-1946   VERIF: UNVERIFIED
    GEOG: MALAYSIA
    SUBJ: LANGUAGE

MOHAMMAD ALIAS   M02011
    KELULUSAN TAK MINJAMIN JADI JURNALIS
        YANG BAIK?
    NADAMINGGU [SUPPLEMENT TO <BERITA MINGGU>]
        (21 MAY 1978).
    ##/MAL-3
                            LANG: MALAY/INDONESIAN
    CHRON: 1970-1980
    GEOG: MALAYSIA
    SUBJ: DEVELOPMENT

MOHD. FAUZI PATEL   M00816
    EDITOR TELLS STORY OF MALAYSIAN STATE'S
        SHUTDOWN OF HIS PAPER
    IPI REPORT 25:2(DEC 1976), 12.
    ##/MAL-2
    CHRON: 1970-1980
    GEOG: MALAYSIA
    SUBJ: CONTROL

MOHR, CHARLES   M02188
    THIS WAR AND HOW WE COVER IT
    DATELINE [OPC, NEW YORK] X:1(1966), 19-22.
    CHRON: 1960-1970
    GEOG: VIETNAM   TAIWAN
    SUBJ: FOR CORR

MONTEIRO, SWITHIN   M00814
     WHAT TV VIEWERS CAN EXPECT IN THE FUTURE
     MALAY MAIL 18 JUNE 74
     ##/MAL-2
     MEDIUM: ELECTRONIC
     CHRON: 1970-1980
     GEOG: MALAYSIA
     SUBJ: DESCRIPTION

MOODY, RANDALL J.   M00815
     PRESERVING THE IMAGE IN VIETNAM
     FOI CENTER REPORT NO. 0010(AUG 1970).
     ##/VN
     MEDIUM: GENERAL
     CHRON: 1970-1980
     GEOG: VIETNAM   U.S.
     SUBJ: FOR CORR   CONTROL   DESCRIPTION

MOON, EUGENE UI   M02237
     HISTORY OF NEWS AGENCIES IN KOREA
     MASTERS THESIS, UNIVERSITY OF MISSOURI, 1963.
     CHRON: SURVEY
     METH: HISTORICAL
     GEOG: EAST ASIA
     SUBJ: FLOW/AGENCY JRN HISTORY

MOORAD, GEORGE L.   M01593
     CHINESE TALKIES
     ASIA 35:10(OCT 1935), 614-19.
     ##/CHIN-4
     MEDIUM: FILM
     CHRON: 1910-1946
     GEOG: CHINA
     SUBJ: JRN HISTORY DESCRIPTION

MOORAD, GEORGE L.   M01674
     WHEN CHINA GOES TO PRESS
     THE CHINA JOURNAL XXVII:1(JULY 1937), 22-8.
     ##/CHIN-5
     CHRON: 1910-1946
     GEOG: CHINA
     SUBJ: DESCRIPTION

MOORE, HARRIET   M01850
     THE SOVIET PRESS AND JAPAN'S WAR ON CHINA
     PACIFIC AFFAIRS 11:1(MAR 1938), 44-51.
     ##/RUSS
     CHRON: 1910-1946
     METH: CONTENT ANALYSIS
     GEOG: CHINA   EAST ASIA   RUSSIA
     SUBJ: PROPAGANDA DESCRIPTION

MORGAN, JAMES   M00818
     MEDIUM, NOT THE MESSAGE
     FEER LXXII:20(15 MAY 1971), 8, 11.
     ##/SIN
     CHRON: 1970-1980
     GEOG: SINGAPORE
     SUBJ: CONTROL

MORGAN, JAMES   M00820
     LITTLE RED KORAN
     FEER 78:53(30 DEC 1972), 23.
     ##/MAL-2
     CHRON: 1970-1980
     GEOG: MALAYSIA
     SUBJ: CONTROL

MORGAN, JAMES   M00819
     LETTER FROM KUALA LUMPUR
     FEER 76:23(3 JUNE 1972), 44.
     ##/MAL-2; ADVERTISING.
     CHRON: 1970-1980
     GEOG: MALAYSIA
     SUBJ: OTHER JRN

MORGAN, JOE W.   M02189
     HOW THE WAR LOOKS FROM THE DESK
     DATELINE [OPC, NEW YORK] X:1(1966), 80-1.
     MEDIUM: GENERAL
     CHRON: 1960-1970
     GEOG: VIETNAM   U.S.
     SUBJ: FOR CORR   FLOW/AGENCY

MORITZ, FREDERIC   M00821
     CHINESE COMICS TEACH MAO'S LESSONS
     CSM 15 AUG 1973
     ##/CHIN
     CHRON: 1970-1980
     GEOG: CHINA
     SUBJ: PROPAGANDA   DEVELOPMENT

MORITZ, FREDERIC A.   M00822
     THE FILM MAKERS OF HONG KONG LOOK INTO CHINA
     CSM 27 APR 1977
     ##/CHIN-3
     MEDIUM: FILM
     CHRON: 1970-1980
     GEOG: HONG KONG   CHINA
     SUBJ: DESCRIPTION

MORITZ, FREDERIC A.   M01409
    CHINA CLOSES DOOR TO CRITICAL NEWSMAN
    CSM 28 NOV 1977
    ##/CHIN-5; MUNRO.
    CHRON: 1970-1980
    GEOG: CHINA
    SUBJ: FOR CORR   CONTROL   DESCRIPTION

MORRI, YASOTARO   M01594
    PRESS IN WARTIME ASSUMES IMPORTANT ROLE
    THE PEIPING CHRONICLE 21 APR 1940
    CHRON: 1910-1946
    GEOG: EAST ASIA
    SUBJ: CONTROL   PROPAGANDA DESCRIPTION

MORRIS, JOHN G.   M02193
    THE NEW PICTURES: BLOOD AND GORE FOR BREAKFAST
    DATELINE [OPC, NEW YORK] 13:1(APR 1969), 56-7.
    MEDIUM: FILM
    CHRON: 1960-1970
    GEOG: VIETNAM
    SUBJ: FOR CORR   LAW/ETHICS

MORRIS, JOHN R.   M02528
    COVERING THE WAR AGAINST JAPAN
    IN MOTT M02529, PP. 67-71.
    CHRON: 1910-1946
    GEOG: EAST ASIA   SEV ASIA
    SUBJ: FOR CORR

MORRIS, JOHN R.   M01851
    FIRST CHINESE CLASS IN JOURNALISM
    EDITOR & PUBLISHER (17 JUNE 1922), 7.
    ##/CHIN-6
    CHRON: 1910-1946
    GEOG: CHINA
    SUBJ: EDUCATION

MORROW, MIKE   M01595
    ASIAN JOURNALISM: THE STRUGGLE FOR SURVIVAL
    MEDIA [HONG KONG] 4:9-10(SEPT-OCT 1976), 41.
    CHRON: 1970-1980
    GEOG: SEV ASIA
    SUBJ: DESCRIPTION

MOSEL, JAMES N.   M00823
    THE 'VERSE EDITORIAL' IN THAI JOURNALISM
    JQ 39:1(WINTER 1962), 70-4.
    ##/THAI
    CHRON: 1960-1970
    GEOG: THAILAND
    SUBJ: DESCRIPTION

MOSEL, JAMES N.   M02652
    COMMUNICATION PATTERNS AND POLITICAL
        SOCIALIZATION IN TRANSITIONAL THAILAND
    IN PYE P02658, PP. 184-228.
    MEDIUM: GENERAL
    CHRON: 1960-1970
    METH: OTHER OR COMB
    GEOG: THAILAND
    SUBJ: DEVELOPMENT POLIT SCI

MOSES, SIR CHARLES AND   M02619
        CRISPIN MASLOG
    MASS COMMUNICATION IN ASIA A BRIEF HISTORY
    SINGAPORE, AMIC, 1978.
    MEDIUM: GENERAL
    CHRON: SURVEY
    METH: OTHER OR COMB
    GEOG: SEV ASIA
    SUBJ: JRN HISTORY

MOSLEM WORLD, THE   M01596
    NEWSPAPER PROPAGANDA
    XV:1(JAN 1925), 76.
    ##/SIN-2
    CHRON: 1910-1946
    GEOG: SINGAPORE
    SUBJ: PROPAGANDA

MOTT, FRANK LUTHER, EDITOR.   M02529
    JOURNALISM IN WARTIME
    AMERICAN COUNCIL ON PUBLIC AFFAIRS,
        WASHINGTON, D. C., 1943.
    #3
    CHRON: 1910-1946
    GEOG: SEV ASIA
    SUBJ: FOR CORR   DESCRIPTION

MOTT, JOHN R., EDITOR.   M02012
    THE MOSLEM WORLD OF TODAY
    NEW YORK, GEORGE H. DORAN, 1925.
    ##/ASIA
    CHRON: 1910-1946
    GEOG: MALAYSIA   INDONESIA   CHINA
    SUBJ: DESCRIPTION

MOWLANA, HAMID   M01597
     POLITICAL AND SOCIAL IMPLICATIONS OF
          COMMUNICATION SATELLITE APPLICATIONS IN
          DEVELOPED AND DEVELOPING COUNTRIES
     IN RUBEN R02564, PP. 427-38.
     MEDIUM: GENERAL
     CHRON: 1970-1980
     GEOG: WORLD
     SUBJ: FLOW/AGENCY CROSS CULTU

MOY, E. K.   M02194
     A SCHOOL OF JOURNALISM FOR CHINA IN PEIPING
     THE CHINA WEEKLY REVIEW 48:12(18 MAY 1929),
          519, 524.
     CHRON: 1910-1946
     GEOG: CHINA
     SUBJ: EDUCATION

MUNRO, ROSS H.   M00827
     JOURNALIST JOINS CHINA'S TOILING PEASANT
          MASSES
     CSM 27 JULY 1976
     ##/CHIN-2
     CHRON: 1970-1980
     GEOG: CHINA
     SUBJ: FOR CORR

MUNRO, ROSS H.   M00828
     HOW PEKING EDITORS SNIP HISTORY
     CSM 7 JAN 1977
     ##/CHIN-2
     MEDIUM: FILM
     CHRON: 1970-1980
     GEOG: CHINA
     SUBJ: CONTROL   DESCRIPTION

MURDOCK, VICTOR   M02043
     CHINESE PRINTERS MUST KNOW 10,000 LETTERS
     THE INLAND PRINTER 59:1(APR 1917), 91-2.
     ##/CHIN-7
     CHRON: 1910-1946
     GEOG: CHINA
     SUBJ: PRINTING

MURRAY, J. EDWARD   M02750
     FOUR THOUSAND MILES ACROSS CHINA
     DETROIT, DETROIT FREE PRESS, 1972.
     REPRINT OF SIX ARTICLES FROM <FREE PRESS>;
          29 OCT TO 3 NOV 1972.
     CHRON: 1970-1980   VERIF: UNVERIFIED
     GEOG: CHINA
     SUBJ: OTHER JRN   OTHER NON-J

MURTHY, P. A. NARASHIMA   M02620
    CHINA'S OTHER TRADE
    CHINA REPORT VI:5(SEPT/OCT 1970), 13-15.
    CHRON: 1970-1980
    GEOG: CHINA
    SUBJ: PROPAGANDA   PUBLISHING

MYERS, GILBERT H.   M02314
    POLICE TAKE LAW INTO OWN HANDS, SUSPEND
        PAPER SUMMARILY
    THE CHINA WEEKLY REVIEW 102:9(27 JULY 1946),
        197-8.
    <WEN HUI PAO>
    CHRON: 1946-1960
    GEOG: CHINA
    SUBJ: CONTROL   LAW/ETHICS

MYO NYUNT, MAUNG   M00830
    A CONTENT ANALYSIS OF 3 SOURCES OF PRINTED
        COMMUNICATION DEALING WITH THE MILITARY
        CARETAKER REGIME IN BURMA, . . .
    MASTERS THESIS, CORNELL UNIVERSITY, 1962.
    CHRON: 1946-1960   VERIF: UNVERIFIED
    METH: CONTENT ANALYSIS
    GEOG: BURMA
    SUBJ: SOCIO/ANTHR

NADAMINGGU   N02013
    FILEM MELAYU KEMBALI PULIH SEMULA
    21 MAY 1978
    ##/MAL-3; SUPPLEMENT WITH <BERITA MINGGU>.
    MEDIUM: FILM   LANG: MALAY/INDONESIAN
    CHRON: 1970-1980
    GEOG: MALAYSIA
    SUBJ: DESCRIPTION OTHER JRN

NAFZIGER, RALPH O., COMPILER.   N00832
    INTERNATIONAL NEWS AND THE PRESS:
        COMMUNICATIONS, . . .: A BIBLIOGRAPHY
    NEW YORK, H. W. WILSON, 1940.
    REPRINTED BY ARNO PRESS 1972
    MEDIUM: GENERAL
    CHRON: SURVEY
    GEOG: WORLD
    SUBJ: RESEARCH

NAM, SUNWOO   N02559
    NEWSPAPERS UNDER TRIBULATION: THE
        PRESENT-DAY KOREAN PRESS?
    GAZETTE XXIV:2(1978), 109-20.
    CHRON: 1970-1980
    GEOG: EAST ASIA
    SUBJ: CONTROL   DESCRIPTION

NAM, SUNWOO   N01045
THE FLOW OF INTERNATIONAL NEWS INTO KOREA
GAZETTE XVI:1(1970), 14-26.
MEDIUM: GENERAL
CHRON: 1970-1980
METH: CONTENT ANALYSIS
GEOG: EAST ASIA   WORLD
SUBJ: FLOW/AGENCY

NAM, SUNWOO   N01650
THE TAMING OF THE KOREAN PRESS
COL JRN REVIEW XVI:6(MAR/APR 1978), 43-5.
CHRON: 1970-1980
GEOG: EAST ASIA
SUBJ: CONTROL

NAM, SUNWOO   N01044
A COMPARATIVE STUDY OF FREEDOM OF THE PRESS
      IN KOREA, TAIWAN (NATIONALIST CHINA) AND
      THE PHILIPPINES
COLUMBIA, MO., U. OF MISSOURI, SCHOOL OF
      JOURNALISM, 1969.
##/FREE; MIMEO, 40 PP.
CHRON: 1960-1970
METH: OTHER OR COMB
GEOG: PHILIPPINES TAIWAN   EAST ASIA
SUBJ: CONTROL

NAM, SUNWOO   N01047
EDITORIAL DECISIONS IN THE UNITED STATES: A
      COMPARISON WITH THE JAPANESE AND
      KOREAN PAPERS
GAZETTE XXII:2(1976), 91-105.
CHRON: 1970-1980
METH: OTHER OR COMB
GEOG: EAST ASIA   U.S.
SUBJ: DESCRIPTION

NAM, SUNWOO   N01046
EDITORIALS AS AN INDICATOR OF PRESS FREEDOM
      IN THREE ASIAN COUNTRIES
JQ 48:4(WINTER 1971), 730-40.
CHRON: 1970-1980
METH: OTHER OR COMB
GEOG: PHILIPPINES TAIWAN   EAST ASIA
SUBJ: CONTROL

NARAIN, PREM   N02621
THE ETHOS OF THE INDIAN LANGUAGE PRESS
      AFTER THE REPEAL (1882) OF THE VERNACULAR
      PRESS ACT
QUARTERLY REVIEW OF HISTORICAL STUDIES
      15:2(1975-6), 77-89.
CHRON: BEFORE 1910   VERIF: UNVERIFIED
METH: HISTORICAL
GEOG: SO/WEST ASI
SUBJ: JRN HISTORY

NARAYAN, S. V.   N00833
    SAMACHAR: THE THIRD WORLD'S FIRST
        INTERNATIONAL AGENCY?
    IPI REPORT 25:5(MAY 1976), 1, 8-9.
    MEDIUM: GENERAL
    CHRON: 1970-1980
    GEOG: SO/WEST ASI WORLD
    SUBJ: FLOW/AGENCY

NASH, VERNON   N00834
    CHINESE JOURNALISM IN 1931
    JQ VIII:4(DEC 1931), 446-52.
    ##/CHIN
    CHRON: 1910-1946
    GEOG: CHINA
    SUBJ: DESCRIPTION

NASH, VERNON   N01598
    TRADE OR PROFESSIONAL SCHOOLS FOR JOURNALISTS?
    THE NEW CHINA [PEKING] (JUNE 1931), 194-5.
    #3/NEW CHINA
    CHRON: 1910-1946
    GEOG: CHINA
    SUBJ: EDUCATION

NASH, VERNON   N01347
    PROBLEMS OF THE PRESS IN CHINA
    IN CHINA PRESS C02568, P. 86.
    ##/FILM
    CHRON: 1910-1946
    GEOG: CHINA
    SUBJ: DESCRIPTION

NASH, VERNON   N02315
    FREEDOM WITHIN THE PRESS
    THE CHINA WEEKLY REVIEW 77:9(1 AUG 1936), 312.
    CHRON: 1910-1946
    GEOG: CHINA
    SUBJ: CONTROL

NASH, VERNON   N00835
    JOURNALISM IN CHINA: 1933
    JQ X:4(DEC 1933), 316-22.
    ##/CHIN
    CHRON: 1910-1946
    GEOG: CHINA
    SUBJ: DESCRIPTION

NASH, VERNON AND RUDOLF LOWENTHAL   N02195
    RESPONSIBLE FACTORS IN CHINESE JOURNALISM
    DIGEST OF THE SYNODAL COMMISSION (CATHOLIC
        CHURCH IN CHINA) 9:12(DEC 1936),
        1043-8.
    FROM <THE CHINESE SOCIAL AND POLITICAL SCIENCE
        REVIEW> NASH N0023
    CHRON: 1910-1946
    GEOG: CHINA
    SUBJ: DESCRIPTION LAW/ETHICS

NASH, VERNON AND RUDOLF LOWENTHAL   N01023
    RESPONSIBLE FACTORS IN CHINESE JOURNALISM
    THE CHINESE SOCIAL AND POLITICAL SCIENCE
        REVIEW XX:3(OCT 1936), 420-6.
    ##/CHIN-4; REPRINTED IN NASH N02195.
    CHRON: 1910-1946
    GEOG: CHINA
    SUBJ: DESCRIPTION LAW/ETHICS

NATARAJAN, LAKSHMI   N00836
    UTUSAN CHIEF WINS APPEAL IN SEDITION CASE
    MALAY MAIL 1 NOV 1971
    ##/MALSP
    CHRON: 1970-1980
    GEOG: MALAYSIA
    SUBJ: LAW/ETHICS

NATION, THE   N01852
    ASIA'S FOURTH ESTATE
    86:2238(21 MAY 1908), 460-1.
    ##/CHIN-5
    CHRON: 1910-1946
    GEOG: CHINA
    SUBJ: CONTROL   DESCRIPTION

NATION, THE   N01599
    MUZZLE IN CHINA
    129:3346(21 AUG 1929), 185-6.
    ##/CHIN-5
    CHRON: 1910-1946
    GEOG: CHINA
    SUBJ: CONTROL

NATIONS, RICHARD   N01970
    COMRADES' WAR OF WORDS AND HORROR
    FEER 99:4(27 JAN 1978), 10-12.
    ##/VN
    MEDIUM: GENERAL
    CHRON: 1970-1980
    GEOG: VIETNAM   CAMBODIA
    SUBJ: PROPAGANDA

NEVIN, JAMES   N00837
      INDIA'S TV PROJECT MAY HERALD 'SCREEN
         REVOLUTION' IN THIRD WORLD
      CSM 4 AUG 1977
      ##/SWAS
      MEDIUM: ELECTRONIC
      CHRON: 1970-1980
      GEOG: SO/WEST ASI
      SUBJ: DEVELOPMENT DESCRIPTION

NEW CHINA, THE [PEKING]   N02690
      JAPAN ADVERTISER REAPPEARS
      I:4(FEB 1931), 102.
      CHRON: 1910-1946
      GEOG: EAST ASIA
      SUBJ: DESCRIPTION

NEW CHINA, THE [PEKING]   N02687
      NEW 'REGISTRATION' ORDER ISSUED
      I:4(FEB 1931), 101.
      CHRON: 1910-1946
      GEOG: CHINA
      SUBJ: CONTROL

NEW CHINA, THE [PEKING]   N02686
      ALL NEWSPAPERS MUST REGISTER
      I:4(FEB 1931), 101.
      CHRON: 1910-1946
      GEOG: CHINA
      SUBJ: CONTROL

NEW CHINA, THE [PEKING]   N02675
      PRESS MESSAGE GIVEN EQUAL STANDING WITH
         COMMERCIAL
      I:2(DEC 1930), 52.
      CHRON: 1910-1946
      GEOG: CHINA
      SUBJ: OTHER JRN

NEW CHINA, THE [PEKING]   N02653
      JAPAN ADVERTISER WILL ASSUME PUBLICATION
      I:2(DEC 1930), 51.
      CHRON: 1910-1946
      GEOG: EAST ASIA
      SUBJ: DESCRIPTION

NEW CHINA, THE [PEKING]   N02698
    EARLY AMERICAN NEWSPAPER IN CHINA
    I:6(APR 1931), 160, 162.
    <THE SHANGHAI NEWSLETTER>; SEE <THE CHINA
        WEEKLY REVIEW> 56:5(4
        APR 1931), 145-6.
    CHRON: BEFORE 1910
    GEOG: CHINA
    SUBJ: JRN HISTORY

NEW CHINA, THE [PEKING]   N02706
    'N. Y. TIMES' CORRESPONDENT EXPLAINS
    I:7(MAY 1931), 190.
    HALLETT ABEND
    CHRON: 1910-1946
    GEOG: CHINA
    SUBJ: FOR CORR   DESCRIPTION

NEW CHINA, THE [PEKING]   N02645
    CHINESE JOURNALISM BEGAN BEFORE TANG PERIOD
    I:2(DEC 1930), 49.
    CHRON: SURVEY
    METH: HISTORICAL
    GEOG: CHINA
    SUBJ: JRN HISTORY

NEW CHINA, THE [PEKING]   N02708
    NEW WEEKLY APPEARS IN PEIPING
    I:8(JUNE 1931), 212.
    <CHINA IN BRIEF>
    CHRON: 1910-1946
    GEOG: EAST ASIA
    SUBJ: DESCRIPTION

NEW CHINA, THE [PEKING]   N02707
    C. W. REVIEW COMMENTS ON BRITISH ADVERTISING
    I:8(JUNE 1931), 212.
    CHRON: 1910-1946
    GEOG: CHINA
    SUBJ: OTHER JRN

NEW CHINA, THE [PEKING]   N02705
    J. C. SUN ADDRESSES FU JEN JOURNALISM CLUB
    I:7(MAY 1931), 190.
    CHRON: 1910-1946
    GEOG: CHINA
    SUBJ: DESCRIPTION

NEW CHINA, THE [PEKING]   N02704
    PRESS CENSORSHIP AGAIN
    I:7(MAY 1931), 190.
    CHRON: 1910-1946
    GEOG: CHINA
    SUBJ: CONTROL

NEW CHINA, THE [PEKING]   N02703
    DR. WU PRESENTS LIONS, GETS L. L. D.
    I:7(MAY 1931), 190.
    CHRON: 1910-1946
    GEOG: CHINA   U.S.
    SUBJ:. DESCRIPTION EDUCATION

NEW CHINA, THE [PEKING]   N02702
    NEW CHINESE DAILY FOR SHANGHAI
    I:7(MAY 1931), 189.
    CHRON: 1910-1946
    GEOG: CHINA
    SUBJ: DESCRIPTION

NEW CHINA, THE [PEKING]   N02701
    INFLUENCE OF THE PRESS IN SHANGHAI
    I:7(MAY 1931), 188.
    CHRON: 1910-1946
    GEOG: CHINA
    SUBJ: DESCRIPTION

NEW CHINA, THE [PEKING]   N02700
    INACCURATE REPORTING OR PREJUDICE
    I:7(MAY 1931), 188.
    CHRON: 1910-1946
    GEOG: CHINA   EAST ASIA
    SUBJ: CONTROL   PROPAGANDA DESCRIPTION

NEW CHINA, THE [PEKING]   N02699
    SOME CRITICISM OF EDUCATION FOR JOURNALISM
    I:6(APR 1931), 138-9.
    CHRON: 1910-1946
    GEOG: CHINA
    SUBJ: EDUCATION

NEW CHINA, THE [PEKING]   N02688
    OFFICIAL MAKES RECKLESS CHARGES
    I:4(FEB 1931), 101.
    CHRON: 1910-1946
    GEOG: CHINA
    SUBJ: DESCRIPTION

NEW CHINA, THE [PEKING]   N02696
    IMPROVING NEWS TRANSMISSION
    I:6(APR 1931), 160.
    CHRON: 1910-1946
    GEOG: CHINA
    SUBJ: FLOW/AGENCY

NEW CHINA, THE [PEKING]   N02676
    CONTROL BY REGISTRATION IN PLACE OF
        CENSORSHIP
    I:2(DEC 1930), 52.
    CHRON: 1910-1946
    GEOG: CHINA
    SUBJ: CONTROL

NEW CHINA, THE [PEKING]   N02677
    MANCHURIA TO ERECT PAPER MILL
    I:2(DEC 1930), 52.
    CHRON: 1910-1946
    GEOG: CHINA
    SUBJ: OTHER JRN

NEW CHINA, THE [PEKING]   N02697
    GOVERNMENT ATTEMPTS TO RESTRICT PRESS
    I:6(APR 1931), 160.
    CHRON: 1910-1946
    GEOG: CHINA
    SUBJ: CONTROL

NEW CHINA, THE [PEKING]   N02692
    DAILY NEWS AGENCY TO 'GO'
    I:4(FEB 1931), 102.
    <CHICAGO DAILY NEWS>
    CHRON: 1910-1946
    GEOG: EAST ASIA
    SUBJ: DESCRIPTION

NEW CHINA, THE [PEKING]   N02691
    PAO MOST POPULAR NAME
    I:4(FEB 1931, 102.
    CHRON: 1910-1946
    GEOG: CHINA
    SUBJ: DESCRIPTION LANGUAGE

NEW CHINA, THE [PEKING]   N02693
    A. P. BUREAU IS ESTABLISHED IN INDIA
    I:4(FEB 1931), 102.
    CHRON: 1910-1946
    GEOG: SO/WEST ASI
    SUBJ: FLOW/AGENCY DESCRIPTION

NEW CHINA, THE [PEKING]   N02695
    NANKING STOPS NEWSPAPER SUBSIDY
    I:6(APR 1931), 159.
    CHRON: 1910-1946
    GEOG: EAST ASIA
    SUBJ: DESCRIPTION

NEW CHINA, THE [PEKING]   N02694
    PROPAGANDA CARRIED OVERSEAS
    I:4(FEB 1931), 104.
    <OVERSEAS NEWS SERVICE>
    CHRON: 1910-1946
    GEOG: CHINA
    SUBJ: PROPAGANDA

NEW CHINA, THE [PEKING]   N02711
    FREEDOM OF PRESS UPHELD IN PEOPLES' MEET
    I:8(JUNE 1931), 214.
    CHRON: 1910-1946
    GEOG: CHINA
    SUBJ: CONTROL

NEW CHINA, THE [PEKING]   N02710
    MILITARY CENSORSHIP IN FORCE
    I:8(JUNE 1931), 213.
    CHRON: 1910-1946
    GEOG: EAST ASIA
    SUBJ: CONTROL

NEW CHINA, THE [PEKING]   N02709
    RENGO'S SIDE OF ITS CHINESE NEWS SERVICE
    I:8(JUNE 1931), 212.
    CHRON: 1910-1946
    GEOG: CHINA   EAST ASIA
    SUBJ: FLOW/AGENCY

NEW CHINA, THE [PEKING]   N02672
    TIMES HAS NEW PEIPING CORRESPONDENT
    I:2(DEC 1930), 51.
    LONDON TIMES, C. M. MC DONALDSON
    CHRON: 1910-1946
    GEOG: CHINA
    SUBJ: FLOW/AGENCY DESCRIPTION

NEW CHINA, THE [PEKING]   N02673
    SON OF EUGENE CHEN FOLLOWS FATHER'S STEP
    I:2(DEC 1930), 51.
    ASSISTANT EDITOR, <MOSCOW NEWS>
    CHRON: 1910-1946
    GEOG: CHINA
    SUBJ: BIOGRAPHY

NEW CHINA, THE [PEKING]   N02712
    HARBIN PAPER ORDERED TO CLOSE
    I:8(JUNE 1931), 214.
    <TUNG SANSHENG SHANGPAO>
    CHRON: 1910-1946
    GEOG: CHINA   EAST ASIA
    SUBJ: CONTROL   FLOW/AGENCY

NEW CHINA, THE [PEKING]   N02682
    PEIPING EDITOR RETURNS AFTER EUROPEAN TOUR
    I:3(JAN 1931), 72.
    CHEN SHEH-WO
    CHRON: 1910-1946
    GEOG: CHINA
    SUBJ: BIOGRAPHY

NEW CHINA, THE [PEKING]   N02684
    WORK GIVEN STUDENTS IN NEWSPAPER OFFICES
    I:3(JAN 1931), 73.
    CHRON: 1910-1946
    GEOG: CHINA
    SUBJ: EDUCATION

NEW CHINA, THE [PEKING]   N02683
    UNITED PRESS CORRESPONDENTS IN ORIENT
        CHANGE POSTS
    I:3(DEC 1930), 72.
    RANDALL GOULD, H. R. EKINS, D. C. BESS
    CHRON: 1910-1946
    GEOG: CHINA
    SUBJ: FLOW/AGENCY BIOGRAPHY

NEW CHINA, THE [PEKING]   N02671
    NEW CHINESE NEWSPAPER PAYS ATTENTION TO
        SCIENCE
    I:2(DEC 1930), 51.
    UNITED PRESS
    CHRON: 1910-1946
    GEOG: CHINA
    SUBJ: DESCRIPTION

NEW CHINA, THE [PEKING]   N02689
    PEOPLE'S TRIBUNE IS SHORT-LIVED
    I:4(FEB 1931), 101.
    CHRON: 1910-1946
    GEOG: CHINA
    SUBJ: DESCRIPTION

NEW CHINA, THE [PEKING]   N02670
    YAO SHIH-FEN SPEAKS AT YENCHING
    I:2(DEC 1930), 51.
    YAO SHEN-FEN
    CHRON: 1910-1946
    GEOG: CHINA
    SUBJ: FLOW/AGENCY DESCRIPTION

NEW CHINA, THE [PEKING]   N02678
    KUOMINTANG LEADERS THINKS PRESS HAS
        IMPROVED
    I:2(DEC 1930), 52.
    CHRON: 1910-1946
    GEOG: CHINA
    SUBJ: CONTROL

NEW CHINA, THE [PEKING]   N02674
    GOVERNMENT ARRESTS EDITOR OF RIVAL PAPER
    I:2(DEC 1930), 52.
    CHU YU-HSIN, <KIANG NAN WAN PAO>
    CHRON: 1910-1946
    GEOG: CHINA
    SUBJ: CONTROL

NEW CHINA, THE [PEKING]   N02795
     HARBIN HERALD CLOSED
     I:6(APR 1931), 159.
     CHRON: 1910-1946
     GEOG: CHINA   EAST ASIA
     SUBJ: CONTROL   DESCRIPTION

NEW CHINA, THE [PEKING]   N02794
     CARTOONS COME TO STAY
     I:4(FEB 1931), 101.
     CHRON: 1910-1946
     GEOG: CHINA
     SUBJ: DESCRIPTION

NEW CHINA, THE [PEKING]   N02713
     C. C. WU GIVEN ADDRESSES AT UNIVERSITY
     I:8(JUNE 1931), 214.
     UNIVERSITY OF MISSOURI
     CHRON: 1910-1946
     GEOG: CHINA   U.S.
     SUBJ: DESCRIPTION

NEW CHINA, THE [PEKING]   N02685
     JEN MIN JIH PAO ISSUES ENGLISH SUPPLEMENT
     I:3(JAN 1931), 73.
     CHRON: 1910-1946
     GEOG: CHINA
     SUBJ: DESCRIPTION

NEW CHINA, THE [PEKING]   N02681
     SIMPLE LANGUAGE USED IN CHINESE NEWSPAPER
     I:3(JAN 1931), 72.
     CHRON: 1910-1946
     GEOG: CHINA
     SUBJ: LANGUAGE

NEW CHINA, THE [PEKING]   N02680
     JOURNALIST BECOMES JUDGE
     I:3(JAN 1931), 72.
     LIU NIANG-CHUAN
     CHRON: 1910-1946
     GEOG: CHINA
     SUBJ: BIOGRAPHY

NEW CHINA, THE [PEKING]   N02679
    MINISTRY MAY ORDER SEIZURE OF NEWSPAPER
    I:2(DEC 1930), 52.
    CHRON: 1910-1946
    GEOG: CHINA
    SUBJ: CONTROL

NEW COMMONWEALTH, THE   N02118
    IMPERSONAL RADIO
    28:8(14 OCT 1954), 421.
    MEDIUM: ELECTRONIC
    CHRON: 1960-1970
    GEOG: MALAYSIA
    SUBJ: CONTROL   OTHER JRN

NEW COMMONWEALTH, THE   N02116
    BROADCASTING
    21(APR 1951), 548.
    MEDIUM: ELECTRONIC
    CHRON: 1960-1970
    GEOG: SEV ASIA
    SUBJ: DESCRIPTION

NEW COMMONWEALTH, THE   N02115
    NEWSPRINT
    21(JAN 1951), 312-13.
    CHRON: 1946-1960
    GEOG: SEV ASIA   WORLD
    SUBJ: PRINTING

NEW COMMONWEALTH, THE   N02117
    AERIAL PROPAGANDA
    24:12(8 DEC 1952), 601-2.
    MEDIUM: OTHER
    CHRON: 1960-1970
    GEOG: MALAYSIA
    SUBJ: PROPAGANDA

NEW LEADER, THE   N00839
    REPORTING VIETNAM: EIGHT WAR CORRESPONDENTS
        REBUT S. L. A. MARSHALL'S 'PRESS
        FAILURE IN VIETNAM'
    XLIX:23(21 NOV 1966), 3-16.
    ##/VN; MARSHALL ARTICLE, M00788; BROWNE,
        SHAPLEN, MECKLIN, HUGHES,
        ARNETT, FAAS, NEFF, MINOR.
    MEDIUM: GENERAL
    CHRON: 1960-1970
    GEOG: VIETNAM   U.S.
    SUBJ: FOR CORR   CONTROL

NEW REPUBLIC, THE   N01853
    MR. MOORE'S PRIVATE WAR
    50:645(13 APR 1927), 210-12.
    ##/CHIN-5
    CHRON: 1910-1946
    GEOG: CHINA
    SUBJ: DESCRIPTION BIOGRAPHY

NEWSWEEK   N00841
    REORIENTING THE JOURNAL
    (13 SEPT 1976), 80.
    ##/ASIA
    CHRON: 1970-1980
    GEOG: HONG KONG   SEV ASIA
    SUBJ: DESCRIPTION

NEWSWEEK   N00840
    WALL STREET EAST
    (17 NOV 1975), 23.
    ##/HKG
    CHRON: 1970-1980
    GEOG: HONG KONG
    SUBJ: DESCRIPTION

NEWSWEEK   N01065
    UNPLEASANT TRUTH: EXPULSION OF FRANCOIS
            SULLY FROM SAIGON
    (17 SEPT 1962), 68.
    CHRON: 1960-1970   VERIF: UNVERIFIED
    GEOG: VIETNAM
    SUBJ: FOR CORR   CONTROL   BIOGRAPHY

NG POH TIP   N01264
    WHAT WENT WRONG WITH SMASH HITS OF THE 50'S
    STRAITS TIMES(SUN) 8 OCT 1972
    ##/MAL-2
    MEDIUM: FILM
    CHRON: 1970-1980
    GEOG: MALAYSIA
    SUBJ: DESCRIPTION

NG POH TIP   N01265
    FLICKER OF HOPE ON THE SCREEN
    STRAITS TIMES 9 OCT 1972
    ##/MALSP
    MEDIUM: FILM
    CHRON: 1970-1980
    GEOG: MALAYSIA
    SUBJ: DESCRIPTION

NGO KHAC TINH   N02449
    TOWARDS A RESPONSIVE PRESS POLICY
    SAIGON, VIETNAM COUNCIL ON FOREIGN
        RELATIONS, 1969.
    CHRON: 1960-1970
    GEOG: VIETNAM
    SUBJ: CONTROL   DEVELOPMENT

NGUYEN THAI   N02660
    SOUTH VIETNAM
    IN LENT L00708, PP. 234-254.
    CHRON: SURVEY
    METH: OTHER OR COMB
    GEOG: VIETNAM
    SUBJ: JRN HISTORY DESCRIPTION

NGUYEN THAI   N01275
    'NEWS' IN VIETNAM: A CASE OF UNDERDEVELOPED
        FREEDOM TO KNOW
    NIEMAN REPORTS 17:1(MAR 1963), 19-22.
    ##/VN; FROM AN FOI REPORT.
    MEDIUM: GENERAL
    CHRON: 1960-1970
    GEOG: VIETNAM
    SUBJ: CONTROL   FLOW/AGENCY

NGUYEN VAN THIEU   N01424
    PRESS FREEDOM IN SOUTH VIETNAM
    ASIA PACIFIC RECORD 1:2(MAY 1970), 9-11.
    ##/VN-2
    CHRON: 1970-1980
    GEOG: VIETNAM
    SUBJ: CONTROL

NIEUWENHUIS, J.   N01268
    THE INDONESIAN PRESS INSTITUTE
    GAZETTE I:1(1955), 48-9.
    ##/INDO
    CHRON: 1946-1960
    GEOG: INDONESIA
    SUBJ: DESCRIPTION EDUCATION

NIEUWENHUIS, J.   N01266
    COURSES IN JOURNALISM AT NIJMEGEN CATHOLIC
        UNIVERSITY
    GAZETTE I:1(1955), 49.
    ##/INDO
    CHRON: 1946-1960
    GEOG: INDONESIA
    SUBJ: EDUCATION

NIEVA, G.   N01600
    NEWS COMMUNICATION IN THE PHILIPPINES
    IN WILLIAMS W02587, PP. 190-5.
    CHRON: 1910-1946
    GEOG: PHILIPPINES
    SUBJ: DESCRIPTION

NIK AHMAD B. HAJI NIK HASSAN   N01267
    THE MALAY VERNACULAR PRESS
    B. A. (HONS) THESIS, UNIVERSITY OF MALAYA AT
          SINGAPORE,1958.
    CHRON: SURVEY
    METH: HISTORICAL
    GEOG: MALAYSIA
    SUBJ: DESCRIPTION

NIO, JOE LAN   N01243
    CHINESE NEW YEAR CELEBRATION IN JAVA:
        SPECIAL NEW YEAR NUMBER OF CHINESE WEEKLY
        NEWSPAPER IN THE MALAYAN LANGUAGE
    CHINA JOURNAL 24:3(MAR 1936), 151.
    ##/INDO
    CHRON: 1910-1946
    GEOG: INDONESIA   OTHER
    SUBJ: DESCRIPTION

NOEL, FRANK   N02316
    U. S. WAR CORRESPONDENT DESCRIBES POW CAMP
    THE CHINA WEEKLY REVIEW 123:2(AUG 1952),
        117-21.
    CHRON: 1946-1960
    GEOG: CHINA   EAST ASIA
    SUBJ: FOR CORR

NOOR AZAM, M.   N01854
    TIGA PERISTIWA PENTING YANG BERTALI ERAT
    DEWAN MASYARAKAT 5:9(SEPT 1967), 7-11.
    ##/MAL-3
    MEDIUM: GENERAL   LANG: MALAY/INDONESIAN
    CHRON: 1960-1970
    GEOG: MALAYSIA
    SUBJ: FLOW/AGENCY

NOORDIN SOPIEE   N01269
    SEX, VIOLENCE--AND THE JELAK PRINCIPLE
    STRAITS TIMES(SUN) 1 OCT 1972
    ##/MAL-2; PART 1 OF SERIES OF 3.
    MEDIUM: FILM
    CHRON: 1970-1980
    GEOG: MALAYSIA
    SUBJ: DESCRIPTION

NOORDIN SOPIEE   N00854
   THE BIG QUESTION--TO BAN OR NOT TO BAN?
   STRAITS TIMES 3 OCT 1972
   ##/MALSP; PART 3 OF SERIES OF 3 ARTICLES.
   MEDIUM: FILM
   CHRON: 1970-1980
   GEOG: MALAYSIA
   SUBJ: CONTROL   DESCRIPTION

NOORDIN SOPIEE   N01270
   THE CENSOR
   STRAITS TIMES 2 OCT 1972
   ##/MALSP; PART 2 OF SERIES OF 3.
   MEDIUM: FILM
   CHRON: 1970-1980
   GEOG: MALAYSIA
   SUBJ: CONTROL   DESCRIPTION

NORDIN MOHAMAD   N00856
   3 JENIS FILEM YANG MESTI ADA SARIKATA
   BERITA MINGGU 29 AUG 1976
   ##/MAL
   MEDIUM: FILM
   CHRON: 1970-1980
   GEOG: MALAYSIA
   SUBJ: CONTROL   LAW/ETHICS

NORDIN, MAZLAN   N02530
   A CHANCE FOR MALAY FILMS
   ASIAWEEK 5:5(9 FEB 1979), 50.
   ##/MAL-3
   MEDIUM: ELECTRONIC
   CHRON: 1970-1980
   GEOG: CHINA
   SUBJ: DESCRIPTION

NORTH-CHINA DAILY NEWS & HERALD, LTD.   N01601
   CHINA'S ATTEMPT TO MUZZLE THE FOREIGN PRESS:
         AN ACCOUNT OF THE ENDEAVORS OF NANKING
         TO SUPPRESS THE TRUTH ABOUT . . . CHINA
   SHANGHAI, NORTH-CHINA DAILY NEWS & HERALD,
         1929.
   ##/FILM
   CHRON: 1910-1946
   GEOG: CHINA
   SUBJ: CONTROL

NORTH-CHINA HERALD AND SUPREME COURT   N02119
         CONSULAR GAZETTE, THE
   THE JAPANESE PRESS
   X:319(14 JUNE 1873), 521-2.
   CHRON: BEFORE 1910
   GEOG: EAST ASIA
   SUBJ: DESCRIPTION

NUNN, G. RAYMOND AND DO VAN ANH   N01246
        [COMPILERS]
    VIETNAMESE, CAMBODIAN AND LAOTIAN NEWSPAPERS
        AN INTERNATIONAL UNION LIST
    TAIPEI, CH'ENG-WEN, 1972.
    CHRON: SURVEY
    GEOG: VIETNAM   CAMBODIA   LAOS
    SUBJ: RESEARCH

NUNN, G. RAYMOND [COMPILER]   N01244
    INDONESIAN NEWSPAPERS AN INTERNATIONAL
        UNION LIST
    TAIPEI, CH'ENG-WEN, 1972.
    CHRON: SURVEY
    GEOG: INDONESIA
    SUBJ: RESEARCH

NUNN, G. RAYMOND [COMPILER]   N01245
    BURMESE AND THAI NEWSPAPERS AN INTERNATIONAL
        UNION LIST
    TAIPEI, CH'ENG-WEN, 1972.
    CHRON: SURVEY
    GEOG: BURMA   THAILAND
    SUBJ: RESEARCH

NUNN, G. RAYMOND, COMPILER.   N02531
    SOUTHEAST ASIAN PERIODICALS: AN INTERNATIONAL
        UNION LIST
    LONDON, MANSELL INFORMATION/PUBLISHING, 1977.
    CHRON: SURVEY
    METH: OTHER OR COMB
    GEOG: SEV ASIA
    SUBJ: RESEARCH

NUNN, RAYMOND   N00857
    SOUTHEAST ASIAN PERIODICALS, SOME
        CHARACTERISTICS OF PUBLICATION AND
        DISTRIBUTION TO LIBRARIES
    MEXICO CITY, 30TH INTL. CONGRESS OF HUMAN
        SCIENCES IN ASIA AND NORTH AFRICA, 1976.
    ##/BIB; MIMEO, 5 PP.
    CHRON: 1970-1980
    GEOG: SEV ASIA
    SUBJ: RESEARCH   PRINTING   PUBLISHING

O'LOUGHLIN, PETER   000864
    SAIGON REVISITED: THE PHONE STILL RINGS
    AP LOG (2 MAY 1977), 1, 3.
    ##/VN-2
    MEDIUM: GENERAL
    CHRON: 1970-1980
    GEOG: VIETNAM
    SUBJ: FOR CORR   FLOW/AGENCY DESCRIPTION

O'NEIL, MICHAEL   000866
    CHINA MAIL, 1845-1974
    MEDIA 1:9(SEPT 1974), 22-5.
    ##/HKG
    CHRON: 1970-1980
    GEOG: HONG KONG
    SUBJ: DESCRIPTION

OAKES, VANYA   001709
    THE WRONG NEWS ABOUT CHINA
    ASIA XLIV:4(APR 1944), 149-52.
    CHRON: 1910-1946
    GEOG: EAST ASIA
    SUBJ: FOR CORR

OESTREICHER, J. C.   001855
    SHANGHAI'S STILL SENDING
    THE QUILL 25(SEPT 1937), 12-14.
    ##/CHIN-6
    CHRON: 1910-1946
    GEOG: CHINA
    SUBJ: FOR CORR

OETAMA, JACOB   000858
    THE INDONESIAN PRESS: PROBLEMS AND
        PERSPECTIVES
    QUADRANT 13:5(SEPT/OCT 1969), 82-4.
    ##/INDON
    CHRON: 1960-1970
    GEOG: INDONESIA
    SUBJ: DESCRIPTION

OEY, GIOK-PO   000859
    SURVEY OF CHINESE LANGUAGE MATERIALS ON
        SOUTHEAST ASIA IN THE HOOVER INSTITUTE
        AND LIBRARY
    ITHACA, N. Y. DEPT. OF FAR EASTERN STUDIES,
        SOUTHEAST ASIA PROGRAM,CORNELL U., 1953.
    #3; CORNELL SOUTHEAST ASIA PROGRAM DATA
        RESEARCH PAPER NO. 8.
    CHRON: 1960-1970
    GEOG: SEV ASIA
    SUBJ: RESEARCH

OGATA, TAKETORA   001856
    PUBLIC OPINION AND THE PRESS
    CONTEMPORARY JAPAN [TOKYO] I:1(JUNE 1932),
        68-73.
    CHRON: 1910-1946
    GEOG: EAST ASIA
    SUBJ: OTHER JRN

OH IN-HWAN   001602
     KOREAN JOURNALISTS: THEIR PERCEPTIONS OF
          ROLES
     KOREA JOURNAL 15:3(MAR 1975), 4-12.
     CHRON: 1970-1980
     METH: SURVEY
     GEOG: EAST ASIA
     SUBJ: DESCRIPTION

OH JIN-KWAN   001857
     TOWARD A PRACTICAL APPROACH TO JOURNALISM IN
          DEVELOPING COUNTRIES THE CASE OF
          SOUTH KOREA
     KOREA JOURNAL 15:3(MAR 1975), 13-26.
     MEDIUM: GENERAL
     CHRON: 1970-1980
     GEOG: EAST ASIA
     SUBJ: DEVELOPMENT

OH, JIN HWAN   000860
     TOWARD A PRACTICAL APPROACH TO JOURNALISM
          IN DEVELOPING COUNTRIES: THE CASE OF
          SOUTH KOREA
     PHD DISS, UNIVERSITY OF IOWA, 1974.
     INTL DISS 35 4412A
     CHRON: 1970-1980   VERIF: UNVERIFIED
     METH: OTHER OR COMB
     GEOG: SO/WEST ASI
     SUBJ: DEVELOPMENT

OHLINGER, FRANKLIN   000861
     THE NEW JOURNALISM IN CHINA
     THE WORLD'S WORK XX(OCT 1910), 13529-13534.
     ##/CHIN-3
     CHRON: BEFORE 1910
     GEOG: CHINA
     SUBJ: DESCRIPTION

OKSENBERG, MICHEL   000862
     METHODS OF COMMUNICATION WITHIN THE CHINESE
          BUREAUCRACY
     CHINA QUARTERLY NO. 57(JAN-MAR 1974), 1-39.
     ##/CHIN-2
     MEDIUM: OTHER
     CHRON: 1970-1980
     GEOG: CHINA
     SUBJ: OTHER NON-J

OKULEY, BERT   002196
     VIET NAM IS STILL THERE
     DATELINE [OPC, NEW YORK] 16:1(1972), 1112.
     CHRON: 1970-1980
     GEOG: VIETNAM
     SUBJ: FOR CORR   DESCRIPTION

OLIPHANT, C. A.   000863
    THE IMAGE OF THE UNITED STATES PROJECTED BY
    <PEKING REVIEW>
    JQ 41:3(SUMMER 1964), 416-20, 468.
    ##/CHIN
    CHRON: 1960-1970
    METH: CONTENT ANALYSIS
    GEOG: CHINA   U.S.
    SUBJ: PROPAGANDA

OLREE, C.   002120
    PRINTING IN THAILAND
    THE ASIAN PRINTER 3:2(1960), 64-70.
    CHRON: 1960-1970
    GEOG: THAILAND
    SUBJ: PRINTING

OLSON, LAWRENCE   000865
    WHAT PAPER DO YOU READ?
    AUFS REPORTS, EAST ASIA SERIES IV:8(1955).
    ANALYSIS OF KYOTO NEWSPAPERS
    CHRON: 1946-1960
    METH: CONTENT ANALYSIS
    GEOG: EAST ASIA
    SUBJ: DESCRIPTION

ON PE   002583
    BURMESE FILMS
    EASTERN WORLD III:11(NOV 1949), 6-7.
    MEDIUM: FILM
    CHRON: 1946-1960
    GEOG: BURMA
    SUBJ: DESCRIPTION

ON-LINE SYSTEMS   002534
    SINGAPORE DAILY ORDERS ROCKWELL
    3:12(DEC 1978), 64.
    ##/SIN-2; NANYANG SIANG PAU.
    CHRON: 1970-1980
    GEOG: SINGAPORE
    SUBJ: DESCRIPTION PRINTING

ONE OF THEM   002197
    WORK OF THE FOREIGN NEWSPAPER CORRESPONDENT
        IN CHINA
    THE CHINA WEEKLY REVIEW XLVI:7(10 OCT 1928),
        50-4.
    CHRON: 1910-1946
    GEOG: CHINA
    SUBJ: FOR CORR

ONO, HIDEO   03   002602
    CHUNG WAI PAO YEH SHIH [HISTORY OF CHINESE
        AND FOREIGN JOURNALISM]
    TAIPEI, CHENG CHUNG SHU CHU, 1966.
                               LANG: CHINESE
    CHRON: SURVEY
    METH: HISTORICAL
    GEOG: TAIWAN   CHINA
    SUBJ: JRN HISTORY

ORIENTAL AFFAIRS   001712
    A NEW KINGS REGULATION: CONTROL OF THE PRESS
    11(JAN 1939), 11-2.
    CHRON: 1910-1946   VERIF: UNVERIFIED
    GEOG: EAST ASIA
    SUBJ: CONTROL

ORIENTAL AFFAIRS   001724
    COPYRIGHT INFRINGEMENTS, FURTHER FACTS AND A
        SUGGESTED SOLUTION
    VIII:2(AUG 1937), 71-2.
    CHRON: 1910-1946
    GEOG: CHINA
    SUBJ: DESCRIPTION LAW/ETHICS

ORIENTAL AFFAIRS   001711
    <THE PEOPLE'S TRIBUNE>: SELF-APPOINTED CENSOR
    VIII:1(JULY 1937), 8-10.
    CHRON: 1910-1946
    GEOG: CHINA
    SUBJ: CONTROL   DESCRIPTION

ORIENTAL AFFAIRS   001710
    PRINTING OF COPYRIGHT WORKS, AN EXTENSIVE
        CHINESE INDUSTRY
    VII:3(MAR 1937), 121-2.
    CHRON: 1910-1946
    GEOG: CHINA
    SUBJ: LAW/ETHICS   PRINTING

ORIENTAL ECONOMIC REVIEW, THE   001858
    THE PRESS OF JAPAN
    I:3(10 DEC 1910), 45-7.
    CHRON: BEFORE 1910
    GEOG: EAST ASIA
    SUBJ: DESCRIPTION

ORIENTAL ECONOMIC REVIEW, THE   001870
    JAPAN'S FIRST PHOTOGRAPHER
    I:6(25 JAN 1911), 105.
    RENJO SHIMOOKA
    CHRON: BEFORE 1910
    GEOG: EAST ASIA
    SUBJ: OTHER JRN

ORIENTAL REVIEW, THE   001871
    THE NEWSPAPERS OF JAPAN
    I:12(25 APR 1911), 223-5.
    CHRON: BEFORE 1910
    GEOG: EAST ASIA
    SUBJ: DESCRIPTION

ORSHEFSKY, MILTON   002198
    THE FOREIGN CORRESPONDENT LIVES IT UP (HONG
        KONG STYLE)
    DATELINE [OPC, NEW YORK] 8:1(1964), 32-4.
    CHRON: 1960-1970
    GEOG: HONG KONG
    SUBJ: FOR CORR

ORVIS, PAT   000867
    INSTRUCTION OUTPULLS ENTERTAINMENT ON TV IN
        INDIA
    NYT 18 JULY 1976
    ##/SWAS
    MEDIUM: ELECTRONIC
    CHRON: 1970-1980
    GEOG: SO/WEST ASI
    SUBJ: EDUCATION

OUTLOOK,THE [NEW OUTLOOK]   001872
    THE NATIVE PRESS AND CHINESE CRISIS
    67:4(26 JAN 1901), 188-9.
    ##/CHIN-5
    CHRON: BEFORE 1910
    GEOG: CHINA
    SUBJ: DESCRIPTION

P'AN TZU-HSIN   15   P02121
        AND WU K'O CHIEN AND HSIUNG CHIN TING
    HSIN-HUA JIH PAO TI HUI I [A REMINISCENCE OF
        THE NEW CHINA DAILY]
    CHUNGKING, CHUNG CH'ING REN MIN CHU PAN SHE,
        1959.
    #3
                        LANG: CHINESE
    CHRON: SURVEY
    GEOG: CHINA
    SUBJ: JRN HISTORY

PACIFIC AFFAIRS   P01604
     PRESS IN CHINA--NO FREEDOM OF OPINION
     4:6(JUNE 1931), 532-3.
     FROM OSAKA <MAINICHI>; 11 APR 1931
     CHRON: 1910-1946
     GEOG: CHINA
     SUBJ: CONTROL

PACIFIC AFFAIRS   P01603
     NANKING ABOLISHES PRESS CENSORSHIP
     4:1(31 JAN 1931), 64.
     FROM <CHINESE NATION>, 12 NOV 1930
     CHRON: 1910-1946
     GEOG: CHINA
     SUBJ: CONTROL

PADASIAN, JOHN J.   P00868
     RADIO-TELEVISION MALAYSIA, SABAH IN <SABAH'S
          REVOLUTION FOR PROGRESS>
     KOTA KINABALU, MALAYSIAN INFORMATION
          SERVICE, N. D. [1971?].
     ##/MAL
     MEDIUM: ELECTRONIC
     CHRON: 1970-1980
     GEOG: MALAYSIA
     SUBJ: DEVELOPMENT

PAGET, ROGER K.   P00869
     INDONESIAN NEWSPAPERS, 1965-1967
     INDONESIA NO. 4(OCT 1967), 170-210.
     #3
     CHRON: 1960-1970
     GEOG: INDONESIA
     SUBJ: RESEARCH

PALL MALL GAZETTE, THE   P02199
     JAPANESE AND CHINESE NEWSPAPERS
     XVIII:2642(4 AUG 1873), 10.
     ##/CHIN-7; REPRINTED IN <HONG KONG DAILY
          PRESS> H01808.
     CHRON: BEFORE 1910
     GEOG: CHINA   EAST ASIA
     SUBJ: DESCRIPTION

PAN-PACIFIC UNION   P02014
     FIRST PAN-PACIFIC PRESS CONFERENCE
     HONOLULU, PAN-PACIFIC UNION, 1921.
     CHRON: 1910-1946
     GEOG: SEV ASIA
     SUBJ: DESCRIPTION

PANG CHI-SHIN   12   P01873
    NEWSPAPER CLIPPINGS IN GOVERNMENT SERVICES
    THE CHINESE ADMINISTRATOR I:1(JAN-MAR 1935),
        81-6.
    CHRON: 1910-1946
    GEOG: EAST ASIA
    SUBJ: OTHER JRN

PANG YUET LENG   P00870
    AMINAH, MOTHER OF SEVEN, IS BACK IN FILMS
    STRAITS TIMES 9 NOV 1973
    ##/MALSP
    MEDIUM: FILM
    CHRON: 1970-1980
    GEOG: MALAYSIA   INDONESIA   SEV ASIA
    SUBJ: BIOGRAPHY

PANKINA, OL'GA GEORGIEVNA   P02718
    PECHAT' KITAISKOI NARODNOI RESPUBLIKI V
        PERIOD SOTSIALISTICHESKIKH PREOBRAZOVANII
    MOSKBA, IZDATEL'STVO MOSKOVSKOVO
        UNIVERSITETA, 1961.
                            LANG: RUSSIAN
    CHRON: 1946-1960   VERIF: UNVERIFIED
    GEOG: CHINA
    SUBJ: DESCRIPTION

PAO MING-SHU   05   P02791
    K'ANG CHAN CH'IEN HOU CHE CHIANG TI PAO YEH
        (NEWSPAPERS IN CHEKIANG BEFORE AND
        AFTER THE WAR)
    PAO HSUEH [TAIPEI] II:2(DEC 1957), 83-5.
                            LANG: CHINESE
    CHRON: 1946-1960
    GEOG: CHINA
    SUBJ: JRN HISTORY

PAO HSUEH [TAIPEI]   P02752
    SHAO NIEN CHUNG KUO CHEN PAO WU SHIH NIEN
        CHIEN SHIH (FIFTY YEARS OF THE YOUNG
        CHINA MORNING POST)
    II:7(JULY 1960), 92-9.
                            LANG: CHINESE
    CHRON: SURVEY
    METH: HISTORICAL
    GEOG: OSEAS CHIN U.S.
    SUBJ: JRN HISTORY

PAO HSUEH [TAIPEI]   P02751
    SHIH NIEN LAI TI CH'IAO PAN PAO K'AN (TEN
        YEARS OF OVERSEAS CHINESE NEWSPAPERS)
    II:7(DEC 1960), 74-7.
                            LANG: CHINESE
    CHRON: 1946-1960
    GEOG: OSEAS CHIN
    SUBJ: DESCRIPTION

PAO-HSUEH CHI-K'AN   P02123
    KO-TI HSIN-WEN SHIH-YEH CHIH YEN-KO YU
        CHIN-K'UANG (THE HISTORY OF NEWSPAPERS
        IN VARIOUS CITIES)
    1:2(JAN 1935), 95-114.
    ##/CHIN-7
                            LANG: CHINESE
    CHRON: 1910-1946
    GEOG: CHINA
    SUBJ: JRN HISTORY

PAO-HSUEH CHI-K'AN   P02122
    WO-KUO KO-TI HSIN-WEN-CHIEH TA-SHIH
        JIH-CHIH [A RECORD OF DAILY JOURNALISM
        IN CHINA]
    1:1(OCT 1934), 153-8.
    ##/CHIN-7
                            LANG: CHINESE
    CHRON: 1910-1946
    GEOG: CHINA
    SUBJ: DESCRIPTION

PAPER AND PRINT [LONDON]   P02200
    CHINA'S NEWSPAPERS AT WAR
    17:2 (SUMMER 1944), 90, 92, 94-5.
    ##/CHIN-7
    CHRON: 1910-1946
    GEOG: CHINA
    SUBJ: DESCRIPTION

PARKER, ALVIN P.   P00872
    THE NATIVE PRESS IN SHANGHAI: OUR RELATION
        TO IT AND HOW WE CAN UTILIZE IT
    CHINESE RECORDER 32:12(DEC 1901), 577-89.
    CHIN REC
    CHRON: BEFORE 1910
    GEOG: CHINA
    SUBJ: PROPAGANDA DESCRIPTION

PARKER, DAVID   P00873
    KEEPING NEWS IN THE NATIONAL INTEREST
    FEER 88:25(20 JUNE 1975), 32.
    ##/CHIN-2; NCNA.
    MEDIUM: GENERAL
    CHRON: 1970-1980
    GEOG: CHINA
    SUBJ: CONTROL   FLOW/AGENCY

PARKER, E. H.   P01713
    PAPER AND PRINTING IN CHINA
    ASIATIC QUARTERLY REVIEW XXVI:52(OCT 1908),
        349-57.
    CHRON: SURVEY
    GEOG: CHINA
    SUBJ: PRINTING

PARKER, EDWARD HARPER   P00874
    THE 'PEKING GAZETTE' AND CHINESE POSTING
    LONGMAN'S MAGAZINE [LONDON] XXIX:CLXIX(NOV
        1896), 73-81.
    ##/CHIN-3; ULS 3:2468.
    CHRON: BEFORE 1910
    METH: HISTORICAL
    GEOG: CHINA
    SUBJ: DESCRIPTION

PARKER, ELLIOTT S.   P00875
    PHOTOJOURNALISM EDUCATION IN A DEVELOPING
        COUNTRY: MALAYSIA AS A CASE STUDY
    COLLEGE PARK, MARYLAND, AEJ CONVENTION, 1976.
    ##/MAL; ACCESSIBLE THROUGH ERIC.
    CHRON: 1970-1980
    GEOG: MALAYSIA
    SUBJ: EDUCATION

PARKER, ELLIOTT S.   P01410
    A POTTED HISTORY OF MALAYSIAN JOURNALISM
    LEADER MALAYSIAN JOURNALISM REVIEW 2:3(1973),
        31-2.
    CHRON: SURVEY
    METH: OTHER OR COMB
    GEOG: MALAYSIA   SINGAPORE
    SUBJ: RESEARCH   JRN HISTORY

PARKER, ELLIOTT S.   P02803
    CHINESE NEWSPAPERS IN THE UNITED STATES:
        BACKGROUND NOTES AND DESCRIPTIVE ANALYSIS
    SEATTLE, WASHINGTON, AEJ CONVENTION, 1978.
    MIMEO; ACCESSIBLE THROUGH ERIC.
    CHRON: SURVEY
    METH: OTHER OR COMB
    GEOG: OSEAS CHIN U.S.
    SUBJ: JRN HISTORY DESCRIPTION

PARKER, WILLIAM   P01874
    SHANGHAI PRESS CONFERENCE
    AMERICAN MERCURY XLIV:174(JUNE 1938), 156-61.
    ##/CHIN-6
    CHRON: 1910-1946
    GEOG: CHINA   EAST ASIA
    SUBJ: FOR CORR

PARRISH, FRED   P01605
    LESSONS COME TO LIFE
    HORIZONS [USIS] XVII:11(1968-1970), 54-58.
    MEDIUM: ELECTRONIC
    CHRON: 1960-1970
    GEOG: EAST ASIA
    SUBJ: EDUCATION

PARSONS, CYNTHIA   P00876
    INDONESIA TURNS TO TV TEACHING
    CSM 24 FEB 1975
    ##/INDO
    MEDIUM: ELECTRONIC
    CHRON: 1970-1980
    GEOG: INDONESIA
    SUBJ: EDUCATION

PATRON, JOSEFINA S.   P00877
    MASS COMMUNICATION TEACHING AND TRAINING IN
        THE PHILIPPINES: PROFILES, PROBLEMS,
        PERSPECTIVES AND PROSPECTS
    KUALA LUMPUR, AMIC SEMINAR ON COMMUNICATION
        TEACHING AND TRAINING, 1972.
    ##/PHIL; MIMEO, 31+ PP.
    MEDIUM: GENERAL
    CHRON: 1970-1980
    GEOG: PHILIPPINES
    SUBJ: EDUCATION

PATTERSON, DON D.   P00878
    THE JOURNALISM OF CHINA
    COLUMBIA, MO., U. OF MISSOURI, 1922.
    #3; ULS 3:2698; U. OF MISSOURI BULLETIN,
        JOURNALISM SERIES 26,
        VOL. 23, NO. 34.
    CHRON: SURVEY
    GEOG: CHINA
    SUBJ: JRN HISTORY DESCRIPTION

PATTERSON, JR., RICHARD C.   P02201
    THE CINEMA IN CHINA
    THE CHINA WEEKLY REVIEW XXXX:2(12 MAR 1927),
        48-9.
    MEDIUM: FILM
    CHRON: 1910-1946
    GEOG: CHINA
    SUBJ: DESCRIPTION

PEAKE, CYRUS   P01606
    THE ORIGIN AND DEVELOPMENT OF PRINTING IN
        CHINA IN THE LIGHT OF RECENT RESEARCH
    GUTENBERG-JAHRBUCH 1935, 9-17.
    ##/CHIN-5
    CHRON: BEFORE 1910
    METH: HISTORICAL
    GEOG: CHINA
    SUBJ: PRINTING

PEAKE, CYRUS H.   P01607
    ADDITIONAL NOTES AND BIBLIOGRAPHY ON THE
        HISTORY OF PRINTING IN THE FAR EAST
    GUTENBERG-JAHRBUCH 1939, 55-61.
    ##/ASIA
    CHRON: BEFORE 1910
    METH: HISTORICAL
    GEOG: CHINA   EAST ASIA
    SUBJ: PRINTING

PEARL, CYRIL   P00879
    MORRISON OF PEKING
    RINGWOOD, VICTORIA, AUSTRALIA, PENGUIN, 1970.
    CHRON: BEFORE 1910
    METH: HISTORICAL
    GEOG: CHINA
    SUBJ: JRN HISTORY BIOGRAPHY

PEARN, B. R.   P01326
    BURMESE PRINTED BOOKS BEFORE JUDSON IN <BURMA
        RESEARCH SOCIETY FIFTIETH
        ANNIVERSARY PUBLICATIONS NO. 2>.
    RANGOON, BURMA RESEARCH SOCIETY, 1960.
    ##/BURMA: REPRINTED FROM <JOURNAL OF BURMA
        RES. SOC.> XXX:11, 384-5.
    CHRON: BEFORE 1910
    GEOG: BURMA
    SUBJ: PRINTING   PUBLISHING

PEI K'E [BAKER, RICHARD T.]   07   P01247
    MEI KUO PAO YEH MIEN LIN TE SHE HUI WEN T'I
        [SOCIAL PROBLEMS AND A RESPONSIBLE PRESS]
    TAIPEI, GRADUATE SCHOOL OF JOURNALISM,
        NATIONAL CHENGCHI U., 1969.
    COLLECTION OF ESSAYS
                            LANG: CHINESE
    CHRON: 1960-1970
    GEOG: TAIWAN
    SUBJ: LAW/ETHICS

PEIPING ASSOCIATION OF UNIVERSITY   P02015
        WOMEN
    SIFTED NEWS
    PEKING, PEIPING ASSOCIATION OF UNIVERSITY
        WOMEN, [N. D., 1930'S?].
    ##/CHIN-6
    CHRON: 1910-1946
    GEOG: CHINA
    SUBJ: CONTROL

PEIPING CHRONICLE, THE   P01971
    FACTS DO NOT SPEAK FOR THEMSELVES
    29 JULY 1934
    FROM <PACIFIC AFFAIRS>, SEE LATTIMORE L01830.
    CHRON: 1910-1946
    GEOG: CHINA   WORLD
    SUBJ: FOR CORR   CROSS CULTU

PEIPING CHRONICLE, THE   P01608
    <PEIPING WAN PAO> CELEBRATES COMPLETION OF
        5,000TH ISSUE
    30 DEC 1934
    ##/CHIN-5
    CHRON: 1910-1946
    GEOG: CHINA
    SUBJ: DESCRIPTION

PEIRIS, DENZIL   P00880
    COMMUNICATIONS GAP MAY HINDER INDIA'S FAMILY
        PLANNING GOALS
    THE ASIAN (2 JULY-8 JULY 1972).
    ##/SWAS
    MEDIUM: GENERAL
    CHRON: 1970-1980
    GEOG: SO/WEST ASI
    SUBJ: DEVELOPMENT

PEIRIS, DENZIL   P00901
    INDIRA RELAXES PRESS SQUEEZE
    FEER 94:40(1 OCT 1976),17-18.
    ##/SWAS
    CHRON: 1970-1980
    GEOG: SO/WEST ASI
    SUBJ: CONTROL

PEIRIS, DENZIL   P00900
    TELLING IT LIKE IT SHOULD BE
    FEER 93:33(13 AUG 1976), 23-4.
    ##/AGEN
    CHRON: 1970-1980
    GEOG: WORLD
    SUBJ: FLOW/AGENCY

PEIRIS, DENZIL   P00902
    FREEDOM TO CHOP AND CHANGE
    FEER 96:16(22 APR 1977), 27.
    ##/SWAS
    CHRON: 1970-1980
    GEOG: SO/WEST ASI
    SUBJ: CONTROL

PENGULAS [PSEUD.?]   P00882
    'JELITA' MAJALAH BARU SERBA MEMIKAT
    BERITA MINGGU 1 AUG 1976
    ##/MAL
                                LANG: MALAY/INDONESIAN
    CHRON: 1970-1980
    GEOG: MALAYSIA
    SUBJ: DESCRIPTION

PENNELL, WILFRED V.   P02603
    A LIFETIME WITH THE CHINESE
    HONG KONG, SOUTH CHINA MORNING POST, 1974.
    CHRON: SURVEY
    GEOG: HONG KONG   TAIWAN   CHINA
    SUBJ: FOR CORR   BIOGRAPHY

PENNELL, WILFRED V.   P02604
    THE ROLE OF THE JOURNALIST IN THE
        COMMONWEALTH
    ASIAN REVIEW LX:221(JAN 1964), 1-10.
    ##/ASIA
    CHRON: SURVEY
    GEOG: HONG KONG   TAIWAN   CHINA
    SUBJ: FOR CORR   BIOGRAPHY

PENULIS KHAS   P01875
    KENAPA TAK BOLEH NYANYI LAGU INGGERIS DI TV?
    BERITA HARIAN (SUNDAY, MALAYSIA) 26 FEB 1978
    ##/MAL-3
    MEDIUM: ELECTRONIC   LANG: MALAY/INDONESIAN
    CHRON: 1970-1980
    GEOG: MALAYSIA
    SUBJ: CONTROL

PEOPLE'S TRIBUNE, THE   P01616
    LETTERS OF JUNIUS SINICUS: TO MR. JOHN
        BENJAMIN POWELL
    XXIX N. S.:3 & 4(AUG 1940), 97-104.
    CHRON: 1910-1946
    GEOG: CHINA
    SUBJ: DESCRIPTION

PEOPLE'S TRIBUNE, THE   P01610
    CHINA AND THE SINO-FOREIGN PRESS
    I N. S.:5(16 JAN 1932), 142-3.
    CHRON: 1910-1946
    GEOG: CHINA   WORLD
    SUBJ: FOR CORR   PROPAGANDA DESCRIPTION

PEOPLE'S TRIBUNE, THE   P01609
    JAPANESE PROPAGANDA IN CHINA
    I N. S.:2(26 DEC 1931), 55-8.
    CHRON: 1910-1946
    GEOG: CHINA   EAST ASIA
    SUBJ: PROPAGANDA

PEOPLE'S TRIBUNE, THE   P01614
    BOWDERLIZING NEWS FROM NORTH CHINA
    XX N. S.:5 & 6(MAR 1938), 153-7.
    CHRON: 1910-1946
    GEOG: CHINA
    SUBJ: CONTROL   DESCRIPTION

PEOPLE'S TRIBUNE, THE   P01613
    THE CHINESE FILM INDUSTRY
    IX N. S.:1(1 APR 1935), 25-32.
    ##/CHIN-5
    MEDIUM: FILM
    CHRON: 1910-1946
    GEOG: CHINA
    SUBJ: DESCRIPTION

PEOPLE'S TRIBUNE, THE   P01612
    THIS CENSORSHIP BUSINESS
    VIII N. S.:3(1 FEB 1935), 153-6.
    CHRON: 1910-1946
    GEOG: CHINA
    SUBJ: CONTROL

PEOPLE'S TRIBUNE, THE   P01611
    MR. WOODHEAD'S CHARGES OF INCONSISTENCY
    7 N. S.:2(16 JULY 1934), 55-8.
    CHRON: 1910-1946
    GEOG: CHINA
    SUBJ: CONTROL

PEOPLE'S TRIBUNE, THE   P01615
    GANGSTER JOURNALISM IN SHANGHAI
    XXVII N. S.:1-6(AUG/OCT 1939), 52-4.
    ##/CHIN-5
    CHRON: 1910-1946
    GEOG: CHINA
    SUBJ: DESCRIPTION

PEYTON-GRIFFIN, R. T.   P01876
    WHAT THE SOUND FILM IS DOING
    THE CHINA JOURNAL XI:5(NOV 1929), 215-16.
    MEDIUM: FILM
    CHRON: 1910-1946
    GEOG: CHINA
    SUBJ: DESCRIPTION CROSS CULTU

PHAN NHU MY   P02655
    'THE EVENT OF THE YEAR'
    THE JOURNALIST'S WORLD IV:1(1966), 19-20.
    CHRON: 1960-1970
    GEOG: VIETNAM
    SUBJ: OTHER JRN   OTHER NON-J

PHAN NHU MY   P02654
    PROFESSIONAL TRAINING: ABROAD OR ON
        THE SPOT
    THE JOURNALIST'S WORLD II:3(1964), 10-11.
    CHRON: 1960-1970
    GEOG: VIETNAM
    SUBJ: EDUCATION

PHAN NHU MY   P02656
    VIETNAMESE NEWSMEN UNDER FIRE
    THE JOURNALIST'S WORLD VI:1(1968), 25-6.
    CHRON: 1960-1970
    GEOG: VIETNAM
    SUBJ: FOR CORR   DESCRIPTION

PHILIPPINES PRESS INSTITUTE   P00883
    PHILIPPINES NEWS MEDIA DIRECTORY
    MANILA, 1968.
    CHRON: 1960-1970   VERIF: UNVERIFIED
    GEOG: PHILIPPINES
    SUBJ: RESEARCH

PHILIPPINES. DEPARTMENT OF   P00906
        PUBLIC INFORMATION
    GUIDELINES FOR MASS MEDIA
    BULLETIN OF CONCERNED ASIAN SCHOLARS 5:1
        (JULY 1973), 58.
    ##/PHIL
    MEDIUM: GENERAL
    CHRON: 1970-1980
    GEOG: PHILIPPINES
    SUBJ: CONTROL

PHOENIX, THE   P01714
    MODERN PRINTING IN JAPAN
    II:23(MAY 1872), 191-2.
    CHRON: BEFORE 1910
    GEOG: EAST ASIA
    SUBJ: PRINTING

PHOENIX, THE   P01715
    MISCELLANEOUS NOTES: PERIODICALS IN CHINA,
        JAPAN, SIAM
    I:9(MAR 1871), 156.
    CHRON: 1910-1946
    GEOG: SEV ASIA
    SUBJ: DESCRIPTION

PICKERELL, ALBERT G.   P00884
    THE PRESS OF THAILAND: CONDITIONS AND TRENDS
    JQ 37:1(WINTER 1960), 83-96.
    ##/THAI
    CHRON: 1960-1970
    GEOG: THAILAND
    SUBJ: DESCRIPTION

PIKE, DOUGLAS   P00885
    VIET CONG COMMUNICATION TECHNIQUES
    CAMBRIDGE, CENTER FOR INTERNATIONAL STUDIES,
        MIT, 1966.
    IN PIKE P00886, NO. C/66-11.
    MEDIUM: GENERAL
    CHRON: 1960-1970   VERIF: UNVERIFIED
    GEOG: VIETNAM
    SUBJ: PROPAGANDA DESCRIPTION

PIKE, DOUGLAS   P00886
    VIET CONG: THE ORGANIZATION AND TECHNIQUES OF
        OF SOUTH VIETNAM
    CAMBRIDGE, MIT, 1966.
    CHAPTER ON COMMUNICATION OF IDEAS AND APPENDIX
        ON NLF MASS MEDIA
    MEDIUM: GENERAL
    CHRON: 1960-1970
    GEOG: VIETNAM
    SUBJ: PROPAGANDA

PILLAI, G. PARAMASWARAN   P01716
    THE PRESS IN INDIA: ITS ORIGIN AND GROWTH
    ASIATIC QUARTERLY REVIEW VII 3RD
        SERIES:13(JAN 1899), 16-38.
    CHRON: BEFORE 1910
    METH: HISTORICAL
    GEOG: SO/WEST ASI
    SUBJ: JRN HISTORY

PILLAI, M. G. G.   P00889
    MCA PRESS INTEREST
    FEER 78:53(30 DEC 1972), 38.
    ##/MAL-2
    CHRON: 1970-1980
    GEOG: MALAYSIA
    SUBJ: DESCRIPTION

PILLAI, M. G. G.   P00887
    CHANGING TIMES
    FEER 77:36(2 SEPT 1972), 18.
    ##/MAL-2; I. I. N. A.
    CHRON: 1970-1980
    GEOG: MALAYSIA   WORLD
    SUBJ: FLOW/AGENCY DESCRIPTION

PILLAI, M. G. G.   P00888
    MALAYSIAN PATTERNS
    FEER 78:45(4 NOV 1972), 36, 40.
    ##/MAL-2
    CHRON: 1970-1980
    GEOG: MALAYSIA
    SUBJ: OTHER NON-J

PIROVANO-WANG, NORA   P02622
    JOURNAUX CHINOIS DE CHANGHAI ET MOUVEMENT
         DU 30 MAI 1925: QUELQUES REMARQUES A
         PROPOS D'UN TEXTE
    MOUVEMENT SOCIAL 89(1974), 37-58.
                   LANG: OTHER EUROPEAN
    CHRON: 1910-1946   VERIF: UNVERIFIED
    GEOG: CHINA
    SUBJ: JRN HISTORY

PIXLEY, MORRISSON   P01877
    A CHINESE NEWSPAPER IN AMERICA
    THE WORLD'S WORK 3:6(APR 1902), 1950-3.
    ##/CHIN-US
    CHRON: BEFORE 1910
    GEOG: OSEAS CHIN   U.S.
    SUBJ: DESCRIPTION

PLUVIER, J. M.   P00890
    THE DUTCH PRESS AND THE INDONESIAN QUESTION
    JERNAL SEJARAH [PETALING JAYA] I:3(1962/3)
    CHRON: 1946-1960   VERIF: UNVERIFIED
    GEOG: INDONESIA   EUROPE
    SUBJ: GEN HISTORY

PO T'AO   07   P02124
    PEI-CHING CHIH HSIN-WEN CHIEH [JOURNALISM IN
         PEKING]
    KUO-WEN CHOU-PAO II:13(12 APR 1925), 9-12.
    ##/CHIN-7
                   LANG: CHINESE
    CHRON: 1910-1946
    GEOG: CHINA
    SUBJ: DESCRIPTION

POCKRASS, ROBERT M.   P00891
    THE ORIENT'S LIVELY ENGLISH-LANGUAGE PRESS
    PENN STATE JOURNALIST 10:1(JAN 1968), 6-9.
    ##/ASIA
    CHRON: 1960-1970
    GEOG: OTHER   SEV ASIA
    SUBJ: DESCRIPTION

POLSKY, ANTHONY   P00892
    LEE KUAN YEW VERSUS THE PRESS
    PACIFIC COMMUNITY 3:1(OCT 1971), 183-203.
    ##/SIN
    CHRON: 1970-1980
    GEOG: SINGAPORE
    SUBJ: CONTROL

POOL, ITHIEL DE SOLA   P01617
    COMMUNICATIONS AND DEVELOPMENT
    HORIZONS [USIS] XVIII:8(1968-70), 24-5, 52-3.
    MEDIUM: GENERAL
    CHRON: 1960-1970
    GEOG: WORLD
    SUBJ: DEVELOPMENT

POOLE, FREDERICK K.   P00894
    SINGAPORE: THE NEW QUALITY PRINTING SOURCE
    PUBLISHER'S WEEKLY 210:7(16 AUG 1976), 91-7.
    ##/SIN
    CHRON: 1970-1980
    GEOG: SINGAPORE
    SUBJ: PRINTING   PUBLISHING

POON, DAVID JIM-TAT   P02657
    <TATZEPAO>: ITS HISTORY AND SIGNIFICANCE
        AS A COMMUNICATION MEDIUM
    IN CHU C02273, PP. 184-221.
    MEDIUM: OTHER
    CHRON: SURVEY
    METH: OTHER OR COMB
    GEOG: CHINA
    SUBJ: DESCRIPTION

POPP, RITA A.   P00893
    CHINA PRESS TAKES ORDERS
    GRASSROOTS EDITOR (FALL 1976), 9-10.
    ##/CHIN-4
    CHRON: 1970-1980
    GEOG: CHINA
    SUBJ: CONTROL

POPULAR PHOTOGRAPHY   P01618
    FOR THOSE WHO NEVER CAME HOME
    77:4(OCT 1975), 90-1.
    PHOTO/PJ
    CHRON: 1970-1980
    GEOG: VIETNAM   U.S.
    SUBJ: FOR CORR

POSSIBLE, HENRITA SAKUNTALA   P00895
    THE PRESS AND POLITICAL CHANGE
    KUALA LUMPUR, GRADUATION EXERCISE FOR
        ECONOMICS AT U. OF MALAYA, 1970.
    CHRON: 1970-1980
    GEOG: MALAYSIA
    SUBJ: DEVELOPMENT POLIT SCI

POWELL, J. B.   P02330
    LET THE ADVERTISING LIGHT SHINE OUT IN CHINA
    THE CHINA WEEKLY REVIEW IV:2(9 MAR 1918),
        39-41.
    CHRON: 1910-1946
    GEOG: CHINA
    SUBJ: OTHER JRN

POWELL, J. B.   P01619
    THE JOURNALISTIC FIELD IN <AMERICAN
        UNIVERSITY MEN IN CHINA>
    SHANGHAI, THE COMACRIB PRESS, 1936.
    FILM
    CHRON: 1910-1946
    GEOG: CHINA
    SUBJ: DESCRIPTION BIOGRAPHY

POWELL, J. B.   P01717
    THE PROPOSAL TO LICENSE THE SHANGHAI PRESS
    THE CHINA WEEKLY REVIEW IX:5(5 JULY 1919),
        172-4.
    CHRON: 1910-1946
    GEOG: CHINA
    SUBJ: CONTROL   LAW/ETHICS

POWELL, J. B.   P02202
    WAS CHINA 'SAVED' BY THE FOREIGN NEWSPAPER
        CORRESPONDENTS
    THE CHINA WEEKLY REVIEW XLI:5(2 JULY 1927),
        106-7.
    CHRON: 1910-1946
    GEOG: CHINA
    SUBJ: FOR CORR   DESCRIPTION

POWELL, J. B.   P01718
    THE AMERICAN CORRESPONDENT IN CHINA
    ASIA XXVII:5(MAY 1927), 380-2.
    CHRON: 1910-1946
    GEOG: CHINA
    SUBJ: FOR CORR

POWELL, JOHN B.   P00896
    MISSOURIANS IN CHINA
    MISSOURI HISTORICAL REVIEW 15(1920-21),
        611-16.
    ##/CHIN-4
    CHRON: 1910-1946
    GEOG: CHINA
    SUBJ: DESCRIPTION BIOGRAPHY

POWELL, JOHN B.   P02532
    PUBLISHING IN SHANGHAI
    IN MOTT M02529, PP. 72-6.
    CHRON: 1910-1946
    GEOG: CHINA
    SUBJ: PUBLISHING

POWELL, JOHN BENJAMIN   P01360
    MY TWENTY-FIVE YEARS IN CHINA
    NEW YORK, MACMILLAN, 1945.
    REPRINT AVAILABLE
    CHRON: 1910-1946
    GEOG: CHINA
    SUBJ: JRN HISTORY BIOGRAPHY

POWELL, JOHN W.   P02331
    REPLY TO AN ATTACK ON THE CHINA WEEKLY REVIEW
    THE CHINA WEEKLY REVIEW 117:4(25 MAR 1950),
        54-6.
    CHRON: 1946-1960
    GEOG: CHINA
    SUBJ:

PRAKOSO, MASTINI HARDJO   P02623
    MASS COMMUNICATION IN INDONESIA: AN
        ANNOTATED BIBLIOGRAPHY
    SINGAPORE, AMIC, 1978.
    BIBLIOGRAPHY SERIES 10
    MEDIUM: GENERAL
    CHRON: SURVEY
    GEOG: INDONESIA
    SUBJ: RESEARCH

PRESCOTT, C. LANE   P02332
    PROPAGANDA--ITS USE AND MISUSE
    THE CHINA WEEKLY REVIEW VII:9(1 FEB 1919),
        308-10.
    CHRON: 1910-1946
    GEOG: CHINA
    SUBJ: PROPAGANDA

PRESS INSTITUTE OF INDIA   P00898
    EMERGING ESTATE
    NEW DELHI, ORIENT, LONGMANS, 1966.
    NUC AUTHORS 68-72, 77:231
    CHRON: 1960-1970
    GEOG: SO/WEST ASI
    SUBJ: DESCRIPTION

PRESS UNION   P02588
    THE SHANGHAI INCIDENT MISREPRESENTED:
        SHANGHAI EDITORS DRAW ATTENTION TO
        INCORRECT REPORTS IN AMERICAN PAPERS
    SHANGHAI, PRESS UNION, 1932.
    NUC<56 470:348
    CHRON: 1910-1946
    GEOG: CHINA
    SUBJ: DESCRIPTION

PRINGLE, R.   P00903
    PIECES FROM THE BROOKE PAST IV:
        (PROTO-NEWSPAPERS IN BROOKE SARAWAK)
    SARAWAK GAZETTE XCI:1288(30 JUNE 1965) 186-7.
    ##/MAL
    CHRON: BEFORE 1910
    METH: HISTORICAL
    GEOG: SO/WEST ASI
    SUBJ: JRN HISTORY

PROPAGANDA ANALYSIS   P00904
    WAR IN CHINA
    II:5(FEB 1939), 1-2.
    CHRON: 1910-1946
    GEOG: CHINA   EAST ASIA
    SUBJ: PROPAGANDA

PU SHAO-FU   02   P00905
    T'AN HSIN WEN CHIAO YU (JOURNALISM
        INSTRUCTION)
    HSIN CHUNG-HUA (NEW SERIES, 2ND) 2:4(APR
        1944), 60-69.
                            LANG: CHINESE
    CHRON: 1910-1946   VERIF: UNVERIFIED
    GEOG: CHINA
    SUBJ: EDUCATION

PUBLISHERS' AUXILLARY   P00907
    WALL STREET JOURNAL STUDIES SHOWED ASIAN
        MARKET RIPE FOR NEW EDITION
    9 OCT 1976
    ##/HKG
    CHRON: 1970-1980
    GEOG: HONG KONG   SEV ASIA
    SUBJ: DESCRIPTION

PUBLISHERS' WEEKLY   P02203
     [CHINESE NEWSPAPERS]
     LXXXVII (1915), 797.
     ##/CHIN-7
     CHRON: 1910-1946
     GEOG: CHINA
     SUBJ: DESCRIPTION

PUBLISHERS' WEEKLY, THE   P02065
     JOURNALISTIC NOTES [A CHINESE NEWSPAPER IN
          NEW YORK]
     LXV:1666(2 JAN 1904), 963.
     ##/CHIN-7
     CHRON: BEFORE 1910
     GEOG: OSEAS CHIN   U.S.
     SUBJ: DESCRIPTION

PYE, LUCIAN W.   P02044
     COMMUNICATION AND CHINESE POLITICAL CULTURE
     ASIAN SURVEY XVIII:3(MAR 1978), 221-46.
     ##/CHIN-7
     MEDIUM: GENERAL
     CHRON: SURVEY
     METH: OTHER OR COMB
     GEOG: CHINA
     SUBJ: OTHER JRN

PYE, LUCIAN, EDITOR.   P02658
     COMMUNICATIONS AND POLITICAL DEVELOPMENT
     PRINCETON, N. Y., PRINCETON UNIVERSITY
          PRESS, 1963.
     SEE MOSEL M02652 AND YU Y02666
     MEDIUM: GENERAL
     CHRON: SURVEY
     METH: OTHER OR COMB
     GEOG: WORLD
     SUBJ: DEVELOPMENT OTHER JRN

QUARTERLY REVIEW [LONDON]   Q00908
     TA TSING LEU LU; BEING THE FUNDAMENTAL LAWS,
          AND A SELECTION FROM THE SUPPLEMENTARY
          STATUTES OF THE PENAL CODE IN CHINA
     III:6(MAY 1810), 273-319.
     ##/CHIN-3; FREEDOM OF PRINTING, PRESSES,
          P. 291.
     CHRON: BEFORE 1910
     GEOG: CHINA
     SUBJ: CONTROL   LAW/ETHICS

QUIGLEY, HAROLD S.   Q02203
     FOREIGN NEWSPAPERS AND CHINA'S PROGRESS
     THE CHINA WEEKLY REVIEW XXIV:5(31 MAR 1923),
          170.
     CHRON: 1910-1946
     GEOG: CHINA
     SUBJ: DEVELOPMENT DESCRIPTION

QUILL, THE   Q00909
    POWER OF THE THRONE
    (APR 1976), 12.
    ##/THAI
    CHRON: 1970-1980
    GEOG: THAILAND
    SUBJ: CONTROL

QUINN, THOMAS ANTHONY   Q00910
    REPORTING VIETNAM
    MASTERS THESIS, UNIVERSITY OF TEXAS/AUSTIN,
        1968
    APR 1966-JUNE 1967; CHAPTER ON PRESS HISTORY
        OF VIETNAM.
    CHRON: 1960-1970   VERIF: UNVERIFIED
    GEOG: VIETNAM   U.S.
    SUBJ: FOR CORR

QUIRINO, JOE   Q02549
    FILMS FOR THE NEW YEAR
    ASIAWEEK 5:2(19 JAN 1979), 49.
    ##/PHIL
    MEDIUM: FILM
    CHRON: 1970-1980
    GEOG: PHILIPPINES
    SUBJ: DESCRIPTION

QUIRINO, JOSE A.   Q01620
    A LOOK AT ASIAN FILMS
    HORIZONS [USIS] XVII:11(1968-70), 46-48.
    MEDIUM: FILM
    CHRON: 1960-1970
    GEOG: SEV ASIA
    SUBJ: DESCRIPTION

R., H.   R02238
    DANGLING PARTICULARS
    THE QUILL 66:10(NOV 1978), 11.
    ##/CHIN-8; LETTERS TO EDITOR OF <REN MIN
        JIH PAO>.
    CHRON: 1970-1980
    GEOG: CHINA
    SUBJ: DESCRIPTION

RAFI-ZADEH, HASSAN   R01365
    INTERNATIONAL MASS COMMUNICATIONS: A
        COMPUTERIZED ANNOTATED BIBLIOGRAPHY
    CARBONDALE, ILL., HONORARY RELATION-ZONE,
        1972.
    MEDIUM: GENERAL
    CHRON: SURVEY
    METH: OTHER OR COMB
    GEOG: WORLD
    SUBJ: RESEARCH

RAGSDALE, WILMOTT   R00911
    A PROGRAM FOR DEVELOPING THE MEDIA OF
        SOUTHEAST ASIA
    JQ 37:2(SPRING 1960), 275-9.
    ##/ASIA
    CHRON: 1960-1970
    GEOG: THAILAND   SEV ASIA
    SUBJ: DEVELOPMENT

RAJAGOPAL, D. R.   R00912
    PULLING OUT THE STOPS
    FEER 83:1(18 MAR 1974), 14.
    ##/ASIA
    MEDIUM: GENERAL
    CHRON: 1970-1980
    GEOG: VIETNAM   SEV ASIA
    SUBJ: FOR CORR

RAM, MOHAN   R00914
    HOW GANDHI GAG ORDER WORKED
    CSM 4 AUG 1977
    ##/SwAS
    MEDIUM: GENERAL
    CHRON: 1970-1980
    GEOG: SO/WEST ASI
    SUBJ: CONTROL

RAM, MOHAN   R00913
    INDIA'S PRESS: FREE BUT WARY
    CSM 9 FEB 1977
    ##/SwAS
    CHRON: 1970-1980
    GEOG: SO/WEST ASI
    SUBJ: CONTROL

RAMACHANDRAN, RASU   R00915
    SOURCES OF INFORMATION ON THE PRESS OF SOUTH
        AND SOUTH-EAST ASIA: A BRIEF SURVEY
    AUSTRALIAN ACADEMIC AND RESEARCH LIBRARIES
        5:1(MAR 1974), 29-36.
    ##/BIB
    CHRON: 1970-1980
    GEOG: SEV ASIA
    SUBJ: RESEARCH

RAND, CHRISTOPHER   R00916
    REPORTING IN THE FAR EAST
    NIEMAN REPORTS PART 1, VIII:1(1954), 19-22;
        PART 2 VIII:2(1954), 14-17.
    ##/ASIA
    CHRON: 1946-1960
    GEOG: SEV ASIA
    SUBJ: FOR CORR

RAO, Y. V. LAKSHMANA   R00917
    PROPAGANDA THROUGH THE PRINTED MEDIA IN THE
        DEVELOPING COUNTRIES
    ANNALS OF THE AMERICAN ACADEMY OF POLITICAL
        AND SOCIAL SCIENCE 398(NOV 1971), 93-103.
    ##/OTHR
    CHRON: 1970-1980
    GEOG: WORLD
    SUBJ: PROPAGANDA FLOW/AGENCY

RASBINA H. A.   R02239
    TAK ADA ESOK BAGI INDUSTRI FILEM MELAYU?
    NADAMINGGU (28 MAY 1978), 1, 2.
    ##/MAL-3; SUPPLEMENT TO BERITA HARIAN,
        SUNDAY EDITION.
    MEDIUM: FILM   LANG: MALAY/INDONESIAN
    CHRON: 1970-1980
    GEOG: MALAYSIA
    SUBJ: DESCRIPTION

RASMUSSEN, O. D.   R01973
    THE WORLD OF FLEET STREET
    THE CHINESE NATION II:26(9 DEC 1931),
        898-900, 917.
    FILM
    CHRON: 1910-1946
    GEOG: CHINA   EUROPE
    SUBJ: DESCRIPTION

RASMUSSEN, O. D.   R01972
    FLEET STREET JOURNALISM
    THE CHINESE NATION II:25(21 DEC 1931),
        859, 877.
    FILM
    CHRON: 1910-1946
    GEOG: CHINA   EUROPE
    SUBJ: DESCRIPTION

RAVENHOLT, ALBERT   R00919
    ASIA'S FREE DAILY NEWSPAPERS
    NIEMAN REPORTS 17:3(1963), 28-31.
    ##/ASIA; FROM AUFS REPORT, RAVENHOLT R00918
    CHRON: 1960-1970
    GEOG: SEV ASIA
    SUBJ: CONTROL   DESCRIPTION

RAVENHOLT, ALBERT   R00918
    ASIA'S FREE DAILY NEWSPAPERS
    AUFS REPORTS, SEA SERIES 10:7(1962).
    ##/ASIA
    CHRON: 1960-1970
    GEOG: SEV ASIA
    SUBJ: CONTROL   DESCRIPTION

RAVENHOLT, ALBERT   R00921
    A. V. H. HARTENDORP: MANILA'S DOUGHTY
        SEVENTY-ONE YEAR-OLD AMERICAN EDITOR
    AUFS REPORTS, SEA SERIES XII:13(1964).
    CHRON: 1960-1970
    GEOG: PHILIPPINES
    SUBJ: BIOGRAPHY

RAVENHOLT, ALBERT   R00920
    XATLAO: THE HISTORY AND PROBLEMS OF A
        LAOTIAN NEWSPAPER
    AUFS REPORTS, SEA SERIES XV:4(1967).
    ##/LAOS
    CHRON: 1960-1970
    GEOG: THAILAND
    SUBJ: DESCRIPTION BIOGRAPHY

REA, GEORGE BRONSON   R01879
    ADVENTURE IN AMERICAN JOURNALISM IN THE
        FAR EAST
    FAR-EASTERN REVIEW 27:6(JUNE 1931), 335-7.
    CHRON: 1910-1946
    GEOG: SEV ASIA
    SUBJ: DESCRIPTION

REA, GEORGE BRONSON   R01878
    TWENTY FIVE YEARS: THE AMERICANISM OF THE
        'FAR-EASTERN REVIEW'
    FAR-EASTERN REVIEW 24:4(APR 1928), 145-51.
    CHRON: 1910-1946
    GEOG: SEV ASIA
    SUBJ: DESCRIPTION

REA, GEORGE BRONSON   R01880
    OUR FRIENDSHIP FOR CHINA (THE FAR-EASTERN
        REVIEW ATTACKED IN THE PEOPLE'S TRIBUNE
        AS A PRO-JAPANESE ORGAN)
    FAR-EASTERN REVIEW 28:1(JAN 1932), 6-7.
    EXTRACT FROM <PEOPLE'S TRIBUNE> P01609
    CHRON: 1910-1946
    GEOG: CHINA   EAST ASIA   SEV ASIA
    SUBJ: PROPAGANDA

READ, W. H.   R02016
    AN EDITOR HOAXED
    MALAYA [BRITISH MALAYA, MALAYSIA] (SEPT
        1954), 507-8.
    ##/SIN-2
    CHRON: 1910-1946
    GEOG: SINGAPORE
    SUBJ: DESCRIPTION BIOGRAPHY

REECE, ROBERT   R00923
    ASIAN PRESS IS URGED: 'HELP US TO MODERNIZE'
    THE ASIAN [HONG KONG] (10-16 SEPT 1972).
    ##/ASIA
    CHRON: 1970-1980
    GEOG: SEV ASIA
    SUBJ: DEVELOPMENT

REED, PAUL   R01719
    THE PRESS IN JAPAN
    FAR EASTERN MIRROR 1:7(10 JUNE 1938), 10-14.
    CHRON: 1910-1946
    GEOG: EAST ASIA
    SUBJ: DESCRIPTION

REEVES, RICHARD   R02533
    CHINA BEAMS ABROAD
    ESQUIRE 91:2(30 JAN 1979), 9-10.
    MEDIUM: ELECTRONIC
    CHRON: 1970-1980
    GEOG: CHINA
    SUBJ: DESCRIPTION

REINSH, PAUL SAMUEL   R01327
    INTELLECTUAL AND POLITICAL CURRENTS IN THE
        FAR EAST
    BOSTON, HOUGHTON MIFFLIN, 1911.
    ##/CHIN-4; PP. 159-62.
    CHRON: 1910-1946
    GEOG: CHINA
    SUBJ: DESCRIPTION

REVIEW'S CORRESPONDENT AT CHANCHUN   R02317
    MANCHUKUO INVOKES CRUSHING PRESS LAW
    THE CHINA WEEKLY REVIEW 65:1(12 AUG 1933),
        460.
    CHRON: 1910-1946
    GEOG: CHINA   EAST ASIA
    SUBJ: CONTROL   LAW/ETHICS

REYNOLDS, JACK   R02285
    ANOTHER PEEK THROUGH THE BAMBOO CURTAIN
    NYT 7 JAN 1978
    ##/CHIN-8
    MEDIUM: ELECTRONIC
    CHRON: 1970-1980
    GEOG: CHINA
    SUBJ: FOR CORR   EDUCATION

RHODES, DENNIS E.   R00924
    THE SPREAD OF PRINTING: INDIA, PAKISTAN,
        CEYLON, BURMA, AND THAILAND.
    AMSTERDAM, VANGENDT AND CO., 1969.
    CHRON: SURVEY
    METH: HISTORICAL
    GEOG: SEV ASIA
    SUBJ: JRN HISTORY PRINTING

RIAJANSKY, A. A.   R02318
    MOVIE BUSINESS IN CHINA'S INTERIOR IN
        UNHEALTHY STATE DURING WAR
    THE CHINA WEEKLY REVIEW 104:1(7 DEC 1946),
        17-18.
    MEDIUM: FILM
    CHRON: 1946-1960
    GEOG: CHINA
    SUBJ: DESCRIPTION

RICH, RAYMOND T.   R01881
    HOW TO READ THE NEWS FROM CHINA
    THE OUTLOOK [NEW OUTLOOK] 140:10(8 JULY
        1925), 363-6.
    ##/ChIN-5
    CHRON: 1910-1946
    GEOG: CHINA   U.S.
    SUBJ: PROPAGANDA DESCRIPTION

RICHARDSON, MICHAEL   R01974
    SHAKING OFF A DOSE OF THE FLU
    FEER 99:8(24 FEB 1978), 18-20.
    ##/SIN-2
    CHRON: 1970-1980
    GEOG: SINGAPORE
    SUBJ: CONTROL

RISHER, EUGENE V.   R02125
    QUITE A LITTLE WAR
    DATELINE [OPC, NEW YORK] XII:1(1968), 38-40.
    CHRON: 1960-1970
    GEOG: VIETNAM
    SUBJ: FOR CORR

RITCHIE, ROBERT WELLS   R01882
    THE JAPANESE PRESS
    THE ORIENTAL REVIEW II:10(AUG 1912), 616-19.
    CHRON: 1910-1946
    GEOG: EAST ASIA
    SUBJ: DESCRIPTION

ROBINSON, EDNAH   R01884
    CHINESE JOURNALISM IN AMERICA
    CURRENT LITERATURE [CURRENT OPINION] 32:3(MAR
        1902), 325-6.
    FROM ROBINSON R01883
    CHRON: BEFORE 1910
    GEOG: OSEAS CHIN U.S.
    SUBJ: DESCRIPTION

ROBINSON, EDNAH   R01883
    CHINESE JOURNALISM IN CALIFORNIA
    OUT WEST XVI:1(JAN 1902), 33-42.
    ##/CHIN-US; EXCERPTED IN <CURRENT LITERATURE>
        ROBINSON R01884.
    CHRON: BEFORE 1910
    GEOG: OSEAS CHIN U.S.
    SUBJ: DESCRIPTION

RODERICK, JOHN   R02535
    CHINA-WATCHING FROM THE INSIDE
    AP LOG (8 JAN 1979), 1-2.
    ##/CHIN-8
    MEDIUM: GENERAL
    CHRON: 1970-1980
    GEOG: CHINA
    SUBJ: FOR CORR   FLOW/AGENCY

ROFF, W.   R02624
    MALAY NEWSPAPERS
    IN TREGONNING T02627, PP. 95-7.
    CHRON: SURVEY
    GEOG: MALAYSIA   SINGAPORE
    SUBJ: RESEARCH

ROFF, WILLIAM R.   R00926
    GUIDE TO MALAY PERIODICALS, 1876-1941.
    SINGAPORE, EASTERN UNIVERSITIES PRESS, 1961.
    CHRON: SURVEY
    METH: HISTORICAL
    GEOG: MALAYSIA
    SUBJ: RESEARCH

ROFF, WILLIAM R.   R00929
    CORRESPONDENCE
    JRNL OF SOUTHEAST ASIAN STUDIES VI:2(1975),
        196-7.
    REPLY TO YUSOF TALIB'S REVIEW (SEE Y01207)
        OF ROFF'S BOOK
    CHRON: 1970-1980
    METH: HISTORICAL
    GEOG: MALAYSIA   SINGAPORE
    SUBJ: RESEARCH

ROFF, WILLIAM R.   R00928
    TOWARDS A PRESS IN LINE WITH MALAYSIAN
        SENTIMENTS AND INTERESTS
    MALAYSIAN BUSINESS (OCT 1974), 51-2.
    ##/MAL
    CHRON: 1970-1980
    GEOG: MALAYSIA
    SUBJ: DEVELOPMENT DESCRIPTION

ROFF, WILLIAM R.   R01411
    THE MALAYO-MUSLIM WORLD OF SINGAPORE AT THE
        CLOSE OF THE NINETEENTH CENTURY
    JRNL OF ASIAN STUDIES XXIV:1(NOV 1964), 75-90.
    ##/MAL-3
    CHRON: BEFORE 1910
    METH: HISTORICAL
    GEOG: MALAYSIA   SINGAPORE
    SUBJ: RESEARCH   JRN HISTORY

ROFF, WILLIAM R.   R00927
    THE ORIGINS OF MALAY NATIONALISM
    KUALA LUMPUR, U. OF MALAYA PRESS, 1967.
    CHRON: SURVEY
    METH: HISTORICAL
    GEOG: MALAYSIA   SINGAPORE
    SUBJ: JRN HISTORY

ROGERS, F. THEO   R00930
    LOOKING BACK AT 50 YEARS OF PHILIPPINES
        JOURNALISM
    IN <FOOKIEN TIMES YEARBOOK 1958>.
    CHRON: SURVEY   VERIF: UNVERIFIED
    METH: HISTORICAL
    GEOG: PHILIPPINES
    SUBJ: JRN HISTORY BIOGRAPHY

ROGERS, WALTER S.   R02333
    TINTED AND TAINTED NEWS
    THE CHINA WEEKLY REVIEW 1:12(25 AUG 1917),
        319-23.
    FROM <SATURDAY EVENING POST>
    CHRON: 1910-1946
    GEOG: CHINA
    SUBJ: FOR CORR

ROLNICK, HARRY   R00931
    THE MYSTERIOUS DEATH OF A JOURNALIST
    FEER 84:14(8 APR 1974), 26-7.
    ##/THAI
    CHRON: 1970-1980
    GEOG: THAILAND
    SUBJ: DESCRIPTION

RONQUILLO, BERNARDINO   R00932
    MANAGED MEDIA
    FEER 78:46(11 NOV 1972), 14.
    ##/PHIL
    MEDIUM: GENERAL
    CHRON: 1970-1980
    GEOG: PHILIPPINES
    SUBJ: CONTROL

RONQUILLO, BERNARDINO   R00933
    THE SELF-DISCIPLINED APPROACH TO NEWS
    FEER 86:44(8 NOV 1974), 34.
    ##/PhIL
    CHRON: 1970-1980
    GEOG: PHILIPPINES
    SUBJ: CONTROL

ROSARIO, ERNESTO DEL   R00934
    THE POST-WAR PRESS
    IN FOOKIEN F02714
    CHRON: SURVEY
    GEOG: PHILIPPINES
    SUBJ: JRN HISTORY BIOGRAPHY

ROSE, E. J. B.   R00935
    THE ASIAN PRESS
    IN WINT W02557, PP. 638-43.
    ##/ASIA; ALSO A SECTION ON BROADCASTING.
    CHRON: 1960-1970
    GEOG: SEV ASIA
    SUBJ: DESCRIPTION

ROSE, ERNEST D.   R00936
    IMPRESSIONS FROM INDIA'S NATIONAL FILM
          INSTITUTE
    JRNL OF THE UNIVERSITY FILM ASSOCIATION
          25:4(1973), 76-9, 87.
    ##/SwAS
    MEDIUM: FILM
    CHRON: 1970-1980
    GEOG: SO/WEST ASI
    SUBJ: DESCRIPTION

ROSENBERG, DAVID   R00937
    THE END OF THE FREEST PRESS IN THE WORLD
    BULLETIN OF CONCERNED ASIAN SCHOLARS 5:1(JULY
          1973), 53-8.
    ##/PhIL
    CHRON: 1970-1980
    GEOG:
    SUBJ: CONTROL

ROSENTHAL, A. M.   R02204
    WHAT SUKARNO WANTS, SUKARNO GETS
    DATELINE [OPC, NEW YORK] 7:1(1963), 46-7.
    CHRON: 1960-1970
    GEOG: AUSTRALASIA
    SUBJ: CONTROL   DESCRIPTION

ROSHOLT, MALCOLM   R01348
    AND A 'BABY' <CHINA PRESS> WAS BORN
    IN CHINA PRESS C02568, P. 80.
    ##/FILM
    CHRON: 1910-1946
    GEOG: CHINA
    SUBJ: DESCRIPTION

ROSLEY IBRAHIM   R02205
    RTM BENARKAN UNTUK PROPAGANDA SAJA
    SARINA [KUALA LUMPUR] 3:29(AUG 1978), 64-8.
    ##/MAL-3
    MEDIUM: ELECTRONIC
    CHRON: 1970-1980
    GEOG: MALAYSIA
    SUBJ: PROPAGANDA

ROSS, ALBION   R00939
    ENGLISH-LANGUAGE BIBLIOGRAPHY ON FOREIGN
        PRESS AND COMPARATIVE JOURNALISM
    MILWAUKEE, CENTER FOR THE STUDY OF THE
        AMERICAN PRESS, MARQUETTE U., 1966.
    #3
    CHRON: 1960-1970
    GEOG: WORLD
    SUBJ: RESEARCH

ROTH, ANDREW   R02319
    THE PLACE OF THE PRESS IN COMMUNIST CHINA
    THE CHINA WEEKLY REVIEW 113:10(7 MAY 1949),
        220-1.
    CHRON: 1946-1960
    GEOG: CHINA
    SUBJ: DESCRIPTION

ROWLEY, ANTHONY   R01622
    SINGAPORE NEWSPAPER BARGAINS
    FEER 98:40(7 OCT 1977), 120-1.
    ##/SIN-2
    CHRON: 1970-1980
    GEOG: SINGAPORE
    SUBJ: CONTROL   PUBLISHING

ROWLEY, ANTHONY   R01623
    BUYERS RUSH FOR SIN CHEW SHARES
    FEER 98:44(4 NOV 1977), 64.
    ##/SIN-2
    CHRON: 1970-1980
    GEOG: SINGAPORE
    SUBJ: CONTROL   PUBLISHING

ROWLEY, ANTHONY   R01621
    DETAINEE'S PUBLIC PLEA TO LEE
    FEER 97:31(5 AUG 1977), 26-7.
    ##/PHIL
    CHRON: 1970-1980
    GEOG: SINGAPORE
    SUBJ: CONTROL

RUBEN, BRENT, EDITOR.   R02564
    COMMUNICATION YEARBOOK: AN ANNUAL REVIEW
    NEW BRUNSWICK, N. J., TRANSACTIONS BOOKS,
        1977.
    SEE DE VERNEIL D01474 AND MOWLANA M01597.
    CHRON: 1970-1980
    METH: NUMERICAL
    GEOG: WORLD
    SUBJ: DESCRIPTION OTHER JRN

RUBIN, BARRY   R01624
    INTERNATIONAL NEWS AND THE AMERICAN MEDIA
    BEVERLY HILLS, CALIF., SAGE, 1978.
    MEDIUM: GENERAL
    CHRON: 1970-1980   VERIF: UNVERIFIED
    GEOG: WORLD
    SUBJ: FLOW/AGENCY DESCRIPTION

RUCKER, FRANK W.   R01625
    WALTER WILLIAMS
    COLUMBIA, MO., MISSOURIAN PUB. ASSN., 1964.
    ##/CHIN-5
    CHRON: 1960-1970
    GEOG: CHINA
    SUBJ: DESCRIPTION BIOGRAPHY

RUSSELL, J. T. AND QUINCY WRIGHT   R01885
    NATIONAL ATTITUDES ON THE FAR EASTERN
        CONTROVERSY
    AMERICAN POLITICAL SCIENCE REVIEW
        XXVII:4(AUG 1933), 555-76.
    ##/CHIN-5; <CHINA CRITIC> AND <OSAKA
        MAINICHI>.
    CHRON: 1910-1946
    METH: CONTENT ANALYSIS
    GEOG: CHINA   EAST ASIA
    SUBJ: PROPAGANDA DESCRIPTION CROSS CULTU

RUSSO, FRANK D.   R00942
    A STUDY OF BIAS IN TV COVERAGE OF THE
        VIETNAM WAR: 1969 AND 1970.
    PUB. OPINION QUARTERLY XXXV:4(WINTER 1971-2),
        539-43.
    MEDIUM: ELECTRONIC
    CHRON: 1970-1980
    GEOG: VIETNAM   U.S.
    SUBJ: FOR CORR   LAW/ETHICS

RUSTIN, RICHARD   R00943
    CENSORSHIP AND CAM NE
    COL JRN REVIEW (FALL 1965), 22-3.
    MEDIUM: GENERAL
    CHRON: 1960-1970
    GEOG: VIETNAM   U.S.
    SUBJ: FOR CORR   CONTROL   DESCRIPTION

RYAN, WILLIAM L.   R02126
    THIS IS WHERE THE STORY IS
    DATELINE [OPC, NEW YORK] XII:1(1968), 45-7.
    CHRON: 1960-1970
    GEOG: VIETNAM
    SUBJ: FOR CORR

SAAD, HASHIM   S00944
    RAZAK ON MEDIA'S ROLE
    STRAITS TIMES 12 MAR 1973
    ##/MAL-2
    MEDIUM: GENERAL
    CHRON: 1970-1980
    GEOG: MALAYSIA
    SUBJ: PROPAGANDA DEVELOPMENT

SAFER, MORLEY   S02206
    TELEVISION COVERS THE WAR
    DATELINE [OPC, NEW YORK] X:1(1966), 69-71.
    MEDIUM: ELECTRONIC
    CHRON: 1960-1970
    GEOG: VIETNAM   U.S.
    SUBJ: DESCRIPTION

SAITO, M.   S02447
    PRODUCTION OF THE MAINICHI NEWSPAPERS BY
        JAPANESE MONOTYPES
    THE ASIAN PRINTER 3:1(1960), 42-50.
    CHRON: 1960-1970
    GEOG: EAST ASIA
    SUBJ: PRINTING

SAKURAI, YOSHIKO   S01626
    19TH CENTURY REBEL WITH A CAUSE
    MEDIA [HONG KONG] 4:11(NOV 1976), 6.
    HIKOMA UENO,JAPAN 19TH CENTURY PHOTOGRAPHER.
    MEDIUM: OTHER
    CHRON: 1970-1980
    GEOG: EAST ASIA
    SUBJ: JRN HISTORY DESCRIPTION

SALLOWAY, NITI   S00946
    NEW ARTS IN ANCIENT INDIA
    CSM 6 AUG 1971
    ##/SWAS; 5-PART SERIES.
    MEDIUM: FILM
    CHRON: 1970-1980
    GEOG: SO/WEST ASI
    SUBJ: DESCRIPTION

SAM-O, KIM   S02805
    ELITE INDUSTRY OR JUST ANOTHER PROFIT MAKER?
    FEER 104:20(18 MAY 1979), 59-60.
    ##/EASI
    MEDIUM: GENERAL
    CHRON: 1970-1980
    GEOG: EAST ASIA
    SUBJ: DESCRIPTION OTHER JRN

SAMAD, ISMAIL   S00947
    KAJAI--A GIANT OF HIS TIME
    STRAITS TIMES 10 JUNE 1972
    ##/MALSP; ABDUL RAHIM KAJAI.
    CHRON: 1910-1946
    METH: HISTORICAL
    GEOG: MALAYSIA
    SUBJ: JRN HISTORY BIOGRAPHY

SAMAD, MARINA   S01412
    EARLY MALAY JOURNALISM
    LEADER MALAYSIAN JOURNALISM REVIEW NO.
        1(1972), 18-22.
    CHRON: SURVEY
    METH: HISTORICAL
    GEOG: MALAYSIA   SINGAPORE
    SUBJ: RESEARCH   JRN HISTORY

SANDERS, ALAN   S00948
    LANGUAGE: A CHANGE OF POLICY
    FEER 93:29(16 JULY 1976), 20-2.
    ##/CHIN-2
    MEDIUM: GENERAL
    CHRON: 1970-1980
    GEOG: CHINA
    SUBJ: LANGUAGE

SANGER, J. W.   S02446
     ADVERTISING METHODS IN JAPAN, CHINA, AND
        THE PHILIPPINES
     WASHINGTON, D. C., DEPARTMENT OF COMMERCE,
        BUREAU OF FOREIGN AND DOMESTIC COMMERCE,
        1921.
     SPECIAL AGENTS SERIES NO. 209.
     CHRON: 1910-1946
     GEOG: PHILIPPINES CHINA   EAST ASIA
     SUBJ: OTHER JRN

SARKAR, CHANCHAL   S00950
     THE WESTERN PRESS IN THE REGION DISTORTING
        ASIA
     THE ASIA MAGAZINE (24 MAR 1968), 3, 14-15.
     ##/INTL
     CHRON: 1960-1970
     GEOG: SEV ASIA   WORLD
     SUBJ: FOR CORR   FLOW/AGENCY DESCRIPTION

SARKAR, CHANCHAL   S00949
     REPORTING ASIA
     NIEMAN REPORTS XVIII:3(JUNE 1964), 15-18.
     ##/ASIA
     MEDIUM: GENERAL
     CHRON: 1960-1970
     GEOG: SEV ASIA
     SUBJ: FOR CORR   OTHER JRN

SCANDLEN, GUY B. AND KENNETH WINKLER   S01720
     HOW THAI NEWSPAPERS VIEW THEMSELVES
     NIEMAN REPORTS XXXI:2/3(SUMMER/AUTUMN 1977),
        57-60.
     ##/THAI
     CHRON: 1970-1980
     METH: CONTENT ANALYSIS
     GEOG: THAILAND
     SUBJ: DESCRIPTION

SCHECTER, JERROLD L.   S00951
     REPORTER'S SECOND LOOK
     TIME (10 APR 1972), 34-9.
     NOTHING ON MEDIA
     CHRON: 1970-1980
     GEOG: CHINA   U.S.
     SUBJ: FOR CORR   OTHER NON-J

SCHELL, ORVILLE   S02560
     CHINESE FIGURES IN A BORROWED LANDSCAPE
     COL JRN REVIEW XVIII:1(MAY/JUNE 1979),
        42-3.
     MEDIUM: ELECTRONIC
     CHRON: 1970-1980
     GEOG: CHINA   U.S.
     SUBJ: FOR CORR

SCHOOL AND SOCIETY [INTELLECT]   S01886
    EDUCATIONAL MOTION PICTURES IN CHINA
    XLIV:1126(25 JULY 1936), 109-10.
    MEDIUM: FILM
    CHRON: 1910-1946
    GEOG: CHINA
    SUBJ: EDUCATION

SCHRAMM, WILBUR   S00953
    TELEVISION RECONSIDERED
    SINGAPORE, AMIC, 1972.
    ##/MISC; MIMEO.
    MEDIUM: ELECTRONIC
    CHRON: 1970-1980
    GEOG: SEV ASIA
    SUBJ: DEVELOPMENT

SCHRAMM, WILBUR, ET AL.   S02580
    INTERNATIONAL NEWS WIRES AND THIRD WORLD
        NEWS IN ASIA (A FIRST STAGE REPORT)
    HONG KONG, CENTRE FOR COMMUNICATION STUDIES,
        CHINESE UNIVERSITY OF HONG KONG, 1978.
    CHRON: 1970-1980
    METH: CONTENT ANALYSIS
    GEOG: SEV ASIA
    SUBJ: DESCRIPTION

SCHUMAN, JULIAN   S00954
    THOSE INTREPID U. S. NEWSMEN IN CHINA: A
        POST-MORTEM
    FEER LXXVI:18(29 APR 1972), 16-7.
    ##/CHIN
    MEDIUM: GENERAL
    CHRON: 1970-1980
    GEOG: CHINA
    SUBJ: FOR CORR

SCHUMAN, JULIAN   S00955
    SERVING THE REVOLUTION WITH WORDS
    FEER LXXV:4(22 JAN 1972), 8, 19.
    ##/CHIN
    CHRON: 1970-1980
    GEOG: CHINA
    SUBJ: CONTROL   PROPAGANDA

SCHWARZ, HENRY G.   S00956
    THE <TS'AN-K'AO HSIAO-HSI>: HOW WELL
        INFORMED ARE CHINESE OFFICIALS ABOUT THE
        OUTSIDE WORLD?
    THE CHINA QUARTERLY NO. 27(JULY-SEPT 1966),
        54-83.
    ##/CHIN
    CHRON: 1960-1970
    GEOG: CHINA   WORLD
    SUBJ: CONTROL   DESCRIPTION POLIT SCI

SCIENTIFIC AMERICAN SUPPLEMENT   S02128
     SOME CURIOUS PHASES OF CHINESE JOURNALISM
     NO. 1793(14 MAY 1910), 315-16.
     ##/CHIN-7
     CHRON: BEFORE 1910
     GEOG: CHINA
     SUBJ: DESCRIPTION

SCOTT, ANNE   S01887
     THE CHALLENGE OF BEING FAIR
     MEDIA [HONG KONG] (FEB 1978), 16.
     ##/HKG; <FEER>.
     CHRON: 1970-1980
     GEOG: SEV ASIA
     SUBJ: DESCRIPTION

SCOTT, GAVIN   S00957
     VIETNAM: ON THE SHELF IN SAIGON
     DATELINE [OPC, NEW YORK] 18:1(1974), 66-8.
     ##/VIET
     MEDIUM: GENERAL
     CHRON: 1970-1980
     GEOG: VIETNAM   U.S.
     SUBJ: FOR CORR

SEARLE, PAUL   S02017
     THE MALAYAN FILM UNIT'S SUCCESSES
     MALAYA [BRITISH MALAYA, MALAYSIA] (JULY
          1956), 30-2.
     MEDIUM: FILM
     CHRON: 1946-1960
     GEOG: MALAYSIA
     SUBJ: DESCRIPTION

SELANGOR JOURNAL, THE   S01413
     ADVERTISING IN THE VERNACULAR
     II:23(27 JULY 1894), 372-3.
     ##/MAL-3; <BINTANG TIMOR>.
     CHRON: BEFORE 1910
     GEOG: MALAYSIA   SINGAPORE
     SUBJ: DESCRIPTION OTHER JRN

SENKUTTUVAN, ARUN   S00958
     SINGAPORE PROVIDES THE CONNECTION
     FEER 93:27(2 JULY 1976), 9-10.
     ##/SIN
     CHRON: 1970-1980
     GEOG: MALAYSIA   SINGAPORE
     SUBJ: FOR CORR   OTHER NON-J

SERDT, MICHEL   S00959
    HERE A MAO, THERE A MAO
    ATLAS WORLD PRESS REVIEW 21:6(JULY 1974),
        56-7.
    ##/CHIN; FROM <LE QUOTIDIEN DE PARIS>.
    MEDIUM: GENERAL
    CHRON: 1970-1980
    GEOG: CHINA
    SUBJ: PROPAGANDA

SETON-KARR, W. S.   S01721
    THE NATIVE PRESS OF INDIA
    ASIATIC QUARTERLY REVIEW VIII(JULY 1889),
        41-63.
    CHRON: BEFORE 1910
    GEOG: SO/WEST ASI
    SUBJ: DESCRIPTION

SEVAREID, ERIC   S01627
    CENSORS IN THE SADDLE
    THE NATION 160:15(14 APR 1945), 415-17.
    ##/CHIN-5
    CHRON: 1910-1946
    GEOG: CHINA
    SUBJ: CONTROL

SHAN, SHEN   S00960
    TAIWAN AND ITS PRESS
    NIEMAN REPORTS XIV:3(JULY 1960), 7-22.
    ##/TAI
    CHRON: 1960-1970
    GEOG: TAIWAN
    SUBJ: DESCRIPTION

SHANG YUEH-HENG   11   S00961
    T'UNG MENG HUI SHIH TAI <MIN PAO> CHIH
        YEN CHIU (MIN PAO [PEOPLE'S NEWS] AT THE
        TIME OF THE T'UNG MENG HUI)
    UNPUB MASTERS THESIS IN JOURNALISM, 1965.
    SKINNER S00982 II:46403
                        LANG: CHINESE
    CHRON: BEFORE 1910   VERIF: UNVERIFIED
    METH: HISTORICAL
    GEOG: CHINA
    SUBJ: JRN HISTORY

SHANG-HAI T'UNG SHE, EDITOR.   03   S02607
    SHANG-HAI YEN CHIU TZU LIAO HSU CHI
        (SUPPLEMENTARY RESEARCH MATERIALS ON
        SHANGHAI)
    SHANGHAI, CHUNG-HUA SHU CHU, 1939.
                        LANG: CHINESE
    CHRON: 1910-1946
    GEOG: CHINA
    SUBJ: DESCRIPTION

SHANG-HAI WEN HUA   03   S02129
    HSIAO-PAO HUA CHOU-K'AN WEN-T'I TSO-T'AN-HUI
        (WHY TABLOIDS BECOME WEEKLIES: A
        DISCUSSION)
    NO. 4(1 MAY 1946), 15-17.
    ##/CHIN-7
                                LANG: CHINESE
    CHRON: 1910-1946
    GEOG: CHINA
    SUBJ: DESCRIPTION

SHANGHAI PRESS UNION   S02207
    THE SINO-JAPANESE CONFLICT: THE SITUATION
        REVIEWED BY AMERICAN AND BRITISH EDITORS
        IN CHINA
    SHANGHAI, THE PRESS UNION, 1932.
    CHRON: 1910-1946
    GEOG: CHINA
    SUBJ: DESCRIPTION OTHER JRN

SHAO LI-TZU   08   S00962
    SHIH NIEN LAI TI CHUNG-KUO HSIN WEN SHIH YEH
        (JOURNALISM IN CHINA DURING THE PAST
        DECADE)
    IN CHUNG-KUO 04C02591, PP. 481-502.
                        LANG: CHINESE
    CHRON: 1910-1946   VERIF: UNVERIFIED
    METH: HISTORICAL
    GEOG: CHINA
    SUBJ: JRN HISTORY

SHAO NIEN CHUNG-KUO CH'EN PAO WU SHIH   S02019
        NIEN CHI NIEN CHUAN K'AN
    PIEN YIN WEI YUAN HUI [YOUNG CHINA MORNING
        PAPER, 60TH ANNIVERSARY]
    SAN FRANCISCO, YOUNG CHINA MORNING PAPER,
        1971.
                                LANG: CHINESE
    CHRON: SURVEY
    GEOG: OSEAS CHIN U.S.   OTHER
    SUBJ: JRN HISTORY

SHAO NIEN CHUNG-KUO CH'EN PAO WU SHIH   S02018
        CHOU NIEN CHI NIEN CHUAN K'AN
    PIEN YIN WEI YUAN HUI [YOUNG CHINA MORNING
        PAPER, 50TH ANNIVERSARY]
    SAN FRANCISCO, YOUNG CHINA MORNING PAPER,
        1960.
                                LANG: CHINESE
    CHRON: SURVEY
    GEOG: OSEAS CHIN U.S.   OTHER
    SUBJ: JRN HISTORY

SHAPLEN, ROBERT   S00964
    THE CHALLENGE AHEAD
    COL JRN REVIEW IX:4(WINTER 1970-1), 40-6.
    CHRON: 1970-1980
    GEOG: VIETNAM
    SUBJ: FOR CORR   OTHER NON-J

SHAPLEN, ROBERT   S00963
    SOME OF MY BEST FRIENDS WERE PIRATES: THE
        STORY OF CONSUL REEVES OF MACAO
    NIEMAN REPORTS 2:3(JULY 1948), 15-6.
    ##/HKG
    CHRON: 1910-1946
    METH: HISTORICAL
    GEOG: HONG KONG   MACAO
    SUBJ: BIOGRAPHY

SHARP, EUGENE WEBSTER   S00965
    INTERNATIONAL NEWS COMMUNICATION
    COLUMBIA, MO., U. OF MISSOURI, 1927.
    U. OF MISSOURI BULLETIN, 28:3., 43 PP.
    CHRON: 1910-1946
    GEOG: WORLD
    SUBJ: FLOW/AGENCY

SHARP, ILSA   S00966
    SINGAPORE WAVES THE MUZZLE
    FEER 84:15(15 APR 1974), 16.
    ##/SIN
    CHRON: 1970-1980
    GEOG: SINGAPORE
    SUBJ: CONTROL   LAW/ETHICS

SHASTRI, H. P.   S01722
    THE PRESS AND DEMOCRACY IN JAPAN
    THE CHINA WEEKLY REVIEW VI:5(5 OCT 1918),
        176-8.
    CHRON: 1910-1946
    GEOG: EAST ASIA
    SUBJ: DESCRIPTION

SHAW, ERNEST T.   S01723
    RADIO BROADCASTING IN CHINA
    ASIA XXXV:I(JAN 1935), 19-23.
    MEDIUM: ELECTRONIC
    CHRON: 1910-1946
    GEOG: CHINA
    SUBJ: DESCRIPTION

SHECKLEN, GEORGE F.   S02320
    RADIO ANSWERS THE SKEPTICS
    THE CHINA WEEKLY REVIEW 51:7(18 JAN 1930),
        245-6.
    MEDIUM: ELECTRONIC
    CHRON: 1910-1946
    GEOG: CHINA
    SUBJ: DESCRIPTION

SHECKLEN, GEORGE F.   S02208
    MODERN CHINA WILL COMMUNICATE BY RADIO
    THE CHINA WEEKLY REVIEW XLVI:7(10 OCT 1928),
        57-8.
    MEDIUM: ELECTRONIC
    CHRON: 1910-1946
    GEOG: CHINA
    SUBJ: DEVELOPMENT DESCRIPTION

SHECKLEN, GEORGE F.   S00967
    RADIO CENTRAL, SHANGHAI
    THE CHINA WEEKLY REVIEW L:12(16 NOV. 1929),
        412.
    ##/CHIN-3
    MEDIUM: ELECTRONIC
    CHRON: 1910-1946
    GEOG: CHINA
    SUBJ: DESCRIPTION

SHEN PAO   S02130
    IN COMMEMORATION OF THE SHUN PAO'S GOLDEN
        JUBILEE, 1872-1922 [WU SHIH NIEN LAI
        CHUNG KUO NUNG YEH SHIH]
    SHANGHAI, SHEN PAO, 1923.
    NEWSPAPERS, PART III, PP. 1-15.
                              LANG: CHINESE
    CHRON: SURVEY
    GEOG: CHINA
    SUBJ: DESCRIPTION

SHEN, C. Y. [CHENG YEE]   S01888
    LIANG CHI-CHAO AND HIS TIMES
    PHD DISS, UNIVERSITY OF MISSOURI, 1953.
    DISS. ABS. 14:11(1954)
    CHRON: BEFORE 1910   VERIF: UNVERIFIED
    METH: HISTORICAL
    GEOG: CHINA
    SUBJ: BIOGRAPHY

SHEN, JAMES C. Y.   S01271
    THE LAW AND MASS MEDIA IN HONG KONG
    HONG KONG, MASS COMMUNICATIONS CENTRE,
        CHINESE U. OF HONG KONG, 1972.
    ##/HKG
    MEDIUM: GENERAL
    CHRON: 1970-1980
    GEOG: HONG KONG
    SUBJ: LAW/ETHICS

SHENG, TSUNG-LIN, COMPILER.   07   S02020
    HSIN WEN HSUEH LI LUN [MASS COMMUNICATION
        THEORY]
    TAIPEI, T'AI WAN HSUEH SHENG SHU CHU, 1973.
                              LANG: CHINESE
    CHRON: SURVEY
    GEOG: CHINA
    SUBJ: DESCRIPTION

SHEWMAKER, KENNETH E.   S00968
    THE MANDATE OF HEAVEN VS. U. S. NEWSMEN IN
        CHINA, 1941-45
    JQ 46:2(SUMMER 1969), 274-80.
    ##/CHIN
    CHRON: 1910-1946
    METH: HISTORICAL
    GEOG: CHINA
    SUBJ: FOR CORR   JRN HISTORY

SHIEH, MILTON   S00969
    RED CHINA PATTERNS CONTROLS OF PRESS ON
        RUSSIAN MODEL
    JQ 28:1(WINTER 1951), 74-80.
    ##/CHIN
    CHRON: 1946-1960
    METH: HISTORICAL
    GEOG: CHINA
    SUBJ: CONTROL

SHIEH, MILTON J. T.   S00970
    TOWARDS A BETTER PRESS
    FREE CHINA REVIEW XIX:10(OCT 1969), 45-6.
    ##/CHIN-3
    CHRON: 1960-1970
    GEOG: TAIWAN
    SUBJ: DEVELOPMENT EDUCATION

SHIEH, MILTON J. T. [HSIEH, JAN-CHIH]   S01889
    THE PRESS OF FREE CHINA
    TAIPEI, SHIN SHENG PAO DAILY, 1959.
    ##/VF
    CHRON: SURVEY
    GEOG: TAIWAN   CHINA
    SUBJ: CONTROL   PROPAGANDA   JRN HISTORY

SHIH CHAO-HSI   10   S00971
    T'AI-PEI KO PAO CH'U LI TSUI O HSIN WEN CHIH
        PI CHIAO YEN CHIU
    UNPUB MASTERS THESIS IN JOURNALISM, 1959.
    (A COMPARATIVE STUDY OF CRIMINAL-CASE
        REPORTING IN TAIPEI NEWSPAPERS);
        SKINNER S00982 II:46546.
                         LANG: CHINESE
    CHRON: 1946-1960   VERIF: UNVERIFIED
    METH: OTHER OR COMB
    GEOG: TAIWAN
    SUBJ: DESCRIPTION

SHIH I-WEI   10   S00972
    I NIEN LAI CHIH TIEN HSIN CHIEN SHE KAI
        SHU' (THE DEVELOPMENT TELECOMMUNICATIONS
        DURING THE PAST YEAR)
    CHUNG-KUO CHIEN SHE 15:5(MAY 1937), 1-12.
    SKINNER S00982 II:41866
    MEDIUM: ELECTRONIC   LANG: CHINESE
    CHRON: 1910-1946   VERIF: UNVERIFIED
    GEOG: CHINA
    SUBJ: DESCRIPTION

SHIH K'UN-SUNG   10   S00973
    T'AI-WAN WAN PAO TI FA CHAN CHIH YEN CHIU
        (THE DEVELOPMENT OF EVENING PAPERS IN
        TAIWAN)

    UNPUB MASTERS THESIS IN JOURNALISM, 1968.
                        LANG: CHINESE
    CHRON: SURVEY   VERIF: UNVERIFIED
    METH: HISTORICAL
    GEOG: TAIWAN
    SUBJ: JRN HISTORY DESCRIPTION

SHIH KANG   S02131
    KU-CH'ENG PAO-YEH NIAO-K'AN (A BIRD'S EYE
        VIEW OF THE NEWSPAPERS IN PEKING)
    FU-NU WEN-HUA 2:1(JAN 1947), 14-15.
    ##/CHIN-7
                        LANG: CHINESE
    CHRON: 1910-1946
    GEOG: CHINA
    SUBJ: DESCRIPTION

SHIH SHAO-HUA   S02132
    VIGOROUSLY DEVELOPING AFRO-ASIAN JOURNALISM
    THE AFRO-ASIAN JOURNALIST 9:2(JUNE 1972), 4-5.
    CHRON: 1970-1980
    GEOG: SEV ASIA
    SUBJ: DESCRIPTION

SHIH YUNG KUEI   05   S01890
    CH'UAN PO YU SHENG HUO [MASS COMMUNICATIONS
        AND SOCIETY]
    TAIPEI, LI MING WEN HUA SHIH YEH, 1975.
    MEDIUM: GENERAL   LANG: CHINESE
    CHRON: 1970-1980
    GEOG: CHINA
    SUBJ: OTHER JRN

SHIH, MEI-CHING   S01630
    TYPOGRAPHY
    TAIPEI, COMMERCIAL PRESS, 1963.
                        LANG: CHINESE
    CHRON: 1960-1970   VERIF: UNVERIFIED
    GEOG: TAIWAN   CHINA
    SUBJ: PRINTING

SHIMABUKURO, BETTY   S01414
    WALL STREET JOURNAL ASIAN OFFSPRING
    WICI NATIONAL NEWSLETTER 10:2(NOV 1977), 6.
    CHRON: 1970-1980
    GEOG: HONG KONG   SEV ASIA
    SUBJ: DESCRIPTION

SHRIDHAR, DEV   S01631
    A CENTER FOR MASS COMMUNICATIONS
    HORIZONS [USIS] XVII:11(1968-70), 44-45.
    MEDIUM: GENERAL
    CHRON: 1960-1970
    GEOG: SEV ASIA
    SUBJ: DESCRIPTION

SHU HSIN-CH'ENG   12   S00974
    I NIEN LAI CHIH WO KUO CH'U PAN SHIH YEH
        (CHINA'S PUBLISHING INDUSTRY DURING THE
        PAST YEAR)
    WEN HUA CHIEN SHE 1:3(DEC 1934), 101-13.
    SKINNER S00982 II:41867; ULS 5:4772.
                            LANG: CHINESE
    CHRON: 1910-1946   VERIF: UNVERIFIED
    GEOG: CHINA
    SUBJ: PUBLISHING

SHUN, YU-HSIU, EDITOR.   S01632
    HISTORY OF CHINESE PRINTING
    TAIPEI, COMMERCIAL PRESS, 1964.
                            LANG: CHINESE
    CHRON: 1960-1970   VERIF: UNVERIFIED
    METH: HISTORICAL
    GEOG: CHINA
    SUBJ: JRN HISTORY PRINTING

SILVA, FATHER   S01633
    A PHILIPPINE VERSION OF VILLAGE 'DAZIBAO'
    MEDIA [HONG KONG] 1:10(OCT 1975), 27.
    MEDIUM: OTHER
    CHRON: 1970-1980
    GEOG: PHILIPPINES
    SUBJ: DESCRIPTION

SILVA, FATHER   S00975
    THE WALL NEWSPAPERS OF MOALBOAL
    ATLAS WORLD PRESS REVIEW 22:5(MAY 1975), 54.
    ##/PHIL; FROM <MEDIA>, OCT 1974, SILVA S01633.
    MEDIUM: OTHER
    CHRON: 1970-1980
    GEOG: PHILIPPINES
    SUBJ: DESCRIPTION

SILVA, MERVYN DE   S01975
    A MINORITY OF ONE
    FEER 99:1(6 JAN 1978), 13.
    ##/ASIA
    MEDIUM: GENERAL
    CHRON: 1970-1980
    GEOG: SEV ASIA
    SUBJ: FLOW/AGENCY

SILVER, GERALD A.   S00976
    ESTIMATING IN THE FAR EAST
    GRAPHIC ARTS MONTHLY 47:4(APR 1975), 78-9.
    ##/PRIN
    CHRON: 1970-1980
    GEOG: SEV ASIA
    SUBJ: PRINTING   PUBLISHING

SILVER, GERALD A.   S00977
    ESTIMATING IN ASIA
    GRAPHIC ARTS MONTHLY PART 1, 48:5(MAY 1976),
        74, 6; PART 2, 48:6(JUNE 1976), 84;
        PART 3, 48:7(JULY 1976), 62.
    ##/PRIN
    CHRON: 1970-1980
    GEOG: SEV ASIA
    SUBJ: PRINTING   PUBLISHING

SIMMONS, WALTER   S02334
    SHANGHAI
    THE CHINA WEEKLY REVIEW 117:4(25 MAR 1950),
        54.
    CHRON: 1946-1960
    GEOG: CHINA
    SUBJ: PROPAGANDA

SIMONS, PAUL   S00978
    PRESS FREEDOM IN ASIA
    FEER XLVIII:3(APR 1965), 157-9.
    CHRON: 1960-1970
    GEOG: SEV ASIA
    SUBJ: CONTROL

SIN CHEW JIH POH   09   S00979
    HUA-WEN TSA-CHIH [CHINESE MAGAZINES]
    12 APR 1975
    ##/SINSP
                            LANG: CHINESE
    CHRON: 1970-1980
    GEOG: MALAYSIA   OTHER
    SUBJ: DESCRIPTION

SINENSIS [PSEUD.]   S01307
    THE CHINESE PRESS
    THE TIMES [LONDON] (30 OCT 1895), 6.
    LT; LETTER TO EDITOR.
    CHRON: BEFORE 1910
    GEOG: CHINA
    SUBJ: DESCRIPTION

SING PIN JIH PAO, EDITOR.   09   S01634
    (SING PIN JIH PAO SILVER JUBILEE SOUVENIR
        BOOK, 1939-1964)
    PENANG, SING PIN JIH PAO, 1964.
                            LANG: CHINESE
    CHRON: 1960-1970
    GEOG: MALAYSIA
    SUBJ: JRN HISTORY DESCRIPTION

SINGH, GEETANJALI   S01635
    NOW IT CAN BE SHOWN . . .
    FEER 97:37(16 SEPT 1977); 24-5.
    ##/SWAS; <KISSA KURSEE KAA>.
    MEDIUM: FILM
    CHRON: 1970-1980
    GEOG: SO/WEST ASI
    SUBJ: DESCRIPTION

SINGH, KHUSHWANT   S00980
    'WE SELL THEM DREAMS'
    NYT MAGAZINE (31 OCT 1976), 42-3, 89-98.
    ##/SWAS
    MEDIUM: FILM
    CHRON: 1970-1980
    GEOG: SO/WEST ASI
    SUBJ: DESCRIPTION

SIRIWARDENE, REGGIE   S01260
    FILM-MAKERS LOOK FOR AN AUDIENCE
    FEER 95:2(14 JAN 1977), 35.
    ##/SWAS
    MEDIUM: FILM
    CHRON: 1970-1980
    GEOG: SO/WEST ASI
    SUBJ: DESCRIPTION

SKACHKOV, PETR EMEL'IANOVICH   S02719
    BIBLIOGRAFIA KITAIA
    MOSKVA, GOSUDARSTVENNOIE COTSIAL'NO
        EKONOMICHESKOE IZDATEL'STVO, 1960.
                            LANG: RUSSIAN
    CHRON: SURVEY
    GEOG: CHINA
    SUBJ: RESEARCH

SKINNER, G. WILLIAM   S00981
    REPORT ON THE CHINESE IN SOUTH EAST ASIA
    ITHACA, CORNELL U., DEPT. OF FAR EASTERN
        STUDIES, 1950.
    ##/ASIA; MIMEO, 91 PP.; SECTIONS ON PAPERS
        IN SEA COUNTRIES;
        APPENDIX OF CHINESE NEWSPAPERS.
    CHRON: 1946-1960
    GEOG: OTHER   SEV ASIA
    SUBJ: DESCRIPTION

SKINNER, G. WILLIAM, ET AL., EDITORS.   S00982
    MODERN CHINESE SOCIETY: AN ANALYTICAL
        BIBLIOGRAPHY
    STANFORD, STANFORD U. PRESS, 1973, 3 VOLS.
    VOL. 1 LISTS ENGLISH CITATIONS, VOL. 2
        LISTS CHINESE CITATIONS,
        VOL. 3 LISTS JAPANESE CITATIONS.
    MEDIUM: GENERAL
    CHRON: SURVEY
    METH: OTHER OR COMB
    GEOG: TAIWAN   CHINA
    SUBJ: RESEARCH

SLOBODIANIUK, IVAN NIKIFOROVICH   S02720
    PECHAT' NOVOGO KITAIA
    KIEV, IZDATEL'STVO KIEVSKOVO
        GOSUDARSTVENNOVO UNIVERSITETA, 1958.
                    LANG: RUSSIAN
    CHRON: 1946-1960
    GEOG: CHINA
    SUBJ: DESCRIPTION

SLOMKOWSKI, ZYGMUNT   S00984
    THE PRESS IN ASIA
    INTERNATIONAL REVIEW OF JOURNALISTS NO.
        1(1966), 61-71.
    EMPHASIS ON INDIA
    CHRON: 1960-1970
    GEOG: SO/WEST ASI SEV ASIA
    SUBJ: DESCRIPTION

SMALLWOOD, H. ST. CLAIR   S01891
    MODERN PRESS IN CHINA
    GREAT BRITAIN AND THE EAST 49(5 AUG 1937),
        202-3.
    ##/CHIN-6
    CHRON: 1910-1946
    GEOG: CHINA
    SUBJ: DESCRIPTION

SMEDLEY, AGNES C.   S01892
    CORRUPT PRESS IN CHINA
    THE NATION 141:3652(3 JULY 1935), 8-10.
    ##/CHIN-5
    CHRON: 1910-1946
    GEOG: CHINA
    SUBJ: DESCRIPTION

SMITH, EDWARD CECIL   S00985
    A HISTORY OF NEWSPAPER SUPPRESSION IN
        INDONESIA, 1949-65.
    MASTERS THESIS, UNIVERSITY OF IOWA, 1969.
    CHRON: SURVEY   VERIF: UNVERIFIED
    GEOG: INDONESIA
    SUBJ: CONTROL

SNIDER, PAUL B.   S01002
    EXPERIENCES OF A JOURNALISM TEACHER IN
        AFGHANISTAN
    JQ 45:2(SUMMER 1968), 316-8.
    ##/SwAS
    CHRON: 1960-1970
    GEOG: SO/WEST ASI
    SUBJ: EDUCATION

SNOW, EDGAR   S01893
    THE WAYS OF THE CHINESE CENSOR
    CURRENT HISTORY AND FORUM 42(JULY 1935),
        381-6.
    ##/CHIN-6
    CHRON: 1910-1946
    GEOG: CHINA
    SUBJ: CONTROL

SOGA, Y.   S00986
    JAPANESE PRESS IN HAWAII
    IN WILLIAMS W01152, PP. 449-53.
    #3
    CHRON: 1910-1946
    GEOG: U.S.   OTHER
    SUBJ: DESCRIPTION

SOH TIANG KENG   S01636
    A SURVEY OF NEWSPAPERS IN SINGAPORE TODAY
    COMMENTARY [SINGAPORE] 4:1(SEPT 1971), 3-20.
    ##/SIN-2
    CHRON: 1970-1980
    GEOG: SINGAPORE
    SUBJ: DESCRIPTION

SOLOMON, RICHARD   S00987
    COMMUNICATION PATTERNS AND THE CULTURAL
        REVOLUTION
    THE CHINA QUARTERLY NO. 32(OCT-DEC 1967),
        88-110.
    ##/CHIN-2
    MEDIUM: OTHER
    CHRON: 1960-1970
    METH: OTHER OR COMB
    GEOG: CHINA
    SUBJ: OTHER JRN   OTHER NON-J

SOMMERLAD, ERNEST LLOYD   S00988
    THE PRESS IN DEVELOPING COUNTRIES
    MELBOURNE, SYDNEY U. PRESS, 1966.
    CHRON: 1960-1970
    GEOG: WORLD
    SUBJ: DEVELOPMENT DESCRIPTION

SOON, LAU TEIK   S00989
     SINGAPORE AND POLITICAL STABILITY
     PACIFIC COMMUNITY 3:1(JAN 1972), 378-88.
     ##/SIN; HERALD/NANYANG.
     CHRON: 1970-1980
     GEOG: SINGAPORE
     SUBJ: CONTROL

SOONG, JAMES CHU-YUL [COMPILER]   S00990
     THE RED FLAG (HUNG CH'I), 1958-1968: A
          RESEARCH GUIDE
     WASHINGTON, D. C., CENTER FOR CHINESE
          RESEARCH MATERIALS, 1969.
     CHRON: SURVEY
     GEOG: CHINA
     SUBJ: RESEARCH

SOU TUN   15   S02753
     TSUI TSAO TI NEI MU HSIN WEN--SHE HUI HSIN
          WEN ('THE SOCIAL NEWS'-- AN EARLY
          PUBLICATION ON INSIDE NEWS)
     PAO HSUEH III:8(JUNE 1967), 94-6.
                              LANG: CHINESE
     CHRON: SURVEY
     METH: HISTORICAL
     GEOG: CHINA
     SUBJ: JRN HISTORY

SOUTH EAST ASIA PRESS CENTRE   S02816
     THE PRESS AND BROADCASTING MEDIA IN
          SINGAPORE
     KUALA LUMPUR, SOUTH EAST ASIA PRESS CENTRE,
          [1973?].
     MEDIUM: GENERAL
     CHRON: 1970-1980
     METH: OTHER OR COMB
     GEOG: SINGAPORE
     SUBJ: DESCRIPTION

SOUTHERLAND, DANIEL   S00991
     FREE-SWINGING PRESS KEEPS SAIGON DUCKING
     CSM 18 SEPT 1970
     ##/VN
     CHRON: 1970-1980
     GEOG: VIETNAM
     SUBJ: CONTROL   DESCRIPTION

SOUTHERLAND, DANIEL   S00992
     INDONESIAN PRESS PUT UNDER TIGHT LEASH
     CSM 13 AUG 1974
     ##/INDON
     CHRON: 1970-1980
     GEOG: INDONESIA
     SUBJ: CONTROL

SOUTHERLAND, DANIEL   S00994
    HOW CHINA PUBLIC GETS WORLD NEWS
    CSM 14 MAY 1976
    ##/CHIN; REFERENCE NEWS.
    CHRON: 1970-1980
    GEOG: CHINA
    SUBJ: CONTROL   DESCRIPTION

SOUTHERLAND, DANIEL   S00993
    INDONESIAN PRESS FLEXES MUSCLES
    CSM 19 MAR 1976
    ##/INDON
    CHRON: 1970-1980
    GEOG: INDONESIA
    SUBJ: CONTROL   DESCRIPTION

SPECIAL CORRESPONDENT   S02240
    CORRESPONDENT IS A DIRTY WORD IN MANILA
    MEDIA [HONG KONG] NO. 12 (OCT 1978), 1, 4-5.
    ##/PHIL
    CHRON: 1970-1980
    GEOG: PHILIPPINES
    SUBJ: FOR CORR   CONTROL

SPURR, RUSSELL   S00995
    THE BEEB IS LOOKING FOR A NEW HOME
    FEER 86:45(15 NOV 1974), 30.
    ##/MAL-2
    MEDIUM: ELECTRONIC
    CHRON: 1970-1980
    GEOG: MALAYSIA
    SUBJ: DESCRIPTION

SPURR, RUSSELL   S00996
    BEAMING IN TO THE WORLD
    FEER 91:5(30 JAN 1976), 20-1.
    ##/CHIN
    MEDIUM: ELECTRONIC
    CHRON: 1970-1980
    GEOG: CHINA
    SUBJ: DESCRIPTION

SPURR, RUSSELL ET AL.   S02561
    TV IS ESSENTIALLY AN ENTERTAINMENT MEDIUM
        . . .YET MOST GOVERNMENTS FEAR ITS
        POLITICAL INFLUENCE
    FEER 103:1(5 JAN 1979), 24-33.
    ##/ASIA
    MEDIUM: ELECTRONIC
    CHRON: 1970-1980
    GEOG: SEV ASIA
    SUBJ: CONTROL   DESCRIPTION

SRIBURATHAM, ARRY   S00997
    THE BANGKOK 'WORLD'
    FOI CENTER REPORT PUBLICATION NO. 113 (NOV
        1963).
    ##/THAI
    CHRON: SURVEY
    METH: HISTORICAL
    GEOG: THAILAND
    SUBJ: JRN HISTORY DESCRIPTION

STANDING, PERCY CROSS   S01894
    JOURNALISM IN THE FAR EAST
    SATURDAY REVIEW [OF POLITICS, LITERATURE,
        SCIENCE AND ART. LONDON] 86(16 JULY
        1898), 79.
    ##/THAI; LETTER TO EDITOR; SEE LILLIE L01836.
    CHRON: BEFORE 1910
    GEOG: THAILAND
    SUBJ: CONTROL   LAW/ETHICS

STANFORD U. CHINA 'PROJECT   S01024
    PROPAGANDA AND PUBLIC INFORMATION IN <NORTH
        CHINA>, HRAF [COMPILER], VOL. 2, 597-633.

    ##/CHIN-4; 1956; HRAF SUBCONTRACTORS
        MONOGRAPHS, 27; STANFORD 1.
    MEDIUM: GENERAL
    CHRON: 1946-1960
    GEOG: CHINA
    SUBJ: DESCRIPTION

STANFORD U. CHINA PROJECT   S01028
    PUBLIC INFORMATION IN <TAIWAN(FORMOSA)>,
        HRAF[COMP.], VOL. 1, 207-21.

    ##/TAI; HRAF SUBCONTRACTORS MONOGRAPHS,
        31; STANFORD 5; ALSO
        SEE 'PROPAGANDA' IN VOL. 2, 429-36.
    MEDIUM: GENERAL
    CHRON: 1946-1960
    GEOG: TAIWAN
    SUBJ: CONTROL   PROPAGANDA   PUBLISHING

STANFORD U. CHINA PROJECT   S01025
    PROPAGANDA AND PUBLIC INFORMATION IN
        <CENTRAL SOUTH CHINA>, HRAF [COMPILER],
        VOL. 2, 547-86.

    ##/CHIN-4; 1956; HRAF SUBCONTRACTORS
        MONOGRAPHS, 28; STANFORD 2.
    MEDIUM: GENERAL
    CHRON: 1946-1960
    METH: CONTENT ANALYSIS
    GEOG: CHINA
    SUBJ: CONTROL   PROPAGANDA   PUBLISHING

STANFORD U. CHINA PROJECT   S01026
    PROPAGANDA AND PUBLIC INFORMATION IN <EAST
        CHINA>, HRAF [COMP.], VOL. 2, 610-69.

    ##/CHIN-4; 1956; HRAF SUBCONTRACTORS
        MONOGRAPHS, 29; STANFORD 3.
    MEDIUM: GENERAL
    CHRON: 1946-1960
    METH: CONTENT ANALYSIS
    GEOG: CHINA
    SUBJ: CONTROL   PROPAGANDA   PUBLISHING
318   ASIAN JOURNALISM

STANFORD U. CHINA PROJECT   S01027
    PROPAGANDA AND PUBLIC INFORMATION IN
        <SOUTHWEST CHINA>, HRAF [COMP.], VOL. 2,
        606-81.

    ##/CHIN-4; 1956; HRAF SUBCONTRACTORS
        MONOGRAPHS, 30; STANFORD 4.
    MEDIUM: GENERAL
    CHRON: 1946-1960
    METH: CONTENT ANALYSIS
    GEOG: CHINA
    SUBJ: CONTROL   PROPAGANDA   PUBLISHING

STAR, THE [PENANG]   S02134
    30 MASS MEDIA SPECIALISTS FOR CONFERENCE
    17 AUG 1974
    CHRON: 1970-1980
    GEOG: MALAYSIA
    SUBJ: DESCRIPTION PRINTING

STAR, THE [PENANG]   S02135
    MASS COMMUNICATION EXPERT JOINS
        SCIENCE VARSITY
    19 AUG 1974
    CHRON: 1970-1980
    GEOG: MALAYSIA
    SUBJ: PRINTING

STAR, THE [PENANG]   S02133
    THE STAR TAKES OVER KWONG WAH
    15 AUG 1974
    ##/MAL-3; SPECIAL SUPPLEMENT.
    CHRON: SURVEY
    GEOG: MALAYSIA
    SUBJ: DESCRIPTION OTHER JRN

STARNER, FRANCIS   S01637
    REPORTING ON VIETNAM : IGNORING ALL THE
        FACTS?
    MEDIA [HONG KONG] 4:4(APR 1977), 23.
    MEDIUM: GENERAL
    CHRON: 1970-1980
    GEOG: VIETNAM
    SUBJ: FOR CORR

STAUBER, ROSE   S01029
    VIETNAM'S CONTROLLED PRESS
    FOI CENTER REPORT NO. 207(AUG 1968).
    ##/VN
    CHRON: 1960-1970
    GEOG: VIETNAM
    SUBJ: CONTROL

STEAD, HENRY   S01030
     THE PRESS AND PEACE IN THE PACIFIC
     IN WILLIAMS W01152, PP. 481-5.
     #3
     CHRON: 1910-1946
     GEOG: SEV ASIA
     SUBJ: FLOW/AGENCY DESCRIPTION

STEIN, GUENTHER   S01638
     THROUGH THE EYES OF A JAPANESE NEWSPAPER
          READER
     PACIFIC AFFAIRS IX:2(JUNE 1936), 177-90.
     CHRON: 1910-1946
     GEOG: EAST ASIA
     SUBJ: DESCRIPTION

STEIN, GUNTHER   S01896
     NEWS FROM JAPAN
     LIVING AGE 350:4434(MAR 1936), 12-14.
     ##/CHIN-6; FROM <SPECTATOR> [LONDON].
     CHRON: 1910-1946
     GEOG: EAST ASIA
     SUBJ: FOR CORR

STEINLE, PEGGY   S01031
     'YOU LIKE IT RAW, WE LIKE IT COOKED'
     NYT 16 AUG 1970
     ##/VN
     MEDIUM: ELECTRONIC
     CHRON: 1970-1980
     GEOG: VIETNAM
     SUBJ: DESCRIPTION

STELLMANN, LOUIS J.   S01895
     YELLOW JOURNALISM, SAN FRANCISCO'S ORIENTAL
          NEWSPAPERS
     SUNSET 24:2(FEB 1910), 197-201.
     ##/CHIN-US
     CHRON: BEFORE 1910
     GEOG: OSEAS CHIN U.S.
     SUBJ: DESCRIPTION

STEVENS, FREDERICK W.   S01897
     PUBLIC OPINION AS A FORCE IN CHINA
     THE CHINESE SOCIAL AND POLITICAL SCIENCE
          REVIEW VII:1(JAN 1923), 44-55.
     CHRON: 1910-1946
     GEOG: CHINA
     SUBJ: OTHER JRN

STEVENSON, H. L.   S01898
    UPI DELEGATION TO CHINA, MAY 12-JUNE 2
    UPI REPORTER (27 APR 1978), 1.
    ##/CHIN-6
    MEDIUM: GENERAL
    CHRON: 1970-1980
    GEOG: U.S.
    SUBJ: FLOW/AGENCY

STEVENSON, H. L.   S02536
    AN INSTANT PRESS CORPS IN PEKING
    UPI REPORTER (11 JAN 1979), 1-2.
    ##/CHIN-8
    MEDIUM: GENERAL
    CHRON: 1970-1980
    GEOG: CHINA
    SUBJ: FLOW/AGENCY

STEVENSON, H. L.   S02538
    UPI'S PEKING TEAM: CRABBE AND MOSBY
    UPI REPORTER (22 MAR 1979), 1-2.
    ##/CHIN-8
    MEDIUM: GENERAL
    CHRON: 1970-1980
    GEOG: CHINA
    SUBJ: FOR CORR   FLOW/AGENCY BIOGRAPHY

STEVENSON, H. L.   S02537
    A NEW LOOK FOR NEWS FROM CHINA
    UPI REPORTER (8 MAR 1979), 1-2.
    ##/CHIN-8
    MEDIUM: GENERAL
    CHRON: 1970-1980
    GEOG: CHINA
    SUBJ: FLOW/AGENCY

STEVENSON, H. L.   S02045
    CHINA REVISITED: A 17-DAY NEW LOOK
    UPI REPORTER (1 JUNE 1978), 1-2.
    ##/CHIN-7
    MEDIUM: GENERAL
    CHRON: 1970-1980
    GEOG: CHINA   U.S.
    SUBJ: FLOW/AGENCY DESCRIPTION OTHER JRN

STEVENSON, H. L.   S02021
    CHINA REVISITED: A REVOLUTION IN PR
    UPI REPORTER (8 JUNE 1978), 1-2.
    ##/CHIN-6
    MEDIUM: GENERAL
    CHRON: 1970-1980
    GEOG: CHINA
    SUBJ: DESCRIPTION OTHER JRN

STEVENSON, REX   S01032
    CINEMAS AND CENSORSHIP IN COLONIAL MALAYA
    JOURNAL OF SOUTHEAST ASIAN STUDIES V:2(SEPT
        1974), 208-24.
    ##/MAL
    MEDIUM: FILM
    CHRON: SURVEY
    METH: HISTORICAL
    GEOG: MALAYSIA   SINGAPORE
    SUBJ: CONTROL

STIER, W. RUDOLF   S02136
    THE ATTITUDES OF THE AMERICAN PRESS TO JAPAN
        AND THE JAPANESE
    MASTERS THESIS, COLUMBIA UNIVERSITY, 1917.
    CHRON: BEFORE 1910
    METH: OTHER OR COMB
    GEOG: EAST ASIA   U.S.
    SUBJ: OTHER JRN

STILLMAN, DON   S01034
    TONKIN: WHAT SHOULD HAVE BEEN ASKED
    COL JRN REVIEW IX:4(WINTER 1970-1), 21-5.
    MEDIUM: GENERAL
    CHRON: 1970-1980
    GEOG: VIETNAM   U.S.
    SUBJ: FOR CORR   LAW/ETHICS

STOCKWIN, HARVEY   S01036
    COMMUNICATIONS GAP ON SUMMIT ISLAND
    FEER 91:11(12 MAR 1976), 30.
    ##/INDO
    MEDIUM: GENERAL
    CHRON: 1970-1980
    GEOG: INDONESIA
    SUBJ: FOR CORR

STOCKWIN, HARVEY   S01035
    PLAYING A VITAL ROLE
    FEER 82:49(10 DEC 1973), 28-9.
    ##/THAI
    CHRON: 1970-1980
    GEOG: THAILAND
    SUBJ: CONTROL

STOCKWIN, HARVEY   S01037
    THE POLITICS OF DETENTION
    FEER 93:27(2 JULY 1976), 10, 15.
    ##/SIN
    CHRON: 1970-1980
    GEOG: SINGAPORE
    SUBJ: CONTROL

STOCKWIN, HARVEY   S01038
    COMMENT
    FEER 94:40(1 OCT 1976), 18-19.
    ##/PHIL
    CHRON: 1970-1980
    GEOG: PHILIPPINES
    SUBJ: FOR CORR   CONTROL

STONG, PHIL D.   S02022
    KING OF SIAM'S DAILY AMERICANIZED BY NEW YORK
        NEWSPAPER MAN
    EDITOR & PUBLISHER (11 AUG 1928), 16.
    ##/THAI; ANDREW FREEMAN.
    CHRON: 1910-1946
    GEOG: THAILAND
    SUBJ: DESCRIPTION BIOGRAPHY

STRAITS TIMES   S02023
    HOW THE PUBLIC RELATIONS MEN CAN HELP FIGHT
        POLLUTION
    19 MAR 1978
    ##/MAL-3; SUNDAY, MALAYSIA EDITION.
    CHRON: 1970-1980
    GEOG: MALAYSIA
    SUBJ: DEVELOPMENT OTHER JRN

STRAITS TIMES   S02066
    WORK TOWARDS UNITED NATION, PRESS TOLD
    2 APR 1978
    ##/MAL-3; SUNDAY, MALAYSIA EDITION.
    CHRON: 1970-1980
    GEOG: MALAYSIA
    SUBJ: DEVELOPMENT

STRAITS TIMES   S02068
    LOCAL WOMEN APPOINTED DIRECTORS OF SRM
    16 APR 1978
    ##/MAL-3; SUNDAY, MALAYSIA EDITION.
    MEDIUM: OTHER
    CHRON: 1970-1980
    GEOG: MALAYSIA
    SUBJ: OTHER JRN

STRAITS TIMES   S02067
    CO-OPERATION BETWEEN POLICE AND PRESS VITAL
    16 APR 1978
    ##/MAL-3; SUNDAY, MALAYSIA EDITION.
    CHRON: 1970-1980
    GEOG: MALAYSIA
    SUBJ: DEVELOPMENT

```
STRAITS TIMES                                      S02540
    BERNAMA PLANS TO INTRODUCE PHOTO SERVICE NEXT
        YEAR
    22 OCT 1978
    ##/MAL-4; SUNDAY, MALAYSIAN EDITION.
    CHRON: 1970-1980
    GEOG:  MALAYSIA
    SUBJ:  DESCRIPTION


STRAITS TIMES                                      S02539
    'PLAN MEDIA CONCEPT TO SUIT LOCAL NEEDS'
    22 OCT 1978
    ##/MAL-4; SUNDAY, MALAYSIA EDITION.
    MEDIUM:  GENERAL
    CHRON: 1970-1980
    GEOG:  MALAYSIA       SEV ASIA
    SUBJ:  DEVELOPMENT


STRAITS TIMES                                      S02137
    'NO MOVE TO ROB OTHERS OF RIGHTS'
    21 MAY 1978
    ##/MAL-3; SUNDAY, MALAYSIA EDITION.
    CHRON: 1970-1980
    GEOG:  MALAYSIA
    SUBJ:  FOR CORR       CONTROL


STRAITS TIMES                                      S02138
    WHY SWITCH TO COLOUR TV IS TIMELY MOVE
    21 MAY 1978
    ##/MAL-3; SUNDAY, MALAYSIA EDITION.
    MEDIUM:  ELECTRONIC
    CHRON: 1970-1980
    GEOG:  MALAYSIA
    SUBJ:  OTHER JRN


STRAITS TIMES                                      S02241
    PERAK MB'S NEW RULING ON PRESS STATEMENTS
    ##/MAL-3; SUNDAY, MALAYSIA EDITION.
    MEDIUM:  GENERAL
    CHRON: 1970-1980
    GEOG:  MALAYSIA
    SUBJ:  CONTROL


STRAITS TIMES                                      S02242
    MB ON THAT DON'T TALK TO PRESS DIRECTIVE
    27 AUG 1978
    ##MAL-3; SUNDAY, MALAYSIA EDITION.
    MEDIUM:  GENERAL
    CHRON: 1970-1980
    GEOG:  MALAYSIA
    SUBJ:  CONTROL
```

STRAITS TIMES   S01900
    TRAINING FOR ASEAN JOURNALISTS
    5 FEB 1978
    ##/ASIA; SUNDAY, MALAYSIA EDITION.
    CHRON: 1970-1980
    GEOG: MALAYSIA   SEV ASIA
    SUBJ: EDUCATION

STRAITS TIMES   S01899
    PERTAMA URGED: GO FOR REGIONAL EXCHANGE
    5 MAR 1978
    ##/MAL-2; SUNDAY, MALAYSIA EDITION.
    CHRON: 1970-1980
    GEOG: MALAYSIA
    SUBJ: DEVELOPMENT

STRANAHAN, SUSAN AND SIMON LI   S02541
    WIRE SERVICES DUCK NEW PE(C)KING ORDER
    APME NEWS NO. 113(JAN 1979), 12.
    ##/CHIN-8
    CHRON: 1970-1980
    GEOG: CHINA
    SUBJ: FLOW/AGENCY LANGUAGE

STRAND, DAVID   S02243
    [REVIEW OF POWELL <MY TWENTY FIVE YEARS IN
        CHINA> REPRINT P01360]
    THE CHINA QUARTERLY NO. 74(JUNE 1978), 422-3.
    ##/CHIN-8
    CHRON: 1910-1946
    GEOG: CHINA
    SUBJ: DESCRIPTION OTHER JRN

SUBBIAH, RAMA   S01328
    TAMIL MALAYSIANA: A CHECKLIST OF TAMIL
        BOOKS AND PERIODICALS PUBLISHED IN
        MALAYSIA AND SINGAPORE
    KUALA LUMPUR, U. OF MALAYA LIBRARY, 1968.
    CHRON: 1970-1980
    GEOG: MALAYSIA   SINGAPORE
    SUBJ: RESEARCH

SUGIMURA, K.   S01639
    JOURNALISTIC EDUCATION IN JAPAN AND CHINA
    IN WILLIAMS W02587, PP. 215-7.
    CHRON: 1910-1946
    GEOG: CHINA   EAST ASIA
    SUBJ: EDUCATION

SULAIMAN, RAJA   S01039
    REGENT AND CONSORT DROP IN FOR A CLOSER LOOK
    STRAITS TIMES 15 DEC 1972
    ##/MAL-2
    CHRON: 1970-1980
    GEOG: MALAYSIA
    SUBJ: DESCRIPTION

SULLIVAN, JOHN H.   S01040
    THE PRESS AND POLITICS IN INDIA
    JQ 44:1(SPRING 1967), 99-106.
    ##/INDO
    CHRON: 1960-1970
    GEOG: SO/WEST ASI
    SUBJ: CONTROL

SULLY, FRANCOIS   S01041
    VIETNAM: NEW AMERICAN DILEMMA
    NIEMAN REPORTS 17:2(JAN 1963), 3-5.
    NOTHING ON PRESS
    CHRON: 1960-1970
    GEOG: VIETNAM   U.S.
    SUBJ: OTHER NON-J

SULLY, FRANCOIS   S02209
    WHERE COLD WAR IS HOTTEST: VIETNAM
    DATELINE [OPC, NEW YORK] 9:1(1965), 31-5.
    MEDIUM: GENERAL
    CHRON: 1960-1970
    GEOG: VIETNAM
    SUBJ: FOR CORR

SUN JU LING   10   S01901
    PAO HSUEH YEN CIU [JOURNALISM RESEARCH]
    TAIPEI, HSUEH SHENG SHU CHU, 1976.
                            LANG: CHINESE
    CHRON: 1970-1980
    METH: OTHER OR COMB
    GEOG: TAIWAN
    SUBJ: OTHER JRN

SUN JU-LING   10   S02754
    CHUNG KUO CH'U CH'I HSIN WEN SHIH YEH TI YEN
        CHIN (THE DEVELOPMENT OF CHINESE PRESS
        IN EARLY STAGE)
    PAO HSUEH [TAIPEI] II:2(DEC 1957), 76-9.
                            LANG: CHINESE
    CHRON: SURVEY
    METH: HISTORICAL
    GEOG: CHINA
    SUBJ: JRN HISTORY

SUN, J. C.   S01361
    NEW TRENDS IN THE CHINESE PRESS
    PACIFIC AFFAIRS 8:1(MAR 1935), 56-65.
    ##/CHIN-5
    CHRON: 1910-1946
    GEOG: CHINA
    SUBJ: DESCRIPTION

SUN, J.C.   S01640
    THE FUTURE OF THE CHINESE PRESS
    THE NEW CHINA [PEIPING] I:2(DEC 1930), 30-33.
    #3/NEW CHINA
    CHRON: 1910-1946
    GEOG: CHINA
    SUBJ: DESCRIPTION

SUNG CH'UAN YU   07   S01902
    CHUNG KUO MIN YI YU HSIN WEN TZU YU FA CHAN
         SHIH [HISTORY OF CHINESE PUBLIC OPINION
         AND PRESS FREEDOM]
    TAIPEI, CHENG CHUNG SHU CHU, 1974.
    MEDIUM: GENERAL   LANG: CHINESE
    CHRON: SURVEY
    METH: HISTORICAL
    GEOG: TAIWAN   CHINA
    SUBJ: CONTROL   OTHER JRN

SUNG CHIN   07   S02755
    WO KUO KU-TAI CHIH YU LUN (THE PUBLIC
         OPINION IN ANCIENT CHINA)
    PAO HSUEH II:3(AUG 1958), 16-18.
                          LANG: CHINESE
    CHRON: BEFORE 1910
    METH: HISTORICAL
    GEOG: CHINA
    SUBJ: JRN HISTORY

SUNG HAN-CHANG   07   S01042
    PAO CHIH KUANG KAO CHIH FA LU TSE JEN
         (LEGAL LIABILITY OF OF NEWSPAPER
         ADVERTISING)
    UNPUB MASTERS THESIS IN JOURNALISM, 1964.
    SKINNER S00982 II:41012
    CHRON: 1960-1970   VERIF: UNVERIFIED
    METH: OTHER OR COMB
    GEOG: TAIWAN
    SUBJ: LAW/ETHICS

SUNG I-CHUNG   07   S01043
    PUBLICATIONS CHRONICLE
    T'IEN HSIA MONTHLY V:2(SEPT 1937), 185-92.
    TH
    CHRON: 1910-1946
    GEOG: CHINA
    SUBJ: DESCRIPTION

SUNG I-CHUNG   07   S01273
PUBLICATIONS CHRONICLE
T'IEN HSIA MONTHLY 3:5(NOV 1936), 477-85.
TH
CHRON: 1910-1946
GEOG: CHINA
SUBJ: DESCRIPTION

SUNG I-CHUNG   07   S01641
SOME PUBLICATION TENDENCIES IN CHINA
THE CHINA CRITIC XII:10(5 MAR 1936), 226-9.
##/FILM
CHRON: 1910-1946
GEOG: CHINA
SUBJ: DESCRIPTION PUBLISHING

SUNG SHAN LIANG (TRANS.)   07   S01903
JIH PAO CH'I K'AN SHIH [HISTORY OF
    NEWSPAPERS AND PERIODICALS]
[PEKING?], SHANG WU YIN SHU KUAN, 1940.
TRANS. OF WEILL, G. J. <LE JOURNAL;
    EVOLUTION ET ROLE DE LA PRESSE
    PERIODIQUE>
                        LANG: CHINESE
CHRON: SURVEY
GEOG: WORLD
SUBJ: JRN HISTORY   .

SURYADINATA, LEO   S01048
THE PRE-WORLD WAR II PERANAKAN CHINESE PRESS
    IN JAVA: A PRELIMINARY SURVEY
ATHENS, OH., OHIO UNIVERSITY, CENTER FOR
    INTERNATIONAL STUDIES, 1971.
SEA SERIES 18.
CHRON: SURVEY
METH: HISTORICAL
GEOG: INDONESIA   OTHER
SUBJ: JRN HISTORY

SUSANTO, ASTRID S.   S01049
PLENARY SESSION ON THE REVISION OF CURRICULA
    THE SUB-CONSORTIUM FOR SOCIAL
    SCIENCES/HUMANITIES SECTION FOR
    JOURNALISM/COMMUNICATION SCIENCES
KUALA LUMPUR, JOURNALISM EDUCATION IN ASIA,
    1973[?].
##/INDO; MIMEO, 6 PP.
CHRON: 1970-1980
GEOG: INDONESIA
SUBJ: EDUCATION

SUSSMAN, LEONARD R.   S01050
SAIGON'S REFUGEE NEWSMEN
CSM 18 JULY 1975
CHRON: 1970-1980
GEOG: VIETNAM   WORLD
SUBJ: FOR CORR   DESCRIPTION

SYLVESTER, ARTHUR   S02210
     TELEVISION COVERS THE WAR
     DATELINE [OPC, NEW YORK] X:1(1966), 66-7.
     MEDIUM: ELECTRONIC
     CHRON: 1960-1970
     GEOG: VIETNAM   U.S.
     SUBJ: FOR CORR   DESCRIPTION

T'AI PEI SHIH HSIN WEN CHI CHE   T01052
     KUNG HUI, EDITOR.
     HSIN WEN CHIAO YU P'IEN (JOURNALISM
          INSTRUCTION IN THE REPUBLIC OF CHINA)
     IN T'AI-PEI T02800, PP. 1-39.
     SKINNER S00982 II:44177.
                          LANG: CHINESE
     CHRON: 1960-1970   VERIF: UNVERIFIED
     GEOG: TAIWAN
     SUBJ: EDUCATION

T'AI-PEI SHIH HSIN WEN CHI CHE   14   T01053
     KUNG HUI, EDITOR.
     HSIEN CHUANG P'IEN (PRESENT CONDITIONS)
     IN T'AI-PEI T02800, PP. 1-114.
                          LANG: CHINESE
     CHRON: 1960-1970   VERIF: UNVERIFIED
     GEOG: TAIWAN
     SUBJ: DESCRIPTION

T'AI-PEI SHIH HSIN WEN CHI CHE   T02800
     KUNG HUI, EDITOR.
     CHUNG-HUA MIN KUO HSIN WEN NIEN CHIEN
          (YEARBOOK OF JOURNALISM IN THE
          REPUBLIC OF CHINA)
     TAIPEI, T'AI-PEI SHIH HSIN WEN CHI CHE
          KUNG HUI, 1961.
                          LANG: CHINESE
     CHRON: 1960-1970   VERIF: UNVERIFIED
     GEOG: TAIWAN
     SUBJ: DESCRIPTION

T'AI-WAN HSIN SHENG PAO, EDITOR.   14   T02574
     T'AI-WAN SHIH NIEN [TEN YEARS IN TAIWAN]
     TAIPEI, T'AI-WAN HSING SHENG PAO SHE, 1955.
     SEE HSIEH H01999, WEN 12W02725, WU 07W02726
                          LANG: CHINESE
     CHRON: 1946-1960
     GEOG: TAIWAN
     SUBJ: DESCRIPTION

T'ANG LEANG-LI   T01951
     THE BAN ON 'ORIENTAL AFFAIRS'
     THE PEIPING CHRONICLE 11 JULY 1934
     ##/CHIN-6
     CHRON: 1910-1946
     GEOG: CHINA
     SUBJ: CONTROL

T'IEN SHENG   T02140
    CHUNG-KUO CHIH HSIN-WEN HSUEH (JOURNALISM
        IN CHINA)
    KUO-WEN CHOU-PAO 2:6(22 FEB 1925), 13-16.
    ##/CHIN-7
                              LANG: CHINESE
    CHRON: 1910-1946
    GEOG: CHINA
    SUBJ: DESCRIPTION

TACHIBANA, TAKASHIRO   T01904
    THE CINEMA IN JAPAN
    CONTEMPORARY JAPAN [TOKYO] I:1(JUNE 1932),
        117-24.
    MEDIUM: FILM
    CHRON: 1910-1946
    GEOG: EAST ASIA
    SUBJ: DESCRIPTION

TADOKORO, IZUMI   T01051
    JAPAN'S ANXIETIES OVER BROADCASTING
        FREQUENCIES ALLAYED
    IPI REPORT 25:5(MAY 1976), 10-11.
    MEDIUM: ELECTRONIC
    CHRON: 1970-1980
    GEOG: EAST ASIA
    SUBJ: DESCRIPTION

TAI FENG   17   T02756
    SAO TANG PAO HSIAO SHIH (A SHORT HISTORY OF
        THE SAO TANG PAO)
    PAO HSUEH II:7(DEC 1960), 87-8.
                              LANG: CHINESE
    CHRON: SURVEY
    METH: HISTORICAL
    GEOG: CHINA
    SUBJ: JRN HISTORY

TALBERT, ANSEL   T02211
    ALONG THE 38TH PARALLEL
    DATELINE [OPC, NEW YORK] X:1(1966), 62-3.
    MEDIUM: GENERAL
    CHRON: 1960-1970
    GEOG: EAST ASIA
    SUBJ: FOR CORR

TAMNEY, JOSEPH B.   T01054
    THE <SINGAPORE HERALD> AFFAIR
    ASIAN STUDIES [U. OF PHILIPPINES] (AUG 1972),
        256-61.
    ##/SIN; NST 1:489.
    CHRON: 1970-1980
    GEOG: SINGAPORE
    SUBJ: CONTROL

TAN JU-CHIEN   19   T02757
    SSU SHIH CH'I NIEN LAI KUANG TUNG PAO YEH
        SHIH KAI LUEH (THE HISTORY OF THE PRESS
        IN KUANGTUNG DURING THE LAST 47 YEARS)
    PAO HSUEH III:8(JUNE 1967), 76-83.
                        LANG: CHINESE
    CHRON: SURVEY
    METH: HISTORICAL
    GEOG: CHINA
    SUBJ: JRN HISTORY

TAN PENG SIEW   T02659
    MALAYSIA AND SINGAPORE
    IN LENT L00708, PP. 179-190.
    CHRON: SURVEY
    METH: OTHER OR COMB
    GEOG: SINGAPORE   INDONESIA
    SUBJ: JRN HISTORY DESCRIPTION

TAN TAT SENG   11   T01055
    HSING MA-WU WEN PAO YEH PAI NIEN SHU
        [ONE HUNDRED YEARS OF THE MALAY PRESS IN
        SINGAPORE]
    TUNG-NAN YA YEN CHIU [JOURNAL OF SOUTHEAST
        ASIAN RESEARCHES] V(1969),147-59.
    ##/SIN; NST IV:5878.
                        LANG: CHINESE
    CHRON: SURVEY
    METH: HISTORICAL
    GEOG: MALAYSIA   SINGAPORE
    SUBJ: DESCRIPTION

TAN, CHENG GUAN   T01415
    A RESPONSIBLE PRESS
    COMMENTARY [SINGAPORE] 4:1(SEPT 1971), 21-3.
    ##/SIN-2
    CHRON: 1970-1980
    GEOG: SINGAPORE
    SUBJ: CONTROL   LAW/ETHICS

TAN, S. H.   T02625
    A NOTE ON MALAYAN CHINESE NEWSPAPERS
    IN TREGONNING T02627, PP. 93-4.
    CHRON: SURVEY
    GEOG: MALAYSIA   SINGAPORE
    SUBJ: RESEARCH   JRN HISTORY

TANG CHI-CHIN   T01416
    THE PRESS
    IN <THE CHINESE YEARBOOK 1944-1945>,
        PP. 811-21.
    ##/CHIN-5
    CHRON: 1910-1946
    GEOG: CHINA
    SUBJ: DESCRIPTION

TANG, JANE AND JAMES SHEN   T01642
    FIRST JOURNALISM WEEK IN CHINA HELD AT
        YENCHING UNIVERSITY
    THE NEW CHINA [PEIPING] (APR 1931), 157-9.
    #3/NEW CHINA
    CHRON: 1910-1946
    GEOG: CHINA
    SUBJ: DESCRIPTION EDUCATION

TANG, T. C.   T02286
    NANKING PUBLISHER RAPS CHINESE PRESS
    THE CHINA PRESS (3 MAR 1936), 7, 14.
    CHEN MING-TEH
    CHRON: 1910-1946
    GEOG: CHINA
    SUBJ: LAW/ETHICS

TANG, THOMAS   T01056
    HISTORY OF CHINESE BOOK ILLUSTRATION
    ARTS OF ASIA 2:2(MAR/APR 1972), 47-53.
    CHRON: SURVEY
    METH: HISTORICAL
    GEOG: CHINA
    SUBJ: PRINTING   PUBLISHING

TAO WEI-LIEN   T02335
    WESTERN PRESS DISTORTS CHINA NEWS
    THE CHINA WEEKLY REVIEW 118:3(17 JUNE 1950),
        44-6.
    CHRON: 1946-1960
    GEOG: CHINA
    SUBJ: LAW/ETHICS

TARANTINO, ANTHONY GEORGE   T01336
    CHINESE MEDIA OF COMMUNICATION: THEIR HISTORY
        AND POLITICAL IMPACT IN RESPECT TO WESTER
        DEVELOPMENTS
    PHD DISS, UNIVERSITY OF CALIFORNIA/IRVINE,
        1975.
    INTL. DISS. 36 7716A
    CHRON: SURVEY
    METH: HISTORICAL
    GEOG: CHINA
    SUBJ: OTHER JRN   OTHER NON-J

TARZIAN, JEAN   T02046
    CHINESE REFUGEE SIFTS FACTS FROM PROPAGANDA
    EDITOR & PUBLISHER (21 SEPT 1963), 36.
    #8/CHIN-US
    CHRON: 1960-1970
    GEOG: CHINA   U.S.   OTHER
    SUBJ: DESCRIPTION

TASKER, RODNEY   T01651
    JOURNALIST VINDICATED
    FEER 97:26(1 JULY 1977), 14.
    ##/PHIL
    CHRON: 1970-1980
    GEOG: PHILIPPINES
    SUBJ: CONTROL

TASKER, RODNEY   T01253
    HEARING BECOMES A TEST-CASE
    FEER 95:10(11 MAR 1977), 10.
    ##/PHIL; B. WIDEMAN.
    CHRON: 1970-1980
    GEOG: PHILIPPINES
    SUBJ: FOR CORR   CONTROL

TASKER, RODNEY   T01250
    FOREIGN PRESS UNDER SCRUTINY?
    FEER 94:46(12 NOV 1976), 22-4.
    ##/PHIL
    CHRON: 1970-1980
    GEOG: PHILIPPINES
    SUBJ: FOR CORR   CONTROL

TASKER, RODNEY   T01251
    AFTER ZEITLIN, ASSURANCES
    FEER 94:47(19 NOV 1976), 18-9.
    CHRON: 1970-1980
    GEOG: PHILIPPINES
    SUBJ: FOR CORR   CONTROL

TASKER, RODNEY   T01652
    REBUILDING THE PRESS FOUNDATION
    FEER 97:31(5 AUG 1977), 24-5.
    ##/PHIL
    CHRON: 1970-1980
    GEOG: PHILIPPINES SEV ASIA
    SUBJ: DESCRIPTION

TASKER, RODNEY   T01252
    REPORTER'S VISA PROBE
    FEER 95:9(4 MAR 1977), 8-9.
    ##/PHIL; B. WIDEMAN.
    CHRON: 1970-1980
    GEOG: PHILIPPINES
    SUBJ: FOR CORR   CONTROL

TAY, B. H.   15   T01057
    HSIN-CHIA-P'O HUA WEN PAO YEH SHIH 1881-1972
        (HISTORY OF CHINESE NEWSPAPERS IN
        SINGAPORE 1881-1972)
    SINGAPORE, HSIN MA PUB. CO., 1973.
    AUTHOR IS CHENG IN WADE-GILES
                            LANG: CHINESE
    CHRON: SURVEY
    METH: HISTORICAL
    GEOG: SINGAPORE
    SUBJ: JRN HISTORY

TAY, LOUISE   T01058
    A DIRECTOR'S SURPRISE VISIT SHOT ANITA TO
        STARDOM
    MALAY MAIL 8 NOV 1973
    ##/MALSP
    MEDIUM: FILM
    CHRON: 1970-1980
    GEOG: MALAYSIA
    SUBJ: BIOGRAPHY

TAYLOR, CARSON   T01059
    HISTORY OF THE PHILIPPINE PRESS
    MANILA, MANILA DAILY BULLETIN PRESS, 1927.
    NUC L. C. CATALOG OF PRINTED CARDS 146:163.
    CHRON: 1910-1946
    METH: HISTORICAL
    GEOG: PHILIPPINES
    SUBJ: JRN HISTORY

TAYLOR, CHARLES   ·T01060
    REPORTER IN RED CHINA
    NEW YORK, RANDOM HOUSE, 1966.
    CHRON: 1960-1970
    GEOG: CHINA
    SUBJ: FOR CORR   DESCRIPTION

TEGJEU, BILL   T01061
    BUILDING UP NATIONAL UNITY THROUGH TV
    STRAITS TIMES (SUNDAY) 20 OCT 1974
    ##/MALSP
    MEDIUM: ELECTRONIC
    CHRON: 1970-1980
    GEOG: MALAYSIA
    SUBJ: CONTROL   DEVELOPMENT

TEIXEIRA, PE. MANUEL   T01653
    A IMPRENSA PERIODICA PORTUGUESA NO
        EXTREMO-ORIENTE
    MACAO, NOTICIAS DE MACAU, 1965.
                            LANG: OTHER EUROPEAN
    CHRON: 1960-1970
    GEOG: MACAO   SEV ASIA
    SUBJ: DESCRIPTION

TENG SSU-YU AND KNIGHT BIGGERSTAFF   T01725
     [COMPILERS]
AN ANNOTATED BIBLIOGRAPHY OF SELECTED
     CHINESE REFERENCE WORKS
CAMBRIDGE, HARVARD U. P., 1950.
INDEXES TO PERIODICALS AND NEWSPAPERS,
     PP. 95-105.
CHRON: 1946-1960
GEOG: CHINA
SUBJ: RESEARCH

TENG YENG-LIN   15   T01062
A PRELIMINARY LIST OF PERIODICALS AND SERIALS
     IN WESTERN LANGUAGES PUBLISHED IN CHINA
QUARTERLY BULLETIN OF CHINESE BIBLIOGRAPHY
     I(1934), 184-98.
##/BIB; THE NATIONAL LIBRARY OF PEKING, ED.,
     REPRINTED BY KRAUSE, 1968.
CHRON: SURVEY
GEOG: CHINA
SUBJ: RESEARCH

TENGKU MOHAMED   T01066
NEW AGENCY MUST WIELD INFLUENCE, SAYS TENGKU
STRAITS TIMES 17 AUG 1972
##/MALSP
CHRON: 1970-1980
GEOG: MALAYSIA
SUBJ: FLOW/AGENCY

TEOH, JOHN   T01067
FINDING THE RIGHT ANSWERS
STRAITS TIMES(SUN) 4 NOV 1973
##/MAL-2
CHRON: 1970-1980
GEOG: MALAYSIA
SUBJ: DESCRIPTION

TERZANI, TIZIANO   T01654
INDOCHINA WATCHERS HAVE SOME HOMEWORK TO DO
MEDIA [HONG KONG] 3:8(AUG 1976), 9.
MEDIUM: GENERAL
CHRON: 1970-1980
GEOG: VIETNAM   SEV ASIA
SUBJ: DESCRIPTION

TETERS, BARBARA   T02572
PRESS FREEDOM AND THE <26TH CENTURY>
     AFFAIR IN MEIJI JAPAN
MODERN ASIAN STUDIES 6:3(1972), 337-51.
##/EASI
CHRON: BEFORE 1910
METH: HISTORICAL
GEOG: EAST ASIA
SUBJ: CONTROL   JRN HISTORY

THACKREY, T. O.   T02661
    CENSORSHIP IN CHINA
    EDITOR & PUBLISHER 67:47(6 APR 1935), 37.
    LETTER TO EDITOR
    CHRON: 1910-1946
    GEOG: CHINA
    SUBJ: CONTROL

THAI NOI, (PSEUD.)   T02139
    NUNG SATTAWAY NANGSUPHIM THAI
    BANGKOK, N. P., 1967.
                              LANG: OTHER ASIAN
    CHRON: SURVEY   VERIF: UNVERIFIED
    GEOG: THAILAND
    SUBJ: DESCRIPTION

THAN, U BA   T01068
    THE PRESS--EARLIER NEWSPAPERS IN BURMA IN
        <BURMESE YEARBOOK: 1957-1958>, 29-31, 33.
    RANGOON, STUDENT PRESS, 1957.
    ##/BURMA
    CHRON: BEFORE 1910
    GEOG: BURMA
    SUBJ: JRN HISTORY

THAYER, NATHANIEL   T01069
    A TRIBUTE TO A REPORTER
    JOURNAL OF INTERNATIONAL AFFAIRS 26:2(1972),
        154-9.
    ##/FOCO; SPENCER DAVIS/AP.
    CHRON: 1970-1980
    GEOG: SEV ASIA   WORLD
    SUBJ: FOR CORR   BIOGRAPHY

THIEN, TON THAT   T01070
    SOUTH VIETNAM: CREATING AN IMAGE
    FEER 53:2(JULY 1966), 53-4.
    CHRON: 1960-1970
    GEOG: VIETNAM
    SUBJ: PROPAGANDA

THOM, WAH-DING   T02212
    NEW WIRELESS STATION AT CANTON
    THE CHINA WEEKLY REVIEW XLII:4(24 SEPT
        1927), 98, 100.
    MEDIUM: ELECTRONIC
    CHRON: 1910-1946
    GEOG: CHINA
    SUBJ: DESCRIPTION

THOMPSON, HUNTER S.   T02562
    INTERDICTED DISPATCH FROM THE GLOBAL AFFAIRS
        DESK
    ROLLING STONE NO. 187(22 MAY 1975), 32-4.
    ##/VN-2
    MEDIUM: GENERAL
    CHRON: 1970-1980
    GEOG: VIETNAM
    SUBJ: FOR CORR

THOMPSON, SCOTT   T01071
    MUZZLING THE PRESS MAY HURT MARCOS
    CSM 8 AUG 1974
    ##/PHIL
    CHRON: 1970-1980
    GEOG: PHILIPPINES
    SUBJ: CONTROL

THOMPSON, VIRGINIA   T01080
    THAILAND: THE NEW SIAM
    NEW YORK, MACMILLAN, 1941.
    ##/THAI; HISTORY OF PRESS CENSORSHIP,
        PP. 788-800.
    CHRON: SURVEY
    GEOG: THAILAND
    SUBJ: CONTROL

THU VIEN QUOC GIA   T01726
    MUC-LUC BAO-CHI VIET-NGU 1865-1965
        [VIETNAMESE NEWSPAPERS 1865-1965]
    SAIGON, THU VIEN QUOC GIA, 1966.
                        LANG: OTHER ASIAN
    CHRON: SURVEY
    METH: HISTORICAL
    GEOG: VIETNAM
    SUBJ: JRN HISTORY

THUNG, YVONNE AND JOHN M. ECHOLS   T02760
    A GUIDE TO INDONESIAN SERIALS (1945-1965) IN
        THE CORNELL UNIVERSITY LIBRARY
    ITHACA, SOUTHEAST ASIA PROGRAM, CORNELL
        UNIVERSITY, 1966.
    CHRON: SURVEY
    METH: OTHER OR COMB
    GEOG: INDONESIA
    SUBJ: RESEARCH

TIEDE, TOM   T02213
    PROFILE OF THE PIO
    DATELINE [OPC, NEW YORK] X:1(1966), 84-6.
    MEDIUM: GENERAL
    CHRON: 1960-1970
    GEOG: VIETNAM   U.S.
    SUBJ: FOR CORR   CONTROL   DESCRIPTION

TIENTSIN CORRESPONDENT   T02321
    HOW JAPANESE CREATE 'NEWS' AND DISTORT
        FACTS IN NORTH CHINA
    THE CHINA WEEKLY REVIEW 75:2(14 DEC 1935), 58.
    CHRON: 1910-1946
    GEOG: CHINA   EAST ASIA   OTHER
    SUBJ: PROPAGANDA

TIME   T01074
    OUT OF THE ZOO
    (28 SEPT 1959), 61.
    CHIN-3
    CHRON: 1946-1960
    GEOG: CHINA
    SUBJ: FOR CORR   CONTROL

TIME   T01076
    PRESS LORD WITHOUT PORTFOLIO
    (31 MAY 1971), 31.
    ##/SIN; NANYANG SIANG PAU AFFAIR.
    CHRON: 1970-1980
    GEOG: SINGAPORE
    SUBJ: CONTROL

TIME   T01075
    FOREIGN CORRESPONDENTS: THE VIEW FROM SAIGON
    (20 SEPT 1963), 62.
    ##/VN-2
    CHRON: 1960-1970
    GEOG: VIETNAM
    SUBJ: FOR CORR

TIMES, THE [LONDON]   T01078
    JOURNALISTS ACCUSED OF COMMUNIST PLOT
    23 JUNE 1976
    ##/SIN
    CHRON: 1970-1980
    GEOG: SINGAPORE
    SUBJ: CONTROL   LAW/ETHICS

TIMES, THE [LONDON]   T01077
    SINGPORE EDITOR 'TRIED TO UNDERMINE RELIGION'
    29 JUNE 1976
    ##/SIN
    CHRON: 1970-1980
    GEOG: SINGAPORE
    SUBJ: CONTROL   LAW/ETHICS

TIMES, THE [LONDON]   T01306
    IMPERIAL AND FOREIGN INTELLIGENCE: ATTITUDE
        OF THE PRESS
    (8 NOV 1911), 5.
    #=
    CHRON: BEFORE 1910
    GEOG: CHINA
    SUBJ: DESCRIPTION

TIMES, THE [LONDON]   T01305
    CHINESE PRESS SUBSIDIES
    (3 MAY 1910), 7.
    #=
    CHRON: BEFORE 1910
    GEOG: CHINA
    SUBJ: DESCRIPTION

TIMES, THE [LONDON]   T01296
    THE PRESS IN CHINA
    (31 DEC 1892), 4.
    #=; IMBAULT-HUARD SPEECH.
    CHRON: BEFORE 1910
    GEOG: CHINA
    SUBJ: DESCRIPTION

TIMES, THE [LONDON]   T01294
    AN OLD CHINESE PRINTING ESTABLISHMENT
    (15 FEB 1888), 4.
    #=
    CHRON: BEFORE 1910
    GEOG: CHINA
    SUBJ: PRINTING

TIMES, THE [LONDON]   T01292
    AN ENGLISH NEWSPAPER IN CHINA
    (28 DEC 1886), 7.
    #=; <CHINESE TIMES>, TIENTSIN.
    CHRON: BEFORE 1910
    GEOG: CHINA
    SUBJ: DESCRIPTION

TIMES, THE [LONDON]   T01282
    ENGLISH NEWSPAPERS IN CHINA
    (19 OCT 1842), 7.
    #=
    CHRON: BEFORE 1910
    GEOG: CHINA
    SUBJ: DESCRIPTION

TIMES, THE [LONDON]   T01283
     NEWSPAPERS TO CHINA
     (17 JAN 1844), 4.
     #=
     CHRON: BEFORE 1910
     GEOG: CHINA
     SUBJ: DESCRIPTION OTHER NON-J

TIMES, THE [LONDON]   T01290
     CHINESE NEWSPAPERS
     (19 MAR 1881), 6.
     #=
     CHRON: BEFORE 1910
     GEOG: CHINA
     SUBJ: DESCRIPTION

TIMES, THE [LONDON]   T01281
     [<THE EVANGELIST AND MISCELLANEA SINICA>]
     (24 OCT 1833), 3.
     #=
     CHRON: BEFORE 1910
     GEOG: CHINA
     SUBJ: DESCRIPTION

TIMES, THE [LONDON]   T01286
     CHINA [A NEWSPAPER IN SHANGHAI]
     (28 MAY 1876), 6.
     #=
     CHRON: BEFORE 1910
     GEOG: CHINA
     SUBJ: DESCRIPTION

TIMES, THE [LONDON]   T01285
     [NEW DAILY CHINESE NEWSPAPER]
     (1 APR 1874), 6.
     #=
     CHRON: BEFORE 1910
     GEOG: CHINA
     SUBJ: DESCRIPTION

TIMES, THE [LONDON]   T01302
     THE VERNACULAR PRESS OF CHINA
     (19 FEB 1910), 5.
     #=
     CHRON: BEFORE 1910
     GEOG: CHINA
     SUBJ: DESCRIPTION

TIMES, THE [LONDON]   T01301
    CHINESE PRESS REGULATIONS
    (13 FEB 1908), 5.
    #=
    CHRON: BEFORE 1910
    GEOG: CHINA
    SUBJ: CONTROL

TIMES, THE [LONDON]   T01289
    CHINA [THE PEKIN GAZETTE]
    (18 AUG 1879), 11.
    #=
    CHRON: BEFORE 1910
    GEOG: CHINA
    SUBJ: JRN HISTORY DESCRIPTION

TIMES, THE [LONDON]   T01297
    THE CHINESE GOVERNMENT AND THE PRESS
    (9 SEPT 1903), 3.
    #=
    CHRON: BEFORE 1910
    GEOG: CHINA
    SUBJ: CONTROL

TIMES, THE [LONDON]   T01288
    CHINESE NEWSPAPERS
    (31 JULY 1877), 8.
    #=
    CHRON: BEFORE 1910
    GEOG: CHINA
    SUBJ: DESCRIPTION

TIMES, THE [LONDON]   T01303
    CHINA: OFFICIALS AND THE PRESS
    (10 MAR 1910), 5.
    #=
    CHRON: BEFORE 1910
    GEOG: CHINA
    SUBJ: DESCRIPTION

TIMES, THE [LONDON]   T01304
    THE INDIAN PRESS ACT
    (10 MAR 1910), 5.
    #=
    CHRON: BEFORE 1910
    GEOG: SO/WEST ASI
    SUBJ: DESCRIPTION LAW/ETHICS

TIMES, THE [LONDON]   T01284
    CHINA AND JAPAN
    (27 JUNE 1867), 12.
    #=
    CHRON: BEFORE 1910
    GEOG: CHINA
    SUBJ: CONTROL   DESCRIPTION

TIMES, THE [LONDON]   T01293
    A CHINESE AGONY COLUMN
    (21 JULY 1887), 10.
    #=
    CHRON: BEFORE 1910
    GEOG: CHINA
    SUBJ: DESCRIPTION

TIMES, THE [LONDON]   T01300
    DR. MORRISON CHINESE REFORMS
    (6 NOV 1907), 12.
    #=
    CHRON: BEFORE 1910
    GEOG: CHINA
    SUBJ: DESCRIPTION

TIMES, THE [LONDON]   T01291
    THE CHINESE NATIVE PRESS
    (7 AUG 1885), 13.
    #=
    CHRON: BEFORE 1910
    GEOG: CHINA
    SUBJ: DESCRIPTION

TIMES, THE [LONDON]   T01298
    JAPAN AND CHINA
    (26 JUNE 1906), 19.
    #=
    CHRON: BEFORE 1910
    GEOG: CHINA   EAST ASIA
    SUBJ: DESCRIPTION

TIMES, THE [LONDON]   T01299
    THE CHINESE PRESS
    (29 AUG 1906), 7.
    #=
    CHRON: BEFORE 1910
    GEOG: CHINA
    SUBJ: DESCRIPTION

TIMES, THE [LONDON]   T01287
     CHINESE NEWSPAPERS
     (7 APR 1877), 10.
     #=
     CHRON: BEFORE 1910
     GEOG: CHINA
     SUBJ: JRN HISTORY DESCRIPTION

TIMES,THE [LONDON]   T01295
     THE STYLE OF THE <PEKIN GAZETTE>
     (16 APR 1888), 9.
     #=
     CHRON: BEFORE 1910
     GEOG: CHINA
     SUBJ: DESCRIPTION

TIMES,THE [LONDON]   T01280
     JOURNALISM IN RANGOON
     (20 APR 1937), 30.
     ##/BURMA
     CHRON: SURVEY
     GEOG: BURMA
     SUBJ: JRN HISTORY DESCRIPTION

TIMPERLEY, H. J.   T01254
     THE BEGINNINGS OF JOURNALISM IN CHINA
     PEIPING, N. P., 1930.
     GIVEN BEFORE THE <THINGS CHINESE> SOCIETY OF
          PEKING, 25 NOV 1930;
          16 PP. AND BIBLIOGRAPHY.
     CHRON: SURVEY   VERIF: UNVERIFIED
     GEOG: CHINA
     SUBJ: JRN HISTORY

TIMPERLY, H. J.   T01079
     MAKERS OF PUBLIC OPINION ABOUT THE FAR EAST
     PACIFIC AFFAIRS IX:2(JUNE 1936), 221-30.
     ##/ASIA
     MEDIUM: GENERAL
     CHRON: 1910-1946
     GEOG: SEV ASIA
     SUBJ: FLOW/AGENCY OTHER JRN

TIN-MOUNG   T01081
     CONTEMPORARY BURMESE PRESS UNDERGOING AN
          EVOLUTION
     JQ 24:2(1947), 139-42.
     ##/BURMA
     CHRON: 1946-1960
     GEOG: BURMA
     SUBJ: DESCRIPTION

TING KUANG-HUA   02   T02759
SUI CHUN JEN YUEH PEI K'UN CHI (I WAS A WAR
     CORRESPONDENT IN VIETNAM)
PAO HSUEH [TAIPEI] II:1(JUNE 1957), 63-5.
                              LANG: CHINESE
CHRON: 1946-1960
GEOG: VIETNAM
SUBJ: FOR CORR   BIOGRAPHY

TING KUANG-HUA   02   T02758
KUNG FEI PAO WEN CHU PAN SHIH YEH TI P'OU
     PAN (AN ANALYSIS OF NEWS PUBLICATIONS
     UNDER THE CHINESE REDS)
PAO HSUEH II:10(AUG 1962), 82-98.
                              LANG: CHINESE
CHRON: 1960-1970
METH: OTHER OR COMB
GEOG: CHINA
SUBJ: DESCRIPTION

TING SHU-CH'I   02   T01082
CHUNG-KUO KUNG CH'AN TI TI I KO CHI KUAN PAO
     <HSIANG TAO> (THE FIRST JOURNAL OF THE
     CHINESE COMMUNIST PARTY: <HSIANG TAO>)
HSIN WEN CHAN HSIEN 1(DEC 1957), 55-67.
SKINNER S00982 II:46505; REPRINT AVAILABLE.
                              LANG: CHINESE
CHRON: 1910-1946   VERIF: UNVERIFIED
METH: HISTORICAL
GEOG: CHINA
SUBJ: JRN HISTORY

TING WANG   02   T01084
CHUNG WEN PAO CHIH CH'U LI 'TA LU HSIN WEN'
     TI WEN T'I
MING 'PAO YUEH K'AN 6:2(FEB 1971), 31-9.
##/CHIN-4; (THE HANDLING OF 'MAINLAND NEWS BY
     CHINESE-LANGUAGE
     NEWSPAPERS [IN HONG KONG]);
     NST 50-70, III:3817.
                              LANG: CHINESE
CHRON: 1970-1980
METH: CONTENT ANALYSIS
GEOG: HONG KONG   CHINA
SUBJ: DESCRIPTION

TING WANG   02   T01905
CHUNG WEN PAO CHIH CH'U LI 'TA LU HSIN WEN'
     TI WEN T'I
HONG KONG, CONTEMPORARY CHINA RESEARCH
     INSTITUTE, 1971.
##/CHIN-4; [THE HANDLING OF 'MAINLAND
     NEWS' BY CHINESE LANGUAGE
     PAPERS (IN HONG KONG)];
     REPRINT OF TING 02T01084.
                              LANG: CHINESE
CHRON: 1970-1980
METH: CONTENT ANALYSIS
GEOG: HONG KONG   CHINA
SUBJ: DESCRIPTION

TING, LEE-HSIA HSU   T01083
GOVERNMENT CONTROL OF THE PRESS IN MODERN
     CHINA, 1900-1912
CAMBRIDGE, HARVARD U. PRESS, 1974.
CHRON: SURVEY
METH: HISTORICAL
GEOG: CHINA
SUBJ: CONTROL

TING, WANG, EDITOR   02   T02025
     CHUNG-KUO TA LU HSIN EN CHIEH WEN HUA TA KO
     MING TZU LIAO HUI PIEN (COMP. . . .
     ARTICLES ON NEWS POLICY DURING
     THE CULTURAL REVOLUTION
HONG KONG, CHINESE UNIVERSITY OF HONG KONG,
     1973.
                         LANG: CHINESE
     CHRON: 1960-1970
     GEOG: CHINA
     SUBJ: CONTROL   DESCRIPTION

TOKYO GAZETTE   T01906
     BROADCASTING IN THE CURRENT EMERGENCY
     17(NOV 1938), 5-10.
     MEDIUM: ELECTRONIC
     CHRON: 1910-1946
     GEOG: EAST ASIA
     SUBJ: DESCRIPTION

TONG HOLLINGTON KONG   13   T02141
     HSIN WEN HSUEH LUN CHI [JOURNALISM ANTHOLOGY]
     TAIPEI, CHUNG HWA WEN HUA CHU PAN SHIH YEH,
     1955.
     #3
                         LANG: CHINESE
     CHRON: SURVEY
     GEOG: TAIWAN   CHINA
     SUBJ: JRN HISTORY DESCRIPTION

TONG, H. K.   T01655
     NEW JOURNALISM IN CHINA
     LIVING AGE 313:4057(8 APR 1922), 83-6.
     ##/CHIN-5
     CHRON: 1910-1946
     GEOG: CHINA
     SUBJ: DESCRIPTION

TONG, HOLLINGTON K.   T01729
     THE NEW TENDENCY OF JOURNALISM IN CHINA
     THE CHINA WEEKLY REVIEW XX:6(11 FEB 1922),
     454-6.
     CHRON: 1910-1946
     GEOG: CHINA
     SUBJ: DESCRIPTION

TONG, HOLLINGTON K.   T01087
     DATELINE: CHINA
     NEW YORK, ROCKPORT PRESS, 1950.
     CHRON: 1946-1960
     GEOG: CHINA
     SUBJ: DESCRIPTION

TONG, HOLLINGTON K.   T01086
    CHINA AND THE WORLD PRESS
    NANKING, N. P., 1948.
    NUC AUTHORS 42-62 134:366
    CHRON: 1910-1946
    GEOG: CHINA
    SUBJ: FLOW/AGENCY DESCRIPTION

TONG, HOLLINGTON K.   T01085
    OPEN DIPLOMACY, THE HOPE OF THE PACIFIC PRESS
    IN WILLIAMS W01152, PP. 445-9.
    #3
    CHRON: 1910-1946
    GEOG: SEV ASIA
    SUBJ: DESCRIPTION OTHER JRN

TONG, HOLLINGTON K.   T01727
    PRESIDENT OF WORLD CONGRESS IN CHINA
    THE CHINA WEEKLY REVIEW XIX:2(10 DEC 1921),
        57-60.
    WALTER WILLLIAMS
    CHRON: 1910-1946
    GEOG: CHINA
    SUBJ: DESCRIPTION

TONG, HOLLINGTON K.   T01728
    CHINA'S PARTICIPATION IN THE WORLD PRESS
        CONGRESS
    THE CHINA WEEKLY REVIEW XIX:2(10 DEC 1921),
        61-4.
    CHRON: 1910-1946
    GEOG: CHINA
    SUBJ: DESCRIPTION

TONG, HOLLINGTON K.   T02214
    DEVELOPING A MODERN CHINESE NEWSPAPER IN
        SHANGHAI
    THE CHINA WEEKLY REVIEW XLIII:6(7 JAN 1928),
        147.
    THE CHINA TIMES
    CHRON: 1910-1946
    GEOG: CHINA
    SUBJ: DESCRIPTION

TONG, HOLLINGTON K.   T01730
    THE SHANGHAI PRINTED MATTER BYE-LAW
    THE CHINA WEEKLY REVIEW XX:7(15 APR 1922),
        246-8.
    CHRON: 1910-1946
    GEOG: CHINA
    SUBJ: LAW/ETHICS

TONG, TE-KONG   T01088
    RED GUARD NEWSPAPERS
    COLUMBIA FORUM XII:1(SPRING 1969), 38-41.
    ##/CHIN-2
    CHRON: 1960-1970
    GEOG: CHINA
    SUBJ: DESCRIPTION

TOROPTSEV, S.   T01089
    MOVIES SPLICED WITH MAO-THOUGHT
    ATLAS 19:6(SEPT 1970), 55.
    ##/CHIN-2; FROM <HONG KONG STANDARD>.
    MEDIUM: FILM
    CHRON: 1970-1980
    GEOG: CHINA
    SUBJ: PROPAGANDA

TOZER, WARREN W.   T02626
    THE FOREIGN CORRESPONDENTS' VISIT TO YENAN
        IN 1944: A REASSESMENT
    PACIFIC HISTORICAL REVIEW XLI:2(MAY 1972),
        207-224.
    CHRON: 1910-1946
    METH: HISTORICAL
    GEOG: CHINA
    SUBJ: FOR CORR   JRN HISTORY

TRAN TRONG HUNG   T02584
    ASIAN JOURNALISM
    VIETNAM MAGAZINE 4:10(1971), 20-2.
    CHRON: 1970-1980
    GEOG: VIETNAM   SEV ASIA
    SUBJ: DESCRIPTION

TRANS-PACIFIC [TOKYO]   T01656
    AMERICAN NEWS IN CHINA
    13(18 SEPT 1926), 5, 22.
    ##/CHIN-5; FROM <THE CHINA WEEKLY REVIEW>.
    CHRON: 1910-1946
    GEOG: CHINA
    SUBJ: DESCRIPTION

TRAVELER'S TALES   T01092
    [SINGAPORE HERALD]
    FEER LXXII:23(5 JUNE 1971), 13.
    CHRON: 1970-1980
    GEOG: SINGAPORE
    SUBJ: CONTROL

TRAVELER'S TALES   T01091
    [MERGER OF BANGKOK WORLD AND POST]
    FEER LXXII:2(29 MAY 1971), 13.
    ##/THAI
    CHRON: 1970-1980
    GEOG: THAILAND
    SUBJ: DESCRIPTION

TRAVELER'S TALES   T01090
    FEER LXXII:21(22 MAY 1971), 13.
    ##/SIN; HERALD.
    CHRON: 1970-1980
    GEOG: SINGAPORE
    SUBJ: CONTROL

TREASTER, JOSEPH B.   T01093
    SOUTH VIETNAM WORKS TO REVISE OUTMODED
        PRESS LAWS
    NYT 24 MAR 1969
    CHRON: 1960-1970   VERIF: UNVERIFIED
    GEOG: VIETNAM
    SUBJ: LAW/ETHICS

TREAT, PAYSON J.   T02047
    REVIEW OF ROSWELL S. BRITTON'S <THE CHINESE
        PERIODICAL PRESS, 1800-1912>
    PACIFIC HISTORICAL REVIEW III:3(SEPT 1934),
        355-6.
    CHRON: 1910-1946
    GEOG: CHINA
    SUBJ: RESEARCH

TREFFKORN, HANS   T02448
    CHOLLIMA--THE PEGASUS OF THE FAR EAST
    THE DEMOCRATIC JOURNALIST (SEPT 1978), 4-6.
    ##/EASI
    MEDIUM: GENERAL
    CHRON: 1970-1980
    GEOG: EAST ASIA
    SUBJ: DESCRIPTION

TREGASKIS, RICHARD   T02215
    WHY WE COVER WAR
    DATELINE [OPC, NEW YORK] X:1(1966),
        24-5, 27.
    MEDIUM: GENERAL
    CHRON: 1960-1970
    GEOG: VIETNAM   U.S.
    SUBJ: FOR CORR

TREGONNING, K. G., EDITOR.   T02627
    MALAYSIAN HISTORICAL SOURCES
    SINGAPORE, HISTORY DEPARTMENT, UNIVERSITY
        OF SINGAPORE, 1962.
    SEE ROFF R02624 AND TAN T02625
    CHRON: SURVEY
    GEOG: MALAYSIA   SINGAPORE   OTHER
    SUBJ: RESEARCH   JRN HISTORY

TREVELYAN G. M.   T01912
    THE WHITE PERIL
    NINETEENTH CENTURY [TWENTIETH CENTURY]
        50:298(DEC 1901), 1043-55.
    ##/CHIN-6
    CHRON: BEFORE 1910
    GEOG: CHINA
    SUBJ: LAW/ETHICS   CROSS CULTU

TROLLOPE, M. N.   T02026
    BOOK PRODUCTION AND PRINTING IN COREA
    TRANSACTIONS OF THE KOREA BRANCH OF THE
        ROYAL ASIATIC SOCIETY 25(1936), 103-7.
    PRECEDED BY BIBLIOGRAPHICAL NOTE ON PAGE 101.
    CHRON: BEFORE 1910
    METH: HISTORICAL
    GEOG: EAST ASIA
    SUBJ: PRINTING

TRONG NHAN   T02585
    PRESS AGENCIES IN VIETNAM
    VIETNAM MAGAZINE III:4(1970), 21.
    CHRON: 1970-1980
    GEOG: VIETNAM
    SUBJ: FLOW/AGENCY DESCRIPTION

TRUMBULL, ROBERT   T01274
    THE SCRUTABLE EAST: A CORRESPONDENT'S REPORT
        ON SOUTHEAST ASIA
    NEW YORK, DAVID MCKAY, 1964.
    CHRON: SURVEY
    GEOG: SEV ASIA
    SUBJ: FOR CORR   BIOGRAPHY   OTHER NON-J

TS'AO, IGNATIUS J. H.   T02628
    REMOULDING WORLD OUTLOOK AND THE 'RED FLAG'
    STUDIES IN SOVIET THOUGHT 11:2(JUNE 1971),
        113-17.
    ##/CHIN-9
    CHRON: 1970-1980
    METH: OTHER OR COMB
    GEOG: CHINA
    SUBJ: PROPAGANDA

TSENG HSI-CHING   12   T01094
    ON THE QUESTION OF THE PARTY PRESS (TRANS. OF
        KUAN YU CH'UAN TANG PAN PAO WEN T'I IN
        <JEN MIN JIH PAO> 16 JUNE 1960)
    WASHINGTON, D. C., JPRS, 16 JUNE 1960.
    SKINNER I:7015; JPRS 3518; MC 14, 237/1960).
    CHRON: 1960-1970   VERIF: UNVERIFIED
    GEOG: CHINA
    SUBJ: DESCRIPTION

TSENG HSU-PAI, EDITOR.   12   T01095
    CHUNG-KUO HSIN WEN SHIH (HISTORY OF CHINESE
        JOURNALISM)
    TAIPEI, KUO LI CHENG CHIH TA HSUEH, HSIN WEN
        CHIU SO, 1966.
                              LANG: CHINESE
    CHRON: SURVEY
    METH: HISTORICAL
    GEOG: TAIWAN   CHINA   SEV ASIA
    SUBJ: JRN HISTORY

TSENG, H. P.   T02662
    CHINA PRIOR TO 1949
    IN LENT L00708, PP. 31-42.
    CHRON: SURVEY
    METH: HISTORICAL
    GEOG: CHINA
    SUBJ: JRN HISTORY

TSIEN TSUEN-HSUIN   T01096
    CHINA: TRUE BIRTHPLACE OF PAPER, PRINTING AND
        MOVABLE TYPE
    THE UNESCO COURIER (DEC 1972), 4-11.
    ##/CHIN-2
    CHRON: BEFORE 1910
    GEOG: CHINA
    SUBJ: PRINTING

TU HENG   07   T01097
    CINEMA CHRONICLE
    T'IEN HSIA MONTHLY VII:3(OCT 1938), 291-5.
    TH
    MEDIUM: FILM
    CHRON: 1910-1946
    GEOG: CHINA
    SUBJ: DESCRIPTION

TU-SHU YUEH-K'AN [PEIPING]   22   T01657
    CHUNG-KUO HSIN-WEN HSUEH SHU CHIH LUN WEN
        MU-LU [A BIBLIOGRAPHY OF BOOKS ON
        CHINESE JOURNALISM]
    1:10(10 JULY 1932), 28-37.
    ##/BIB; NATIONAL LIBRARY OF PEIPING,
        READERS MONTHLY.
                              LANG: CHINESE
    CHRON: 1910-1946
    GEOG: CHINA
    SUBJ: RESEARCH

TUNKU ABDUL RAHMAN   T01661
    THE PRESS AND SOCIAL CHANGE
    HORIZONS [USIS] XVII:3(1968-1970), 4-5.
    CHRON: 1960-1970
    GEOG: MALAYSIA
    SUBJ: DEVELOPMENT DESCRIPTION

TURNBULL, GEORGE S., JR.   T01099
    REPORTING THE WAR IN INDO-CHINA
    JQ 34:1(WINTER 1957), 87-9.
    ##/VN
    CHRON: 1946-1960
    GEOG: VIETNAM
    SUBJ: FOR CORR   DESCRIPTION

TZU WU   03   T02142
    P'ING CHIN CH'U-PAN CHIEN ERH SAN SHIH [THE
        PUBLISHING WORLD IN PEKING AND TIENTSIN]
    MIN CHU NO. 15 (19 JAN 1946), 384.
    ##/CHIN-7
                              LANG: CHINESE
    CHRON: 1910-1946
    GEOG: CHINA
    SUBJ: DESCRIPTION PRINTING

U. K. PRESS GAZETTE   U02217
    SULTAN BANS ISSUE OF ENGLISH-LANGUAGE DAILY
    (13 AUG 1973), 12.
    CHRON: 1970-1980
    GEOG: BRUNEI
    SUBJ: CONTROL

U. K. PRESS GAZETTE   U02216
    JOURNALIST TOLD TO QUIT SAIGON
    (30 JULY 1973), 16.
    JACQUES LESLIE
    CHRON: 1970-1980
    GEOG: VIETNAM
    SUBJ: FOR CORR   CONTROL

UNESCO   U01158
    WORLD COMMUNICATIONS
    EPPING, ESSEX, ENGLAND, GOWER PUB., 1975.
    MEDIUM: GENERAL
    CHRON: 1970-1980
    GEOG: WORLD
    SUBJ: RESEARCH   DESCRIPTION

UNESCO   U01101
    DEVELOPING MASS MEDIA IN ASIA
    PARIS, UNESCO, 1960.
    REPORTS AND PAPERS ON MASS COMMUNICATIONS
        NO. 30; UNESCO MEETING IN BANGKOK, 1960.
    MEDIUM: GENERAL
    CHRON: 1960-1970
    GEOG: SEV ASIA
    SUBJ: DEVELOPMENT DESCRIPTION

UNESCO   U01102
    MEETING ON DEVELOPMENT OF NEWS AGENCIES IN
        ASIA AND THE FAR EAST, BANGKOK,
        DEC 19-22, 1961.
    PARIS, UNESCO, 1962.
    UNESCO/MC/44
    MEDIUM: GENERAL
    CHRON: 1960-1970   VERIF: UNVERIFIED
    GEOG: SEV ASIA
    SUBJ: FLOW/AGENCY

UNESCO COURIER   U01103
    CHINA, BIRTHPLACE OF PRINTING CENTURIES
        BEFORE GUTENBERG
    25:1(JAN 1972), 18-19.
    ##/CHIN-2
    CHRON: BEFORE 1910
    METH: HISTORICAL
    GEOG: CHINA
    SUBJ: PRINTING

UNION RESEARCH INSTITUTE   U02761
    CATALOGUE OF MAINLAND CHINESE MAGAZINES AND
        NEWSPAPERS HELD BY UNION RESEARCH
        INSTITUTE
    HONG KONG, UNION RESEARCH INSTITUTE, 1968.
    CHRON: SURVEY
    METH: OTHER OR COMB
    GEOG: CHINA
    SUBJ: RESEARCH

UNITED STATES INFORMATION AGENCY   U01660
    BURMA: A COMMUNICATIONS FACT BOOK
    WASHINGTON, D. C., USIA, RESEARCH AND
        REFERENCE SERVICE, 1966.
    ##/BURMA; R-46-66.
    MEDIUM: GENERAL
    CHRON: 1960-1970
    GEOG: BURMA
    SUBJ: DESCRIPTION

UNITED STATES INFORMATION AGENCY   U01658
    INFORMATIONAL INTERESTS AND GENERAL MEDIA
        HABITS OF URBAN CAMBODIAN RADIO-LISTENERS
    WASHINGTON, D. C., USIA, 1961.
    ##/CAMB; SURVEY RESEARCH STUDIES, PMS-56.
    MEDIUM: ELECTRONIC
    CHRON: 1960-1970
    METH: SURVEY
    GEOG: CAMBODIA
    SUBJ: DESCRIPTION

UNITED STATES INFORMATION AGENCY   U01111
    COMMUNICATIONS FACTBOOK: PHILIPPINES
    WASHINGTON, D. C., USIA, 4 JUNE 1962.
    MEDIUM: GENERAL
    CHRON: 1960-1970   VERIF: UNVERIFIED
    GEOG: PHILIPPINES
    SUBJ: DESCRIPTION

UNITED STATES INFORMATION AGENCY   U01110
    COMMUNICATION FACTBOOK: BURMA
    WASHINGTON, D. C., USIA, 9 APR 1962.
    #3; OFFICE OR RESEARCH AND ANALYSIS, R-32-62.
    MEDIUM: GENERAL
    CHRON: 1960-1970
    GEOG: BURMA
    SUBJ: DESCRIPTION

UNITED STATES INFORMATION AGENCY   U01109
    COMMUNICATIONS FACTBOOK: INDONESIA
    WASHINGTON, D. C., USIA, 15 NOV 1960.
    MEDIUM: GENERAL
    CHRON: 1960-1970   VERIF: UNVERIFIED
    GEOG: INDONESIA
    SUBJ: DESCRIPTION

UNITED STATES INFORMATION SERVICE   U01662
        (SAIGON)
    PROCEEDINGS OF THE SAIGON MEDIA SEMINAR
    SAIGON, USIA, MAY 1974.
    MEDIUM: GENERAL
    CHRON: 1970-1980
    GEOG: VIETNAM
    SUBJ: DESCRIPTION

UNITED STATES OFFICE OF STRATEGIC   U01731
        SERVICES/RESEARCH AND ANALYSIS BRANCH
    RADIO BROADCASTING IN JAPAN
    WASHINGTON, D. C., WAR DEPARTMENT, 1945.
    MEDIUM: ELECTRONIC
    CHRON: 1910-1946   VERIF: UNVERIFIED
    GEOG: EAST ASIA
    SUBJ: DESCRIPTION

UPI REPORTER   U01106
    CENSORSHIP STRUGGLE GOES ON IN INDIA
    17 JULY 1975
    ##/SWAS
    MEDIUM: GENERAL
    CHRON: 1970-1980
    GEOG: SO/WEST ASI
    SUBJ: CONTROL

UPI REPORTER   U01108
     EDITING IN CHINA
     10 FEB 1977
     ##/CHIN-2; 'GANG OF FOUR'.
     CHRON: 1970-1980
     GEOG: CHINA
     SUBJ: FOR CORR   CONTROL

UPI REPORTER   U01107
     THE DIFFICULTIES OF REPORTING IN PEKING
     20 MAY 1976
     ##/CHIN
     MEDIUM: GENERAL
     CHRON: 1970-1980
     GEOG: CHINA
     SUBJ: FOR CORR   CONTROL

UPI REPORTER   U01105
     [DIMINISHING RANKS OF SAIGON REPORTERS]
     19 JUNE 1975
     ##/VN
     MEDIUM: GENERAL
     CHRON: 1970-1980
     GEOG: VIETNAM
     SUBJ: FOR CORR

UPI REPORTER   U01104
     [CLOSING OF PNOHM PENH BUREAU]
     24 APRIL 1975
     ##/CAM
     MEDIUM: GENERAL
     CHRON: 1970-1980
     GEOG: CAMBODIA
     SUBJ: FOR CORR   FLOW/AGENCY

UTOMO, JAKOB   U01112
     THE INDONESIAN PRESS AND DEVELOPMENT
     INDONESIAN QUARTERLY I:3(APR 1973), 75-86.
     ##/INDO
     CHRON: 1970-1980
     GEOG: INDONESIA
     SUBJ: DEVELOPMENT

VALENZUELA, JESUS Z.   V01113
     HISTORY OF JOURNALISM IN THE PHILIPPINE
          ISLANDS
     MANILA, GENERAL PRINTING PRESS, 1933.
     CHRON: SURVEY
     GEOG: PHILIPPINES
     SUBJ: JRN HISTORY

VALENZUELA, JESUS Z.   V02244
    HISTORY OF JOURNALISM IN THE PHILIPPINE
        ISLANDS
    MASTERS THESIS, UNIVERSITY OF MISSOURI, 1930.
    CHRON: SURVEY
    METH: HISTORICAL
    GEOG: PHILIPPINES
    SUBJ: JRN HISTORY

VAN NIEL, ROBERT   V01114
    COMMUNICATION EDUCATION IN MALAYSIA
    DEN PASAR, SEMINAR ON COMMUNICATION TEACHING
        AND TRAINING, AMIC, 1972.
    ##/MAL; MIMEO, 4 PP.
    MEDIUM: GENERAL
    CHRON: 1970-1980
    GEOG: MALAYSIA
    SUBJ: EDUCATION

VAN ZANDT, LYDIA   V01115
    YOUNG TAIWANESE WIFE, MOTHER IS FOUNDER,
        EDITOR OF MAGAZINE
    CSM 19 JULY 1976
    ##/TAI
    CHRON: 1970-1980
    GEOG: TAIWAN
    SUBJ: DESCRIPTION BIOGRAPHY

VARIETY   V01116
    MALAYSIA BANNED 80 FILMS IN 1975
    7 APR 1976
    ##/MAL
    MEDIUM: FILM
    CHRON: 1970-1980
    GEOG: MALAYSIA
    SUBJ: CONTROL

VARIETY   V01117
    CHINESE BUY 10 BRITISH PIX, BBC PKG. IN
        UK TREK
    28 JULY 1976
    ##/CHIN
    MEDIUM: FILM
    CHRON: 1970-1980
    GEOG: CHINA
    SUBJ: DESCRIPTION

VATCHAGHANDY, RUSTON N.   V01118
    THE PRESS IN INDIA
    IN WILLIAMS W01152, PP. 530-40.
    #3
    CHRON: 1910-1946
    GEOG: SO/WEST ASI
    SUBJ: DESCRIPTION

VAUGHN, MILES W.   V01119
    COVERING THE FAR EAST
    NEW YORK, COVICI, FRIDE, 1936.
    CHRON: 1910-1946
    GEOG: SEV ASIA
    SUBJ: FOR CORR   DESCRIPTION BIOGRAPHY

VICENCIO, MACARIO T.   V01120
    ASIA'S 'FREE' PRESS
    ATLAS (APR 1964), 228.
    ##/ASIA; FROM <THE ASIA MAGAZINE>.
    CHRON: 1960-1970
    GEOG: SEV ASIA
    SUBJ: CONTROL

VIENET, RENE   V02804
    THE THOUGHTS OF WEI JINGSHENG
    FEER 104:19(11 MAY 1979), 27.
    ##/CHIN-9
    CHRON: 1970-1980
    GEOG: CHINA
    SUBJ: CONTROL

VIETNAM MAGAZINE   V01733
    ASIAN PRESS SEMINAR
    IV:10(1971), 17-19.
    CHRON: 1970-1980
    GEOG: VIETNAM   SEV ASIA
    SUBJ: DESCRIPTION

VIETNAM MAGAZINE   V01732
    ASIAN PRESS SEMINAR '70
    III:4(1970), 11-20.
    CHRON: 1970-1980
    GEOG: VIETNAM   SEV ASIA
    SUBJ: DESCRIPTION

VILANILAM, JOHN V.   V01121
    FOREIGN NEWS IN TWO U. S. NEWSPAPERS AND
        INDIAN NEWSPAPERS DURING SELECTED PERIODS
    GAZETTE XVIII:2(1972), 96-106.
    ##/SWAS
    CHRON: 1970-1980
    METH: CONTENT ANALYSIS
    GEOG: SO/WEST ASI U.S.
    SUBJ: DESCRIPTION

VILENSKII-SIBIRIAKOV, VL.   V02723
    ZHURNALISTIKA V SOVREMENNOM KITAE
    ZHURNALIST 2(1922), 67-68.
                            LANG: RUSSIAN
    CHRON: 1910-1946   VERIF: UNVERIFIED
    GEOG: CHINA
    SUBJ: DESCRIPTION

VILENSKII-SIBIRIAKOV, VL.   V02721
    GAZETA V SOVREMENNOM KITAE
    PECHAT' I REVOLUTSIA 3(1921), 103-109.
                            LANG: RUSSIAN
    CHRON: 1910-1946   VERIF: UNVERIFIED
    GEOG: CHINA
    SUBJ: DESCRIPTION

VILENSKII-SIBIRIAKOV, VL.   V02722
    KITAISKII ZHURNALIST
    ZHURNALIST 2(1922), 68.
                            LANG: RUSSIAN
    CHRON: 1910-1946   VERIF: UNVERIFIED
    GEOG: CHINA
    SUBJ: DESCRIPTION

VIRAVAIDYA, MECHAI   V01663
    GADFLY OF THE AIRWAVES
    HORIZONS [USIS] XIX:6(1968-1970), 46.
    MEDIUM: ELECTRONIC
    CHRON: 1960-1970
    GEOG: PHILIPPINES
    SUBJ: DESCRIPTION BIOGRAPHY

VITTACHI, A. G. TARZIE   V01124
    ASIA FACES A NEWSPAPER REVOLUTION
    NIEMAN REPORTS 17:3(1963), 26-8.
    ##/ASIA
    CHRON: 1960-1970
    GEOG: SEV ASIA
    SUBJ: DESCRIPTION

VITTACHI, TARZIE   V01664
    THE RELUCTANT REVOLUTION
    HORIZONS [USIS] XVII:11(1968-70), 21-24.
    CHRON: 1960-1970
    GEOG: SEV ASIA
    SUBJ: DESCRIPTION

VITTACHI, TARZIE   V01125
    SETTING THE PACE
    INSIGHT 1:7(JULY 1971), 54-5.
    S. KOREAN PRESS AND PRESS ETHICS COMMITTEE
    CHRON: 1970-1980
    GEOG: EAST ASIA
    SUBJ: LAW/ETHICS

VO CONG-TAI   V02143
    DOC VA PHIEN-DICH BAO-CHI ANH-MY
    SAIGON, NAM-SON, 1963.
                             LANG: OTHER ASIAN
    CHRON: 1960-1970
    GEOG: VIETNAM
    SUBJ: DESCRIPTION

VOLKERT, KURT   V02144
    COMBAT CAMERAMAN--VIETNAM
    DATELINE [OPC, NEW YORK] XII:1(1968), 96-9.
    MEDIUM: ELECTRONIC
    CHRON: 1960-1970
    GEOG: VIETNAM
    SUBJ: DESCRIPTION

VOLZ, FRED J.   V02048
    TAIWAN WOOS PRESS WITH 7-DAY JUNKETS
    EDITOR & PUBLISHER (24 JUNE 1978), 22, 36.
    ##/TAI
    CHRON: 1970-1980
    GEOG: TAIWAN
    SUBJ: DESCRIPTION OTHER JRN

VOTAW, MAURICE   V01734
    TOWARD A BETTER JOURNALISM IN CHINA
    THE CHINESE MERCURY I:1(JAN 1937), 21-4.
    CHRON: 1910-1946
    GEOG: CHINA
    SUBJ: DESCRIPTION

WADDELL, J. A. L.   W01907
    SOME THOUGHTS CONCERNING ECONOMICS IN THE
         DEVELOPMENT OF CHINA: DISSEMINATION OF
         CURRENT NEWS, INFORMATION ...
    FAR-EASTERN REVIEW 25:6(JUNE 1929), 253.
    CHRON: 1910-1946
    GEOG: CHINA
    SUBJ: DESCRIPTION

WADDELL, J.A.L.   W01665
    SOME THOUGHTS CONCERNING ECONOMICS IN THE
        DEVELOPMENT OF CHINA: DISSEMINATION OF
        CURRENT NEWS, INFORMATION . . .
    CHINESE SOCIAL AND POLITICAL SCIENCE REVIEW
        13(OCT 1929), 386-9.
    CHRON: 1910-1946
    GEOG: CHINA
    SUBJ: DESCRIPTION

WAIZZA, MAUNG   W02586
    SAYAGYI SHWE U DAUNG'S 30-YEAR-OLD ARTICLE
        ON BURMESE NEWSPAPERS AND BURMESE
        LANGUAGE
    GUARDIAN [RANGOON] 22:1(JAN 1975), 16-18.
    ##/BUR; FROM BA THEIN B02609.
    CHRON: 1970-1980
    GEOG: BURMA
    SUBJ: DESCRIPTION LANGUAGE

WALKER, RICHARD LOUIS   W01666
    WESTERN LANGUAGE PERIODICALS ON CHINA; A
        SELECTIVE LIST
    NEW HAVEN, YALE U.P., 1949.
    CHRON: 1910-1946
    GEOG: CHINA
    SUBJ: RESEARCH

WALTERS, RAY   W02547
    A BILLION POSSIBLE READERS
    THE NEW YORK TIMES BOOK REVIEW (13 MAY 1979),
        15, 32-3.
    ##/CHIN-9
    CHRON: 1970-1980
    GEOG: CHINA
    SUBJ: PUBLISHING LITERATURE

WANG CHIA-YU   W01126
    PEIPING'S 'NEW CHINA NEWS AGENCY' (NCNA)
    ISSUES AND STUDIES II:3(DEC 1965), 7-16.
    ##/CHIN-3
    MEDIUM: GENERAL
    CHRON: 1960-1970
    GEOG: CHINA
    SUBJ: FLOW/AGENCY

WANG CHUN   04   W01667
    CHUNG KUNG TI BAO JIH (CHINESE COMMUNIST
        NEWSPAPERS)
    CHUNG KUNG YEN CHIU (STUDIES ON CHINESE
        COMMUNISM) [TAIPEI] 3:4(APR 1969), 64-5.
    ##/CHIN-5
                        LANG: CHINESE
    CHRON: 1960-1970
    GEOG: CHINA
    SUBJ: DESCRIPTION

WANG CHUNG   04   W01127
    TI I TZ'U KUO NEI KO MING CHAN CHENG SHIH
        CH'I CHUNG YAO TI KO MING PAO CHIH YU
        CH'I K'AN
    TA KUNG PAO (TIENTSIN) 3(AUG 1951).
    (MAJOR REVOLUTIONARY NEWSPAPERS AND JOURNALS
        DURING THE FIRST
        REVOLUTIONARY CIVIL
        WAR [1924-1927]; SKINNER S00982 II:41878.
                          LANG: CHINESE
    CHRON: 1910-1946   VERIF: UNVERIFIED
    METH: HISTORICAL
    GEOG: CHINA
    SUBJ: JRN HISTORY

WANG EN-FAN AND YANG CHAO-TAO   04   W01128
    PAO CHIH TI HSIN WEN FEN HSI (A
        [QUANTITATIVE] ANALYSIS OF NEWS REPORTS)
    CH'ING HUA HSUEH PAO 1:1(JUNE 1924), 119-27.
    ULS 2:1026
                          LANG: CHINESE
    CHRON: 1910-1946
    METH: CONTENT ANALYSIS
    GEOG: CHINA
    SUBJ: DESCRIPTION

WANG HSIN-MIN   04   W01129
    HSIN WEN CHUAN LI SSU SHIH NIEN (FORTY YEARS
        IN JOURNALISM)
    TAIPEI, CHUNG YANG JIH PAO SHE, 1957.
    SKINNER S00982 II:50635
                          LANG: CHINESE
    CHRON: SURVEY   VERIF: UNVERIFIED
    GEOG: CHINA
    SUBJ: DESCRIPTION BIOGRAPHY

WANG HSUEH-WEN   W01130
    A STUDY OF BIG-CHARACTER POSTERS
    ISSUES AND STUDIES XII:4(APR 1976), 1-18.
    MEDIUM: OTHER
    CHRON: 1970-1980
    GEOG: CHINA
    SUBJ: DESCRIPTION

WANG HUNG CHUN   04   W01909
    TA CHUNG CH'UAN PO YU HSIEN TAI SHE HUI
        [MASS COMMUNICATIONS AND CONTEMPORARY
        SOCIETY]
    TAIPEI, FU YUAN YIN SHUA SHIH YEH, 1975, 2 VOL
    MEDIUM: GENERAL   LANG: CHINESE
    CHRON: 1970-1980
    GEOG: WORLD
    SUBJ: OTHER JRN

WANG JUI-CHENG   04   W02762
    JIH PEN MING CHIH SHIH TAI TI HSIN WEN TZU YU
        (FREEDOM OF PRESS DURING MEIJI REIGN IN
        JAPAN)
    PAO HSUEH [TAIPEI] II:2(DEC 1957), 15-20.
                          LANG: CHINESE
    CHRON: BEFORE 1910
    METH: HISTORICAL
    GEOG: EAST ASIA
    SUBJ: CONTROL   JRN HISTORY

WANG LING-LING   W01133
    NEWSPAPERS ON MAINLAND CHINA
    ISSUES AND STUDIES XII:4(APR 1976), 19-43.
    ##/CHIN-2
    CHRON: 1970-1980
    GEOG: CHINA
    SUBJ: DESCRIPTION

WANG MU   04 W01735
    SOME EXPERIENCES IN NEWSPAPER WORK SINCE
        THE GREAT LEAP FORWARD
    EXTRACTS FROM CHINA MAINLAND MAGAZINES NO.196
        (18 JAN 1960), 14-24.
    FROM <HSIN-WEN CHAN-HSIEN> (NEWS FRONT) (24
        SEPT 1959)
    CHRON: 1946-1960
    GEOG: CHINA
    SUBJ: DESCRIPTION

WANG SEE-ZEE   W02322
    WEN WEI PAO TO RESUME PUBLICATION
    THE CHINA WEEKLY REVIEW 110:13(28 AUG 1948),
        353.
    CHRON: 1946-1960
    GEOG: CHINA
    SUBJ: CONTROL

WANG WEN-PIN, EDITOR.   04 W02049
    PAO JEN CHIH LU [JOURNALIST'S ROAD]
    SHANGHAI, SAN HUNG SHU TIEN, 1938.
    CHRON: 1910-1946
    GEOG: CHINA
    SUBJ: DESCRIPTION BIOGRAPHY

WANG YING-CHI   04 W01137
    FAN TSUI HSIN WEN CHIH PAO TAO CHI CH'A FA
        LU TSE JEN (CRIME REPORTING AND LEGAL
        LIABILITY)
    UNPUB MASTERS THESIS IN JOURNALISM, 1964.
    SKINNER S00982 II:46549
                        LANG: CHINESE
    CHRON: 1960-1970   VERIF: UNVERIFIED
    GEOG: TAIWAN
    SUBJ: LAW/ETHICS

WANG YUN-WU   04 W01138
    SHIH NIEN LAI TI CHUNG-KUO CH'U PAN SHIH YEH
        (PUBLISHING IN CHINA DURING THE PAST
        DECADE)
    IN CHUNG-KUO WEN HUA 04C02591, PP. 463-79.
    REPRINT AVAILABLE; SKINNER S00982 II:41884.
                        LANG: CHINESE
    CHRON: 1910-1946   VERIF: UNVERIFIED
    GEOG: CHINA
    SUBJ: PUBLISHING

WANG, BETTY SIAO-MENG   W02145
    A COMPARISON OF AMERICAN AND CHINESE
        JOURNALISM HISTORIES
    MASTERS THESIS, U. CALIFORNIA/LOS ANGELES,
        1934.
    #3
    CHRON: SURVEY
    METH: HISTORICAL
    GEOG: CHINA   U.S.
    SUBJ: JRN HISTORY OTHER JRN

WANG, CHARLES C. S.   W01908
    CHINA HOLDS ITS FIRST JOURNALISM WEEK
    THE CHINA WEEKLY REVIEW 56:7(18 APR 1931),
        230, 238.
    CHRON: 1910-1946
    GEOG: CHINA
    SUBJ: EDUCATION

WANG, CHARLES KILORD ATHEN   W00106
    REACTIONS IN COMMUNIST CHINA: AN ANALYSIS OF
        LETTERS TO NEWSPAPER EDITORS
    LACKLAND AFB, TEXAS; AF PERSONNEL AND
        TRAINING RESEARCH CENTER,AIR R AND D
        COMMAND, 1955.
    #3; U. S. HUMAN RESOURCES RESEARCH INSTITUTE
        TECHNICAL REPORTS NO. 33
        (STUDIES IN CHINESE COMMUNISM,
        SERIES III, NO. 7, 1953).
    CHRON: 1946-1960
    METH: CONTENT ANALYSIS
    GEOG: CHINA
    SUBJ: DESCRIPTION

WANG, F.T.   W01668
    TENDENTIOUS NEWS STORIES
    THE PEOPLE'S TRIBUNE VIII N.S.:6(16 MAR
        1935), 375-6.
    LETTER
    CHRON: 1910-1946
    GEOG: CHINA
    SUBJ: CONTROL

WANG, GEORGE K. T.   W01417
    UNDECLARED 'ETHER WAR' IN MANCHURIA
    THE CHINA WEEKLY REVIEW 71:9(26 JAN 1935),
        300-1.
    MEDIUM: ELECTRONIC
    CHRON: 1910-1946
    GEOG: CHINA
    SUBJ: PROPAGANDA FLOW/AGENCY DESCRIPTION

WANG, JAMES EN-WEI   W01131
    CHINESE NEWSPAPERS IN THE U. S.
    MASTERS THESIS, UNIVERSITY OF MISSOURI, 1968.
    CHRON: 1960-1970
    GEOG: OSEAS CHIN U.S.
    SUBJ: DESCRIPTION

WANG, K. P.   W01132
    GETTING NEWS IN AND OUT OF CHINA
    IN WILLIAMS W01152, PP. 471-9.
    #3
    CHRON: 1910-1946
    GEOG: CHINA
    SUBJ: FOR CORR   FLOW/AGENCY DESCRIPTION

WANG, PAUL HUNG CHEN   W02245
    A HISTORICAL STUDY OF THE CHINESE PRESS OF
        3,000 YEARS
    MASTERS THESIS, UNIVERSITY OF MISSOURI, 1955.
    ##
    CHRON: SURVEY
    METH: HISTORICAL
    GEOG: CHINA
    SUBJ: JRN HISTORY

WANG, THI-WU   W01134
    THE PRESS IN FREE CHINA
    NIEMAN REPORTS XXI:2(JUNE 1967), 26-7.
    ##/TAI
    CHRON: 1960-1970
    GEOG: TAIWAN
    SUBJ: DESCRIPTION

WANG, THI-WU   W01135
    ON THE YUITUNG CASE
    FREE CHINA REVIEW XX:10(OCT 1970), 74-80.
    ##/TAI
    CHRON: 1970-1980
    GEOG: TAIWAN
    SUBJ: CONTROL   LAW/ETHICS

WANG, Y. C.   W02146
    THE <SU-PAO> CASE: A STUDY OF FOREIGN
        PRESSURE, INTELLECTUAL FERMENTATION, AND
        DYNASTIC DECLINE
    MONUMENTA SERICA 24(1965), 84-129.
    CHRON: 1910-1946
    METH: HISTORICAL
    GEOG: CHINA
    SUBJ: CONTROL   LAW/ETHICS

WANG, Y. P.   W01136
    THE RISE OF THE NATIVE PRESS IN CHINA
    NEW YORK, COLUMBIA U. PRESS, 1924.
    BASED ON AUTHORS THESIS
    CHRON: SURVEY
    METH: HISTORICAL
    GEOG: CHINA
    SUBJ: JRN HISTORY

WARD, LEA   W01669
    A QUESTION OF CLASS
    MEDIA [HONG KONG] NO. 3(JAN 1978), 14-5.
    ##/HKG; <ASIAWEEK>.
    CHRON: 1970-1980
    GEOG: HONG KONG
    SUBJ: DESCRIPTION

WARIN, W. J.   W02218
    HOW TO SELL TO MALAYA'S 4,385,000 MARKET
    WORLD'S PRESS NEWS 17:428(13 MAY 1937), IX-X.
    CHRON: 1910-1946
    GEOG: MALAYSIA   SINGAPORE
    SUBJ: OTHER JRN

WARNER, DENIS   W01139
    REPORTING SOUTHEAST ASIA
    SYDNEY, ANGUS & ROBERTSON, 1966.
    CHRON: SURVEY
    GEOG: SEV ASIA
    SUBJ: FOR CORR   DESCRIPTION OTHER NON-J

WATAN [PSEUD. (FATHERLAND)]   W01141
    THE STRAITS TIMES: A SERVILE APOLOGIST FOR
        THE ESTABLISHMENT
    MAHASISWA NEGARA [KUALA LUMPUR] 21 JUNE 1971
    ##/MAL-2
    CHRON: 1970-1980
    GEOG: MALAYSIA
    SUBJ: DESCRIPTION LAW/ETHICS

WATANABE, HARUKO   W01142
    SOUTH KOREAN PRESS
    FOI CENTER PUB. NO. 119(1964).
    ##/EASI
    CHRON: 1960-1970
    GEOG: EAST ASIA
    SUBJ: DESCRIPTION

WATTS, RONALD A.   W02664
    ASIAN JOURNALISM: DYNAMIC, DEVELOPING
    THE JOURNALIST'S WORLD I:4(1964), 8-9.
    CHRON: 1960-1970
    GEOG: SEV ASIA
    SUBJ: DEVELOPMENT DESCRIPTION

WATTS, RONALD A.   W02663
     ASIAN JOURNALISTS' UNIONS SEEK SUCCESS
          FORMULA
     THE JOURNALIST'S WORLD NO. 3(JULY-SEPT
          1963), 5.
     CHRON: 1960-1970
     GEOG: SEV ASIA
     SUBJ: OTHER JRN

WAY, EUGENE IRVING [COMPILER]   W01671
     MOTION PICTURES IN CHINA
     WASHINGTON, D.C., FOREIGN AND DOMESTIC
          COMMERCE BUREAU, 1930.
     TRADE INFORMATION BULLETIN 722; C18.25:722.
     MEDIUM: FILM
     CHRON: 1910-1946
     GEOG: CHINA
     SUBJ: DESCRIPTION

WAY, EUGENE IRVING [COMPILER]   W01670
     MOTION PICTURES IN JAPAN, PHILIPPINE ISLAND,
          NETHERLANDS EAST INDIES, SIAM, BRITISH
          MALAYA, AND FRENCH INDO-CHINA
     WASHINGTON, D.C., FOREIGN AND DOMESTIC
          COMMERCE BUREAU, 1929.
     TRADE INFORMATION BULLETIN 634; C18.25:634.
     MEDIUM: FILM
     CHRON: 1910-1946
     GEOG: SEV ASIA
     SUBJ: DESCRIPTION

WEAIT, R. H.   W01418
     THE ORIENT AND THE CINEMA
     BRITISH MALAYA VIII:11(MAR 1934), 231-2, 245.
     ##/MAL-3; SEE BILAINKIN B01367 AND
          HARLOFF H01392.
     MEDIUM: FILM
     CHRON: 1910-1946
     GEOG: MALAYSIA   SINGAPORE   SEV ASIA
     SUBJ: DESCRIPTION CROSS CULTU

WEALE, PUTNAM [PSEUD. OF BERTRAM   W01419
          LENOX SIMPSON]
     WHY CHINA SEES RED
     NEW YORK, DODD, MEAD, 1925.
     ##/CHIN-5; THE MIRROR OF THE CHINESE PRESS,
          PP. 118-45.
     CHRON: 1910-1946
     GEOG: CHINA
     SUBJ: DESCRIPTION

WEBB, ALVIN B.   W01910
     [<BIG STORY>]
     UPI REPORTER (9 MARCH 1978), 1, 4.
     ##/VN-2
     MEDIUM: GENERAL
     CHRON: SURVEY
     GEOG: VIETNAM   U.S.
     SUBJ: FOR CORR   FLOW/AGENCY

WEBSTER, NORMAN   W01143
    WHAT'S PLAYING IN PEKING, IF NIXON HAS TIME
        FOR A MOVIE
    CSM 23 JULY 1971
    ##/CHIN-2
    MEDIUM: FILM
    CHRON: 1970-1980
    GEOG: CHINA
    SUBJ: DESCRIPTION

WEI, MICHAEL AND TIMOTHY LIGHT   W02287
    A NEWSPAPER'S VOCABULARY--A RAW FREQUENCY
        COUNT OF THE WORDS IN THE SOUTH CHINA
        MORNING POST
    HONG KONG, CHINESE UNIVERSITY OF HONG KONG,
        1973.
    CHRON: 1970-1980   VERIF: UNVERIFIED
    GEOG: HONG KONG
    SUBJ: EDUCATION   LANGUAGE

WEI, MICHAEL TA-KUNG   W02246
    A SURVEY OF PERIODICALS IN TAIWAN, 1959.
    MASTERS THESIS, UNIVERSITY OF MISSOURI, 1960.
    CHRON: 1946-1960
    METH: SURVEY
    GEOG: TAIWAN
    SUBJ: DESCRIPTION

WEINER, ALAN   W01144
    INDONESIA: PRESS AND POLITICS
    FOI CENTER PUB. NO. 138 (1965).
    ##/INDON
    CHRON: 1960-1970
    GEOG: INDONESIA
    SUBJ: CONTROL   DESCRIPTION POLIT SCI

WEINRAUB, BERNARD   W01145
    INDIAN PRESS HAS LOST TOUCH WITH READERS
    STRAITS TIMES (NYT) 22 DEC 1973
    ##/SWAS
    CHRON: 1970-1980
    GEOG: SO/WEST ASI
    SUBJ: DESCRIPTION

WEINTRAUB, PETER   W02542
    LEE'S ISLANDS OF FREEDOM
    FEER 102:48(1 DEC 1978), 37.
    ##/SIN-2; LIM HOCK SIEW, SAID ZAHARI.
    CHRON: 1970-1980
    GEOG: SINGAPORE
    SUBJ: CONTROL

WEINTRAUB, PETER   W01675
    LEARNING TO LIVE WITH ASIA
    FEER 97:38(23 SEPT 1977), 35-6.
    ##/HKG; <THE ASIAN WALL STREET JOURNAL>.
    CHRON: 1970-1980
    GEOG: HONG KONG   SEV ASIA
    SUBJ: DESCRIPTION

WEINTRAUB, PETER   W01976
    BURMA SPREADS THE WORD
    FEER 100:15(14 APR 1978), 48.
    ##/BURMA
    MEDIUM: ELECTRONIC
    CHRON: 1970-1980
    GEOG: BURMA
    SUBJ: CONTROL   DESCRIPTION

WEN CH'UNG-HSIN   12   W02725
    SHIH NIEN LAI T'AI WAN TI CHU PAN CHIEH [TEN
        YEARS OF CHINA'S PUBLISHING INDUSTRY]
    IN T'AI-WAN 14T02574, PP. 276-9.
                          LANG: CHINESE
    CHRON: SURVEY
    GEOG: TAIWAN
    SUBJ: PUBLISHING

WEN, Y. C.   W01349
    WIRE AND RADIO COMMUNICATIONS
    IN CHINA PRESS C02568, PP. 132-3, 167.
    ##/FILM
    MEDIUM: ELECTRONIC
    CHRON: 1910-1946
    GEOG: CHINA
    SUBJ: DESCRIPTION

WERNER, JOHN R.   W02050
    JAPANESE NEWSPAPERS USE ADVANCED TECHNOLOGY
    EDITOR & PUBLISHER (24 JUNE 1978), 17-18.
    ##/EASI
    CHRON: 1970-1980
    GEOG: EAST ASIA
    SUBJ: DESCRIPTION PRINTING

WHANG, PAUL K.   W02323
    THE PROBLEM OF THE FREEDOM OF THE PRESS IN
        CHINA
    THE CHINA WEEKLY REVIEW 70:9(27 OCT 1934),
        300.
    CHRON: 1910-1946
    GEOG: CHINA
    SUBJ: CONTROL

WHEELER, GEOFFREY   W01146
    PROPAGANDA IN ASIA: DISCUSSION GROUP WITH A
          PAPER BY GEOFFREY WHEELER
    ASIAN AFFAIRS 63(NEW SERIES VOL. VII),
          PART 2(JUNE 1976), 183-9.
    MEDIUM: GENERAL
    CHRON: 1970-1980
    GEOG: SEV ASIA
    SUBJ: PROPAGANDA

WHITE, EDWIN Q.   W02543
    ASIA WAR COVERAGE LARGELY IS LONG DISTANCE
    AP LOG (5 MAR 1979), 1, 4.
    ##/CHIN-9
    MEDIUM: GENERAL
    CHRON: 1970-1980
    GEOG: VIETNAM   CHINA
    SUBJ: FOR CORR   FLOW/AGENCY

WHITE, EDWIN Q.   W02219
    ASSOCIATED PRESS STRAIGHT LINE TO SAIGON
    DATELINE [OPC, NEW YORK] XI:1(1967), 52.
    MEDIUM: GENERAL
    CHRON: 1960-1970
    GEOG: VIETNAM   U.S.
    SUBJ: FLOW/AGENCY

WHITE, JAMES D.   W01913
    CHINESE PRESS GOES AMERICAN
    EDITOR & PUBLISHER (13 APR 1935), 10, 12.
    ##/CHIN-6
    CHRON: 1910-1946
    GEOG: CHINA
    SUBJ: DESCRIPTION

WILCOX, DENNIS   W01148
    ENGLISH-LANGUAGE NEWSPAPERS ABROAD
    DETROIT, GALE RESEARCH, 1967.
    CHRON: 1960-1970
    GEOG: OTHER   WORLD
    SUBJ: DESCRIPTION

WILLIAMS, ALDEN   W01149
    UNBIASED STUDY OF TELEVISION NEWS BIAS
    JRNL OF COMMUNICATION 25:4(AUTUMN 1975),
          190-9.
    ##/VN
    MEDIUM: ELECTRONIC
    CHRON: 1970-1980
    METH: OTHER OR COMB
    GEOG: VIETNAM   U.S.
    SUBJ: RESEARCH   LAW/ETHICS

WILLIAMS, DEAN [WALTER]   W01952
    'THE CORRUPT PRESS IN CHINA'
    THE CHINA CRITIC X:6(8 AUG 1935), 123-4.
    FILM
    CHRON: 1910-1946
    GEOG: CHINA
    SUBJ: DESCRIPTION

WILLIAMS, FREDERICK WELLS   W01676
    THE LIFE AND LETTERS OF SAMUEL WELLS
        WILLIAMS, LL. D.
    NEW YORK, G. P. PUTNAM'S SONS, 1889.
    CHRON: BEFORE 1910
    METH: HISTORICAL
    GEOG: CHINA
    SUBJ: JRN HISTORY

WILLIAMS, MRS. WALTER   W01736
    WALTER WILLIAMS, WORLD JOURNALIST
    THE CHINESE MERCURY I:2(FALL 1937), 10-13.
    CHRON: 1910-1946
    GEOG: CHINA
    SUBJ: DESCRIPTION BIOGRAPHY

WILLIAMS, SARA LOCKWOOD   W01914
    TWENTY YEARS OF EDUCATION FOR JOURNALISM
    COLUMBIA, MISSOURI, E. W. STEPHENS, 1929.
    ##/CHIN-5
    CHRON: 1910-1946
    GEOG: CHINA
    SUBJ: BIOGRAPHY

WILLIAMS, WALTER   W01329
    A NEW JOURNALISM IN A NEW FAR EAST
    COLUMBIA, MO., U. OF MISSOURI, 1928.
    ##/ASIA; U. OF MISSOURI BULLETIN, JOURNALISM
        SERIES 52, VOL. 29, NO. 45, PP. 3-17.
    CHRON: 1910-1946
    GEOG: SEV ASIA
    SUBJ: DESCRIPTION

WILLIAMS, WALTER   W01425
    DEAN WILLIAMS ON CHINESE JOURNALISM
    THE CHINA WEEKLY REVIEW XLV:11(11 AUG 1928),
        353.
    ##/CHIN-5
    CHRON: 1910-1946
    GEOG: CHINA
    SUBJ: DESCRIPTION EDUCATION

WILLIAMS, WALTER   W01153
    THE JOURNALISM OF CHINA
    JAPAN OVERSEAS TRAVEL MAGAZINE XVIII:IV(APR
        1929), 34-5, 39-40.
    ##/CHIN-3; ULS 3:2153.
    CHRON: 1910-1946
    GEOG: CHINA
    SUBJ: DESCRIPTION

WILLIAMS, WALTER, EDITOR.   W01152
    PRESS CONGRESS OF THE WORLD IN HAWAII
    COLUMBIA, MO., E. W. STEPHENS, 1922.
    CHRON: 1910-1946
    GEOG: WORLD
    SUBJ: DESCRIPTION

WILLIAMS, WALTER, EDITOR.   W02587
    PRESS CONFERENCE OF THE WORLD IN SWITZERLAND
    COLUMBIA, MISSOURI, E. W. STEPHENS, 1928.
    CONFERENCE HELD IN 1926
    CHRON: 1910-1946
    GEOG: SEV ASIA   WORLD
    SUBJ: DESCRIPTION

WILLIAMSON, LENORA   W01915
    JAPAN JOURNAL FORMS NEWS SYNDICATE
    EDITOR & PUBLISHER (6 MAY 1978), 53.
    ##/EASI
    CHRON: 1970-1980
    GEOG: EAST ASIA
    SUBJ: DESCRIPTION OTHER JRN

WILLIAMSON, LENORA   W02545
    U. S. WIRE SERVICES STAFF PEKING BUREAUS
    EDITOR & PUBLISHER (24 MAR 1979), 9.
    ##/CHIN-8
    MEDIUM: GENERAL
    CHRON: 1970-1980
    GEOG: CHINA   U.S.
    SUBJ: FOR CORR   FLOW/AGENCY BIOGRAPHY

WILLIAMSON, LENORA   W02544
    CHINA-VIET WAR POSES PROBLEMS FOR REPORTERS
    EDITOR & PUBLISHER (10 MAR 1979), 11, 44.
    ##/CHIN-8
    MEDIUM: GENERAL
    CHRON: 1970-1980
    GEOG: VIETNAM   CHINA
    SUBJ: FOR CORR   FLOW/AGENCY

WILLYOUNG, A. K.   W01916
    CHINESE JOURNALISM
    AMERICAN PRESS 52(MAY 1934), 20.
    ##/CHIN-6
    CHRON: 1910-1946
    GEOG: CHINA
    SUBJ: DESCRIPTION

WILSON, DICK   W01160
    A LONG VIEW--OR BOGEY?
    FEER LXXIII:32(7 AUG 1971), 30, 33.
    ##/SIN; HERALD.
    CHRON: 1970-1980
    GEOG: SINGAPORE
    SUBJ: CONTROL

WILSON, QUINTUS C.   W01161
    WHAT JAPAN READS ABOUT AMERICA
    NIEMAN REPORTS IX:4(OCT 1955), 22-9.
    ##/EASI
    CHRON: 1946-1960
    GEOG: EAST ASIA   U.S.
    SUBJ: FOR CORR   FLOW/AGENCY DESCRIPTION

WILSON, W. ARTHUR   W01162
    MALAYAN PRESS
    BRITISH MALAYA 20:12(APR 1946), 297-8, 302,
        PART 1; 21:1(MAY 1946),7-8, 11, PART 2;
        21:4(AUG 1946), 55-8, PART 3.
    ##/MAL-2; ULS 1:788; AUTHOR WAS EDITOR OF
        <MALAYA TRIBUNE> AND
        <FREE PRESS>/SINGAPORE.
    CHRON: SURVEY
    GEOG: MALAYSIA   SINGAPORE
    SUBJ: JRN HISTORY DESCRIPTION BIOGRAPHY

WILSON, W. ARTHUR   W01421
    A MALAYAN JINGLE: JUST A JOURNALIST
    BRITISH MALAYA III:9(JAN 1929), 245.
    ##/MAL-3
    CHRON: 1910-1946
    GEOG: MALAYSIA   SINGAPORE
    SUBJ: DESCRIPTION OTHER JRN

WILSON, W. ARTHUR   W01420
    MALAYAN JINGLES: THE PRESS
    BRITISH MALAYA II:10(FEB 1928), 254.
    ##/MAL-3
    CHRON: 1910-1946
    GEOG: MALAYSIA   SINGAPORE
    SUBJ: DESCRIPTION OTHER JRN

WINDER, DAVID   W01163
     TV TO LINK VILLAGES IN INDIA
     CSM 27 JUNE 1972
     ##/SWAS
     MEDIUM: ELECTRONIC
     CHRON: 1970-1980
     GEOG: SO/WEST ASI
     SUBJ: DEVELOPMENT DESCRIPTION

WINKLER, MANFRED   W01164
     PLASTIC DREAMS IN INDIA
     ATLAS 20:2(FEB 1971), 52-3.
     FROM <FRANKFURTER ALLGEMEINE ZEITUNG>
     MEDIUM: GENERAL
     CHRON: 1970-1980
     GEOG: SO/WEST ASI
     SUBJ: DESCRIPTION

WINT, GUY, EDITOR.   W02577
     ASIA: A HANDBOOK
     NEW YORK, PRAEGER, 1966.
     SEE ROSE R00935.
     CHRON: 1960-1970
     GEOG: SEV ASIA
     SUBJ: DESCRIPTION

WITCOVER, JULES   W01165
     WHERE WASHINGTON REPORTING FAILED
     COL JRN REVIEW IX:4(WINTER 1970-1), 7-13.
     CHRON: 1970-1980
     GEOG: VIETNAM   U.S.
     SUBJ: FOR CORR   OTHER NON-J

WONG, DAVID TZI KI   W02147
     A VALUE-ANALYSIS OF SOME ASIAN NEWSPAPERS
     MASTERS THESIS, STANFORD, 1953.
     <HINDUSTAN TIMES>, <PAKISTAN TIMES>,
          <TIMES OF INDONESIA>,
          <MANILA CHRONICLE>, <SHANGHAI TIMES>,
          <NIPPON TIMES>.
     CHRON: 1946-1960
     METH: OTHER OR COMB
     GEOG: SEV ASIA
     SUBJ: OTHER JRN

WONG, HIN   W01350
     HISTORY OF JOURNALISM IN CHINA
     IN CHINA PRESS C02568, PP. 83-5.
     ##/FILM
     CHRON: SURVEY
     METH: HISTORICAL
     GEOG: CHINA
     SUBJ: JRN HISTORY

WONG, KEN   W02220
     TIME ON HIS HANDS
     FEED/BACK [SAN FRANCISCO] IV:11(WINTER
          1978), 10-11.
     ##/CHIN-US
     CHRON: 1970-1980
     GEOG: OSEAS CHIN U.S.
     SUBJ: DESCRIPTION BIOGRAPHY

WONG, PAUL   W01167
     STORAGE AND RETRIEVAL OF DATA ON COMMUNIST
          CHINA
     ASIAN SURVEY VIII:5(MAY 1968), 378-83.
     CHRON: 1960-1970
     GEOG: CHINA
     SUBJ: RESEARCH

WONG, PAUL   W01166
     CODING AND ANALYSIS OF DOCUMENTARY MATERIALS
          FROM COMMUNIST CHINA
     ASIAN SURVEY VIII:3(MAR 1967), 198-211.
     CHRON: 1960-1970
     METH: CONTENT ANALYSIS
     GEOG: CHINA
     SUBJ: RESEARCH

WONG, V. L.   W01737
     MOTION PICTURES TODAY IMPORTANT AGENCY IN
          EDUCATION OF OLD AND YOUNG
     THE CHINA WEEKLY REVIEW 101:11(11 MAY 1946),
          230-1.
     MEDIUM: FILM
     CHRON: 1910-1946
     GEOG: CHINA
     SUBJ: DESCRIPTION EDUCATION

WONG, Y. W.   W01338
     PUBLICATIONS
     IN <THE CHINESE YEARBOOK 1936>, PP. 533-40.
     ##/CHIN-5
     CHRON: 1910-1946
     GEOG: CHINA
     SUBJ: DESCRIPTION

WONG, Y. W.   W01337
     PUBLICATIONS, PP. 535-41; NEWSPAPERS AND
          MAGAZINES, PP. 541-7
     IN <THE CHINESE YEARBOOK 1936/1937>
     ##/CHIN-5
     CHRON: 1910-1946
     GEOG: CHINA
     SUBJ: DESCRIPTION

WONG, Y. W.   W01330
    PUBLICATIONS
    IN <THE CHINESE YEARBOOK 1937>, PP. 1101-10.
    ##/CHIN-5
    CHRON: 1910-1946
    GEOG: CHINA
    SUBJ: DESCRIPTION

WOO KOVAI   W02817
    LE JOURNALISME EN CHINE
    THESIS, FONTENAY-AUX-ROSES, 1928.
    CATALOGUE GENERAL . . .BIBLIOTHEQUE
        NATIONALE 226:847
                            LANG: OTHER EUROPEAN
    CHRON: 1910-1946   VERIF: UNVERIFIED
    GEOG: CHINA
    SUBJ: DESCRIPTION

WOO KYATANG   W01351
    HISTORIAN AND FRIEND
    IN CHINA PRESS C02568, P. 80.
    ##/FILM
    CHRON: 1910-1946
    GEOG: CHINA
    SUBJ: DESCRIPTION BIOGRAPHY

WOO, LYON   W02820
    SHOWCASE IN CELLULOID
    ASIAWEEK 5:28(20 JULY 1979), 14-15.
    ##/HKG
    MEDIUM: FILM
    CHRON: 1970-1980
    GEOG: HONG KONG   SEV ASIA
    SUBJ: DESCRIPTION

WOOD, CHARLES W.   W02148
    CHINA THROUGH THE EYES OF AN AMERICAN
        NEWSPAPERMAN
    THE FAR EASTERN REPUBLIC II:11(AUG 1920),
        217-18.
    CHRON: 1910-1946
    GEOG: CHINA
    SUBJ: DESCRIPTION BIOGRAPHY

WOOD, NAT   W02069
    THE CHINATOWN PRESS: A MYSTERIOUS REVOLUTION
    THE QUILL 54:8(AUG 1966), 27-8.
    ##/CHIN-7
    CHRON: 1960-1970
    GEOG: OSEAS CHIN U.S.
    SUBJ: DESCRIPTION

WOODBRIDGE, ISETT S.   W01168
    DANGEROUS JOURNALISM
    CHINESE RECORDER XXXV:3(MAR 1904), 112-16.
    ##/CHIN-3
    CHRON: BEFORE 1910
    GEOG: CHINA
    SUBJ: CONTROL   DESCRIPTION

WOODBRIDGE, S. I.   W01422
    CHINESE NEWSPAPERS
    THE CHINA WEEKLY REVIEW IV:2(9 MAR 1918),
        41-2.
    ##/CHIN-5; FROM <ENCYCLOPAEDIA SINICA>.
    CHRON: 1910-1946
    METH: HISTORICAL
    GEOG: CHINA
    SUBJ: JRN HISTORY

WOODHEAD, H. G. W.   W01169
    ADVENTURES IN FAR EASTERN JOURNALISM:
        A RECORD OF 33 YEARS' EXPERIENCE
    TOKYO, HOKUSEIDO, 1935.
    PUB. IN LONDON AS <A JOURNALIST IN CHINA>;
        NUC<56 165:436.
    CHRON: SURVEY
    GEOG: CHINA
    SUBJ: FOR CORR   BIOGRAPHY

WOODHEAD, HENRY G. W.   W01917
    SHANGHAI RED WEEKLY PROTESTED BY CHINESE
    TRANS-PACIFIC [TOKYO] 20(4 AUG 1932), 6, 19.
    ##/CHIN-6; <CHINA FORUM>.
    CHRON: 1910-1946
    GEOG: CHINA   EAST ASIA
    SUBJ: CONTROL

WOODRUFF, LANCE R.   W01170
    BIRTH OF THE NATION
    INSIGHT (AUG 1971), 54-5.
    ##/THAI
    CHRON: 1970-1980
    GEOG: THAILAND
    SUBJ: DESCRIPTION

WOOLLACOTT, MARTIN   W01173
    THIRD WORLD: REPORTERS UNWELCOME
    COL JRN REVIEW XV:3(SEPT/OCT 1976), 12.
    ##/INTL; FROM ARTICLE IN <JOURNALISM STUDIES
        REVIEW>, SEE W01172.
    MEDIUM: GENERAL
    CHRON: 1970-1980
    GEOG: WORLD
    SUBJ: FOR CORR   CONTROL   FLOW/AGENCY

WOOLLACOTT, MARTIN   W01172
    WESTERN NEWS-GATHERING: WHY THE THIRD WORLD
        HAS REACTED
    JOURNALISM STUDIES REVIEW I:1(JUNE 1976),
        12-14.
    ##/INTL
    MEDIUM: GENERAL
    CHRON: 1970-1980
    GEOG: WORLD
    SUBJ: FOR CORR   CONTROL   FLOW/AGENCY

WOOLLACOTT, MARTIN   W01171
    'PRIESTS' OF THE PRINTED WORD IN PEKING
    STRAITS TIMES(THE GUARDIAN) 17 NOV 1972
    ##/CHIN
    CHRON: 1970-1980
    GEOG: CHINA
    SUBJ: CONTROL   DESCRIPTION

WORD, THE [BOMBAY]   W01677
    PRESS IN INDONESIA LINKS EDUCATED AND
        UNEDUCATED
    (DEC 1964), 52.
    CHRON: 1960-1970
    GEOG: INDONESIA
    SUBJ: DEVELOPMENT DESCRIPTION

WORLD NEWSPAPERS CONFERENCE   W01339

    TOKYO, ASAHI SHIMBUN, 1967.
    CONFERENCE IN JAPAN, 1967
    CHRON: 1960-1970
    GEOG: CHINA   EAST ASIA
    SUBJ: DESCRIPTION

WORLD'S PRESS NEWS   W02221
    ENGLISH DAILIES COVER THE PENINSULA
    17:428 (MALAYA SUPPLEMENT) (13 MAY 1937),
        VIII, XIV.
    CHRON: 1910-1946
    GEOG: MALAYSIA
    SUBJ: DESCRIPTION

WRIGHT, ARNOLD   W01331
    BABOO ENGLISH AS 'TIS WRIT: BEING
        CURIOSITIES OF INDIAN JOURNALISM
    LONDON, T. FISHER UNWIN, 1891.
    CHRON: BEFORE 1910
    GEOG: SO/WEST ASI
    SUBJ: DESCRIPTION LANGUAGE

WRIGHT, ARNOLD   W01678
    TWENTIETH CENTURY IMPRESSIONS OF BURMA: ITS
        HISTORY, PEOPLE, COMMERCE, INDUSTRIES,
        AND RESOURCES
    LONDON, LLOYDS GREATER BRITAIN, 1910.
    ##/BURMA; PP. 132-9; FOR OTHERS IN SERIES,
        SEE WRIGHT W01174, W01175
        W02565, W02589; ALSO HAS COPY OF WRIGHT
        (SIAM) W01174 CHAPTER ON PRESS.
    CHRON: BEFORE 1910
    METH: HISTORICAL
    GEOG: BURMA
    SUBJ: JRN HISTORY DESCRIPTION

WRIGHT, ARNOLD, EDITOR.   W01174
    TWENTIETH CENTURY IMPRESSIONS OF SIAM: ITS
        HISTORY, PEOPLES, COMMERCE, INDUSTRIES,
        AND RESOURCES
    LONDON, LLOYDS GREATER BRITAIN, 1908.
    ##/THAI; PP. 293-7; FOR OTHERS IN SERIES,
        SEE WRIGHT W01175, W01678,
        W02565, W02589.
    CHRON: BEFORE 1910
    GEOG: THAILAND
    SUBJ: JRN HISTORY DESCRIPTION

WRIGHT, ARNOLD, EDITOR.   W01175
    TWENTIETH CENTURY IMPRESSIONS OF BRITISH
        MALAYA: ITS HISTORY, PEOPLE, COMMERCE,
        INDUSTRIES, AND RESOURCES
    LONDON, LLOYDS GREATER BRITAIN, 1908.
    ##/MAL-2; PP. 35-8, 56-7, 62; FOR OTHERS
        IN THIS SERIES, SEE
        WRIGHT W01174, W01678, W02565, W02589.
    CHRON: BEFORE 1910
    GEOG: MALAYSIA   SINGAPORE
    SUBJ: JRN HISTORY DESCRIPTION

WRIGHT, ARNOLD, EDITOR.   W02565
    TWENTIETH CENTURY IMPRESSIONS OF NETHERLANDS
        INDIA
    LONDON, LLOYDS GREATER BRITAIN PUB. CO.,
        1909 [1910 ON BINDING].
    SEE DEKKER D01017
    CHRON: SURVEY
    GEOG: INDONESIA
    SUBJ: JRN HISTORY DESCRIPTION

WRIGHT, ARNOLD, EDITOR.   W02589
    TWENTIETH CENTURY IMPRESSIONS OF HONG KONG,
        SHANGHAI, AND OTHER TREATY PORTS OF CHINA
    LONDON, LLOYDS GREATER BRITAIN, 1908.
    SEE DONALD D01238
    CHRON: BEFORE 1910
    GEOG: HONG KONG   CHINA
    SUBJ: DESCRIPTION

WRIGHT, JAMES D.   W01176
    <LIFE>, <TIME> AND THE FORTUNES OF WAR
    TRANSACTION 9:3(JAN 1972), 42-52.
    CHRON: 1970-1980
    METH: CONTENT ANALYSIS
    GEOG: VIETNAM   U.S.
    SUBJ: FOR CORR   DESCRIPTION

WU HSI TSE   07   W02726
     SHIH NIEN LAI TI T'AI WAN HSIN WEN SHIH YEH
          [TEN YEARS IN TAIWAN JOURNALISM]
     IN T'AI-WAN 14T02574, PP. 273-5.
                         LANG: CHINESE
     CHRON: SURVEY
     GEOG: TAIWAN
     SUBJ: JRN HISTORY DESCRIPTION

WU MING-KUN   07   W01918
     THE CHINESE PRESS IN JAVA
     DIGEST OF THE SYNODAL COMMISSION (CATHOLIC
          CHURCH IN CHINA) 10:2(FEB 1937),
          163-9.
     ##/INDO-2; ULS 2:945.
     CHRON: 1910-1946
     GEOG: INDONESIA   OSEAS CHIN
     SUBJ: DESCRIPTION

WU PA-LING   08   W01180
     KUANG-TUNG CHIH HSIN WEN SHIH YEH
          (JOURNALISM IN KWANGTUNG)
     IN KUANG-TUNG 15K02590, PP. 755-90.
     #3
                         LANG: CHINESE
     CHRON: 1910-1946
     GEOG: CHINA
     SUBJ: DESCRIPTION

WU PAO-FENG   08   W01181
     SHIH NIEN LAI TI CHUNG-KUO KUANG PO SHIH YEH
          (BROADCASTING IN CHINA)
     IN CHUNG-KUO 04C02591, PP. 693-737.
     (CHINA DURING THE PAST DECADE);
          SKINNER S00982 II:41887.
     MEDIUM: ELECTRONIC   LANG: CHINESE
     CHRON: 1910-1946   VERIF: UNVERIFIED
     GEOG: CHINA
     SUBJ: DESCRIPTION

WU T'IEH-SHENG   08   W01182
     WO KUO CH'U PAN CHIEH TI HSIEN TSAI YU
          CHIANG LAI (THE PUBLISHING WORLD IN
          CHINA AND ITS FUTURE)
     HSIN CHUNG-HUA 2(NEW 2ND SERIES):11(NOV
          1944), 21-30.
     SKINNER S00982 II:41888
                         LANG: CHINESE
     CHRON: 1910-1946   VERIF: UNVERIFIED
     GEOG: CHINA
     SUBJ: PUBLISHING

WU, K. T.   07   W01679
     PUBLISHING BUSINESS IN CHINA
     THE CHINA CRITIC XV:13(24 DEC 1936), 297-9.
     ##/FILM
     CHRON: 1910-1946
     GEOG: CHINA
     SUBJ: PUBLISHING

WU, KUANG-CH'ING   W02027
    MING PRINTING AND PRINTERS
    HARVARD JOURNAL OF ASIATIC STUDIES 7:3(FEB
        1943), 203-60.
    ##/CHIN-7
    CHRON: BEFORE 1910
    GEOG: CHINA
    SUBJ: PRINTING

WU, KUANG-CHING   W01177
    THE DEVELOPMENT OF PRINTING IN CHINA
    T'IEN HSIA MONTHLY 3:2(SEPT 1936), 137-60.
    TH
    CHRON: BEFORE 1910
    METH: HISTORICAL
    GEOG: CHINA
    SUBJ: PRINTING

WU, KUANG-CHING   W01179
    COLOUR PRINTING IN THE MING DYNASTY
    T'IEN HSIA MONTHLY XI:1(AUG-SEPT 1940),
        30-44.
    TH
    CHRON: BEFORE 1910
    METH: HISTORICAL
    GEOG: CHINA
    SUBJ: PRINTING

WU, KUANG-CHING   W01178
    THE CHINESE BOOK: ITS EVOLUTION AND
        DEVELOPMENT
    T'IEN HSIA MONTHLY 3:1(AUG 1936), 25-33.
    TH
    CHRON: BEFORE 1910
    METH: HISTORICAL
    GEOG: CHINA
    SUBJ: PRINTING

WU, YUAN-LI   W01183
    PRESS REGULATION IN MAO'S CHINA
    PROBLEMS OF COMMUNISM VI:4(JULY-AUG 1957),
        33-40.
    ##/CHIN-2
    CHRON: 1946-1960
    GEOG: CHINA
    SUBJ: CONTROL

WURTZBURG, C. E.   W01184
    THE BAPTIST MISSION PRESS AT BENCOOLEN
    JOURNAL OF THE MALAYAN BRANCH, RAS XXIII PART
        3(1950), 136-42.
    ##/INDON
    CHRON: BEFORE 1910
    METH: HISTORICAL
    GEOG: INDONESIA
    SUBJ: JRN HISTORY PRINTING

WYNAR, LUBOMYR R. AND ANNA T. WYNAR   W02247
    ENCYCLOPEDIC DIRECTORY OF ETHNIC NEWSPAPERS
        AND PERIODICALS IN THE UNITED STATES
    LIBRARIES UNLIMITED, LITTLETON, COLORADO,
        1976.
    ##/BIB
    CHRON: SURVEY
    METH: SURVEY
    GEOG: OSEAS CHIN
    SUBJ: RESEARCH

Y., P. [PATRICK YEOH?]   Y02028
    THE CINEMAS ARE HERE TO STAY
    STRAITS TIMES 26 MAR 1978
    ##/MAL-3; SUNDAY, MALAYSIAN EDITION.
    MEDIUM: FILM
    CHRON: 1970-1980
    GEOG: MALAYSIA
    SUBJ: DESCRIPTION OTHER JRN

Y., Z. K.   Y01738
    A CHINESE EDITOR ON JOURNALISM
    THE CHINA WEEKLY REVIEW XVI:2(12 MAR 1921),
        114.
    BOOK REVIEW
    CHRON: 1910-1946
    GEOG: CHINA
    SUBJ: DESCRIPTION

YAMAGATA, I.   Y01185
    JOURNALISM IN KOREA
    IN WILLIAMS W01152, PP.456-9.
    #3
    CHRON: 1910-1946
    GEOG: EAST ASIA
    SUBJ: DESCRIPTION

YAMAMOTO, FUMIO   Y01186
    THE ASIAN EDITORS CONFERENCE
    GAZETTE II:2(1956), 119.
    IPI CONFERENCE, 1956
    CHRON: 1946-1960
    GEOG: SEV ASIA
    SUBJ: DESCRIPTION

YANG HSIA YUNG   13   Y01919
    CH'UAN PO YEN CHIU YU SHE HUI TS'AN YU [MASS
        COMMUNICATIONS AND ITS PLACE IN SOCIETY]
    TAIPEI, HUA HSIN WEN HUA SHIH YEH
        CHUNG HSIN, 1974.
    MEDIUM: GENERAL   LANG: CHINESE
    CHRON: SURVEY
    METH: OTHER OR COMB
    GEOG: WORLD
    SUBJ: OTHER JRN

YANG SHOU-JUNG, EDITOR.   13   Y02051
    ABSTRACTS OF COMMUNICATION RESEARCH PAPERS
        (III)
    TAIPEI, KUO LI CHENG CHI DA HSUEH, 1974.
    MEDIUM: GENERAL   LANG: OTHER OR COMB.
    CHRON: SURVEY
    METH: OTHER OR COMB
    GEOG: TAIWAN   CHINA
    SUBJ: RESEARCH

YANG, G. K.   Y01977
    BRITISH CORRESPONDENTS IN CHINA
    THE CHINESE NATION I:19(22 OCT 1930),
        387, 402.
    CHRON: 1910-1946
    GEOG: CHINA   EUROPE
    SUBJ: FOR CORR

YANG, SHOU-JANG   Y02629
    MASS COMMUNICATION IN TAIWAN: AN
        ANNOTATED BIBLIOGRAPHY
    SINGAPORE, AMIC, 1977.
    BIBLIOGRAPHY SERIES 5
    MEDIUM: GENERAL
    CHRON: SURVEY
    GEOG: TAIWAN
    SUBJ: RESEARCH

YANG, SHOU-JUNG   Y01187
    THE RELATIONSHIP OF COMMUNICATION BEHAVIOR
        AND MODERNIZATION OF RESIDENTS OF TAIPEI
    THE NATIONAL CHENCHI U. JOURNAL 31(MAY 1975),
        185-212.
    MEDIUM: GENERAL   LANG: CHINESE
    CHRON: 1970-1980
    METH: OTHER OR COMB
    GEOG: TAIWAN
    SUBJ: DEVELOPMENT

YAO HSIN-NUNG   09   Y01188
    CHINESE MOVIES
    T'IEN HSIA MONTHLY IV:4(APR 1937), 393-400.
    MEDIUM: FILM
    CHRON: 1910-1946
    GEOG: CHINA
    SUBJ: DESCRIPTION

YAO, IGNATIUS PENG   Y01189
    THE NEW CHINA NEWS AGENCY: HOW IT SERVES THE
        PARTY
    JQ 40:1(WINTER 1963), 83-6.
    ##/CHIN
    MEDIUM: GENERAL
    CHRON: 1960-1970
    GEOG: CHINA
    SUBJ: PROPAGANDA FLOW/AGENCY

YAO, RAYMOND   Y01259
    ONE MAGAZINE FOR THE TWO CHINAS
    FEER 96:21(27 MAY 1977), 20-1.
    ##/CHIN-4; <HUANG HO>.
    CHRON: 1970-1980
    GEOG: HONG KONG   TAIWAN   CHINA
    SUBJ: DESCRIPTION

YAO, RAYMOND   Y01258
    CURTAIN CALL FOR COMMUNIST FILMS
    FEER 96:15(15 APR 1977), 18-9.
    ##/CHIN-4
    MEDIUM: FILM
    CHRON: 1970-1980
    GEOG: HONG KONG   CHINA
    SUBJ: CONTROL   DESCRIPTION

YAO, RAYMOND   Y01256
    BOX-OFFICE BY THE LEFT
    FEER 94:47(19 NOV 1976), 9.
    ##/HKG
    MEDIUM: FILM
    CHRON: 1970-1980
    GEOG: HONG KONG   CHINA
    SUBJ: DESCRIPTION

YAO, RAYMOND   Y01255
    A TESTING TIME ON THE CAMPUS
    FEER 93:29(16 JULY 1976), 26-7.
    ##/HKG
    CHRON: 1970-1980
    GEOG: HONG KONG
    SUBJ: CONTROL   EDUCATION

YAO, RAYMOND   Y01680
    FIXING THE DRUG TRADE EMPIRES
    FEER 97:36(9 SEPT 1977), 19-20.
    ##/HKG; <ORIENTAL DAILY NEWS>.
    CHRON: 1970-1980
    GEOG: HONG KONG
    SUBJ: DESCRIPTION

YATES, RONALD   Y01190
    GUNS FIRE PAPER ON QUEMOY
    PHILADELPHIA INQUIRER (CHICAGO TRIBUNE)
         23 NOV 1975
    ##/VN
    MEDIUM: OTHER
    CHRON: 1970-1980
    GEOG: TAIWAN   CHINA
    SUBJ: PROPAGANDA

YEE SIEW-PUN   Y01191
    AN INDEX TO CHINESE-LANGUAGE NEWSPAPER
        REPORTING ON SINGAPORE AND
        MALAYSIAN AFFAIRS
    SINGAPORE, NANYANG UNIVERSITY, 1973.
    CHRON: 1970-1980
    METH: CONTENT ANALYSIS
    GEOG: MALAYSIA   SINGAPORE   OSEAS CHIN
    SUBJ: RESEARCH

YEH TSUNG-K'UEI   12   Y01192
    HSIEN CHANG CHENG TS'E HSIA TI HSIN WEN CH'U
        LI WEN T'I (PROBLEMS OF NEWS TREATMENT
        UNDER THE PAGE LIMITATION POLICY)
    UNPUB MASTERS THESIS IN JOURNALISM, 1959.
    SKINNER S00982 II:46550.
                         LANG: CHINESE
    CHRON: 1946-1960   VERIF: UNVERIFIED
    GEOG: TAIWAN
    SUBJ: DESCRIPTION

YEH, WEN-HSING   Y02149
    WANG KAN-NIEN AND THE REFORM MOVEMENT OF
        LATE CHING CHINA
    MASTERS THESIS, UNIVERSITY OF
        SOUTHERN CALIFORNIA, 1975.
    CHRON: BEFORE 1910
    METH: OTHER OR COMB
    GEOG: CHINA
    SUBJ: JRN HISTORY BIOGRAPHY

YEN CHING HWANG   Y02605
    THE OVERSEAS CHINESE AND THE 1911 REVOLUTION
        WITH SPECIAL REFERENCE TO SINGAPORE AND
        MALAYA
    KUALA LUMPUR, OXFORD UNIVERSITY PRESS, 1976.
    PP. 100-17.
    CHRON: 1910-1946
    METH: HISTORICAL
    GEOG: MALAYSIA   SINGAPORE
    SUBJ: JRN HISTORY

YEN HSIN-HENG   16   Y02786
    HAN TAI MIN YI TI HSING CHENG YU CH'I TUI
        CHENG CHIH CHIH YING HSIANG
    PAO HSUEH [TAIPEI] II:7(DEC 1960), 24-51.
    (THE FORMATION OF PUBLIC OPINION IN HAN
        DYNASTY AND ITS INFLUENCE ON POLITICS)
    MEDIUM: GENERAL   LANG: CHINESE
    CHRON: BEFORE 1910
    METH: HISTORICAL
    GEOG: CHINA
    SUBJ: JRN HISTORY OTHER JRN

YIN, SHERMAN KUANG-YING   Y02248
    <THE CHINA WEEKLY REVIEW>
    MASTERS THESIS, UNIVERSITY OF MISSOURI, 1962.
    CHRON: SURVEY
    METH: HISTORICAL
    GEOG: CHINA
    SUBJ: JRN HISTORY DESCRIPTION

YOON, SUTHICHAI   Y01681
    AN EDITOR SPEAKS HIS MIND
    HORIZONS [USIS] XX:12(1971), 48-51.
    CHRON: 1970-1980
    GEOG: THAILAND
    SUBJ: DESCRIPTION

YORRO, DIONISIO K.   Y01194
    30 YEARS OF PHILIPPINES JOURNALISM
    IN FOOKIEN TIMES YEARBOOK 1957
    NUC 56-67, 37:182
    CHRON: SURVEY   VERIF: UNVERIFIED
    METH: HISTORICAL
    GEOG: PHILIPPINES
    SUBJ: JRN HISTORY

YOSHIDA, KENSEI   Y01195
    THE JAPANESE REPORTERS CLUBS
    FOI CENTER REPORT NO. 268 (1971).
    ##/EASI
    CHRON: 1970-1980
    GEOG: EAST ASIA
    SUBJ: FOR CORR   CONTROL   DESCRIPTION

YOSHIMURA, YOSUKE   Y02665
    A LESSON FROM JAPAN
    THE JOURNALIST'S WORLD IV:2(1966), 21-2.
    CHRON: 1960-1970
    GEOG: EAST ASIA
    SUBJ: DESCRIPTION

YOUNG, A. MORGAN   Y01683
    THE PRESS AND JAPANESE THOUGHT
    PACIFIC AFFAIRS X(DEC 1937), 412-19.
    CHRON: 1910-1946
    GEOG: EAST ASIA
    SUBJ: DESCRIPTION CROSS CULTU

YOUNG, A. MORGAN   Y01682
    JAPANESE PRESS CENSORSHIP
    ASIA XXXV:8(AUG 1935), 474-5, 7.
    ##/EASI
    CHRON: 1910-1946
    GEOG: EAST ASIA
    SUBJ: CONTROL

YOUNG, A. MORGAN   Y01739
    COLLISION WITH JAPANESE AUTHORITY
    ASIA XXXVII:10(OCT 1937), 703-6; PART 2,
           XXXVII:11(NOV 1937), 753-6.
    CHRON: 1910-1946
    GEOG: EAST ASIA
    SUBJ: CONTROL

YOUNG, C. KUANGSON   Y01352
    SHANGHAI'S 1ST SUNDAY PAPER
    IN CHINA PRESS C02568, P. 150.
    ##/FILM
    CHRON: 1910-1946
    GEOG: CHINA
    SUBJ: DESCRIPTION

YOUNG, M. C. KUANGSON   Y02809
    LA PRESSE EN CHINE ET SES SERVICES ETRANGERS
    PRESSE PUBLICITE 2(15 AUG 1938), 7-8.
    ##/CHIN-9
                          LANG: OTHER EUROPEAN
    CHRON: 1910-1946
    GEOG: CHINA
    SUBJ: DESCRIPTION

YOUNG, PERRY DEANE   Y01193
    TWO OF THE MISSING
    NEW YORK, COWARD, MCCANN AND GEOGHEGAN, 1975.
    CHRON: 1970-1980
    GEOG: VIETNAM   U.S.
    SUBJ: FOR CORR   BIOGRAPHY

YOUR READER   Y02324
    KUNMING PAPERS BANNED
    THE CHINA WEEKLY REVIEW 102:12(17 AUG 1946),
        267.
    LETTER TO EDITOR
    CHRON: 1946-1960
    GEOG: CHINA
    SUBJ: CONTROL

YU CH'ANG-CH'IN AND YU HUI-YIN   03   Y01196
    CH'UAN TANG PAN PAO TI HSIN FA CHAN' (THE NEW
        DEVELOPMENT IN PARTY- OPERATED NEWSPAPERS
    JEN MIN JIH PAO 11 JUNE 1960
    SKINNER S00982 II:48477; TRANS. <PARTY
        CONTROL OF COMMUNICATION MEDIA>,
        USJPRS, 18 AUG 1960 (JPRS 5260; MC
        15,821/1960).
    MEDIUM: GENERAL
    CHRON: 1960-1970   VERIF: UNVERIFIED
    GEOG: CHINA
    SUBJ: CONTROL

YU CHEN-MING   09   Y01197
     PRESS CHRONICLE
     T'IEN HSIA IX:2(SEPT 1939), 176-9.
     TH
     CHRON: 1910-1946
     GEOG: CHINA
     SUBJ: DESCRIPTION

YU CHEN-MING   09   Y01198
     PRESS CHRONICLE
     T'IEN HSIA MONTHLY XI:1(AUG-SEPT 1940), 63-6.
     TH
     CHRON: 1910-1946
     GEOG: CHINA
     SUBJ: DESCRIPTION

YU CHEN-MING   09   Y01199
     PRESS CHRONICLE
     T'IEN HSIA MONTHLY XII:1(AUG-SEPT 1941), 71-4.
     CHRON: 1910-1946
     GEOG: CHINA
     SUBJ: DESCRIPTION

YU FEI-P'ENG   09   Y01200
     SHIH NIEN LAI TI CHUNG-KUO TIEN HSIN SHIH YEH
          (TELECOMMUNICATIONS IN CHINA DURING THE
          PAST DECADE)
     IN CHUNG-KUO WEN HUA 04C02591, PP. 364-401.
     MEDIUM: ELECTRONIC   LANG: CHINESE
     CHRON: 1910-1946   VERIF: UNVERIFIED
     GEOG: CHINA
     SUBJ: DESCRIPTION

YU HSIEH-LUN   12   Y02789
     T'AN MIN CH'U HAN K'OU LIANG CHIA HSIAO PAO
          (TWO SMALL PAPERS IN HANKOW)
     PAO HSUEH [TAIPEI] II:7(DEC 1960), 79-80.
                              LANG: CHINESE
     CHRON: SURVEY
     METH: HISTORICAL
     GEOG: CHINA
     SUBJ: DESCRIPTION

YU HSIEH-LUN   12   Y02788
     T'AN SHANG HAI SZE MIN PAO (THE SZE MIN PAO
          IN SHANGHAI)
     PAO HSUEH [TAIPEI] II:4(FEB 1958), 136-8.
                              LANG: CHINESE
     CHRON: SURVEY
     METH: HISTORICAL
     GEOG: CHINA
     SUBJ: JRN HISTORY

YU HSIEH-LUN   12   Y02787
    T'AN HAN K'OU HSIN WEN CHIEH TI 'CH'I JEN
        T'UAN' (SEVEN MAN GROUP OF NEWSPAPERMEN
        IN HANKOW)
    PAO HSUEH [TAIPEI] II:1(JUNE 1957), 135-7.
                        LANG: CHINESE
    CHRON: 1946-1960
    METH: HISTORICAL
    GEOG: CHINA
    SUBJ: BIOGRAPHY

YU PI-TA   07   Y01203
    CHUNG-KUO KO SHENG NUNG YEH K'AN WU CHIA
        TIAO CH'A (SURVEY OF PERIODICALS IN
        VARIOUS CHINESE PROVINCES)
    NUNG SHIH YUEH K'AN 4:11(MAY 1926), 63-70.
    SKINNER S00982 II:41892
                        LANG: CHINESE
    CHRON: 1910-1946   VERIF: UNVERIFIED
    GEOG: CHINA
    SUBJ: DESCRIPTION

YU SHEN-MING   09   Y01204
    PRESS CHRONICLE
    T'IEN HSIA MONTHLY VII:1(AUG 1938), 89-93.
    TH
    CHRON: 1910-1946
    GEOG: CHINA
    SUBJ: DESCRIPTION

YU WAH   Y02336
    NEW CHINA NEWS AGENCY--YENAN TO PEKING
    THE CHINA WEEKLY REVIEW 117:3(18 MAR 1950),
        40.
    CHRON: 1946-1960
    GEOG: CHINA
    SUBJ: FLOW/AGENCY JRN HISTORY

YU, FREDERICK AND JOHN LUTER   Y01201
    THE FOREIGN CORRESPONDENT AND HIS WORK
    COL JRN REVIEW (SPRING 1964), 5-12.
    ##/FOCO
    MEDIUM: GENERAL
    CHRON: 1960-1970
    GEOG: WORLD
    SUBJ: FOR CORR

YU, FREDERICK T. C.   Y01202
    PERSUASIVE COMMUNICATIONS DURING THE CULTURAL
        REVOLUTION
    GAZETTE XVI:2(1970), 73-87 (PART 1);
        XVI:3(1970), 137-148 (PART 2).
    ##/CHIN-2
    MEDIUM: GENERAL
    CHRON: 1960-1970
    GEOG: CHINA
    SUBJ: PROPAGANDA

YU, FREDERICK T. C.   Y02152
    HOW ASIANS SEE INDIA
    MONTANA JOURNALISM REVIEW NO. 5(1962), 26-9.
    CHRON: 1960-1970
    METH: OTHER OR COMB
    GEOG: CHINA   SO/WEST ASI
    SUBJ: DESCRIPTION OTHER JRN

YU, FREDERICK T. C.   Y02151
    LITTLE ROCK EPISODE IN CHINESE NEWSPAPERS
    MONTANA JOURNALISM REVIEW NO. 2(SPRING 1959),
        24-8.
    CHRON: 1946-1960
    METH: OTHER OR COMB
    GEOG: CHINA   U.S.
    SUBJ: DESCRIPTION OTHER JRN

YU, FREDERICK T. C.   Y02150
    RADIO PROPAGANDA IN COMMUNIST CHINA
    MONTANA JOURNALISM REVIEW NO. 1(1958), 20-26.
    MEDIUM: ELECTRONIC
    CHRON: 1946-1960
    GEOG: CHINA
    SUBJ: DESCRIPTION

YU, FREDERICK T. C.   Y02666
    COMMUNICATIONS AND POLITICS IN COMMUNIST
        CHINA
    IN PYE P02658, PP. 259-297.
    MEDIUM: GENERAL
    CHRON: SURVEY
    METH: OTHER OR COMB
    GEOG: CHINA
    SUBJ: DEVELOPMENT OTHER JRN

YU, HELEN Y. Y.   Y02052
    FORMOSA'S ENGLISH-LANGUAGE NEWSPAPER:
        <CHINA POST>
    MASTERS THESIS, U. OF MISSOURI, 1958.
    #3
    CHRON: 1960-1970
    METH: OTHER OR COMB
    GEOG: TAIWAN
    SUBJ: JRN HISTORY

YU, HUNG-HAI   Y02153
    MU CH'IEN T'AI-PEI SHIH CHU-YAO JIH PAO
        HSIN-WEN NEI-JUNG LEI T'UNG CH'ENG-TU
        CHI CH'I YUAN-YIN
    MASTERS THESIS, CHENG CHI TA HSUEH, 1972.
                        LANG: CHINESE
    CHRON: 1970-1980
    METH: OTHER OR COMB
    GEOG: TAIWAN
    SUBJ: DESCRIPTION

YU, P. K. [PING-KUEN], EDITOR.   Y01684
RESEARCH MATERIALS ON TWENTIETH-CENTURY
    CHINA: AN ANNOTATED LIST OF CCRM
    PUBLICATIONS
WASHINGTON, D. C., CCRM/ASSOCIATION OF
    RESEARCH LIBRARIES, 1975.
#3; NEWSPAPERS, PP. 1-40.
CHRON: SURVEY
GEOG: CHINA
SUBJ: RESEARCH

YU, PING-KUEN   Y01920
A NOTE ON HISTORICAL PERIODICALS OF
    TWENTIETH-CENTURY CHINA
JOURNAL OF ASIAN STUDIES XXIII:4(AUG 1964),
    581-90.
CHRON: SURVEY
GEOG: CHINA
SUBJ: RESEARCH   OTHER JRN

YU, TIMOTHY L. M., COMPILER.   Y01249
MASS COMMUNICATION IN HONG KONG AND MACAO:
    AN ANNOTATED BIBLIOGRAPHY
SINGAPORE, AMIC, 1976.
BIBLIOGRAPHY SERIES 3
MEDIUM: GENERAL
CHRON: 1970-1980
GEOG: HONG KONG   MACAO
SUBJ: RESEARCH

YUAN CH'ANG-CH'AO   10   Y01205
CHUNG-KUO PAO YEH HSIAO SHIH (BRIEF HISTORY
    OF JOURNALISM IN CHINA)
HONG KONG, HSIN WEN T'IEN TI SHE, 1957.
CHRON: SURVEY
GEOG: CHINA
SUBJ: JRN HISTORY

YUAN LIANG   10   Y01206
CHUNG-MEI PAO CHIH PIEN TS'AI CHIH TU CHIH
    PI CHIAO YEN CHIU (CHINESE AND AMERICAN
    NEWSPAPERS: A COMPARATIVE STUDY OF REPORT
    REPORTING AND EDITING)
UNPUB MASTERS THESIS IN JOURNALISM, 1962.
SKINNER S00982 II:46551
                        LANG: CHINESE
CHRON: 1960-1970   VERIF: UNVERIFIED
METH: OTHER OR COMB
GEOG: TAIWAN   U.S.
SUBJ: DESCRIPTION

YUAN TUNG-LI, COMPILER.   Y01921
CHINA IN WESTERN LITERATURE
NEW HAVEN, FAR EASTERN PUBLICATIONS,
    YALE U. P., 1958.
CHRON: SURVEY
GEOG: CHINA
SUBJ: RESEARCH

YUAN, L. Z.   Y02667
    NEW CHINESE PRESS LAW PROHIBITS ATTACKS
        ON NATIONALIST PARTY
    EDITOR & PUBLISHER 63:40(21 FEB 1931), 44.
    CHRON: 1910-1946
    GEOG: CHINA
    SUBJ: CONTROL   LAW/ETHICS

YUI, MASASHI   Y01740
    THE REGIMENTED PRESS OF JAPAN
    THE CHINA WEEKLY REVIEW 93:11(10 AUG 1940),
        396-7.
    CHRON: 1910-1946
    GEOG: EAST ASIA
    SUBJ: CONTROL

YUN, ART   Y02325
    CHINA IN MANHATTAN'S PRESS
    THE CHINA WEEKLY REVIEW 55:5(3 JUNE 1931),
        180-2.
    CHRON: 1910-1946
    GEOG: CHINA   U.S.
    SUBJ: DESCRIPTION OTHER JRN

YUSOF A. TALIB   Y01207
    CORRESPONDENCE
    JRNL OF SOUTHEAST ASIAN STUDIES VI:2(1975),
        198-9.
    ##/MAL; REPLY TO ROFF; SEE ROFF R00929.
    CHRON: SURVEY
    GEOG: MALAYSIA   SINGAPORE
    SUBJ: RESEARCH

YUSOF A. TALIB   Y01208
    <BIBLIOGRAPHY OF MALAY AND ARABIC
        PERIODICALS IN THE STRAITS SETTLEMENTS
        AND PENINSULAR MALAY STATES, 1876-1941>
    JOURNAL OF SOUTHEAST ASIAN STUDIES V:2(SEPT
        1974), 279-82.
    ##/MAL; REVIEW OF ROFF'S BOOK; SEE Y01207 AND
        R00929.
    CHRON: SURVEY
    METH: HISTORICAL
    GEOG: MALAYSIA   SINGAPORE
    SUBJ: RESEARCH

ZAILAH ISMAIL   Z01209
    TURNING TO OUR OWN LEGENDS TO DELIGHT THE
        CHILDREN
    STRAITS TIMES (SUN) 21 OCT 1973
    ##/MAL-2
    MEDIUM: OTHER
    CHRON: 1970-1980
    GEOG: MALAYSIA
    SUBJ: LITERATURE

ZAINAL ABIDIN B. AHMAD [ZA'BA]   Z01210
    MALAY JOURNALISM IN MALAYA
    JOURNAL MALAYAN BRANCH, RAS 19 PART 2(1941),
        244-50.
    ##/MAL
    CHRON: SURVEY
    GEOG: MALAYSIA
    SUBJ: JRN HISTORY

ZEITUNGSWISSENSCHAFT   Z02810
    EIN NEUES PRESSGESETZ
    5:1(15 JAN 1930), 44-5.
    ##/CHIN-9
                              LANG: OTHER EUROPEAN
    CHRON: 1910-1946
    GEOG: CHINA
    SUBJ: PROPAGANDA DESCRIPTION

ZIA, FRANCIS   Z01741
    DR. WALTER WILLIAM'S MESSAGE TO
        JOURNALISTIC CHINA
    THE CHINA WEEKLY REVIEW XIX:3(17 DEC 1921),
        99-101.
    CHRON: 1910-1946
    GEOG: CHINA
    SUBJ: DESCRIPTION

ZUMOTO, MOTSSADA   Z01922
    AMERICAN AND JAPANESE NEWPAPERS
    THE ORIENTAL REVIEW II:4(FEB 1912), 206-10.
    CHRON: 1910-1946
    GEOG: EAST ASIA   U.S.
    SUBJ: DESCRIPTION

ZWEMER, S.   Z01211
    THE NATIVE PRESS OF THE DUTCH EAST INDIES
    MOSLEM WORLD 13(1923), 39-49.
    ##/INDO
    CHRON: 1910-1946
    GEOG: INDONESIA
    SUBJ: DESCRIPTION

APPENDIX

THE CHINA WEEKLY REVIEW

ONE OF THE MOST NOTEWORTHY EXAMPLES OF AN
ENGLISH-LANGUAGE ACCESS POINT TO A PERIOD OF
ASIAN JOURNALISM IS <THE CHINA WEEKLY REVIEW>.
BECAUSE OF THE EDITOR'S INTEREST, NOT
ONLY IN THE CONTENT, BUT IN THE PROCESS
OF JOURNALISM, THE MAGAZINE OFFERS A COHERENT,
IF UNAVOIDABLY PERSONAL, VIEW OF JOURNALISM
IN CHINA ALMOST CONTINUOUSLY FROM 1917 TO
1953.
FOUNDED BY THOMAS MILLARD AS <MILLARD'S
REVIEW OF THE FAR EAST>, IN 1917, IT WAS
RENAMED IN 1922 WHEN MILLARD SOLD HIS INTEREST
TO JOHN B. POWELL WHO BECAME EDITOR AND
CHANGED THE NAME TO <THE CHINA WEEKLY REVIEW>.
POWELL WAS IMPRISONED BY THE JAPANESE AND THE
MAGAZINE SUSPENDED PUBLICATION FROM 1941 TO 1945.
POWELL'S SON, JOHN WILLIAM POWELL, RESUMED
PUBLICATION IN 1945. IN 1950 IT BECAME <THE CHINA
MONTHLY REVIEW>. THE FINAL ISSUE WAS PUBLISHED
IN JULY 1953.
AS PROBABLY THE MOST SUBSCRIBED-TO PUBLICATION
ABOUT CHINA IN THE UNITED STATES, <THE CHINA
WEEKLY REVIEW> IS READILY AVAILABLE IN BOUND
VOLUMES IN MANY LIBRARIES. IT IS ALSO AVAILABLE
IN MICROFORM. IT CAN USUALLY BE FOUND CATALOGED
AS <CHINA WEEKLY REVIEW>.
THE COMPREHENSIVE HISTORY OF THE <REVIEW> AND
POWELL'S INFLUENCE IS FOUND IN SHERMAN KUANG-JUNG
YIN'S THESIS Y02248.
THE <REVIEW> CARRIED BOTH EDITORIALS AND
ARTICLES, SIGNED AND UNSIGNED. A PERUSAL OF THE
ARTICLE TITLES IS A CAPSULE OUTLINE OF THE
CONCERNS OF A WORKING JOURNALIST OVER 30 YEARS IN
CHINA. THE FIRST SECTION BELOW LISTS UNSIGNED
ARTICLES IN CHRONOLOGICAL ORDER. THE SECOND LIST
IS A COMPILATION OF SIGNED ARTICLES FOR WHICH THE
FULL CITATION CAN BE FOUND IN THE BODY OF THIS
BIBLIOGRAPHY.

'THE WICKED CORRESPONDENTS AND THE CRITICS'
2:7(13 OCT 1917), 186-88.
FROM <JAPAN CHRONICLE>

THE DEPORTATION OF GILBERT REID
3:5(29 DEC 1917), 129-33.
EDITOR OF <PEKING POST>

CHINESE WOMEN NOW HAVE A 'LADIES HOME JOURNAL'
VI:3(21 SEPT 1918), 112.

THE JAPANESE ANTI-AMERICAN PRESS CAMPAIGN
VIII:6(5 APR 1919), 218-22.

PRESS CENSORSHIP BYE-LAWS CARRIED BY JAPANESE VOTE
IX:6(12 JULY 1919), 235.

PRESS COMMENT ON CENSORSHIP LAW
IX:7(19 JULY 1919), 268-70.

MISS WONG CHEN QUAN EDITS WOMEN'S WEEKLY
X:6(11 OCT 1919), 248-9.

THE CHURCH PRESS ON THE EASTERN SITUATION
X:11(15 NOV 1919), 473-77.

A MAGAZINE FOR CHINESE WOMEN
XVI:10(7 MAY 1921), 520-2.
<THE NEW WOMAN>

REVIEWS CANTON CORRESPONDENT RELEASED
XXIII:13(24 FEB 1923), 524-5.

STATEMENT OF THE AMERICAN LEGATION REGARDING THE
    WIRELESS CONTROVERSY
XXIV:6(7 APR 1923), 192-3.

THE JAPANESE PROTEST AGAINST ERECTION IN CHINA OF
    AMERICAN RADIO
XXIV:6(7 APR 1923), 193-4.

CHINESE IN THE FIELD OF JOURNALISM
XXIV:12(19 MAY 1923), 418-20.

CENSORSHIP AS AGENCY TO MISLEAD THE PUBLIC
XXV:3(16 JUNE 1923), 66.

DR. CRANE, AMERICAN JOURNALIST, IN ORIENT
XXV:8(21 JULY 1923), 260.

FEDERAL RADIO CONTRACT GOES THROUGH
XXV:10(4 AUG 1923), 314-5.

THE FORMATION OF A SCHOOL OF JOURNALISM AT PEKING
    UNIVERSITY OF M. E. MISSION IS FALSELY
    REPORTED
XXV:10(4 AUG 1923), 324.

SCHOOLS OF JOURNALISM FOR CHINA
XXVI:1(1 SEPT 1923), 3-4.

THE JOURNALIST'S CREED
XXVI:1(1 SEPT 1923), 4.

THERE'S ONLY ONE GENUINE 'WHO'S WHO IN CHINA'
XXVI:1(1 SEPT 1923), 4.

RADIO COMMUNICATION BETWEEN CHINA AND AMERICA
XXVII:12(16 FEB 1924), 409-10.

THE BATTLE OF THE NEWS AGENCIES
XXXVIII:3(18 SEPT 1926), 60-1.

THE CONFERENCE ON BETTER NEWS FACILITIES
XXXIII:10(8 AUG 1925), 181-2.

SURVEY SHOWS GROWTH OF CHINESE NEWSPAPER
    ADVERTISING
XXXVI:8(24 APR 1926), 200-1.

JAPANESE AND CHINESE NEWS AGENCIES
XXXVI:10(8 MAY 1926), 245.

THE GREATEST NEED OF THE AMERICAN COMMUNITY AT
    SHANGHAI
XXXVI:8(24 APR 1926), 187-8.

STATUS OF THE AMERICAN NEWSPAPER SITUATION AT
    SHANGHAI
XXXVI:9(1 MAY 1926), 215-6.

AMERICAN PAPERS EVERYWHERE EXCEPT IN SHANGHAI
XXXVI:10(8 MAY 1926), 243.

THE BRITISH VS. THE AMERICAN NEWSPAPER EDITORS
XXXVI:11(15 MAY 1926), 285-6.

THE OWNERSHIP OF THE 'AMERICAN' PAPER
XXXVII:1(5 JUNE 1926), 1-2.

THE MOVE TO ESTABLISH AN AMERICAN NEWSPAPER
XXXVII:3(19 JUNE 1926), 53.

THE PLAN FOR A NEW AMERICAN NEWSPAPER IN SHANGHAI
XXXVII:4(26 JUNE 1926), 83-4.

CHANG CHUNG-CHANG SHOOTS ANOTHER EDITOR
XXXVII:12(21 AUG 1926), 289-90.

BY THEIR NEWS SHALL YOU KNOW THEM
XXXVII:12(21 AUG 1926), 290.

CHINA MUST NOT OPERATE HER OWN WIRELESS STATION
XXXVIII:4(25 SEPT 1926), 90.

THE BRITISH AND THE AMERICAN PRESS IN CHINA
XXXVIII:12(20 NOV 1926), 317.

THE FUTURE OF FOREIGN NEWSPAPERS IN CHINA
XXXX:8(23 APR 1927), 196.

WHAT THE AMERICAN PRESS THINKS ABOUT IT!
XLI:1(4 JUNE 1927), 6.
POWELL AND SHANGHAI CHAMBER OF COMMERCE

SOME COMMENTS ON THE SHANGHAI PRESS
XLI:3(18 JUNE 1927), 63.

SOME WISDOM FROM A FRENCH EDITOR
XLI:4(25 JUNE 1927), 76.

ALSO SOME WISDOM FROM A BRITISH EDITOR
XLI:4(25 JUNE 1927), 76.

THE SHANGHAI NEWSPAPERS AND THE NEWS
XLI:7(16 JULY 1927), 157-8.

HAS SHANGHAI A FREE PRESS?
XLI:13(27 AUG 1927), 331.
FROM <BOSTON HERALD.> 9 JULY 1927.

NEWS WHICH DIDN'T APPEAR IN SHANGHAI NEWSPAPERS
XLIII:1(3 DEC 1927), 1.

NEWS WHICH DOES NOT APPEAR IN SHANGHAI PAPERS
XLIII:2(10 DEC 1927), 30.

ANOTHER CHAPTER IN THE RADIO TANGLE
XLIII:4(24 DEC 1927), 92.

THE CHANGING NEWSPAPER SITUATION AT SHANGHAI
XLIII:9(28 JAN 1928), 210-11.

AMERICAN ADVERTISING AND AN AMERICAN PRESS IN CHINA
XLIV:4(24 MAR 1928), 85-79

S. M. C. POLICE SLAM THE CHINESE PRESS!
XLIV:6(7 APR 1928), 161.

AN AMERICAN NEWSPAPER FOR SHANGHAI!
XLIV:8(21 APR 1928), 213.
CARL CROW; THE EVENING NEWS

FOREIGN DIE-HARD PRESS BLAMES CHINESE
XLIV:11(12 MAY 1928), 305-6.

GREAT NEED OF A CHINESE NEWS SERVICE!
XLIV:3(16 JUNE 1928), 76-7.

THE NORTH-CHINA DAILY NEWS AND THE YELLOW TAXIS
XLV:3(16 JUNE 1928), 80.

FOREIGN NEWS AGENCY PROPAGANDA
XLV:10(4 AUG 1928), 314.

PROBLEM OF FREE PRESS AND NEWS SERVICE
XLV:12(18 AUG 1928), 379-80.

THE PRESS IN CHINA
XLV:12(18 AUG 1928), 384, 402.
FROM <THE LITERARY DIGEST>, SEE L01063

WHERE THE FOREIGN PRESS OBTAINS CHINESE NEWS
XLV:13(25 AUG 1928), 412-13.

CHINA'S COMPLICATED RADIO TELEGRAPH AND CABLE
      SITUATION
XLVI:1(1 SEPT 1928)8 5-6.

THE FOOLISH DEADLOCK OF RADIO DEVELOPMENT
XLVI:2(8 SEPT 1928), 37-8.

NATIONAL GOVERNMENT AND CHINESE NEWSPAPERS
XLVI:11(10 NOV 1928), 348-9.

SETTLEMENT OF THE RADIO DEADLOCK
XLVI:11(10 NOV 1928)8 352-3.

NEWSPAPER CORRESPONDENTS AS DIPLOMATS
XLVII:5(29 DEC 1928), 189.

JOURNALISTIC ETHICS
FROM <THE CHINA CRITIC>
XLVII:5(29 DEC 1928), 192.

THE PROPOSAL FOR A LAW GOVERNING THE PRESS
XLVII:6(5 JAN 1929), 225.

DR. FERGUSON'S SALE OF THE SIN WAN PAO
XLVII:8(19 JAN 1929), 309-10.

SOMETHING OUGHT TO BE DONE ABOUT PEIPING'S NEWS
XLVII:9(26 JAN 1929)8 355.

PRIVATE CONFIDENTIAL-NOT FOR THE PRESS
XLVII:11(9 FEB 1929), 440.

EDITOR WANTS TO KNOW WHY HE WAS SUPPRESSED
XLVII:12(16 FEB 1929), 476.
C. J. FOX, NORTH CHINA STAR

THE NEED FOR A MODERN PUBLICATION LAW
XLVIII:(16 MAR 1929), 85-6.

THE SUDDEN POPULARITY OF AMERICAN NEWS
XLVIII:6(6 APR 1929), 220-1.

THE PRESS AND THE CONFERENCE ON PACIFIC RELATIONS
XLVIII:8(20 APR 1929), 311-2.

THE KUOMINTANG ACTION AGAINST MR. SOKOLSKY AND THE
      NORTH CHINA DAILY NEWS
XLVIII:9(27 APR 1929), 352-4.

THE EVENING POST'S ATTACK ON THE SHANGHAI POLICE
    DEPARTMENT
XLVIII:11(11 MAY 1929), 446-8.

WHAT ANOTHER BRITISH PAPER THINKS OF NCDN CASE
XLIX:1(1 JUNE 1929), 1.
THE STRAITS TIMES

A CASE OF CONTEMPIBLE REPORTING
XLIX:1(1 JUNE 1929), 29

HAS THE NCDN PROMISED TO BE GOOD
XLIX:3(15 JUNE 1929), 98-100.

NANKING ASKS DEPORTATION OF HALLETT ABEND
XLIX:6(6 JULY 1929)8 266.

THE NEW YORK TIMES AND ITS CHINA CORRESPONDENTS
XLIX:7(13 JULY 1929)8 283-4.

THE US NEWSPAPERS PARTY AND JAPANESE PROPAGANDA
XLIX:10(3 AUG 1929), 409-10.

MORE LIGHT ON JOURNALISTS TOUR AND PROPAGANDA
L:1(7 SEPT 1929), 37-8.

PASSING OF CENSORSHIP
L:2(14 SEPT 1929), 78.

PRESS CENSORSHIP ABOLISHED
L:2(14 SEPT 1929), 108.

SOME FRUITS OF CARNEGIE 'GOOD WILL' TOUR
L:4(28 SEPT 1929), 153.

DESPICABLE REPORTING BY THE SHANGHAI TIMES
L:4(28 SEPT 1929), 153-4.

MISSOURI SCHOOL SEEKS JOURNALISM MEMORIAL FROM
    CHINA
L:10(9 NOV 1929), 379.

WE ARE ACCUSED
L:11(16 NOV 1929), 408-9.

MR. WOODHEAD'S VIEWS--AND HIS ACTIONS
51:9(1 FEB 1930), 305.

WOODHEAD'S PAPER BANNED FROM MAILS
51:11(15 FEB 1930), 385.

THE SHANGHAI EVENING POST AND THE CHINESE POSTAL
    BAN
LII:2(8 MAR 1930), 79.

WHO'S WHO IN CHINA <P'AN KUNG-PI>
52:5(30 MAR 1930), 186..
GENERAL MANAGER OF <CHINA TIMES>

THE SOPHER BROTHERS AND THE KEMMERER REPORT
FOREIGN VS. THE CHINESE MOVIE CENSORSHIP
LII:6(5 APR 1930), 198-9.

DEAN WALTER WILLIAMS HEADS UNIVERSITY OF MISSOURI
52:7(12 APR 1930), 237.

WHO'S WHO IN CHINA [T. B. CHANG]
52:7(12 APR 1930), 262.

NEW CHINESE PAPER OPENS IN CHICAGO--TYPE BOUGHT IN
    SHANGHAI
52:9(26 APR 1930), 341.
FROM <EDITOR & PUBLISHER>; <SAN MIN>.

THE 'ERA OF WEEKLIES' COMES TO CHINA
52:10(3 MAY 1930), 353.

HAROLD LLOYD FILMS ALL BANNED
52:11(10 MAY 1930), 430.

THE MAGAZINE WRITERS USED BETTER JUDGEMENT
52:12(17 MAY 1930), 435.

SHANGHAI <MERCURY> GOES INTO VOLUNTARY LIQUDATION
53:2(14 JUNE 1930), 79.

<CHINA TIMES> CONDUCTS TRADE-MARK CONTEST
53:2(14 JUNE 1930), 79.

THE <CHINESE NATION>, WEEKLY PAPER, MAKES FIRST
    APPEARANCE
53:4(28 JUNE 1930), 152.

THE DEPARTURE OF EDITOR GREEN OF THE N. C. D. N.
53:5(5 JULY 1930), 169-70.

FOREIGN NEWSPAPER CORRESPONDENTS ON TRIP TO HONAN
    FRONT
53:5(5 JULY 1930), 187.

ENFORCING MORALITY ON CHINESE PAPERS, BUT . . .
53:9(2 AUG 1930), 320-21.

SOME INTERESTING FAKERY BY PUTNAM WEALE
53:10(9 AUG 1930), 359-60.

SHANGHAI <EVENING POST> AND SHANGHAI <MERCURY>
    MERGE
53:10(9 AUG 1930), 393.

TWO-YEAR OLD <POST> BUYS 51-YEAR-OLD <MERCURY>
53:11(16 AUG 1930), 397-8.

BRITISH-AMERICAN NEWSPAPER 'AMENITIES' AT SHANGHAI
53:12(23 AUG 1930), 437-40.

LENNOX SIMPSON 'EXPLAINS' THE 'FAKE' PICTURES
53:12(23 AUG 1930), 467.

BAD YEAR FOR AMERICAN NEWSPAPERS IN FAR EAST
54:11(15 NOV 1930), 381-2.

THE MARKET SPOILED FOR CHINA WAR PICTURES
54:12(22 NOV 1930), 417-8.

WHO'S WHO IN CHINA [KWEI CHUNG-SHU (KUEI
    CHUNG-SHU)]
54:13(29 NOV 1930), 486.

CHINA'S FIRST ALL-TALKING FILM PRODUCED AT
    SHANGHAI
54:13(29 NOV 1930), 480.

'MOSQUITO' PAPERS ARE ORDERED TO REGISTER
55:9(31 JAN 1931), 336.

NATIONAL GOVERNMENT'S NEW PRESS LAW
55:12(21 FEB 1931), 422-3.

THE CHINESE CONTROL OF <THE CHINA PRESS>
55:13(28 FEB 1931), 441-2.

EARLY AMERICAN NEWSPAPER ISSUED IN SHANGHAI
56:5(4 APR 1931), 145-6.
<THE SHANGHAI NEWSLETTER> 1867-1869

JAPANESE NEWS AGENCY UNDER CHINESE BAN
56:6(11 APR 1931), 217.

A FURTHER CHAPTER IN THE 'RENGO' NEWS AGENCY CASE
56:8(25 APR 1931), 263-4.

DESPICABLE CASE OF NEWS AGENCY PROPAGANDA
56:11(16 MAY 1931), 369-70.

CHINA AT THE UNIVERSITY OF MISSOURI
56:11(16 MAY 1931), 370-71.

HARBIN PAPER SUPPRESSED FOR EXAGGERATING
      ANTI-CHIANG MOVEMENT IN CANTON
56:11(16 MAY 1931), 395.

CHARGE OF UNFAIRNESS MADE AGAINST 'REUTERS' NEWS
      SERVICE
56:11(16 MAY 1931), 395.

SOME BRITISH ADVERTISING PRACTICES IN CHINA
56:12(23 MAY 1931), 408-10.

THE CASE OF THE CHINESE REPUBLIC VERSUS THE NEW
      YORK TIMES
56:13(30 MAY 1931), 453-5.

<CHINA PRESS> CELEBRATES TWENTIETH ANNIVERSARY
58:3(19 SEPT 1931), 119.

DR. FARRINGTON DISCUSSES CHINESE-AMERICAN NEWS
      SERVICES
58:9(31 OCT 1931), 353.

MUZZLING THE PRESS IN THE FRENCH CONCESSION
59:3(19 DEC 1931), 72.

FRANK L. MARTIN COMING TO YENCHING UNIVERSITY
59:3(19 DEC 1931), 95.

RIVAL 'UNITED CHINA' PUBLICATIONS
59:4(26 DEC 1931), 123.

JAPANESE BURN DOWN CHINESE NEWSPAPER OFFICE AT
      TSINGTAO, JAPANESE MARINES LANDED
59:7(16 JAN 1932), 228.

SHANGHAI BECOMES WORLD NEWS DISTRIBUTING CENTER
60:1(5 MAR 1932), 25.
LIST OF CORRESPONDENTS

JAPANESE ATTEMPT TO 'BUY-UP' SHANGHAI NEWSPAPERS
60:3(19 MAR 1932), 67-8.

DEATH OF KANG TUNG-I, <SHUN PAO'S> CHIEF REPORTER
60:10(7 MAY 1932), 338.

JAPANESE ARREST THE HEARST CORRESPONDENT AT HARBIN
60:13(28 MAY 1932), 422.
EDWARD HUNTER

STRIKING PRINTERS TIE UP CHINESE NEWSPAPERS
61:2(11 JUNE 1932), 40.

RABID FILM CENSORSHIP OPPOSED BY AMERICAN IN
    SHANGHAI
70:12(17 NOV 1934), 483-4.

NO EFFORTS SHOULD BE SPARED TO SOLVE SZE LIANG
    TSAI MURDER
70:13(24 NOV 1934), 417-18.
EDITOR OF SHUN PAO

REGISTRATION OF NEWSPAPERS IN CHINA
71:1(1 DEC 1934), 2.

JAPANESE NAVAL MEN DETAIN AMERICAN
    REPORTER-PHOTOGRAPHER IN SHANGHAI
71:4(22 DEC 1934), 112-3.

HOLLINGTON TONG RESIGNS AS MANAGING DIRECTOR OF
    THE <CHINA PRESS>
71:6(5 JAN 1935), 202.

PUBLIC ADMINISTRATION DISCUSSED IN NEW PUBLICATION
71:10(2 FEB 1935), 313.
<THE CHINESE ADMINISTRATOR>, KAN NAI-KUANG, EDITOR

MYSTERIOUS PLOT AGAINST ARIYOSHI AND THE
    CENSORSHIP SITUATION
72:4(23 MAR 1935), 107-9.

TOKYO DEFIES NANKING ON NEWS-COMMERCIAL CENSORSHIP
72:8(20 APR 1935), 240-1.

LACK OF CENSORSHIP ON JAP CABLE CAUSE OF DISTORTED
    NEWS
72:9(27 APR 1935), 274-5.

UNCENSORED JAP CABLES CHARGE CHIANG'S DRIVE
    FAILING
72:10(4 MAY 1935), 307-8.

MORE UNCENSORED JAPANESE CABLES ON YUNNAN
    POLITICAL SITUATION
72:11(11 MAY 1935), 343-4.

TRYING TO PLUG JAPANESE LEAK IN CENSORSHIP
73:1(1 JUNE 1935), 1-2.

ANTI-FOREIGNISM PROHIBITED: EDITOR'S APPEAL DENIED
73:9(27 JULY 1935), 280-1.

WALTER WILLIAMS' INFLUENCE ON EASTERN JOURNALISM
73:10(3 AUG 1935), 317-18.

JAPAN BARS BOOKS, PAPERS, AND TWO JOURNALISTS
74:1(7 SEPT 1935), 1-2.

SMEDLEY-BURTON CONTROVERSY AND <THE REVIEW>
74:1(7 SEPT 1935), 2.

JAPANESE PRESS AND ORGANIZATIONS CHALLENGE
    BRITISH CONTROL IN SHANGHAI
74:2(14 SEPT 1935), 45-6.

STRANGE SIMILARITY IN CASES OF DR. MINOBE AND
    EDITOR TU
74:4(28 SEPT 1935), 109.

CENSORSHIP SHOULD BE CONDUCTED INTELLIGENTLY OR
    ABOLISHED ENTIRELY
74:7(19 OCT 1935), 216-18.

HOW JAPANESE PRESSURE AND CHINESE CENSORSHIP ARE
    KILLING THE CHINESE PRESS
74:9(2 NOV 1935), 289-90.

JAPANESE THREAT TO 'KILL' REUTERS NEWS SERVICE
74:11(16 NOV 1935), 365-66.

WHY WASHINGTON GOT ITS CHINA NEWS REPORTS FROM
    TOKYO
74:12(23 NOV 1935), 405-6.

<TA KUNG PAO> CENSORSHIP CASE AND SUNG CHEH-YUAN'S
    ATTITUDE ON INDEPENDENCE
75:2(14 DEC 1935), 38-40.

<RENGO'S> SWAN SONG - SWALLOWED UP IN <NEWSPAPER
    ALLIANCE>
75:3(21 DEC 1935), 74.

<CATHAY COSMOPOLITAN> NEW SHANGHAI MAGAZINE VENTURE
75:7(18 JAN 1936), 239.

HOW 'MANCHURIA DAILY NEWS' AND 'KOKUTSU' DISTORTED
    THE NEWS
76:7(18 APR 1936), 232.

JAPAN BANS PAPERS CONTAINING REPORTS OF TOKYO
    REBELLION
76:5(4 APR 1936), 145-6.

RECENT SIGNIFICANT NEWSPAPER DEVELOPMENTS IN CHINA
76:6(11 APR 1936), 182.

ARE AMERICANS 'ANTI-CHINESE' A REPLY TO LO
    CHUAN-FANG IN THE CHINA CRITIC
76:10(9 MAY 1936), 327-331.

JAPANESE DEPORT JOURNALIST AT RESUMPTION OF
    NAKAYAMA CASE-ANOTHER FRAME UP?
76:10(9 MAY 1936), 331-5.
NOBUKAZU TACHIBANA

FIFTH ANNUAL JOURNALISM INSTITUTE HELD AT
    YENCHING UNIVERSITY
76:13(30 MAY 1936), 453.

AMERICAN JOURNALISTS AND THEIR WORKS IN CHINA
77:3(20 JUNE 1936), 76-8.

RENGO-NIPPON DEMPO MERGER MARKED END OF INDEPENDENT
    JOURNALISM IN JAPAN
77:12(20 AUG 1936), 410-12.

MORE EVIDENCE ON OBJECTIVES OF JAPANESE NEWS
    MONOPOLY
78:1(5 SEPT 1936), 2-3.

PRESS SURVEY REVEALS SERIOUS ANTI-CHINESE ATTITUDE
    OF JAPANESE OFFICIALS AND GOVERNMENT
78:5(3 OCT 1936), 146-9.

HOLLINGTON TONG SEVERS NEWSPAPER CONNECTIONS
79:2(12 DEC 1936), 63.

JOINT PRESS MANIFESTO ISSUED BY 157 CHINESE
    NEWSPAPERS
79:3(19 DEC 1936), 108.

A PLEA FOR CORDIALITY BETWEEN THE PRESS OF
    JAPAN AND CHINA
79:5(2 JAN 1937), 146.

VIEW OF INTERIOR OF JAPANESE BARRACKS IN SHANGHAI--
    PHOTOGRAPHER WHO TOOK PICTURE WAS EXECUTED
79:5(2 JAN 1937), 159.

GERMANS HELP JAPANESE PRODUCE <NEW EARTH>,
    MANCHUKUO PROPAGANDA FILM
80:7(17 APR 1937), 240-2.

PUBLISHER OF TWO NEWSPAPERS IN KIANGSI ARRESTED
80:8(24 APR 1937), 307.
<SHAN PAO>, <KIEN PAO>

JOURNALISTIC ETHICS AND SANCTITY OF RED CROSS
    FLAGS
82:1(4 SEPT 1937), 1-2.

WHOLESALE SUSPENSION OF CHINESE NEWSPAPERS
    FOLLOWS EXTENSION OF JAPANESE RULE
83:1(4 DEC 1937), 2-5.

CORRESPONDENTS ASKED TO HELP PREVENT NECESSITY
    FOR CENSORSHIP
83:1(4 DEC 1937).

CHINESE EDITORS AND THE WAR
SUPPLEMENT (4 DEC 1937), 20-1.

JAPANESE CENSOR HOLDS UP ALL REPORTS OF ATROCITIES
83:8(22 JAN 1938), 199-200.

WHY SO MANY JAPANESE NEWSPAPERMEN HAVE BEEN KILLED
83:11(12 FEB 1938), 284-5.

SAD STORY OF THE MAGDALENES-CAMERAMEN MISSED IT!
83:12(19 FEB 1938), 312.

HEADS FALL, GRENADES EXPLODE AS TERRORISTS
    ATTACK NEWSPAPERS
83:12(19 FEB 1938), 320-1.

POLICE PROMOTIONS PRECIPITATE PRESS POLEMICS
83:13(26 FEB 1938), 348.

FOREIGN WRITERS NOT BRIBED BY CHINA - JAPANESE
    REPORT
84:5(2 APR 1938), 116.

JAPAN'S 'THOUGHT CONTROL' IN NORTH CHINA
84:12(21 MAY 1938), 346-7.

CALIFORNIA EDITOR WAS DEEPLY INTERESTED IN ORIENT
85:4(25 JUNE 1938), 109.
V.S. MCCLATCHY

SHANGHAI EVENING POST AND THE SITUATION AT TSINGTAO
85:7(16 JUL 1938), 211.

CHINESE EDITORS DEFY CENSORSHIP PRESERVE BEST
    TRADITIONS OF FREE PRESS
85:7(16 JUL 1938), 214-17.

REUTERS HARD HIT BY JAPANESE CENSORS
86:7(15 OCT 1938), 234.

JAPANESE PRESS WARNS NATION TO BE READY IN NEW
    SOVIET CRISIS
87:2(10 DEC 1938), 43.

SHANGHAI EVENING POST DROPS UNITED PRESS
87:6(7 JAN 1939), 180.

NIPPO REPLACED BY NEW JAPANESE DAILY
87:6(7 JAN 1939), 181.

PUPPETS PUBLISH TWENTYEIGHT NEWSPAPERS
88:4(25 MAR 1939), 105.

TOKYO JOURNALIST DIES IN BATTLE ON HAINAN
88:9(29 APR 1939), 282.
MUSATSUGU TAKETA

CHIANG ORDERS SPECIAL PROTECTION FOR NEWSMEN
88:9(29 APR 1939), 282.

ENGLISH JOURNALISM ALSO 'GOES WEST' IN WAR-TIME
    CHINA
88:10(6 MAY 1939), 292.

CHINESE NEWS DISSEMINATORS GET REBUKE OVER FALSE
    NANCHANG STORY
·88:10(6 MAY 1939), 307.

ANTI-BRITISH CAMPAIGN AND SUPPRESSION OF CHINESE
    NEWSPAPERS
88:13(27 MAY 1939), 399-401.

FOREIGN CORRESPONDENTS WITNESS BIG BATTLES ON THE
    MANCHUKUO FRONTIER
89:7(15 JULY 1939), 220.

PRESS REPORTS HINT AT OUTCOME OF PARLEYS IN TOKYO
89:8(22 JULY 1939), 234-5.

CHINESE NEWSPAPERS MOVE TO COLONY OF HONGKONG
89:11(12 AUG 1939), 327.

FOREIGN PRESSMEN VISIT NANKING
92:5(30 MAR 1940), 157-8.

AMERICAN NEWSPAPER PLANT BOMBED IN NEW WAVE OF
    TERRIORISM HERE
92:10(4 MAY 1940), 342.

S. M. C. CENSORS LOCAL VERNACULAR ORGAN
93:12(17 AUG 1940), 438.
<CHINESE-AMERICAN DAILY NEWS>

NEWSMEN FACE MORE AND MORE RESTRICTION; HARRY
    STUCKGOLD VIGOROUSLY CRITICIZES SHANGHAI
    POLICE
94:13(30 NOV 1940), 427, 434.

BRITISH PRESS IN HANKOW PARALYZED
97:9(2 AUG 1941), 279.

AN OLD LADY DISCOVERS THE BENEFITS OF
    ITALIAN FASCISM
97:9(2 AUG 1941), 260.
NORTH-CHINA DAILY NEWS?

WOODHEAD ARTICLE CAUSES TROUBLE FOR THE POST
97:10(9 AUG 1941), 300.

PUPPETS, JAPANESE HOLD CONFERENCE OF PRESS
    IN CANTON; WANG ATTENDS
97:10(9 AUG 1941), 308.

SHANGHAI WAR ANNIVERSARY MARKED BY BURNING
    OF PUPPET NEWSPAPER
97:11(16 AUG 1941), 332.
<CENTRAL-CHINA DAILY NEWS>

LOCAL NEWSPAPERS IN VERBAL WAR ON RESPONSIBILITY
    FOR TERRORISM
98:5(4 OCT 1941), 138.

FOREIGN NEWSMEN FLOCK TO CHUNGKING
98:12(22 NOV 1941), 342.

CENSORSHIP IN CHINA
100:6(5 JAN 1946), 90-1.

INDIRECT CENSORSHIP
100:7(12 JAN 1946), 109.

IRRESPONSIBLE JOURNALISM
100:8(19 JAN 1946), 127-8.

DEATH OF A JOURNALIST
100:8(19 JAN 1946), 129.

CENSORSHIP AGAIN
101:7(13 APR 1946), 138.

NEWSPAPER HEADACHES
101:9(27 APR 1946), 181.

CENSORSHIP BY ADVERTISERS?
101:10(4 MAY 1946), 204.

NEWSPAPER BANNED
102:1(1 JUNE 1946), 14.
HSIAO HSI WEEKLY

FREEDOM OF THE PRESS
102:6(6 JUL 1946), 116-17.

J.B. POWELL TESTIFIES AT TOKYO WAR TRIAL
102:11(10 AUG 1946), 255.

CHUNGKING PAPER OFFICES WRECKED
103:8(26 OCT 1946), 241.
KUO MIN KUNG PAO

COPYRIGHTS AND TRADE MARKS
104:6(11 JAN 1947), 164-5.

ANOTHER REPORTER ARRESTED
104:7(18 JAN 1947), 189-90.
TING WEN-CHIH

CONSERVATION OR CENSORSHIP
104:10(8 FEB 1947), 267-8.

BROADCASTING IN CHINA
104:12(22 FEB 1947), 313-14.

BOOKS AND NEWSPRINT
104:12(22 FEB 1947), 314.

'J.B.' POWELL PASSES
105:2(8 MAR 1947), 33-4.

CENSORSHIP IN TAIWAN
105:11(10 MAY 1947), 285-6.

CENSORSHIP DENIED
106:7(19 JUL 1947), 192-3.

CENSORSHIP AGAIN?
107:7(18 OCT 1947), 217-18.

THE PRESS IS NOT FREE
107:10(8 NOV 1947), 313-15.

NEWSPRINT CONTROL
108:4(27 DEC 1947), 107-8.

CENSORSHIP AGAIN DENIED
108:12(21 FEB 1948), 339-40.

CENSORSHIP AGAIN?
111:7(16 OCT 1948), 173-75.

KOREA'S 'FREE' PRESS
111:9(30 OCT 1948), 226-7.

UNITED STATES INFORMATION SERVICE IN CHINA
111:11(13 NOV 1948), 281.

NEWSMAN'S VISA CANCELLED
112:13(26 FEB 1949), 310.
WALTER BRIGGS IN INDO-CHINA

NEWS OF THE WEEK: FREEDOM OF THE PRESS
113:2(12 MAR 1949), 40.

CENSORSHIP PROBLEMS
113:10(7 MAY 1949), 213.

SHANGHAI'S FOREIGN PRESS
114:4(25 JUNE 1949), 70-2.

WHO'S NOT PERMITTING WHAT?
115:5(1 OCT 1949), 60.

NEWS OF THE WEEK: FILM INDUSTRY PLAN
116:10(4 FEB 1950), 159.

CHINA STORY KILLED OR DISTORTED BY AMERICAN PRESS
117:6(8 APR 1950), 104.

SHANGHAI'S NEW PAPER
118:3(17 JUNE 1950), 40.
<THE SHANGHAI NEWS>

MOVIE REGULATIONS
118:8(22 JUL 1950), 137.

MOVIES GAIN IN POPULARITY
123:2(AUG 1952), 154-55.

BARUNG B02288
BRYAN B02326
C. C02289
CASEY C01372
CHANG C02290
CHANG 11C01006
CHANG C02327
CHEN C02168
CHEN C02328
CHEN C02291
CHENG C02166
CHIEN C02329
CONLU C02169
DEANE D02292
DEANE L02293
FALCONER F02294
FANG F02295
FOOCHOW F02296
GINSBORG G02297
GOULD G02188
HARBIN H02298
HENDRICK H02299
HOBEN H02300
HU H02301
HWANG H02302
J. J01821
JEE J02194
JEE J02195
JEN 06J02638
JOHNSTON J01700
JOHNSTON J01701
KEITH K01702
KUNG K02303
KUO 11K01829
KUO K01395
KUO K02646
LEE L02304
LEE L01832
LEE L02305
LI L02306
LIANG L02307
LIN 08L01400
LING L02648
LU L02308
LUAN L02309
MA M02184

MC KENZIE M00801
MENG M02310
MENG M02311
MENG M02312
MENG M02313
MYERS M02314
NASH N02315
NOEL N02316
ONE OF THEM 002197
PATTERSON P02201
POWELL P02330
POWELL P01717
POWELL P02202
POWELL P02331
PRESCOTT P02332
QUIGLEY Q02203
REVIEW'S R02317
RIAJANSKY R02318
ROGERS R02333
ROTH R02319
SHASTRI S01722
SHECKLEN S02208
SHECKLEN S00967
SHECKLEN S02320
SIMMONS S02334
TAO T02335
THOM T02212
TONG T01727
TONG T01728
TONG T01729
TONG T01730
TONG T02114
WANG W01908
WANG W01417
WANG W02322
WHANG W02323
WILLIAMS W01425
WONG W01737
WOODBRIDGE W01422
Y. Y01738
YOUR READER Y02324
YU Y02336
YUI Y01740
YUN Y02325
ZIA Z01741

Index

THE INDEX IS DIVIDED INTO TWO PARTS. IN THE FIRST PART, THE CITATIONS FOR EACH COUNTRY ARE LISTED ACCORDING TO THE 'CHRONOLOGICAL' DESCRIPTOR AND IN THE SECOND PART, EACH COUNTRY IS DIVIDED BY THE 'SUBJECT' DESCRIPTOR.
AN EXPLANATION OF THESE DESCRIPTORS AND CAUTIONS IN THEIR USE IS FOUND IN THE INTRODUCTION AND EXPLANATORY NOTES.
THE INDIVIDUAL INDEX ENTRIES ARE COMPOSED OF THE FIRST CHARACTERS OF THE MAIN ENTRY AND THE CITATION NUMBER FROM THE BODY OF THE BIBLIOGRAPHY.

F01485 FLUG, K. K.
G01489 GILES, LIONEL
G00527 GOODRICH, L. CA
G00528 GOODRICH, L. CA
G00529 GOODRICH, L. CA
H01808 HONG KONG DAILY
H00597 HUANG, PAUL T.
I01818 INDEPENDENT, TH
I02041 INLAND PRINTER,
I02042 INLAND PRINTER,
I02039 INLAND PRINTER,
I02040 INLAND PRINTER,
I02032 INLAND PRINTER,
I02058 INLAND PRINTER,
I02038 INLAND PRINTER,
I02036 INLAND PRINTER,
I02034 INLAND PRINTER,
I02062 INLAND PRINTER,
10K00653 KAO LIANG-TSO
K00675 KING, FRANK H.
L01577 LAUFER, BERTHOL
08L02526 LIN YUAN-CH'I
08L02748 LIN YU-LAN
L02236 LU, DAVID CHI-H
M00782 MALCOLM, ELIZAB
M01281 MAULE, GEORGE B
M00795 MAYERS, WILLIAM
M01408 MESNY'S CHINESE
N02698 NEW CHINA, THE
O00861 OHLINGER, FRANK
O01872 OUTLOOK,THE [NE
P02199 PALL MALL GAZET
P00872 PARKER, ALVIN P
P00874 PARKER, EDWARD
P01607 PEAKE, CYRUS H.
P01606 PEAKE, CYRUS
P00879 PEARL, CYRIL
G00908 QUARTERLY REVIE
S02128 SCIENTIFIC AMER
11S00961 SHANG YUEH-HENG
S01888 SHEN, C. Y. [CH
S01307 SINENSIS [PSEUD
07S02755 SUNG CHIN
T01281 TIMES, THE [LON
T01299 TIMES, THE [LON
T01284 TIMES, THE [LON
T01301 TIMES, THE [LON
T01291 TIMES, THE [LON
T01297 TIMES, THE [LON
T01292 TIMES, THE [LON
T01298 TIMES, THE [LON
T01296 TIMES, THE [LON
T01285 TIMES, THE [LON
T01286 TIMES, THE [LON
T01306 TIMES, THE [LON
T01287 TIMES, THE [LON
T01294 TIMES, THE [LON
T01289 TIMES, THE [LON
T01283 TIMES, THE [LON
T01305 TIMES, THE [LON
T01293 TIMES, THE [LON
T01303 TIMES, THE [LON
T01300 TIMES, THE [LON
T01290 TIMES, THE [LON
T01302 TIMES, THE [LON
T01288 TIMES, THE [LON
T01282 TIMES, THE [LON

T01295 TIMES,THE [LOND
T01912 TREVELYAN G. M.
T01096 TSIEN TSUEN-HSU
U01103 UNESCO COURIER
W01676 WILLIAMS, FREDE
W01168 WOODBRIDGE, ISE
W02589 WRIGHT, ARNOLD,
W02027 WU, KUANG-CH'IN
W01179 WU, KUANG-CHING
W01177 WU, KUANG-CHING
W01178 WU, KUANG-CHING
Y02149 YEH, WEN-HSING
16Y02786 YEN HSIN-HENG

1910-1946

A01744 ABEND, HALLETT
A01345 ALCOTT, C. D.
A01745 ALCOTT, CAROLL
A01780 AMERASIA
A01425 AMERASIA
A01424 AMERASIA
A01426 AMERASIA
A01781 AMERICAN JOURNA
A01982 AMERICAN REVIEW
06A01782 AN I
09A00119 ANG, PSEUD.
B02077 BANNING, WILLIA
B02288 BARUNG, E. U.
B01783 BETTS, T. J.
B00738 BIGGERSTAFF, KN
B01672 BOJESEN, C. C.
B00180 BOOKER, EDNA LE
B01689 BRILLER, BERT
B00189 BRITTON, ROSWEL
B00191 BRITTON, ROSWEL
B02326 BRYAN, R. J., J
B01690 BURTON, WILBUR
C02289 C., G. F.
C00208 CAMERON, W. H.
C01372 CASEY, JOHN H.
C02080 CELESTIAL EMPIR
C02083 CELESTIAL EMPIR
C02082 CELESTIAL EMPIR
C02085 CELESTIAL EMPIR
C02084 CELESTIAL EMPIR
C02154 CELESTIAL EMPIR
11C02090 CH'EN LANG
11C01815 CH'EN CHI-YING
11C00237 CH'EN TZU HSIAN
11C00231 CH'EN CHI-YING
11C00230 CH'EN CHI-YING
11C01375 CH'EN, HUNG-SHU
12C01007 CH'ENG CH'ANG-P
C02596 CH'ENG SHE-WO
C02595 CH'ENG CH'I-HEN
C02594 CH'ENG CHI-HENG
11C02089 CHANG JO-YIN
11C02088 CHANG I-WEI
C02087 CHANG HSIAO-LU
C02167 CHANG T'IEN-HU
C02593 CHANG CHING-LU
07C01691 CHANG CHING LU
C00487 CHANG CHI-LUAN
11C01318 CHANG PEI-HEI
C02327 CHANG, Y. L.
14C02793 CHAO CHAN-YUAN

F02296 FOOCHOW CORRESP	L01835 LIANG, HUBERT S
F01486 FOREIGN CORRESP	L01399 LIANG, HUBERT S
G02297 GINSBOURG, ANNA	L01353 LIANG, HUBERT S
G01490 GINSBOURG, ANNA	L01834 LIANG, HUBERT S
G01954 GOULD, RANDALL	L02307 LIANG, HUBERT S
G01742 GOULD, RANDALL	L02005 LIANG, H. S.
G02188 GOULD, RANDALL	08L01524 LIN YUTANG
G01277 GOULD, RANDALL	08L01523 LIN YU
G01492 GOULD, RANDALL	08L01400 LIN YU-TANG
G01322 GREEN, O. M. [O	L01837 LIN YU
G01493 GRIGGS, (DAVID)	08L00740 LIN YUTANG
G01570 GROFF, SAMUEL	L01648 LIN, MOUSHENG
H01341 HAMMOND, JAMES	L01580 LINDT, A. R.
H02298 HARBIN CORRESPO	L02648 LING, C. P.
H01497 HAUSER, ERNEST	L01841 LITERARY DIGEST
H02613 HAZAMA, NAOKI	L01846 LITERARY DIGEST
07H02741 HO TSANG-HSU	L01839 LITERARY DIGEST
H02300 HOBEN, LINDSAY	L01838 LITERARY DIGEST
H01807 HONG KONG DAILY	L01840 LITERARY DIGEST
H02192 HSIAO CHI'EN	L01063 LITERARY DIGEST
H00831 HSIEH, WINSTON	15L02176 LIU HOH-HSUAN A
13H02102 HSIN HUA JIH PA	15L00748 LIU PU-T'UNG
H02103 HSING CHENG YUA	L01842 LIVING AGE
H01393 HSU CHAO-YUNG	19L00752 LO CHIA-LUN
10H01572 HSU, PAO-HUANG	L00757 LOWENTHAL, RUDO
H00586 HSU, JABIN	L01359 LOWENTHAL, RUDO
H02193 HU LIN	L01405 LOWENTHAL, RUDO
09H01574 HU TAO-CHING	L01529 LOWENTHAL, RUDO
H02301 HU CHENG	L02181 LOWENTHAL, RUDO
09H00587 HU SHIH	L00758 LOWENTHAL, RUDO
09H00596 HU TAO-CHING	L02180 LOWENTHAL, RUDO
09H01573 HU TAO-CHING	L01707 LOWENTHAL, RUDO
09H01503 HUNG, FREDERICK	L01706 LOWENTHAL, RUDO
H01811 HUNTER, DARD	L01528 LOWENTHAL, RUDO
H01817 HUNTER, EDWARD	L02182 LOWENTHAL, RUDO
H01812 HUNTER, DARD	L01527 LOWENTHAL, RUDO
HU2302 HWANG CHING-SHU	L01950 LOWENTHAL, RUDO
I01819 ISHIBASHI, TANZ	L02183 LOWENTHAL, RUDO
I02728 ISHII, AKIRA	L01403 LOWENTHAL, RUDO
I02642 IWANAGA, Y.	L01404 LOWENTHAL, RUDO
J01821 J., J. A.	L02179 LOWENTHAL, RUDO
J02195 JEE, LUTHER M.	L01019 LOWENTHAL, RUDO
J02194 JEE, LUTHER M.	L01018 LOWENTHAL, RUDO
06J02638 JEN, RICHARD	L01020 LOWENTHAL, RUDO
J01508 JEN, RICHARD L.	L00760 LU, DAVID CHI-H
J01507 JEN, RICHARD L.	L02308 LU, DAVID CHI-H
J02639 JOHNSON, ALBIN	L02309 LUAN, JOSEPH I.
J01700 JOHNSTON, WILLI	M01325 MA YIN-LIANG
K01510 KAIM, J. R.	M02184 MA, W. Y.
K01394 KAO, Y.	M00773 MA, HSIN-YE WEI
K02799 KORNER, FRITZ	M00769 MA, HSIN YE WEI
05K02173 KU T'ING-CH'ANG	M00771 MA, HSIN-YE WEI
15K02590 KUANG-TUNG WEN	M00772 MA, HSIN-YE WEI
K01828 KUNAU, JOHN A.	M00770 MA, SHIN-YE WEI
K01395 KUO WEI-HUNG	M01843 MAC NAIR, H. F.
11K02646 KUO, WEI-HUNG	M02640 MARTIN, DUDLEY
K02108 KUO-WEN CHOU-PA	M01533 MASON, ISAAC
K01516 KWEI, CHUNGSHU	M01534 MASON, ISAAC
16L00688 LAI KUANG-LIN	M00791 MATEER, ADA HAV
L01517 LASKER, BRUNO A	M01847 MC KENZIE, VERN
L01830 LATTIMORE, OWEN	M00801 MC KENZIE, VERN
L02304 LEE, B. Y.	M00800 MC KENZIE, VERN
L01832 LEE, EDWARD BIN	M01591 MEI CHI-CHU
L02305 LEE, T. T.	M02313 MENG, C. Y. W.
07L00731 LI LUNG-MU	M02312 MENG, C. Y. W.
L02599 LI YU-NING	M02310 MENG, C. Y. W.
L01355 LI, TI-TSUN	M02311 MENG, C. Y. W.
11L02174 LIANG CHI-CHAO	M01346 MILLARD, THOMAS

T02286 TANG, T. C.
T02661 THACKREY, T. O.
T02212 THOM, WAH-DING
T02321 TIENTSIN CORRES
02T01082 TING SHU-CH'I
T01730 TONG, HOLLINGTO
T01655 TONG, H. K.
T01727 TONG, HOLLINGTO
T01729 TONG, HOLLINGTO
T01728 TONG, HOLLINGTO
T02214 TONG, HOLLINGTO
T01086 TONG, HOLLINGTO
T02626 TOZER, WARREN W
T01656 TRANS-PACIFIC [
T02047 TREAT, PAYSON J
07T01097 TU HENG
22T01657 TU-SHU YUEH-K'A
03T02142 TZU WU
V02722 VILENSKII-SIBIR
V02723 VILENSKII-SIBIR
V02721 VILENSKII-SIBIR
V01734 VOTAW, MAURICE
W01907 WADDELL, J. A.
W01665 WADDELL, J.A.L.
W01666 WALKER, RICHARD
04W01128 WANG EN-FAN AND
04W01127 WANG CHUNG
04W01138 WANG YUN-WU
04W02049 WANG WEN-PIN, E
W01908 WANG, CHARLES C
W01417 WANG, GEORGE K.
W02146 WANG, Y. C.
W01668 WANG, F.T.
W01132 WANG, K. P.
W01671 WAY, EUGENE IRV
W01419 WEALE, PUTNAM [
W01349 WEN, Y. C.
W02323 WHANG, PAUL K.
W01913 WHITE, JAMES D.
W01952 WILLIAMS, DEAN
W01153 WILLIAMS, WALTE
W01914 WILLIAMS, SARA
W01736 WILLIAMS, MRS.
W01425 WILLIAMS, WALTE
W01916 WILLYOUNG, A. K
W01330 WONG, Y. W.
W01337 WONG, Y. W.
W01338 WONG, Y. W.
W01737 WONG, V. L.
W02817 WOO KOVAI
W01351 WOO KYATANG
W02148 WOOD, CHARLES W
W01422 WOODBRIDGE, S.
W01917 WOODHEAD, HENRY
08W01182 WU T'IEH-SHENG
08W01180 WU PA-LING
08W01181 WU PAO-FENG
07W01679 WU, K. T.
Y01738 Y., Z. K.
Y01977 YANG, G. K.
09Y01188 YAO HSIN-NUNG
Y01352 YOUNG, C. KUANG
Y02809 YOUNG, M. C. KU
09Y01199 YU CHEN-MING
09Y01200 YU FEI-P'ENG
09Y01197 YU CHEN-MING
09Y01204 YU SHEN-MING
07Y01203 YU PI-TA

09Y01198 YU CHEN-MING
Y02667 YUAN, L. Z.
Y02325 YUN, ART
Z02810 ZEITUNGSWISSENS
Z01741 ZIA, FRANCIS

1946-1960

07C02192 CHANG CHING-LU,
C00241 CHENG CHU-YUAN
09C01692 CHIANG KUEI-LIN
C00249 CHIANG YEN, MA
08C01450 CHIN TA-K'AI
C00253 CHINA NEWS ANAL
C00255 CHINA NEWS ANAL
C00254 CHINA NEWS ANAL
C00261 CHINA NEWS ANAL
C00260 CHINA NEWS ANAL
C00259 CHINA NEWS ANAL
C00258 CHINA NEWS ANAL
C00257 CHINA NEWS ANAL
C00256 CHINA NEWS ANAL
06C00348 CHUNG-CH'UNG, P
D02716 DELYUSIN, L.
F02294 FALCONER, ALUN
H00574 HO LIN
H02224 HSI, KUNG K'AI
H00585 HSU HSU
H02575 HSU HSU
10H02745 HSU YUNG-PING
01I00606 I CHIH [PSEUD]
01I00605 I CHIH [PSEUD.]
I00632 ISAACS, HAROLD
06J01506 JEN CHUNG
06J01505 JEN CHUNG
K02303 KUNG MIN-CHUNG
K00685 KURODA, KAZUO
L02306 LI CHUNG-FA
L00736 LIEBERMAN, HENR
08L01705 LO LIEH
L02717 LO LE
M00789 MARTIN, ROBERT
M02314 MYERS, GILBERT
N02316 NOEL, FRANK
P02718 PANKINA, OL'GA
05P02791 PAO MING-SHU
P02331 POWELL, JOHN W.
R02318 RIAJANSKY, A. A
R02319 ROTH, ANDREW
S00969 SHIEH, MILTON
S02334 SIMMONS, WALTER
S02720 SLOBODIANIUK, I
S01024 STANFORD U. CHI
S01025 STANFORD U. CHI
S01026 STANFORD U. CHI
S01027 STANFORD U. CHI
T02335 TAO WEI-LIEN
T01725 TENG SSU-YU AND
T01074 TIME
T01087 TONG, HOLLINGTO
04W01735 WANG MU
W02322 WANG SEE-ZEE
W00106 WANG, CHARLES K
W01183 WU, YUAN-LI
Y02324 YOUR READER
12Y02787 YU HSIEH-LUN
Y02336 YU WAH
Y02151 YU, FREDERICK T

E00432 ENGLISH, JOHN
F02517 FANTANANGE, ST
F01483 FAR EASTERN EC
F00461 FAR EASTERN EC
F00475 FAR EASTERN EC
F02223 FRASER, JOHN
F00501 FREE CHINA WEE
F02520 FREE CHINA WEE
F00502 FREE CHINA WEE
F02521 FREE CHINA WEE
F01994 FREE CHINA WEE
F02518 FREE CHINA WEE
G02606 GOODMAN, DAVID
H01494 HALBERSTAM, DA
H00557 HAYES, HAROLD
H02523 HILL, I. WILLI
H00578 HOHENBERG, JOH
H00601 HUGHES, JOHN
H00693 HUGHES, RICHAR
H02637 HWANG, JOHN C.
100634 ISAACS, NORMAN
K01825 KEHL, FRANK
K01515 KULKARNI, V. G
L02563 LEE, MARY
L00734 LIAO, KUAN-SHEN
L01590 LIEBERTHAL, KEN
L00745 LIU, ALAN P. L.
L00744 LIU, ALAN P. L.
L01157 LIU, ALAN P. L.
L02235 LONDON, MIRIAM
L02616 LUNG CHUNG
M02007 MA, T. C., EDIT
M00775 MACFARQUHAR, RO
M00774 MACFARQUHAR, RO
M02618 MIYOSHI, OSAMU
M00821 MORITZ, FREDERI
M01409 MORITZ, FREDERI
M00822 MORITZ, FREDERI
M00828 MUNRO, ROSS H.
M00827 MUNRO, ROSS H.
M02750 MURRAY, J. EDWA
M02620 MURTHY, P. A. N
N02530 NORDIN, MAZLAN
O00862 OKSENBERG, MICH
P00873 PARKER, DAVID
P00893 PUPP, RITA A.
R02238 R., H.
R02533 REEVES, RICHARD
R02285 REYNOLDS, JACK
R02535 RODERICK, JOHN
S00948 SANDERS, ALAN
S00951 SCHECTER, JERRO
S02560 SCHELL, ORVILLE
S00955 SCHUMAN, JULIAN
S00954 SCHUMAN, JULIAN
S00959 SERDT, MICHEL
05S01890 SHIH YUNG KUEI
S00994 SOUTHERLAND, DA
S00996 SPURR, RUSSELL
S02021 STEVENSON, H. L
S02538 STEVENSON, H. L
S02536 STEVENSON, H. L
S02537 STEVENSON, H. L
S02045 STEVENSON, H. L
S02541 STRANAHAN, SUSA
02T01905 TING WANG
02T01084 TING WANG
T01089 TOROPTSEV, S.

T02628 TS'AO, IGNATIUS
U01108 UPI REPORTER
U01107 UPI REPORTER
V01117 VARIETY
V02804 VIENET, RENE
W02547 WALTERS, RAY
W01130 WANG HSUEH-WEN
W01133 WANG LING-LING
W01143 WEBSTER, NORMAN
W02543 WHITE, EDWIN Q.
W02545 WILLIAMSON, LEN
W02544 WILLIAMSON, LEN
W01171 WOOLLACOTT, MAR
Y01259 YAO, RAYMOND
Y01256 YAO, RAYMOND
Y01258 YAO, RAYMOND
Y01190 YATES, RONALD

SURVEY

A00112 ALLEN, T. HARRE
A02156 ARLINGTON, L. C
B00165 BERNSTEIN, STAN
B01432 BERTON, PETER A
B00177 BONAVIA, DAVID
11C02259 CH'EN KUO-CH'IN
16C00251 CH'IEN CH'I-CH'
11C01006 CHANG T. B.
07C02193 CHANG CHING-LU
C01363 CHANG, RAYMOND
14C00224 CHAO, THOMAS MI
14C01443 CHAO, MIN-HENG
11C02731 CHEN SHENG-SHIH
12C02732 CHENG CHANG-PO
15C01749 CHENG JEN MING
C02811 CHIEN, HSUIN YU
C02568 CHINA PRESS, TH
C01988 CHINA TODAY
C01779 CHOU, ERIC
06C01960 CHU CH'UAN-YU
C00358 CONTEMPORARY CH
C00363 COOLING, SAMUEL
C01989 CROW, CARL
D00408 DIZARD, WILSON
F01696 FAIRBANK, JOHN
04F02055 FANG PAI
F00480 FASS, JOSEF
12F00485 FENG AI-CHUN LE
F00505 FREEDOM OF INFO
G00522 GILES, HERBERT
G00526 GOODMAN, DAVID
H00573 HIRTH, F.
H02225 HSIAO, I-WEN
07H02743 HSING SUNG-WEN
H02104 HSING CHENG YUA
09H02798 HU SHIH
09H02797 HU SHIH
12H00598 HUANG T'IEN-P'E
09H00602 HUNG KUEI-CHI
H00603 HUNTER, WILLIAM
I02579 IRICK, ROBERT L
I02615 ISHIJIMA, NORIY
J01343 JEN, RICHARD L.
K02228 KAO, IRVING KE-
K01344 KAO, Y.
K00676 KING, VINCENT V
K00680 KO KUNG-CHEN
L00691 LANNING, GEORGE

N02712 NEW CHINA, THE
N02653 NEW CHINA, THE
N02690 NEW CHINA, THE
N02710 NEW CHINA, THE
N02700 NEW CHINA, THE
N02708 NEW CHINA, THE
N02709 NEW CHINA, THE
N02695 NEW CHINA, THE
001709 OAKES, VANYA
001856 OGATA, TAKETORA
001712 ORIENTAL AFFAIR
12P01873 PANG CHI-SHIN
P01874 PARKER, WILLIAM
P01609 PEOPLE'S TRIBUN
P00904 PROPAGANDA ANAL
R01880 REA, GEORGE BRO
R01719 REED, PAUL
R02317 REVIEW'S CORRES
R01882 RITCHIE, ROBERT
R01885 RUSSELL, J. T.
S02446 SANGER, J. W.
S01722 SHASTRI, H. P.
S01896 STEIN, GUNTHER
S01638 STEIN, GUENTHER
S01639 SUGIMURA, K.
T01904 TACHIBANA, TAKA
T02321 TIENTSIN CORRES
T01906 TOKYO GAZETTE
U01731 UNITED STATES O
W01917 WOODHEAD, HENRY
Y01185 YAMAGATA, I.
Y01682 YOUNG, A. MORGA
Y01683 YOUNG, A. MORGA
Y01739 YOUNG, A. MORGA
Y01740 YUI, MASASHI
Z01922 ZUMOTO, MOTSSAD

1946-1960

A02213 ALLEN, LAFE FRA
A02450 ASIAN PRINTER,
A02075 ASIAN PRINTER,
B00154 BEECH, KEYES
B00153 BEECH, KEYES
B00152 BEECH, KEYES
B02160 BEECH, KEYES
C02216 CHANG, YONG
C02715 COUGHLIN, WILLI
C00362 COUGHLIN, WILLI
D02292 DEANE, HUGH
D02293 DEANE, HUGH
K00685 KURODA, KAZUO
N02316 NOEL, FRANK
000865 OLSON, LAWRENCE
W01161 WILSON, QUINTUS

1960-1970

A02076 ASIAN PRINTER,
B02214 BOROP, MIRIAM JI
C01442 CHANG YONG
G00508 GALLAGHER, CHARI
G00510 GARVER, RICHARD
G00511 GARVER, RICHARD
H00544 HALLORAN, RICHA
H01495 HAN KI-UK
H00575 HOBERECHT, EARN
J02640 JOURNALIST'S WO

K01511 KANG HUI-SU
K02641 KASAGI, MASAAKI
K01512 KOH MYUNG-SHIK
K00681 KOJIMA, HARUKO
L01518 LEE SANG-HI
M01592 MIN BYONG-GI
N01044 NAM, SUNWOO
P01605 PARRISH, FRED
S02447 SAITO, M.
T02211 TALBERT, ANSEL
W01142 WATANABE, HARUK
W01339 WORLD NEWSPAPER
Y02665 YOSHIMURA, YOSU

1970-1980

A02071 AFRO-ASIAN JOUR
A02802 ASIAWEEK
A01953 AWANOHARA, SUSU
C01454 CHOI CHANG-SUP
C01455 CHONG YUN-MU
D00385 DAVIES, DEREK
F00458 FAR EASTERN ECO
F00656 FORBIS, WILLIAM
G00530 GOW, GORDON
H00547 HANI, GYO
H00583 HORSLEY, WILLIA
H01501 HUGHES, RICHARD
L00687 LACHICA, EDUAR
M01844 MALCOLM, ANDREW
M02618 MIYOSHI, OSAMU
N01045 NAM, SUNWOO
N01650 NAM, SUNWOO
N01047 NAM, SUNWOO
N01046 NAM, SUNWOO
N02559 NAM, SUNWOO
001602 OH IN-HWAN
001857 OH JIN-KWAN
S01626 SAKURAI, YOSHIK
S02805 SAM-O, KIM
T01051 TADOKORO, IZUMI
T02448 TREFFKORN, HANS
V01125 VITTACHI, TARZI
W02050 WERNER, JOHN R.
W01915 WILLIAMSON, LEN
Y01195 YOSHIDA, KENSEI

SURVEY

C02507 CARROLL, JOHN
H02614 HUFFMAN, JAMES
I02615 ISHIJIMA, NORIY
K02644 KUWABARA, TAKEO
L00704 LENT, JOHN A.
M02237 MOON, EUGENE UI

EUROPE

BEFORE 1910

C00291 CHINESE REPOSIT
C00287 CHINESE REPOSIT

C00208 CAMERON, W. H.
F02099 FOWLER, JOHN A.
H01496 HARAHAP, PARADA
I02106 INGLESON, JOHN
L00755 LOON, G. VAN
M02012 MOTT, JOHN R.,
N01243 NIO, JOE LAN
07W01918 WU MING-KUN
Z01211 ZWEMER, S.

1946-1960

H00555 HASIBUAN, ADAHA
06H02792 HSING SUNG-WEN
K00683 KROEF, JUSTUS M
L00762 LUBIS, MOCHTAR
N01266 NIEUWENHUIS, J.
N01268 NIEUWENHUIS, J.
P00890 PLUVIER, J. M.

1960-1970

A00654 ADINEGORO, DJAM
A00104 AGASSI, JUDITH
A02724 AKKEREN, DR. PH
A02074 ASIAN-AFRICAN J
17C02739 CHUNG KWANG-HSI
C00364 CRAWFORD, ROBER
D02096 DJASWADI,SOEPRA
D02095 DJAWADI SUPRAPT
K00667 KERTAPATI, TON
L00686 LACEY, JOSEPH
L00764 LUBIS, MOCHTAR
L01324 LUBIS, MOCHTAR
O00858 OETAMA, JACOB
P00869 PAGET, ROGER K.
U01109 UNITED STATES I
W01144 WEINER, ALAN
W01677 WORD, THE [BOMB

1970-1980

A01309 ADJI, OEMAR SEN
A02072 AFRO-ASIAN JOUR
A00117 ANDELMAN, DAVID
A00118 ANDELMAN, DAVID
A01984 ANWAR, ROSIHAN
A01311 ANWAR, H. ROSIH
A00138 ASSEGAFF, D. H.
A00137 ASSEGAFF, D. H.
B01814 BERITA HARIAN
C00213 CHANDRA, A. M.
D00384 DAVIES, DEREK A
D02220 DEVOSS, DAVID
D01475 DJAJANTO, WARIE
E00419 EAPEN, K. E.
E00418 EAPEN, K. E.
G01334 GARIS BESAR PER
G00525 GOLDSTONE, ANTH
H00559 HAYWARD, HENRY
H00558 HAYWARD, HENRY
I00627 IPI REPORT
J01966 JENKINS, DAVID
J01965 JENKINS, DAVID
J02815 JENKINS, DAVID
J01964 JENKINS, DAVID
J00641 JENKINS, DAVID
J00697 JENKINS, DAVID

J00696 JENKINS, DAVID
J00698 JENKINS, DAVID
K01824 KAMM, HENRY
L02110 LINANG, W.
L00763 LUBIS, MOCHTAR
M02113 MARTONO
M02114 MAWATARI, T.
M00799 MC ELHENY, VICT
M00813 MOHAMAD, GOENAW
P00870 PANG YUET LENG
P00876 PARSONS, CYNTHI
S00993 SOUTHERLAND, DA
S00992 SOUTHERLAND, DA
S01036 STOCKWIN, HARVE
S01049 SUSANTO, ASTRID
U01112 UTOMO, JAKOB

SURVEY

C02635 CRAWFORD, ROBER
D01017 DEKKER, DOUWES
F00436 FABER, G. H. VO
G00531 GRAFF, H. J. DE
I01335 ISA, ZUBAIDAH
K00658 KATALOGUS SURAT
K00670 KHOUW GIOK PO [
M00802 MC MURTRIE, DOU
N01244 NUNN, G. RAYMON
P02623 PRAKOSO, MASTIN
S00985 SMITH, EDWARD C
S01048 SURYADINATA, LE
I02659 TAN PENG SIEW
T02760 THUNG, YVONNE A
W02565 WRIGHT, ARNOLD,

LAOS

1946-1960

A02450 ASIAN PRINTER,
B00488 BUREAU OF SOCIA

1960-1970

H01810 HUNTER, DARD
M00784 MALLOY, MICHAEL

1970-1980

A01261 ARNETT, PETER
E01481 EVERINGHAM, JOH
E00433 EVERINGHAM, JOH
H00694 HUGHES, RICHARD
I00629 IPI REPORT
L00711 LENT, JOHN A.
L01263 LENT, JOHN A.

SURVEY

N01246 NUNN, G. RAYMON

D01471 DAS, K.
E01391 EDITOR & PUBLIS
F00456 FAR EASTERN ECO
F01482 FAR EASTERN ECO
F00468 FAR EASTERN ECO
F00469 FAR EASTERN ECO
F00448 FAR EASTERN ECO
G02813 GLATTBACH, JACK
G00539 GUIMARY, DONALD
G00541 GUNARATNE, SHEL
H00545 HANCOCK, ALAN
H00550 HARBEN, AYESHA
H00549 HARBEN, AYESHA
H00571 HILL, R. D.
H02631 HITCHCOCK, DAVI
H01499 HORIZONS [USIS]
I00604 IBRAHIM HAMID
I00618 IPI REPORT
I00635 ISMAIL HUSSEIN
I00636 ISMAIL HUSSEIN
J01823 JUSOF MANAF
K00647 KAM, JOHN
K00646 KAM, JOHN
K00665 KELANA, C. M.
K00669 KHOO BOON CHOO
L00721 LENT, JOHN, A.
L00714 LENT, JOHN A.
L00722 LENT, JOHN A.
L01833 LENT, JOHN A.,
L00719 LENT, JOHN A.
L00715 LENT, JOHN A.
L00717 LENT, JOHN A.
L00716 LENT, JOHN A.
L02109 LENT, JOHN A.
L01519 LETCHMIKANTHAN,
L01521 LETCHMIKANTHAN,
L01520 LETCHMIKANTHAN,
L01241 LIM HUCK TEE, C
L00767 LUM, MAGDALENE
L00765 LUM, MAGDALENE
L00766 LUM, MAGDALENE
M01242 MALAYSIAN BUSIN
M02011 MOHAMMAD ALIAS
M00816 MOHD. FAUZI PAT
M00814 MONTEIRO, SMITH
M00820 MORGAN, JAMES
M00819 MORGAN, JAMES
N02013 NADAMINGGU
N00836 NATARAJAN, LAKS
N01265 NG POH TIP
N01264 NG POH TIP
N01270 NOORDIN SOPIEE
N00854 NOORDIN SOPIEE
N01269 NOORDIN SOPIEE
N00856 NORDIN MOHAMAD
P00868 PADASIAN, JOHN
P00870 PANG YUET LENG
P00875 PARKER, ELLIOTT
P00882 PENGULAS [PSEUD
P01875 PENULIS KHAS
P00889 PILLAI, M. G. G
P00887 PILLAI, M. G. G
P00888 PILLAI, M. G. G
P00895 POSSIBLE, HENRI
R02239 RASBINA H. A.
R00929 ROFF, WILLIAM R
R00928 ROFF, WILLIAM R
R02205 ROSLEY IBRAHIM

S00944 SAAD, HASHIM
S00958 SENKUTTUVAN, AR
09S00979 SIN CHEW JIH PO
S00995 SPURR, RUSSELL
S02135 STAR, THE [PENA
S02134 STAR, THE [PENA
S01899 STRAITS TIMES
S02067 STRAITS TIMES
S02066 STRAITS TIMES
S02241 STRAITS TIMES
S02242 STRAITS TIMES
S02138 STRAITS TIMES
S02068 STRAITS TIMES
S02137 STRAITS TIMES
S02023 STRAITS TIMES
S02540 STRAITS TIMES
S02539 STRAITS TIMES
S01900 STRAITS TIMES
S01328 SUBBIAH, RAMA
S01039 SULAIMAN, RAJA
T01058 TAY, LOUISE
T01061 TEGJEU, BILL
T01066 TENGKU MOHAMED
T01067 TEOH, JOHN
V01114 VAN NIEL, ROBER
V01116 VARIETY
W01141 WATAN [PSEUD. (
Y02028 Y., P. [PATRICK
Y01191 YEE SIEW-PUN
Z01209 ZAILAH ISMAIL

SURVEY

A00142 AVELING, HARRY
C00228 CHEESEMAN, H. A
C00238 CHEN YUN-LO
11H02744 HSU YUN-CHIAO
I02060 IBNU HANIFFAH
I02107 ISKANDAR HAJI A
L01341 LIM, PUI HUEN P
M02617 MALAY MAIL [MAL
N01267 NIK AHMAD B. HA
P01410 PARKER, ELLIOTT
R02624 ROFF, W.
R00927 ROFF, WILLIAM R
R00926 ROFF, WILLIAM R
S01412 SAMAD, MARINA
S02133 STAR, THE [PENA
S01032 STEVENSON, REX
11T01055 TAN TAT SENG
T02625 TAN, S. H.
T02627 TREGONNING, K.
W01162 WILSON, W. ARTH
Y01207 YUSOF A. TALIB
Y01208 YUSOF A. TALIB
Z01210 ZAINAL ABIDIN B

OTHER

1910-1946

B02077 BANNING, WILLIAM
B02288 BARUNG, E. U.
C02081 CELESTIAL EMPIRE
F01990 FAR EASTERN INFO

1960-1970

A00136 ASPIRAS, JOSE D
A00135 ASPIRAS, JOSE D
B00150 BAUTISTA, JOSE
C00211 CASTRO, JOSE LU
L00686 LACEY, JOSEPH
L00705 LENT, JOHN A.
M00790 MASLOG, CRISPIN
N01044 NAM, SUNWOO
P00883 PHILIPPINES PRE
R00921 RAVENHOLT, ALBE
U01111 UNITED STATES I
V01663 VIRAVAIDYA, MEC

1970-1980

A00123 AP LOG
A02255 ASIAWEEK
A02257 ASIAWEEK
A02256 ASIAWEEK
C02508 CORRESPONDENT
D01798 DE LA CRUZ, JR.
D00405 DIARIO, RUBEN
D00406 DIBBLE, ARNOLD
E01480 ESPIE, STEPHEN
F02272 FAR EASTERN ECO
F00454 FAR EASTERN ECO
G00516 GEORGE, T. J. S
G00517 GEORGE, T. J. S
G00515 GEORGE, T. J. S
G00537 GUILLERMO, ARTE
H00560 HAYWARD, HENRY.
H02631 HITCHCOCK, DAVI
I00625 IPI REPORT
J00640 JEFFRES, LEO W.
L00707 LENT, JOHN A.
L00706 LENT, JOHN A.
L00723 LENT, JOHN A.
L00713 LENT, JOHN A.
M00787 MARQUEZ, FLORDE
M00808 MISA, VERONICA
N01046 NAM, SUNWOO
P00877 PATRON, JOSEFIN
P00906 PHILIPPINES. DE
G02549 QUIRINO, JOE
R00932 RONQUILLO, BERN
R00933 RONQUILLO, BERN
R00937 ROSENBERG, DAVI
S01633 SILVA, FATHER
S00975 SILVA, FATHER
S02240 SPECIAL CORRESP
S01038 STOCKWIN, HARVE
T01252 TASKER, RODNEY
T01651 TASKER, RODNEY
T01253 TASKER, RODNEY
T01250 TASKER, RODNEY
T01652 TASKER, RODNEY
T01251 TASKER, RODNEY
T01071 THOMPSON, SCOTT

SURVEY

A01427 AMERICAN UNIVER
B00175 BOGUSLAV, DAVID
B02550 BRESNAHAN, MARY
C00214 CHANG, CHUH-HA
C00250 CHICO, SILVANO

F02714 FOOKIEN TIMES,
H00554 HARTENDORP, A.
L02647 LENT, JOHN A.
L00703 LENT, JOHN A.
L00709 LENT, JOHN A.
R00930 ROGERS, F. THEO
R00934 ROSARIO, ERNEST
V01113 VALENZUELA, JES
V02244 VALENZUELA, JES
Y01194 YORRO, DIONISIO

RUSSIA

1910-1946

L01830 LATTIMORE, OWEN
L02182 LOWENTHAL, RUDO
M01850 MOORE, HARRIET

1946-1960

L00736 LIEBERMAN, HENR

1960-1970

M01532 MARKHAM, JAMES

SEVERAL ASIA

BEFORE 1910

C01446 CHATURVEDI, RAM
C00284 CHINESE REPOSIT
C00296 CHINESE REPOSIT
C00295 CHINESE REPOSIT
12F00489 FENG TZU-YU

1910-1946

B01431 BELL, HENRY HES
B01367 BILAINKIN, GEOR
C02289 C., G. F.
C01794 CROW, CARL
F01801 FAIRPLAY
F00495 FORD, ALEXANDER
G01587 GOLDEN, NATHAN
H00556 HAUSER, ERNEST
H02300 HOBEN, LINDSAY
I02727 INSTITUTE OF PA
K01702 KEITH, ORRIN
K02004 KOREA REVIEW
K01262 KUO, HELENA [CH
08L01522 LIN YU
L01529 LOWENTHAL, RUDO
M02640 MARTIN, DUDLEY
M02528 MORRIS, JOHN R.
M02529 MOTT, FRANK LUT
P02014 PAN-PACIFIC UNI
P01715 PHOENIX, THE
R01880 REA, GEORGE BRO
R01879 REA, GEORGE BRO
R01878 REA, GEORGE BRO

S01030 STEAD, HENRY
T01079 TIMPERLY, H. J.
T01085 TONG, HOLLINGTO
V01119 VAUGHN, MILES W
W01670 WAY, EUGENE IRV
W01418 WEAIT, R. H.
W02587 WILLIAMS, WALTE
W01329 WILLIAMS, WALTE

1946-1960

H01356 HOBBS, CECIL
I00615 INTERNATIONAL P
K00682 KRAUSZ, GEORGE
N02115 NEW COMMONWEALT
R00916 RAND, CHRISTOPH
S00981 SKINNER, G. WIL
W02147 WONG, DAVID TZI
Y01186 YAMAMOTO, FUMIO

1960-1970

A00128 ASIA FOUNDATION
A02074 ASIAN-AFRICAN J
B02164 BURROWS, LARRY
C00210 CARBALLO, TITO
F00481 FELICIANO, GLOR
F00490 FERNANDEZ, T.
F00491 FEUEREISEN, FR
H00577 HOHENBERG, JOHN
I01240 INTERNATIONAL P
K01575 KERR, FRANCES
L01530 LUBIS, MOCHTAR
M01535 MATIENZO, LORET
N02116 NEW COMMONWEALT
O00859 OEY, GIOK-PO
P00891 POCKRASS, ROBER
Q01620 QUIRINO, JOSE A
R00911 RAGSDALE, WILMO
R00919 RAVENHOLT, ALBE
R00918 RAVENHOLT, ALBE
R00935 ROSE, E. J. B.
S00950 SARKAR, CHANCHA
S00949 SARKAR, CHANCHA
S01631 SHRIDHAR, DEV
S00978 SIMONS, PAUL
S00984 SLOMKOWSKI, ZYG
T01653 TEIXEIRA, PE. M
U01102 UNESCO
U01101 UNESCO
V01120 VICENCIO, MACAR
V01664 VITTACHI, TARZI
V01124 VITTACHI, A. G
W02663 WATTS, RONALD A
W02664 WATTS, RONALD A
W02577 WINT, GUY, EDIT

1970-1980

A00107 ALPHA MONTHLY
A02073 ALVAREZ, MAX
A01213 ASIAN MASS COMM
A01215 ASIAN MASS COMM
A01214 ASIAN MASS COMM
A00134 ASIAN PRESS, TH
A02502 ASIAWEEK
A00141 ATLAS WORLD PRE
B00148 BARBER, STEPHEN

B02162 BLACKMAN, SAMUE
B00194 BROWNE, DONALD
C01440 CAREEM, NICKY
C01438 CAREEM, NICKY
C00593 CHANG, JOSEPHIN
C00331 CHOWDHURY, AMIT
C00357 COMMUNICATION A
D00370 DAHLAN, M. ALWI
D00439 DALTON, JAMES J
D00371 DANIELS, JOSEPH
D00383 DAVIES, DEREK
D00382 DAVIES, DEREK
D00381 DAVIES, DEREK
D00380 DAVIES, DEREK A
D00394 DAVIES, DEREK
D00396 DAVIES, DEREK
D02557 DAVIES, DEREK
D02173 DAY, BILLIE
D02513 DEEN, THALIF
D01645 DEVOSS, DAVID
E01477 ELEGANT, ROBERT
E02187 ELEGANT, ROBERT
F00440 FAR EASTERN ECO
F00459 FAR EASTERN ECO
F00450 FAR EASTERN ECO
F01586 FAR HORIZONS
F02223 FRASER, JOHN
G01488 GALLINER, PETER
G00533 GRISOLA, MICHEL
H01239 HALE, KATHLEEN,
H01804 HILL, I. WILLIA
H01500 HSUEH, CHUN-TU
I00612 INSIGHT
I00621 IPI REPORT
J00639 JEBB, MARCIA
K00666 KENNARD, ALLING
K01827 KIRKHAM, BARRY
K01514 KULKARNI, V. G.
L00690 LANIAUSKAS, VIC
L00720 LENT, JOHN A.
L00712 LENT, JOHN A.
L02525 LENT, JOHN A.
L00710 LENT, JOHN A.
M00792 MATIENZO, LORET
M01595 MORROW, MIKE
N00841 NEWSWEEK
N00857 NUNN, RAYMOND
P00870 PANG YUET LENG
P00907 PUBLISHERS' AUX
R00912 RAJAGOPAL, D. R
R00915 RAMACHANDRAN, R
R00923 REECE, ROBERT
S00953 SCHRAMM, WILBUR
S02580 SCHRAMM, WILBUR
S01887 SCOTT, ANNE
S02132 SHIH SHAO-HUA
S01414 SHIMABUKURO, BE
S01975 SILVA, MERVYN D
S00977 SILVER, GERALD
S00976 SILVER, GERALD
S02561 SPURR, RUSSELL
S02539 STRAITS TIMES
S01900 STRAITS TIMES
T01652 TASKER, RODNEY
T01654 TERZANI, TIZIAN
T01069 THAYER, NATHANI
T02584 TRAN TRONG HUNG
V01733 VIETNAM MAGAZIN

V01732 VIETNAM MAGAZIN
W01675 WEINTRAUB, PETE
W01146 WHEELER, GEOFFR
W02820 WOO, LYON

SURVEY

A00133 ASIAN MASS COMM
A01747 AUSTRALIAN NATI
B00196 BRYANT, CHARLES
C00212 CENTER FOR RESE
C01459 CREWDSON, JOHN
D01472 DATELINE: ASIA,
F02519 FARIS, BARRY
12F01698 FENG AI-CHUN [E
H00657 HART, DONN VORH
H01571 HORNE, NORMAN P
H02814 HUGHES, RICHARD
I00613 INTERNATIONAL C
K02063 KAY, CHARLES S.
15L00699 LAU TZU-CHING
L02746 LENT, JOHN A.
L00708 LENT, JOHN A.,
L00718 LENT, JOHN A.
L01323 LIM, PUI HUEN P
15L00750 LIU TZU CHENG
M02619 MOSES, SIR CHAR
N02531 NUNN, G. RAYMON
R00924 RHODES, DENNIS
T01274 TRUMBULL, ROBER
12T01095 TSENG HSU-PAI,
W01139 WARNER, DENIS

SINGAPORE

BEFORE 1910

A01315 ASIATIC JOURNAL
B00169 BIRCH, E. W.
B00207 BYRD, CECIL K.
C00234 CHEN MONG HOCK
G00521 GIBSON-HILL, C.
R01411 ROFF, WILLIAM R
S01413 SELANGOR JOURNA
W01175 WRIGHT, ARNOLD,

1910-1946

A00114 ALSAGOFF, HUSSE
A02158 AW BOON HAW
B01370 BRITISH MALAYA
C00208 CAMERON, W. H.
C02170 CURRIE, J.
F02099 FOWLER, JOHN A.
G01995 GERMAN, R. L.,
M00781 MAKEPEACE, W. E
M00780 MAKEPEACE, WALT
M01596 MOSLEM WORLD, T
R02016 READ, W. H.
W02218 WARIN, W. J.
W01418 WEAIT, R. H.
W01420 WILSON, W. ARTH
W01421 WILSON, W. ARTH
Y02605 YEN CHING HWANG

1946-1960

B00197 BUREAU OF SOCIA
11C02730 CHEN HSIAO-CHI
G00512 GASPARD, ARMAND

1960-1970

B00166 BETTS, RUSSELL

1970-1980

A00115 ANDELMAN, DAVID
A00116 ANDELMAN, DAVID
A01583 ASIAWEEK
A02537 ASIAWEEK
A02819 ASIAWEEK
A02552 AWANOHARA, SUSU
B00160 BERITA HARIAN
B00158 BERITA HARIAN
B00167 BHATHAL, R. S.
B00184 BORDWELL, CONST
B00413 BOWRING, PHILIP
C01155 CASADY, SIMON
C01456 CHAN, HENG CHEE
C01456 CHOPRA, PRAN
D00379 DAS, K.
D00397 DAVIES, DEREK
D00395 DAVIES, DEREK
D00393 DAVIES, DEREK
D00392 DAVIES, DEREK
D00391 DAVIES, DEREK
D00389 DAVIES, DEREK
D00401 DELIKHAN, GERA
E02098 EDITOR & PUBLIS
F00446 FAR EASTERN ECO
F00445 FAR EASTERN ECO
F00470 FAR EASTERN ECO
F00447 FAR EASTERN ECO
F00455 FAR EASTERN ECO
F00473 FAR EASTERN ECO
F00474 FAR EASTERN ECO
F00441 FAR EASTERN ECO
F00476 FAR EASTERN ECO
F00443 FAR EASTERN ECO
F00452 FAR EASTERN ECO
F00442 FAR EASTERN ECO
F02806 FAR EASTERN ECO
F00493 FONG, LESLIE
G00507 GALE, JOHN
G00514 GEORGE, T. J. S
H00571 HILL, R. D.
H01500 HSUEH, CHUN-TU
12H02274 HUANG HO
I00611 INSIGHT
I00616 INTERNATIONAL P
J00643 JOSEY, ALEX
K00668 KHAW, AMBROSE
K01513 KOH TAI ANN
K02598 KUO, EDDIE C. Y
K01396 KWA, CHONG GUAN
L01578 LEE KUAN YEW
L01967 LEE MAU-SENG
L01423 LEE KUAN YEW
L02279 LEE, MARY
L01156 LENT, JOHN A.
M00818 MORGAN, JAMES
O02534 ON-LINE SYSTEMS

P00902 PEIRIS, DENZIL
R00913 RAM, MOHAN
R00914 RAM, MOHAN
R00936 ROSE, ERNEST D.
S00946 SALLOWAY, NITI
S00980 SINGH, KHUSHWAN
S01635 SINGH, GEETANJA
S01260 SIRIWARDENE, RE
U01106 UPI REPORTER
V01121 VILANILAM, JOHN
W01145 WEINRAUB, BERNA
W01163 WINDER, DAVID
W01164 WINKLER, MANFRE

SURVEY

K00671 KHURSHID, A. S.

TAIWAN

1910-1946

11C00231 CH'EN CHI-YING
C02596 CH'ENG SHE-WO

1946-1960

11C00232 CH'EN CHIH-P'IN
11C00235 CH'EN SHENG-SHI
11C02729 CHEN CHIH-PING
09C00247 CHIANG CHAN-K'U
08C02737 CHOU SHENG-SHEN
06C02093 CHU HSU-PAI
C00340 CHU, AUGUSTUS F
10H00588 HSI KEN-LIN
H02226 HUANG, NANCY LA
L02230 LAI, LESLIE K.
L02232 LEW TIEN
15L01582 LIU, WEI-SEN
L02234 LONG, HWA SHU
M02185 MAC GREGOR, GR
10S00971 SHIH CHAO-HSI
S01028 STANFORD U. CHI
14T02574 T'AI-WAN HSIN S
W02246 WEI, MICHAEL TA
12Y01192 YEH TSUNG-K'UEI

1960-1970

11C01449 CH'EN, SHIH-AN
11C01584 CHANG, LI-HSIUN
16C00240 CHENG CHEN-MING
16C00239 CHENG CHEN-MING
10C02735 CHIN PAO-MIN
08C02736 CHOU HSIAO-HUNG
06C00347 CHU YU-LUNG
06C00346 CHU WEI-YU
C00341 CHU CHI-YING
04C00349 CHUNG-KUO KUO M
17H02101 HSIEH, JAN-CHIH
10K00652 KAO FENG-JUNG
L02231 LEE HSING-CHU
07L00732 LI SHENG-WEN
07L00729 LI CHAN
07L02576 LI CHAN

15L02233 LIU KUANG-YEN
15L02111 LIU KUANG-YEN
07L00761 LU K'ANG-YU
16L00759 LU CHIH-CH'U
12L00768 LUNG CH'UNG-KUA
M02187 MC LAUGHLIN, J
08M00807 MING CHIEN-HUA
M02188 MOHR, CHARLES
N01044 NAM, SUNWOO
07P01247 PEI K'E LBAKER,
S00960 SHAN, SHEN
S00970 SHIEH, MILTON J
S01630 SHIH, MEI-CHING
07S01042 SUNG HAN-CHANG
T01052 T'AI PEI SHIH H
14T01053 T'AI-PEI SHIH H
T02800 T'AI-PEI SHIH H
04W01137 WANG YING-CHI
W01134 WANG, THI-WU
Y02052 YU, HELEN Y. Y.
10Y01206 YUAN LIANG

1970-1980

A00126 ARMBRUSTER, WIL
A00125 ARMBRUSTER, WIL
A00412 ARMBRUSTER, WIL
A02801 ASIAWEEK
11C01376 CH'EN YUAN-HSIU
08C00328 CH'IU JUNG-KUAN
13C01585 CHENG HENG-HSIU
C00345 CHU, JAMES C. Y
F00460 FAR EASTERN ECO
F00466 FAR EASTERN ECO
F01962 FAR EASTERN ECO
F02520 FREE CHINA WEEK
F02521 FREE CHINA WEEK
F00503 FREE CHINA WEEK
F01994 FREE CHINA WEEK
F00500 FREE CHINA WEEK
F02518 FREE CHINA WEEK
F00501 FREE CHINA WEEK
17H01979 HSIEH, JAN-SHIH
10H01809 HSU YUNG P'ING
I00619 IPI REPORT
I00626 IPI REPORT
I00659 IPI REPORT
J00637 JACOBS, J. BRUC
K02276 KAZER, BILL
K02524 KAZER, BILL
K00679 KLIMLEY, APRIL
K00678 KLIMLEY, APRIL
07L02277 LAI MING-CHI
07L02281 LI CHAN
L00733 LI TZE-CHUNG
07L00730 LI CHAN
15L02600 LIU CHIEN-SHUN
L01525 LIU, MELINDA
L00746 LIU, HAN C. AND
L01526 LIU, MELINDA
L01581 LIU, HENRY Y.
L01968 LIU, MELINDA
L01969 LIU, MELINDA
L02283 LIU, MELINDA
L02064 LIU, MELINDA
M02007 MA, T. C., EDIT
N01046 NAM, SUNWOO
10S01901 SUN JU LING

VIETNAM

1946-1960

H02299 HENDRICK, J.
02T02759 TING KUANG-HUA
T01099 TURNBULL, GEORG

1960-1970

A02191 ARNETT, PETER
B00146 BAILEY, GEORGE
B02159 BALK, ALFRED
B02214 BOROP, MIRIAM J
B00187 BOYLAN, JAMES
B02578 BOYLE, RICHARD
B02556 BRAESTRUP, PETE
B00188 BRAESTRUP, PETE
B01368 BRAESTRUP, PETE
B00195 BROWNE, MALCOLM
B02164 BURROWS, LARRY
C00350 CLANCY, PHYLLIS
C00353 COLUMBIA JOURNA
C00352 COLUMBIA JOURNA
C00354 COLUMBIA JOURNA
C01458 COSTENOBLE, EAR
D00399 DAVISON, W. PHI
D02174 DEEPE, BEVERLY
F00497 FOX, TOM
G00520 GERSHEN, MARTIN
G00519 GERSHEN, MARTIN
H00543 HALBERSTAM, DAV
H02189 HALBERSTAM, DAV
H00564 HERR, MICHAEL
H00565 HERR, MICHAEL
H00566 HERR, MICHAEL
H01364 HERR, MICHAEL
H00576 HOFFER, THOMAS
H02191 HOFFMAN, FRED S
H01810 HUNTER, DARD
J00881 JOHNSON, DEWAYN
K02171 KALB, MARVIN
K00661 KARNOW, STANLEY
K02172 KEARNS, FRANK
M00788 MARSHALL, S. L.
M02186 MC ANDREW, WIL
M02187 MC LAUGHLIN, J
M00803 MC NULTY, THOMA
M02188 MOHR, CHARLES
M02189 MORGAN, JOE W.
M02193 MORRIS, JOHN G.
N00839 NEW LEADER, THE
N01065 NEWSWEEK
N02449 NGO KHAC TINH
N01275 NGUYEN THAI
P02654 PHAN NHU MY
P02655 PHAN NHU MY
P02656 PHAN NHU MY
P00885 PIKE, DOUGLAS
P00886 PIKE, DOUGLAS
Q00910 QUINN, THOMAS A
R02125 RISHER, EUGENE
R00943 RUSTIN, RICHARD
R02126 RYAN, WILLIAM L
S02206 SAFER, MORLEY
S01029 STAUBER, ROSE
S01041 SULLY, FRANCOIS
S02209 SULLY, FRANCOIS

S02210 SYLVESTER, ARTH
T01070 THIEN, TON THAT
T02213 TIEDE, TOM
T01075 TIME
T01093 TREASTER, JOSEP
T02215 TREGASKIS, RICH
V02143 VO CONG-TAI
V02144 VOLKERT, KURT
W02219 WHITE, EDWIN Q.

1970-1980

A02070 AFRO-ASIAN JOUR
A01261 ARNETT, PETER
A01643 ARNETT, PETER
A00129 ARNETT, PETER
A00127 ASIAN, THE
A02503 ASIAWEEK
B01644 BRAESTRUP, PETE
B02163 BRANNIGAN, BILL
C00245 CHERRY, BENJAMI
C00355 COLUMBIA JOURNA
D02512 DAWSON, ALAN
D00404 DIAMOND, EDWIN
D02054 DUDMAN, RICHARD
E01479 ELLITHORPE, HAR
E01478 ELLITHORPE, HAR
E02222 ERLANGER, STEVE
F01362 FAAS, HORST
F00506 FRIENDLY, FRED
G01996 GIDLUND, CARL A
G00538 GUIMARY, DONALD
H01494 HALBERSTAM, DAV
H01392 HALBERSTAM, DAV
H02190 HANGEN, PAT
H00561 HAYWARD, HENRY
H00567 HERR, MICHAEL
H00568 HERR, MICHAEL
H01647 HERR, MICHAEL
I00607 INDOCHINA SOLID
L00702 LEFEVER, ERNEST
L02178 LOVING, GEORGE
M00797 MC CARTNEY, JAM
M00798 MC NULTY, THOMA
M00815 MOODY, RANDALL
N01970 NATIONS, RICHAR
N01424 NGUYEN VAN THIE
O00864 O'LOUGHLIN, PET
O02196 OKULEY, BERT
P01618 POPULAR PHOTOGR
R00912 RAJAGOPAL, D. R
R00942 RUSSO, FRANK D.
S00957 SCOTT, GAVIN
S00964 SHAPLEN, ROBERT
S00991 SOUTHERLAND, DA
S01637 STARNER, FRANCI
S01031 STEINLE, PEGGY
S01034 STILLMAN, DON
S01050 SUSSMAN, LEONAR
T01654 TERZANI, TIZIAN
T02562 THOMPSON, HUNTE
T02584 TRAN TRONG HUNG
T02585 TRONG NHAN
U02216 U. K. PRESS GAZ
U01662 UNITED STATES I
U01105 UPI REPORTER
V01733 VIETNAM MAGAZIN
V01732 VIETNAM MAGAZIN

W02543 WHITE, EDWIN Q.
W01149 WILLIAMS, ALDEN
W02544 WILLIAMSON, LEN
W01165 WITCOVER, JULES
W01176 WRIGHT, JAMES D
Y01193 YOUNG, PERRY DE

SURVEY

D00407 DINH, TRAN VAN
E00431 EMERSON, GLORIA
F00498 FRANK, ROBERT S
H00546 HANGEN, PATRICI
K02229 KENNEDY, WILLIA
N02660 NGUYEN THAI
N01246 NUNN, G. RAYMON
T01726 THU VIEN QUOC G
W01910 WEBB, ALVIN B.

WESTERN HEMISPHERE

1970-1980

H00557 HAYES, HAROLD

SURVEY

L02790 LO, KARL AND H

WORLD

BEFORE 1910

I02058 INLAND PRINTER,

1910-1946

D02184 DIGEST OF THE S
G01587 GOLDEN, NATHAN
K01702 KEITH, ORRIN
L01830 LATTIMORE, OWEN
M02640 MARTIN, DUDLEY
P01971 PEIPING CHRONIC
P01610 PEOPLE'S TRIBUN
S00965 SHARP, EUGENE W
W02587 WILLIAMS, WALTE
W01152 WILLIAMS, WALTE

1946-1960

I00614 INTERNATIONAL P
K00664 KAYSER, JACQUES
N02115 NEW COMMONWEALT

1960-1970

A00113 ALMANEY, ADNAN
B00174 BOGART, LEO
B02164 BURROWS, LARRY
B00205 BUSINESS WEEK
F00504 FREEDOM OF INFO
F02056 FULBRIGHT, NEWT

H02105 HUGHES, PENNETH
I00617 INTERNATIONAL P
L00700 LEE, JOHN
07L01579 LI, CHAN
P01617 POOL, ITHIEL DE
R00939 ROSS, ALBION
S00950 SARKAR, CHANCHA
S00956 SCHWARZ, HENRY
S00988 SUMMERLAD, ERNE
W01148 WILCOX, DENNIS
Y01201 YU, FREDERICK A

1970-1980

A01980 AFRO-ASIAN JOUR
A00592 ALIAS RAHIM
A02073 ALVAREZ, MAX
B02162 BLACKMAN, SAMUE
B00171 BLOCKER, JOEL
B02505 BRINK, DIRK
C00217 CHANG, JOSEPHIN
D00386 DAVIES, DEREK
D01474 DE VERNEIL, AND
G01488 GALLINER, PETER
G00518 GERBNER, GEORGE
G00523 GOLDING, PETER
G00532 GRIMES, PAUL
H00542 HAISMAN, STEPHE
H00552 HARIHARAN, A.
H00569 HESTER, AL
H01589 HILL, I. WILLIA
H00582 HORNIK, ROBERT
17H01979 HSIEH, JAN-SHIH
I00608 INGRAM, DEREK
K00672 KIHSS, PETER
L01423 LEE KUAN YEW
L00724 LENT, JOHN A.
M00805 MERRILL, JOHN C
M00806 MERRILL, JOHN C
M01597 MOWLANA, HAMID
N01045 NAM, SUNWOO
N00833 NARAYAN, S. V.
P00900 PEIRIS, DENZIL
P00887 PILLAI, M. G. G
R00917 RAO, Y. V. LAKS
R02564 RUBEN, BRENT, E
R01624 RUBIN, BARRY
S01050 SUSSMAN, LEONAR
T01069 THAYER, NATHANI
U01158 UNESCO
04W01909 WANG HUNG CHUN
W01173 WOOLLACOTT, MAR
W01172 WOOLLACOTT, MAR

SURVEY

06C01960 CHU CH'UAN-YU
12F01698 FENG AI-CHUN [E
K00676 KING, VINCENT V
L00735 LIBRARY OF CONG
N00832 NAFZIGER, RALPH
P02658 PYE, LUCIAN, ED
R01365 RAFI-ZADEH, HAS
07S01903 SUNG SHAN LIANG
13Y01919 YANG HSIA YUNG

LANGUAGE

B02609 BA THEIN, U
W02586 WAIZZA, MAUNG

LITERATURE

B02609 BA THEIN, U

SOCIOLOGY, ANTHROPO

M00830 MYO NYUNT, MAUN

CAMBODIA

FOREIGN CORRESPONE

A01261 ARNETT, PETER
A02503 ASIAWEEK
D00398 DAVIS, NEIL
G02522 GRAY, DENIS
U01104 UPI REPORTER

CONTROL OF PRESS

B00145 BACZYNSKYJ, BOR

PROPAGANDA

F01646 FOSTER, DOUGLAS
N01970 NATIONS, RICHAR

RESEARCH

N01246 NUNN, G. RAYMON

SERIALS

H01997 HOC, KIM CHHEAN

FLOW/AGENCY

G02522 GRAY, DENIS
U01104 UPI REPORTER

DESCRIPTION

F01646 FOSTER, DOUGLAS
H01997 HOC, KIM CHHEAN
U01658 UNITED STATES I

PRINTING

H01810 HUNTER, DARD

CHINA

P02331 POWELL, JOHN W.
P02331 POWELL, JOHN W.

FOREIGN CORRESPOND

A01745 ALCOTT, CAROLL
A01426 AMERASIA
A01425 AMERASIA
A01424 AMERASIA
A00124 AP LOG
A00122 AP LOG
A02501 AP LOG
A01746 AP WORLD, THE
B01279 BOCCARDI, LOUIS
B00176 BONAVIA, DAVID
B00179 BONAVIA, DAVID
B00178 BONAVIA, DAVID
B00177 BONAVIA, DAVID
B02555 BONAVIA, DAVID
B00180 BOOKER, EDNA LE
C01372 CASEY, JOHN H.
C01998 CHANCE, NORMAN,
C01933 CHINA CRITIC, T
C00265 CHINA NEWS ANAL
C01788 CHRISTIANSEN, S
C02510 CRABBE, ROBERT
C01796 CROW, CARL
C01797 CROW, CARL
D00388 DAVIES, DEREK
D02512 DAWSON, ALAN
D00403 DIAL, ROGER L.
E02221 EDITOR & PUBLIS
E01401 EDITOR & PUBLIS
E00432 ENGLISH, JOHN W
F00475 FAR EASTERN ECO
F01486 FOREIGN CORRESP
F02223 FRASER, JOHN
F02520 FREE CHINA WEEK
F02521 FREE CHINA WEEK
F02518 FREE CHINA WEEK
F00502 FREE CHINA WEEK
G01322 GREEN, O. M. [O
H01494 HALBERSTAM, DAV
H01497 HAUSER, ERNEST
H02523 HILL, I. WILLIA
H02300 HOBEN, LINDSAY
H00578 HOHENBERG, JOHN
H01817 HUNTER, EDWARD
I00632 ISAACS, HAROLD
I00634 ISAACS, NORMAN
K00660 KARNOW, STANLEY
K01825 KEHL, FRANK
K00685 KURODA, KAZUO
L01830 LATTIMORE, OWEN
L00736 LIEBERMAN, HENR
L01580 LINDT, A. R.
L00744 LIU, ALAN P. L.
L01842 LIVING AGE
L00754 LO HUI-MIN, EDI
M00789 MARTIN, ROBERT
M00796 MC CABE, ROBERT
M01409 MORITZ, FREDERI
M00827 MUNRO, ROSS H.
N02706 NEW CHINA, THE
N02316 NOEL, FRANK
O01855 OESTREICHER, J.

S01027 STANFORD U. CHI
S01025 STANFORD U. CHI
S01026 STANFORD U. CHI
07S01902 SUNG CH'UAN YU
T01951 T'ANG LEANG-LI
T02661 THACKREY, T. O.
T01074 TIME
T01301 TIMES, THE [LON
T01297 TIMES, THE [LON
T01284 TIMES, THE [LON
02T02025 TING, WANG, EDI
T01083 TING, LEE-HSIA
U01108 UPI REPORTER
U01107 UPI REPORTER
V02804 VIENET, RENE
W02322 WANG SEE-ZEE
W02146 WANG, Y. C.
W01668 WANG, F.T.
W02323 WHANG, PAUL K.
W01168 WOODBRIDGE, ISE
W01917 WOODHEAD, HENRY
W01171 WOOLLACOTT, MAR
W01183 WU, YUAN-LI
Y01258 YAO, RAYMOND
Y02324 YOUR READER
03Y01196 YU CH'ANG-CH'IN
Y02667 YUAN, L. Z.
T02335 TAO WEI-LIEN

PROPAGANDA

A01744 ABEND, HALLETT
A01980 AFRO-ASIAN JOUR
A01780 AMERASIA
B02258 BONAVIA, DAVID
B01689 BRILLER, BERT
B00192 BROMAN, BARRY M
B00199 BURNS, JOHN
B00203 BURNS, JOHN
B00206 BUTTERFIELD, FO
C01998 CHANCE, NORMAN,
C02611 CHANG P'ENG-YUA
14C01444 CHAO, THOMAS MI
C02630 CHEN, HERMIA
C00241 CHENG CHU-YUAN
C00243 CHENG, PHILIP H
C01939 CHINA CRITIC, T
C00258 CHINA NEWS ANAL
C00262 CHINA NEWS ANAL
C01956 CHINESE NATION,
C01959 CHINESE NATION,
C01457 CHU, JAMES C. Y
C00343 CHU, GODWIN C.
C01123 COCKBURN, ALEXA
C00366 CURRENT SCENE
D00408 DIZARD, WILSON
E00420 ECO, UNBERTO
F00475 FAR EASTERN ECO
F01483 FAR EASTERN ECO
F01802 FAR EASTERN REV
F02521 FREE CHINA WEEK
H02298 HARBIN CORRESPO
H01497 HAUSER, ERNEST
H00557 HAYES, HAROLD B
H02613 HAZAMA, NAOKI
H00601 HUGHES, JOHN

I01819 ISHIBASHI, TANZ
J01821 J., J. A.
06J02638 JEN, RICHARD
L01517 LASKER, BRUNO A
L01832 LEE, EDWARD BIN
L02599 LI YU-NING
L01590 LIEBERTHAL, KEN
08L00739 LIN YUTANG
L01840 LITERARY DIGEST
L01841 LITERARY DIGEST
L00745 LIU, ALAN P. L.
L00741 LIU, ALAN PING-
L02616 LUNG CHUNG
M02311 MENG, C. Y. W.
M01850 MOORE, HARRIET
M00821 MORITZ, FREDERI
M02620 MURTHY, P. A. N
N02694 NEW CHINA, THE
N02700 NEW CHINA, THE
O00863 OLIPHANT, C. A.
P00872 PARKER, ALVIN P
P01609 PEOPLE'S TRIBUN
P01610 PEOPLE'S TRIBUN
P02332 PRESCOTT, C. LA
P00904 PROPAGANDA ANAL
R01880 REA, GEORGE BRO
R01881 RICH, RAYMOND T
R01885 RUSSELL, J. T.
S00955 SCHUMAN, JULIAN
S00959 SERDT, MICHEL
S01889 SHIEH, MILTON J
S02334 SIMMONS, WALTER
S01027 STANFORD U. CHI
S01025 STANFORD U. CHI
S01026 STANFORD U. CHI
T02321 TIENTSIN CORRES
T01089 TOROPTSEV, S.
T02628 TS'AO, IGNATIUS
W01417 WANG, GEORGE K.
Y01189 YAO, IGNATIUS P
Y01190 YATES, RONALD
Y01202 YU, FREDERICK T
Z02810 ZEITUNGSWISSENS

DEVELOPMENT

C01569 CHENG HSI CHANG
C00242 CHENG HUAN
15C02734 CHIEH FU
C00344 CHU, GODWIN
C00367 CURRENT SCENE
H00584 HOWSE, HUGH
K02573 KLATT, WERNER,
L00741 LIU, ALAN PING-
L00742 LIU, ALAN P. L.
L01157 LIU, ALAN P. L.
M01346 MILLARD, THOMAS
M00821 MORITZ, FREDERI
Q02203 QUIGLEY, HAROLD
S02208 SHECKLEN, GEORG
Y02666 YU, FREDERICK T
N02673 NEW CHINA, THE

RESEARCH

B00692 BENNETT, ADRIAN

B01333 BENNETT, ADRIAN
B00156 BENNETT, ADRIAN
B00155 BENNETT, ADRIAN
B00190 BRITTON, ROSWEL
C00208 CAMERON, W. H.
11C02059 CH'EN CHI-YING
16C00251 CH'IEN CH'I-CH'
C02611 CHANG P'ENG-YUA
11C00221 CHANG MING-FANG
07C01691 CHANG CHING LU
14C00224 CHAO, THOMAS MI
14C01443 CHAO, MIN-HENG
C01748 CHENG, JASON (J
15C00248 CHIANG SHEN-WU
09C01692 CHIANG KUEI-LIN
C02811 CHIEN, HSUIN YU
C02568 CHINA PRESS, TH
06C02738 CHU CHUAN-YU
06C01237 CHU CHUANG-YU
06C02030 CHU CH'UAN-YU
C00363 COULING, SAMUEL
C02612 COX, THOMAS R.
C01989 CROW, CARL
D01473 DAVIES, DEREK
D00272 DURDIN, F. T.
E01476 ELDERLY CHINA H
F02558 FAIRBANK, JOHN
12F00485 FENG AI-CHUN [E
12F00489 FENG TZU-YU
F01340 FISHER, W. E. J
G00522 GILES, HERBERT
H02613 HAZAMA, NAOKI
H02225 HSIAO, I-WEN
07H02743 HSING SUNG-WEN
H02104 HSING CHENG YUA
09H02798 HU SHIH
12H00598 HUANG T'IEN-P'E
H00597 HUANG, PAUL T.
09H00602 HUNG KUEI-CHI
01I00605 I CHIH [PSEUD.]
01I00606 I CHIH [PSEUD]
I02058 INLAND PRINTER,
I02615 ISHIJIMA, NORIY
J01343 JEN, RICHARD L.
10K00653 KAO LIANG-TSO
K01344 KAO, Y.
K02228 KAO, IRVING KE-
K00680 KO KUNG-CHEN
L00691 LANNING, GEORGE
L01831 LAU WEI-SAN
L01577 LAUFER, BERTHOL
07L00731 LI LUNG-MU
L00728 LIANG, HUBERT S
08L02748 LIN YU-LAN
08L02526 LIN YUAN-CH'I
L02649 LIU, ALAN P. L.
L00754 LO HUI-MIN, EDI
L02236 LU, DAVID CHI-H
M01325 MA YIN-LIANG
M00782 MALCOLM, ELIZAB
M02808 MAYER, NORBERT
M00795 MAYERS, WILLIAM
M01022 MICHENER, CARRO
M01593 MOORAD, GEORGE
N02645 NEW CHINA, THE
N02698 NEW CHINA, THE
03O02602 ONO, HIDEO
15P02121 P'AN TZU-HSIN

05P02791 PAO MING-SHU
P02123 PAO-HSUEH CHI-K
P00878 PATTERSON, DON
P00879 PEARL, CYRIL
P02622 PIROVANO-WANG,
P01360 POWELL, JOHN BE
11S00961 SHANG YUEH-HENG
08S00962 SHAO LI-TZU
S00968 SHEWMAKER, KENNI
S01889 SHIEH, MILTON J
S01632 SHUN, YU-HSIU,
15S02753 SOU TUN
10S02754 SUN JU-LING
07S02755 SUNG CHIN
17T02756 TAI FENG
19T02757 TAN JU-CHIEN
T01287 TIMES, THE [LON
T01289 TIMES, THE [LON
T01254 TIMPERLEY, H. J
02T01082 TING SHU-CH'I
13T02141 TONG HOLLINGTON
T02626 TOZER, WARREN W
12T01095 TSENG HSU-PAI,
T02662 TSENG, H. P.
04W01127 WANG CHUNG
W01136 WANG, Y. P.
W02145 WANG, BETTY SIA
W02245 WANG, PAUL HUNG
W01676 WILLIAMS, FREDE
W01350 WONG, HIN
W01422 WOODBRIDGE, S.
Y02149 YEH, WEN-HSING
16Y02786 YEN HSIN-HENG
Y02248 YIN, SHERMAN KU
12Y02788 YU HSIEH-LUN
Y02336 YU WAH
10Y01205 YUAN CH'ANG-CH'

DESCRIPTION

A01426 AMERASIA
A01983 AMERICAN REVIEW
A01982 AMERICAN REVIEW
06A01782 AN I
A00122 AP LOG
A02156 ARLINGTON, L. C
B02077 BANNING, WILLIA
B00149 BAROOAH, RENEE
B02288 BARUNG, E. U.
B00151 BEAGARIE, MAX
B02161 BERGER, VIRGIL
B00165 BERNSTEIN, STAN
B01783 BETTS, T. J.
B00738 BIGGERSTAFF, KN
B01279 BOCCARDI, LOUIS
B00176 BONAVIA, DAVID
B00179 BONAVIA, DAVID
B00177 BONAVIA, DAVID
B00178 BONAVIA, DAVID
B02258 BONAVIA, DAVID
B02554 BONAVIA, DAVID
B00180 BOOKER, EDNA LE
B01317 BOX, ERNEST
B00191 BRITTON, ROSWEL
B00189 BRITTON, ROSWEL
B00203 BURNS, JOHN
B00202 BURNS, JOHN

C00317 CHINESE REPOSIT
C00316 CHINESE REPOSIT
C00315 CHINESE REPOSIT
C00314 CHINESE REPOSIT
C00313 CHINESE REPOSIT
C00312 CHINESE REPOSIT
C00311 CHINESE REPOSIT
C00310 CHINESE REPOSIT
C00308 CHINESE REPOSIT
C00304 CHINESE REPOSIT
C00303 CHINESE REPOSIT
C00302 CHINESE REPOSIT
C00307 CHINESE REPOSIT
C00306 CHINESE REPOSIT
C00305 CHINESE REPOSIT
C00301 CHINESE REPOSIT
C00298 CHINESE REPOSIT
C00300 CHINESE REPOSIT
C00299 CHINESE REPOSIT
C00290 CHINESE REPOSIT
C00289 CHINESE REPOSIT
C00288 CHINESE REPOSIT
C00297 CHINESE REPOSIT
C00294 CHINESE REPOSIT
C00293 CHINESE REPOSIT
C00292 CHINESE REPOSIT
C01779 CHOU, ERIC
06C01960 CHU CH'UAN-YU
C02273 CHU, GODWIN C.,
C01457 CHU, JAMES C. Y
C00343 CHU, GODWIN C.
C01789 CHU, B. F.
06C00348 CHUNG-CH'UNG, P
04C02086 CHUNG-KUO CH'IN
04C02591 CHUNG-KUO WEN H
C01791 CLAYTON, CHARLE
C00351 COLQUHOUN, ARCH
C01813 COLQUHOUN, ARCH
C01816 COLQUHOUN, ARCH
C00361 CORNABY, W. ART
C01695 CORRESPONDENT I
C01961 CORRESPONDENT,
C01793 COVENTRY-ISLAND
C02509 CRABBE, ROBERT
C01797 CROW, CARL
C01796 CROW, CARL
C01794 CROW, CARL
C01989 CROW, CARL
C01464 CURRENT SCENE
C01463 CURRENT SCENE
C01462 CURRENT SCENE
C01461 CURRENT SCENE
C01466 CURRENT SCENE
C01467 CURRENT SCENE
C00365 CURRENT SCENE
C00366 CURRENT SCENE
C00369 CURRENT SCENE
C00368 CURRENT SCENE
C01468 CURRENT SCENE
C01469 CURRENT SCENE
C01390 CURZON, GEORGE
D00373 DARROCH, J.
D00390 DAVIES, DEREK
C00400 DEKA [PSEUD.?]
D02716 DELYUSIN, L.
D02182 DIGEST OF THE S
D02181 DIGEST OF THE S
D02183 DIGEST OF THE S

D02186 DIGEST OF THE S
D02179 DIGEST OF THE S
D01238 DONALD, W. H.
D00411 DONOVAN, JOHN P
D02097 DUDMAN, RICHARD
D00415 DUDMAN, RICHARD
D00272 DURDIN, F. T.
E00420 ECO, UNBERTO
E00421 EDELSTEIN, ALEX
E00426 EDITOR & PUBLIS
E02516 EDITOR & PUBLIS
E00425 EDITOR & PUBLIS
E00427 EDITOR & PUBLIS
F01801 FAIRPLAY
F02294 FALCONER, ALUN
F02295 FANG FU-AN
04F02055 FANG PAI
F02517 FANTANANGE, STE
F01990 FAR EASTERN INF
F01803 FAR EASTERN REV
F01340 FISHER, W. E. J
F01486 FOREIGN CORRESP
F02518 FREE CHINA WEEK
F02520 FREE CHINA WEEK
F02521 FREE CHINA WEEK
F00505 FREEDOM OF INFO
F02056 FULBRIGHT, NEWT
G01742 GOULD, RANDALL
G01492 GOULD, RANDALL
G01954 GOULD, RANDALL
G01277 GOULD, RANDALL
G02188 GOULD, RANDALL
G01493 GRIGGS, (DAVID)
H01341 HAMMOND, JAMES
07H02741 HO TSANG-HSU
H02300 HOBEN, LINDSAY
H01807 HONG KONG DAILY
H01808 HONG KONG DAILY
H00584 HOWSE, HUGH
H02224 HSI, KUNG K'AI
H02192 HSIAO CHI'EN
H00589 HSIEH, ALICE LA
07H02743 HSING SUNG-WEN
H02103 HSING CHENG YUA
H02575 HSU HSU
H01393 HSU CHAO-YUNG
H00585 HSU HSU
10H01572 HSU, PAO-HUANG
H00586 HSU, JABIN
09H00596 HU TAO-CHING
09H00587 HU SHIH
09H01573 HU TAO-CHING
H02301 HU CHENG
09H01574 HU TAO-CHING
09H01503 HUNG, FREDERICK
H02637 HWANG, JOHN C.
I01818 INDEPENDENT, TH
I02032 INLAND PRINTER,
I02039 INLAND PRINTER,
I02041 INLAND PRINTER,
I02062 INLAND PRINTER,
I02034 INLAND PRINTER,
I02038 INLAND PRINTER,
I02042 INLAND PRINTER,
I01819 ISHIBASHI, TANZ.
I02728 ISHII, AKIRA
J01821 J., J. A.
J02194 JEE, LUTHER M.

CROSS CULTURAL

A00112 ALLEN, T. HARRE
B02555 BONAVIA, DAVID
B01690 BURTON, WILBUR
C01945 CHINA CRITIC, T
C02612 COX, THOMAS R.
F02223 FRASER, JOHN
09H01503 HUNG, FREDERICK
M02640 MARTIN, DUDLEY
P01971 PEIPING CHRONIC
P01876 PEYTON-GRIFFIN,
R01885 RUSSELL, J. T.
T01912 TREVELYAN G. M.

EDUCATION

C00487 CHANG CHI-LUAN
C01569 CHENG HSI CHANG
C01748 CHENG, JASON (J
C01923 CHINA CRITIC, T
C01931 CHINA CRITIC, T
C00262 CHINA NEWS ANAL
D02176 DIGEST OF THE S
D02180 DIGEST OF THE S
E02515 EDITOR & PUBLIS
E02668 EDITOR & PUBLIS
E01800 EDITOR & PUBLIS
F00461 FAR EASTERN ECO
H02193 HU LIN
L01835 LIANG, HUBERT S
L01399 LIANG, HUBERT S
15L02176 LIU HOH-HSUAN A
08L01705 LU LIEH
M02007 MA, T. C., EDIT
M01851 MORRIS, JOHN R.
M02194 MOY, E. K.
N01598 NASH, VERNON
N02703 NEW CHINA, THE
N02699 NEW CHINA, THE
N02684 NEW CHINA, THE
02P00905 PU SHAO-FU
R02285 REYNOLDS, JACK
S01886 SCHOOL AND SOCI
S01639 SUGIMURA, K.
T01642 TANG, JANE AND
W01908 WANG, CHARLES C
W01425 WILLIAMS, WALTE
W01737 WONG, V. L.

PRINTING

B02610 BARNETT, SUZANN
B01672 BOJESEN, C. C.
B01437 BRITTON, ROSWEL
11C02259 CH'EN KUO-CH'IN
C01363 CHANG, RAYMOND
C00252 CHIN, CHIEN
C01787 CHINA JOURNAL,
C00260 CHINA NEWS ANAL
C01694 CHINA PICTORIAL
C00278 CHINESE REPOSIT
C00281 CHINESE REPOSIT
C00287 CHINESE REPOSIT
C00309 CHINESE REPOSIT
C00288 CHINESE REPOSIT

C00291 CHINESE REPOSIT
C00363 COULING, SAMUEL
C00365 CURRENT SCENE
D01470 DALAND, JUDSON
D02053 DAVIS, JOHN K.
D01280 DILKE, CHARLES
E01799 EDKINS, J.
F01485 FLUG, K. K.
F00501 FREE CHINA WEEK
G00528 GOODRICH, L. CA
G00529 GOODRICH, L. CA
G00527 GOODRICH, L. CA
H00573 HIRTH, F.
H00603 HUNTER, WILLIAM
H01811 HUNTER, DARD
H01812 HUNTER, DARD
I02032 INLAND PRINTER,
I02042 INLAND PRINTER,
I02040 INLAND PRINTER,
I02034 INLAND PRINTER,
I02036 INLAND PRINTER,
L01577 LAUFER, BERTHOL
L02304 LEE, B. Y.
L01019 LOWENTHAL, RUDO
M00775 MACFARQUHAR, RO
M01281 MAULE, GEORGE B
M02043 MURDOCK, VICTOR
O01710 ORIENTAL AFFAIR
P01713 PARKER, E. H.
P01606 PEAKE, CYRUS
P01607 PEAKE, CYRUS H.
S01630 SHIH, MEI-CHING
S01632 SHUN, YU-HSIU,
T01056 TANG, THOMAS
T01294 TIMES, THE [LON
T01096 TSIEN TSUEN-HSU
03T02142 TZU WU
U01103 UNESCO COURIER
W01177 WU, KUANG-CHING
W02027 WU, KUANG-CH'IN
W01179 WU, KUANG-CHING
W01178 WU, KUANG-CHING

PUBLISHING

09A00119 ANG, PSEUD.
B02610 BARNETT, SUZANN
B00149 BAROOAH, RENEE
07C02193 CHANG CHING-LU
07C02192 CHANG CHING-LU
C02593 CHANG CHING-LU
C02327 CHANG, Y. L.
C00334 CHINA NEWS ANAL
C00270 CHINA NEWS ANAL
C00269 CHINA NEWS ANAL
C00261 CHINA NEWS ANAL
C00260 CHINA NEWS ANAL
C00278 CHINESE REPOSIT
C00363 COULING, SAMUEL
C01465 CURRENT SCENE
09F00438 FAN WEI, ET AL.
F00501 FREE CHINA WEEK
K01828 KUNAU, JOHN A.
K02303 KUNG MIN-CHUNG
M02620 MURTHY, P. A. N
P02532 POWELL, JOHN B.
12S00974 SHU HSIN-CH'ENG

S01027 STANFORD U. CHI
S01026 STANFORD U. CHI
S01025 STANFORD U. CHI
07S01641 SUNG I-CHUNG
T01056 TANG, THOMAS
W02547 WALTERS, RAY
04W01138 WANG YUN-WU
08W01182 WU T'IEH-SHENG
07W01679 WU, K. T.

LANGUAGE

B02553 BONAVIA, DAVID
B02215 BUTTERFIELD, FO
C02337 CHINA NEWS ANAL
C00330 CHOU, NELSON
D02185 DIGEST OF THE S
D02183 DIGEST OF THE S
F01994 FREE CHINA WEEK
09H02798 HU SHIH
09H02797 HU SHIH
07L02747 LI TIEN-YI
08L01400 LIN YU-TANG
L00749 LIU SHIH-HONG
M00791 MATEER, ADA HAV
N02691 NEW CHINA, THE
N02681 NEW CHINA, THE
S00948 SANDERS, ALAN
S02541 STRANAHAN, SUSAI

OTHER JOURNALISM

A01980 AFRO-ASIAN JOUR
B02288 BARUNG, E. U.
B00192 BROMAN, BARRY M
B02326 BRYAN, R. J., J
C02289 C., G. F.
C02291 CHEN, PAUL
C02168 CHEN, KINGLU S.
09C02091 CHENG CHIH
07C01750 CHIN HSIANG LIN
C02265 CHINA PRESS, THI
C00326 CHINESE ECONOMI'
06C02738 CHU CHUAN-YU
C02511 CRANZ, GALEN
C01989 CROW, CARL
C01460 CROW, CARL
C01795 CROW, CARL
D02181 DIGEST OF THE S
F02295 FANG FU-AN
F01803 FAR EASTERN REV
G01489 GILES, LIONEL
G01570 GROFF, SAMUEL
H02224 HSI, KUNG K'AI
H02637 HWANG, JOHN C.
06J01506 JEN CHUNG
06J02638 JEN, RICHARD
K01515 KULKARNI, V. G.
K02108 KUO-WEN CHOU-PA
L02563 LEE, MARY
L00727 LEWIS, JOHN WIL
L02648 LING, C. P.
L02308 LU, DAVID CHI-H
M00774 MACFARQUHAR, RO
M01591 MEI CHI-CHU
M00810 MITCHELL, JOHN

M02750 MURRAY, J. EDWAI
N02707 NEW CHINA, THE
N02677 NEW CHINA, THE
N02675 NEW CHINA, THE
P02330 POWELL, J. B.
P02044 PYE, LUCIAN W.
S02446 SANGER, J. W.
S02207 SHANGHAI PRESS
05S01890 SHIH YUNG KUEI
S00987 SOLOMON, RICHAR
S01897 STEVENS, FREDER
S02045 STEVENSON, H. L
S02021 STEVENSON, H. L
S02243 STRAND, DAVID
07S01902 SUNG CH'UAN YU
T01336 TARANTINO, ANT
W02145 WANG, BETTY SIA
16Y02786 YEN HSIN-HENG
Y02152 YU, FREDERICK T
Y01920 YU, PING-KUEN
Y02151 YU, FREDERICK T
Y02666 YU, FREDERICK T
Y02325 YUN, ART

LITERATURE

C00256 CHINA NEWS ANAL
C00255 CHINA NEWS ANAL
C00258 CHINA NEWS ANAL
C00261 CHINA NEWS ANAL
C00269 CHINA NEWS ANAL
C00334 CHINA NEWS ANAL
C00294 CHINESE REPOSIT
C01466 CURRENT SCENE
L00691 LANNING, GEORGE
08L01524 LIN YUTANG
W02547 WALTERS, RAY

POLITICAL SCIENCE

C00343 CHU, GODWIN C.
C00344 CHU, GODWIN
D00403 DIAL, ROGER L.
H00589 HSIEH, ALICE LA
L00727 LEWIS, JOHN WIL
L00734 LIAO, KUAN-SHEN
L01590 LIEBERTHAL, KEN
L00745 LIU, ALAN P. L.
L00744 LIU, ALAN P. L.
S00956 SCHWARZ, HENRY

SOCIOLOGY, ANTHRO

M00810 MITCHELL, JOHN

OTHER NON-JOURNAL

C02630 CHEN, HERMIA
C00344 CHU, GODWIN
F00461 FAR EASTERN ECO
M02750 MURRAY, J. EDWA
O00862 OKSENBERG, MICH
S00951 SCHECTER, JERRO
S00987 SOLOMON, RICHAR

T01336 TARANTINO, ANT
T01283 TIMES, THE [LON
P02331 POWELL, JOHN W.

EAST ASIA
H02570 HOARE, J. E.
H02570 HOARE, J. E.
H02570 HOARE, J. E.

FOREIGN CORRESPOND

A01745 ALCOTT, CAROLL
B00152 BEECH, KEYES
B00153 BEECH, KEYES
B00154 BEECH, KEYES
B02160 BEECH, KEYES
D00385 DAVIES, DEREK
D02293 DEANE, HUGH
D02292 DEANE, HUGH
F00656 FORBIS, WILLIAM
H00544 HALLORAN, RICHA
H01497 HAUSER, ERNEST
H00575 HOBERECHT, EARN
H01501 HUGHES, RICHARD
H01817 HUNTER, EDWARD
K01826 KENNEDY, M. D.
K02003 KOREA REVIEW
K00685 KURODA, KAZUO
L01842 LIVING AGE
M02528 MORRIS, JOHN R.
N02316 NOEL, FRANK
O01709 OAKES, VANYA
P01874 PARKER, WILLIAM
S01896 STEIN, GUNTHER
T02211 TALBERT, ANSEL
W01161 WILSON, QUINTUS
Y01195 YOSHIDA, KENSEI

CONTROL OF PRESS

C02081 CELESTIAL EMPIRI
C02216 CHANG, YONG
C01944 CHINA CRITIC, TI
C01927 CHINA CRITIC, TI
C01942 CHINA CRITIC, TI
C01959 CHINESE NATION,
C02715 COUGHLIN, WILLI
D02292 DEANE, HUGH
D02293 DEANE, HUGH
F00458 FAR EASTERN ECO
F01992 FAR EASTERN INF
H00544 HALLORAN, RICHA
H01817 HUNTER, EDWARD
K00681 KOJIMA, HARUKO
K02001 KOREA JOURNAL
L01842 LIVING AGE
M01592 MIN BYONG-GI
M02618 MIYOSHI, OSAMU
M01594 MORRI, YASOTARO
N01046 NAM, SUNWOO
N01650 NAM, SUNWOO
N02559 NAM, SUNWOO
N01044 NAM, SUNWOO

N02712 NEW CHINA, THE
N02710 NEW CHINA, THE
N02795 NEW CHINA, THE
N02700 NEW CHINA, THE
O01712 ORIENTAL AFFAIR
R02317 REVIEW'S CORRES
T02572 TETERS, BARBARA
04W02762 WANG JUI-CHENG
W01917 WOODHEAD, HENRY
Y01195 YOSHIDA, KENSEI
Y01682 YOUNG, A. MORGA
Y01739 YOUNG, A. MORGA
Y01740 YUI, MASASHI

PROPAGANDA

A01780 AMERASIA
B01689 BRILLER, BERT
C01939 CHINA CRITIC, T
C01956 CHINESE NATION,
C01959 CHINESE NATION,
F01802 FAR EASTERN REV
H01497 HAUSER, ERNEST
H02613 HAZAMA, NAOKI
I01819 ISHIBASHI, TANZ
J01821 J., J. A.
L01517 LASKER, BRUNO A
M01708 MENEFEE, SELDEN
M01850 MOORE, HARRIET
M01594 MORRI, YASOTARO
N02700 NEW CHINA, THE
P01609 PEOPLE'S TRIBUN
P00904 PROPAGANDA ANAL
R01880 REA, GEORGE BRO
R01685 RUSSELL, J. T.
T02321 TIENTSIN CORRES

DEVELOPMENT

C01455 CHONG YUN-MU
G00508 GALLAGHER, CHAR
G00511 GARVER, RICHARD
H01495 HAN KI-UK
H02614 HUFFMAN, JAMES
M01592 MIN BYONG-GI
O01857 OH JIN-KWAN

FLOW/AGENCY

A00111 ALLEN, RILEY .
C01939 CHINA CRITIC, T
C01959 CHINESE NATION,
C01956 CHINESE NATION,
F01992 FAR EASTERN INF
I02642 IWANAGA, Y.
M02237 MOON, EUGENE UI
N01045 NAM, SUNWOO
N02712 NEW CHINA, THE
N02709 NEW CHINA, THE
W01161 WILSON, QUINTUS

JOURNALISM HISTORY

A01745 ALCOTT, CAROLL

EDUCATION

A02450 ASIAN PRINTER,
K01511 KANG HUI-SU
K02004 KOREA REVIEW
L01518 LEE SANG-HI
P01605 PARRISH, FRED
S01639 SUGIMURA, K.

PRINTING

A02450 ASIAN PRINTER,
A02076 ASIAN PRINTER,
D01470 DALAND, JUDSON
G00528 GOODRICH, L. CA
H01811 HUNTER, DARD
K02641 KASAGI, MASAAKI
P01607 PEAKE, CYRUS H.
P01714 PHOENIX, THE
S02447 SAITO, M.
T02026 TROLLOPE, M. N.
W02050 WERNER, JOHN R.

OTHER JOURNALISM

A02802 ASIAWEEK
C02079 CELESTIAL EMPIR
F01803 FAR EASTERN REV
K02029 KOREA REVIEW
K02004 KOREA REVIEW
M01844 MALCOLM, ANDREW
O01856 OGATA, TAKETORA
O01870 ORIENTAL ECONOM
12F01873 PANG CHI-SHIN
S02805 SAM-O, KIM
S02446 SANGER, J. W.
S02136 STIER, W. RUDOL
W01915 WILLIAMSON, LEN

EUROPE

FOREIGN CORRESPOND

Y01977 YANG, G. K.

CONTROL OF PRESS

I00607 INDOCHINA SOLID
L02306 LI CHUNG-FA

PROPAGANDA

H00557 HAYES, HAROLD B
H02299 HENDRICK, J.
I00607 INDOCHINA SOLID

DESCRIPTION

I00607 INDOCHINA SOLID

R01972 RASMUSSEN, O. D
R01973 RASMUSSEN, O. D

PRINTING

C00291 CHINESE REPOSIT
C00287 CHINESE REPOSIT

GENERAL HISTORY

P00890 PLUVIER, J. M.

PROPAGANDA

L02616 LUNG CHUNG
N02673 NEW CHINA, THE

DESCRIPTION

L02616 LUNG CHUNG

BIOGRAPHY

N02673 NEW CHINA, THE

HONG KONG

FOREIGN CORRESPOND

A00124 AP LOG
A00122 AP LOG
D02171 DATELINE LOPC,
D00388 DAVIES, DEREK
E01477 ELEGANT, ROBERT
E00432 ENGLISH, JOHN W
K00660 KARNOW, STANLEY
O02198 ORSHEFSKY, MILT
P02603 PENNELL, WILFRE
P02604 PENNELL, WILFRE

CONTROL OF PRESS

C00219 CHANG KUO-SIN
D00388 DAVIES, DEREK
E00432 ENGLISH, JOHN W
Y01258 YAO, RAYMOND
Y01255 YAO, RAYMOND

DEVELOPMENT

B01436 BORSUK, RICHARD
M00811 MITCHELL, ROBER

RESEARCH

C02261 CHENG, PAUL P.

SOCIOLOGY, ANTHRO

M00811 MITCHELL, ROBER

OTHER NON-JOURNAL

C00356 COMMUNICATION A
F00461 FAR EASTERN ECO
F00496 FOX, RICHARD W.

INDONESIA

FOREIGN CORRESPOND

S01036 STOCKWIN, HARVE

CONTROL OF PRESS

A02072 AFRO-ASIAN JOUR
A01984 ANWAR, ROSIHAN
B01814 BERITA HARIAN
D00384 DAVIES, DEREK A
D02220 DEVOSS, DAVID
G00525 GOLDSTONE, ANTH
I00627 IPI REPORT
J00698 JENKINS, DAVID
J00697 JENKINS, DAVID
J01965 JENKINS, DAVID
J01964 JENKINS, DAVID
J01966 JENKINS, DAVID
K01824 KAMM, HENRY
L00764 LUBIS, MOCHTAR
M02113 MARTONO
S00985 SMITH, EDWARD C
S00992 SOUTHERLAND, DA
S00993 SOUTHERLAND, DA
W01144 WEINER, ALAN

PROPAGANDA

L02110 LINANG, W.

DEVELOPMENT

A02500 AHMAT, ADAM
A00118 ANDELMAN, DAVID
E00419 EAPEN, K. E.
K00683 KROEF, JUSTUS M
U01112 UTOMO, JAKOB
W01677 WORD, THE [BOMB

RESEARCH

K00658 KATALOGUS SURAT
K00670 KHOUW GIOK PO [
N01244 NUNN, G. RAYMON
P00869 PAGET, ROGER K.
P02623 PRAKOSO, MASTIN
T02760 THUNG, YVONNE A

FLOW/AGENCY

E00418 EAPEN, K. E.

JOURNALISM HISTORY

A02500 AHMAT, ADAM
C00208 CAMERON, W. H.
C02635 CRAWFORD, ROBER
D01017 DEKKER, DOUWES
F00436 FABER, G. H. VO
I02106 INGLESON, JOHN
L00755 LOON, G. VAN
S01048 SURYADINATA, LE
T02659 TAN PENG SIEW
W02565 WRIGHT, ARNOLD,
W01184 WURTZBURG, C. E

DESCRIPTION

A00654 ADINEGORO, DJAM
A02072 AFRO-ASIAN JOUR
A00104 AGASSI, JUDITH
A00118 ANDELMAN, DAVID
A01310 ANETA
A02074 ASIAN-AFRICAN J
C00208 CAMERON, W. H.
C00213 CHANDRA, A. N.
17C02739 CHUNG KWANG-HSI
C00364 CRAWFORD, ROBER
C02635 CRAWFORD, ROBER
D01017 DEKKER, DOUWES
D02220 DEVOSS, DAVID
F00436 FABER, G. H. VO
G01334 GARIS BESAR PER
H00555 HASIBUAN, ADAHA
H00559 HAYWARD, HENRY
H00558 HAYWARD, HENRY
06H02792 HSING SUNG-WEN
J00641 JENKINS, DAVID
J02815 JENKINS, DAVID
J00696 JENKINS, DAVID
K00667 KERTAPATI, TON
K00683 KROEF, JUSTUS M
L00686 LACEY, JOSEPH
L00755 LOON, G. VAN
L01324 LUBIS, MOCHTAR
L00762 LUBIS, MOCHTAR
M00799 MC ELHENY, VICT
M00813 MOHAMAD, GOENAW
M02012 MOTT, JOHN R.,
N01268 NIEUWENHUIS, J.
N01243 NIO, JOE LAN
O00858 OETAMA, JACOB
S00993 SOUTHERLAND, DA
T02659 TAN PENG SIEW
U01109 UNITED STATES I
W01144 WEINER, ALAN
W01677 WORD, THE [BOMB
W02565 WRIGHT, ARNOLD,
07W01918 WU MING-KUN
Z01211 ZWEMER, S.

LAW, ETHICS

A01309 ADJI, OEMAR SEN
H01496 HARAHAP, PARADA
06H02792 HSING SUNG-WEN
L00764 LUBIS, MOCHTAR

BIOGRAPHY

A02724 AKKEREN, DR. PH
L00764 LUBIS, MOCHTAR
L00763 LUBIS, MOCHTAR
P00870 PANG YUET LENG

EDUCATION

A00654 ADINEGORO, DJAM
A01311 ANWAR, H. ROSIH
A00138 ASSEGAFF, D. H.
A00137 ASSEGAFF, D. H.
K00667 KERTAPATI, TON
L01324 LUBIS, MOCHTAR
N01266 NIEUWENHUIS, J.
N01268 NIEUWENHUIS, J.
P00876 PARSONS, CYNTHI
S01049 SUSANTO, ASTRID

PRINTING

D01475 DJAJANTO, WARIE
D02096 DJASWADI,SOEPRA
D02095 DJAWADI SUPRAPT
G00531 GRAFF, H. J. DE
I01335 ISA, ZUBAIDAH
J02815 JENKINS, DAVID
M02114 MAWATARI, T.
M00802 MC MURTRIE, DOU
W01184 WURTZBURG, C. E

PUBLISHING

I01335 ISA, ZUBAIDAH

OTHER JOURNALISM

F02099 FOWLER, JOHN A.

GENERAL HISTORY

P00890 PLUVIER, J. M.

POLITICAL SCIENCE

A00117 ANDELMAN, DAVID
W01144 WEINER, ALAN

LAOS

FOREIGN CORRESPOND

A01261 ARNETT, PETER
E00433 EVERINGHAM, JOH
E01481 EVERINGHAM, JOH
H00694 HUGHES, RICHARD

CONTROL OF PRESS

E01481 EVERINGHAM, JOH
I00629 IPI REPORT
L01263 LENT, JOHN A.

RESEARCH

N01246 NUNN, G. RAYMON

DESCRIPTION

B00488 BUREAU OF SOCIA
E00433 EVERINGHAM, JOH
L00711 LENT, JOHN A.
L01263 LENT, JOHN A.
M00784 MALLOY, MICHAEL

BIOGRAPHY

M00784 MALLOY, MICHAEL

EDUCATION

A02450 ASIAN PRINTER,

PRINTING

A02450 ASIAN PRINTER,
H01810 HUNTER, DARD

OTHER JOURNALISM

B00488 BUREAU OF SOCIA

POLITICAL SCIENCE

B00488 BUREAU OF SOCIA

MACAO

FOREIGN CORRESPOND

C01788 CHRISTIANSEN, S

RESEARCH

K00675 KING, FRANK H.
Y01249 YU, TIMOTHY L.

FLOW/AGENCY

A01212 AP LOG
C01788 CHRISTIANSEN, S

DESCRIPTION

C00308 CHINESE REPOSIT
C00302 CHINESE REPOSIT
C00298 CHINESE REPOSIT
C00290 CHINESE REPOSIT
I00622 IPI REPORT
T01653 TEIXEIRA, PE. M

BIOGRAPHY

C00302 CHINESE REPOSIT
S00963 SHAPLEN, ROBERT

MALAYSIA

FOREIGN CORRESPOND

A01685 AMAT MAT TOP
E00424 EDITOR & PUBLIS
S00958 SENKUTTUVAN, AR
S02137 STRAITS TIMES

CONTROL OF PRESS

A00131 ASIAN ALMANAC
A02502 ASIAWEEK
B00157 BERITA HARIAN
B00160 BERITA HARIAN
B00158 BERITA HARIAN
C00244 CHEONG MEI SUI
D00377 DAS, K.
D00374 DAS, K.
D00375 DAS, K.
D00376 DAS, K.
E01391 EDITOR & PUBLIS
F01482 FAR EASTERN ECO
F00468 FAR EASTERN ECO
I00604 IBRAHIM HAMID
I00618 IPI REPORT
L00714 LENT, JOHN A.
L00716 LENT, JOHN A.
L01833 LENT, JOHN A.,
L01519 LETCHMIKANTHAN,
L00765 LUM, MAGDALENE
M00816 MOHD. FAUZI PAT
M00820 MORGAN, JAMES
N02118 NEW COMMONWEALT
N00854 NOORDIN SOPIEE
N01270 NOORDIN SOPIEE

N00856 NORDIN MOHAMAD
P01875 PENULIS KHAS
S01032 STEVENSON, REX
S02137 STRAITS TIMES
S02241 STRAITS TIMES
S02242 STRAITS TIMES
T01061 TEGJEU, BILL
V01116 VARIETY

PROPAGANDA

C02170 CORRIE, J.
D00378 DAS, K.
D00379 DAS, K.
F00469 FAR EASTERN ECC
H02100 HARIMAU [PSEUD.
K00646 KAM, JOHN
N02117 NEW COMMONWEALT
R02205 ROSLEY IBRAHIM
S00944 SAAD, HASHIM

DEVELOPMENT

A02155 ABDUL MANAF SUL
B01369 BRITISH MALAYA
G00539 GUIMARY, DONALD
H02631 HITCHCOCK, DAVI
K00646 KAM, JOHN
K00669 KHOO BOON CHOO
L01833 LENT, JOHN A.,
M01407 MALAYSIA [BRITI
M02011 MOHAMMAD ALIAS
P00868 PADASIAN, JOHN
P00895 POSSIBLE, HENRI
R00928 ROFF, WILLIAM R
S00944 SAAD, HASHIM
S02539 STRAITS TIMES
S02066 STRAITS TIMES
S01899 STRAITS TIMES
S02023 STRAITS TIMES
S02067 STRAITS TIMES
T01061 TEGJEU, BILL
T01661 TUNKU ABDUL RAH

RESEARCH

B00166 BETTS, RUSSELL
C00228 CHEESEMAN, H. A
H00571 HILL, R. D.
L01241 LIM HUCK TEE, C
L01341 LIM, PUI HUEN P
M02617 MALAY MAIL [MAL
P01410 PARKER, ELLIOTT
R01411 ROFF, WILLIAM R
R00926 ROFF, WILLIAM R
R00929 ROFF, WILLIAM R
R02624 ROFF, W.
S01412 SAMAD, MARINA
S01328 SUBBIAH, RAMA
T02625 TAN, S. H.
T02627 TREGONNING, K.
Y01191 YEE SIEW-PUN
Y01208 YUSOF A. TALIB
Y01207 YUSOF A. TALIB

B00160 BERITA HARIAN
B00158 BERITA HARIAN
B00163 BERNAMA
C00227 CHEAH, FREDDIE
C00226 CHEAH, FREDDIE
C00594 CHEAH, FREDDIE
C00595 CHEONG MEI SUI
C00244 CHEONG MEI SUI
D00376 DAS, K.
D00377 DAS, K.
E01391 EDITOR & PUBLIS
F00448 FAR EASTERN ECO
F01482 FAR EASTERN ECO
H01743 HARLOFF, A. J.
L00701 LEEPER, ETHEL M
L01519 LETCHMIKANTHAN,
L00767 LUM, MAGDALENE
L00766 LUM, MAGDALENE
L00765 LUM, MAGDALENE
N00836 NATARAJAN, LAKS
N00856 NORDIN MOHAMAD
W01141 WATAN [PSEUD.

BIOGRAPHY

D00375 DAS, K.
J01509 JOHNSON, MARTIN
P00870 PANG YUET LENG
S00947 SAMAD, ISMAIL
T01058 TAY, LOUISE
W01162 WILSON, W. ARTH

CROSS CULTURAL

H01743 HARLOFF, A. J.
H02631 HITCHCOCK, DAVI
W01418 WEAIT, R. H.

EDUCATION

B01986 BERITA HARIAN
C02217 CHEE OI CHIN
C00329 CHOOI, BEBE
H00545 HANCOCK, ALAN
H01499 HORIZONS [USIS]
K00647 KAM, JOHN
L00701 LEEPER, ETHEL M
P00875 PARKER, ELLIOTT
S01900 STRAITS TIMES
V01114 VAN NIEL, ROBER

PRINTING

B00207 BYRD, CECIL K.
C00278 CHINESE REPOSIT
H01498 HOLBERT, JOHN
S02135 STAR, THE [PENA
S02134 STAR, THE [PENA

PUBLISHING

C00278 CHINESE REPOSIT
H01498 HOLBERT, JOHN

L01520 LETCHMIKANTHAN,

LANGUAGE

A00483 A. GHANI ISMAIL
G00540 GULLICK, J. M.
K00665 KELANA, C. M.
M00812 MOHAMED TAIB OS

OTHER JOURNALISM

A01981 AHMAD A. HAMID
A02253 ASIAWEEK
B00159 BERITA HARIAN
B01371 BUCHLER, WALTER
B00197 BUREAU OF SOCIA
C02170 CORRIE, J.
F02099 FOWLER, JOHN A.
M00819 MORGAN, JAMES
N02013 NADAMINGGU
N02118 NEW COMMONWEALT
S01413 SELANGOR JOURNA
S02133 STAR, THE [PENA
S02138 STRAITS TIMES
S02023 STRAITS TIMES
S02068 STRAITS TIMES
W02218 WARIN, W. J.
W01421 WILSON, W. ARTH
W01420 WILSON, W. ARTH
Y02028 Y., P. [PATRICK

LITERATURE

A00483 A. GHANI ISMAIL
A00103 ADIBAH AMIN
A00142 AVELING, HARRY
B00157 BERITA HARIAN
B00161 BERITA HARIAN
B01371 BUCHLER, WALTER
C00244 CHEONG MEI SUI
G00540 GULLICK, J. M.
I00635 ISMAIL HUSSEIN
I00636 ISMAIL HUSSEIN
Z01209 ZAILAH ISMAIL

GENERAL HISTORY

A00103 ADIBAH AMIN
K00665 KELANA, C. M.

POLITICAL SCIENCE

P00895 POSSIBLE, HENRI

OTHER NON-JOURNAL

B00197 BUREAU OF SOCIA
F00469 FAR EASTERN ECO
F00456 FAR EASTERN ECO
L01354 LIN YU, EDITOR.
P00888 PILLAI, M. G. G
S00958 SENKUTTUVAN, AR

OTHER

```
11L02175 LIANG, WILLIAM        L00723 LENT, JOHN A.
08L01522 LIN YU                L00713 LENT, JOHN A.
   L00751 LIU TZU-CHENG        N01044 NAM, SUNWOO
   L00755 LOON, G. VAN         N01046 NAM, SUNWOO
   L01402 LOWENTHAL, RUDO      P00906 PHILIPPINES. DE
   M02010 MARSDALE, JAMES      R00932 RONQUILLO, BERN
   P02751 PAO HSUEH [TAIP      R00933 RONQUILLO, BERN
   P02803 PARKER, ELLIOTT      S02240 SPECIAL CORRESP
   P01877 PIXLEY, MORRISS      S01038 STOCKWIN, HARVE
   P02065 PUBLISHERS' WEE      T01252 TASKER, RODNEY
   R01884 ROBINSON, EDNAH      T01250 TASKER, RODNEY
   R01883 ROBINSON, EDNAH      T01651 TASKER, RODNEY
   S01895 STELLMANN, LOUI      T01253 TASKER, RODNEY
   W01131 WANG, JAMES EN-      T01251 TASKER, RODNEY
   W02220 WONG, KEN            T01071 THOMPSON, SCOTT
   W02069 WOOD, NAT
07W01918 WU MING-KUN
                               DEVELOPMENT

          LAW, ETHICS          A00135 ASPIRAS, JOSE D
                               H02631 HITCHCOCK, DAVI
06H02792 HSING SUNG-WEN        L00707 LENT, JOHN A.
12H02274 HUANG HO
J01701 JOHNSTON, WILLI.
                                     RESEARCH

          BIOGRAPHY            A01427 AMERICAN UNIVER
                               H00591 HART, DONN V. A
11C02730 CHEN HSIAO-CHI        P00883 PHILIPPINES PRE
   W02220 WONG, KEN
                                    FLOW/AGENCY
          PRINTING
                               A00123 AP LOG
   I02031 INLAND PRINTER,
   I02033 INLAND PRINTER,
                                JOURNALISM HISTORY

          PUBLISHING           B00175 BOGUSLAV, DAVID
                               C00214 CHANG, CHUH-HA
F02806 FAR EASTERN ECO         C00250 CHICO, SILVANO
                               H00554 HARTENDORP, A.
                               L00709 LENT, JOHN A.
          LANGUAGE             L02647 LENT, JOHN A.
                               L00703 LENT, JOHN A.
A02819 ASIAWEEK                R00930 ROGERS, F. THEO
                               R00934 ROSARIO, ERNEST
                               T01059 TAYLOR, CARSON
     OTHER JOURNALISM          S02240 SPECIAL CORRESP
                               S01038 STOCKWIN, HARVE
A02802 ASIAWEEK                T01252 TASKER, RODNEY
                               T01251 TASKER, RODNEY
                               T01253 TASKER, RODNEY
     OTHER NON-JOURNAL         T01250 TASKER, RODNEY

L01354 LIN YU, EDITOR.
                                CONTROL OF PRESS

                               A00123 AP LOG
                               C01946 CHINA CRITIC, T
PHILIPPINES                    D00405 DIARIO, RUBEN
                               D00406 DIBBLE, ARNOLD
                               F02272 FAR EASTERN ECO
     FOREIGN CORRESPOND        G00516 GEORGE, T. J. S
                               G00517 GEORGE, T. J. S
A00123 AP LOG                  G00515 GEORGE, T. J. S
B00193 BROWN, CHARLES          H00560 HAYWARD, HENRY.
I00625 IPI REPORT              I00625 IPI REPORT
```

V01113 VALENZUELA, JES
V02244 VALENZUELA, JES
Y01194 YORRO, DIONISIO

DESCRIPTION

A00120 ARNALDO, CARLOS
A02257 ASIAWEEK
A02256 ASIAWEEK
A02255 ASIAWEEK
A00136 ASPIRAS, JOSE D
B00150 BAUTISTA, JOSE
C00303 CHINESE REPOSIT
C02169 CONLU, DR. FRAN
C02508 CORRESPONDENT
E01480 ESPIE, STEPHEN
F00454 FAR EASTERN ECO
F02714 FOOKIEN TIMES,
G00515 GEORGE, T. J. S
G00537 GUILLERMO, ARTE
J00640 JEFFRES, LEO W.
L00686 LACEY, JOSEPH
L00707 LENT, JOHN A.
L00705 LENT, JOHN A.
L00706 LENT, JOHN A.
L02647 LENT, JOHN A.
M01021 MANGAHAS, FEDER
M00787 MARQUEZ, FLORDE
M00790 MASLOG, CRISPIN
N01600 NIEVA, G.
Q02549 QUIRINO, JOE
S01633 SILVA, FATHER
S00975 SILVA, FATHER
T01652 TASKER, RODNEY
U01111 UNITED STATES I
V01663 VIRAVAIDYA, MEC

LAW, ETHICS

A01003 AMBION, B. C.
F02272 FAR EASTERN ECO

BIOGRAPHY

B00175 BOGUSLAV, DAVID
C00214 CHANG, CHUH-HA
F02714 FOOKIEN TIMES,
M00790 MASLOG, CRISPIN
M00808 MISA, VERONICA
R00921 RAVENHOLT, ALBE
R00930 ROGERS, F. THEO
R00934 ROSARIO, ERNEST
V01663 VIRAVAIDYA, MEC

CROSS CULTURAL

H02631 HITCHCOCK, DAVI
M00787 MARQUEZ, FLORDE

EDUCATION

C00211 CASTRO, JOSE LU
P00877 PATRON, JOSEFIN

PRINTING

D01798 DE LA CRUZ, JR.

PUBLISHING

D01798 DE LA CRUZ, JR.

LANGUAGE

B02550 BRESNAHAN, MARY
J00640 JEFFRES, LEO W.

OTHER JOURNALISM

A02255 ASIAWEEK
A02256 ASIAWEEK
A02257 ASIAWEEK
F02714 FOOKIEN TIMES,
M00787 MARQUEZ, FLORDE
S02446 SANGER, J. W.

RUSSIA

FOREIGN CORRESPOND

L01830 LATTIMORE, OWEN
L00736 LIEBERMAN, HENR

PROPAGANDA

M01850 MOORE, HARRIET

DESCRIPTION

L00736 LIEBERMAN, HENR
L02182 LOWENTHAL, RUDO
M01532 MARKHAM, JAMES
M01850 MOORE, HARRIET

SEVERAL ASIA

FOREIGN CORRESPOND

A02073 ALVAREZ, MAX
A00128 ASIA FOUNDATION
B00148 BARBER, STEPHEN
B02162 BLACKMAN, SAMUE
B02164 BURROWS, LARRY
C00210 CARBALLO, TITO
D01472 DATELINE: ASIA,
D00396 DAVIES, DEREK
E02187 ELEGANT, ROBERT
E01477 ELEGANT, ROBERT
F02519 FARIS, BARRY

F02223 FRASER, JOHN
H00556 HAUSER, ERNEST
H01804 HILL, I. WILLIA
H02300 HOBEN, LINDSAY
H00577 HOHENBERG, JOHN
H02814 HUGHES, RICHARD
K01702 KEITH, ORRIN
K00682 KRAUSZ, GEORGE
K01262 KUO, HELENA [CH
L00690 LANIAUSKAS, VIC
M02528 MORRIS, JOHN R.
M02529 MOTT, FRANK LUT
R00912 RAJAGOPAL, D. R
R00916 RAND, CHRISTOPH
S00949 SARKAR, CHANCHA
S00950 SARKAR, CHANCHA
T01069 THAYER, NATHANI
T01274 TRUMBULL, ROBER
V01119 VAUGHN, MILES W
W01139 WARNER, DENIS

CONTROL OF PRESS

A02502 ASIAWEEK
B01367 BILAINKIN, GEOR
C00210 CARBALLO, TITO
C00331 CHOWDHURY, AMIT
D02557 DAVIES, DEREK
D01645 DEVOSS, DAVID
G01488 GALLINER, PETER
H01500 HSUEH, CHUN-TU
I00621 IPI REPORT
L00690 LANIAUSKAS, VIC
L02525 LENT, JOHN A.
R00918 RAVENHOLT, ALBE
R00919 RAVENHOLT, ALBE
S00978 SIMONS, PAUL
S02561 SPURR, RUSSELL
V01120 VICENCIO, MACAR

PROPAGANDA

B00148 BARBER, STEPHEN
C01459 CREWDSON, JOHN
R01880 REA, GEORGE BRO
W01146 WHEELER, GEOFFR

DEVELOPMENT

A00133 ASIAN MASS COMM
D00382 DAVIES, DEREK
D00380 DAVIES, DEREK A
D00381 DAVIES, DEREK
L01530 LUBIS, MOCHTAR
R00911 RAGSDALE, WILMO
R00923 REECE, ROBERT
S00953 SCHRAMM, WILBUR
S02539 STRAITS TIMES
U01101 UNESCO
W02664 WATTS, RONALD A

RESEARCH

A00133 ASIAN MASS COMM

A01215 ASIAN MASS COMM
A01214 ASIAN MASS COMM
A01213 ASIAN MASS COMM
A01747 AUSTRALIAN NATI
B00196 BRYANT, CHARLES
C00212 CENTER FOR RESE
C01794 CROW, CARL
F00481 FELICIANO, GLOR
H01239 HALE, KATHLEEN,
H00657 HART, DONN VORH
H01356 HOBBS, CECIL
H01571 HORNE, NORMAN P
K00666 KENNARD, ALLING
L00718 LENT, JOHN A.
L02746 LENT, JOHN A.
L00712 LENT, JOHN A.
L00708 LENT, JOHN A.,
L00720 LENT, JOHN A.
L01323 LIM, PUI HUEN P
L01529 LOWENTHAL, RUDO
N02531 NUNN, G. RAYMON
N00857 NUNN, RAYMOND
O00859 OEY, GIOK-PO
R00915 RAMACHANDRAN, R

FLOW/AGENCY

A02502 ASIAWEEK
B00148 BARBER, STEPHEN
B02162 BLACKMAN, SAMUE
D02557 DAVIES, DEREK
D00394 DAVIES, DEREK
D02513 DEEN, THALIF
F01586 FAR HORIZONS
F00490 FERNANDEZ, T.
F00495 FORD, ALEXANDER
H00556 HAUSER, ERNEST
I00613 INTERNATIONAL C
I00615 INTERNATIONAL P
K01702 KEITH, ORRIN
S00950 SARKAR, CHANCHA
S01975 SILVA, MERVYN D
S01030 STEAD, HENRY
T01079 TIMPERLY, H. J.
U01102 UNESCO

JOURNALISM HISTORY

C01446 CHATURVEDI, RAM
12F01698 FENG AI-CHUN [E
12F00489 FENG TZU-YU
15L00699 LAU TZU-CHING
15L00750 LIU TZU CHENG
M02619 MOSES, SIR CHAR
R00924 RHODES, DENNIS
12T01095 TSENG HSU-PAI,

DESCRIPTION

A00107 ALPHA MONTHLY
A00128 ASIA FOUNDATION
A00134 ASIAN PRESS, TH
A02074 ASIAN-AFRICAN J
A00141 ATLAS WORLD PRE
B01431 BELL, HENRY HES

C00357 COMMUNICATION A
D00439 DALTON, JAMES J
F00440 FAR EASTERN ECO
F00450 FAR EASTERN ECO
N02115 NEW COMMONWEALT
N00857 NUNN, RAYMOND
R00924 RHODES, DENNIS
S00977 SILVER, GERALD
S00976 SILVER, GERALD

PUBLISHING

C00357 COMMUNICATION A
D00439 DALTON, JAMES J
F00450 FAR EASTERN ECO
F00440 FAR EASTERN ECO
N00857 NUNN, RAYMOND
S00976 SILVER, GERALD
S00977 SILVER, GERALD

LANGUAGE

K02063 KAY, CHARLES S.

OTHER JOURNALISM

C02289 C.,.G. F.
D01472 DATELINE: ASIA,
K02004 KOREA REVIEW
S00949 SARKAR, CHANCHA
T01079 TIMPERLY, H. J.
T01085 TONG, HOLLINGTO
W02663 WATTS, RONALD A
W02147 WONG, DAVID TZI

POLITICAL SCIENCE

H00577 HOHENBERG, JOHN

OTHER NON-JOURNAL

F00482 FELLNER, FREDER
T01274 TRUMBULL, ROBER
W01139 WARNER, DENIS

SINGAPORE

FOREIGN CORRESPOND

B00413 BOWRING, PHILIP
D00392 DAVIES, DEREK
D00393 DAVIES, DEREK
D00395 DAVIES, DEREK
D00391 DAVIES, DEREK
F00473 FAR EASTERN ECO
F00470 FAR EASTERN ECO
F00474 FAR EASTERN ECO
F00476 FAR EASTERN ECO
J00643 JOSEY, ALEX

S00958 SENKUTTUVAN, AR

CONTROL OF PRESS

A00115 ANDELMAN, DAVID
A00116 ANDELMAN, DAVID
A01315 ASIATIC JOURNAL
A01583 ASIAWEEK
A02537 ASIAWEEK
B00160 BERITA HARIAN
B00158 BERITA HARIAN
B00167 BHATHAL, R. S.
B00413 BOWRING, PHILIP
C01155 CASADY, SIMON
C01456 CHOPRA, PRAN
D00392 DAVIES, DEREK
D00393 DAVIES, DEREK
D00395 DAVIES, DEREK
D00391 DAVIES, DEREK
D00397 DAVIES, DEREK
D00401 DELIKHAN, GERA
F00443 FAR EASTERN ECO
F00445 FAR EASTERN ECO
F00442 FAR EASTERN ECO
F00441 FAR EASTERN ECO
F00452 FAR EASTERN ECO
F00474 FAR EASTERN ECO
F00473 FAR EASTERN ECO
F00447 FAR EASTERN ECO
F00446 FAR EASTERN ECO
F00470 FAR EASTERN ECO
F00476 FAR EASTERN ECO
G00507 GALE, JOHN
G00512 GASPARD, ARMAND
H01500 HSUEH, CHUN-TU
I00611 INSIGHT
I00616 INTERNATIONAL P
J00643 JOSEY, ALEX
K00668 KHAW, AMBROSE
L01967 LEE MAU-SENG
L01423 LEE KUAN YEW
L01578 LEE KUAN YEW
L01156 LENT, JOHN A.
M00818 MORGAN, JAMES
P00892 POLSKY, ANTHONY
R01974 RICHARDSON, MIC
R01623 ROWLEY, ANTHONY
R01622 ROWLEY, ANTHONY
R01621 ROWLEY, ANTHONY
S00966 SHARP, ILSA
S00989 SOON, LAU TEIK
S01032 STEVENSON, REX
S01037 STOCKWIN, HARVE
T01054 TAMNEY, JOSEPH
T01415 TAN, CHENG GUAN
T01076 TIME
T01077 TIMES, THE (LON
T01078 TIMES, THE (LON
T01090 TRAVELER'S TALE
T01092 TRAVELER'S TALE
W02542 WEINTRAUB, PETE
W01160 WILSON, DICK

PROPAGANDA

C02170 CURRIE, J.

W01162 WILSON, W. ARTH

CROSS CULTURAL

W01418 WEAIT, R. H.

EDUCATION

B00184 BORDWELL, CONST

PRINTING

B00207 BYRD, CECIL K.
E02098 EDITOR & PUBLIS
O02534 ON-LINE SYSTEMS
P00894 POOLE, FREDERIC

PUBLISHING

F02806 FAR EASTERN ECO
P00894 POOLE, FREDERIC
R01623 ROWLEY, ANTHONY
R01622 ROWLEY, ANTHONY

LANGUAGE

A02819 ASIAWEEK
A02552 AWANOHARA, SUSU
K02598 KUO, EDDIE C. Y

OTHER JOURNALISM

B00197 BUREAU OF SOCIA
C02170 CURRIE, J.
F02099 FOWLER, JOHN A.
L02279 LEE, MARY
S01413 SELANGOR JOURNA
W02218 WARIN, W. J.
W01420 WILSON, W. ARTH
W01421 WILSON, W. ARTH

OTHER NON-JOURNAL

B00197 BUREAU OF SOCIA
S00958 SENKUTTUVAN, AR

SOUTH/WEST ASIA
P00898 PRESS INSTITUTE
P00898 PRESS INSTITUTE

FOREIGN CORRESPOND

B00181 BORDERS, WILLIA
K01272 KAMM, HENRY
L00737 LIFSHULTZ, LAWR

CONTROL OF PRESS

A02250 ALI, SALAMAT
A02249 ALI, SALAMAT
A01428 ARNOT, SANDFORD
A01313 ASIATIC JOURNAL
A01312 ASIATIC JOURNAL
A02254 ASIAWEEK
B01688 BANGALORE CORRE
B00170 BIRD, KAI
B00181 BORDERS, WILLIA
B00183 BORDERS, WILLIA
B01911 BORDERS, WILLIA
C02269 CHINOY, MICHAEL
F00465 FAR EASTERN ECO
F02270 FAR EASTERN ECO
F00467 FAR EASTERN ECO
F01991 FAR EASTERN INF
F00494 FONGALLAND, GUY
G01963 GHAURI, S. R.
H00553 HARIHARAN, A.
I00608 INGRAM, DEREK
I00630 IRANI, C. R.
J02227 JABLONS, PAMELA
J00695 JAYEWARDENE, B.
L00737 LIFSHULTZ, LAWR
P00902 PEIRIS, DENZIL
P00901 PEIRIS, DENZIL
R00913 RAM, MOHAN
R00914 RAM, MOHAN
S01040 SULLIVAN, JOHN
U01106 UPI REPORTER

PROPAGANDA

F01697 FAR EASTERN FOR

DEVELOPMENT

B00183 BORDERS, WILLIA
F00462 FAR EASTERN ECO
M00777 MADDOX, BRENDA
M00778 MADDOX, BRENDA
N00837 NEVIN, JAMES
O00860 OH, JIN HWAN
P00880 PEIRIS, DENZIL
W01163 WINDER, DAVID

FLOW/AGENCY

A00102 ABU-LUGHOD, IBR
C00359 COOLEY, JOHN
N00833 NARAYAN, S. V.
N02693 NEW CHINA, THE

JOURNALISM HISTORY

G02569 GUPTA, UMA DAS
K00671 KHURSHID, A. S.
N02621 NARAIN, PREM
P01716 PILLAI, G. PARA
P00903 PRINGLE, R.

S01889 SHIEH, MILTON J
S01028 STANFORD U. CHI
Y01190 YATES, RONALD

DEVELOPMENT

06C00346 CHU WEI-YU
H02226 HUANG, NANCY LA
S00970 SHIEH, MILTON J
Y01187 YANG, SHOU-JUNG

RESEARCH

13C01585 CHENG HENG-HSIU
I00631 IRICK, ROBERT L
J00637 JACOBS, J. BRUC
J00644 JU, WILLIAM C.
L01581 LIU, HENRY Y.
S00982 SKINNER, G. WIL
13Y02051 YANG SHOU-JUNG,
Y02629 YANG, SHOU-JANG

FLOW/AGENCY

C01988 CHINA TODAY
07L00761 LU K'ANG-YU

JOURNALISM HISTORY

06C02733 CHENG YI
16C00240 CHENG CHEN-MING
10H00588 HSI KEN-LIN
H02225 HSIAO, I-WEN
17H01999 HSIEH, JAN-SHIH
H02104 HSING CHENG YUA
09H02275 HUNG KUEI-CHI
09H00602 HUNG KUEI-CHI
03002602 ONO, HIDEO
S01889 SHIEH, MILTON
10S00973 SHIH K'UN-SUNG
13T02141 TONG HOLLINGTON
12T01095 TSENG HSU-PAI,
07W02726 WU HSI TSE
Y02052 YU, HELEN Y. Y.

DESCRIPTION

A02801 ASIAWEEK
11C00235 CH'EN SHENG-SHI
11C00232 CH'EN CHIH-P'IN
11C01376 CH'EN YUAN-HSIU
C02596 CH'ENG SHE-WO
08C00328 CH'IU JUNG-KUAN
11C02731 CHEN SHENG-SHIH
11C02729 CHEN CHIH-PING
15C01749 CHENG JEN MING
12C02732 CHENG CHANG-PO
09C00247 CHIANG CHAN-K'U
10C02735 CHIN PAO-MIN
08C02737 CHOU SHENG-SHEN
08C02736 CHOU HSIAO-HUNG
06C01960 CHU CH'UAN-YU
C00341 CHU CHI-YING

06C00347 CHU YU-LUNG
06C02093 CHU HSU-PAI
C00345 CHU, JAMES C. Y
04C00349 CHUNG-KUO KUO M
C02634 CLAYTON, CHARLE
F02521 FREE CHINA WEEK
F02520 FREE CHINA WEEK
F02518 FREE CHINA WEEK
F00503 FREE CHINA WEEK
F00500 FREE CHINA WEEK
10H00588 HSI KEN-LIN
17H02101 HSIEH, JAN-CHIH
17H01979 HSIEH, JAN-SHIH
H02226 HUANG, NANCY LA
10K00652 KAO FENG-JUNG
K02524 KAZER, BILL
K00678 KLIMLEY, APRIL
K00679 KLIMLEY, APRIL
07L02277 LAI MING-CHI
L02230 LAI, LESLIE K.
L02231 LEE HSING-CHU
L02232 LEW TIEN
07L00730 LI CHAN
07L00732 LI SHENG-WEN
L00733 LI TZE-CHUNG
15L02600 LIU CHIEN-SHUN
15L02111 LIU KUANG-YEN
15L01582 LIU, WEI-SEN
L01526 LIU, MELINDA
L00746 LIU,' HAN C. AND
L02234 LONG, HWA SHU
12L00768 LUNG CH'UNG-KUA
M02185 MAC GREGOR, GR
M02187 MC LAUGHLIN, J
S00960 SHAN, SHEN
10S00973 SHIH K'UN-SUNG
10S00971 SHIH CHAO-HSI
T02800 T'AI-PEI SHIH H
14T01053 T'AI-PEI SHIH H
14T02574 T'AI-WAN HSIN S
13T02141 TONG HOLLINGTON
V01115 VAN ZANDT, LYDI
V02048 VOLZ, FRED J.
W01134 WANG, THI-WU
W02246 WEI, MICHAEL TA·
07W02726 WU HSI TSE
Y01259 YAO, RAYMOND
12Y01192 YEH TSUNG-K'UEI
Y02153 YU, HUNG-HAI
10Y01206 YUAN LIANG

LAW, ETHICS

A00412 ARMBRUSTER, WIL
11C01584 CHANG, LI-HSIUN
F00466 FAR EASTERN ECO
07L02281 LI CHAN
07L02576 LI CHAN
07L00729 LI CHAN
15L01582 LIU, WEI-SEN
16L00759 LU CHIH-CH'U
M02187 MC LAUGHLIN, J
07P01247 PEI K'E [BAKER,
07S01042 SUNG HAN-CHANG
04W01137 WANG YING-CHI
W01135 WANG, THI-WU

E00423 EDITOR & PUBLIS
E00433 EVERINGHAM, JOH
E00434 EVERINGHAM, JOH
E00435 EVERS, HANS-DIE
F01484 FAR EASTERN ECO
F00471 FAR EASTERN ECO
F00453 FAR EASTERN ECO
H00548 HANNA, WILLARD
H01502 HULSTON, LINDA
J00638 JACOBS, MILTON
K02000 KAVIYA, SOMKUAN
M00787 MARQUEZ, FLORDE
M00809 MITCHELL, JOHN
M02651 MITCHELL, JOHN
M00823 MOSEL, JAMES N.
P00884 PICKERELL, ALBE
R00920 RAVENHOLT, ALBE
R00931 ROLNICK, HARRY
S01720 SCANDLEN, GUY B
S00997 SRIBURATHAM, AR
S02022 STONG, PHIL D.
T02139 THAI NOI, (PSEU
T01091 TRAVELER'S TALE
W01170 WOODRUFF, LANCE
W01174 WRIGHT, ARNOLD,
Y01681 YOON, SUTHICHAI

LAW, ETHICS

F00472 FAR EASTERN ECO
S01894 STANDING, PERCY

BIOGRAPHY

D00372 DANIELS, JOSEPH
F01487 FREEMAN, ANDREW
H00548 HANNA, WILLARD
M00776 MACDONALD, ALEX
R00920 RAVENHOLT, ALBE
S02022 STONG, PHIL D.

CROSS CULTURAL

A01430 AYER, FREDERIC
M00787 MARQUEZ, FLORDE

PRINTING

H01588 HANSEN, CARL C.
O02120 OLREE, C.

PUBLISHING

E00423 EDITOR & PUBLIS

OTHER JOURNALISM

A01430 AYER, FREDERIC
J01504 JACOBS, MILTON
J00638 JACOBS, MILTON
M00787 MARQUEZ, FLORDE

POLITICAL SCIENCE

M02652 MOSEL, JAMES N.

SOCIOLOGY, ANTHROPO

E00435 EVERS, HANS-DIE

OTHER NON-JOURNAL

J00638 JACOBS, MILTON

UNITED STATES

FOREIGN CORRESPOND

A01685 AMAT MAT TOP
A01643 ARNETT, PETER
A02191 ARNETT, PETER
B02159 BALK, ALFRED
B02555 BONAVIA, DAVID
B01644 BRAESTRUP, PETE
B02556 BRAESTRUP, PETE
B00188 BRAESTRUP, PETE
B01368 BRAESTRUP, PETE
B00193 BROWN, CHARLES
B00195 BROWNE, MALCOLM
C01933 CHINA CRITIC, T
C00353 COLUMBIA JOURNA
C00354 COLUMBIA JOURNA
D00399 DAVISON, W. PHI
D02174 DEEPE, BEVERLY
D00404 DIAMOND, EDWIN
D02054 DUDMAN, RICHARD
E02221 EDITOR & PUBLIS
E00431 EMERSON, GLORIA
F00497 FOX, TOM
F00498 FRANK, ROBERT S
H01364 HALBERSTAM, DAV
H01392 HALBERSTAM, DAV
H00543 HALBERSTAM, DAV
H00546 HANGEN, PATRICI
H02190 HANGEN, PAT
H00556 HAUSER, ERNEST
H01364 HERR, MICHAEL
H02523 HILL, I. WILLIA
H02191 HOFFMAN, FRED S
I00634 ISAACS, NORMAN
J00881 JOHNSON, DEWAYN
K00661 KARNOW, STANLEY
K02172 KEARNS, FRANK
K02229 KENNEDY, WILLIA
K02003 KOREA REVIEW
L02178 LOVING, GEORGE
M00788 MARSHALL, S. L.
M00797 MC CARTNEY, JAM
M00803 MC NULTY, THOMA
M00798 MC NULTY, THOMA
M00815 MOODY, RANDALL
M02189 MORGAN, JOE W.
N00839 NEW LEADER, THE

M02186 MC ANDREW, WIL
M00803 MC NULTY, THOMA
M00815 MOODY, RANDALL
N01047 NAM, SUNWOO
N02713 NEW CHINA, THE
N02703 NEW CHINA, THE
P02803 PARKER, ELLIOTT
P01877 PIXLEY, MORRISS
P02065 PUBLISHERS' WEE
R01881 RICH, RAYMOND T
R01884 ROBINSON, EDNAH
R01883 ROBINSON, EDNAH
R00943 RUSTIN, RICHARD
S02206 SAFER, MORLEY
S00986 SOGA, Y.
S01895 STELLMANN, LOUI
S02045 STEVENSON, H. L
S02210 SYLVESTER, ARTH
T02046 TARZIAN, JEAN
T02213 TIEDE, TOM
V01121 VILANILAM, JOHN
W01131 WANG, JAMES EN-
W01161 WILSON, QUINTUS
W02220 WONG, KEN
W02069 WOOD, NAT
W01176 WRIGHT, JAMES D
Y02151 YU, FREDERICK T
10Y01206 YUAN LIANG
Y02325 YUN, ART
Z01922 ZUMOTO, MOTSSAD

LAW, ETHICS

A01685 AMAT MAT TOP
A01781 AMERICAN JOURNAI
G00519 GERSHEN, MARTIN
G00520 GERSHEN, MARTIN
J01701 JOHNSTON, WILLI
L02178 LOVING, GEORGE
M02186 MC ANDREW, WIL
R00942 RUSSO, FRANK D.
S01034 STILLMAN, DON
W01149 WILLIAMS, ALDEN

BIOGRAPHY

C01748 CHENG, JASON (JI
H02190 HANGEN, PAT
W02545 WILLIAMSON, LEN
W02220 WONG, KEN
Y01193 YOUNG, PERRY DE

CROSS CULTURAL

A00112 ALLEN, T. HARRE
B02555 BONAVIA, DAVID

EDUCATION

C01748 CHENG, JASON (J
N02703 NEW CHINA, THE

PRINTING

I02033 INLAND PRINTER,
I02031 INLAND PRINTER,

OTHER JOURNALISM

B02159 BALK, ALFRED
E00431 EMERSON, GLORIA
L02308 LU, DAVID CHI-H
M00798 MC NULTY, THOMA
S02045 STEVENSON, H. L
S02136 STIER, W. RUDOL
W02145 WANG, BETTY SIA
Y02151 YU, FREDERICK T
Y02325 YUN, ART

OTHER NON-JOURNALIS

S00951 SCHECTER, JERRO
S01041 SULLY, FRANCOIS
W01165 WITCOVER, JULES

VIETNAM
F00498 FRANK, ROBERT S

FOREIGN CORRESPOND

A01261 ARNETT, PETER
A01643 ARNETT, PETER
A00129 ARNETT, PETER
A02191 ARNETT, PETER
A00127 ASIAN, THE
A02503 ASIAWEEK
B02159 BALK, ALFRED
B00187 BOYLAN, JAMES
B02578 BOYLE, RICHARD
B02556 BRAESTRUP, PETE
B00188 BRAESTRUP, PETE
B01644 BRAESTRUP, PETE
B01368 BRAESTRUP, PETE
B02163 BRANNIGAN, BILL
B00195 BROWNE, MALCOLM
B02164 BURROWS, LARRY
C00354 COLUMBIA JOURNA
C00353 COLUMBIA JOURNA
C01458 COSTENOBLE, EAR
D00399 DAVISON, W. PHI
D02512 DAWSON, ALAN
D02174 DEEPE, BEVERLY
D00404 DIAMOND, EDWIN
D02054 DUDMAN, RICHARD
E01478 ELLITHORPE, HAR
E00431 EMERSON, GLORIA
E02222 ERLANGER, STEVE
F01362 FAAS, HORST
F00497 FOX, TOM
F00498 FRANK, ROBERT S
H02189 HALBERSTAM, DAV
H00543 HALBERSTAM, DAV
H01494 HALBERSTAM, DAV
H01392 HALBERSTAM, DAV

W02543 WHITE, EDWIN Q.
W02544 WILLIAMSON, LEN

JOURNALISM HISTORY

A01643 ARNETT, PETER
B01644 BRAESTRUP, PETE
N02660 NGUYEN THAI
T01726 THU VIEN QUOC G

DESCRIPTION

A02070 AFRO-ASIAN JOURI
A00127 ASIAN, THE
B00146 BAILEY, GEORGE
B02214 BOROP, MIRIAM J
B00195 BROWNE, MALCOLM
C00352 COLUMBIA JOURNA
C00355 COLUMBIA JOURNA
C01458 COSTENOBLE, EAR
E01479 ELLITHORPE, HAR
E02222 ERLANGER, STEVE
F01362 FAAS, HORST
F00506 FRIENDLY, FRED
G00538 GUIMARY, DONALD
H01392 HALBERSTAM, DAV
H00543 HALBERSTAM, DAV
H00561 HAYWARD, HENRY
H01647 HERR, MICHAEL
H00576 HOFFER, THOMAS
I00607 INDOCHINA SOLID
K00661 KARNOW, STANLEY
K02172 KEARNS, FRANK
L00702 LEFEVER, ERNEST
M02186 MC ANDREW, WIL
M02187 MC LAUGHLIN, J
M00803 MC NULTY, THOMA
M00815 MOODY, RANDALL
N02660 NGUYEN THAI
O00864 O'LOUGHLIN, PET
O02196 OKULEY, BERT
P02656 PHAN NHU MY
P00885 PIKE, DOUGLAS
R00943 RUSTIN, RICHARD
S02206 SAFER, MORLEY
S00991 SOUTHERLAND, DA
S01031 STEINLE, PEGGY
S01050 SUSSMAN, LEONAR
S02210 SYLVESTER, ARTH
T01654 TERZANI, TIZIAN
T02213 TIEDE, TOM
T02584 TRAN TRONG HUNG
T02585 TRONG NHAN
T01099 TURNBULL, GEORG
U01662 UNITED STATES I
V01732 VIETNAM MAGAZIN
V01733 VIETNAM MAGAZIN
V02143 VO CONG-TAI
V02144 VOLKERT, KURT
W01176 WRIGHT, JAMES D

LAW, ETHICS

E01478 ELLITHORPE, HAR
G00519 GERSHEN, MARTIN

G00520 GERSHEN, MARTIN
L02178 LOVING, GEORGE
M02186 MC ANDREW, WIL
M02187 MC LAUGHLIN, J
M02193 MORRIS, JOHN G.
R00942 RUSSO, FRANK D.
S01034 STILLMAN, DON
T01093 TREASTER, JOSEP
W01149 WILLIAMS, ALDEN

BIOGRAPHY

D00407 DINH, TRAN VAN
H02190 HANGEN, PAT
N01065 NEWSWEEK
02T02759 TING KUANG-HUA
Y01193 YOUNG, PERRY DE

EDUCATION

P02654 PHAN NHU MY

PRINTING

H01810 HUNTER, DARD

OTHER JOURNALISM

B02159 BALK, ALFRED
E00431 EMERSON, GLORIA
M00798 MC NULTY, THOMA
P02655 PHAN NHU MY

OTHER NON-JOURNAL

H00565 HERR, MICHAEL
H00564 HERR, MICHAEL
H00566 HERR, MICHAEL
P02655 PHAN NHU MY
S00964 SHAPLEN, ROBERT
S01041 SULLY, FRANCOIS
W01165 WITCOVER, JULES

WESTERN HEMISPHERE

PROPAGANDA

H00557 HAYES, HAROLD B

RESEARCH

L02790 LO, KARL AND H.

JOURNALISM HISTORY

L02790 LO, KARL AND H.

WORLD

FOREIGN CORRESPONDE

CONTROL OF PRESS

PROPAGANDA

DEVELOPMENT

RESEARCH

FLOW/AGENCY

JOURNALISM HISTORY

DESCRIPTION

BIOGRAPHY

06C01960 CHU CH'UAN-YU
T01069 THAYER, NATHANI

CROSS CULTURAL

M02640 MARTIN, DUDLEY
M01597 MOWLANA, HAMID
P01971 PEIPING CHRONIC

EDUCATION

H02105 HUGHES, PENNETH
I00617 INTERNATIONAL P

PRINTING

N02115 NEW COMMONWEALT

OTHER JOURNALISM

A01980 AFRO-ASIAN JOUF
D01474 DE VERNEIL, AND
P02658 PYE, LUCIAN, ED
R02564 RUBEN, BRENT, E
04W01909 WANG HUNG CHUN
13Y01919 YANG HSIA YUNG

POLITICAL SCIENCE

F00504 FREEDOM OF INFO
S00956 SCHWARZ, HENRY

GENERAL HISTORY

P00890 PLUVIER, J. M.

CONTROL OF PRESS

R00937 ROSENBERG, DAVI